TWENTIETH CENTURY FOX

The original painting of the Twentieth Century Fox logo by Emil Kosa, Jr. Five additional moving spotlights and a triumphant brass fanfare composed by Alfred Newman would be added to complete the now-famous introduction that has greeted audiences since 1935.

TWENTIETH CENTURY FOX

A CENTURY OF ENTERTAINMENT

Michael Troyan

Jeffrey Paul Thompson ~ Stephen X. Sylvester

Guilford, Connecticut

All seven stories of a Parisian tenement were built at Fox's Western Avenue studio in Hollywood for the silent film classic *7th Heaven* (1927) so that Chico (Charles Farrell) could ascend the staircase in one take. Director Frank Borzage, second from left, and other production staff pose on the second floor of the elaborate set.

FOR THOSE WHO WILL CLIMB IT, THERE IS A LADDER LEADING FROM THE DEPTHS TO THE HEIGHTS . . . THE LADDER OF COURAGE.

—*7TH HEAVEN* (1927)

For William Fox, Joseph Schenck, and Darryl F. Zanuck,
all individual champions of the motion picture industry, whose
creation of Twentieth Century Fox inspired a century of
extraordinary filmmaking.

Alice Faye (with large fur collar) walks through a maze of lights, cameras, and cords for a scene in *On the Avenue* (1937).

Henry Fonda and Claudette Colbert get some direction from John Ford, center, during the wedding scene in *Drums Along the Mohawk* (1939).

RIGHT: The cast of *Springtime in the Rockies* (1942) following an old Fox lot tradition: being photographed walking arm-in-arm across the lot. In this case they are walking in between Bldg. 31 and Bldg. 88. From left to right: Charlotte Greenwood, Carmen Miranda, Cesar Romero, Betty Grable, John Payne, Helen Forrest, and Harry James.

BOTTOM: The cast of *All About Eve* (1950) walking past Stages Ten and Eleven. From left to right: Gary Merrill, Bette Davis, George Sanders, Anne Baxter, Hugh Marlowe, and Celeste Holm.

OPPOSITE: The cast of *The Towering Inferno* (1974) walking up the east side of the lot (note the Century City high-rise condos in the background). From left to right: Steve McQueen, Robert Wagner, Faye Dunaway, William Holden, Jennifer Jones, Fred Astaire, Paul Newman, Richard Chamberlain, Robert Vaughn, and O.J. Simpson.

$\mathcal{C}$ONTENTS

View of the Twentieth Century Fox lot looking northeast taken in 2007 with Pico Boulevard running along the bottom.

FOREWORD

When I was growing up in New York, every Sunday afternoon my grandfather, a first generation Greek immigrant who spoke barely any English, would take me to the movies, so he could spend some quality time with me, and so he could learn the language of his new country. He loved the movies—all of them—and his passion was contagious. We saw everything, from cartoons to classic westerns, war films, romances and thrillers. (My grandfather wasn't particularly discerning in his choices and often he was guided as much by the proximity to a theater than by what was playing.)

The whole world seemed to be up there on the screen, especially worlds beyond our own, populated by swashbuckling pirates, mysterious aliens and femme fatales. To a pre-teen kid from Brooklyn, it was heaven! I spent the long days between Sundays imagining I could talk to the animals like *Doctor Dolittle,* or go on a *Fantastic Voyage* with Raquel Welch.

I wasn't a ten year-old kid on a subway; I was one of the *Those Magnificent Men in Their*

Flying Machines. I was Frank Sinatra in *Von Ryan's Express*, Paul Newman in *Hombre*, Charlton Heston in *The Agony and the Ecstasy*, and Brooklyn was Arabia, Siberia, the moon.

Now, many years later, in a turn of events right out of a Hollywood script, I spend many more of my days watching movies. As Chairman and CEO of Twentieth Century Fox, I am in the business of helping a new generation explore new worlds and appreciate their own, through the timeless magic of film.

I am incredibly honored and grateful to be working on one of the great, legendary Hollywood movie lots. When I look out my window I see the sound stages where Julie Andrews sang, as Maria Von Trapp, "Do-Re-Mi" in *The Sound of Music*, and Peter Boyle as The Monster in *Young Frankenstein* croaked out "Puttin' on the Ritz." I see the stages where decades of incredibly talented actors, cameramen, musicians, costume designers and so many other artisans turned dreams into movies, and I see the home base for the legendary writers and directors behind such classic films as *Star Wars* and *Avatar*.

I walk down the magnificent New York street built for *Hello, Dolly!*, past a bungalow once occupied by Shirley Temple and the old dressing room buildings frequented by stars like Marilyn Monroe. I eat lunch at our commissary, where, in 1959, Nikita Khrushchev engaged in a lively debate with then Fox President Spyros Skouras over communism vs. capitalism (after Frank Sinatra invited Khrushchev to Stage 8 to visit the set of *Can-Can*). As I walk back to my office, I look upward at the source of the giant shadow cast across the lot and see "Nakatomi Plaza," where *Die Hard*'s John McClane crawled through ventilation ducts—in what is actually the nearby office tower known as Fox Plaza. I stroll past the two story Swiss chalet now known as the Old Writers' Building, and think of authors like John Steinbeck and F. Scott Fitzgerald and their contributions to some of Fox's most famous films. I work at a true dream factory, a place where, for me, every day feels a little bit like a Sunday afternoon in 1965.

This book imbues the reader with that kind of feeling. Also, it offers the opportunity to spend some time here at Fox, exploring its backlot looking for treasures and memories, rummaging through its corners for glimpses of the past, and sneaking peeks at its future. It's a passport to a place where everything is possible, where people conjure whole new realities into being every day. A place that can take you anywhere. A world full of wonderful worlds.

Jim Gianopulos, Chairman and CEO, Twentieth Century Fox

PREFACE

My interest in the Twentieth Century Fox Studio started with a visit to the lot. Unfortunately, my visit didn't take place when the studio was Zanuck's playground—when the backlot was still intact.

No, my first visit came three decades later, in the mid-1980s.

As I entered the studio entrance off Pico Boulevard, I was thrilled to see the famous *Hello, Dolly!* set from 1968, still standing in all its faded glory. Back in those days, the guard shack was way up by the administration building, so you could park and walk around about 70 percent or more of that amazing set without a studio pass. But after an hour or two of exploring, I wanted to see more.

Several months later I came back, this time I went to examine the rest of the *Hello, Dolly!* set,

discover the inside of the Café de Paris, inspect remnants of TV's *Peyton Place* set and the Gotham City Plaza set from TV's *Batman*, explore a Western street used in *Butch Cassidy and the Sundance Kid*, and then end my visit in the auditorium of the Darryl F. Zanuck Theatre.

Yet, as informative as that day was, I still wanted to learn more.

So years later I jumped at the chance to be part of the Friends of Fox campaign, set up to illustrate for the studio neighbors the positive benefits of an expanded and refurbished studio versus a

RIGHT: Original 1934 caption: "DOLL HOUSE—Sally Eilers at the door of the doll house-like dressing room which, moved from stage to stage, saves her many steps and the studio much time which, otherwise, would be taken up by trips to her permanent dressing room suite. She is shown here in one of the costumes she wears in Fox Film's *3 On A Honeymoon*." The cute dressing room hung around for years.

massive cluster of upscale condominiums and the heavy traffic associated with them. We were given a tour of the studio, lunch in the Café de Paris, and an impressive packet of well-researched information on the studio's history. Despite all that, I still wanted to learn more about the studio—specifically, about the famous backlot, now fully consumed by Century City real estate development.

That desire motivated me as I helped do some of the research for this book. I learned more than I ever imagined possible.

Here is a small sample:

Movie industry pioneer and dynamo William Fox invented the star system, championed an early sound-on-film technology that became the industry standard, and created a chain of beautiful movie palaces, with many still in use today. Darryl F. Zanuck was the most talented of the Hollywood movie moguls, a unique combination of M-G-M's Louis B. Mayer's administrative skills and Irving Thalberg's artistic sensibilities. Zanuck's military-service experience during World War II made him more in touch with the changing tastes of postwar movie audiences. He lived to see the death of the powerful studio system he'd had a major role in creating, and while the movie studios fought home video for years, Zanuck correctly predicted the big profits it would deliver.

By sheer size and scope, Twentieth Century Fox had the best backlot of the Hollywood studios, and it housed the most authentic and extensive of the standing exterior sets. The studio made successful movies with adult themes, including economic inequality, anti-Semitism, bigotry, and mental health. Yet at the same time, they also excelled in big, glossy Technicolor musical extravaganzas. And when the box office started to wane with competition from television, they successfully reinvigorated moviegoing with the introduction of wide-screen CinemaScope.

Contrary to popular belief, the studio had originally planned to develop their backlot into Century City themselves, and only after a series of financial mishaps were they forced to sell it to outside developers.

I learned from legendary Marilyn Monroe photographer Lawrence Schiller that to help create the infamous Monroe hip-based sashay, Marilyn had an eighth of an inch shaved off the heel of her right shoe!

It has been an amazing journey of discovery. I hope that between the covers of this book, you, the reader, will experience and enjoy an interesting journey of discovery as well.

A book of this scope and magnitude requires the collaboration of many, and a small army helped make it all happen. Michael Troyan and his single-minded passion for classic movies and movie stars brought multiple layers to this endeavor. Living in Hollywood, I have met many classic movie lovers over the years, but none match Mike's focused obsession. Fox archivist Jeffrey Thompson was a constant support and supplier of material that only a studio archivist would know where to find.

Many thanks to Jaime Larkin at the Motion Picture & Television Fund, Ray Courts, Oscar Arslanian, Don Berry, Joel Rogosin, Fabian Forte, Don Murray, Leslie Mann, Marlene Sharp, Austin "Rocky" Kalish, and Irma Kalish. Final round of gratitude goes to Hope M. Parrish, Dennis J. Parrish, Fred J. Koenekamp, Joseph Musso, Mike Malone, Kari E. Johnson, Robert Vaughn and the American Film Institute, Christy Johnson McAvoy and Historic Resources Group, Escott O. Norton and the Los Angeles Historic Theatre Foundation, Keith C. Anderson, Brian Leon and Yale Film & Video, Stacey Behlmer, David Greim, Robert J. Holmes, Ruth A. Holmes, Paul A. Grimm, and Edward M. and Bobbie Johnson.

And last, but certainly not least, thanks to Twentieth Century Fox for supplying a century of entertainment.

Cheers!

Stephen X. Sylvester

The cast in the finale of *There's No Business Like Show Business* (1954): Johnnie Ray, Mitzi Gaynor, Dan Dailey, Ethel Merman, Donald O'Connor, and Marilyn Monroe.

View of the new "Fox Movietone City" looking northeast taken on October 18, 1929 with Pico Boulevard running along the bottom.

INTRODUCTION AND ACKNOWLEDGMENTS:
"Once in a Hundred Years"

Come with me to sing the songs for those who have forgotten. It is good for people to change, but not to forget.

—When the Legends Die *(1972)*

In 1951 Twentieth Century Fox released *Once in 3,000 Years*, a promotional featurette for its religious epic, *David and Bathsheba* (1951). Today, it reflects the studio at its most golden, with enduring stars of the magnitude of Gregory Peck and Susan Hayward discussing the film in front of the studio's commissary. Peck offers precious glimpses of that fabled lot and its now-legendary top craftsmen at work, from director Henry King in the administration building and art director Lyle Wheeler in the mill, to costume designer Charles LeMaire in Women's Wardrobe and screenwriter Philip Dunne in the Old Writers' Building.

This book, the first official history of Twentieth Century Fox ever released, is meant to offer an even better look over the studio walls to celebrate a unique company at its centenary. For this anniversary, the complete story—bookended by empire builders William Fox and Rupert Murdoch—is shared. Or, to borrow the titles of some classic Fox films, we offer you a *Hollywood Cavalcade* (1939) and *The Best of Everything* (1959). With unique access to the studio's materials we discovered, as studio executive David Brown once said, that "the myth of Hollywood is far less than the reality."

Fox has been unique for its century's worth of filmmaking art, that historic fourth network, and bold, technological breakthroughs, from sound on film, widescreen, and stereo sound, to cutting-edge 3-D and digital effects technology. Besides having the first sex symbol (Theda Bara), the first Western star (Tom Mix), and the most popular child star (Shirley Temple), and musical star (Betty Grable), the studio's contributions to the science fiction genre is second to none. It has been an important distributor of animated films since 1933, and even its output in the horror genre includes Hollywood's two best ghost stories.

> *"You can wipe out a generation of people; you can burn their homes to the ground and somehow they'll still come back. But if you destroy their achievements—their history— then it's like they never existed. It's just ash floating."*
>
> —George Clooney in The Monuments Men (2014)

The pattern for this book was set by MGM: Hollywood's Greatest Backlot, with me as the primary writer and co-author Stephen X. Sylvester. For this book Stephen and I have been fortunate to have the help of Jeffrey Thompson, photo archivist at Twentieth Century Fox, who has vitally contributed in every way, from choosing the photos and checking our facts to contributing to the commissary, Fox music, and portrait studio sections as well as supplying many of the captions. This book simply would not exist without him. As with the MGM book, we are proud to offer another studio tour, "archiving" for posterity Twentieth Century Fox's production facilities in California.

> *Have fun storming the castle!*
> —Billy Crystal in The Princess Bride (1987)

So much of Hollywood has been disastrously transitory. For example, Fox suffered the most devastating nitrate fire in American history in July of 1937, in a warehouse in Little Ferry, New Jersey. Forty-two film vaults containing three-quarters of the company's product were destroyed, much of it lost forever. Happily, Fox still calls its historic West Los Angeles studio home, and we hope the tour provided in this book inspires an appreciation for its precious history.

Because this tour cannot encapsulate all one hundred years of the studio's history, I have developed a variety of interactive pieces to make up the whole. Besides the corporate history sections there are "featurettes" that explore, in further anecdotal

The lower third of the main lot was originally used as a backlot during the 1920s and 1930s. This photo, taken in 1935, shows the Berkeley Square set, the lower London set, and the Ocean Liner set, among others.

View looking southeast taken in the summer of 1936. The permanent facilities on the lot were greatly expanded under Darryl Zanuck and included the construction of Stages 14, 15, and 16, a new administration building, a prop building, and a new dressing room building for major stars.

detail, the studio's other lots, key movies and people. The appendices offer a studio filmography that honors those who earned Academy Awards and Emmys for the studio, and a good sampling of what was shot on various sound stages and outdoor sets.

"Every journey begins with a first step. May the Good Lord be with us. Onward!"
—*Sir Oliver (James Mason)*, Journey to the Center of the Earth *(1959)*

When one thinks of Twentieth Century Fox, its magnificent logo and accompanying fanfare surely come to mind. But it is first and foremost the people who worked for the company, and work for it still, that make it what it is. We wish to thank and honor them.

Our journey began with Jean Yuan, a good friend and executive director, Creative Department Worldwide Marketing, who introduced us to the studio's state-of-the-art archives. This is where we first discussed the project in 2011, with Rob

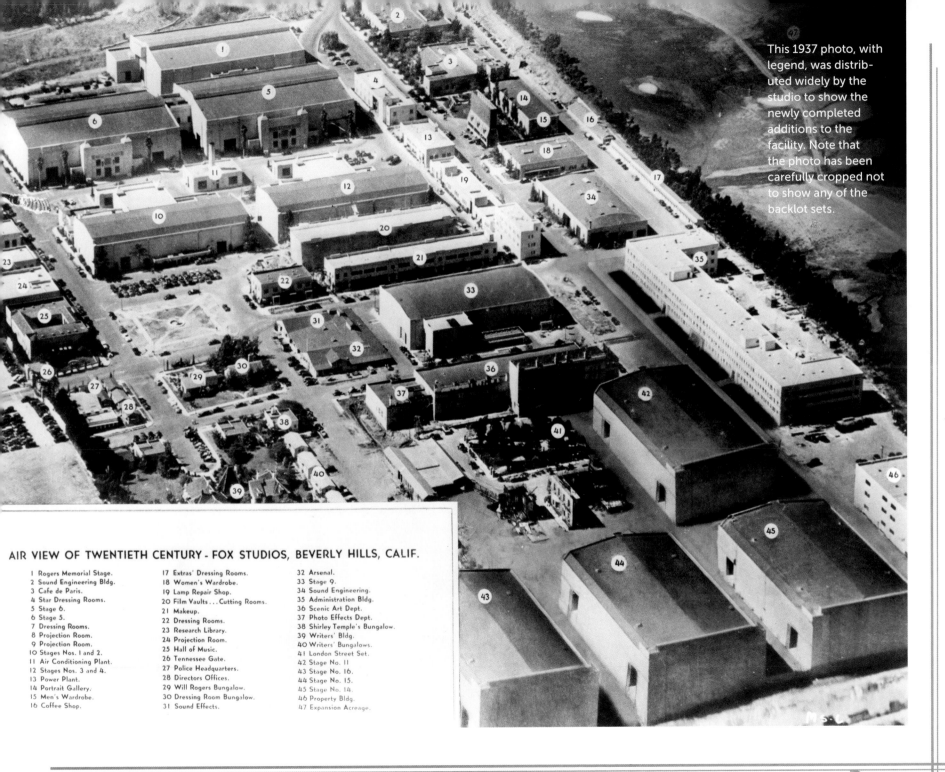

This 1937 photo, with legend, was distributed widely by the studio to show the newly completed additions to the facility. Note that the photo has been carefully cropped not to show any of the backlot sets.

AIR VIEW OF TWENTIETH CENTURY - FOX STUDIOS, BEVERLY HILLS, CALIF.

1 Rogers Memorial Stage.	17 Extras' Dressing Rooms.	32 Arsenal.
2 Sound Engineering Bldg.	18 Women's Wardrobe.	33 Stage 9.
3 Cafe de Paris.	19 Lamp Repair Shop.	34 Sound Engineering.
4 Star Dressing Rooms.	20 Film Vaults . . . Cutting Rooms.	35 Administration Bldg.
5 Stage 6.	21 Makeup.	36 Scenic Art Dept.
6 Stage 5.	22 Dressing Rooms.	37 Photo Effects Dept.
7 Dressing Rooms.	23 Research Library.	38 Shirley Temple's Bungalow.
8 Projection Room.	24 Projection Room.	39 Writers' Bldg.
9 Projection Room.	25 Hall of Music.	40 Writers' Bungalows.
10 Stages Nos. 1 and 2.	26 Tennessee Gate.	41 London Street Set.
11 Air Conditioning Plant.	27 Police Headquarters.	42 Stage No. 11
12 Stages Nos. 3 and 4.	28 Directors Offices.	43 Stage No. 16.
13 Power Plant.	29 Will Rogers Bungalow.	44 Stage No. 15.
14 Portrait Gallery.	30 Dressing Room Bungalow.	45 Stage No. 14.
15 Men's Wardrobe.	31 Sound Effects.	46 Property Bldg.
16 Coffee Shop.		47 Expansion Acreage.

FAR RIGHT: View looking north taken in the late 1950s. This was the Fox lot at its largest at almost 300 acres encompassing all of the land between Santa Monica Boulevard and Pico Boulevard (at bottom) and Century Park East and Century Park West.

Easterla, former director of the photo archive, and Jeffrey Thompson. When Rick Rinehart, director of editorial acquisitions, of Rowman & Littlefield Publishers, Inc., showed faith in the project it was Joshua Izzo, director of licensing, Global Publishing, who formed our dream-come-true partnership with Twentieth Century Fox. Nicole Spiegel, manager of Global Product Development, helped navigate our way to key personnel and materials, and Jeff James on the Fox Consumer Products Support Team was also helpful.

We owe the largest thanks to Ed Hutson, who managed the studio's celebrated art department for many years, not only for his memories and adherence to the truth (invaluable to film historians in the ballyhoo that is Hollywood), but also for pointing us toward his department files that built the book's appendices. His work allowed for the plaques on the Century City lot's stages, noting key productions made there. Studio manager Hal Haenel helped Jeffrey Thompson and I further expand them in this book into the twenty-first century.

Robert Anger, retired grip department head, Fox Studios Operations, was equally generous in showing us the lot, sharing his memories, and patiently answering a lot of e-mailed questions. Victor Villegas, Rich Greene, and Stephaine Boltjes of the Fox Photography Club, shot new photos of the lot for us. The following people also generously shared information or their memories about Twentieth Century Fox: Oscar Arslanian, Diane Baker, Don Berry, David Boyd, Mel Brooks, John Candreva, Angela Cartwright, Ray Courts, Audrey Dalton, Fabian Forte, Austin "Rocky" Kalish, Irma Kalish, Robert Kinoshita, Sharon Leib, Alan Loeb, Leslie Mann, Roddy McDowall, Jeanne Moffat, Terry Moore, Don Murray, Joe Musso, Joel Parham, Dennis Parrish, Susan Perkins, Jeff Powers, Preston Reese, Joel Rogosin, Susan Fox Rosellini, Marlene Sharp, Robert Wagner, Alicia Williams, and Jane Withers.

We offer thanks to the many Fox documentarians who came before us. Besides the seminal works on the studio by Aubrey Solomon and Tony Thomas, and Christy Johnson McAvoy's Historic Resources Group's careful examination and survey of the Westwood lot, no one has documented a studio and its many facets over the years as entertainingly as Kevin Burns and his staff. Similarly, Nick Redman's work with Fox Music and his collaboration with Brian Jamieson on Twilight Time releases of Fox classics, is second to none in the industry—particularly with that interchangeable team of his including Julie Kirgo, John Burlingame, and Rudy Behlmer. In addition, by some great stroke of luck, Turner Classic Movies began programming Fox movies shortly after we started this project. Fox's own promotional material, like *Life*

ABOVE LEFT: View looking northwest circa 1966.

ABOVE RIGHT: View looking north: the prison set for *Von Ryan's Express* (1965) can be seen with Century City rising in the background.

RIGHT: View looking south, the dotted line shows the footprint of the Fox lot at its largest while the solid line shows what remained after the backlot was torn down in 1961.

after Film School and Tom Rothman's *Fox Legacy*, from the Fox Movie Channel, were also helpful.

Beyond the studio's walls we thank Stacey Behlmer and the staff of the Academy of Motion Picture Arts and Sciences Margaret Herrick Library, and the American Film Institute and its gloriously informative website. Mike Malone, park ranger/volunteer program manager for the Santa Monica Mountains National Recreation Area, generously shared research material about the old Century Ranch in Malibu, and took us on a tour we will never forget.

Likewise, although eighty years have passed since Will Rogers welcomed guests to his lovely

186-acre Santa Monica ranch, warm hospitality is still a trademark out there. We enjoyed our tour at the Will Rogers State Historic Park, and highly recommend a visit to the home of this great American.

Although we are thrilled that the photos in this book are from the studio's own photo archive—many never before published—we thank Lawrence Schiller for his unique photo of Marilyn Monroe. Jessica Bean was the art director for the cover design. From the American Film Institute Louis B. Mayer Library we accessed the oral history interviews conducted by Thomas R. Stempel in 1970–1971 for the Darryl F. Zanuck Research Project. These included Charles G. Clarke, Philip Dunne, Nunnally Johnson, Henry King, Barbara McLean, and Robert D. Webb. Barbara Bogart accessed Henry King's unpublished autobiography for us at the University of Wyoming. More thanks to Jaime Larkin at the Motion Picture & Television Fund. Miles Kreuger, president of the Institute of the American Musical, was our guide for our study of the Fox musical. Disney archivist emeritus David R. Smith and Warner Bros. corporate archivist Leith Adams were invaluable support, as always. Also gratitude to Hope M. Parrish, Dennis J. Parrish, Fred J. Koenekamp, Kari E. Johnson, Robert Vaughn, Escott Norton, the Los Angeles Historic Theatre Foundation, Keith C. Anderson, Brian Leon and Yale Film & Video, David Greim, Robert

TOP: View looking northwest taken in 1970 with Pico Boulevard running along the bottom.

BOTTOM: View looking northeast taken in 1970.

RIGHT: View looking southeast taken in 2007 with Olympic Boulevard running along the bottom.

J. Holmes, Ruth A. Holmes, Paul A. Grimm, and Edward M. Johnson.

Many thanks to staff members at the DeGolyer Library at Southern Methodist University, who allowed us to review their oral history #158 with Cesar Romero, done on February 26, 1979. This collection is now housed at the Margaret Herrick Library. We accessed the Mahonri M. Young Papers, L. Tom Perry Special Collections Library, at the Harold B. Lee Library of Brigham Young University in Provo, Utah. Lisa Dale, director of the Folsom Public Library, had such supportive staff, particularly Julie Rinaldi, Phyllis Bulaga, and Regina Maduell. Similarly, Jamie Finlay helped us at the Roseville and Maidu Public Libraries in Roseville, California.

Much thanks to my family for their support all along this journey. My good friends Tyler Feser and Giovanni Secchi significantly contributed to the research and writing phase. Jack L. Parker and Chris Enss, my favorite authors, are morale boosters like no other. In fact, it was Chris who introduced me to Rowman & Littlefield Publishers,

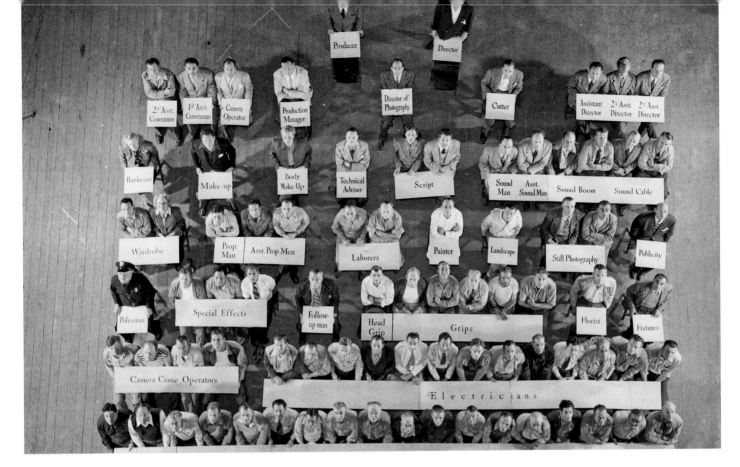

The photo contains the following labels: 2ⁿᵈ Asst. Cameraman, 1ˢᵗ Asst. Cameraman, Camera Operator, Production Manager, Producer, Director, Director of Photography, Cutter, Assistant Director, 2ⁿᵈ Asst. Director, 2ⁿᵈ Asst. Director, Hairdresser, Make-up, Body Make-Up, Technical Adviser, Script, Sound Man, Asst. Sound Man, Sound Boom, Sound Cable, Wardrobe, Prop. Man, Asst. Prop Men, Laborers, Painter, Landscape, Still Photography, Publicity, Policeman, Special Effects, Follow-up-man, Head Grip, Grips, Florist, Fixtures, Camera Crane Operators, Electricians.

LEFT: It takes many people to make a movie as this 1947 photo illustrates. Note Darryl Zanuck holding the producer sign.

SHOWTIME, KID!

—*PREDATOR* (1987)

Inc. At Rowman & Littlefield Melissa Hayes was our book's very patient editor and fact-checker, and Lynda Chilton provided its design. Also much thanks to: Cecelia Feser, Pat Figley, Carolyn Freeman, Shahzeb Kazi, Tess Navarro, Phoebe Palmer, Alura Raetz, Rob Roberts, Richard Saenz, Blake and Shirlee Scribner, Lisa Stevenson, Brian and Mary Beth Verhunce, and Masato Yoshida. My friend Tomas Overbai became my "IT" guy, setting up the computer on which I wrote this book, and generally keeping me in the twenty-first century.

A historical note: In 1985 the company officially removed the original hyphen from Twentieth Century-Fox. Thus, to avoid confusion as we zigzag through history, I have omitted the hyphen throughout the text.

So "chalk up" this effort as another success story for Miss Dove (*Good Morning, Miss Dove*, 1955) and as they say in *Centennial Summer* (1946): "Ladies and gentlemen, on with the magic!"

—Michael Troyan

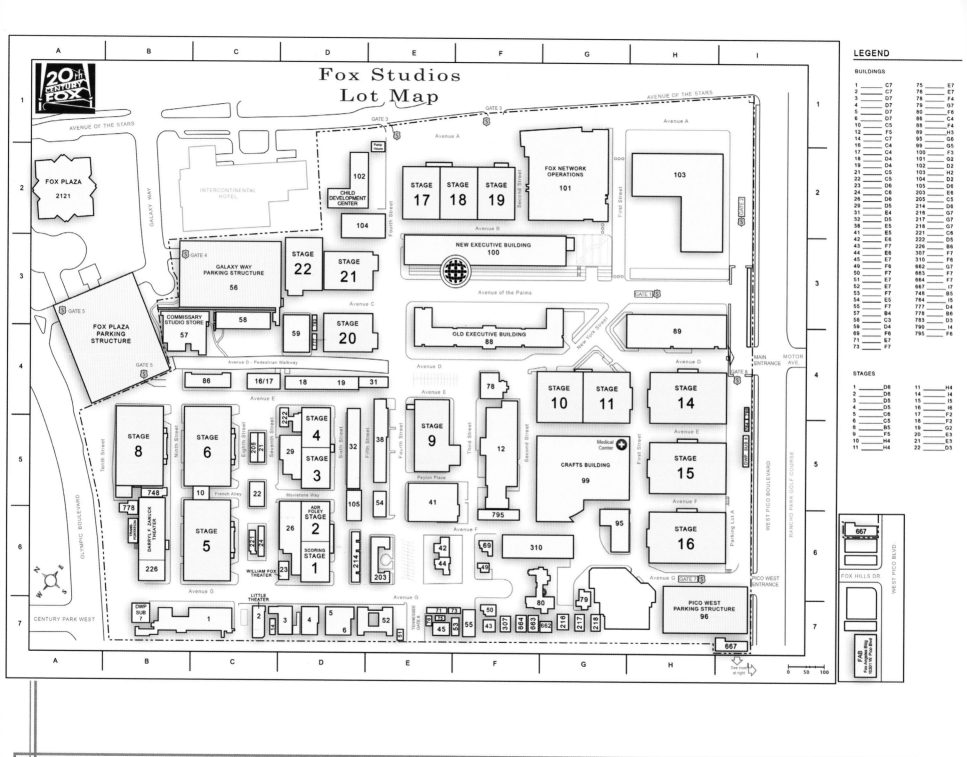

Fox Studios
Lot Map

20th CENTURY FOX

FOX PLAZA 2121

INTERCONTINENTAL HOTEL

GALAXY WAY

Avenue of the Stars

GATE 3

GATE 3

Avenue of the Stars

Avenue A

Avenue A

Pump House

CHILD DEVELOPMENT CENTER

102

104

STAGE 17

STAGE 18

STAGE 19

Second Street

FOX NETWORK OPERATIONS 101

First Street

103

Fourth Street

GATE 4

GALAXY WAY PARKING STRUCTURE 56

STAGE 22

STAGE 21

NEW EXECUTIVE BUILDING 100

Avenue B

GATE 2

GATE 5

FOX PLAZA PARKING STRUCTURE

COMMISSARY STUDIO STORE 57

58

59

STAGE 20

Avenue C

OLD EXECUTIVE BUILDING 88

Avenue of the Palms

New York Street

89

GATE 1

GATE 5

Avenue D - Pedestrian Walkway

86

16/17

18

19

31

Avenue D

Avenue D

GATE 8

MAIN ENTRANCE

MOTOR AVE

Tenth Street

Ninth Street

Eighth Street

Seventh Street

Avenue E

205 21

STAGE 222

STAGE 4

STAGE 3

29

32

38

78

Avenue E

STAGE 10

STAGE 11

STAGE 14

West Pico Boulevard

Rancho Park Golf Course

STAGE 8

STAGE 6

Sixth Street

Fifth Street

Fourth Street

Third Street

STAGE 9

Second Street

12

Medical Center

CRAFTS BUILDING 99

STAGE 15

Avenue E

10

French Alley

22

Movietone Way

26

ADR FOLEY STAGE 2

105

54

Peyton Place

41

First Street

Avenue F

748

778

TRANS-PORTATION

DARRYL F. ZANUCK THEATER

221 24

23

SCORING STAGE 1

214

203

795

42 44

69

49

310

95

STAGE 16

STAGE 5

226

WILLIAM FOX THEATER

Avenue F

80

79

Avenue G

GATE 7

PICO WEST ENTRANCE

Century Park West

Avenue G

LITTLE THEATER

DWP SUB 7

1

2

3

4

5

6

52

51

Tennessee GATE 6

Avenue G

78 75

71 73

45 53 55

50 43

307 664 663 662 216 217 218

80

79

PICO WEST PARKING STRUCTURE 96

Olympic Boulevard

N W E S

667

667

PICO WEST ENTRANCE

FOX HILLS DR

West Pico Blvd

667

FAB Fox Angeles Bldg 10301 W. Pico Blvd

See insert at right

0   50   100

LEGEND

BUILDINGS

1	C7	75	E7
2	C7	76	E7
3	D7	78	F4
4	D7	79	G7
5	D7	80	F6
6	D7	86	C4
10	C5	88	F4
12	F5	89	H3
14	C7	95	G6
16	C4	99	G5
17	C4	100	F3
18	D4	101	G2
19	D4	102	D2
21	C5	103	H2
22	C5	104	D2
23	D6	105	D6
24	C6	203	E6
26	D6	205	C5
29	D5	214	D6
31	E4	216	G7
32	D5	217	G7
38	E5	218	G7
41	E5	221	C6
42	E6	222	D5
43	F7	226	B6
44	E6	307	G7
45	E7	310	F7
49	F6	662	G7
50	F7	663	F7
51	E7	664	F7
52	E7	667	I7
53	F7	748	B5
54	E5	764	I5
55	F7	777	D4
57	B4	778	B6
58	C3	783	D3
59	D4	790	I4
69	F6	795	F6
71	E7		
73	F7		

STAGES

1	D6	11	H4
2	D6	14	I4
3	D5	15	I5
4	D5	16	I6
5	C6	17	F2
6	C5	18	F2
8	B5	19	G2
9	F5	20	E3
10	H4	21	E3
11	H4	22	D3

667

FAB Fox Angeles Bldg 10301 W. Pico Blvd

THE STUDIO TOUR

It's called an industry. Perfect. No factory could present a more industrious atmosphere. A closer view would delight any surrealist. Behind the gates and walls of a film studio, the serious business of make-believe is carried on with a hard-hat discipline any steel mill might envy. All the muses corralled, protected, surrounded with a coven of Magic Makers in every field of technological art. Craft?

—June Havoc, *actress*

Now listen to me. That door is the looking glass, and inside it is Wonderland. Have faith, Alice. Close your eyes and enjoy.

—The Stunt Man *(1980)*

Brad Pitt as Mr. Smith: "Ready?"
Angelina Jolie as Mrs. Smith: "Ready!"

—Mr. & Mrs. Smith *(2005)*

GOOD MORNING, MR. GATE MAN!

—365 NIGHTS IN HOLLYWOOD (1934)

We begin our tour where it all began. The restored Tennessee Gate (now Gate 6) has served as the original main entrance to the studio from the time it opened as Movietone City in 1928. Built to impress—in contrast with the Western Avenue Studio that Jane Withers remembered as "very intimate and quiet and very different"—this lot was the result of the collaborative efforts of William Fox; Winfield Sheehan; architects C. H. Mulldorfer, William H. Werner, and George E. Miller; chief construction engineer H. Keith Weeks; and an estimated 2,700 laborers.

TENNESSEE AVENUE GATE ENTRANCE

The *Los Angeles Times* was impressed enough to consider it proof that Hollywood was now the international center of the film industry. Employees, guests, and hopeful actors seeking the Casting Department in the early days could access a small gate farther north to enter the old administration building from a parking lot that is now a residential

TOP RIGHT: One of the studio's feline residents gazes in through the Tennessee Gate from its namesake Tennessee Avenue, 2015. This was the main drive-on entrance to the studio in the 1920s and 1930s.

BOTTOM RIGHT: Although the gates haven't greeted visitors for decades, the old guard house still stands at right, 2015.

district. Flanking the entrance is the original Fox police department gatehouse (BLDG. 51) and the employee time clock to the left, and an original Craftsman bungalow that predates the studio to the right, used as the home and hospital (Bldg. 45) of the studio's first doctor, C. A. Seyfarth. Another staff doctor was gossip columnist Louella Parsons's husband. Studio police—later headquartered in Bldg. 45, and once publicized as forty-two men strong—had an honorary member who initiated the Shirley Temple Police Force, dispensing toy badges both for infractions (such as flubbing a line) as well as for rewarding good behavior.

TOP LEFT: Shirley Temple is greeted at the Tennessee Gate circa 1936.

BOTTOM LEFT: A guard stands to ensure that only authorized personnel enter the studio, 1934. The Tom Mix barn can be seen in the distance.

View of the main entrance of the original administration building as seen from Orton Avenue, 1934. Following the construction of Building 88 as the new administration building, this entrance was fenced off and hasn't been used since.

"If there were any clouds, they drifted far too high to obscure the brilliance of that January day in 1934 when I marched onto Fox studio property as a regular employee," Shirley Temple recalled. "Everywhere was bustle, glitter, excitement, and a cavalcade of strangers. Grips and gaffers, costume and makeup people, and executives in matching coats and pants hustled purposefully by. Despite all the waved hands, smiles, and apparent camaraderie, I sensed the studio lot was strange territory, filled with potholes for the unwary."

Bldg. 1: The Original Administration Building) (1928)

We find the lot's very first administration building at the northern end of Mel Brooks Boulevard, the former Avenue G that was dedicated to him in October of 2014. "Now fans can walk all over me!" Brooks exclaimed of the street that is still recognizable from the 1960s *Batman* and *Green Hornet* TV shows, made here.

Designed in the Spanish Colonial Revival style by architect William H. Werner—with its

ABOVE LEFT: View of the back of the Administration Building in 1934.

ABOVE: View of back in 2015.

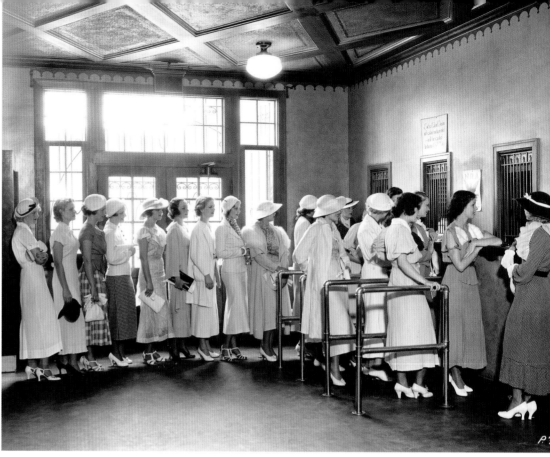

ABOVE: This arcade gallery, connecting the two wings, and skylights are original features of the building.

RIGHT: Contract players stand in line in the south wing lobby for their paychecks, early 1930s.

three wings for the executive, administration, and casting (north wing) divisions of the company—the building's doors were officially opened on June 3, 1928. Beyond the reception room in the early days were offices for the studio business manager, legal counsel, transportation, and location departments. The publicity department managed the "casting gate." The studio post office, telephone switchboard, and employee credit union (founded in Room 38 in 1933) were also located here.

Winfield Sheehan's big office was at the south end of the second floor. Shirley Temple thought he looked like Santa Claus—which was appropriate, since he approved the first contract she signed on December 21, 1933. " 'Winnie' Sheehan drove through to fame and fortune across the picaresque years in which the motion picture became an art and an industry," the *Motion Picture Herald* observed. "He was adventurer, explorer and motivator through both of the inter-linked evolutions."

When Darryl Zanuck arrived he took the

office of Ben Jacksen, former head of the music department and then general superintendent of the studio, on the first floor. Within a month he knew he needed more room, and made plans for a general update and expansion of the lot, including Bldg. 88. When he moved out his old office was turned into a dressing room; in fact, Jane Withers asked to use it in order to take advantage of the then-enclosed patio for her many pets. The fountain located there, between Bldg. 1 and Bldg. 2, was recently restored and is now operational again. In Withers's day it teemed with goldfish that she

View of the backlot
from the tower of Bldg.
1 looking north, circa
1929.

named after her starry friends on the lot, like Henry Fonda. She recalled that the actor would stop by and ask: "How's Henry doing?"

In the late 1960s the north end of the first floor was occupied by the still department, with the still lab for black-and-white photos located outside, on the northwest corner of the lot.

The building's status as the Television Building —used by producers like Irwin Allen (who occupied Sheehan's old office), Paul Monash *(Peyton Place),*

ABOVE: View from the Bldg. 1 tower looking north where backlot sets like the Colonial Home (left) and Chateau Tokay (right) can be seen, 1934.

LEFT: View from the Bldg. 1 tower looking north, 2015.

and Stephen Bochco—continues to this day, with production offices for *Bones* and *Modern Family* and FX Productions.

FAR LEFT: During the mid-twentieth century Fox maintained a photo lab in Bldg. 1 housed in the north end of the first floor. A few of the many millions of photographs produced here can be seen.

LEFT: Darryl Zanuck (and an unidentified visitor) stands outside the entrance to the office he assumed on the south side of the building when he was put in charge of production after the merger of Fox Film Corporation and Twentieth Century Pictures. When he vacated this office for his suite in Building 88, Jane Withers inherited his office as her dressing room.

BOTTOM: The restored patio and pool beside Bldg. 1 currently hosts social events on the lot.

ABOVE: The former Selig Studio became the first Fox studio in California in December of 1915 at 1845 Glendale Boulevard.

RIGHT: The Fox Film Corporation building located on the corner of 10th Avenue and 55th Street in New York City circa 1921.

THE CORPORATE HISTORY PART ONE: THE FANTASTIC MR. FOX (1879-1935)

When I entered, actively, the producing field of motion pictures I was actuated by a double motive. The so-called features that I had been selecting with all the care possible for my theatres did not fill my ideals of the highest standard possible in motion pictures. Therefore, I was fairly driven, in the interest of my patrons, and also as a secondary consideration in the belief that there was immense demand for really good pictures, into the manufacturing end of the business . . . I decided to carry out, in my motion picture–producing career, the same ideals as I had introduced at the Academy of Music. That is to say . . . that the public insistently demands photoplay features by great and world-famous authors, featuring celebrated dramatic stars . . . What concerned me . . . was to make a name that would stand for the finest in entertainment the world over.

—William Fox, founder (1915 press release)

ABOVE: William Fox

The drive for success that transformed William Fox into the Hollywood mogul who forged the foundations for Twentieth Century Fox was evident to his father, Michael Fuchs, a Jewish émigré from Tulcheva, Hungary, and mother Anna (Fried) from an early age. In fact by the age of eleven young William, the eldest of thirteen raised in bitter poverty in the Lower East Side immigrant ghettos of New York, was the main family breadwinner.

He left the Sheriff Street public school to work twelve hours a day as a coat liner at D. Cohen & Sons, a garment center sweatshop. One day, riding to work in an ice wagon, he fell out and broke his left arm in three places. His parents did not have the money for a specialist, and the elbow never healed

TOP: F. W. Murnau

MIDDLE: John Ford

BOTTOM: Frank Borzage

correctly. If William Fox the child was determined to succeed, William Fox the man, left with an infirmity for the rest of his life, was even more tenacious.

Working his way up at G. Lippman & Sons—he was foreman at thirteen—granted him the financial security to marry Eve Leo, the daughter of a clothing manufacturer, on New Year's Eve 1899 at twenty. They had two daughters, Caroline and Isabelle. Fox soon opened his first business, the Knickerbocker Cloth Examining and Shrinking Company, and by the time he sold out in 1904, he had earned a profit of $50,000.

By then show business was pulling him away from the thriving garment industry sweatshops. To earn extra income as a child Fox had performed a comedy routine in vaudeville and he'd always been intrigued by how such places were managed. An even greater allure was the magic of nickelodeons, which presented motion pictures for a nickel. Convincing two partners to join him, Fox purchased a Brooklyn nickelodeon at 200 Broadway, and then another, until they had fifteen of them. This allowed him to purchase his first large theater—the Gaiety—at 194 Grand Street, Brooklyn. He renamed it "The Comedy Theatre." By 1908, from an office at 24 Union Square, William Fox was offering the potent combination of vaudeville and movies in Manhattan and Brooklyn, all the while distributing films to other theaters through his own Greater New York Film Rental Company. Two

years later he leased the prestigious New York Academy of Music building, at 14th Street and Irving Place in Manhattan, that became the William Fox Theatre and hosted the Prince of Wales in 1921.

His menu for success was to make entertainment affordable for everyone by offering "popular prices," and by polling his audiences to discover what it was they wanted, he made a fascinating discovery: "I sent out 10,000 cards requesting patrons to say what part of the performance they liked best," he told a journalist in 1912. "Fifty-five percent of the answers were in favor of moving pictures . . . more than the vaudeville acts. The only explanation I can find is that motion pictures, perhaps, realize the American idea of speed and activity."

No two words better describe William Fox's meteoric rise in the burgeoning entertainment industry. Nothing was going to stop him—not even an American legend like Thomas Alva Edison. After inventing the technology that made movies possible, Edison and the reigning motion picture studios of the time formed the Motion Picture Patents Company, virtually monopolizing the production of movies. Their General Film Company similarly attempted to monopolize distribution. When they offered to buy Fox's Greater New York Film Rental Company for $75,000, Fox impudently countered with $750,000. When they deprived him of access to their films, he sued under the newly enacted Sherman Antitrust Act, and won.

This pioneering fight with future moguls Adolph Zukor (Paramount) and Carl Laemmle (Universal) ended Edison's monopoly and allowed Fox the freedom to interlock production distribution and exhibition, thereby giving birth to the Hollywood studio system.

Fox wasted no time in expanding the distribution of films from his new offices at 116 East Street, including contracting out all the films produced by the Balboa Amusement Producing Company in Long Beach, California. Then he was ready to form his own company, introducing Box Office Attractions, Inc., in 1914, headquartered at the recently purchased Éclair studio in Fort Lee, New Jersey. From there he introduced his very first movie—an orphan's tale called *Life's Shop Window* on November 19, 1914, directed by J. Gordon Edwards and starring Claire Whitney.

The Fox Film Corporation was born on February 1, 1915, absorbing Box Office Attractions, Inc. From its first headquarters in the Leavitt Building at 130 West Forty-Sixth Street, Fox oversaw films like director Raoul Walsh's *Regeneration* (1915), the first feature-length gangster film. The most important men in his growing ranks were Winfield R. Sheehan and Sol M. Wurtzel. Wurtzel was his private secretary, involved in all aspects of production, and Sheehan—a power in New York journalism and politics—became general manager, building up the company's star roster, film production, and network of domestic and European distribution.

Creating their first constellation of stars required pioneering methods of advertising and marketing. Theodosia Goodman was their greatest success, debuting as "Miss Theda Bara" in *A Fool There Was* (1915). She was the first publicity-made star and sex symbol on the American screen, popularizing the seductive—and destructive—"vamp," making thirty-nine additional films in four years. Although Fox publicists insisted her name was created from an anagram for "Arab Death," it was in fact the name of her maternal Swiss grandfather, Francis Bara de Coppet.

Witnessing her popularity, Fox soon cast Valeska Surratt, Virginia Pearson, and Betty Blythe to follow Bara's lead. The company's first athlete-turned-movie-star was former champion long-distance swimmer, Annette Kellerman, who starred in the company's first million-dollar production, *A Daughter of the Gods* (1916). The enormously popular William Farnum appeared in the studio's first adaptations of *Les Miserables* (1918) and *Riders of the Purple Sage* (1918). Farnum's brother Dustin also starred in numerous Fox films until 1924, a year longer than his brother. Raoul Walsh's brother George and wife Miriam Cooper were also among the company's earliest stars.

To make his films William Fox utilized a variety of studios on the East Coast between 1915 and

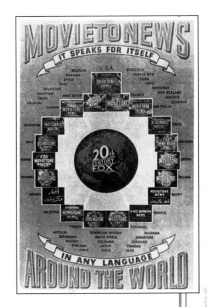

The Fox Movietonews cameramen traveled the world capturing current events on film from the 1920s through the 1960s. It was the biggest and best newsreel outfit producing more newsreel footage than any of its competitors.

RIGHT: Movietone City officially opens on October 28, 1928, with 30 buildings at a cost of more than $12 million.

1919, including nine in New Jersey, four in Manhattan, Scott's Farm on Staten Island, and others in Brooklyn, the Bronx, and Yonkers. He established others in Miami, Florida, and Kingston, Jamaica, and leased the former Colonel William N. Selig Studios in the Los Angeles, California, suburb of Edendale, across the street from the Max Sennett Studios in 1915. While visiting his new acquisition the following year—and deeming it too small for

his needs—he met and signed Selig's Tom Mix, the first cowboy movie star, and acquired five and a half acres of land on the southwest corner of Sunset Boulevard and Western Avenue in Hollywood. He then purchased an additional eight acres across the street to start a new studio. Sol Wurtzel was promoted and dispatched to run what became known as the Western Avenue Studio in 1917.

In 1918 Fox and Sheehan developed the

company's first series of studio brands for their films to help develop stars, including Standard (the highest quality, often historical films), Victory (the second tier, often action films), Excel (for new talent), and Sunshine (for comedies). The following year Sheehan opened offices overseas for film distribution, talent scouting, and the realization of another Fox dream: a division for the making of Fox newsreels. They quickly became the best in the business, with cameramen sent literally around the world to supply theaters with footage of current events.

Squeezed out of the Leavitt Building, the pair supervised construction of a three-floor studio to centralize their far-flung holdings in 1919. At a cost of $2.5 million, it was the largest yet built in the world under one roof, an imposing brick building that filled a square block between Fifty-Fifth and Fifty-Sixth Streets along Tenth Avenue in Manhattan.

From the main entrance the corporate offices—including the sales, distribution, advertising, and accounting departments—were accessed on the first and second floors. The film lab was split between the two floors, along with twelve screening rooms. The grandest of these screening rooms was on the second floor with the wardrobe and art departments, set construction, dressing rooms, and the commissary. The third floor accommodated twenty silent-film companies and star dressing rooms. The building later housed both Fox News and Hearst Metrotone News. Fox also leased the old Kelly-Springfield tire factory one block south on Tenth Avenue and Fifty-Fourth Street, for more room, including space for the East Coast story department and paint and sign shop.

In 1920 Fox celebrated his success with the purchase of an estate at Woodmere, Long Island, where he could rule his family, too. Many of his family members were involved within the corporation. While his wife Eve helped to select scripts, supervise some of the productions, and design Fox theaters, her brothers Jack and Joe ran domestic distribution of the films and Fox Theatres, respectively, and her brother Aaron headed the film lab.

In 1923, with the Western Avenue Studio bursting at the seams, William Fox expanded his southern California land holdings by purchasing 99.34 acres of low rolling hills to the west of the small community of Beverly Hills, from the Janss family. Industry insiders mocked him for making this trek into the wilderness and giving Winfield Sheehan $2 million to transform it into Fox Hills, "the Greatest Outdoor Studio."

As part of an industry trend, Fox was slowly phasing out moviemaking on the East Coast. Such prestigious efforts as Emmett Flynn's *East Lynne* (1925) and Raoul Walsh's World War I epic, *What Price Glory* (1926), were now coming out of

TOP: Edward R. Tinker

MIDDLE: Sidney Kent

BOTTOM: Harley Clarke

California. *Glory* made stars of Edmund Lowe and Victor McLaglen, who reprised their roles in films like *The Cock-Eyed World* (1929), *Women of All Nations* (1931), and *Hot Pepper* (1933).

By 1926 Fox had Sheehan as senior studio executive, with Sol Wurtzel second in command of eleven production teams. His demand that they upgrade the quality of their directors and stars ushered in the studio's first golden age of filmmaking. There were three star directors: Frank Borzage, F. W. Murnau, and John Ford. After directing half a dozen films for the studio, Borzage, known as Hollywood's great romanticist, made *7th Heaven* (1927), which became a major success, launching the careers of wholesome Charles Farrell and Janet Gaynor, the most popular romantic team of the silent and early sound era.

F. W. Murnau's *Sunrise: A Song of Two Humans* (1928) is regarded as the greatest silent film ever made. Remarkably, Janet Gaynor starred in this milestone, as well, opposite George O'Brien. *Sunrise* earned rave critical reviews, but was not a hit at the box office. Winfield Sheehan's interference to correct this "fault" in Murnau's subsequent films, *4 Devils* (1929 and *City Girl* (1929), caused the director to leave the studio—but not before profoundly affecting the way Fox films were made.

Among Murnau's greatest admirers was John Ford. Combining Borzage's sentiment with Murnau's art, Ford's silent-film work presages his great work to come. From his first effort, *Just Pals* (1920), starring Buck Jones, came a distinguished line of films about worthy but often unassuming or misunderstood men, including *Doctor Bull* (1933), *Judge Priest* (1934), *Steamboat Round the Bend* (1935), *The Prisoner of Shark Island* (1936), and *Young Mr. Lincoln* (1939). From the epic *The Iron Horse* (1925) came *Drums Along the Mohawk* (1939) and *My Darling Clementine* (1946). From family dramas like *Four Sons* (1928) came *Pilgrimage* (1933), *The Grapes of Wrath* (1940), and *How Green Was My Valley* (1941).

William Fox leapt ahead of competing studios that were unsure about "talking pictures" by forming the Fox-Case Corporation with inventor Theodore Case, to perfect sound on film. His was the only Hollywood studio maintaining its own research facilities for such a purpose. The result, patented as Movietone, became the industry standard.

He kept his newsreel at the forefront, too, by adding sound to them first beginning in the spring of 1927. By the fall of 1928, $10 million had been spent to transform Fox Hills into Movietone City, the first studio built solely for sound pictures in Southern California. On October 28, Winnie Sheehan presided at the official opening, and Fox was present via a special wire hookup to New York.

Movietone City was so named because the plant—the majority of which was built between 1928 and 1932—was indeed laid out like one. There was a "factory" area comprised of unique and grand Assyrian/Mesopotamian-looking soundstages and Spanish Colonial Revival offices, and there was a quiet "residential" area made up of service buildings and bungalows in Period Revival and other styles for directors, actors, and writers.

By the end of the year the new studio had released John Ford's *Four Sons* (1928), Frank Borzage's *Street Angel* (1928), and Raoul Walsh's *The Red Dance* (1928), all box office winners. The company was now second only to Loews Incorporated, parent company of Metro-Goldwyn-Mayer.

For its fifteenth anniversary the company introduced a milestone motion picture featuring dazzling new technology, and scored the coup of signing the most beloved man in America to a contract. With its unique state-of-the-art newsreel field equipment, only Fox could have made *In Old Arizona* (1929), the first all-talking feature made outdoors. Its star, Warner Baxter, earned an Academy Award and a long career at the studio.

The technological leap was introducing 70mm film as "Fox Grandeur" with the *Fox Movietone Follies of 1929,* in fifty-fifty partnership with financier Harley Clarke, president of General Theaters Equipment. And it was Winnie Sheehan who proudly signed Will

Rogers to a studio contract. Rogers made his debut at the studio in his first "talkie" (he dubbed them "noisies"), *They Had to See Paris* (1929). His films continued to be welcome box-office hits. Commenting on Hollywood in that era, he reported: "Everybody that can't sing has a double that can, and everybody that can't talk is going right on and proving it. Everyone is so busy enunciating that they pay no attention to what they are saying."

Back in 1925 William Fox had formed the Fox Theatres Corporation to strengthen his company's exhibition arm and to compete with Adolph Zukor's Paramount, which led the industry with the greatest number of theaters. By 1929 Fox had surpassed Zukor, with a network of over 1,500 theaters including the prestigious Fox Metropolitan Playhouses

Cavalcade (1933) became Fox's first Best Picture winner due to the contributions of (left to right) stars Clive Brook and Diana Wynyard, producer Winfield Sheehan, and director Frank Lloyd.

ABOVE: The fledgling Twentieth Century Pictures got a big boost by teaming up with the luminaries at United Artists in 1933. Back Row (left to right): Charlie Chaplin, Darryl Zanuck, Samuel Goldwyn. Front row: Mary Pickford, Joseph Schenck, Douglas Fairbanks.

Inc. circuit, encompassing the four largest boroughs of New York; the Roxy circuit, including the Roxy Theatre—the largest in the world—in Manhattan; the Wesco theaters in California; Fox Midwesco in Illinois and Wisconsin; the New England Poli theater chain; and interests in Gaumont–British Picture Corporation Ltd. in England.

As the largest movie theater owner in New York, Fox turned offices in the Roxy into his world headquarters. By the spring of 1929 he owned the controlling share of prestigious Loews Incorporated, with its own theater chain and MGM. Estimated at a value of $300 million, the fifty-one-year-old mogul's empire was at its height. In his biography of Fox, Upton Sinclair reeled at his success and grand-scale ambition, noting that he

"planned to get all the moving picture theatres in the United States under his control sooner or later . . . I think also that he planned to have the making of moving pictures entirely in his own hands."

Then fate, for once, took a dramatic turn against William Fox. As MGM mogul Louis B. Mayer sought to break the Loews deal by appealing to President Hoover and his antitrust division of the Justice Department, Fox was involved in a serious automobile accident on July 17, 1929. He was headed to a golf match at the Lakeview Country Club on Long Island, in an effort to strengthen his ties with Loews New York man Nick Schenck, when his chauffeur got lost and was hit by another car that sent them careening into a ditch on Old Westbury Road. The chauffeur was killed, and it took Fox three months to recover from his injuries. Five days after his return to his office, the stock market crash struck another lethal blow to his company. When bankers demanded payment for the money he'd borrowed to build his empire, Fox was unable to comply.

Whether due to L. B. Mayer's efforts or not, on November 27, 1929, the US attorney general filed an antitrust suit, and William Fox's situation worsened. A few days later, on December 3, he got a loan by forming a five-year trusteeship co-administered by Halsey, Stuart, & Co. and John Otterson of the American Telephone and Telegraph Company (AT&T), with whom he had partnered for the development of sound motion pictures. He put his controlling shares in Fox Film and Fox Theaters up for collateral.

Finding the partnership unsupportive, Fox sought refinancing elsewhere. The resulting litigation upheld the original trust that wanted him out and the company in receivership. Even Winfield Sheehan aligned himself against him. There was no one to help him from defaulting on his interest payments, and on April 1, 1930, he finally admitted defeat. He sold his controlling shares for $15 million to Harley L. Clarke and General Theaters Equipment, Inc., on April 6, and could only serve as a director and chairman of an advisory board to help put it back on a sound financial basis. This he accomplished in five years. The Loews merger collapsed after less than a year, and Fox Grandeur proved to be a short-lived luxury exhibitors could not afford during the Depression.

Management of Fox Film passed to Harley Clarke, and box-office profits plummeted from the $9.5 million of William Fox's last year in 1930, to a loss of more than $4 million in 1931. Edward R. Tinker, board chairman of Chase National, replaced Clarke in November. By 1932, when the Depression had dragged most of the Hollywood studios down into the red, Fox was at the bottom. Tinker brought in Paramount sales chief Sidney R. Kent to take his job when he retired. Kent in turn hired his brother-in-law, Paramount's head of production, Jesse L.

Lasky. A further boost came when Charles Skouras, along with younger brothers Spyros and George, stepped in to restore the Fox West Coast theater chain as the National Theaters Corporation when it toppled into bankruptcy in February of 1933.

William Fox's Hollywood studios remained a problem. All the creative excitement he had generated by developing a team of quality studio technicians and stars in the 1920s faded. His strong leadership skills were also missed. Hit hard by the stock market crash and the stress of running a studio for a rudderless company, Winfield Sheehan became seriously ill in 1930. His famed energetic management abilities never returned. Sol Wurtzel fared no better amid the company's wretched state.

Their decentralized producer system failed partly because Sheehan did not get along with the new ones, including Jesse Lasky and Broadway imports Buddy DeSylva and George White. Lasky's quality films added class when the company needed it, but when they were successful, it was abroad, not at home. Disastrously, the lots began to depopulate.

Raoul Walsh left after making one of Laurence Olivier's earliest Hollywood films (*The Yellow Ticket*, 1931). Frank Borzage turned down the opportunity to direct Sheehan's next big project, *Cavalcade*, to move to Paramount and direct *A Farewell to Arms* (1932).

Those who chose to stay included Frank Lloyd, who took up *Cavalcade*. It was Edward Tinker's

wife who purchased the screen rights to Noel Coward's enormously successful play and songs. Winfield Sheehan broadened its scope and box office by bringing the story up to the present day, offering a hopeful ending to a country shattered by the Depression. Released in 1933—a milestone year for the company, with *The Power and the Glory, Berkeley Square,* and *State Fair,* the first Fox film to open at Radio City Music Hall—*Cavalcade* earned the company its first Best Picture Academy Award.

Sheehan also picked up distribution of Earle W. Hammons's Educational Pictures that year, which included Paul Terry's pioneering Terrytoons. When Educational Pictures folded in 1938, Fox continued to release Terrytoons until 1968. In all, Paul Terry would produce more than 1,100 cartoons featuring such popular characters as Mighty Mouse and Heckle and Jeckle from a converted Knights of Columbus hall in New Rochelle, New York.

Although Sidney Kent had great hopes for Fritz Lang's *Liliom* when it premiered in Paris in April of 1934, it remains only a sparkling remnant of his dream for Fox studios in France, Britain, and Germany, headed by producer (and brother-in-law) Robert T. Kane.

Fortunately there was that amazing five-year-old who auditioned at Movietone City that winter. She made her studio debut in *Carolina* (1934) with Janet Gaynor, followed by the star-making *Stand Up and Cheer!* (1934) and *Baby Take a Bow* (1934). Coached by her mother to "Sparkle!," her ebullience and good cheer charmed everyone on the lot, and then the world. The legendary career of Shirley Temple had begun.

The timing was not lost on Winfield Sheehan. Not only did he desperately need more stars, but he needed ones that were appropriate for a new Hollywood. The Motion Picture Producers and Distributors of America (MPPA), formed in 1922, had tightened their regulation of the Motion Picture Production Code because of public outcry over the increasingly tasteless material issuing from Hollywood. Family films and child stars were in.

In this, Sheehan was also fortunate to gain another extraordinary tot named Jane Withers, who rocketed to fame playing Temple's nemesis with delightful relish in Sol Wurtzel's *Bright Eyes* (1934). Temple's now-iconic rendition of "On the Good Ship Lollipop" sold four hundred thousand copies of sheet music and hit number three on the charts.

All this was not enough to stave off threats of foreclosure from the studio's creditors. While he looked for a new production executive, Sidney Kent held merger discussions with MGM and Warner Bros.

Meanwhile, at the United Artists studio, Nicholas Schenck's brother Joseph and a thirty-two-year-old producer named Darryl F. Zanuck were releasing a steady line of quality hit films under the banner of Twentieth Century Pictures. After a mere seven months, the company was among the most profitable in Hollywood. Both men had stellar reputations. Joseph had risen to chairman of the board of United Artists, and Zanuck had been head of production at Warner Bros., encouraging the studio's pioneering efforts with sound and establishing its rich tradition for gangster films, musicals, and social-conscience pictures.

Schenck and Zanuck had received a $100,000 check of support from MGM's Louis B. Mayer, with the proviso that Mayer's son-in-law, William E. Goetz, became Zanuck's executive assistant. The tie with Hollywood's greatest studio gave the fledgling company the enviable boost of access to their stars. It was another assistant named Samuel Engel who came up with the name "Twentieth Century Pictures, Inc." Landscape painter and matte artist Emil Kosa Jr. devised the logo, and Alfred Newman composed the fanfare.

Intrigued, Sidney Kent met with Joseph Schenck for lunch at the Grill of the Plaza Hotel in Manhattan in the spring of 1935. He offered to purchase Twentieth Century Pictures. When Schenck declined, Kent agreed to a merger. The deal was closed on May 23, and signed on May 28. Kent wanted to call the company Fox-Twentieth Century. Schenck wanted to call it the Twentieth Century Fox Film Corporation, and so it was officially named, on July 19.

Fighting the merger with a lawsuit to no avail were William and Eve Fox, who contended that Fox stockholders were being shortchanged. Weakened by a stroke, Fox died at Doctors Hospital in New York on May 8, 1952, having never returned to the industry. His funeral was held at Temple Emanu-El, on Fifth Avenue.

The trade ad placed in *Variety* that week by Twentieth Century Fox read in part: "His daring, initiative, and courage enabled him to make a significant contribution to the growth and development of the motion picture industry. From the beginnings of his career he engaged in the production of films of magnitude and scope, and blazed a trail for the industry in providing box-office attractions of wide popular appeal. He was truly a pioneer in foreseeing the present status of the screen as a medium of popular entertainment."

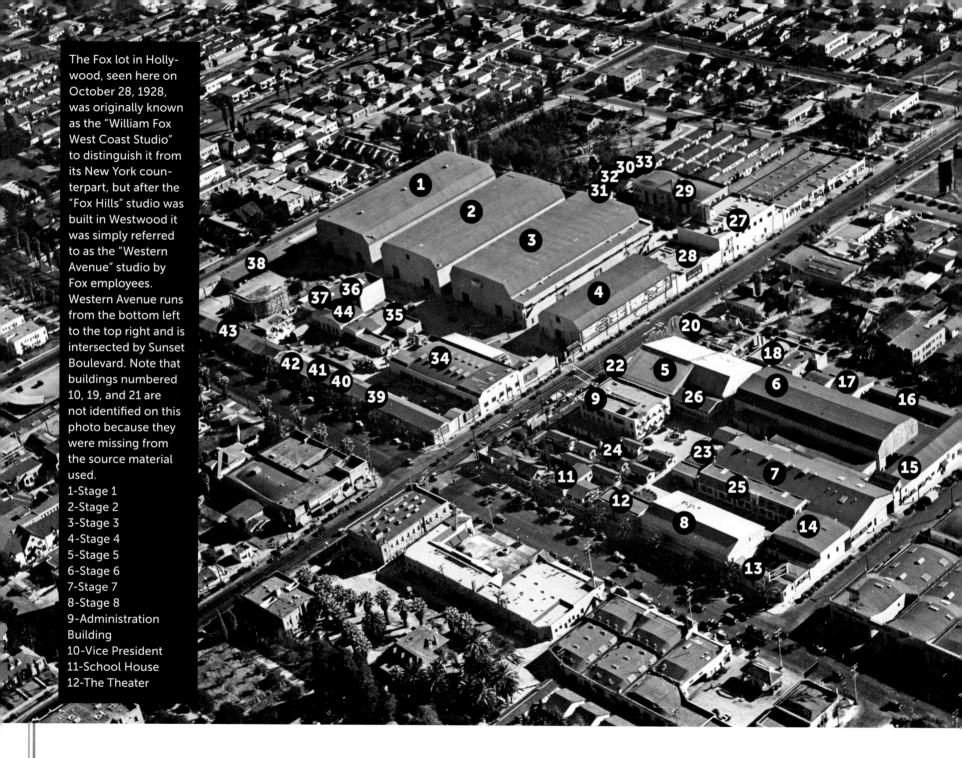

The Fox lot in Holly-wood, seen here on October 28, 1928, was originally known as the "William Fox West Coast Studio" to distinguish it from its New York coun-terpart, but after the "Fox Hills" studio was built in Westwood it was simply referred to as the "Western Avenue" studio by Fox employees. Western Avenue runs from the bottom left to the top right and is intersected by Sunset Boulevard. Note that buildings numbered 10, 19, and 21 are not identified on this photo because they were missing from the source material used.
1-Stage 1
2-Stage 2
3-Stage 3
4-Stage 4
5-Stage 5
6-Stage 6
7-Stage 7
8-Stage 8
9-Administration Building
10-Vice President
11-School House
12-The Theater

THE WESTERN AVENUE STUDIO (1916–1971)

[William] Fox sent for me and asked me what I remembered about the corner of Sunset and Western Avenue in Hollywood. I thought for a while and finally came up with the not very brilliant remark that it was central. Why?

Fox: We're building there, self-contained modern, the works. I want you to go out to the Coast and christen it.

Me: When?

Fox: I have just paid too much money for a script called The Honor System. *You'll direct it.*

—*Raoul Walsh,* Each Man in His Time: The Life Story of a Director

No Fox facility better represents the evolution of the motion picture industry than this one at 1401 N. Western Avenue in Los Angeles. William Fox purchased the ranch of Thomas Dixon—where he wrote the novel that D. W. Griffith shaped into *The Birth of a Nation* (1915)—amid alfalfa and orange and lemon groves in 1916 for $180,000.

By the time Raoul Walsh arrived to direct *The Honor System* (1917), William Fox had placed Sol Wurtzel in charge of the studio. He was expected to roll out sixty to seventy films a year (a new movie released to theaters each week), with final script approval and the final cut made in New York by Fox himself.

Wurtzel's big release the following year was *Cleopatra* (1918), Theda Bara's first film made in California. Hollywood's first "vampire" married lot director Charles J. Brabin and was driven about in a chauffeured white Rolls-Royce. Even easier to spot on the lot was the company's other major star riding around in his black Locomobile, trimmed

in red, with a gleaming white ten-gallon hat. Tom Mix made more than eighty films for Fox over eleven years. He moved here from the Selig Studio, but made his films at the twelve-acre Winna Brown Ranch in Edendale (known as "Mixville") until 1925, when he consolidated everything at the "Mix Rancho" in West Los Angeles. This became Movietone City in 1928 when his contract expired.

Besides Mix's surviving films, his greatest legacy was bringing along future Hollywood Western stars. In the early 1920s he hired George O'Brien as an assistant cameraman. O'Brien would do similar work for Buck Jones, Fox's other Western star, as well as stunt and bit work before winning the starring role in John Ford's epic, *The Iron Horse* (1925). Thereafter he reigned as a brawny hero of Fox films for more than a decade.

Marion Robert "Duke" Morrison also apprenticed here, forging what would become a legendary partnership with no less a mentor than John Ford, when Mix gave him summer employment in order to get box seats for the 1926–1927 season of the University of Southern California's football team. Earning his first screen credit in *Words and Music* (1929), the "Duke" was spotted by Raoul Walsh while working in the property department on this lot. Walsh then cast him to star in *The Big Trail* (1930) as John Wayne—a name Walsh claims to have come up with—over at Movietone City. Of the lot's transition from silent to sound filmmaking, Fox star Madge Bellamy observed: "There was panic, bedlam and enthusiasm." In 1916 Earl Sponable had joined Theodore Case in the development of Movietone sound motion pictures. As part of that effort, a $500,000 "sound laboratory" of Spanish Colonial Revival design was dedicated here on June 29, 1928, as part of the latest studio retrofit. Sponable later became head of the studio's research and development unit, the wellspring of technological innovation at the company for many years.

Grand spectacle has always been part of the Hollywood landscape as evidenced by this enormous set built for *Queen of Sheba* (1921). Constructed on the northern end of the East Lot, Sunset Boulevard is just on the other side of the two-story structure on the left.

The retrofit included a lab for the pioneering Fox Nature Color film in partnership with Eastman Kodak, which became another victim of the studio's financially unstable times. The ten stages of the silent-film days (two of glass, two of wood, and six open-air) made way for soundstages. Stage Three, known as the largest in the world at 300 by 190 feet, incorporated a three-story building housing eighty-eight dressing rooms. Stages One and Two were rebuilt to equal its size. Stage Two contained the primary and largest theater set used for

ABOVE LEFT: Theda Bara was Fox's biggest star in its first decade. Here she appears in *Cleopatra* (1918), her first film made at the Western Avenue studio.

LEFT: Dancers practice their routine for *Queen of Sheba* (1921).

RIGHT: Looking north along Western Avenue to the Hollywood Hills, the William Fox sign and the huge stages of the East Lot are clearly visible, mid-1920s.

BELOW RIGHT: A very early view looking south down Western Avenue when Hollywood still had orchards, circa 1921. The house where the book that became *The Birth of a Nation* (1915) was written can be seen on the West Lot.

Aerial view looking east of the East and West Lots (Sunset Boulevard runs from top to bottom at left; Western Avenue runs from left to right), circa early 1920s. Note the abundance of sets built on the East Lot.

decades for musicals and theatrical presentations, while Stage Five housed the ship dock used over the years for many of those farewell and reunion scenes. The Grandeur Room, specially built to screen Grandeur films, was used for more sound-stage space.

Until the dawn of Movietone, the West and East lots had distinct personalities. Abraham Carlos and then Sol Wurtzel were in charge of the entire operation, but the East lot was initially run independently by Henry "Pathe" Lehrman, who produced the two-reel Sunshine Comedies. George Marshall, who supervised the similar Imperial comedies, subsequently ran the comedy division. Their popularity peaked—fifty-two produced a year—in 1927, before the shorts division was shut down in 1929 with the arrival of sound.

The lot included a backlot with a cyclorama and sky backing, the studio water tower (emblazoned with "William Fox Studio"), and the production and casting building. Sol Wurtzel's bungalow was nearby, presided over by his secretary, Anna Snyder. His first bungalow would move to Movietone City and become the production bungalow. The second would find its way to Fox Hills's Suburban Street. Stage Four incorporated the test department, where all film tests were done. The makeup department was incorporated into Stage Five. Along the north side was the plaster shop, and in the northwest corner was the scenic department building, with a large skylight for painting backings, portraits, and all special-effects work, such as matte and glass shots. Trick photography had its own department

Visitors entered the more-impressive West Lot through a reception building that ran along Western Avenue between De Longpre Avenue and Sunset Boulevard. Beyond the entrance of hand-tooled art stone, over which hung the studio's electric sign, was a lobby and information desk. It was built in 1926—a big year for studio expansion, with the addition of a still portrait studio, wardrobe building, a schoolhouse with resident teacher Z. A. Ferrell, and an administration building. The latter, a sixty-room Spanish-styled structure, housed the business manager, screenwriters, and directors on the first floor, with the art department, technical staff, and research library located on the second

F.W. Murnau created his masterpiece *Sunrise* (1927) within the soundstages of the Western Avenue studio lot.

floor. It replaced Thomas Dixon's thirty-seven-year-old Victorian farmhouse, built by early Hollywood settler W. C. Frye.

The old home had been used as a boarding-house and later, offices, including Sol Wurtzel's on the lower floor. Besides a small backlot of outdoor sets running east and west, this lot also contained the sheet-metal works, the arsenal and effects department, the test and film stock library, a large wardrobe building, two film vaults, and the services of police chief Captain Tod F. McAdam, fire chief Harry Seigal, and Dr. F. A. Skaletar.

The film lab at the south end of the lot could handle a million feet of film each week, and much of the studio's process work. Release prints were then sent out to theaters from the adjacent shipping

room. This studio also pioneered color stills for publicity, and the lab was the first to duplicate color transparencies in quantity. Mrs. Eve Fox herself purchased furniture and art objects to begin the company's "prop shop."

"The Munchers" commissary, where "Fox stars munch their lunch . . . amidst artistic surroundings" near Stage Eight, was managed by William Barnes, and was indeed decorated with studio artwork by its artists. Looking after it all was chief watchman Joseph Collingwood.

That the studio had lost prestige as the primary center of filmmaking activity—a transition that began when Movietone City opened and talent like Janet Gaynor went over there—became evident when it was nearly abandoned twice. In those heady early months of 1929, when William Fox acquired Loews Inc., he had planned to shut this studio down and move everything to the MGM lot. The dissolution of his empire precluded that, but then Harley L. Clarke proposed saving money by consolidating the Western Avenue Studio and

Movietone City by January 1, 1931. Everything was shut down except the film lab, which was taken over in March of 1932 by Deluxe Laboratories.

The lot reopened in May of 1933, and its survival was ensured when Sidney Kent placed Sol Wurtzel, who had been enjoying the freedom of making films on both lots, back in charge. Although he still had ambitious plans—producing three Will Rogers films and *Dante's Inferno* (1935) here—Wurtzel's lot evolved into the company's "B" unit, with the formation of Twentieth Century Fox. He made it among the best in town, initiating the very first Fox franchises with the well-made Charlie Chan, Mr. Moto, Jones family, Cisco Kid, Michael Shayne, and Laurel and Hardy films.

Then there was Jane Withers. Always proud to be queen of the "B" pictures made here, her fans ranged from FDR to Gandhi. She also contributed to Wurtzel's famed production efficiency—reaching a high point when ten pages of script that usually took a day and a half were shot in one five-minute take for *The Girl from Avenue A* (1940), with

ABOVE LEFT: This attractive building, built in the mid-1920s on the East Lot, housed the wardrobe and drapery departments. The signs on either side of the main door say "General Wardrobe" and "Studio Modiste."

ABOVE RIGHT: A multitude of plaster props created at the Western Avenue studio, 1920s.

her handpicked production unit—and encouraged future stars like the young dancer who debuted in *Charlie Chan in Egypt* (1935), who became Rita Hayworth.

Wurtzel moved into independent production in 1944—replaced by Bryan Foy of vaudeville's famous "Seven Little Foys"—releasing eighteen films through Fox. By the 1940s there were at least twenty Wurtzels making contributions throughout the company. Sol's nephew Paul would be the last to retire, from the special effects department, in February of 1984.

Darryl Zanuck's edict, on December 31, 1944—that the company would make only "A" pictures—effectively ended the golden era of "B" picture–making here. After that it was known only as an adjunct to the Westwood lot.

Spyros Skouras and Darryl Zanuck were as excited about their bold foray into the world of wide-screen as they were antagonistic toward the rival technology of television that had brought it about. Stage Two was renovated to serve the crucial purpose of introducing CinemaScope, with its forty-five-foot-wide screen and new stereo rerecording room, first to Fox's producers and writers in March of 1953, and then to other studios, the press, and exhibitors from all over the world. But it was television that kept this studio running. *My Blue Heaven* (1950) provides a fascinating look at

these changing times. Betty Grable and Dan Dailey play radio performers in the "broadcast studio" on Stages Two and Three who transition to television. The couple presaged later TV families like *Father Knows Best* (whose stars Jane Wyatt and Elinor Donahue are in this film). The movie also pokes fun at TV ads, with one for "Cosmo Cosmetics," performed by nineteen-year-old Mitzi Gaynor in her film debut on Stage Two. Fox's "Golden Girl" was another to credit Jane Withers as an inspiration. The film contains a parody of Rodgers and Hammerstein 1949 Broadway hit *South Pacific* starring Mary Martin. Gaynor reprised Martin's role on film in 1958—not only making the role her own, but making it an extraordinary capstone to an extraordinary career at the studio.

My Blue Heaven also addressed the Baby Boom and the burgeoning of suburbia as causes for the drop in attendance at movie theaters, which led studio manager Harold Lewis to convert and partition three of his stages on the East lot into nine for Twentieth Century Fox Television (TCF-TV) production by September of 1955. The little backlot on the West side was refurbished as the Western town for the first two shows put into production: *My Friend Flicka* (1956–58), and the first episode for *The 20th Century-Fox Hour* (1955–57), "The Ox Bow Incident." This series, produced on both lots and hosted by General Electric on CBS, continued to present teleplays of the studio's classic films, with *Cavalcade* the appropriate first televised installment.

RIGHT: The interiors for the 1953 version of *Titanic* were built on Stage One, including the grand dining room. Here from left to right are Clifton Webb, Robert Wagner, Frances Bergen, Brian Aherne, and Barbara Stanwyck.

FAR RIGHT: Stage One provided the setting for the Sarah Siddons Society annual banquet where Eve Harrington (Anne Baxter) received the theater world's most prestigious award and where we start learning *All About Eve* (1950).

BOTTOM LEFT: Expensive sets built for A-list movies like *Titanic* (1953) were often used again to save money on future productions. Such was the case for *Dangerous Crossing* (1953) which used the dining room and grand staircase but updated them to look like an elegant 1950s liner for this thriller starring Jeanne Crain.

BOTTOM RIGHT: Gene Tierney as Laura Hunt and Clifton Web as Waldo Lydecker perform on the set of Waldo's apartment on Stage One for *Laura* (1944).

"Back then working in television was always touted as being a hindrance to your career," recalled Audrey Dalton who appeared in *The 20th Century-Fox Hour,* "only a small step above doing commercials. The premise being that if you did either you'd never be cast in motion pictures. But the fact that Twentieth Century Fox was producing added some luster. It was sold to me by my agent that this was the beginning of a new era. The pace was definitely faster, and there was an eagerness to prove that good filmmaking was possible under a tighter schedule. An atmosphere of pioneering something new prevailed. And everyone worked together to make it happen. Everyone on the set was a hero if only one take was needed. How quickly that standard became routine in the business!"

More television shows followed on both lots. As the popularity of Erle Stanley Gardner's *Perry Mason* (1957–66) grew to extraordinary heights, it moved from here to the Westwood lot, and then to Charlie Chaplin's old studio on La Brea Avenue in 1959. By then Fox was producing its first original hit series, *James A. Michener's Adventures in Paradise* (1959–62). Despite the success, Buddy Adler was forced to lease the lot to Four Star Television, moving TCF-TV to Westwood in 1959. *The Many*

ABOVE LEFT: This is the permanent theater set on Stage Two. Here Tyrone Power and Alice Faye are on stage for the finale of *Alexander's Ragtime Band* (1938).

ABOVE RIGHT: Setting up for the elaborate production number "The Sheik of Araby" in *Tin Pan Alley* (1940) on Stage Two.

RIGHT: Rex Harrison as Sir Alfred de Carter conducts an orchestra in Preston Sturges' black comedy *Unfaithfully Yours* (1948). This scene provides a great view of the auditorium with its balconies.

BELOW RIGHT: *Footlight Serenade* (1942) was almost completely shot on Stage Two and, hence, offers a great view of the stage set. Here Betty Grable (second from right on stairs) receives instructions in the wings of the backstage. Co-star Carole Landis stands next to Betty.

Loves of Dobie Gillis (1959–63) featured Darryl Hickman's (*Leave Her to Heaven*, 1945) younger brother Dwayne as Dobie Gillis, with up-and-comer Tuesday Weld. There was *The Green Hornet* (starring Van Williams and Bruce Lee, 1966–67), *Felony Squad* (1966–69), *The Ghost and Mrs. Muir* (1968–70), *Bracken's World* (1969–70), and *Room 222* (1969–74). *Batman* (1966–68), shot on the stages here and using the Westwood lot for exteriors, had an extraordinary guest-star list, including many Fox vets. Everyone wanted to be on the show—even Frank Sinatra and Robert Kennedy.

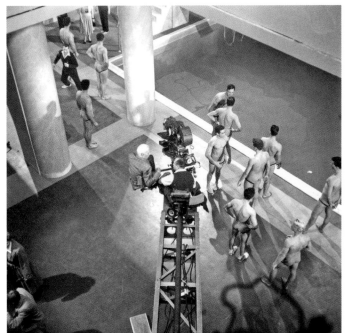

By 1966, TCF-TV had hit series on all three networks: *Peyton Place* (1964–69), *Batman* and *Voyage to the Bottom of the Sea* (1964–68) on ABC, *Lost in Space* (1965–68) set in the faraway year of 1997 on CBS, and *Daniel Boone* (1964–70), the last production shot here, on NBC.

In May of 1971 Lewis N. Wolff, head of the company's realty development, negotiated to lease the property as a cost-cutting measure. Deluxe Laboratories remained at the back of the property, reminding movie buffs of its storied past until it closed on May 9, 2014, a victim of another of Hollywood's transitions from film to digital technology. It seems the lot could only survive so many of them.

RIGHT: View of the West Lot along Western Avenue, late 1920s. The door with the flag above it was the entrance to the Publicity Department; the pitched roof belonged to Stage Five.

BELOW LEFT: Exterior of the Munchers restaurant, located on the northwest corner of the West Lot, which served as the studio commissary.

BELOW RIGHT: Original 1920s caption: "MUNCHER'S, WHERE FOX STARS MUNCH THEIR LUNCH". For ten years extras and stars on the Fox Hollywood lot have dined beneath paintings by James Montgomery Flagg, Henry Clive, Clarence Underwood, Arthur William Brown, William Darling, Leon Gordon, Tatsuo Itoh, at Muncher's, now owned by William Barnes."

FAR LEFT: View of the southwest corner of the intersection of Sunset Boulevard (running across the bottom of the photo) and Western Avenue. Note the "Fox News" sign.

LEFT: Original 1920s caption: "PROJECTION ROOM 1, at Fox Film's Hollywood studio . . . where Producers Sol M. Wurtzel and John Stone view rushes of Fox Hollyood productions." This small theater was located on the West Lot. Stage 8 can be seen behind it.

BOTTOM LEFT: The gate to the West Lot, late 1920s. The Administration building is on the right and Stage 5 is on the left.

BOTTOM RIGHT: View of the plaza on the West Lot looking north to the Hollywood Hills with the Administration Building to the right. Several of the small bungalows seen behind the fountain would eventually be moved to the Pico lot.

RIGHT: Charlie Chan (Warner Oland), at right, is up to something clever in *Charlie Chan's Chance* (1932).

FAR RIGHT: Charlie Chan (Warner Oland) and Son Number One (Keye Luke) are locked up in *Charlie Chan at Monte Carlo* (1938). Cinematographer Dan Clark is peering through the camera, and director Eugene Forde is at left.

BOTTOM RIGHT: The permanent dock set on Stage Five used in this case in *Charlie Chan's Murder Cruise* (1940).

BOTTOM LEFT: Strolling arm-in-arm on the East Lot by Stage One are, from left to right, Cesar Romero, Sally Blane, Pauline Moore, and Sidney Toler during the making of *Charlie Chan on Treasure Island* (1939).

FAR LEFT: Peter Lorre, who rose to stardom at Fox, was perfectly cast as the enigmatic world traveler and explorer Mr. Moto.

ABOVE: A behind-the-scenes shot from *Mr. Moto's Last Warning* (1939).

LEFT: Peter Lorre and Norman Foster (at right) welcome the author and creator of Mr. Moto, J.P. Marquand, to the set of *Mysterious Mr. Moto* (1938).

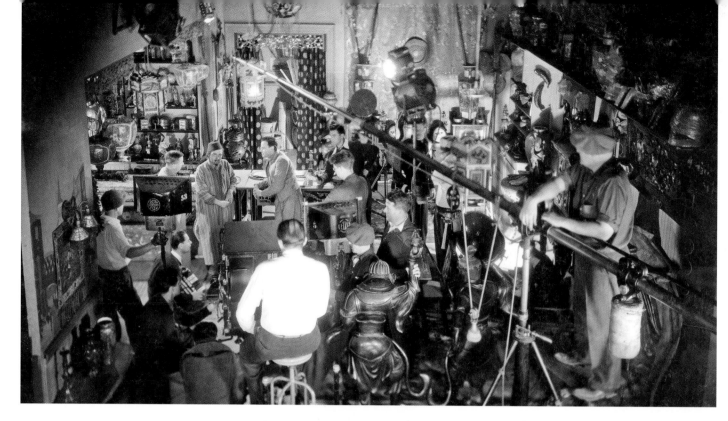

RIGHT: Peter Lorre as the Japanese supersleuth receiving direction from director Norman Foster (who is just right of Lorre) for *Think Fast, Mr. Moto* (1937).

BOTTOM LEFT: Original 1937 caption: "It's wedding day for the Jones family, on parade on the lot, for *Borrowing Trouble* (1937). Pictured are: [starting at left] Jed Prouty and Spring Byington (Mr. & Mrs. John Jones), Kenneth Howell (Jack Jones) and June Carlson (Lucy Jones), Russell Gleason (the groom) and Shirley Deane (the bride Bonnie Jones), together with George Ernest (Roger Jones) and Florence Roberts (Granny Jones)." This was taken on the East Lot in front of Stages One, Two, and Three.

BOTTOM RIGHT: The Jones family in *Big Business*, directed by Frank A. Strayer, who is seated beside the camera. The interior of the Jones home was on Stage Three.

FAR LEFT: Original 1935 caption: "EASTER DISGUISE—Jane Withers had to present her Fox Film pass when her favorite gateman, Jett Fore, pretended not to recognize her in the Easter rabbit get-up, en route to surprise Claire Trevor and Spencer Tracy, with whom she plays in Fox Film's *Dante's Inferno*. [Note that Jane Withers did not appear in *Dante's Inferno*.]"

LEFT: Rita Cansino (later Hayworth), Jane Withers, and director Lewis Seiler on the set of *Paddy O'Day* (1936).

BOTTOM LEFT: Original 1937 caption: "Jane Withers tries to cheer up Una Merkel and patch up her romance with Stuart Erwin in that classic of the turf, *Checkers* (1937), directed by H. Bruce "Lucky" Humberstone, seated beside the camera. He received that nickname on the lot for walking away from a serious car accident."

BOTTOM RIGHT: Jane Withers (right) walks and reads comics with her stand-in Gloria Fischer at the Western Avenue studio during the filming of *This is the Life* (1935).

TOP LEFT: Movie audiences got their first substantial look at Marilyn Monroe as a waitress in Sol Wurtzel's *Dangerous Years* (1947) made on this lot.

TOP RIGHT: The Hollywood community is invited to see a demonstration of CinemaScope.

BOTTOM LEFT: The dotted-line shows the dimensions of the standard movie screen compared to the grandeur of CinemaScope. Only the largest theaters in the biggest cities would be outfitted like this one: most theaters did not have a curved screen or a stereo speaker system. The "Marvel You See Without Glasses" was a direct jab at the 3-D process championed by Warner Bros.

BOTTOM RIGHT: Dan Dailey, in costume for *What Price Glory* (1952), gets chummy with Marilyn Monroe on the East Lot between Stage 3 and 4.

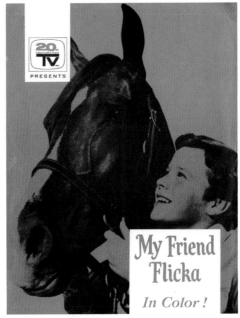

FAR LEFT: Mitzi Gaynor, in her film debut as Gloria Adams, performs a commercial for a fake product before a fake studio audience in *My Blue Heaven* (1950). The film took some satirical jabs at the encroaching influence of television on the film industry.

LEFT: Like other studios, Fox turned movie hits into television series including *How to Marry a Millionaire, 5 Fingers*, and *The Long Hot Summer*, among others. One of their most successful ventures was *My Friend Flicka* (1956). Thinking ahead the studio produced the series in color in an era of black-and-white.

BOTTOM RIGHT: Michael Wilding and Merle Oberon starred in the "Cavalcade" episode of *The 20th Century Fox Hour* (1955). Fox's first Best Picture Oscar winner was adapted into the studio's first TV series. This cast included Michael Wilding and Merle Oberon as the Marryotts who experience the tumultuous early years of the twentieth century.

TOP LEFT: View looking southeast of the East lot, 1960s.

TOP RIGHT: View of the façade on Western Avenue. With the construction of four new sound stages at the Westwood lot in 1966, television production was consolidated there, and the Western Avenue studio was slowly phased out. It was leased for development in May of 1971, closed on June 20, and torn down that summer.

MIDDLE: Bob Denver, Dwayne Hickman, and Tuesday Weld, at center, filming the episode "Greater Love Hath No Man" for one of Fox's most popular early TV shows *The Many Loves of Dobie Gillis* (1959-1963).

BOTTOM LEFT: Dwayne Hickman, at left, Tuesday Weld, and a young Warren Beatty receive instructions during the filming of the *Dobie Gillis* episode "Sweet Singer of Central High."

BOTTOM RIGHT: Bob Denver and Dwayne Hickman are filmed outdoors on the East Lot for the episode "The Big Question" for *Dobie Gillis* (1959-63).

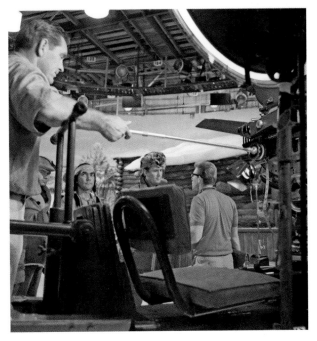

FAR LEFT: Before making it big in martial arts films of the 1970s, Bruce Lee was cast as Kato, a sidekick to the Green Hornet. Here he is demonstrating his martial arts abilities.

LEFT: The cast of *Daniel Boone* (1964-70) on set going over the script for "A Rope for Mingo."

BOTTOM LEFT: Wende Wagner and Van Williams prepare for a scene during the filming of *The Green Hornet* (1966-67) episode "Programmed for Death."

BOTTOM MIDDLE: Ed Ames as Taramingo and Fess Parker as Daniel Boone filming the episode "The Christmas Story."

BOTTOM RIGHT: On Western Avenue *Daniel Boone* star Ed Ames strikes a pose in front of the studio's sign.

RIGHT: Exterior of the Little Theater, 2015.

FAR RIGHT: Interior of the Little Theater, 2015.

BLDG. 2: THE LITTLE THEATER (1928) (PROJECTION ROOM 1)

The studio's 120-seat primary screening room has been used for everything from screenings for the press and special groups to the viewing of screen tests, "dailies," and preview trailers. There are too many examples of stars discovered and actors and roles matched in Fox screening rooms to list them here. To name a few, Tyrone Power acknowledged his debt to Alice Faye, who had coached and supported him in his rise to fame on the lot, by appearing in her test for *In Old Chicago* (1938), and Robert Wagner credited Helena Sorrell for convincing Darryl Zanuck to give his screen test a second look. Other actors, like Gene Tierney, considered this building a unique classroom where they could study films in the Fox library late into the night.

A producer like Richard Zanuck had so many special memories here that he asked the studio to name the theater after him, but it was decided there would be confusion with the Zanuck name on two theaters. Directors like George Stevens invited their casts to watch the dailies here each evening, as in the case of *The Diary of Anne Frank* (1959). Of course, it has also served as a movie set. Watch for its interior as a theater in *Dreamboat* (1952), *Vicki* (1953), and *The Three Faces of Eve* (1957). This is also the theater where Julie Andrews as Gertrude Lawrence watches a newsreel of her life produced by filmmaker Jerry Paul in *Star!* (1968). Assistant editor Bill Gordean recalled that whenever Mel Brooks completed a reel of *Young Frankenstein* (1973), he would gather up studio employees—not executives—to watch and truly judge his work here.

In 1989 Matt Groening had to retool *The Simpsons* ("the most agonizing week of my life") after a disastrous first screening to make his case to pull it away from *The Tracey Ullman Show*. Many of the creators had never worked in animation, including Groening himself, and it was considered a risky venture to bring animation back to prime-time television, where it had not flourished since the 1960s. There was consternation, too, when James Cameron pitched the $237 million-dollar gamble that was *Avatar* (2009). Jim Gianopulos recalled: "There was that moment when he first mentioned 10-foot blue people with tails..." Likewise the fate of *Life of Pi* (2012), already in preproduction in Taiwan—a location that had not been used for a major film since *The Sand Pebbles* (1966)—literally rested on Ang Lee's presentation of it here on the lot as the budget escalated.

These screening rooms are of course the domain of the projectionist, a position held by generations on the Fox lot. Some, like Don Berry,

did more than one job. Besides running all sorts of screenings, most often in the Darryl Zanuck Theatre, Berry would also be sent to executives' homes to run film, and because of his expertise, project rear screen on the soundstages of *The Love Boat, Charlie's Angels, The Fall Guy, M*A*S*H,* and *Dynasty.* His favorite memory? Having Marlon Brando come up into the booth and introduce himself.

Bldg. 3: The Research Library (1928)

Boy! Look at that library. I wonder if they have Superman *or* Dick Tracy?
—*Stan Laurel in* The Dancing Masters *(1943)*

If you have enjoyed *Desk Set* (1957), you have a good idea of what happened in here. The difference was, the Research Library—formed in 1923,

ABOVE: This was the bookplate used by the library for many years.

BOTTOM LEFT: The Research Library as it appeared in 1937 .

BOTTOM RIGHT: After a half century of collecting research materials, the Research Library was bursting at the seams in this small building in the late 1970s. The collection was relocated to the basement of Bldg. 89 where it has operated ever since. The building was converted to production offices and for many years hosted Glen A. Larson.

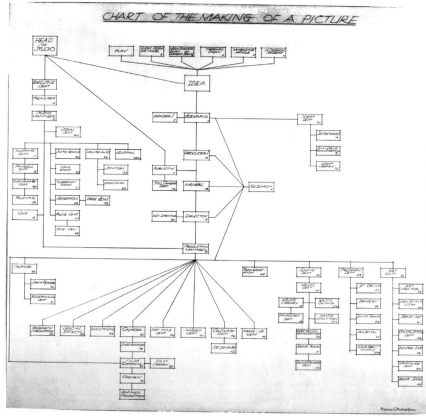

the second such facility created in Hollywood after Cecil B. De Mille's in 1916—was strictly for motion picture research for sets, costumes, and so forth. It began with the extensive library of retired English actor George Ingleton, who served as its first librarian, and resided on the second floor of the administration building at the Western Avenue Studio, across the hall from the art department.

Frances Cary Richardson, from the art and music department of the Los Angeles Public Library, took over the department in January of 1928. Under her direction the library grew from 5,000 volumes and half a million clippings to more than 40,000 books, 100 periodicals, and enough pictures and clippings to fill twenty-three four-drawer steel cabinets, representing every field of knowledge. Her staff included four researchers, a cataloger, and three assistants.

In December of 1931 they moved to this location. The librarian on Richardson's staff was Ruth Fox, who also handled all the incoming and outgoing items for research purposes, often delivered by studio

motorcycle. Among Richardson's most unique challenges when it came to living by her credo—"Just ask us anything!"—was for *Thanks for Everything* (1938), when the property man burst in with the director's last-minute request for a dog. Her own Scottie "Wendy" was promptly sent to the soundstage.

Richardson retired in 1970, and like many studio departments, the Research Library was threatened with closure—three times in this case. Fortunately, the library's rare materials (dating back to the 1700s) eventually moved to Bldg. 89 in 1980, where they continue to be accessed for films and television shows. This building has served as production offices ever since, most notably for television producer Glen A. Larson.

LEFT: Librarian Frances Richardson shows some of the research used for the production of *In Old Chicago* (1938).

BOTTOM LEFT: A librarian shows (L-R) Lee J. Cobb, Vincent Price, Charles Dingle, and Aubrey Mather the research binder prepared for the production design of *The Song of Bernadette* (1943). The library still retains these binders prepared for classic Fox films.

BOTTOM RIGHT: Director Otto Preminger goes over the research binders prepared for his film *Forever Amber* (1947) in his office in Building 88.

BELOW: Looking north down Avenue G (now Mel Brooks Boulevard) circa 1929.

Bldg. 4: Film Editorial (1928)

This building was used for the editing of foreign versions of Fox films. In the silent days movies could easily be played around the world, but the dawn of sound presented problems. Besides providing subtitles, Fox, like other studios, produced foreign-language versions of their films. Winfield Sheehan created a department, headed by John Stone, to bring Spanish, German, French, Italian, and Scandinavian talent to the lot to make them. Only the Spanish films were made from 1930 to 1935, with their contingent of actors, writers, and directors set up in "Latin Quarters" here on the lot.

By the 1950s, the international department was responsible for shipping completed films that were edited and rerecorded with sound effects and music tracks to foreign offices, along with a script in the appropriate language ready for lip-sync dubbing. This required writers like Fred Zinnemann—who produced dialogue for the German version of *The Big Trail* (1930), and later became the acclaimed director of *A Hatful of Rain* (1957) and *Julia* (1977)—to create foreign-language scripts. Musicals generally were not popular overseas, and frequently their songs were cut except of course in the case of *The Sound of Music* (1965) which was the first Fox musical to have its songs dubbed into different languages—thirty in all.

Bldg. 5: Projection Rooms 2 and 3 (1928), and Bldg. 6: Music Vault (1928)

[We] find on our right a battery of projection rooms, where the daily 'rushes' are shown night and morning for inspection of the progress of films in the making. The word was derived from the marking of this newly made film 'rush,' for development and printing and showing."

—1933 studio tour

Besides housing the original studio projection rooms 2 and 3, this building also contained offices for the music department, including arranging, and the acting or talent school.

ABOVE: Maureen O'Hara and John Payne in costume for *To the Shores of Tripoli* (1942) walk down Avenue G which stood in for a Marine base for that film.

FAR LEFT: Façade of Building 4 in 2015.

LEFT: Façade of Building 5 in 2015.

ABOVE: The most elegant building on the lot, the Hall of Music glistens after a rain storm in 2015.

RIGHT: The courtyard as it appeared in the 1930s. The fountain statue is the "Muse of Music" sculpted by Mahonri Young.

FAR RIGHT: Looking out from the courtyard in the 1930s.

BLDG. 52: THE HALL OF MUSIC (1929)

Along with most of the buildings on Movietone City's original main street, including the first stars' dressing rooms (Bldg. 54), William H. Werner also designed this one, complete with a Greco-Roman courtyard. Winfield Sheehan commissioned renowned sculptor Mahonri Young (grandson of Brigham Young) to adorn it with both medallions, which are still there, depicting, from left to right, profiles of Grieg, Mozart, Sullivan, Debussy, Tchaikovsky, Liszt, Beethoven, and Verdi, and a marble statue to the spirit of harmony and a bronze bust of Victor Herbert, which are not. In all, Young created nineteen pieces for the Fox studio during the summer of 1929, including a life-size bronze statue for *Seven Faces* (1929) that later graced Madison Square Garden.

Young also created the rooster bas-relief for the facade of the Café de Paris. Although the courtyard originally contained a fountain, also created

RIGHT: The large rehearsal hall on the south end of the building was actually used in this scene with Oliver Hardy from *The Dancing Masters* (1943).

MIDDLE RIGHT: The Hall of Music was also home to the Printing Department for many years.

BOTTOM RIGHT: The Hall of Music once housed the Mail Department. This is just a sampling of the thousands of fan letters sent to the studio on behalf of the movie stars pictured above in 1938.

by Young, known as the "Muse of Music," its current replacement was purchased for *Hello, Dolly!* (1969) as a model for the two larger ones made for the film.

After dedication day (September 22, 1929), the building was used to store music scores and act as a rehearsal hall (most memorably in Laurel and Hardy's *The Dancing Masters,* 1943), with separate sides for men and women.

Buddy Ebsen never forgot the lesson in professionalism he received here from Shirley Temple during rehearsals for *Captain January* (1937). She arrived in a limousine with an assistant director and carefully watched Ebsen and choreographer Jack Donohue's performance. She asked if it were all completely worked out. When Ebsen admitted it was not, she climbed back into the limousine, saying she would be back when they were ready.

Betty Grable admitted that musicals were the hardest movies to make, and always gave a lot of credit to the choreographer. Fox certainly had many of the best. When cinematographer Peverell Marley stepped in to teach Linda Darnell the dance steps for *The Gang's All Here* (1943), the couple fell in love. After she sprained her ankle during those rehearsals, they eloped, and Sheila Ryan replaced her in the film.

The unique design of the building—like many others on the lot—allowed it to be dual-purposed

for both functional usage and as a movie set. It is a nightclub in *To the Shores of Tripoli* (1942), the Pasadena Playhouse in *Beloved Infidel* (1959), and the Monterey Inn, where James Garner checks in two wives, Doris Day and Polly Bergen, in *Move Over, Darling* (1963). It can also be seen as the funeral home in *Hush . . . Hush, Sweet Charlotte* (1964), and was used for a variety of sets in television shows, including *Room 222, Hart to Hart,* and *The Fall Guy.*

Since the 1950s the building has variously housed the script department, print shop, copy center, and mailroom, as well as production offices. Today Twentieth Century Fox Animation is located here.

FAR LEFT: Occasionally used as a film set, the Hall of Music doubled for the Pasadena Playhouse in *Beloved Infidel* (1959) with Gregory Peck and Deborah Kerr playing F. Scott Fitzgerald and Sheilah Graham.

LEFT: The Hall of Music became the Monterey Inn in *Move Over, Darling* (1963). It also appeared as the mortuary in *Hush. . . Hush, Sweet Charlotte* (1964).

LOWER LEFT: The original fountain with the "Muse of Music" disappeared prior to the mid-1960s but was eventually replaced by a fountain created for the film *Hello, Dolly!* (1969) which was still present in 2015.

Director/Writer Bungalows

At the crossroads of Mel Brooks Boulevard and Fourth Street, and spread the length of the Boulevard, are bungalows from the Western Avenue Studio that were used in the early days by directors and writers. For example Bldg. 75 housed director Frank Lloyd and later George White (yes, it was known as the "White House"). When Howard Hawks brought William Faulkner to the lot for *The Road to Glory* (1936), the writer told Darryl Zanuck that he could not work in his assigned bungalow, and wanted to work at home. Assuming he had a rented place in Beverly Hills, Zanuck agreed. Imagine his surprise when Faulkner went back to Oxford, Mississippi.

Bldg. 203: New Writers' Building (1925)

William Fox believed in "motion picture parks, not motion picture lots," and recent restoration and landscaping efforts reveal the beauty of that original design. However, all that remains of the paved-over Tennessee Park is the fountain in front of this building, now filled with koi fish. Moved here from the Western Avenue Studio in 1937, a second floor was added in the 1950s for more offices for directors and, of course, screenwriters. Richard Zanuck went from college to an office here representing DFZ Productions during his father's independent filmmaking years, headquartered on the Rue la Boétie in Paris. Look for the building in many films and television shows, including *To the Shores of Tripoli* (1942), as the Dixie Motel in *The Three Faces of Eve* (1957), and in *Perry Mason* and *Charlie's Angels*.

ABOVE LEFT: The building in 2007. The large fountain hosts a koi pond.

ABOVE RIGHT: An aerial view circa 1929 of Tennessee Park.

LEFT: Original 1931 caption: "'These women drivers!' mutters Alfred Santell as Janet Gaynor tries out the speed possibilities of Santell's electric 'scooter' at the Fox Films studio. Santell is directing 'Daddy Long Legs' in which Miss Gaynor and Warner Baxter are co-starred." They are driving past Tennessee Park with its fountain.

RIGHT: Jean Harlow and Warren Hymer in a scene from *Goldie* (1931).

FAR RIGHT: Ernest Lehman stands in front of the fountain. Lehman penned the scripts for three of the most famous Fox musicals: *The King and I* (1956), *The Sound of Music* (1965), and *Hello, Dolly!* (1969).

BOTTOM LEFT: The New Writers' Building originally was only one story high before the second story was added in the early 1950s.

BOTTOM RIGHT: As the Dixie Motel in *The Three Faces of Eve* (1957) where Eve (Joanne Woodward) is slowly sauntering in.

959-x-89

Bldg. 54: Dressing Rooms A (1929)

William Fox also said, "A comfortable player is a productive player," and these dressing rooms are proof of a more-gracious era of Hollywood film-making. Now occupied by Twentieth Century Fox TV Production Accounting, they are an appropriate spot to consider the constellation of Fox stars (circa 1927–35) for which they were designed.

Besides the aforementioned ones, there were Lois Moran, Earle Fox, J. Farrell MacDonald, Dolores Del Rio, Alma Rubens, Olive Borden, Rex Bell, and Caryl Lincoln. Jane Alice Peters became

Carol Lombard while under contract in 1925–1927. Carol added the "e" to her name in 1930, and rose to fame elsewhere. Harlean Carpenter got started at Fox in 1928, and was on the rise as Jean Harlow by the time she made her last film here (*Goldie* in 1931). Marilyn Monroe so admired the star's career that she later attempted to produce a film about her. Spencer Tracy and Humphrey Bogart made their film debuts on the lot in John Ford's *Up the River* (1930), and Tracy went on to make twenty films under contract that decade. Neither remembers that difficult period—after William Fox

departed and before Darryl Zanuck arrived—fondly. Fellow contract player Claire Luce remembered they all made bets as to who would break their contract first.

Although Winfield Sheehan failed to reignite the stardom of Clara Bow when he brought her to the lot in the early 1930s, his production of *Call Her Savage* (1932) remains a quintessential Fox Pre-Code melodrama. Equally melodramatic is the mysterious death of Bow's co-star Thelma Todd three years later. The actress was having an affair with on-the-rocks former Fox director Roland West who was married to former Fox siren Jewel Carmen. All three managed Thelma Todd's Sidewalk Café in Pacific Palisades. Todd's body was found in her car in Carmen's garage near the eatery, a supposed victim of carbon monoxide poisoning. The restaurant's unsavory underworld clientele and West himself remain suspects in what many still consider an unsolved murder case.

Star sisters Constance and Joan Bennett

and Claire Trevor weathered the period better than most. Constance starred in the big 1930 hit *Common Clay,* and Joan came back in the early 1940s. Trevor—who made her film debut in *Life in the Raw* (1933), and costarred with one of the media events of the decade, the Dionne Quintuplets, in the last of their three films for Fox, *Five of a Kind* (1938)—enjoyed a long career through the Zanuck era, all the way to a *Love Boat* episode in 1983.

Intriguingly, Sidney Kent sought to sign Charlie Chaplin's ex-wife Lita Grey Chaplin and her two sons. The ex-husband would have none of it. Then Kent hired Broadway stage director Edward Curtis to form the Fox Film Stock Company, to hire and train new Fox stars. Of this group only Lynn Bari made it. The bottom floor's six suites, for prestigious stars with sitting room, bedroom, and bath, remain intact today. Lesser stars were housed in the twelve single rooms above, with their own bathroom. In later years the *M*A*S*H* TV stars were housed here.

Madge Bellamy

Claire Trevor

Edmund Lowe

George O'Brien

Constance Bennett

Lois Moran

Mary Duncan

John Boles

Marguerite Churchill

Myrna Loy

James Dunn & Sally Eilers

Alan Dinehart

J. Farrell MacDonald

Paul Muni

Joan Bennett

Warner Baxter

Elissa Landi

Earle Fox

Dolores del Rio

Victor McLaglen

BLDG. 38: MAKEUP AND HAIRDRESS-ING DEPT./DRESSING ROOMS B (1929)

The eyebrows are too low and too thick. We'll have to raise them. Give her some eyelashes and shadow. I think we better raise her cheek-bones. She looks too well-fed. Can you do anything with her nose? There is nothing to work on . . .

—Second Fiddle *(1939)*

What more appropriate spot to bring up this delightful send-up of Hollywood than the birth-place of so much of that famed Twentieth Century Fox glamour? Although used for dressing rooms for lesser stars—the second floor locker room for chorus boys and male extras was at the east end while the women's locker room was at the west end—this building's fame rests upon its use as the studio's makeup and hairdressing department during Hollywood's Golden Age. There was even a makeup lab at the southwest corner. Whether it was here or, then as now, in a honeywagon or on a soundstage, this is where an actor's day begins.

Fox's female stars showed up at five o'clock in the morning to have their hair set, done, and dressed; body and face makeup was carefully applied, and then wardrobe. Men could hit the bar-bershop run by Sam Silver at the northeast corner before makeup and wardrobe. You were expected to be on the set with your lines learned by eight-thirty or nine o'clock.

Although Alice Faye launched the studio's tradition of the glamorous Fox blonde, the depart-ment's greatest achievement was helping to create Twentieth Century Fox's most popular male star.

After Darryl Zanuck saw Tyrone Edmund Power Jr.'s screen test ("He looks like a frightened monkey!") in 1936, the latest discovery of Fox scout Joe Pincus was sent here to makeup man Ray Sebastian, who did the trick with his eye-brow plucker. Ernie Westmore headed the makeup department then.

By the 1940s, when Guy Pearce was in charge, it was Gene Tierney who owed a debt to this department. She remembered that it was her hairdresser, Marie Walters, who encouraged her to stick with *Laura* (1944) through its troubled produc-tion. Another trusted associate of Tierney's was makeup artist Allan Snyder, popularly known as "Whitey," who supervised the cosmetics for Alice Faye, Betty Grable, Linda Darnell, and Marilyn Monroe, among others.

Although Loretta Young reveled in the process of makeup and wardrobe, saying she never grew out of the enjoyment of "dress-up," Betty Grable never got used to getting up "at this unearthly hour." Dorothy McGuire simply avoided the department after they rec-ommended that she shave her eyebrows. Ethel Merman

View of Building 38 looking west in the early 1930s. The large ocean liner set built for *So This is London* (1930) rises in the background on the future site of Building 88.

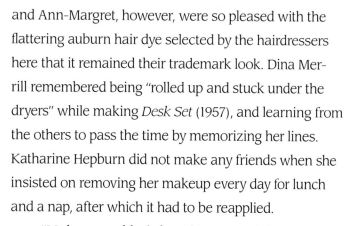

and Ann-Margret, however, were so pleased with the flattering auburn hair dye selected by the hairdressers here that it remained their trademark look. Dina Merrill remembered being "rolled up and stuck under the dryers" while making *Desk Set* (1957), and learning from the others to pass the time by memorizing her lines. Katharine Hepburn did not make any friends when she insisted on removing her makeup every day for lunch and a nap, after which it had to be reapplied.

"Makeup and hairdressing were right next to each other," recalled Audrey Dalton. "One just walked from one to the other, and unlike the hairdressing, the makeup was done in small individual rooms with a barbershop-type chair in front of a large bulb-lighted mirror (just like in the movies!). Big stars like my costar in *My Cousin Rachel,* Olivia de Havilland, would also have their hairdressing done privately in rooms like these. Minor players—but those ranked above small part actors and extras—all had their hair done in a large well-lighted room with maybe ten or twelve 'stations.' Depending on what time of the morning you were there, you might run into June Haver, Debra Paget, Terry Moore, or even once, as she wafted by, Marilyn Monroe. I never spoke to her, but the buzz in the room was very apparent."

Ben Nye Sr. headed the department from 1944 to 1967. He began his career as a copier of sheet music in the music building in 1932. Three years later he left to become a makeup apprentice for David O. Selznick's studio. Returning to the lot in 1937, he began crafting his now-legendary movie magic in this building, working on more than five hundred films. His art included transforming Al (David) Hedison into *The Fly* (1958). Costar Patricia Owens said she was never afraid of insects after that; she only saw them as Hedison in a new role.

Another groundbreaking milestone came in late 1965 when Richard Zanuck approved a makeup

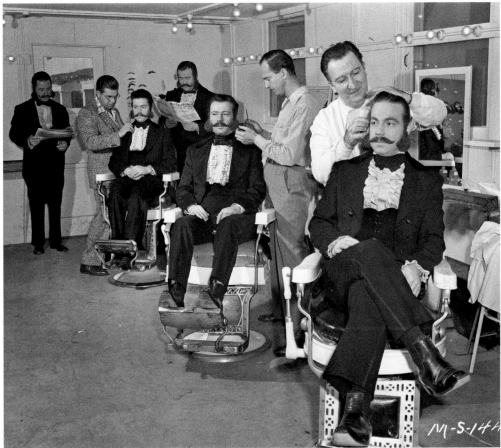

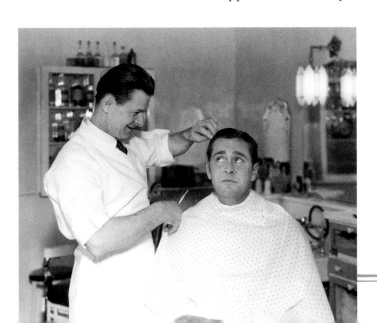

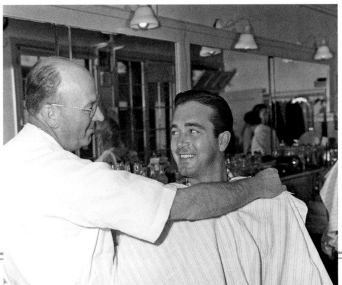

ABOVE: Extras get expertly groomed facial hair for a period piece, 1950.

FAR LEFT: James Dunn, apparently still afraid of scissors, sits for a haircut in the barber shop in the mid-1930s.

LEFT: John Payne gets a trim in the barber shop in 1944.

RIGHT: Original 1933 caption: "THE MAKEUP CAR is Hollywood's latest convenience for stars on location. It is an innovation introduced by the Fox studios. Joan Blondell is shown looking out of the car just after she finished making up for a scene of *Broadway Bad* [1933]. Far from being just a luxury, the makeup car is a great efficiency aid, Fox executives declare. Stars spend far less time making up and do better jobs of it."

FAR RIGHT: Director Joshua Logan contemplates how short they should cut Mitzi Gaynor's hair for her role in *South Pacific* (1958) during this media event on January 27, 1958.

BOTTOM: Jeanne Crain gets her hair set in the salon with the help of her son, 1950.

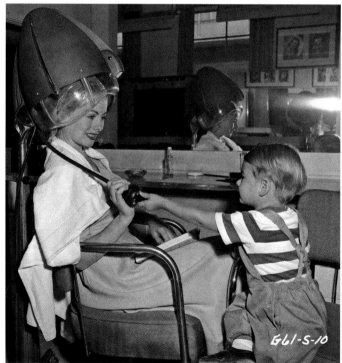

test to see whether Pierre Boulle's *La Planète des Singes (Planet of the Apes,* 1968) could be adapted for the screen. John Chambers recalled getting the call from Ben Nye to do the makeup and being so unimpressed with the title of the project that he only did it because Nye was his friend. Although successful, it was not until another sci-fi effort, *Fantastic Voyage,* became a hit that Richard Zanuck gave the green light. Chambers received an honorary Academy Award from Walter Matthau and a real live tuxedoed chimp for his achievement that continues to inspire.

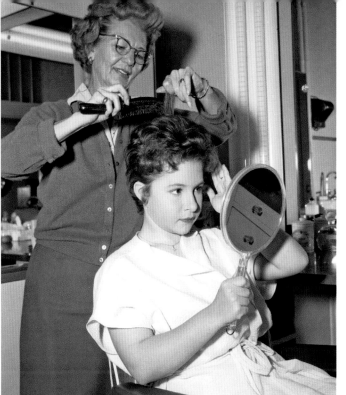

FAR LEFT: Joanne Woodward gets an elegant coiffure for her role in *From the Terrace* (1960).

LEFT: Helen Turpin prepares pop singer Brenda Lee for her film debut in *Two Little Bears* (1961). Between 1954 and 1965, Helen supervised the hairstyling for 129 Fox films.

BOTTOM LEFT: Ann-Margret, making her film debut in *State Fair* (1962), holds a placard indicating the scene when she would wear this hairstyle.

BOTTOM RIGHT: Ann-Margret was transformed from brunette to titian-red for her role in *State Fair* in the salon in Building 38. She liked the color so much she retained it for her entire career. This portrait was taken for *Stagecoach* (1966).

RIGHT: Ape hair can be so difficult! Studio stylists try to figure out appropriate hairstyles in the salon for *Planet of the Apes* (1968).

BELOW: For large productions with casts of hundreds, the hair and makeup departments would do a large set up on a soundstage such as this one for *Forever Amber* (1947).

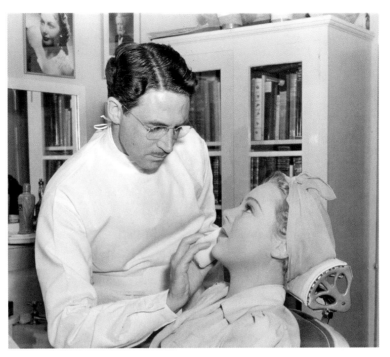

FAR LEFT: Linda Darnell's exquisite face gets touched up, early 1940s.

LEFT: Sonja Henie gets her makeup done for *Everything Happens at Night* (1939).

BOTTOM LEFT: In the most luxurious trailer we've ever seen, Buddy Westmore, one of the famed Westmore brothers who made their way into almost every Hollywood studio, makes up Binnie Barnes for *Frontier Marshal* (1939).

Despite its glamorous past, the building imitated a military base in *To The Shores of Tripoli* (1942), and currently has a statue of Napoleon Dynamite in front of it, complete with a tetherball stand. Dedicated on June 9, 2014, the statue is located at the southeast corner and commemorates the twentieth anniversary of Fox Searchlight Pictures, now housed here, and its most financially successful film. John Davis of Davis Entertainment also has his office here.

RIGHT: Plaster casts of actors faces were made so that the makeup artists could design and practice applying makeup, late 1930s.

FAR RIGHT: Rex Harrison is made up for *Anna and the King of Siam* (1948).

BOTTOM LEFT: Even in the makeup chair, Pat Boone wears his signature white buckskin shoes during the making of *Bernardine* (1957).

BOTTOM RIGHT: Charlton Heston arrived early in the morning to begin the transformation into Andrew Jackson for his role in *The President's Lady* (1953).

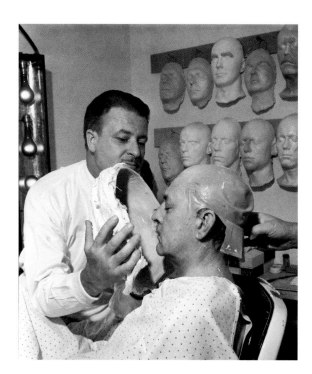

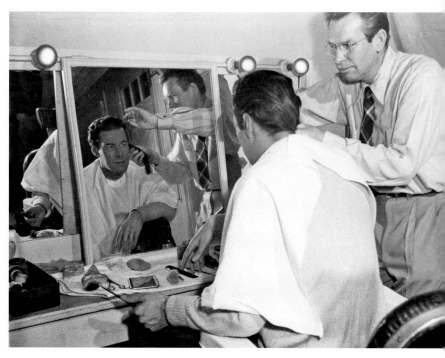

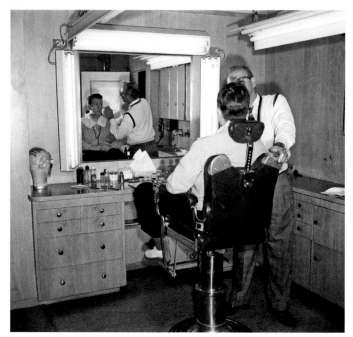

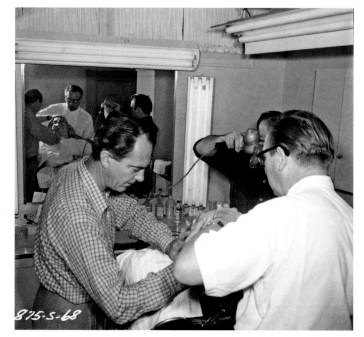

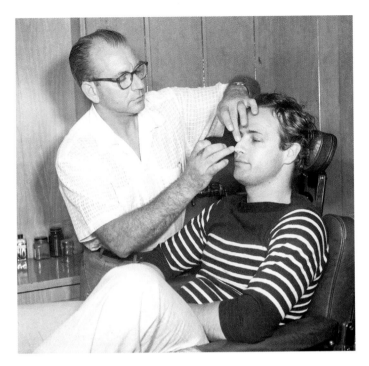

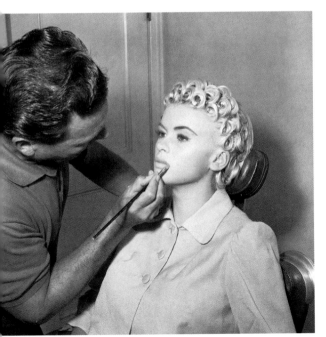

FAR LEFT: Marlon Brando getting a new nose for his role as Napoleon Bonaparte in *Désirée* (1954).

LEFT: Famed makeup man Ben Nye worked at Fox from 1937 until 1968 garnering over 400 film credits to his name.

BOTTOM LEFT: Jayne Mansfield is prepared for *The Girl Can't Help It* (1956).

BOTTOM RIGHT: The offices for Fox Searchlight now occupy the building and in honor of their most financially-successful film, *Napoleon Dynamite* (2004), this statue of the titular character was erected complete with a tether ball. Cast members from the film were present for the dedication. From left to right: Haylie Duff, Shondrella Avery, Carmen Brandy, Diedrich Bader, Jon Heder, Sandy Martin, Jared Hess, Tina Majorino, Efren Ramirez.

TOP: Weir Building.

ABOVE: Colonel Jason Joy.

Bldg. 214: The Weir Building (1928)

This building with the mysterious name, originally built as directors' offices at the Western Avenue studio, was moved here in 1935. It has housed the public relations office run by Colonel Jason S. Joy, the location department, and the studio mailroom.

Initially hired by Fox to run the story department in 1934, Joy later acted as the studio's intermediary for the Production Code with his experience as head of the Studio Relations Committee of the Motion Picture Producers and Distributors of America.

The mail and script department, which moved here from Bldg. 222 in the 1950s, was the birthplace of many a studio career. Seventeen-year-old Richard Jaeckel (*Guadalcanal Diary,* 1943) was one. Alan Buckhanse, a survivor of a Nazi concentration camp, directed many Little Theater presentations for the Studio Club on the lot before becoming a television director. William Jurgenson became the first cameraman on the *M*A*S*H* TV series, and Ronnie Browne became the first cameraman for the *Mission: Impossible* TV series.

Lee MacGregor graduated from Darryl Zanuck's personal mail boy to contract player in *Margie* (1946), *Scudda Hoo! Scudda Hay!* (1948), and *Twelve O'Clock High* (1949). Allan Balter wrote more than twenty scripts for Irwin Allen's *Voyage to the Bottom of the Sea* TV series. Tenacious Jeff Maxwell made a beeline from here to the *M*A*S*H* TV set whenever he could, first as a frequent stand-in, and then playing the running part of Igor the mess hall attendant.

Most famous of all are Roger Corman and John Landis. Corman, who started in the mailroom in the early 1940s, remembers the Fox lot being something between a campus and a factory. Although he rose to story analyst, recommending films like *The Gunfighter* (1950), he found success elsewhere as a purveyor of horror films, often starring Fox vet Vincent Price. He later directed *The St. Valentine's Day Massacre* (1967) and *Frankenstein Unbound* (1990), and nurtured future Fox talent like Jack Nicholson, Francis Ford Coppola, Irvin Kirshner, James Cameron, Ron Howard, and Sandra Bullock. Landis carried mail here in the late 1970s before launching his career as a director at Universal.

More recently the building has served as offices for Fox Television and postproduction. Look for this

unique structure in *The Right Approach* (1961).

And what of the building's name? We know that the names of all the studio's buildings were in place by the middle of the twentieth century. Was this building named for some long-forgotten Fox film, like *North of 53* (1917), starring the popular screen team of Dustin Farnum and Winifred Kingston, in which Kingston's character's name was Hazel Weir?

Our guess is that, like the Urban Building, it a tribute to an artist(s) by the art department. Julian Alden Weir, his father Robert Weir, and half brother John Weir were all noted American painters. Jack Otterson, who got his start in the art department,

had a personal connection, since he received a Yale scholarship named after John Weir. Then there is Julian's daughter, Dorothy, who married studio sculptor Mahonri Young in 1931.

A studio lot as old as this one has yet to give up all its secrets.

Bldg. 32: Film Editorial Building (1936)

Resembling a ship with decks, and specially fire-proofed for its original purpose of storing nitrate film, the Film Editorial Building housed six projection rooms on the first floor (still in use), eighteen

cutting rooms on the second floor (now sound editorial), and fifty-eight film vaults (now empty) on the third. On the west end of the first floor was film receiving and the dock.

If this building were to be dedicated to one person, it should be Darryl Zanuck's favorite film editor, Barbara McLean. A pioneer in the field, McLean became an assistant editor in 1924 at the Western Avenue Studio, and then came here with Zanuck from United Artists. She recalled editing films by day and then sitting through Zanuck's notorious all-night editing sessions, knowing that a scene needed help just by the way Zanuck brushed her arm.

She worked for the studio for forty years, eventually running the department and film vaults.

Among the studio records she set were editing twenty-five Henry King films, thirty of Darryl Zanuck's personal productions, and earning seven Academy Award nominations, including a win for *Wilson* (1944). McLean ensured that the Fox editorial department was one of the best in Hollywood. Her staff members recall John Ford as the most serious transgressor, with his lit pipe among so much nitrate film, insisting no editing was neccecessary for his films.

In 1975 sixty-year lab veteran Henry Goldfarb was summoned back to work by Sid Samuels, director of worldwide print operations, to examine and catalog all the nitrate film stored here so that it could be moved off the lot, preserving the studio's legacy—and his own.

FAR LEFT: Rex Harrison tries his hand at editing during the filming of *Unfaithfully Yours* (1948).

LEFT: Director Preston Sturges (left) looks down from the second story balcony during the production of *Unfaithfully Yours* (1948).

BOTTOM LEFT: One of the projection rooms on the first floor was actually used as a projection room for this scene with Sharon Tate as Jennifer North in *Valley of the Dolls* (1967) where she screens her adult film.

BOTTOM RIGHT: Shirley MacLaine in costume for *What a Way to Go!* (1964) rides past Building 32.

Bldg. 105: Richard D. Zanuck Production Building (2014)

This 15,000-square-foot postproduction facility, designed by Gensler Architects, includes a ninety-four-seat theater with a state-of-the-art Dolby Atmos sound system and projection booth. Bryan Singer was among the first to use the building to edit *X-Men: Days of Future Past* (2014). It was dedicated on February 25, 2014, by a contingent that included Richard Zanuck's wife Lili, his sons and grandsons, as well as Jim Gianopulos, Shirley MacLaine, and Barbara Davis, widow of Marvin Davis.

"For those of us that work at Fox—he was family," said Gianopulos. "He was an integral part of our legacy. He was like a paterfamilias to us. We waited to try and find a building worthy of Dick. We couldn't, so we built one."

ABOVE: The Richard D. Zanuck Production Building, 2015.

RIGHT: Screening Room, 2015.

Bldg. 222: The Lionel Newman Music Building (1946)

This building was dedicated on November 21, 2013, in honor of Lionel Newman. Two plaques were placed here to commemorate his forty-five-year musical legacy with the company. Older brother Alfred brought Lionel into the studio fold in 1943 as a rehearsal pianist. He worked his way up to songwriter with hits including "Again," sung by Ida Lupino for *Road House* (1948) that rose to number two in the country via Doris Day's interpretation in 1949, and "Kiss," sung by Marilyn Monroe in *Niagara* (1953).

Besides conducting he also headed the burgeoning television music department which was housed here, and in 1963 became head of the entire music department. He would ultimately conduct, compose, or score more than 250 films, earning eleven Oscar nominations and a win for *Hello, Dolly!* (1969). On dedication day Steven Spielberg remembered him as a force of nature you did not want to contradict. To do that was to risk a legendary torrent of language. "I never learned to swear until I came to Fox!" Spielberg said.

John Williams was among the composers with offices here, first working with Lionel Newman for *Lost in Space*. Here he wrote the seminal scores for *Jaws* (1975, Universal), *Raiders of the Lost Ark* (1981, Paramount) and the *Star Wars* films. Williams recalled that most of the best music issued from the building between the hours of five and seven in the evening when Newman hosted cocktails. Chernin Entertainment now has offices in this building.

FAR LEFT: The Lionel Newman Music Building on dedication night, November 21, 2013.

LEFT: On dedication night from left to right: Danielle Diego, EVP Fox Music; Randy Newman; John Williams, Stephen Spielberg; Joey Newman, and Jim Gianopulos.

TOP: Lionel Newman with one of his Oscars.

ABOVE: The building as the mailroom.

ABOVE LEFT: The exterior of Stages Three and Four, 2007.

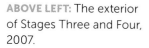

ABOVE RIGHT: Edna May Oliver and Tyrone Power in *Second Fiddle* (1939). It appears that Irving Berlin wrote the song "White Christmas" for this scene but, ultimately, it wasn't used.

STAGES THREE AND FOUR (1928)

Can you imagine *Gone with the Wind* (1939) being made on these stages? Darryl Zanuck was indeed the first to offer to purchase the screen rights to the most popular novel ever written, but David O. Selznick's bid was higher. Nevertheless, Zanuck managed to profit from the flurry of interest by producing films like *Second Fiddle* (1939) here that parodies the making of *Gone with the Wind*. It also features songs by Irving Berlin, and would be more famous today if "White Christmas" had been introduced in it. Miles Kreuger, president of the Institute of the American Musical, suspects this song was written for the movie. It was written at this time, and it certainly explains the reference to Southern California in the introduction of the song.

In 1956 Darryl Zanuck tried again to bring *Gone with the Wind* into the Fox fold as a musical by hiring poet Richard Wilbur, who had adapted Voltaire's *Candide* as a musical on Broadway, and composer Leonard Bernstein and playwright Lillian Hellman. The project was abandoned. Likewise, an effort at a sequel was attempted and abandoned by Richard Zanuck and David Brown in 1975 as a Universal/MGM co-venture.

You can trace Vincent Price's career from dramatic actor to horror star on this very stage. He appeared here in his Fox debut in *Brigham Young* (1940), returned for *Hudson's Bay* (1941), and then those prototype horror roles in *Dragonwyck* (1946) and *Shock* (1946). Enthusiastically throwing himself into *Dragonwyck,* his first directorial effort, Joe

Mankiewicz asked his cameraman Arthur Miller for his viewfinder and found that he could not see a thing. Miller politely informed him he was looking through the wrong end. Watch for that same comment in Mankiewicz's *All About Eve* (1950).

Also starring in *Shock* was Lynn Bari at her femme fatale best. Everyone's favorite Fox villainess in the 1940s would recall that during her studio years, her characters always seemed to have a gun, which she was frightened of; she seemed to go from stage to stage, movie to movie, using it, or trying to steal someone else's husband.

America's top teen idols in the 1950s, Elvis Presley and Pat Boone, made their first movies on Stage Four. Terry Moore had the choice of appearing with Presley in *Love Me Tender* (1956), in which this was the interior of the Reno farmhouse, but chose *Bernardine* (1957) with Boone (this was the Beaumont kitchen) because the studio had more faith in Boone's cinematic possibilities, and thus gave the film a bigger budget to film in color.

Fox crews enjoyed having the gregarious Elvis on the lot, remembering that in short order he knew everyone's name, their families, and what kind of cars they drove. He was back here for a love scene with Hope Lange for *Wild in the Country* (1961). Philip Dunne considered himself unique "as the only director ever to make Elvis Presley listen to Bach on the set. As a matter of fact, he loved it."

ABOVE: Vincent Price and Lynn Bari in *Shock* (1946).

LEFT: Vincent Price, Gene Tierney, and Joseph Mankiewicz, have a wardrobe conference with a costume designer for *Dragonwyck* (1946).

Presley's Fox films reflect his wish to be a serious actor, but his manager Colonel Tom Parker saw more money in lightweight musicals, and took him elsewhere. Boone remained under contract, achieving his dream to make musicals "like Bing Crosby" in a series of well-loved films.

From a technical standpoint, these stages once housed the battery room, test stages at each end of the second floor that were the last home of the studio's talent school, and music cutting on Stage Three. They were combined in November 1999 for post-production facilities. These include the Howard Hawks, John Ford, and Robert Wise dubbing stages. Wise christened his for *A Storm in Summer* (2000, Showtime). Sound designers Andy Nelson and Anna Behlmer were the first to mix a Fox feature film here (*Anna and the King,* 1999). With room to expand, the unfinished area on the second floor has been dubbed "Middle Earth" by employees.

STAGES ONE AND TWO (1928)

Stages One through Six carry a restored frieze over every stage entrance of the Movietone logo framed by Pan, symbolic, of course, of sound. C. H. Muldorfer designed the first four, and W. Asa Hudson designed the fifth and sixth. Built of steel and reinforced concrete, they are all in fact housed within a larger building to further keep out noise. Outside the soundstage doors are small lobbies with restrooms.

Historically Stage One always served multiple uses, with projection rooms and facilities for sound effects, trailer narration, and music scoring. There was even a Wurlitzer organ. Among the earliest motion picture work done at Movietone City were "short subjects" featuring Chic Sale, and the team of Clark & McCullough. Even as the screen was learning how to talk Fox was contributing to the Great American Songbook. *What Price Glory* (1926) set an industry trend by featuring the studio's first hit song "Charmaine" by Erno Rapee with lyrics by Lew Pollack. The pair followed it up with the evergreen "Diane" for *7th Heaven* (1927). The first feature films with dialogue sequences were *The Air Circus* (1928) and *Mother Knows Best* (1928). John Ford's three-reeler *Napoleon's Barber* (1929) was the first all-talking film on the lot. *In Old Arizona* (1929) is credited as the studio's first full-length sound feature film.

There were challenges to be faced when Movietone allowed for the creation of the Fox musical with *Fox Movietone Follies of 1929*. Despite William Fox getting into the act by hiring Edward Royce and Dave Stamper, who had produced the shows of Florenz Ziegfeld, and prolific Broadway songwriters B. G. "Buddy" DeSylva, Lew Brown, and Ray Henderson, the studio's initial efforts looked like static photographed stage plays immobilized by the bulky early sound equipment. Legendary musical talents like John McCormack and Jeanette MacDonald were brought to Movietone City only to have MacDonald—who prerecorded her debut opera performance

TOP: Sheet music for "Charmaine" from *What Price Glory* (1926)

ABOVE: Sheet music for "Diane" from *7th Heaven* (1927).

RIGHT: Scoring *Metropolitan* (1935).

"Liebestod" from Richard Wagner's *Tristan und Isolde* for *Oh, for a Man!* (1930)—complain, "What the people at this studio knew about music could be played with one hand on a toy piano!"

More work and a further infusion of talent by Winfield Sheehan changed all that. DeSylva's experiments with the genre produced *Sunnyside Up* (1929), the company's biggest hit up to that time, with the unbeatable team of Janet Gaynor and Charles Farrell, the truly bizarre *Just Imagine* (1930), the studio's first venture into science fiction as a musical set in faraway 1980, the buoyant Hollywood satire *Bottoms Up* (1934), and five hit Shirley Temple films.

No less than the greatest talent on Broadway was invited to contribute to the growth of the Fox musical, including the Gershwins, with *Delicious* (1931), George White and his *Scandals* (1934), (the first of five proposed films) with Alice Faye, and Irving Berlin with *On the Avenue* (1937), *Alexander's Ragtime Band* (1938), *Second Fiddle* (1939), *Call Me Madam* (1953), and *There's No Business Like Show Business* (1954). Ethel Merman came to belt many of those Berlin tunes and found the Fox star treatment "unbelievable! Anything you wanted was given to you—down to a pedicure. Such treatment was undreamed of in the theater." In this early period there was even a Fox Movietone record label (1933–37) featuring songs from Fox movies, sold only at Fox Theaters.

The fact that Darryl Zanuck hired Alfred Newman to be his general music director in late 1939 reveals the mogul's underrated understanding of the importance and use of music. Theirs was a unique partnership. Although Zanuck had final say over the editing, mixing, and scoring, he allowed Newman to fully unleash his enormous talents, not only to compose and conduct, but also to independently manage the department's army of staff

ABOVE LEFT: Buddy DeSylva, right, listens as one of his tunes is sung by Pat Paterson, on the set of *Bottoms Up* (1934).

ABOVE MIDDLE: Jeanette MacDonald, 1930.

ABOVE RIGHT: Guy Bolton (left), George Gershwin, and Ira Gershwin.

composers, orchestrators, arrangers, music copyists, and, of course, the orchestra, all under contract—in all, sixty-three employees, including the legal staff for music clearances.

For his work Newman won nine Oscars out of an unprecedented forty-five nominations during his Hollywood career. He composed his first motion picture score for Samuel Goldwyn's *Street Scene* (1931), and its theme would be reprised memorably in Twentieth Century Fox films. Newman was a pioneer in the field, and proved how important the use of music can be to a film. Filmmakers were initially nervous to have their films scored, fearing audiences would wonder where the music was coming from.

Even as late as the 1940s Alfred Hitchcock brought this up for his *Lifeboat* (1944), set completely out at sea. Newman logically replied: "The music is coming from the same place your camera comes from!"

"The sound that Newman achieved in *The Song of Bernadette* and on many of his finest scores was a mysterious alchemy," noted Newman scholar Jon Burlingame, "involving his unparalleled abilities as a conductor; his penchant for endless rehearsals and attention to the most minute details of orchestrations and nuance in performance. The score is the result of experienced writing and accomplished playing and the wonderful never-duplicated aural characteristics of Stage One."

Newman's pioneering mixture of tracks before traditional stereophonic recording resulted in such striking works as the harpsichords (two tracks), a woman's voice (third track), and a chorus (fourth track) for the penultimate ghost sequence in *Dragonwyck* (1946). His efforts culminated in the groundbreaking stereo score for *The Robe* (1953), recorded here in July and August of 1953. At that time he also updated his composition of the studio's fanfare with a CinemaScope extension. The Newman System—allowing a composer to match his music to the film with an exact time measurement—was another leap in musical technology.

BOTTOM LEFT: David Raksin, visiting Gene Tierney on the set of *Dragonwyck* (1946), shows her the sheet music for the surprise hit he wrote for *Laura* (1944).

BOTTOM RIGHT: One of the most prolific composers ever to come out of Hollywood, Harry Warren wrote several songs for Fox films that have become standards such as "There Will Never Be Another You" and "At Last."

RIGHT: Glenn Miller
with Tex Beneke and the
Modernaires give a
concert on Stage One
during the making of
Orchestra Wives (1941).

BOTTOM LEFT: Betty
Grable listens to husband
Harry James practicing
his trumpet for *Do You
Love Me* (1946) while
Alfred Newman looks on.

BOTTOM RIGHT: Stage
One during the early
1940s.

He scored many of the important Fox pictures
himself, and supervised all the rest by choosing
composers for them. He hired Hollywood veterans like Arthur Lange, David Buttolph, and Cyril
J. Mockridge, who composed scores for 180 films.
He also nurtured talent like Hugo Friedhofer, who
started here as an arranger, and David Raksin, who
developed the legendary seventy-two-note theme
for *Laura* (1944). When Raksin received more than
1,700 fan letters, Johnny Mercer was hired to write
the lyrics. To date there have been at least four
hundred recordings of the song and score.

Alfred Newman's invitation to Bernard Herrmann to work at Fox led to a brilliant fifteen-year collaboration, beginning with *Jane Eyre* (1944).

Darryl Zanuck brought new energy to the Fox musical, experimenting to find new formulas just as he had done with noted success at Warner Bros. Typical of this period was *Pigskin Parade* (1936), marking the feature film debut of teenage vaudevillian Judy Garland. Another rising talent in that film was Betty Grable. Talk about perserverance —she debuted on the lot at thirteen in *Happy Days* (1930) and continued to show up now and then in a big film like *Fox Movietone Follies* (1930) and as the visible "girl on the couch" in *Cavalcade* (1933) before finally earning stardom in *Down Argentine Way* (1940) aided by the memorable score by Harry Warren. Both would, under Darryl Zanuck's guidance, help make Fox a top producer of musicals.

Among the first of those wonderful Big Bands to perform here was Grable's boyfriend (later husband) Harry James and his Music Makers featured in *Springtime in the Rockies* (1942). "I Had the Craziest Dream" became the theme song for wartime America's favorite couple. Benny Goodman showed up for *Sweet and Low-Down* (1944). The Glenn Miller Orchestra headlined two definitive Big Band musicals: *Sun Valley Serenade* (1941) and *Orchestra Wives* (1942). For their classic "Chattanooga-Choo-Choo" production number, brothers

Fayard and Harold Nicholas suggested that Harold's love interest (and later wife) Dorothy Dandridge dance with them. It was the birth of a film career that included her unforgettable performance in the title role of Oscar Hammerstein's *Carmen Jones* (1954), inspiring and opening doors for future talents like Angela Bassett, Whitney Houston, Jada Pinkett Smith, and Halle Berry.

Darryl Zanuck enlisted more African-American performers to join the historic cast of *Stormy Weather* (1943), including Lena Horne (who sang the title song and made it her own) and Thomas "Fats" Waller.

Watch Betty Grable perform "Don't Bet on Men" for *Meet Me after the Show* (1951), and you witness a significant transition—a shift in style for a new decade of Fox musicals more appropriate for Marilyn Monroe, who replaced Grable in Howard Hawks's *Gentlemen Prefer Blondes* (1953).

That same year director Walter Lang let loose the extraordinary talents of Ethel Merman, Donald O'Connor, and Vera-Ellen in *Call Me Madam* (1953). Things had come full circle for Vera-Ellen, who by then had done some of her best work at the studio, since Robert Alton, who choreographed *Call Me Madam*, had given her a start on Broadway. Fred Astaire got Johnny Mercer back to write the words and music for his only Fox musical, *Daddy Long Legs* (1955), including his favorite song, "Dream."

Since it was common from the earliest days of sound motion pictures for actors/singers to prerecord their voices here for playback and lip-syncing on the set, this stage has stacked up a legendary list of performers too long to list here. It was equally common for actors who could not sing to be dubbed. Lynn Bari was dubbed by Pat Friday, Marilyn Horne dubbed Dorothy Dandridge for *Carmen Jones* (1954), and Connie Francis dubbed Jayne Mansfield in *The Sheriff of Fractured Jaw* (1958).

The most memorable event of this kind occurred here in May 1951 when singer Jane Froman met Susan Hayward, the actress she had chosen to play her in *With a Song in My Heart* (1952).

"When I recorded my songs for the picture, Susan was always around," recalled Froman. "She sat on the set day after day, three and four hours at a time, watching every move I made as I sang, watching, always watching. Susan struck me as being a strange girl, so sensational in appearance, so quiet of voice and manner."

While performing in a USO tour in 1945, Froman had inspired a shell-shocked young soldier to come out of his trance-like state. With his star-making skill, Darryl Zanuck saw an opportunity, and threw new contract player Robert Wagner into the part. Hayward remembered the film as "one of the greatest emotional experiences of my life," and received an Oscar nomination, and Wagner got noticed.

Richard Rodgers and Oscar Hammerstein's immortal melodies were first recorded here for *State Fair* (1945). In retrospect it is clear that no Hollywood studio was better prepared to produce their films than Twentieth Century Fox, with their technical wizardry and the added benefit of Alfred Newman, who had worked with Rodgers on two Broadway shows. Newman would share an Oscar nomination with the prolific Charles Henderson, whose talent as vocal arranger graced two hundred movies in thirty years. *State Fair* also best displays the work of studio orchestrator Edward Powell, another valued member of the Newman team. Ken Darby assumed Henderson's role in 1949, beginning a twenty-two-year partnership with Alfred Newman as an assisting choirmaster, choral arranger, composer, lyricist, and conductor. He revised the old ballad "Aura Lee" with new lyrics and a new title, *Love Me Tender* (1956), which certainly furthered the career of Elvis Presley.

True-life events inspired more Fox music when Dr. Elizabeth Comber's (pen name Han Suyin) international bestseller, *A Many-Splendored Thing*, about her affair with a married Korean War correspondent, was acquired by Buddy Adler. Sammy Fain and Paul Francis Webster's first three attempts to write a love song were turned down.

Webster complained the title was too "Elizabethan" for popular music, until he came up with the introductory "Love Is . . ." Webster and Fain then produced the song in one hour.

Adler approved, but Spyros Skouras complained it was too long for theater marquees. No one wanted to record it, either—an essential promotional component prior to the film's release. Webster recalled that sixteen record companies and everyone from Nat King Cole to next-door-neighbor Doris Day turned it down. Even Frank Sinatra, who had just recently crooned "Three Coins in the Fountain" for Fox, said no.

Fortunately, The Four Aces—who had enjoyed a hit with their recording of "Three Coins in a Fountain"—agreed to record it. The Decca recording was an immediate hit when it was released in August 1955, hitting number one for six weeks. Ultimately

ABOVE: Sheet music for "Love is a Many-Splendored Thing," (1955).

RIGHT: Recording the soundtrack for *South Pacific* (1958); from left to right: director Joshua Logan, Oscar Hammerstein, Alfred Newman, Jack Bean (Mitzi Gaynor's husband), John Kerr, and Mitzi Gaynor.

250 recordings were made of the song by various artists, and it was named one of America's all-time top-five standards. Fain and Webster did it again for *April Love* (1957), with that million-seller title tune sung in the movie by two of the finest singers ever to perform here: Pat Boone and Shirley Jones.

In contrast, have you ever heard of these love songs: "I'll Get No Good Behavior, Baby, If I Keep Thinking of You," and "No Lights on the Christmas Tree, Mother, They're Using the Electric Chair Tonight"? These were playfully composed for *The Girl Can't Help It* (1956). Often regarded as the best rock 'n' roll film ever made, the movie featured

legends like Fats Domino and Little Richard. Jayne Mansfield performed "Rock around the Rock Pile Blues," for the movie here, showing herself and this stage off in its prime.

There were more Rodgers and Hammerstein hits: *Carousel* (1956), *The King and I* (1956) and *South Pacific* (1958). Among *Carousel's* performers was Barbara Ruick who married studio session pianist John Williams. Encouraged by Alfred and then Lionel Newman he found fame composing for Fox television and then film. With such mentoring how appropriate that it was Williams who surpassed Alfred Newman's record of Oscar nominations in 2005—earning forty-nine to date.

ABOVE LEFT: Lionel Newman conducts the music for *Say One for Me* (1959) with Debbie Reynolds and Bing Crosby.

ABOVE RIGHT: The beautiful theme from *Peyton Place* (1957) got lyrics when it was used again for *Return to Peyton Place* (1961). Here composer Franz Waxman conducts Rosemary Clooney who sang the song over the opening credits while Clooney's husband and director of the film, Jose Ferrer, stands behind her.

LEFT: Scoring *What a Way to Go!* (1964)

ABOVE LEFT: Sammy Cahn (left), Ann-Margret, and Jimmy Van Heusen go over the music for *The Pleasure Seekers* (1964).

ABOVE RIGHT: Louis Armstrong on the stage to record *Hello, Dolly!* (1969).

Dubbing was again in order for *The King and I.* "Marni Nixon was so brilliant at adapting her voice to mine," recalled Deborah Kerr. "It was a fascinating experience to watch Marni; she is an actress with her voice and exquisitely musical and I used to sit with her in the sound booth and marvel at the way she managed it all."

The pair were happy to provide an encore the following year for *An Affair to Remember* (1957). Its famous title song by Harry Warren, with lyrics by Harold Adamson and Leo McCarey, was performed by Vic Damone.

Also in production in 1957 (a month in Hawaii and three weeks at the studio, Fox Ranch and backlot) was *South Pacific.* Giorgio Tozzi received credit for dubbing Rossano Brazzi, but Muriel

Smith, singing for Juanita Hall, and Bill Lee, dubbing John Kerr, did not. It became Hollywood's biggest hit of 1958, and produced a bestselling soundtrack. Andrew Lloyd Webber drew inspiration from it to create his own Broadway-to-film phenomenon *The Phantom of the Opera.*

Harry Belafonte's performance of the title tune he wrote for *Island in the Sun* (1957) helped popularize Calypso music in the U.S. Alfred Newman invited German composer Franz Waxman, who had fled anti-Semitism in Berlin, to score a number of Fox films, including *Peyton Place* (1957), which featured lyrics by Paul Francis Webster for the sequel, *Return to Peyton Place* (1961). It was sung by Rosemary Clooney, wife of its director, Jose Ferrer, and aunt of George Clooney.

Darryl Zanuck resisted having his stars sing on the radio or produce recordings, believing that would limit the number of times audiences would see a film. Although the success of albums for *The Song of Bernadette* (1943) and *The Robe* (1953) prompted the release of more Fox scores, it was not until Zanuck retired as an independent producer that the company launched another record label (1958–82). Its first success was making a Christmas perennial of "The Little Drummer Boy" by the Harry Simeone Chorale. The song had been around since 1941, and its first recording was by the Trapp Family Singers in 1955, but it was the Fox record that landed it near the top of the Billboard

charts for five years in a row, inspiring two hundred further recordings ranging from Andy Williams to Jimi Hendrix to Justin Bieber. The label also mined the studio's catalog, releasing compilations of Shirley Temple film songs and music from the Glenn Miller films.

With the departure of Darryl Zanuck and other friends, Newman left the studio at the end of 1959. His youngest brother Lionel remained and became head of the department by 1963. With such a progressive leader, an extraordinary new generation of composers was encouraged to usher in a new decade of film and television scoring, including Alex North, Leonard Rosenman, and Jerry Goldsmith.

Julie Andrews's work here for *Star!* (1968), along with the recording of the songs and score for *Hello, Dolly!* (1969), marked the end of an era. Future Fox musicals, like Brian De Palma's *Phantom of the Paradise* (1974), starring Paul Williams (who wrote the music) and Jessica Harper (who married Tom Rothman), *The Rocky Horror Picture Show* (1975), and *All That Jazz* (1979) would be made elsewhere.

Meanwhile, the company's record label continued to thrive, with soundtracks including the one from *Cleopatra,* which climbed to number two on the Billboard charts.

Another big hit (Billboard #11) was John Williams's album of music for *Valley of the Dolls,* all the more impressive because the hit theme song sung in the film by Dionne Warwick could not be

included on the album because she was signed to another label. That problem was worked out so Barbra Streisand could appear on the soundtrack to *Hello, Dolly!*—the only album in her career not issued on Columbia Records.

The label also cultivated pop music talent, and had a Billboard Top Ten hit with Diane Renay's "Navy Blue," perhaps the perkiest under-the-weather song ever recorded. Lena Horne, after a long tenure at RCA, came and recorded her most provocative album, *Here's Lena Now!* Al Martino, Kitty Kallen, Gogi Grant, Mary Wells, and Hugo Montenegro, among others, also made albums for Fox. Martino encored by singing "Hush…Hush, Sweet Charlotte" in the film.

The label diversified with spoken word, comedy, and live performances; the best were the memorial *John F. Kennedy: The Presidential Years 1960–1963,* with sound clips mined from the Movietone newsreels, and a compilation of comedy greats called *My Favorite Story,* including Lucille Ball, George Burns, Jack Benny, Bob Hope, and Art Linkletter, who also provided a primer to kids about the birds and the bees in his album, *Where Did You Come From?* Jayne Mansfield recorded a live album of her *House of Love* show at the Dunes Hotel, which was released as *Jayne Mansfield Busts Up Las Vegas.*

From the 1970s through the 1990s composers like Johnny Mandel and Mark Snow brought their magic to the studio's television shows. Mandel wrote the theme song for *M*A*S*H,* with lyrics by Michael Altman. Altman made more than $2 million in royalties—first from the film, and then from the TV series—while his father, who directed the film, remained annoyed that all he received was his salary of $75,000. Altman later wrote lyrics for episodes of *The Simpsons.* Besides contributing to such Spelling-Goldberg Productions hits as *Starsky & Hutch* (1977–79), *Love Boat* (1977–86) *Hart to Hart* (1979–84), and *Dynasty* (1981–89), Snow scored Chris Carter's *The X-Files* (1993–2002).

By now, the studio's record label was releasing twenty albums a year, including those by Barry White, Dan McCann, Stephanie Mills, Genya Ravan, Leon Haywood, M'Lady, Cut Glass, Edwin Starr, Jim Photoglo, the Dells, the Chi-Lites, Carl Carlton, and Betty Everett. The title song from *The Poseidon Adventure* boosted Maureen McGovern's career when "The Morning After" became a number-one hit and won Best Song at the Oscars.

All of this success attracted other top talent and seventies' classics such as Dan Hill's "Sometimes When We Touch" and Kenny Nolan's "I Like Dreamin.'" The latter hit gold status, selling a million copies in 1977, the same year the *Star Wars IV* soundtrack, composed by John Williams, went triple platinum, selling three million copies and becoming the first orchestral work to jump onto national music charts.

The last major hit was Stephanie Mills's "Never Knew Love like This Before" in 1981. The following June, as Lionel Newman was named senior vice president of the department, Marvin Davis sold Fox's music publishing companies to Warner Bros. Music. Gone were over twenty thousand copyrights to the music composed and performed here, including the studio's own fanfare by Alfred Newman. That fanfare would have to be paid for in the future. Gone, too, was the record label, sold to Polygram.

It took a musical force of nature like Bette Midler to breathe life back into the Fox musical, and the unique creativity of Baz Luhrmann to reinvent it. Midler did it with *The Rose* (1979) and *For the Boys* (1991), and Luhrmann produced *Moulin Rouge* (2001), the third feature in a theatricalized style he had dubbed the "Red Curtain" trilogy, launched with *Strictly Ballroom* (1992, Miramax) and *Romeo + Juliet* (1996).

Throughout the 1980s the stage continued to be used only for feature films and the most popular television shows. Dialogue looping artist Marlene Sharp recalled the awe workers always felt working here. Looping could be done just about anywhere by that time, but for her "Loop Group"—recording crowd noises or lines of dialogue not delivered by a star—there was a special feeling here that no rental lot could duplicate.

Of his score for *Die Hard* (1988), Michael Kamen noted: "You have to give credit where credit is due: to Beethoven and John McTiernan. McTiernan insisted on using Beethoven's *Ninth* despite my objections. I thought it was sacrilege to use

ABOVE: Dolly Parton records the theme song for *9 to 5* (1980).

Beethoven in this action movie. I told McTiernan, 'I'll make mincemeat out of Wagner and Strauss for you, but why Beethoven?' McTiernan explained that Beethoven's *Ninth* was the theme to underscore the ultra-violence in Stanley Kubrick's *A Clockwork Orange.*"

Kamen agreed, and worked on subsequent *Die Hard* films as well as composed the score for *X-Men* (2000)

The studio's record label was relaunched in 1992, but then closed down in 1995. The catalog became part of the Universal Music Group, except for the Fox film and TV soundtracks that Fox Music has managed since its inception in 2000. The studio fanfare was purchased back in 1996.

Meanwhile, the Newman tradition continued. Alfred Newman's brother Emil, and sons David and younger brother Thomas, composed and conducted feature film and television scores on the stage. A favorite Newman family story is the time Emil conducted scoring in his bathrobe because his clothes were lost in a fire that destroyed his Malibu beach house. In June of 1994 Alfred Newman's fanfare was rerecorded here by David, who began as a violinist in the 1970s, with a ninety-piece orchestra conducted by Bruce Broughton, to update it for the summer release of *True Lies* (1994).

The studio completed a $3.2 million renovation combining Stages One and Two, which always shared an entrance, as postproduction facilities by September of 1997. Besides the Jane Russell Foley Stage (to create sound effects), the Marilyn Monroe ADR Stage (for "Automated Dialogue Replacement"), the similar Marge Simpson ADR Stage, a greenroom, edit bays, and video and projection departments, the historic scoring stage, now Suite One, was dedicated as the Newman Scoring Stage in January of 1998.

The main floor where the orchestra plays (with a capacity of up to 150 musicians) was restored to its original 99.5-foot-by-74.5-foot dimensions. The structure of the room—which included the hardwood floors and even the interior walls put up by Newman himself—was left mostly untouched, so as to retain the unique acoustic qualities that made the room special. The first recording was, appropriately, another update of the studio fanfare conducted by David Newman for *Anastasia* (1997), which also happily relaunched Fox musicals being made here. *Rio* (2011) and *Rio 2* (2014) continued that tradition. Alfred's nephew Randy Newman and Lionel's grandson Joey continue to compose music for film and television.

James Horner's career as one of the studio's finest composers, beginning in the 1990s with such masterworks as his scoring for *Titanic* (1997), was cut tragically short by his death in a plane crash in 2015. One of the most unique instruments ever to be brought in here that decade was the forty-foot-long beam requested by Hans Zimmer for his score for *The*

Thin Red Line (1998). Producer Grant Hill remembers that studio sound technicians were very concerned that it was going to affect the stage structurally because it gave off such powerfully resonant notes.

With pieces like "Ballet Suburbia" and "Chimp Symphony, Op. 37,"—names as whimsical as his music—Danny Elfman scored Tim Burton's *Edward Scissorhands* (1990), *Planet of the Apes* (2001), and *Hitchcock* (2012) here, recalling the Newman and Herrmann sound of the 1930s and '40s.

John Williams returned to score *The Book Thief* (2013). The extraordinary, intertwining legacy of the Newman Stage continues when, due to illness, he was replaced by Thomas Newman for *Bridge of Spies* (2015).

ABOVE: The William Fox Theater and Stages One and Two viewed from the roof of Bldg. 1 in 2015.

RIGHT: Interior of the William Fox Theater, 2015.

BLDG. 23: THE WILLIAM FOX THEATER (1933)

Another of the studio's screening rooms, this smaller, fifty-three-seat Spanish Colonial Revival theater continues to be used by Fox executives today. It was built in the early 1930s for sound re-recording.

LEFT: Batman and the Green Hornet get in a car accident on the Gotham City set during the filming of *Batman* (1966). This façade covered the William Fox Theater.

BOTTOM LEFT: The mod Gotham City plaza built for the *Batman* TV show and movie was between the William Fox Theater and Stage Five.

BOTTOM RIGHT: The Gotham City set on the façade of Stage Five.

RIGHT: Looking west down Ninth Street towards Building 1. Before the Darryl Zanuck Theatre was built, Old Park Row and an executive bungalow were located here.

FAR RIGHT: Old Park Row

BOTTOM: The Darryl F. Zanuck Theatre exterior circa 1962.

BLDG. 226: THE DARRYL F. ZANUCK THEATRE (1957)

It seems fitting that the site of a memorial to Darryl F. Zanuck should be a motion picture theater. In his lifetime, he was totally committed to the making of outstanding films; thus, what better place to perpetuate his work and his memory than in the Twentieth Century Fox theatre, where so many of his productions have entertained literally hundreds of thousands?

—Dennis C. Stanfill, on dedication day, April 16, 1980

This 476-seat theater, unique on the lot for its stage, curtain, sound booth, removable CinemaScope screen, four projection rooms, storage vaults, and four rerecording rooms, was built in 1957. It also housed the studio's talent school—a last effort by Spyros Skouras, Buddy Adler, producer/acting coach Ben Bard, executive casting director Billy Gordon, and casting director Owen McLean to perpetuate its contract star system.

Bard, a contract player in the 1930s, ran the school after years of success with private training. Applicants were whittled down and trained by Bard for three months, and then offered an audition in dramatic shows here for Fox film and TV executives. Among the alumni were Dolores Michaels, Barbara Eden, and Alan Ladd's daughters, Alana and Carol Lee Ladd. Their brother Alan Ladd Jr. would appear on the scene nearly two decades later.

The first four actors to successfully audition under the new program and appear on television were Michael Sargeant, Richard Gardner, Michael Galloway, and Jane Liddell. The talent school lasted another decade on Stage Two as the New Talent

ABOVE LEFT: The New Talent School performs on the stage before the huge CinemaScope screen circa 1957.

ABOVE MIDDLE: Sophia Loren leans forward to greet a guest at the screening of her first English film *Boy on a Dolphin* (1957).

ABOVE RIGHT: Children of employees got to meet Batman and Robin IN PERSON at this screening in 1966.

School, run by studio dialogue coach Pamela Danova until 1971. Among its last graduates were Raquel Welch, Tom Selleck, Sam Elliott, and Lyle Waggoner.

When the sound department moved in here, post-dubbing was done in the basement. Yves Montand, on his first English-language film, *Let's Make Love* (1960), preferred to call it "dumbing," to his costars' amusement.

When the theatre was dedicated to Darryl Zanuck, a bust of the mogul created by Italian sculptor Tamassy was installed in the lobby. There is also a glass display case containing the Oscars for sound design and for Cinemascope. The theatre remains in use today for employee screenings, with an updated, state-of-the-art sound mixing board that is the largest in the United States. Look for the lobby interior in *Beloved Infidel* (1959), the auditorium in *All Hands on Deck* (1961), and the exterior as the Black Cow parking lot for *Bernardine* (1957) and *Madison Avenue* (1962), *The Stripper* (1963), and the "Hollywood A.D." episode of *The X-Files* (2000).

Narrow windows were recently added on the west end of the building when the space was renovated for offices.

Ladies and gentlemen . . . and newspapermen.
—Wake Up and Live *(1937)*

Two buildings from the Western Avenue Studio were originally located on this spot. Bldg. 215, with its unlucky thirteen offices, was used by producers like Al Rockett (*Soup to Nuts,* 1930) and Robert T. Kane (*George White's Scandals,* 1934) in the early days, and the construction department by the 1960s. Although Bldg. 77 was used for a time by songwriters (and thus called the studio's "Tin Pan Alley"), as well as directors and their assistants, the one-story U-shaped building with eighteen offices was best known as "Park Row" by the New York writers who inhabited it, named for the famous street in Lower Manhattan where American journalism was born.

They included Ralph Block, formerly of the *New York Herald Tribune,* Dudley Nichols, of the *New York World,* and E. Lloyd Sheldon, of the *New York Globe.* They even brought over the gag signpost out front noting "Park Row/Piccadilly." Look for it as barracks for *The Young Lions* (1957), the exterior of a hospital in *A Private's Affair* (1959), and a motel in *Wild in the Country* (1961). "Old Park Row" later moved down to the southwest corner of the lot near the Lasky Building, but was torn down when satellites were installed on the site in the 1990s.

BOTTOM LEFT: The interior of the Darryl F. Zanuck Theatre, 2015.

BOTTOM RIGHT: The lobby of the theatre as it appeared in 2015. The display case on the left holds the studio's Oscars for sound as well as the special Oscar for the introduction of Cinemascope. Photos from famous Fox films hang on the walls.

RIGHT: French Alley in 2015.

BOTTOM LEFT: French Alley as it was used for *Johnny Apollo* (1940).

BOTTOM RIGHT: Debbie Reynolds and Robert Wagner have just exited the church set after getting married in *Say One for Me* (1959). The tower of Bldg. 1 can be seen in the distance.

BLDG. 22: HEATING AND REFRIGERATION PLANT (1928)

Has any company's heating and air-conditioning plant ever looked as exotic as this one? It remains one of the lot's most striking and easily recognizable architectural features.

FRENCH ALLEY

Although the alley between Stages Five and Six has been used as the site of a factory or prison since the early days, for films like *The Holy Terror* (1937), *One Mile From Heaven* (1937), *Johnny Apollo* (1940), and *Tonight We Raid Calais* (1943), it gained its permanent name as French Alley as part of the larger "French Street" that ran along Ninth Street for the length of the two stages, beginning in 1963.

The "Street" began with a church for *Say One for Me* (1959), and later the French sets purchased from United Artists's *Irma La Douce* (1963) were incorporated into it. The street and alley can be seen in *Take Her, She's Mine* (1963) and *Do Not Disturb* (1965). The alley became the "Peyton Mills" in *Peyton Place* (1964–69), the first prime-time soap opera credited for building ABC into a major network. Its charming town square set was over by the Café de Paris (as the Peyton Place Inn) and incorporated the sound building (the town hall) and the stars' dressing rooms building. The show also used the POW village (currently the site of Buildings 102 and 104) from *Von Ryan's Express* (1965) as the wharf.

Appropriately there was plenty of romance on and off this *Peyton Place* set. Ryan O'Neal married costar Leigh Taylor-Young, and pointed out Frank Sinatra (working on *Von Ryan*) to costar Mia Farrow, which led to their marriage. The square was also used for David Gerber's *Cade's County* (1970–71) starring Glenn Ford, who made his film debut on the lot in *Heaven with a Barbed Wire Fence* (1939), and *Johnny Dangerously* (1984).

Without a doubt the most unusual use of this square was for the pilot of *The Fall Guy* (1981–86), in which Lee Majors in drag (!) crashes into a watermelon festival. Significantly, he meets real-life wife Farrah Fawcett in the scene. She debuted at Fox in *Myra Breckinridge* (1970), and the lot had another blonde sex symbol when she starred in *Charlie's Angels* (1976–77). Through Majors she met Ryan O'Neal, and thus began a "very real love affair," as celebrity gossip columnist Liz Smith described it, which endured until Fawcett's death in 2009.

Several sets for the *Batman* TV series (1966–68) were built on the lot, including the Gotham City Plaza (in front of Stages One and Two), as well as various storefronts and shops along Mel Brooks Boulevard, including the north wall of Stages One

RIGHT: The set became "French" when it was transformed into Paris for *Take Her, She's Mine* (1963).

FAR RIGHT: Looking east down Ninth Street. The top of the Gothic arch of the church from *Say One for Me* (1959) can be seen on the left; the entrance to Stage Eight juts out a bit further down.

BOTTOM LEFT: The French Alley set along the back of Stage Six, looking east along Ninth Street.

BOTTOM RIGHT: The French Alley set along the back of Stage Five looking west.

and Two. The facade of Stage Five served as the Gotham City Municipal Library. Establishing shots of downtown Gotham City and the courthouse were filmed on the Desilu Lot in Culver City. The famous bat-cave entrance was the entrance of the Bronson Cave in Los Angeles's Griffith Park.

FAR LEFT: Philippe Forquet sings along with Sandra Dee in *Take Her, She's Mine* (1963) on the French Alley set.

LEFT: Things get a little out of hand with a chimp during this scene from *What a Way to Go!* (1964) with Shirley MacLaine and Paul Newman.

BOTTOM LEFT: Doris Day, at right, gets ready to walk down the French Alley set in the spy-spoof *Caprice* (1967).

BOTTOM RIGHT: French Alley was the exit for the secret garage where *The Green Hornet* (1966) kept his special car named Black Beauty.

RIGHT: Bldg. 86 became French for *What a Way to Go!* (1964) when the dome of the Sacre Coeur basilica was placed on top to create a trompe l'oeil effect looking down Ninth Street.

FAR RIGHT: The west façade of Bldg. 86 also served as the hospital in *Peyton Place* (1964-69). Star Barbara Parkins is getting out of the car.

BOTTOM LEFT: Bldg. 86 as it was incorporated into the *Peyton Place* (1964-69) TV show set as the Peyton Place Banking and Trust Company, complete with New England snow.

BOTTOM RIGHT: The commissary (now the entrance to the Studio Store) became the Peyton Place Inn for the television show; even the interior was used. Stars Mia Farrow (left), Dorothy Malone, and Gyl Roland stand out front.

ABOVE: Peyton Place square looking southwest.

ABOVE RIGHT: Leslie Nielsen had a recurring role on *Peyton Place* (1964) and stands here in front of the studio fire station which also served as the Peyton Place fire station.

RIGHT: Fox movie stars prepare for a group portrait in front of the Sound Building standing in for Peyton Place Town Hall, 1964. Front row: (L-R) James Stewart, unidentified woman, Tony Curtis; Second row: Mia Farrow, Glynis Johns, Joseph Cotten; Third row: Victor Buono, Pamela Tiffin, Ann-Margret.

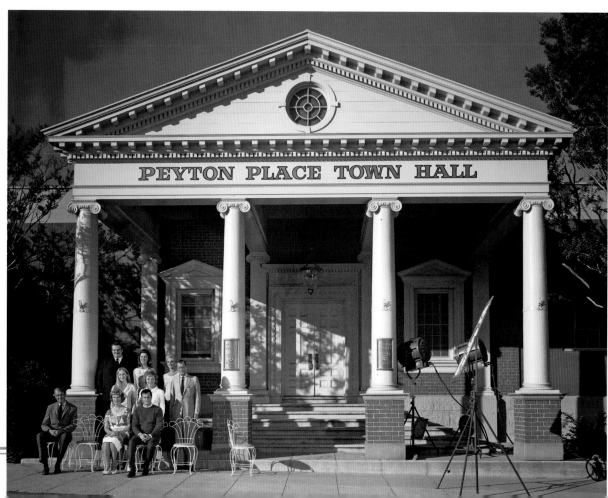

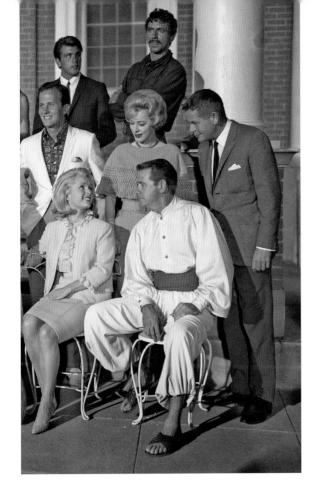

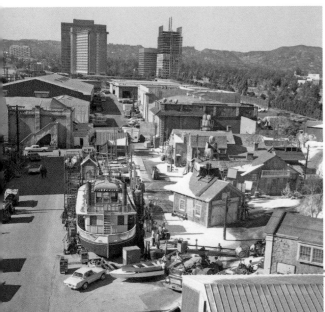

FAR LEFT: Movie stars on the lot getting ready for a group portrait in front of the Sound Building standing in as Peyton Place Town Hall, 1964. Front row (L-R): Debbie Reynolds, Richard Crenna; Second row: Pat Boone, Eleanor Parker, Glenn Ford; Third row: Fabian, Anthony Franciosa.

LEFT: The Sound Building dressed as the Peyton Place Town Hall became the hospital in *Hush . . . Hush, Sweet Charlotte* (1964) where Miriam (Olivia de Havilland, at center) exchanges harsh words with Jewel (Mary Astor) who is accompanied by her chauffeur (Bill Walker).

BELOW FAR LEFT: *Peyton Place* (1964) wharf takes over the prison camp set from *Von Ryan's Express* (1965) with the new Century City rising in the background.

BELOW LEFT: Raquel Welch adds some visual interest to the Peyton Place wharf in this portrait taken during the filming of *Fantastic Voyage* (1966).

STAGE FIVE (1930)

I'll be all around in the dark—I'll be everywhere. Wherever you can look—wherever there's a fight, so hungry people can eat, I'll be there. Wherever there's a cop beating up a guy—I'll be there. I'll be in the way guys yell when they're mad. I'll be there in the way kids laugh when they're hungry, and they know supper's ready, and when the people are eatin' the stuff they raised, living in the houses they build—I'll be there too.

—Henry Fonda as Tom Joad to Jane Darwell
as Ma Joad in The Grapes of Wrath *(1940),*
screenplay by Nunnally Johnson

This scene, among the most memorable in cinema history, was directed here by John Ford. Looking forward to the important scene Fonda recalled that he and Darwell were so well prepared that they performed it in one take. What film better represents Darryl Zanuck's Twentieth Century Fox? Once he believed in its indictment of the plight of the Oklahoma migrant workers—sending his own detective into the camps of California to discover that conditions were even worse than author John Steinbeck described in his book—Zanuck made the film, despite the incendiary feeling that caused him to name it *Highway 66*, while second unit director Otto Brower shot away from the protected confines of the studio.

To the surprise of many it was the studio's biggest hit of 1940. Jane Darwell led Fox's outstanding stock company in those days along with John Carradine, Sara Allgood, Nigel Bruce, Edna May Oliver, Sig Rumann, Jean Hersholt, Arthur Treacher, Joan Davis, Charles Coburn, John Sutton, Anne Revere, Sir Cedric Hardwicke, Spring Byington, Mary Nash, Thomas Mitchell, Reginald Gardner, Dorothy Adams, William Bendix, Lee J. Cobb, Charlotte Greenwood, and Helen Westley.

Besides this stage W. Asa Hudson contributed the [Joseph] Urban Building, the Jesse Lasky Building, the William Fox Theater, and the second of the stars' dressing rooms, among others. Stages Five, Six, and Eight are the largest on the Fox lot, at 30,000 square feet, with forty-foot ceilings. Stages

737-S-68

Five and Six contain upstairs rooms that have been used for everything from rehearsals for the musicals of Shirley Temple, Alice Faye, and Betty Grable to a gathering place for the science-fiction artists who developed *Alien* (1979).

It was a proud moment for Rita Hayworth when she played the Spanish temptress who seduced Tyrone Power in *Blood and Sand* (1941). That her work in this and *My Gal Sal* (1942) and *Tales of Manhattan* (1942) made her a star was ironic—and no doubt enraged Darryl Zanuck—since it was Harry Cohn's Columbia that would benefit. Of course the mogul had only himself to blame. Completely wasted when she was under contract here, while Winfield Sheehan was running the lot, Zanuck, too, had turned down her last-ditch effort for the lead in his prestige project, *Ramona* (1936). She would be back as an even better actress in Clifford Odets's *The Story on Page One* (1959).

Henry Fonda and Dana Andrews were surprised when they showed up here on *Daisy Kenyon's* (1947) apartment set and found that their costar had set the soundstage temperature to 58 degrees. Joan Crawford good-naturedly provided each with a pair of long underwear the following day.

Henry Hathaway made one of his best westerns, the tension-filled *Rawhide* (1950), starring Tyrone Power and Susan Hayward as captives in the "Rawhide Station" almost entirely here. Such thriftiness became lot legend. When directors argued with him about the importance of going on location Darryl Zanuck would also point out Stage Sixteen where Hathaway made almost all of *Diplomatic Courier* (1952).

Fox employees recall that Jean Peters preferred to be apart, quietly eating, picnic-style, on deserted sets with her makeup girl, Maureen McDermott, her hairdresser, Peanuts Ugrin, or her wardrobe girl, Gertie Casey. *Three Coins in the Fountain* (1954), made here, was her favorite film. For fans she retired too early from films and public view when she married Howard Hughes. The couple divorced in 1971, and toward the end of the year she married Fox executive Stanley Hough, whom she had known since her very first film, *Captain from Castile* (1947). By the 1970s Hough had risen to vice president in charge of studio operations, and he'd come to value her opinion of the films produced at the studio. She remained an influence at Fox even if she never granted herself a comeback. She remained married to Hough until his death in 1990.

Among Peters's costars in *Coins* was Clifton Webb, who was too ill to appear as Professor Oliver Lindenbrook in the studio's classic 1959 adaptation of Jules Verne's *Journey to the Center of the Earth*. James Mason was cast instead. Although Carlsbad Caverns National Park was utilized, Stages Five and Six held much of that spectacular underground

ABOVE: One of the massive caverns built for *Journey to the Center of the Earth* (1959).

LEFT: Jean Peters gets her makeup retouched during the filming of *Three Coins in the Fountain* (1954). Maggie McNamara sits to the left.

world that serves as another reminder of the stunning artistry at work on the lot. After launching their quest from the professor's home (also built here), the actors' adventures included Pat Boone narrowly avoiding asphyxiation when several hundred pounds of gypsum crystals fell on him.

Dale Hennesy, who won an Oscar as part of the team who designed the human lung set built here for *Fantastic Voyage* (1966), later created the atmospheric castle set (fifteen thousand square feet and thirty-five feet high) here for *Young Frankenstein*. The west side of the stage, appropriately facing Mel Brooks Boulevard, has a painting of the

ABOVE: Mel Brooks and the mural honoring *Young Frankenstein* (1974) on the west wall of Stage Five.

RIGHT: Director Mel Brooks directs a scene from *Young Frankenstein* (1974).

creation sequence from the film, dedicated in the fall of 2014.

Aaron Spelling's success updating *Dragnet* for the counterculture age with *The Mod Squad* (1968–73), produced primarily at Paramount but also on this stage, offered a first-time positive view of this younger generation and managed to draw these Baby Boomers back to television. Thereafter the stage witnessed a remarkable period of TV filmmaking. Besides Steven Bochco's multi-Emmy winner *L.A. Law* (1986–94), Chris Carter brought *The X-Files* (1993–2002) here after five seasons in Vancouver, Canada.

LEFT: The cast of *L.A. Law* (1986-94).

BOTTOM: David Duchovny directing the "Hollywood A.D." episode of *The X-Files* (1993-2002). (Front row L-R) Tea Leoni (Duchovny's wife), Gillian Anderson, Duchovny, and guest star Garry Shandling.

Joan Fontaine on the set of *Jane Eyre* (1944), one of the very best screen adaptions of the Charlotte Bronte novel.

STAGE SIX (1930)

Rebecca of Sunnybrook Farm (1938) was made here starring Shirley Temple. The impish Temple recalled that her directors tried various methods to keep her on the set, including a duck call that initially brought her running but later turned into a game of hide-and-seek. Costar Gloria Stuart adored her and shared the rest of the lot's awe for her talent. She remembered a director could always find extras from the crowd gathered around whatever set Temple and "Bojangles" Robinson

were working on. Unhappy with her "B" career at Universal in the mid-1930s (mostly "B-minuses," as she referred to them), she made such "A" pictures for Fox as John Ford's *The Prisoner of Shark Island* (1936). Stuart was featured, sixty years later, aboard *Titanic* (1997).

The loveliest and most talented sisters to work at Fox were Joan Fontaine and Olivia de Havilland, and some of their greatest work was performed on stages such as this one where Fontaine made *Jane Eyre* (1944), and de Havilland made *The Snake Pit* (1948), *My Cousin Rachel* (1952) and *Hush...Hush,*

ABOVE LEFT: The exterior of Stage Six, 2007.

ABOVE RIGHT: Portrait of Shirley Temple and Gloria Stuart taken for *Rebecca of Sunnybrook Farm* (1938). Over half a century later, Gloria would become famous again playing "Old Rose" in *Titanic* (1997).

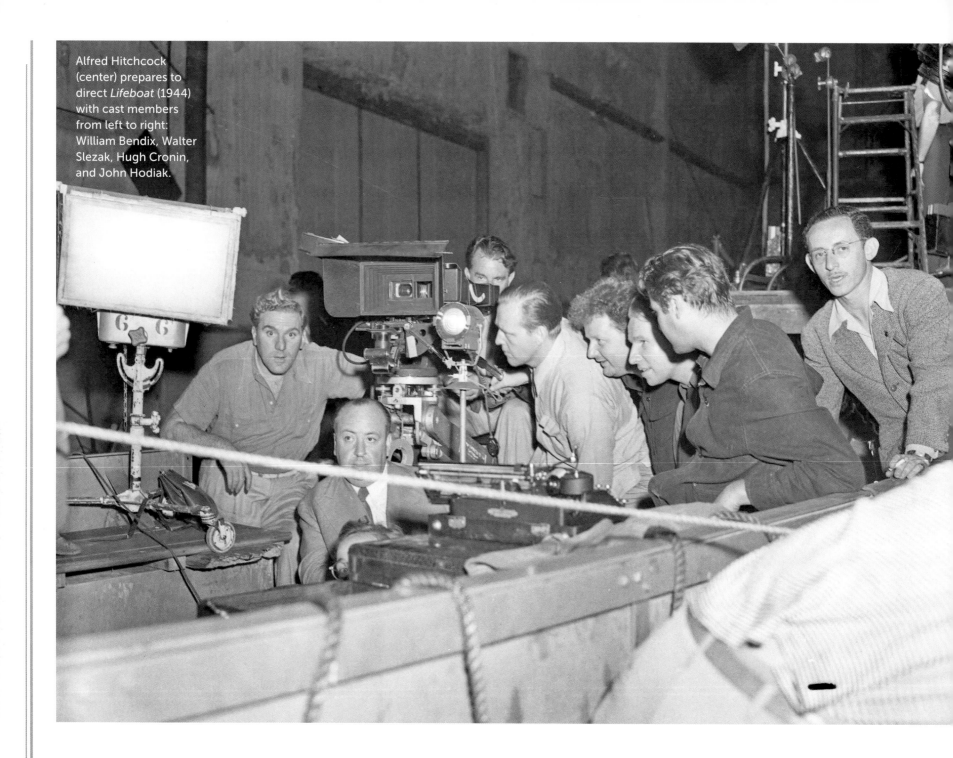

Alfred Hitchcock (center) prepares to direct *Lifeboat* (1944) with cast members from left to right: William Bendix, Walter Slezak, Hugh Cronin, and John Hodiak.

FAR LEFT: The Woodrow Wilson family arrives at the White House in *Wilson* (1944).

LEFT: Mr. Belvedere (Clifton Webb) as babysitter in *Sitting Pretty* (1948).

BELOW LEFT: The massive rocking ship in *Down to the Sea in Ships* (1949).

BELOW RIGHT: Richard Widmark, Dean Stockwell, and Jay C. Flippen in *Down to the Sea in Ships* (1949). Although the criminal parts he played made him a star at Fox, Widmark declared "enough" and broke the pattern with this film. "He was one of the best actors," said Jules Dassin.

RIGHT: "Shall We Dance" from the *King and I* (1956) with Yul Brynner and Deborah Kerr. Such spectacular sets as this ballroom; the throne room, temple and banquet hall on Stage Six; the harem gardens set on Stage Fourteen; the palace courtyard, schoolroom and pool on Stage Fifteen; and Anna's apartment, King's study, and presentation room on Stage Sixteen earned an Academy Award.

FAR RIGHT: The elegant Promenade Room set for *The Towering Inferno* (1974).

BOTTOM: The upside-down main dining room set from *The Poseidon Adventure* (1972).

Sweet Charlotte (1964), directed by Robert Aldrich. The historic Houmas House plantation in Mississippi was recreated at Fox for that film.

"Everybody should do a biblical picture—once," Aldrich said of *The Last Days of Sodom and Gomorrah* (1961). "The Hebraic tribes wouldn't work on Saturday. The Italians wouldn't work on Sunday. Sergio Leone was second-unit director and he was loafing and was terrible...I called him and I said, 'Get your ticket and go back to Rome; you're through.' He went back to Rome, and they had no director for the first Clint Eastwood picture and that's why he's a zillionaire and I'm broke."

After Darryl Zanuck's ambitious *Wilson* (1944), with its costly interiors of the White House, the stage resorted to a household kitchen for *Sitting Pretty* (1948), and the classic scene in which Clifton Webb, as babysitter Mr. Belvedere, dumps a bowl of oatmeal on his young charge. Anticipating the baby's violent reaction, the crew nailed his chair to the floor, tied him in and fastened the bowl to his head, and only then began pouring the mush. Everyone was mystified when his reaction instead was laughter—laughter that only became tears when the lights of the stage were shut off and his mother called "Good-bye."

Recalled producer Samuel Engel: "After the first smash reviews of *Sitting Pretty* came in, I approached our star, Clifton Webb, and said, 'Well, now that you're such a success, I suppose you won't talk to us.' Clifton replied, 'My dear boy, I have always been a success. One more hit will not unsettle me.' "

The full-scale whaling ship for Henry Hathaway's *Down to the Sea in Ships* (1949) was built on hydraulics left over from *The Sea Wolf* (1930). The film featured Dean Stockwell, who literally grew up in significant Fox films. He was eleven when he made *Gentleman's Agreement* (1948), twelve when he made *Down to the Sea in Ships*, twenty-two when he made *Compulsion* (1959), twenty-three when he made *Sons and Lovers* (1960), and twenty-eight when he made *Rapture* (1965).

You're in the Navy Now (1952) featured the film debuts of more important talent: Charles Bronson, Lee Marvin and Jack Warden.

The climactic "Shall We Dance" ballroom sequence was shot here for *The King and I* (1956). Despite the heat—the enormous set required a record 58,000 amps—and physical challenges—Deborah Kerr's enormous hoopskirts bruised her legs, and Yul Brynner required an oxygen tank because he had only one lung—everyone involved with the production remember it as an extraordinary experience. The multimillion-dollar production was the costliest film at Twentieth Century Fox up to that time. *Variety* called it "one of the all-time greats, socko in all departments . . . as the King

ABOVE: Spencer Tracy as Richard and Katharine Hepburn as Bunny stand in front of the modern EMMARAC computer (supplied by IBM) meant to replace the human researchers at a major corporation in the delightful *Desk Set* (1957). Neva Patterson as the efficiency expert stands behind them.

himself might say, et cetera, et cetera, et cetera."

The research department set for *Desk Set* (1957), starring Spencer Tracy and Katharine Hepburn, was here. It was a replica of the Broadway original, including the enormous Emmarac computer whose noises were developed by Fox soundman Ralph Hickey, and later incorporated into *Fantastic Voyage* (1966), TV series *The Time Tunnel* (1966–67), and numerous other science-fiction films and television shows. The computer "Emmy" turns up in *The Fly* (1958), the sequel, and the 1961 film and television series, *Voyage to the Bottom of the Sea* (1964-68). Tracy was later considered for *Ten North Frederick* (1958) with Suzy Parker and a remake of *The Blue Angel* (1959) with Marilyn Monroe.

Joan Collins recalled that when she rehearsed here for her role as a stripper in *Seven Thieves* (1960), the stage became remarkably popular with male personnel who found the excuse of using it as a shortcut to Stages Four or Five, or even the commissary.

Launching a four-and-a-half-month shoot, Ronald Neame directed Gene Hackman, Ernest Borgnine, Carol Lynley, Shelley Winters, Roddy McDowall, and Stella Stevens here in the enormous interior set of the *Poseidon* for Irwin Allen's *The Poseidon Adventure* (1972). By the time cast and crew returned to this stage after a week on the *Queen Mary,* the set had been turned spectacularly

upside down. The film spawned fan clubs, a sequel, a 2006 remake by Warner Bros., television movies, and the even grander, even more profitable *The Towering Inferno* (1974). That all-star cast showed up for this stage's last burst of old Hollywood glamour as the Promenade Room decorated with the fountain used in the Harmonia Gardens Scene of *Hello, Dolly!* (1969). In all there were fifty-seven sets—the most ever built for a Fox film to date.— Ten 1,000-gallon dump tanks were used for the final dousing of this set.

"The first problem with fire was how to keep it from setting off the sprinklers in the soundstages," recalled production designer William Creber. "So at the meeting I said, 'That's easy; we'll just turn the valve off.' The Fire Department said shutting off the sprinkler system with the express intent of setting a fire was considered arson. So we had a fireman with a thermometer, and whenever it would get to be 145 degrees he would shut the company down."

These two epics marked the end of an era for the Century City lot. Never again would the studio be the primary center of Fox filmmaking. Producers increasingly preferred to make their films else-where for financial and artistic reasons. Instead, television production began filling the soundstages, like the Spelling-Goldberg hit *Starsky & Hutch* shot here (and on Stage Twenty) from 1975 to 1979.

The site of a modern office building set circa

1957 (Desk Set) became the site of an office set, circa 1980, for 9 to 5. After Jane Fonda heard stories about the bad treatment secretaries receive, she and Bruce Gilbert decided to produce a serious film on the subject. Then, during script preparations, she enjoyed Lily Tomlin's hilarious one-woman show and heard Dolly Parton on the radio, and decided to turn it into a comedy. Parton in turn was inspired to write the theme song with the help of the women on the set. The film and then the TV series marked Fonda's debut as a producer on the lot. She always marveled at just how unique it was. From the organizing effort came the movie that built the movement and the United Public Service Employees Union. The song, of course, became the anthem of that movement.

Having missed out on the opportunity to release the Geroge Lucas/Steven Spielberg *Indiana Jones* films, Fox put into production John Carpenter's cult classic *Big Trouble in Little China* (1986). Although establishing shots were done in downtown Los Angeles, the moment Kurt Russell turns his truck into a narrow foggy alleyway, he is on this stage—the same one he had been on as a guest star of *Lost in Space* in 1966. It was one of many fantastically elaborate sets built on the lot by production designer John Lloyd in the fall of 1985. Among the impressed visitors were Michael Jackson and his sister Janet Jackson, who used them for a music video. Also appearing in *Big Trouble* in her first credited big-screen role is Richard Burton's daughter, Kate Burton, who later appeared in *Judging Amy* (1999–2005) and *127 Hours* (2010).

ABOVE LEFT: The look of the American office had changed dramatically by the time Judy Bernly (Jane Fonda, sitting at left) and Violet Newstead (Lily Tomlin, standing) entered the work force in *9 to 5* (1980).

ABOVE RIGHT: The massive set of the Jeffersonian in the TV show *Bones*. Emily Deschanel as Temperance Brennan is at the right of the car.

The Welsh village from *How Green Was My Valley* (1941) was transformed into a Norwegian town that suffers under Nazi occupation in *The Moon is Down* (1943).

THE CENTURY RANCH

There is no fence nor hedge 'round time that is gone. You can go back and have what you like of it if you can remember. So I can close my eyes on my valley as it is today and it is gone, and I see it as it was when I was a boy . . .

—Introduction to How Green Was My Valley *(1941), screenplay by Nunnally Johnson*

Thirty miles from the urban sprawl of Los Angeles that surrounds the Westwood studio, off Highway 101 at the Las Virgenes Road exit, are 2,403 historic acres recognizable around the world, thanks to Darryl Zanuck's Twentieth Century Fox. At first, it was known as the "Brent's Crag Location," named for one of the property's most prominent geographical features, in the early years when it was used for *Chicken Wagon Family* (1939), *Brigham Young* (1940), *The Mark of Zorro* (1940), and *Belle Star* (1941). The production of *How Green Was My Valley* (1941) forever immortalized these Malibu hills when Richard Day designed that impressive eighty-acre Welsh village and coal mining set.

That it was made there was a unique twist of fate when World War II, and a board of directors that doubted its box office potential, nixed Darryl Zanuck's grand plans for a Technicolor epic made on location in Wales. John Ford wanted to blacken the hillside with coal, but wartime shortages preempted that, so twenty thousand gallons of black paint had to suffice. Zanuck purchased the property, officially dubbing it the Century Ranch in 1945. The village would appear again as Norway in *The Moon Is Down* (1943)—another ambitious filmization of a John Steinbeck work—and then as part

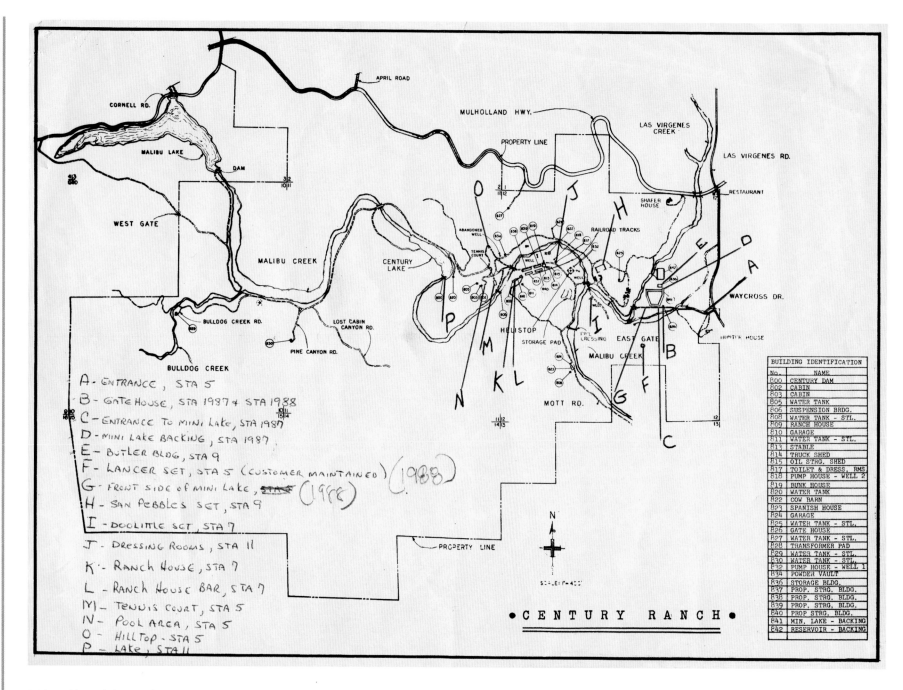

A - ENTRANCE, STA 5
B - GATE HOUSE, STA 1987 & STA 1988
C - ENTRANCE TO MINI LAKE, STA 1987
D - MINI LAKE BACKING, STA 1987
E - BUTLER BLDG, STA 9
F - LANCER SET, STA 5 (CUSTOMER MAINTAINED) (1988)
G - FRONT SIDE OF MINI LAKE, STA 5 (1988)
H - SAN PEBBLES SET, STA 9
I - DOOLITTLE SET, STA 7
J - DRESSING ROOMS, STA 11
K - RANCH HOUSE, STA 7
L - RANCH HOUSE BAR, STA 7
M - TENNIS COURT, STA 5
N - POOL AREA, STA 5
O - HILLTOP - STA 5
P - LAKE, STA 11

BUILDING IDENTIFICATION	
No.	NAME
800	CENTURY DAM
802	CABIN
803	CABIN
805	WATER TANK
806	SUSPENSION BRDG.
808	WATER TANK - STL.
809	RANCH HOUSE
810	GARAGE
811	WATER TANK - STL.
813	STABLE
814	TRUCK SHED
815	OIL STHG. SHED
817	TOILET & DRESS. RMS
818	PUMP HOUSE - WELL 2
819	BUNK HOUSE
820	WATER TANK
822	COW BARN
823	SPANISH HOUSE
824	GARAGE
825	WATER TANK - STL.
826	GATE HOUSE
827	WATER TANK - STL.
828	TRANSFORMER PAD
829	WATER TANK - STL.
830	WATER TANK - STL.
832	PUMP HOUSE - WELL 1
834	POWDER VAULT
836	STORAGE BLDG.
837	PROP. STRG. BLDG.
838	PROP. STRG. BLDG.
839	PROP. STRG. BLDG.
840	PROP STRG. BLDG.
841	MIN. LAKE - BACKING
842	RESERVOIR - BACKING

• C E N T U R Y   R A N C H •

ABOVE: Map of the ranch

of the mission in remotest China for *The Left Hand of God* (1955).

Tierney would remember costar Humphrey Bogart as particularly sympathetic toward her as she began her struggle with mental illness. "I was admitted to three different hospitals—sanitariums, if you prefer—over a period of six years," she said. "So there is hope for everybody."

Witnessing filmmaking at the Ranch at its height in the 1950s was Richard Todd, who Zanuck considered key to the success of *A Man Called Peter* (1955), *The Virgin Queen* (1955), and *D-Day the Sixth of June* (1956).

"The studios were vast in comparison with their counterparts in Europe," he recalled. "At the Fox Ranch there were wood-and-plaster fortresses, stockades, mining townships and ranch buildings used again and again in Westerns, an Indian village left over from a Tyrone Power film, a Mexican village, and what looked to me like part of a medieval English hamlet. California's climate made it possible for these flimsy structures to remain intact for years, something that would have been impossible in Europe."

Zanuck was equally impressed with the Dublin-born matinee idol's heroic service during World War II, and asked him to play himself and re-enact his active part in D-Day, as Captain in the Parachute Regiment (the 6th Airborne) for *The Longest Day* (1962).

ABOVE LEFT: The set of the Welsh village in *How Green Was My Valley* (1941).

ABOVE RIGHT: John Ford gives directions to Maureen O'Hara and Walter Pidgeon in *How Green Was My Valley* (1941).

LEFT: The cast of *How Green Was My Valley* (1941).

ABOVE LEFT: Gene Tierney and Humphrey Bogart are filmed as they stroll along the ranch which doubled for China in *The Left Hand of God* (1955).

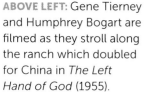

ABOVE RIGHT: That "high and windy hill" was actually in the Santa Monica mountains, not Hong Kong even though many of the on-location shots were made there for *Love is a Many-Splendored Thing* (1955) starring William Holden and Jennifer Jones.

Instead Todd chose to play Major John Howard who speaks to an officer of the Parachute Regiment that would have been young Captain Todd himself.

That ranch or farmhouse set is the one where Cary Grant proposes to Jeanne Crain in the richly comic *People Will Talk* (1951), and where June Haver and Natalie Wood lived in *Scudda Hoo! Scudda Hay!* (1948). That film brought Marilyn Monroe out here for a sequence at Century Lake, all seven acres of it dammed up from Malibu Creek by wealthy businessmen at the turn of the twentieth century as part of Crags Country Club. Marilyn was back during her romance with Elia Kazan while he directed *Viva Zapata!* (1952).

The farmhouse set became the home of the doomed Booths for *Prince of Players* (1955), the Amish for *Violent Saturday* (1955), and Elvis Presley in *Love Me Tender* (1956). He also made *Flaming Star* (1960) and *Wild in the Country* (1961) out here when he was arguably the most famous entertainer in the world. Not famous enough, however, to access the telephone. While making these movies he discovered to his dismay that the ranch had only one phone, and that was at the Torpin home, the caretakers of the property, who were distantly related to the Zanucks. When he showed up there, Mrs. Torpin would not let the star, with his muddy boots, into the house.

For the next fifteen years that remarkable topography of rising cliffs and canyons would substitute for China again, both for the legendary love scene "high on a windy hill" between William Holden and Jennifer Jones, for *Love Is a Many-Splendored Thing* (1955), and as the site of the China Light mission, where seaman Steve McQueen reunites with teacher Candice Bergen in *The Sand Pebbles* (1966). It provided a fantastic setting for Arthur P. Jacobs's *Doctor Dolittle* (1967) and *Planet of the Apes* (1968), and for Paul Newman and Robert Redford's memorable jump in *Butch Cassidy and the Sundance Kid* (1969).

But what brings most fans to the area is the fact that it served as Korea—due to budgetary reasons, Richard Zanuck insisted—for the film and television show based on Dr. H. Richard Hornberger's novel, *MASH: A Novel About Three Army Doctors.* It was Ingo Preminger, brother of Otto, who proposed making the film that Robert Aldrich

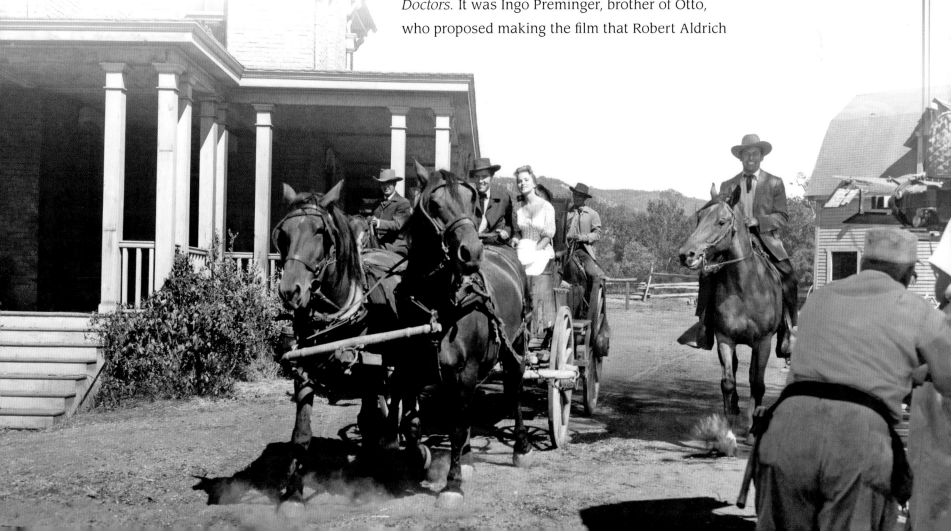

RIGHT: This scene with Robert Redford, left, and Paul Newman from *Butch Cassidy and the Sundance Kid* (1969) was filmed in Utah, but the long shot of the jump that followed was filmed at the ranch.

FAR RIGHT: Batman (Adam West) drives the Batboat in this scene from the *Batman* (1966) movie, which was filmed in the tank on the ranch.

BOTTOM: Lee Meriwether as Catwoman and her daughters in front of the tank used in *Batman* (1966).

turned into a classic. The TV version, using the still-standing sets, was pitched successfully to CBS. Gene Reynolds, whose career at Fox stretched from his child-star days in *In Old Chicago* (1938) to directing *Room 222,* supervised production.

After the Westwood backlot was razed some sets were moved here, including railroad cars, and a water tank was built for filming *Cleopatra*'s (1963) miniatures. It became the second [Fred] Sersen Lake featuring sloped sides that allowed trucks to access the bottom for set placement. The tank held three million gallons, with a sump behind the backing capable of storing four million gallons.

The pump could fill the lake in one hour and forty minutes, and it could be drained back into the sump in fifty minutes. The front of the tank was 198 feet wide. The backing faced south, toward the sun, and was 366 feet wide and 85 feet high. The top tilted away 14 degrees from the bottom to the top to better catch the sunlight. Over this a heavy canvas that could be painted was nailed to the ply-wood. The tank was also used for *Batman* (1966), and emptied to hold models and the forty-foot-high mock-up for stunt people for *The Towering Inferno* (1974).

Although merger plans in May of 1963 between

ABOVE LEFT: The ape village for *Planet of the Apes* (1968) was built at the ranch.

ABOVE RIGHT: Other scenes from *Planet of the Apes* (1968) were also shot on the ranch including at the rock pool where the astronauts swim. (L-R) Charlton Heston, Robert Gunner, and Jeff Burton.

LEFT: Things get a bit tense in the ape village built on the ranch.

TOP: Filming the opening sequence of *M*A*S*H* (1970) at the ranch.

ABOVE: Donald Sutherland (far left) and Elliott Gould receive instructions during the filming *of M*A*S*H* (1970) which was shot on the ranch. Director Robert Altman is on the far right

ABOVE RIGHT: The *M*A*S*H* (1972-1983) TV show was also camped out here.

Darryl Zanuck, Columbia president A. Schneider, and MGM chief Robert H. O'Brien, including the construction of a "Malibu Studio," proved prohibitively expensive the company did purchase 236 acres from soon-to-be-governor Ronald Reagan in December of 1966. They paid $1.9 million for this land, adjacent to the Ranch, and signed a six-year option to buy Reagan's remaining fifty-four acres, although the option was never exercised.

In 1974 Twentieth Century Fox sold the property to the state for $4.8 million under a lease-back agreement in order to continue filmmaking there. Malibu Creek State Park was opened in 1976. In October of 1982 a devastating fire, believed to be arson, destroyed the *M*A*S*H* camp, except for one tent. Filming for the last seven episodes was subsequently adjusted. Although it remains a popular site for filming, Walter Pidgeon's words for *How Green Was My Valley* (1941) are apt: "Something has gone out of this valley that may never be replaced."

LEFT: The exterior of Stage Eight, 2015.

BELOW LEFT: Shirley Temple unveils the plaque at the dedication of Stage Eight to Will Rogers in 1935.

BELOW RIGHT: The Fox Fire Department in front of the fire station that was located on the east side of Stage Eight with Olympic Boulevard just beyond, 1945.

STAGE EIGHT (1935)

Helping to build this stage was Ed Conlon, whose father was fire chief in the station that once neighbored it. Hugh Conlon was in charge of the studio's forty-seven volunteer firemen, shared with the Western Avenue Studio. The Conlons came here in June of 1926 when a friend sold Fox a fire truck and told them they needed someone to run the department. For two months their first home was a closed-in Tom Mix set, with plumbing installed, until the station and a permanent residence was built (Bldg. 139). Ed remembered that after building Stage Eight he worked in the mill before joining the fire department in 1938. He was made captain in 1961 when his father retired, and then chief of plant protection by Richard Zanuck in 1966. Father and son prided themselves that, until economic cutbacks, the Los Angeles Fire Department never had to lay a section of hose on the lot.

Stage Eight was dedicated to Will Rogers upon his death. Shirley Temple presided over the memorial service on November 15, 1935, and unveiled a copper plate that exists at the entrance to this day.

> You made the whole world laugh
> and made the whole world love you.
> 1879–1935

Interesting trivia for *Batman* fans: The 1966 film was shot on this stage—the same one used for *The Mark of Zorro* (1940). The connection? In the 1986 comic reboot of *Batman,* as the Dark Knight Bruce Wayne's parents go to see *The Mark of Zorro* the night they are killed, Wayne models his costume after Tyrone Power's masked man.

When director Henry Hathaway chose Grace Kelly over Anne Bancroft, he made history here directing her on an office set for *Fourteen Hours* (1951). It was her film debut. Darryl Zanuck signed

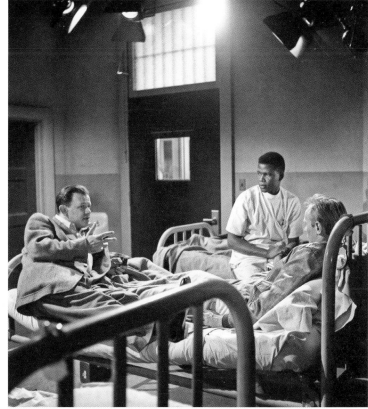

only Bancroft to a studio contract, which he regretted when Kelly became a much bigger star at MGM. Hathaway also regretted Zanuck's decision to give the movie a happy ending. Hathaway had shot the main character (Richard Basehart) jumping to his death, but when Spyros Skouras's daughter actually did jump from a window the day the picture was previewed, Skouras wanted the film destroyed. Six months later Darryl Zanuck added the new ending. Princess Grace of Monaco was later appointed a member of the Fox board of directors by Dennis Stanfill and served from 1976 to 1981.

The County Hospital built here for Joseph Mankiewicz's *No Way Out* (1950) is another historic set. It was the setting for Sidney Poitier's unforgettable film debut as Dr. Luther Brooks, a black intern dealing with a racist patient (Richard Widmark). Poitier never forgot how supportive the cast, particularly Widmark, was. Joseph Mankiewicz and Darryl Zanuck produced it knowing it would not—and indeed, was not—screened below the Mason-Dixon Line. *Ebony* magazine praised it as one of the first honest films ever made about contemporary African-American life. That studio tradition would continue with *The Great White Hope* (1970), *Waiting to Exhale* (1995), and *House M.D.* (2004-12) starring the Image Award-winning Omar Epps as Dr. Eric Foreman. Forest Whitaker has had a productive studio partnership as director (*Waiting to Exhale, Hope Floats*), and actor (*Phone Booth, The Last King of Scotland, Street Kings, Black Nativity, Taken 3*).

Samuel Fuller's *Fixed Bayonets!* (1951) is unique both for its single primary set, and for featuring among its "dogfaces" James Dean. When Ivan Martin complained to Darryl Zanuck that Fuller's habit of shooting off a gun to get his stars' attention was ruining the soundstage roof, Zanuck summoned Fuller to his "Z" Theater for a screening of the film. During a particularly tense scene Zanuck pulled out a gun and fired it. Fuller leapt for the exit, terrified—a lesson learned.

Jayne Mansfield once said: "The quality of making everyone stop in their tracks is what I work at." She certainly did that earning lasting fame for playing, in characteristic over-the-top-yet-knowing style, roles like movie star Rita Marlowe in *Will Success Spoil Rock Hunter?* (1957). This is the stage where she made one of the funniest phone calls in motion picture history, using Tony Randall to make "jungle man" Bobo Branigansky (Mickey Hargitay) jealous. Mansfield and Hargitary wed in real life in January of 1958. After her tragic death she was portrayed in a TV movie by Loni Anderson, and Hargitay, by Austrian muscleman and future Fox star, Arnold Schwarzenegger.

And when Soviet leader Nikita Khrushchev and his wife visited the Bal du Paradis set of

FAR LEFT: Joan Blondell and Tony Randall learn from a master as Jayne Mansfield baits her boyfriend on the telephone in *Will Success Spoil Rock Hunter?* (1957).

LEFT: Raquel Welch hangs on to a wall of lights during the filming of *Fantastic Voyage* (1966).

BOTTOM: Soviet Premier Nikita Krushchev and his wife watch a scene from *Can-Can* (1960) with Frank Sinatra and Juliet Prowse.

Jack Cummings's *Can-Can* (1960), Frank Sinatra informed them: "This is a movie about a lot of pretty girls, and the fellas that like pretty girls."

"Oh, what a day that was," recalled costar Shirley MacLaine. "When I learned I was to be hostess of the whole event, I went over to UCLA to learn the language so I could welcome him properly. I must have been unclear about it, because when he got off the plane I greeted him in Czarist Russian!

"Those costumes were Irene Sharaff originals, and she insisted that they be the original fabric. My velvet costume weighed seventy-five pounds so that it would swirl and be effective. When we made the film we shot little sections, but in front of Khrushchev we had to do the whole dance, and I thought I was going to have a heart attack. During filming I was also witness to Frank falling in love with Juliet Prowse on the afternoon he sang to her, 'It's The Wrong Face.' "

The idol of Sinatra's youth, Bing Crosby, made *Say One for Me* (1959)—the interior of the church—and *High Time* (1960)—his fraternity dorm room—here. The popularity of *High Time*'s "The Second Time Around" led to a Debbie Reynolds/Steve Forrest vehicle called *The Second Time Around* (1962), also made on this stage. All in the family: Crosby's son Gary was under contract and appeared in *Mardi Gras* (1958) and *Holiday for Lovers* (1959), also shot here. Watch for Gavin MacLeod as a member of the faculty in *High Time*. He re-appeared on the lot as the captain of *The Love Boat* (1977–86).

Raquel Welch recalled the science-fiction classic *Fantastic Voyage* (1966), directed by Richard Fleischer, as eight months of hanging from wires on this stage. Tom Mankiewicz dubbed the five women Welch employed for public relations, wardrobe, hair, and makeup "the Raquettes."

Now welcome to the world of the camp classic *Valley of the Dolls* (1967). Like *Peyton Place* it was based on a notorious novel, and the star was the hit television show's Barbara Parkins, who lobbied for the part by going directly to Richard Zanuck's office. Twenty-year-old Patty Duke was playing a part inspired by Judy Garland's career. To complete the triumvirate of women facing show business, Sharon Tate earned the role initially earmarked for Raquel Welch, as the doomed Jennifer. The character was allegedly based on the tragic career of Fox's own Carole Landis. Three years later Tate would be murdered by the Mansons at the age of twenty-six. Thirty years after she had made her feature film debut on the lot, Garland was signed for the role of veteran entertainer Helen Lawson. Parkins remembers working with her here in Lawson's dressing room set until insecurity, medication, and depression over the script caused

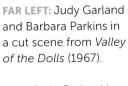

FAR LEFT: Judy Garland and Barbara Parkins in a cut scene from *Valley of the Dolls* (1967).

LEFT: Judy Garland in her film debut, *Pigskin Parade* (1936).

BOTTOM: Bruce Willis in front of the mural on Stage Eight celebrating the successful *Die Hard* franchise.

her to be replaced after only a few days by that old Fox pro, Susan Hayward.

Blake (John Forsythe) and Krystle (Linda Evans) Carrington's mansion interior set was built here for *Dynasty* (1981–89).

To commemorate the twenty-fifth anniversary of the *Die Hard* franchise, and to promote the release of *A Good Day to Die Hard* (2013), a mural depicting Bruce Willis in a scene from the first film was painted on the east side of the building.

RIGHT: Stars' Dressing Rooms, view from north-west corner soon after construction.

BELOW LEFT: View from southwest corner.

BELOW RIGHT: View of east façade.

Bldg. 86: Stars' Dressing Rooms Building (1936)

With the demand for more room for Fox's female stars, this Regency Revival building, by Beverly Hills designer Douglas Honnold, replaced the Café de Paris's formal garden. It was the first built under Darryl Zanuck's expansion plans under the direction of engineer J. A. Barlow. Male stars eventually moved in upstairs and throughout the building, in its fourteen suites lettered "A" through "N."

The building still features decorative gold stars above each window, memorializing Darryl Zanuck's brilliant constellation of talent who once lived within. Alice Faye was the first to receive "M," the largest dressing room in the southeast corner of the building, on the ground floor. While dating Tony Martin, Faye asked neighbor Jane Withers to come over if she knocked on her wall—the signal that Martin's amorous advances were going too far. Betty Grable, Joan Crawford, and Marilyn Monroe later occupied that suite.

When Henry King turned down Don Ameche in favor of Tyrone Power for *Lloyd's of London* (1937), he launched Power's legendary career that included such fringe benefits as the equally spacious "E" suite, directly above on the second floor. Power was introduced to his first wife, actress Annabella, in the hallway here by a wardrobe woman before they began *Suez* (1938). Like other big stars on the lot, Power had his own secretary, stand-in, and wardrobe designer. Zanuck was indulgent and, rare for the mogul, a friend to this star. After Will Rogers was killed he seldom allowed his top talent to fly, but Ty did, flying over the studio late at night with Howard Hughes, and then buying a plane from Hughes to fly elsewhere. When Power playfully carved "DZ" instead of a "Z" in a take for *The Mark of Zorro* (1940), Zanuck got back at him by turning off the heater in the administration building's swimming pool, which he allowed Power to use.

Like Withers, Ethel Merman and Cesar Romero had a lot of fun on this lot. For example, there was the time Harry Brand tried to cook up a romance between them during filming of her Fox debut *Happy Landing* (1938).

"He wasn't free with a buck, to put it mildly," she said. "So every time an item about us appeared, I'd order a beautiful floral arrangement for myself, have his card attached and charge it to his account. Upon its arrival, I'd thank him profusely and he'd sputter, 'I never ordered that.' On one occasion a hearse drew up to collect the body. Guess who was behind all this?"

No one enjoyed his Latin Lover image more than the suave Romero. It showed and audiences loved him for it in more than forty Fox films. No doubt William Dozier's most inspired casting decision for his *Batman* TV series was casting Romero as the Joker.

In the 1940s Gene Tierney proudly led what she dubbed "The Fox Girls"—including best friend Cobina Wright Jr. and Linda Darnell, who brought her pet rooster that showed up in *Chad Hanna* (1940). Among Roddy McDowall's "chums" was Henry Fonda. Their contests to see who could hold their breath longer were recorded on Fonda's dressing room wall. Another handsome face around here was George Montgomery, who can be seen around the lot with "B" favorite Mary Beth Hughes in *The Cowboy and the Blonde* (1941). His wife Dinah Shore later hosted the popular Fox TV show, *Dinah!* (1974–80). Dana Andrews recalled having his apartment next to Alice Faye's and enjoyed spending more time there. Dana's younger brother Steve Forrest debuted in his *Crash Dive* (1943), and later starred in the Spelling/Goldberg hit *S.W.A.T.* (1975–76) on the lot. Jennifer Jones preferred arrangements of lemons rather than flowers in her dressing room. "I'm easy keep," low-maintenance Anne Baxter told the matron who was running this building when she moved in. As persevering as Betty Grable despite unsuccessful bit parts as Frank McCown—try and find him in *Something for the Boys* (1944), *Sunday Dinner for a Soldier* (1944), *The Bullfighters* (1945), and *Nob Hill* (1945)—Rory Calhoun earned a spot in

these hallowed halls playing characters audiences enjoyed rooting for like Jack Stark in *I'd Climb The Highest Mountain* (1951). He dated Jeanne Crain, but she preferred to marry former actor Paul Brinkman. In the 1950s Clifton Webb inherited Tyrone Power's dressing room and was enthroned there as the studio's social lion. "He was very social and very dear in his way," recalled Myrna Loy. "It just had to be his way."

Terry Moore arrived on the lot with fellow Columbia contract player Marilyn Monroe and was established here in 1952 with an apartment on the first floor on the north end. Of the others she remembered seeing in the building—Robert Wagner, Don Murray, Jeffrey Hunter, Jeanne Crain, and Jean Peters—she only had trouble with Peters ("We were all so competitive!"), who was dating Howard Hughes at the same time she was. She married Hughes in 1949, but Hughes publicly married Peters a few years later.

Buddy Adler gave his new contract players Don Murray and Hope Lange a week off in April of 1956 to get married during production of *Bus Stop* (1956). Because his fame preceded hers they shared a dressing room here with his name on it. "It's useful having a husband who rates a lay-out like this," Lange (known as "Hopie" on the lot) said. "I'd just as soon go on using Don's dressing room. Everyone expects me to anyway."

35

NORTH ENTRANCE

| A | JUNE HAVER | | CLIFTON WEBB |
| B | JEANNE CRAIN | | |

WEST ENTRANCE

E	TYRONE POWER		
F			MYRNA LOY
G			BETTE DAVIS
H			BETTY GRABLE
I	SUSAN HAYWARD		ANNE BAXTER

FAR LEFT: The formal garden that existed on the site prior to construction, 1934. The Colonial Home and Chateau Tokay can be seen across Olympic Boulevard.

LEFT: Directory showing who occupied the suites on October 31, 1951.

BELOW: Floorplan showing the layout of the original dressing room suites. The letters by the doors indicate the suite names and the numbers indicate the square footage.

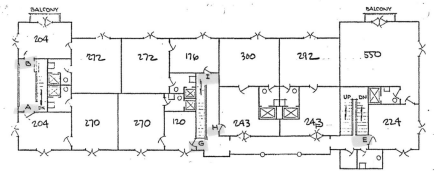

SECOND FLOOR

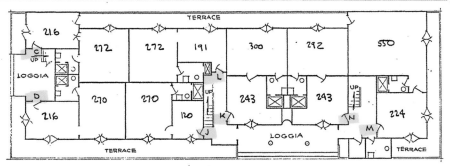

FIRST FLOOR

STARS DRESSING ROOMS №86

SCALE 1/16 = 1'-0"

ABOVE LEFT: The huge dressing room "M" as decorated for Joan Crawford in mid-century modern. It remained much the same when it was Marilyn Monroe's in the 1950s.

ABOVE RIGHT: The sitting room of dressing room "M" as decorated for Joan Crawford in 1947.

RIGHT: The porthole on the east wall of dressing room "M" was removed when the main room was split into two offices. This is how the exterior appeared in 2015.

Dark beauty Dana Wynter ("I pronounce it Donna because that sounds more feminine") made her American film debut in *The View from Pompey's Head* (1955), a quintessential Zanuck 1950s movie mixing soap opera and social conscience in a literary strain.

Russ Tamblyn recalled having a dressing room across from Robert Mitchum while he made *Peyton Place* (1957). In the early mornings, after visiting the makeup department and waiting for shooting to start, he would find Mitchum here with triple-shot vodkas with orange juice for breakfast.

Once, refusing to answer the telephone, Mitchum threw it out the window. "[Mitchum's] air of casualness or, rather, his lack of pomposity is put down as a lack of seriousness, but when I say he's a fine actor, I mean an actor of the caliber of Oliver, Burton, and Brando," said John Huston.

Susan Hayward did some of her best work on this lot, and despite the tough, even manipulative, parts she played that earned her the title "Wayward Hayward," employees recall her with great affection. "The wardrobe girls, the makeup men, the crew—they all seemed to like her very much,"

BOTTOM LEFT: Alice Faye in the huge dressing room "M", 1939.

BOTTOM RIGHT: A chauffeur waits for Loretta Young outside Building 86, 1937.

RIGHT: Betty Grable shows her patriotism with this shirt displaying all of the emblems of the armed forces as she stands in the loggia on the first floor, circa 1945. The black mark indicates that the studio thought that her shirt should be a bit longer.

FAR RIGHT: Betty Grable touches up her makeup in her elegant dressing room, 1946.

BELOW RIGHT: Betty Grable's dressing room decorated in an ornate Victorian style. Note the picture of husband Harry James on the table at left, 1947.

recalled Fox publicist Sonia Wolfson. "I never heard any of them say an unkind thing about her."

By the time the former Queen of the Lot had returned to make *The Marriage-Go-Round* (1960), the building's glamour was fading with the end of the stars-under-contract system. Pat Boone, one of the last to sign a seven-year contract during this period, remembers his apartment as the one closest to the commissary, where the food was.

M.S-12#6

Television stars soon replaced movie stars in the dressing rooms, until they became offices in the mid-1970s. The building was redesigned to its current look for Lawrence Gordon's production company—including enclosing the porches and staircases with steel and glass—in 1986. Chris Columbus's production company, 1492 Productions and Knickerbocker Films Production (*Fight Club*, 1999), have been housed here. Currently the In-Theatre Marketing group resides within. Of course, it has appeared in numerous movies (*Mardi Gras*, 1958), and television shows (*Peyton Place*).

ABOVE LEFT: Maureen O'Hara's dressing room decorated in an 18th century English style, 1947.

ABOVE RIGHT: Maureen O'Hara, standing at the north end of Building 86, apparently doesn't believe that it never rains in southern California, 1941.

RIGHT: Tyrone Power at his vanity in dressing room "E" on the second floor, 1948.

FAR RIGHT: Tyrone Power gets properly fitted in his large dressing room.

BELOW RIGHT: Tyrone Power does some reading in his dressing room.

OPPOSITE LEFT: Ethel Merman in front of Building 86 during the filming of *Call Me Madam* (1953).

OPPOSITE RIGHT: Cesar Romero in a hurry, circa 1939.

872-S-46

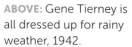

ABOVE: Gene Tierney is all dressed up for rainy weather, 1942.

ABOVE RIGHT: Gene Tierney's room decorated in a Gay Nineties theme, 1947.

RIGHT: Gene Tierney's vanity.

F486-S-1258

ABOVE LEFT: Linda Darnell, seen in the reflection, in her modern dressing room, circa 1947.

ABOVE RIGHT: George Montgomery, 1942.

LEFT: Jennifer Jones stands in the first floor loggia, 1943.

RIGHT: Cary Grant checks out the wig he will wear in *I Was a Male War Bride* (1949).

FAR RIGHT: Richard Burton sits on the north stairs of Building 86, 1954.

BOTTOM LEFT: Lauren Bacall poses in front of one of the concept cars created by Ford for *Woman's World* (1954) at the north end of Building 86.

BOTTOM RIGHT: June Haver in her dressing room, 1952.

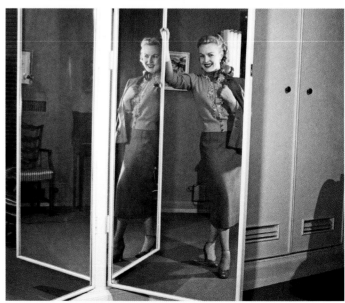

FAR LEFT: Yul Brynner gets his head shaved for his role in *The King and I* (1956) in his Early American dressing room.

LEFT: This is how the dressing room appeared a decade earlier when Douglas Fairbanks, Jr. was there for *That Lady In Ermine* (1948).

BELOW LEFT: Rory Calhoun, 1951.

BOTTOM RIGHT: Jayne Mansfield (performing *Hamlet*???) on the central staircase, circa 1957.

RIGHT: Don Murray and wife Hope Lange in their dressing room, 1958.

FAR RIGHT: Elegant Dana Wynter on the north staircase, 1958.

BOTTOM LEFT: Barbara Eden strikes a fashionable pose outside Building 86, early 1960s.

BOTTOM RIGHT: For decades, the most beautiful women at Fox sat at this dressing table getting ready for their close-ups including Alice Faye, Betty Grable, and Marilyn Monroe. This is how dressing room "M" appeared in the mid-1960s.

ABOVE LEFT: Gene Hackman, in costume for *The Poseidon Adventure* (1972), stands in the doorway of dressing room "C."

ABOVE RIGHT: The bell installed on the east side of Building 86 came from the church that stood on Tombstone Street on the backlot.

LEFT: View of the west façade, 2007.

FOX PLAZA TOWER (1987)

Announced in April of 1984, the Fox Plaza Tower was planned as a new world headquarters for the company. The brainchild of Marvin Davis, the Tower and the adjacent Galaxy Way parking structure and what is now the Intercontinental Hotel

were built by the Miller-Klutznick-Davis-Gray Company, replacing Rehearsal Hall #2, Bldg. 84 (the old coffee shop that had become wardrobe storage), the transportation, grip, and electrical storage departments.

Fortunately that is as far as Davis's plan—to raze the rest of the lot for residential and commercial use—got. On the six-acre site, chosen because of its natural elevation over Olympic Boulevard, architect Scott Johnson of Pereira Associates created the thirty-four-story, 711,000-square-foot tower of coral red granite and blue-tinted glass, with an underground parking garage featuring walls of fluted precast concrete panels as its base. Davis leased the twenty-ninth floor as his headquarters.

Even before it was finished production designer Jackson DeGovia put it in the movies in *Die Hard* (1988). It also appears in *Lethal Weapon 2* (1989, Warner Bros.), *Motorama* (1991, Columbia), *Airheads* (1994), *Speed* (1994), *Tommy Boy* (1995, Paramount), and *Fight Club* (1999). The top floor of the building was leased by the Ronald Reagan Presidential Foundation. Reagan occupied office space here after leaving the White House in January of 1989, until his death in 2001. The building is currently owned by the Irvine Company. Fox rents about half of the floors for departments, including legal, human resources, and home entertainment.

BLDG. 57: THE COMMISSARY (1929)

"We ate out of box lunches in the wilds of Westwood," an unnamed studio vet remarked of the lot's earliest days. "When the Café de Paris opened—well, it was a far cry from the old Munchers on Western Avenue!"

Indeed it was. Inspired by the cafes found in the Bois de Boulogne in Paris—but looking more Mediterranean with its tile roof—it took its name from the famed Cafés de Paris near the casino in Monte Carlo and the famous nightclub in London's West End. To prove that Fox was just as chic, "perambulators" (silver-domed food-service trolleys) were purchased. It was not open to the public, and even employees had to get a special pass. Built during the summer of 1929, the Café was dedicated on September 12 in a ceremony with Will Rogers and actress Fifi D'Orsay as part of their premiere activities for *They Had to See Paris* (1929). Rogers became a regular here, eating hearty meals at a

RIGHT: The Café de Paris as it appeared in the early 1930s. The Sound Building is on the left.

FAR RIGHT: Fifi D'Orsay and Will Rogers, stars of *They Had to See Paris* (1929) dedicated the Café de Paris as part of the premiere activities for the film.

BOTTOM LEFT: The bell from Westphalia.

BOTTOM RIGHT: Interior of the commissary before the mural was painted, looking southwest, circa 1929.

favorite corner table with Coca-Cola, which he dubbed "the champagne of America." Spencer Tracy, who dined with him, recalled that those fortunate enough to do so never paid the check. "Rogers was first to the café," reported Douglas Churchill in the *New York Times*, "and in the parade that paused at his table were some of the great and near-great of the world."

The entrance to the Studio Store was the original main entrance, a porch known as the "Sun Room" that had windows with removable glass panels to allow terrace dining for 150 guests. Later, the front doors were locked, and the Sun Room became a semiprivate dining room called

the Silver Room, used for cocktail parties, press announcements, executive luncheons, and other special functions, like Shirley Temple's birthday parties. The room was completely enclosed in the 1950s, and in the early 1960s it was outfitted with projection equipment so that it could double as a screening room. The Studio Store, selling officially licensed Fox merchandise, opened there in November of 1986.

When it opened in 1929 the main dining room seated three hundred, and was about the size of the sit-down service area of 2015. In fact, the wall separating the cafeteria and the sit-down dining room is approximately where the original south

ABOVE LEFT: Original 1933 caption: " ' Will you have it rare, sir?' asks George O'Brien, Fox Films Western star as he prepares to serve a roast of beef to the British players in *Cavalcade* at the studio café. Those at the table are Herbert Mundin, Merle Tottenham, Frank Lawton, Una O'Connor, and Tempe Piggott, while Janet Chandler is George's decorative assistant." The studio was very proud to have perambulators for food service just like Simpson's in London and Ciro's in Paris.

ABOVE RIGHT: Will Rogers and Shirley Temple, two of the biggest stars at Fox, in the Café de Paris circa 1934.

wall stood. The floors were wood with carpet runners to soften the sound of foot traffic. The ceiling had a large rectangular skylight and alternating, delicate glass pendant light fixtures. Square and round tables covered in white linen and dark bentwood chairs filled the room.

There were two private dining rooms. The one on the east side became known as the Shirley Temple Room, although it was never exclusively hers. In the mid-1930s, etchings of scenes from Henry King's film *Marie Galante* (1935) by French artist Edouard Chimot hung on it walls. Today ten portraits of Shirley Temple hang there. The second private dining room had a beamed ceiling and a fireplace. It disappeared during the 1936 renovation.

The white walls of the main dining room remained unadorned until 1932, when Winfield Sheehan commissioned esteemed Southern California painter Haldane Douglas to paint a mural. Conceived as a tour of the world stopping at all of the studio's major film distribution capitals, it was originally 2,160 feet in length, took four months to paint, and was completed by the end of December. When the mural was restored in 2013, it was discovered that a light brown wash had been applied to it at some point to tone down the colors.

Douglas added several lighthearted items that Sheehan later ordered removed, including a sign pointing "To Reno" in the Hollywood section

(not important enough of a city), gangsters in Chicago, and a battleship in London (the French consultant felt that this left France undefended). Originally there were only two celebrity portraits: Janet Gaynor surfing in Hawaii, and Will Rogers with "Blue Boy" the pig from *State Fair* (1933), in his hometown of Claremore, Oklahoma. When other stars complained, a policy was set that portraits could be added after ten successive box-office hits. Warner Baxter made it, and then Shirley Temple, Warner Oland, Alice Faye, and Darryl Zanuck, who is not surprisingly largest of all.

The mural was enlarged during the 1936 expansion, presumably by Douglas, who was then an art director and color consultant for Fox's foray into Technicolor. There have been minor alterations over the years due to political changes (Palestine became Israel), and the repositioning of walls in the 1976 renovation. Some of the additions do not exactly fit the original theme—no one seems to know why the state seal of New Hampshire was inserted—but overall the changes over the years have been tastefully done to keep the tone and feel of the original.

H. Keith Weeks ran the Café until 1934, when Nick Janios became the Café's general manager and maître d'. This lot legend held restaurant jobs as busboy, waiter, captain, maître d', and catering manager at such Broadway landmarks as

FAR LEFT: Looking into the Silver Room, 1938.

LEFT: Shirley Temple makes her social debut as hostess at her sixth birthday party in 1934 in the Silver Room. This was the first birthday party given to her at Fox and they just kept getting bigger and bigger. In later years, her parties would be held in the main dining room to accommodate the guests.

BOTTOM LEFT: Original 1935 caption: "A FARMER'S BIRTHDAY PARTY—The members of *The Farmer Takes a Wife* company at Fox Film studio give Henry Fonda, new leading man, a birthday party. Left to right, Victor Fleming, director; Henry Fonda, Janet Gaynor, and G. S. Yorke, director of publicity. The party was held at the studio café [in the Silver Room]. The table was decorated in rural style, the menu quite similar to old-fashioned farm proportions, and the favors were packets of garden seeds."

BOTTOM RIGHT: Looking out of the Silver Room, 1938.

RIGHT: Roddy McDowall and his sister Virginia in the Silver Room, 1942.

FAR RIGHT: Steve McQueen is interviewed for *The Sand Pebbles* (1966) in the Silver Room when it was decorated as the Peyton Place Inn for the TV show.

BOTTOM LEFT: Orson Welles, in costume as Rochester from *Jane Eyre* (1944) greets visitors at a luncheon.

BOTTOM RIGHT: Burt Ward and Adam West, stars of the original *Batman* (1966) TV show, exit the Silver Room.

Churchill's and Healy's before being invited to Hollywood in 1927 to manage the world-famous Brown Derby restaurant on Wilshire Boulevard, and then open three more Derbies. He took credit for inventing the Cobb Salad named for the late Derby proprietor, Bob Cobb. Under his management the Café became, according to *Fortune* magazine, "the most luxurious studio restaurant in Hollywood."

With up to four thousand employees during the studio's peak years (1935–49), the commissary served six hundred to twelve hundred of them every day. Staff included a kitchen crew of forty-one, sixteen busboys, two cashiers, three hostesses, thirty-two waitresses, and pastry cook Alfred Ulrich. Ulrich remembered that creamed chicken and peas on toast became a house specialty because it got little Shirley Temple to eat her peas; Tyrone Power loved ox joints; and Betty Grable knew her way around a French menu, inquiring about the *"oefs* [sic] *plat au jambon*: 'What's the idea of putting ham and eggs on the French menu?'" Music editor Len Engel recalled that each department had its own table.

During the lot expansion of 1936, Darryl Zanuck also expanded the Café with a two-story addition at the south end, increasing the footprint of the building by about a third, and allowing for five hundred diners at a time. The main entrance was moved to its current location in the middle of the building. The entrance door, however, was on the right wall at the top of the stairs, where the door now leads to the Commissary Grill. The wood-and-glass doors that lead to the main dining room were installed much later. Inside there was a large cashier counter that sold a wide variety of cigars, cigarettes—smoking was permitted in the dining room until 1993—and candy. A large guestbook was also maintained there that diners were asked to sign. This is where hostess Juanita Brown greeted guests for decades. Behind the counter was a coat and hat rack, currently an opening to the casual seating section.

Two new private dining rooms were also added. What is now the casual dining area with big-screen TVs was originally the "Gold Room," reserved for directors, producers, and top talent. The north wall was enclosed and accessed by French doors in the east wall (now gone). The Gold Room's position made the south end of the Café the most sought-after place to be seated. Howard Hughes occasionally dined in the Gold Room, where he could watch for new conquests among the young actresses.

The second private dining room was built for Darryl Zanuck on the east side of the main dining room, directly across from the Gold Room. There was also a private patio surrounded by foliage. Both are still there and used by top executives. This private dining room was updated in the 1990s with sleek, modern, dark-wood paneling and a mural depicting the career of Rupert Murdoch. The second-story addition contained men's and women's restrooms and a private, three-room apartment for Nick Janios. This was rumored to be a secret rendezvous for Nick's friends for many years. It currently serves as the administrative offices of the commissary.

"Ah, the commissary!" recalled Audrey Dalton. "An actor's day is not only on the set, but in those days you were still 'on' at lunchtime. When lunch was called on the set, your makeup man, and they were always men then, warned you about touching your face and disturbing your makeup, but the hairdresser, perhaps because she was a woman, knew the importance of lunch in the commissary, possibly to your career. After all, the producers and directors also ate there and every actor was on show. In preparation an actress's hair would be beautifully wrapped in mulleen, a very soft, silky, white netting fabric, creating a very flattering turban to hold your hair in place. So you sallied forth to the commissary, makeup perfect, hair covered with the beautiful wrapping, and still in costume. Now the hostess in charge of the dining room seated you according to her private grading of your importance, whether she recognized you, or who accompanied you, and your appearance.

And it was always done in the most gracious way. Service was very good, as nearly everyone there was working on set."

In the 1940s the white linen disappeared in favor of service on the bare wood tables edged with an aluminum trim. The original light fixtures were removed circa late 1946 in favor of "modern" fluorescent lights.

In front of the Café Richard Zanuck peddled the *Saturday Evening Post* at age nine for ten cents. It was his first job at the studio. When he showed his father the $85 he had earned that first day, Darryl questioned how he had managed it. He admitted he had accepted tips—a practice his father stopped. Undeterred, Richard employed his classmates from Pacific Palisades Grammar School to help him. By the time he was in the sixth grade he was reading scripts so that his father could get "a youngster's opinion." During his college years, Richard took jobs at the studio every summer working on the labor gang, constructing sets, working in the cutting room, and reading scripts in the story department. There he met his future partner, David Brown. Richard also wrote press releases in the Fox publicity department under the supervision of Harry Brand. He continued to work his way up from advertising in New York to his father's assistant in Paris.

Over the years the Café was visited by US

presidents Franklin Delano Roosevelt, Harry Truman, John F. Kennedy, Richard Nixon, and Gerald R. Ford. The Shah of Iran and his queen; Prince Philip of Greece; Haile Selassie, Lion of Judah; Prince Charles of Great Britain; President Sukarno of Indonesia; the King and Queen of Greece; and King Saud of Arabia have also visited.

To date, however, the starriest event that ever took place here occurred on September 19, 1959, when Nikita Khrushchev—denied admittance to Disneyland—was honored with a luncheon at the Café. Four hundred and five VIPs attended, including Frank Sinatra, Bob Hope (Mrs. Khrushchev sat between them), and even the reclusive Marilyn Monroe. "You didn't [typically] see Jennifer Jones or Marilyn Monroe around the commissary," recalled David Brown.

It all came to an abrupt end when the commissary was shut down as the studio ran into financial troubles in the early 1960s.

Richard Zanuck recalled that the remaining employees ate in the electricians' shed. No one was happier than his father when the Café reopened—but not to everyone. Kim Hunter recalled that the actors made up for *Planet of the Apes* (1968) were offered free lunches at their makeup table if they stayed away. Jacqueline Bisset (in her first starring role) dined here in *The Sweet Ride* (1968) as

RIGHT: View of the dining room looking northwest, 2015.

BOTTOM LEFT: View of the dining room looking northwest, 1938.

BOTTOM RIGHT and FOLLOWING PAGES: Details of the fabulous mural by Haldane Douglas. Look for Will Rogers in Oklahoma, Shirley Temple in Hollywood, Warner Oland (as Charlie Chan) in Shanghai, Janet Gaynor in Honolulu, and Warner Baxter (as the Cisco Kid) in Madrid.

an actress having lunch with a studio executive (Warren Stevens) and her lover, Michael Sarrazin (in "reel" and real life). She and Raquel Welch were the last major stars nurtured under the Zanuck regime.

From serving intimate meals to VIPs to supplying lunch to a cast of thousands for the "When the Parade Passes By" musical number for *Hello, Dolly!* (1969)—12,000 sandwiches, 6,000 apples and pieces of cake, for ten hours—they could handle anything. The commissary also has a long-held tradition of offering special dishes named for its stars, proving you had "arrived." There was the Henry King cocktail (half tomato juice, half clam juice) that competed with the commissary's signature cocktail (half tomato juice, half sauerkraut juice), and two Tyrone Power salads (one, with cottage cheese and fresh fruit, and the other, similar to a Caesar, but without the garlic croutons, helpful for lovemaking scenes).

The tradition of meals named after current productions goes back at least as far as 1929, when "Sunnyside Up" Eggs were featured at Munchers. Other examples include the Valley of the Dolls Salad, the Flim-Flam Man Hamburger, A Guide to the Married Man Casserole, the Two for the Road Fruit Salad, the Boston Strangler Sandwich, the Butch Cassidy Grilled Filet of Halibut, the Hello, Dolly! Omelet, the M*A*S*H Bowl of Clam Chowder,

and the Escape from the Planet of the Apes Roast Turkey Dinner. The Blood and Guts Minute Steak fortunately changed to the Patton Minute Steak when that film's title changed. Another dud was Batman Ground Round.

It was the end of an era when, again because of the studio's troubles, the Café de Paris closed with Nick Janios's retirement on February 5, 1971. There was even a plan to dismantle and auction the Douglas mural. Fortunately the mural was still there when the Café reopened, but as a cost-cutting measure food was served cafeteria-style by an outside catering service. Decorative arches from the set of *Hello, Dolly!* (1969) were added to guide patrons through the line.

Employees expressed dismay over the death of the old traditions. Burt Reynolds observed, "They wouldn't dare name dishes after stars anymore either because they disappear so quickly." Ed Hutson, who brought his mother [silent film star Eileen Sedgwick], Mrs. Merv Griffin, and Sybil Brand [wife of head of publicity Harry Brand] recalled that those veritable "ladies who lunch" were not pleased to have to stand in line and carry trays to their table when just a few years previously they had been given impeccable table service.

Fox's vice president Bernie Barron remembers that these complaints brought about a complete refurbishment in 1976, which included both sit-down and cafeteria service. The outdoor deck on the south side was built, and the walls of the Gold Room were reconfigured and lined with mirrors to offer a casual dining room for the cafeteria line. Decorative planters were placed to delineate it from the formal sit-down dining area in the main room. Air-conditioning was installed for the first time, and 1970s fluorescent lights replaced the ones from the 1940s. Some large square banquettes with potted palms in the center were installed. The original 1929 chairs were stripped and stained in natural wood tones. Soon daily patronage numbers jumped from 250 back to 1,100. Beer and wine was also made available at lunch for the first time; previously, alcohol was only served on special occasions. However, even more exciting than the availability of booze (if the coverage in the employee newsletter is any indication) was the addition of frozen yogurt to the menu.

In the summer of 1984 the dining room was redecorated with new tables, chairs, carpeting, and dinnerware featuring the new Twentieth Century Fox logo. In 1986 another redecoration returned the dining room to its former Art Deco splendor. The fluorescent lights were removed and, although the original lighting fixtures could not be located, some vintage chandeliers were installed that were very much in line with the original decor. New

ABOVE: More of the original portraits on the café mural that have since been painted over. From top left: Eddie Cantor, Arline Judge, Rochelle Hudson, Frances Drake, Don Ameche, Alice Faye, Jean Hersholt, Sonja Henie; second row: Tyrone Power, Simone Simon, Tony Martin, Claire Trevor, Loretta Young, Gloria Stuart, Michael Whalen; third row: June Lang and Victor McLaglen, 1938.

RIGHT: The cafeteria as it looked in 2015.

FAR LEFT: The Café de Paris during construction. The new addition expanded the main dining room by a third.

LEFT: Looking into the exclusive Gold Room that was created during the addition. A tour of the United States was added to the expanded mural, 1938.

BOTTOM LEFT: The south end of the dining room, 1938. The mural on this wall appears to be part of the original 1932 mural since it fits in geographically with the world tour theme and was kept on the south wall after the expansion of the east and west walls.

BOTTOM MIDDLE: A new entrance was created with the new addition in 1936 and remained like this until the 1970s. You would enter through the door on the right (with bars) and exit through the one on the left.

BOTTOM RIGHT: Closeup of the sign as it appeared on October 31, 1951. Crowds were segregated by whether or not they were working on "shooting companies."

ABOVE LEFT: The cigarette counter, 1938.

ABOVE RIGHT: Warner Baxter pays his bill to cashier Helen Walker, 1936.

RIGHT: Matchbooks.

kelly-green carpet and modern bentwood chairs with matching green upholstery were added as well.

As part of the mid-1980s renovations, the north foyer that existed beyond the double Gothic arches was demolished to make way for the Fox Plaza parking garage. The small chapel-like vestibule, with a vaulted ceiling and elaborate stained-glass windows, had been added in the early 1930s to provide an additional entrance and cashier counter for the Café, as well as access to Nick Janios's office and a telephone booth located just off the foyer.

It was here that the Studio Store had its beginnings in 1976. It later moved to a trailer south of Bldg. 86 from 1984–86 before moving to its present location. The two open arches were filled in to become a solid wall. The sleek *Diana, the Huntress,* a statue from the prop collection that graced numerous films (*Sing Baby, Sing* (1936), *Everything Happens at Night* (1939), *Second Fiddle* (1939), *The Gang's All Here* (1943), *Stormy Weather* (1943), *Quiet Please, Murder* (1943), and *The Dark Corner* (1946)), and then the dining room, was duplicated so there would be one for each alcove.

Although it is impossible to guess just how many actors were cast in roles because they were seen in the commissary, Samuel Fuller remembered choosing Jean Peters for *Pickup on South Street* (1953) while dining with Jeanne Crain, and Tom Mankiewicz wanted Lionel Stander for *Hart to Hart* (1979–84) when he saw him waiting for a table.

As with the rest of the company, Barry Diller was responsible for improvements here. In May of 1988 the studio took back management of the commissary from ARA Services, and its personnel were once again Fox employees. In 1990 he approved an enhanced menu with a category for "junk food"—including a foot-long Lasorda Dog (Fox owned the Los Angeles Dodgers from 1997–2004, and Tommy Lasorda was their manager) and the Fluffer Nutter,

a peanut-butter-and-marshmallow concoction—as well as more health-conscious fare with a calorie count.

The commissary was in need of another makeover by 2013. Structural upgrades and repairs were executed, including replacing a portion of the floor that had warped due to the encroaching roots of trees against the foundation. When the floorboards were torn up, the roots "looked like something out of *Alien*," noted one observer. The interior was redecorated in a new color scheme of deep browns—espresso and chocolate—with new checkered carpet and, most notably, new wood dining chairs with an urbane retro flair. This is only the fourth set of chairs to grace the dining room in its history. Restoration of the mural included installing additional lighting to highlight it. The work was completed by the beginning of 2014.

The northwest corner is now the exclusive one where executives like Rupert Murdoch or Jim Gianopulos sit when they don't require the confines of a private dining room. The friendly staff and the studio's Oscars and Emmys still greet you at the door. Beside the commissary, in place of the original small formal garden, is a lawn used for large film-crew seating and studio events, as well as filming. For example, it was used as the White House Rose Garden in *1600 Penn* (2012), and *Enlisted* (2014) used it for "military drills."

RIGHT: The cast of *Berkeley Square* (1933) dining in what is now the Shirley Temple Room.

BOTTOM: The south end of the Shirley Temple Room, 1935. The etchings on the walls were made by Edouard Chimot as character concept art for the film *Marie Galante* (1934). They remained on the walls until at least the 1970s.

In the early days a giant bronze bell, reputed to have tolled the outbreak of the revolution in Russia in 1917, before the studio acquired it, was placed beside the entrance. Today another bell that once hung in the steeple of the church on Tombstone Street sits across the street. Of course, Avenue D did not originally dead-end here; it used to continue to the north through the studio gate to cross the studio bridge (west of the modern Avenue of the Stars bridge), designed by Joseph Urban and dedicated by Shirley Temple in 1938, to access the backlot. The bridge originally spanned a deep ravine until the late 1930s, when Olympic Boulevard was connected here to Santa Monica Boulevard.

ABOVE LEFT and BOTTOM: The Shirley Temple Room, 2015.

ABOVE: This quaint private dining room disappeared during the 1936 expansion.

ABOVE LEFT: Looking into the Gold Room, circa 1938.

ABOVE RIGHT: Looking into the Gold Room, 2015.

RIGHT: Tyrone Power and Loretta Young are offered a menu by Nick Janios, 1939.

FAR RIGHT: Dorothy McGuire and Cesar Romero, 1943.

ABOVE LEFT: Betty Grable gives her order, perhaps off the French menu.

ABOVE MIDDLE: Nick Janios looks over the menu with Marilyn Monroe, 1954.

ABOVE RIGHT: Robert Wagner, 1959.

FAR LEFT: Deborah Kerr and columnist Sheilah Graham, 1959.

LEFT: Charlton Heston, center, talks to members of the Associated Press about *Planet of the Apes* (1968).

ABOVE LEFT: View of the main dining room circa 1945.

ABOVE RIGHT: View of the main dining room, 2015.

RIGHT: Alice Faye dines with Buck, the star of *Call of the Wild* (1935).

FAR RIGHT: Carmen Miranda and friends.

RIGHT: Richard Greene, left, and Wendy Barrie in costume for *The Hound of the Baskervilles* (1939).

FAR RIGHT: June Haver and Dan Dailey celebrating Dan's birthday.

BELOW LEFT: Maureen O'Hara (left) and Dick Haymes dine with a guest.

BELOW MIDDLE: Richard Burton (center) and Audrey Dalton with hairdo for *My Cousin Rachel* (1952).

BELOW RIGHT: Mitzi Gaynor and William Lundigan.

FAR LEFT: The Pat and Shirley Boone family. Pat is holding future pop singer Debby.

LEFT: Mickey Hargitay (left) and Jayne Mansfield dine with a guest.

BOTTOM LEFT: Tony Curtis and Janet Leigh in costume for *Prince Valiant* (1954).

BOTTOM MIDDLE: William Holden.

BOTTOM RIGHT: Debra Paget and Elvis Presley, in costume for *Love Me Tender* (1956).

RIGHT: Cary Grant and Buddy Adler.

FAR RIGHT: Shirley Jones surrounded by cast members from *The Enemy Below* (1957).

BOTTOM LEFT: John Wayne in costume for *The Comancheros* (1961).

BOTTOM MIDDLE: Doris Day.

BOTTOM RIGHT: Mia Farrow and Barbara Rush.

FAR LEFT: View looking southwest circa 1962.

LEFT: Soviet premier Nikita Krushchev was given the ultimate Hollywood welcome during his visit that culminated with a luncheon at the Café hosted by Spyros Skouras. Frank Sinatra and David Niven are in the foreground.

BOTTOM LEFT: Jacqueline Bisset and Michael Sarrazin in a scene from *The Sweet Ride* (1968), one of only a few times the Commissary has appeared in a movie.

BOTTOM MIDDLE: View looking southwest, 2015.

BOTTOM RIGHT: The menu, February 11, 1969.

RIGHT: The redecorated dining room, 1976.

BOTTOM RIGHT: One of these art deco pendants was found on the lot and several replicas were made to use in the main dining room to replace the fluorescent lighting that had been used for decades. This 1986 redecoration helped bring back the 1920s look to the room.

BOTTOM LEFT: The Commissary Grill as it appeared in 2015.

LEFT: This sleek statue of Diana, Roman goddess of the hunt, dating from the 1930s and a prop in several films, was put on display in the commissary in the 1970s. When the north foyer was razed and the portals filled, a twin was made to fill the opening. She originally had a bow but it has disappeared.

BOTTOM LEFT: Diana appeared in the background of a couple of Sonja Henie's films, including *Second Fiddle* (1939).

BOTTOM RIGHT: Diana is featured in this scene from *Stormy Weather* (1943), when Lena Horne performed "I Can't Give You Anything But Love."

ABOVE LEFT: Looking into the main dining room, this entrance was closed off when the north foyer was torn down in the 1980s.

ABOVE MIDDLE: For years, visitors were asked to sign the guestbook at the entrance, 1930s.

ABOVE RIGHT: Exterior entrance to the north foyer. This served as the main entrance to the Café in the early-to-mid 1930s and was torn down to make way for the Fox Plaza parking structure. This picture is from the 1960s.

BOTTOM LEFT: North foyer looking west. This became the main entrance for a few years in the 1930s.

BOTTOM RIGHT: The studio's Oscars have always been—and still are—housed in the commissary. This was where the Studio Store first opened in the 1970s.

TOP LEFT: The studio's Emmy collection, also on display as you enter, faces the Oscars, 2015.

ABOVE LEFT: The studio's Best Picture Oscars proudly on display as you enter, 2015.

ABOVE MIDDLE: This executive dining room was remodeled in the late 1990s to include a mural depicting Rupert Murdoch's career, and became known as the Rupert Murdoch dining room, 2015.

ABOVE RIGHT: Photo of the Murdoch dining room, circa 1945, with Nick Janios standing ready to serve.

LEFT: The dining room, 2015. The doors lead into the studio store.

Aerial view of the Fox lot taken on November 28, 1928 looking southeast. Santa Monica Boulevard is at the bottom left corner.

THE BACKLOT TOUR

Next time you're at a movie at the Century City shopping center or visiting the Century Plaza Hotel, take a few moments to listen. Perhaps you'll hear the ghosts of such legendary actors as Henry Fonda and Tyrone Power running lines from their memorable roles. During Hollywood's golden era, the backlot of 20th Century Fox spread across Century City. Portions of such films as The Grapes of Wrath *and the 1956 musical* The King and I *were shot here.*

—Susan King, *Los Angeles Times, April 14, 2010*

Welcome to the the Twentieth Century backlot! Sets for William Fox's silent movies would soon appear in the bean fields he had purchased in 1923. The public was officially invited to see them for the first time on Sunday, August 29, 1926, for the opening ceremonies and dedication of "the Greatest Outdoor Studio," Fox Hills. William Fox never did anything in a small way. *Fox Folks,* the New York employee newsletter, reported that thirty thousand people showed up, their parked cars forming a solid line from Beverly Hills to Sawtelle.

Attendees were entertained by the company of US Marines used in *What Price Glory* (1926) and Tom Mix and his "broncho busters" before wandering among the often spectacular sets here, representing more than twenty-five films in or out of production, including: Raoul Walsh's *What Price Glory;* Victor Schertzinger's *The Return of Peter Grimm* (1926) and *Siberia* (1926); John Ford's *Three Bad Men* (1926), *The Blue Eagle* (1926), *Upstream* (1927), and *Mother Machree* (1928); Harry Beaumont's *Womanpower* (1926), starring Margaret Livingston, who was hostess for the event; and Howard Hawks's *Fig*

Leaves (1926), which has to be seen to be believed, with its Adam (George O'Brien) and Eve (Olive Borden) and dinosaur story. To shoot the battle scenes for *What Price Glory* out here, Raoul Walsh claims to be the first to put his camera on a dolly to move along the marines' trench, and remembered that because of powder man Ted Green's dramatic explosions, the company had to pay $75,000 in damages to the owners of neighboring homes.

Expansion came after the Twentieth Century Fox merger, when Joseph Schenck purchased 96.38 acres—half of the eighteen-hole Westwood Golf Public Course, adjacent to the lot—running from Pico Boulevard through what is now Olympic Boulevard. Art director William Creber *(Planet of the Apes, The Towering Inferno)* recalled playing golf there with his father, Lewis H. Creber, also a prolific art director at Fox between 1933 and 1967. Unfortunately, golf balls

BOTTOM: Aerial view of the Fox lot looking south circa 1935. Santa Monica Boulevard is at the bottom of the photo.

were a constant hazard, ruining many a take. In *The Black Swan* (1942), a ball hit a "pirate" during the climactic battle scene on Chicago Lake.

Schenck agreed to let the City of Los Angeles run Olympic Boulevard through the studio completed in 1938. In April of 1946 he authorized the purchase of the second half of the Westwood Golf Course (89.349 acres), running today from Olympic Boulevard north to Santa Monica Boulevard. This brought the studio to its maximum acreage of 286.309. It would be reduced to 265.26 acres for city streets and expansion of Beverly Hills High School the following year.

David Brown tells the possibly apocryphal story that, in the summer of 1953, Darryl Zanuck forwarded him a note from the New York office critical of the high price he paid for a Broadway play. After all, it read, the

RIGHT: Aerial view of the northern section of the backlot taken circa 1935. New England Street and Square is at left, and the Canal set from *The Farmer Takes a Wife* (1935) is in the top right corner. Just below that is Tyrolean Street. The Mill is in the bottom right corner.

company did not own any oil wells. The next week oil, first discovered here in 1908, made a dramatic re-appearance. Oil continues to be pumped, at Olympic Boulevard and Century Park East south of Beverly Hills High School, well past the company's century mark.

"The backlot was never still," remembered Richard Todd. "Even if no exterior scenes were being shot, there was always the light squeak and thudding of 'nodding-donkeys,' the small pumps above miniature oil wells."

Aerial view of the Fox lot looking northeast circa 1937. The newly acquired golf course is being used for *In Old Chicago* (1938). Pico Boulevard runs across the bottom right corner. Note that Olympic Boulevard has yet to punch through the lot.

Aerial view of the Fox lot in 1939. Santa Monica Boulevard is on the left and Pico Boulevard is on the right. Note that some of the backlot sets are labeled with names that were only briefly used, such as Alaskan Town which was more commonly known as the Canal set from *The Farmer Takes a Wife* (1935), Ghost Town which was a remnant of the original Western Street, and German Village, French Montmartre, and European Square which were collectively referred to as Old French Street. Suburban Street, not labeled on the map, was an outgrowth of New England Street.

Aerial view of the southeast quadrant of the Fox lot circa 1941. Pico Boulevard runs along the top right with Hillcrest Country Club on the other side.

Aerial view of the Fox lot looking south when it was at its largest in the 1950s. Santa Monica Boulevard runs along the bottom of the picture.

RIGHT: View of backlot looking north circa 1929.

BELOW LEFT: View of the backlot looking north. In the center is one of the houses that was later incorporated into New England Street.

BELOW RIGHT: Village set that was located in the southeast corner of the north backlot.

FAR LEFT: Village set on backlot.

LEFT: Mansion set on backlot.

BOTTOM LEFT: Filming the trench warfare sequences for *What Price Glory* (1926).

BOTTOM RIGHT: The French village set from *What Price Glory* (1926).

The magnificent Hungarian Chateau Tokay set, built for *Caravan* (1934), would later become the site of the Dutch Moat. The gates to the set were repurposed and became the gates to the backlot in the 1930s. Miraculously, they have hung around the lot ever since. In 2015 they were restored and placed between Stages One/Two and Three/Four with a plaque explaining their history, and the street there was renamed Movietone Way.

THE DUTCH MOAT

The Dutch Moat (mostly used for miniatures) was on the last piece of backlot property the studio owned up until June of 1978, it remained in use for television shows (*Voyage to the Bottom of the Sea*, 1964–68) and films, including the tidal wave and final shot of the upturned ocean liner for *The Poseidon Adventure* (1972).

FAR LEFT: Concept art for the Chateau Tokay

LEFT: Loretta Young and Dudley Digges rehearse a scene for *Caravan* (1934).

BOTTOM LEFT: This Hungarian farmyard, designed by William Darling, was at the rear of the Chateau Tokay set for *Caravan* (1934).

BOTTOM RIGHT: This miniature version of the *Titanic* for the 1953 film is lowered into the Dutch Moat for special effects shots. The Colonial Home can be seen behind it on the right.

BOTTOM: The Permanent Gardens looking west from the terrace.

FAR RIGHT: The Permanent Gardens looking east as they appeared in *Lancer Spy* (1937).

BOTTOM RIGHT: The swimming pool was installed for *Down to Earth* (1932).

THE PERMANENT GARDENS

As you will soon see, it was the movies made for Will Rogers that laid the foundations for the settings of a backlot known and appreciated the world over. The Gardens, for example, were designed by William Darling as his English country estate for *Down to Earth* (1932). There was the façade of his home facing west, manicured gardens and a swimming pool. The eastern façade became the Swedish home for Frank Lloyd's *Servants' Entrance* (1934). Both sides were changed by the time *Lottery Lover* (1935) was filmed. The west facade became a Moroccan French villa seen in *Professional Soldier* (1936). The east side was turned into a neo-classical French home on view in Laurel & Hardy's *The Big Noise* (1944).

Meanwhile the swimming pool, that Betty Grable and Dick Haymes lounge beside to the strains of Haymes's signature tune, "The More I See You " in *Billy Rose's Diamond Horseshoe* (1945), was built to allow underwater photography, allowing us to see young Richard Zanuck, doubling for Alan Ladd, in *Boy on a Dolphin* (1957).

Night scene from *Down to Earth*, (1932) .

BUT-13-P14

ABOVE LEFT: Janet Gaynor and Lew Ayres, standing in front of the garage, star as the attractive help in *Servants' Entrance.* (1934).

ABOVE RIGHT: The east façade became a Swedish country estate for *Servants' Entrance* (1934) complete with a garage at left.

RIGHT: The Swedish manor house was later changed and given a more French look.

ABOVE LEFT: Annabella and William Powell by the pool in *The Baroness and the Butler* (1938).

ABOVE RIGHT: Betty Grable and Dick Haymes in *Billy Rose's Diamond Horseshoe* (1945).

FAR LEFT: Night shot from *Pardon Our Nerve*, (1939).

LEFT: Jean Simmons and Marlon Brando in *Désirée* (1954).

ABOVE: Terry Moore and Robert Wagner in *Between Heaven and Hell* (1956).

RIGHT: Herbert Marshall, Charles Herbert, and Vincent Price find *The Fly* (1958).

THE COLONIAL HOME

Hey, you know something, Tommy boy—I could run guided tours through this joint. It's kind of an educational, kind of historical kind of place. Of course it's not one of them George Washington slept here places. But maybe even better, huh?
—Edmond O'Brien as "Fats" Marty Murdoch
in The Girl Can't Help It *(1956)*

The Colonial Home, built for *Carolina* (1934), was based on a mansion that director Henry King and screenwriter Reginald Berkeley saw in South Carolina. Although dilapidated, as the home of the poverty-stricken, post–Civil War Connellys, it was considerably spruced up when two members of that family (Lionel Barrymore and Shirley Temple) returned for *The Little Colonel* (1935). Temple was back, ready to hold off the Yankees with a sling-shot, in *The Littlest Rebel* (1935). The youngster's dexterity with the weapon was real; she once famously fired it at First Lady Eleanor Roosevelt.

Over the years dormer windows were added and taken off the roof, a new gable was added in the front, and balconies could be installed as needed to the versatile three-sided exterior. Look for it in *Something for the Boys* (1944) as the fixer-upper Magnolia Manor that three unlikely cousins (Carmen Miranda, Phil Silvers, and Vivian Blaine)

The Colonial Home as it appeared in *High Time*, (1960).

E 0 6
SET # 65

RIGHT: The Colonial Home was originally built as a dilapidated southern mansion for *Carolina* (1934).

FAR RIGHT: "There's nothing rational about prejudice." Jeanne Crain in *Pinky* (1949).

BOTTOM LEFT: The Colonial Home was quickly spruced up for two Shirley Temple films including *The Little Colonel* (1935), with Lionel Barrymore.

BOTTOM RIGHT: Allan Dwan, wearing glasses and standing to the rear of the cameraman, directs two Fox stars in their heyday: Don Ameche and Simone Simon in rehearsal for *Josette* (1938).

restore, with the help of the army, and put on a show featuring Perry Como. Mansions like this one can have their dark secrets too. Like the dark and stormy nights when Vincent Price ran it as a sanitarium rife with murder and violent patients roaming the halls in *Shock* (1946).

Nurse Patricia "Pinky" Johnson (Jeanne Crain) bravely transformed it from Miss Em's (Ethel Barrymore) mansion into a clinic and nursery school, despite virulent racial prejudice in the landmark *Pinky* (1949).

The memorable school graduation sequence for *Carousel* (1956) was shot on the lawn.

In its final years this set even appeared in "HorrorScope" for *The Alligator People* (1959). However, perhaps it is best remembered as featured in *Stars and Stripes Forever* (1952), during the most stirring performance of "The Battle Hymn of the Republic" ever committed to film.

ABOVE LEFT: Clifton Webb as John Philip Sousa leads his band for the classic *Stars and Stripes Forever* (1952).

ABOVE MIDDLE: The graduation scene from *Carousel* (1956) with Gordon MacRae was filmed on the lawn in front of the Colonial Home.

ABOVE RIGHT: Suzy Parker and Hope Lange in view of the Colonial Home for the company party sequence for *The Best of Everything* (1959).

LEFT: The Colonial Home stood in for Pebble Beach in this spot promoting the Bing Crosby Golf Tournament in 1959.

TOP RIGHT: The large, wide cityscape built for *Sunrise* (1927).

MIDDLE RIGHT: Backside of the cityscape built for *Sunrise* (1927).

BOTTOM RIGHT: Director F. W. Murnau, at right on steps with hat, directs Janet Gaynor walking down ramp in *Sunrise* (1927).

SUNRISE SET

Although the beach sequence (Coronado Beach) and village (Lake Arrowhead) were filmed elsewhere, the city that the Man (George O'Brien) and his Wife (Janet Gaynor) visit in F. W. Murnau's celebrated *Sunrise: A Song of Two Humans* (1927) was built here. It encompassed an enormous area later taken up by the Lower Moat, Henry King Farm, and Algerian Street.

Gaynor remembered that the elevated set by Murnau's German set designer Rochus Gliese was in forced perspective, enhanced by the the use of children dressed as adults in the background. She also recalled the chilly evenings out here watching the "rushes" in an open-air theater, and the fact that usually around the twentieth take, Murnau, standing behind her, would scratch her head, meaning that was the one he would use. Although planned as a silent film, Murnau was told that his film would be the first to debut using the Movietone sound process, including its first use of human voices.

John Ford subsequently utilized this set for *Four Sons* (1928). Playing the important role of the sons' mother was elderly Margaret Mann, who had persevered for ten years as an extra before landing this part. The very next year this magnificent set was torn down.

Set #63

ALGERIAN STREET

Hidden from the road, by a row of high shrubs, was a land of enchantment. An early middle-eastern set was built for John Ford's *The Black Watch* (1929), and used throughout the early 1930s for films such as Victor Fleming's *Renegades* (1930), and *Chandu the Magician* (1933), starring Bela Lugosi. A new twenty-five-acre set combining Algerian, Tunisian, Turkish, and Arabian architecture was built for Frank Lloyd's *Under Two Flags* (1936). Look for it as "Old Baghdad" in *Ali Baba Goes to Town* (1937), starring Eddie Cantor and featuring the film debut of Louise Hovick.

If that name sounds unfamiliar, it was done on purpose. Darryl Zanuck was concerned that audiences might stay away from a film starring stripper Gypsy Rose Lee, so he billed her by her real name. Lee's semiautobiographical play, *Naked Genius*, was later adapted into *Doll Face* (1946). She also appeared in *The Stripper* (1963). Her affair with Otto

Preminger led to son Erik Preminger, who produced (and had a bit part as a waiter) in *The Heartbreak Kid* (1972). Her sister June Havoc was always an asset to any Fox film in which she appeared.

The movie premiere at the conclusion of *Ali Baba* is actually footage of the premiere of *Wee Willie Winkie* (1937), which was also shot here, starring Shirley Temple. The film, and this set—which she described as "a semi-permanent jumble of minarets and casbah alleys, sun-drenched, dusty, and mysterious"—remained one of her favorites.

Rebuilt for *The Great Commandment,* a Tyrone Power project that was never made, it was suited to World War II adventures such as the North Africa where Kay Francis, Carole Landis, Martha Raye, and Mitzi Mayfair entertain the troops in *Four Jills and a Jeep* (1944). The film celebrated the actresses' actual 1942 USO adventures through England, Ireland, and North Africa. Raye continued this good work through the Korean and Vietnam wars.

After appearing in *David and Bathsheba* (1951), it was remodeled as Cana for *The Robe* (1953), and then appeared as Thebes for *The Egyptian* (1954), civil war–torn China for *The Left Hand of God* (1955), Japan for *The Barbarian and the Geisha* (1958), biblical times again for *The Story of Ruth* (1960), and back to Baghdad for *The Wizard of Baghdad* (1960).

ABOVE LEFT: Richard Burton, center right, in *The Robe* (1953).

ABOVE RIGHT: Algerian Street became the American west for *One Foot in Hell* (1960). Alan Ladd, third from left, observes the duel.

LEFT: Tyrone Power, on horse, received instruction from director Henry King (in ball cap) during the filming of *King of the Khyber Rifles* (1953).

ABOVE LEFT: Spanish Street.

ABOVE MIDDLE: Spanish Street could be dressed for more exotic locales such as those in *China Girl* (1942).

ABOVE RIGHT: Lynn (Loretta Young) and Douglas (Reginald Denny) have just witnessed an execution on Spanish Street in *Four Men and a Prayer* (1938).

RIGHT: Spanish Street stood in for Jerusalem in *The Robe* (1953) where Victor Mature sneaks through the streets.

SPANISH STREET

While there seem to have been Spanish and Italian Streets from the backlot's earliest days, this one, flanked by stuccoed arcades, is best documented and probably created for *Four Men and a Prayer* (1938). The movie was contract player Richard Greene's film debut. The star—who earned the lot nickname of "Bouncer" from John Ford because the dashing young star could not sit still—never forgot the memorable way he received his contract offer from Fox—on Christmas Eve 1937. This set is also the exterior of the Café La Veronica (interior on Stage Eight) where Rita Hayworth danced with Anthony Quinn for *Blood and Sand* (1941).

LEFT: The backlot's original Western Street.

WESTERN STREET A.K.A GHOST TOWN

Besides its use in *In Old Arizona* (1929), this set is notable for having been used by the company's earliest Western stars including Tom Mix, Buck Jones, and George O'Brien. The stables and kennel nearby, built for Buck Jones's horses and dogs, was known by employees as "The Outpost." This set and Tombstone Street have a pedigree later Western sets could not have. The people who used them, like directors Allan Dwan and John Ford, knew historical personages like Wyatt Earp.

"The cowboys [Mix used] were real cowboys who found riding the range in Hollywood movies easier and better-paying than on the Lone Prairie," said Mix co-star Colleen Moore, "It was still really the Old West, not long removed from pioneer days."

THE JUNGLE

The Jungle was built to re-create German West Africa for *Passport to Hell* (1932), where poor Elissa Landi is deported and interned. It later served for many a Fox "B" picture. Chief among those were the Charlie Chan films starring Landi's co-star Warner Oland. He made Chan, America's very first detective, his own in sixteen films based on the novels by Earl Derr Biggers. When he died while *Charlie Chan at the Ringside* was still shooting, it was made over as part of the studio's equally successful Mr. Moto detective series (*Mr. Moto's Gamble*, 1938). Derived from the success of the Chan adventures by novelist John P. Marquand, the Motos (eight films made between 1937 and 1939) remain memorable today chiefly for Peter Lorre's star-making turn as the Japanese detective.

World War II put a stop to them, and Lorre left the studio in July 1939. Director Norman Foster, who made six of the Moto films, was told to revise Lorre's last Moto film into *Charlie Chan in Panama* (1940), bringing the franchises full circle. Sidney

Toler took over the role of Chan in *Charlie Chan in Honolulu* (1938), making ten more Chan films, concluding with *Castle in the Desert* (1942). When James Bond ignited the spy genre in the 1960s, Fox brought back Charlie Chan in *The Return of Mr. Moto* (1965), starring Henry Silva. After directing Fess Parker (as Davy Crockett) and Guy Williams (as Zorro) to fame for Walt Disney, Norman Foster returned to Fox to direct Parker in *Daniel Boone* (1964–70). He also directed *Batman* (1966–68). Williams made his way to the lot to star in *Lost in Space* (1966–68).

Darryl Zanuck's Francophile tendencies brought Jean Renoir out here for his American debut, *Swamp Water* (1941). Darryl Zanuck's other French imports included Simone Simon and Jean Gabin.

LEFT: Original 1932 caption: "AND IT WASN'T MIDNIGHT. Alexander Kirkland and Elissa Landi in one of their scenes in 'Undesirable Lady' [changed to 'Passport to Hell'], the Fox romantic drama directed by Frank Lloyd. This bridge is a part of the extensive jungle set that was built at Movietone City especially for this production, the locale being German West Africa."

BOTTOM LEFT: Walter Pidgeon gets some direction on how to run through the Jungle in *Man Hunt* (1941) from Fritz Lang.

BOTTOM RIGHT: The Jungle was used for the fish market, visited by Irene Dunne, for *Anna and the King of Siam* (1948).

THE LOWER MOAT

This extraordinary area is a good example of just how elaborate the backlot was in the bold days of William Fox. This tank was used for the snowy workers' cabins designed by Harry Oliver for Frank Borzage's *The River* (1929), and as Joseph Wright's Chinese waterfront for Alfred Santell's *The Sea Wolf* (1930). The waterfront structures were torn down in the mid-1930s. The tank continued to be used extensively for productions requiring water and special effects, but only its use for *The Rains Came* (1939) and its remake, *The Rains of Ranchipur* (1955), hinted at past glories.

ABOVE: The cast and crew from *The River* (1929) stand in front of the cabin set.

RIGHT: The rustic cabins were transformed into a Chinese Waterfront for *Shanghai Madness* (1933).

FAR RIGHT: Camera crew getting ready for a closeup of Spencer Tracy in *Shanghai Madness* (1933). Director John Blystone is behind the camera wearing the Panama hat.

LEFT: Later, the Lower Moat was enclosed so that backdrops could be used such as in the mushroom forest sequence for *Journey to the Center of the Earth* (1959).

BOTTOM LEFT: Another view of the Lower Moat, circa 1967.

BOTTOM RIGHT: The Lower Moat as seen in the TV series *Adventures in Paradise* (1959-62).

RIGHT: The King Farm built for *Way Down East* (1936). Both house and barn were built with interiors so filming could be done inside.

BOTTOM LEFT: Detail of barnyard.

BOTTOM MIDDLE: The back side of the set doubled as a general store.

BOTTOM RIGHT: Henry Fonda helps handle the huge fan that was used to blow snow on the heroine played by Rochelle Hudson in *Way Down East* (1936).

THE [HENRY] KING FARM

Perhaps since Henry King was the first to use this ten-acre set built for *Way Down East* (1935), including a farmhouse and a barn (both with interiors), employees always referred to it as his. For his last film as head of production Winfield Sheehan re-teamed *The Farmer Takes A Wife* (1935) stars Janet Gaynor and Henry Fonda. When Gaynor suffered a concussion during filming the always-reliable, and lovely, contract player Rochelle Hudson, by virtue of her rising status working opposite Will Rogers and more recently Shirley Temple, replaced her. Spring Byington played the kindly wife of the farmer who invites Hudson's character in. It was a role Byington was to repeat in her own inimitable way for Fox over the next few years. Interestingly, Sheehan's last film (*Captain Eddie,* 1945) also used this set. Later, this set was the farm Shirley Temple calls home in *Rebecca of Sunnybrook Farm* (1938), the Frake home in *State Fair* (1945), the farm, church and store for *Lure of the Wilderness* (1952), and the country store for *Love Me Tender* (1956). This is the closest Temple got to a certain Kansas farmyard in MGM's *The Wizard of Oz* (1939). Although she was briefly considered for the leading role of Dorothy, her co-star and fellow contract player Jack Haley was borrowed for that film and earned well-deserved screen immortality as the Tin Man.

BOTTOM LEFT: Original 1938 caption: . . . Moviemakers go to the farm for 'Rebecca of Sunnybrook Farm,' Shirley Temple's newest picture at 20th Century-Fox. Here is an interesting behind-the-production scene, showing Shirley Temple, in overalls, at the left. Immediately behind her is Director Allen Dwan. To the right is Gloria Stuart, looking at a script in the hands of Stanley Scheuer, script clerk. To the extreme right is the camera."

BOTTOM RIGHT: Shirley Temple and co-star Jack Haley in *Rebecca of Sunnybrook Farm* (1938).

RIGHT: The King Farm as it appeared in *State Fair* (1945).

FAR RIGHT: Jeanne Crain and screen boyfriend Phil Brown talk on the back porch that appeared to be the King Farm, but was actually recreated on Stage Fourteen.

BOTTOM LEFT: The general store as seen in *Love Me Tender* (1956). Richard Egan is in the center.

BOTTOM RIGHT: Though largely shot on location in the South, the Varner barn in *The Long, Hot Summer* (1958) was on the King Farm.

LEFT: A frame church and general store were later added to the King Farm set as seen here in *Lure of the Wilderness* (1952) with its stars Constance Smith and Jeffrey Hunter.

STAGE A

Sol Wurtzel, responsible for forging the legendary partnership between John Ford and Will Rogers, had first meant to team them for *A Connecticut Yankee* (1931). The spectacular King Arthur's Court became Sylvania for Rogers's *Ambassador Bill* (1931), where he is flown in by a young pilot (the not-yet-famous Ray Milland). This soundstage replaced it, becoming Stage A when Stage Fifteen was built. It continued to be used well into the television era.

OLD FRENCH STREET AND SQUARE

Old French Street and Square, designed by William Darling for *6 Hours to Live* (1932), was a study in contrasts. The Street was a ramshackle alley of half-timber structures while the Square was a formal European plaza of stately buildings. Art director David Hall helped give it a facelift and a church for *Seventh Heaven* (1937). Gordon Wiles designed the neighboring German schloss that was used in *Adorable* (1933), based on a German film written by Billy Wilder. Janet Gaynor's performance as Princess "Mitzi"—singing songs and pretending to be a commoner—inspired Walt Disney to ask for

ABOVE LEFT: Winding street on Old French Street.

ABOVE RIGHT: The elegant city plaza, built to be Geneva, Switzerland, stood in for many European locales.

LEFT: The Old French Street set was originally built for *Six Hours to Live* (1932) starring Warner Baxter as an international diplomat. The film has an interesting early science fiction element to it.

a "Janet Gaynor type" for his *Snow White and the Seven Dwarfs* (1937).

If these atmospheric walls could talk, however, no doubt their most unusual tale would be the making of *Forever Amber,* the studio's biggest grosser of 1947. A cinematic tribute to studio craftsmanship at its height in the 1940s, Linda Darnell's most lavish showcase, and a celebration of the backlot in lush Technicolor, it was a notoriously difficult film to make.

"There was something strange about that picture," said Leon Shamroy, director of photography for the film. "Linda Darnell was burned in the Great Fire of London, and in *Anna and the King of Siam* she was burned to death as a punishment. And she only escaped death in the picture because during the Great Fire, a roof caved in. I pulled the camera back and she just got out with it in time. She was terrified of fire, almost as though she had a premonition."

Indeed, at a friend's apartment during the night of April 8, 1965, after watching herself in *Star Dust* (1940) on television, a fire erupted while she slept. She was burned over 90 percent of her body, and died soon after at the age of forty-one.

FAR LEFT and BELOW LEFT:
Part of Old French Street was rebuilt to more resemble Montmartre for the remake of *7th Heaven* (1937) starring James Stewart.

RIGHT: Filming a scene from *Always Goodbye* (1938) with Barbara Stanwyck (in back seat of car) and Cesar Romero (in top hat).

BELOW RIGHT: Don Ameche strolls down Old French Street as D'Artagnan in *The Three Musketeers* (1939), a musical treatment of the classic Alexandre Dumas tale.

ABOVE LEFT: View of Old French Street.

ABOVE RIGHT: Peggy Ann Garner as *Jane Eyre* (1944) departs her aunt's home.

RIGHT: Linda Darnell and Cornel Wilde seek refuge from the plague in *Forever Amber* (1947). Director Otto Preminger is in the bottom left by the Fox camera.

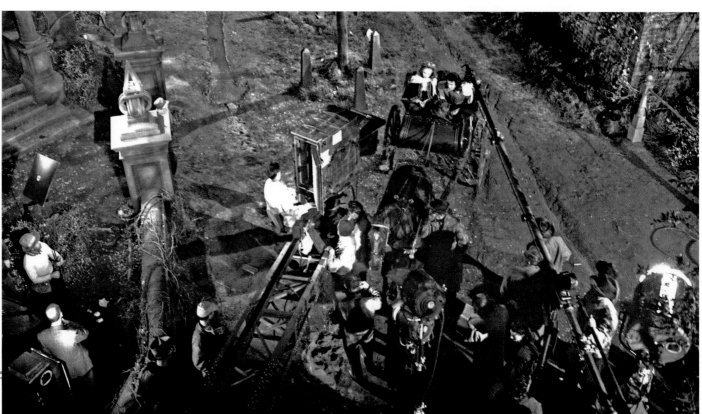

ABOVE LEFT: The Three Stooges perform in *Snow White and the Three Stooges* (1961).

ABOVE RIGHT: Other European sets were built around the Old French Street such as this large palace set for *Adorable* (1933) with Janet Gaynor.

FAR LEFT: The Three Stooges started out as the Five Stooges in their first film *Soup to Nuts* (1931) made at Fox.

LEFT: Janet Gaynor singing "My Heart's Desire" in *Adorable* (1933).

Tyrolean Street as it appeared in *Happy Landing* (1938).

Tyrolean Street

After the success of *Adorable* (1933) Fox brought Billy Wilder to America, launching his legendary Hollywood career. His first project was the Jerome Kern/Oscar Hammerstein II musical *Music in the Air* (1934). Art director Power O'Malley's Irish Street for *Paddy the Next Best Thing* (1933), that was rebuilt by Ernst Stern as a Hungarian village for *Caravan* (1934), became William Darling's Tyrolean Street. Before it was torn down to build Bernadette Street, it appeared in the Shirley Temple classic *Heidi* (1937) and a number of Sonja Henie's films.

ABOVE LEFT: The Tyrolean Street set at the time of *Music in the Air* (1934).

ABOVE RIGHT: Street in the Tyrolean Village.

LEFT: Another view of Tyrolean Village.

ABOVE LEFT: As the set appeared in *Heidi* (1937) starring Shirley Temple.

ABOVE RIGHT: Another view of Tyrolean Village.

RIGHT: Director Erik Charell, at left with megaphone, utilizes the Tyrolean Street for *Caravan* (1934).

Looking down on the Canal. The backlot Cafeteria was incorporated into the set seen in the top right corner."

THE CANAL

ABOVE LEFT: View of the Erie Canal set, looking north, built for *The Farmer Takes a Wife* (1935).

ABOVE RIGHT: The Tyrolean Street village was just beyond this building and shared the belfry tower as part of the church.

RIGHT: *The Farmer Takes a Wife* (1935) was Henry Fonda's first film (second from left). He met young Jane Withers (far right) on his first day and the two became life-long friends.

STAGE B

Among the films shot here was one of the world's classics, *Miracle on 34th Street* (1947). After appearing together in the sleeper hit *Sentimental Journey* (1946), John Payne and Maureen O'Hara were perfectly cast as a couple falling in love and learning to believe in the Santa Claus at the Macy's department store in New York City. Although director George Seaton shot in the actual Macy's in New York—and Edmund Gwenn was coached by the store's own Santa Claus, Charles W. Howard—the interior was also re-created here. In one of the film's most memorable sequences, O'Hara's young, disbelieving daughter, played by Natalie Wood, meets Santa Claus (Edmund Gwenn) and tugs his beard. Finding the beard to be real, she too becomes a believer.

In fact, Wood herself was convinced. "I really did think that Edmund Gwenn was Santa," she recalled. "I had never seen him without his beard, because he used to come in early in the morning and spend several hours putting on this wonderful beard and mustache. And at the end, during the set party, I saw this strange man, without the beard, and I just couldn't get it together."

Gwenn's performance so convinced Hollywood that he earned an Academy Award for Best Supporting Actor for the role.

Although the sequel John Payne wrote was never realized, John Hughes provided the studio with a remake forty-seven years later, with some inspired casting of his own, including Elizabeth Perkins and Dylan McDermott in the Maureen O'Hara and John Payne parts, Mara Wilson replacing Natalie Wood, and Fox veteran Richard Attenborough as Santa Claus.

ABOVE LEFT: Loretta Young gets ready for a scene in *Second Honeymoon* (1937).

ABOVE RIGHT: Spencer Tracy takes a rest after uttering "Dr. Livingstone, I presume" in *Stanley and Livingstone* (1939).

RIGHT: Myrna Loy and Tyrone Power making *The Rains Came* (1939). She recalled him as "a really divine man, perceptive and thoughtful. He had a very strong sense of other people, heightened by a kind of mysticism, a spiritual quality. You saw it in his deep, warm eyes."

THE CYCLORAMA

Built in 1926, this Cyclorama was the largest of its kind in Hollywood, with a treadmill and sky backing on a steel frame, with various levels so that it could be used as a coal mine or for scenes involving water, most famously for the coal-mine sequences in *How Green Was My Valley* (1940).

ABOVE LEFT: The cast on the Cyclorama set for *The Grapes of Wrath* (1940).

LEFT: John Ford, at left in the fedora hat, directs Walter Pidgeon and Roddy McDowall as they come out of the mine set for *How Green Was My Valley* (1941).

BLDG. 115: THE MILL

The mill of the gods may run slowly, but not the mill at Twentieth Century Fox. There, millions of feet of lumber are transformed into the beautiful interior and mammoth exterior sets you see on the screen.

—1937 Fox promotional exhibitors' film

This huge building housed the mill on one side and prop miniatures and action props departments on the other. In its heyday the mill employed eighty people in the tool, cabinet, blacksmith, glass, hardware, and saw-filing departments. Stacks of lumber were stored in an adjacent shed before being cut and assembled for the construction department, run by Sol Wurtzel's brother Ben for twenty-seven years, from an office atop the building.

In all, Ben Wurtzel was responsible for twelve departments, including all construction areas, scenic artists, grips, special effects, landscape department, laborers, painters, and the soundstages. He would also advise the art department on methods of building sets, costs involved, and the time that construction would take.

Sol also brought two of their other brothers into the company: Harry was an agent, representing the likes of John Ford and Henry King, and Sam, the youngest, was a unit manager who had been the first in the family to get a job at Fox in New York, and was actually responsible for getting Sol his job there.

Besides Sol's son Paul and Ben's son Paul, there were three more nephews on the lots that caused all kinds of confusion. Besides Saul and Dan, there was a third Paul, who got a job in the grip department in 1945, through Dan. That Paul eventually headed the special effects department, supervising the extraordinary work done on *Tora! Tora Tora!* (1970), *The Poseidon Adventure* (1972), and *The Towering Inferno* (1974). Of course, there were a lot of jokes on the lot, like: "Pick up any two-by-twelve and there is another Wurtzel," and "Things are getting Wurtzel and Wurtzel around here."

"The lot was really different then," recalled Ben's granddaughter Leslie. "Everyone felt like family. The guard at the Pico gate not only knew everyone by name, but he also knew your spouse and kids. It began to change when the backlot was sold off. We felt an integral part of that family was gone."

After Ivan Martin took over the mill, it reached a peak of eight hundred employees when he supervised the construction of the *Hello, Dolly!* (1969) street set. Martin remembered his most difficult task, however, as the technical work necessary for *Tora! Tora! Tora! (*1970), including the re-creation to five-eighths size of the *USS Arizona;* seven additional ships, including twelve for the Japanese; and some forty P-40 airplanes, to scale.

Joe Holster, a talented jeweler for forty-two years, recalled repairing at least fifty thousand watches and designing pieces for Betty Grable, Gene Tierney, and Ethel, John, and Lionel Barrymore. Pete Peterson was another jeweler renowned on the lot for creating everything from the code machine for *Tora! Tora! Tora!* to the military medals for *Patton* (1970), and Derek Flint's wristwatch for *Our Man Flint* (1966). Charles Ryan, brother-in-law to Richard Nixon, ran the fixtures department. The mill's last great achievement was the twenty-six-foot-tall Christmas tree for *The Poseidon Adventure* (1972).

ABOVE: Interior of the mill circa 1936.

FAR LEFT: Outside the Mill, the chassis of the Fox-built locomotive "Emma Sweeney" is prepared for shipment to Colorado for its debut in *A Ticket to Tomahawk* (1950).

LEFT: Walter Pullman, head of props and miniatures, and art directors Lyle Wheeler and Ben Hayne in the interior of the Mill with the "Emma Sweeney."

RIGHT: Brownstones on Old New York Street.

FAR RIGHT: Jane Withers as a milk can stowaway in a scene from *Paddy O'Day* (1936). Director Lewis Seiler is at extreme right lifting the lid.

BOTTOM LEFT: The street came complete with an elevated train.

BOTTOM RIGHT: Original 1936 caption: "Tyrone Power, who plays one of the leads in *Love is News* [1937] is shown here with the Cord used in this grand newspaper story.' (Note to Exhibitor. Take this still to your nearest Cord dealer and arrange a window display.)"

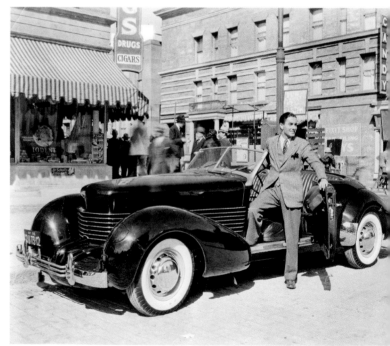

OLD NEW YORK STREET

Although it had an antecedent, a modern city block built in 1926 replacing the old French village from *What Price Glory* (1926), Old New York Street is the primary urban setting for decades' worth of Fox films. Designed by William Darling for Frank Borzage's *Bad Girl* (1930), starring James Dunn and Sally Eilers, the four-story set extended three blocks in one direction, one block in another, and had half-block extensions off all the intersecting streets, with three streetcars, an elevated railroad, and subway entrances. A theater facade with marquee was built with an interior lobby to match the lobby of the theater set on Stage Two at Western Avenue.

Can you imagine finding Alice Faye walking up and down the street with a placard advertising Tony Romano "The Spaghetti King?" She did it to pay for her dinner there after introducing the title song for *You Can't Have Everything* (1937). Jimmy Durante found similar unglamorous work cleaning the streets for *Sally, Irene and Mary* (1938), starring Alice Faye and new husband (1937-41) and early Fox crooner Tony Martin. The couple first met on this set for *Sing, Baby, Sing* (1936).

"Our fans were so anxious to see us together," recalled Faye, "that they made that so-so film a major box office smash."

Tales of Manhattan (1942), made here, left a lasting impression on a youth who saw it in Dallas, Texas. Aaron Spelling came to Hollywood with $200 from his parents, and found work in films that used this very set, like *Vicki* (1953) and *Black Widow* (1954), before being hired by Dick Powell as a writer for his *Zane Grey Theatre* (1956–61) TV show.

Powell, who had been featured in Fox films since 1932, and was signed by Buddy Adler to a contract as a producer-director (*The Enemy Below,* 1957, and *The Hunters,* 1958), became the first major movie star to embrace television with his Four Star Productions that used the stages of the Western Avenue Studio. Years later, many of Spelling's hit shows, like *The Love Boat* (1977–86) and *Dynasty* (1981–89), were filmed on the Century City lot, carrying on the traditions he learned in *Tales of Manhattan,* with its glamour and multiple storylines.

The Love Boat, shot on Stages Ten and Eleven, ran for nine years, offering cruises to exotic locales with guest stars like Fox vets Janet Gaynor, Don Ameche, Alice Faye, Ginger Rogers, and Hope Lange. Spelling's five-year hit *Hart to Hart* (1979–84) was a fortuitous blending of old and new at the studio with Robert Wagner and Tom Mankiewicz involved. Although Spelling suggested Natalie Wood as his co-star, Wagner chose Stefanie Powers. Wood appeared in the pilot for fun, billed under her real name, Natasha Gurdin, as an actress on the Peyton Place square set. Another Fox veteran Jill St. John, featured in the pilot, married

ABOVE LEFT: This hotel façade, at the south end of Old New York Street, was used frequently in the late 1930s as seen here in *Charlie Chan in City in Darkness* (1939).

ABOVE RIGHT: Old New York Street became the avenue in *On the Avenue* (1937). Dick Powell (in top hat) is flanked by Alice Faye on the right and Madeleine Carroll on the left. The Ritz Brothers round out the group.

Wagner after Wood's death. Spelling produced *Mr. Mom* (1983), and his first show for Fox was *Beverly Hills 90210* (1990) followed by the popular spin-off *Melrose Place* (1992).

The set was enlarged and forever immortalized as the setting of Elia Kazan's *A Tree Grows in Brooklyn* (1945). The production ideally suited Kazan's directorial debut since he was an immigrant himself who had come to America around the same time the movie takes place. Kazan always credited Leon Shamroy with teaching him

the ropes, and Peggy Ann Garner as "the little miracle" that made the film great. It must have seemed as much a miracle to James Dunn, who was back on the set after alcoholism destroyed the promise of his Fox career. His performance earned him an Academy Award. Playing his wife was Dorothy McGuire. "It is interesting to learn that Dorothy went to a convent because it did leave its mark on her," said fellow actor Norman Lloyd. "There was something when she worked in rehearsal and particularly studying alone one appreciated the concentration she brought and the absorption and the dedication. She was absolutely committed. I've worked with a lot of people in this business but none as warm, as welcoming, as lovely, as admirably a human being—none more than Dorothy."

Director Bruce Humberstone and cinematographer Edward Cronjager produced a striking look for Betty Grable's *I Wake Up Screaming* (1941) that helped to define the film noir genre and the future of this set. Although the film is regarded as Fox's first effort at the genre, *Johnny Apollo* (1940) is an interesting antecedent featuring Lloyd Nolan, who began appearing in the studio's Michael Shayne detective series the same year. Then, for the rest of the decade, he appeared in some of the finest film noir efforts here including *Circumstantial Evidence* (1945), *Somewhere in the Night* (1946) with no less than Lee Strasberg and W. Somerset Maugham contributing to its screenplay, and *The Street With No Name* (1948).

Although Raymond Chandler's *The High Window* was adapted into a Michael Shayne film, *A Time to Kill (*1942), George Montgomery played Chandler's detective Philip Marlowe in *The Brasher Doubloon* (1947) as well. Then there was Otto Preminger's *Fallen Angel* (1945), and Fred Kohlmar's *The Dark Corner* (1946) starring his protégée Lucille Ball, and containing Clifton Webb's deathless line:

"The enjoyment of art is the only remaining ecstasy that's neither immoral nor illegal."

Fox film noir really kicked violently into gear with Richard Widmark's bloodcurdling performance—and laugh—in his Oscar-nominated film debut, *Kiss of Death* (1947). Although primarily shot on location in New York, the film's dramatic final sequence was shot here. Similarly, the excellent *Call Northside 777* (1948) and *Cry of the City* (1948) also had sequences shot here,

Joseph Mankiewicz's *House of Strangers* (1949) told the dark tale of the powerful Monetti banking family starring noir favorite Richard Conte. It was revised and moved over to Tombstone Street by Richard Murphy as *Broken Lance* (1954). Ted Sherdeman updated it as *The Big Show* (1961), filmed in Munich, with Cliff Robertson and Esther Williams.

The tables were turned on Widmark when he encountered Marilyn Monroe as a psychotic woman in the McKinley Hotel (on Stage Three at the Western Avenue Studio) in *Don't Bother to Knock* (1952). Monroe's acting coach Natasha Lytess appeared in the noir-ish *House on Telegraph Hill* (1951). Valentina Cortesa and Richard Basehart, whose love is doomed in that film, got married in real life. The set rounded out its film noir credits with a remake of *I Wake Up Screaming* renamed *Vicki* (1953) and Nunnally Johnson's CinemaScope entry *Black Widow* (1954).

Don Ameche and Alice Faye on a stroll in *Hollywood Cavalcade* (1939). Santa Monica Boulevard and the Los Angeles Country Club are at the end of the street.

Making her debut in *Don't Bother to Knock* (1952) was contract player Anne Bancroft. Her second film was with Dan Dailey, who lived here with another of those extraordinary Fox child stars, Billy Chapin, playing *The Kid from Left Field* (1953). Bancroft married Mel Brooks, a successful creative partnership that ended with her death in 2005.

In *The Model and the Marriage Broker* (1951), the model (Jeanne Crain) lives in an apartment here that she dubs "Wuthering Depths," before the marriage broker (Thelma Ritter) matches her with Scott Brady. Susan Hayward and Dan Dailey were an even more ambitious pair, plotting in a restaurant here in *I Can Get It for You Wholesale* (1951). Nearby June Haver and William Lundigan ran a cozy boardinghouse at 337 Gramercy Place, where Marilyn Monroe lodged in *Love Nest* (1952).

That same year the great Charles Laughton strolled the length of the street and eventually due to movie magic ran into Marilyn playing a streetwalker on Midwestern Street who is touched by his gallantry when he calls her a "lady." It is one

ABOVE LEFT: Charles Boyer and Rita Hayworth star in the first of five vignettes about a tuxedo in *Tales of Manhattan* (1942).

ABOVE RIGHT: Aaron Spelling in the creepy film *Vicki* (1953).

RIGHT: Betty Grable (center, with co-star Victor Mature) took on a rare non-musical part as the sister of a murdered woman (Carole Landis, on the floor) in *I Wake Up Screaming* (1941).

FAR RIGHT: Things go awry in this prison break scene from *Johnny Apollo* (1940) with Edward Arnold (left) and Tyrone Power.

BOTTOM LEFT: Lloyd Nolan at his best in the Michael Shayne detective series.

BOTTOM RIGHT: Lucille Ball, at her best before *I Love Lucy* in *The Dark Corner* (1946).

episode in the blindingly all-star *O. Henry's Full House* (1952), the kind of film that could only have been made at Fox, with its literary aspirations—not to mention John Steinbeck as its narrator.

The most beloved story in the mix is "The Gift of the Magi," featuring Jeanne Crain and Farley Granger as a young couple living near the set's elevated railway, whose sacrifices lead up to a memorable Christmas Eve. Another of the stories, "The Last Leaf," stars Anne Baxter who is abandoned by her lover on this snowy street. The man who left her was contract player Bert Hicks, whose daughter, future Fox actress Dolores Hart, was schooled at Marymount College in the hills above nearby UCLA. She later entered the Community of the Abbey of Regina Laudis in Bethlehem, Connecticut, whose founding was dramatized as *Come to the Stable* (1949).

ABOVE: Don't blink or you might miss Shelley Winters in the quintessential film noir *Cry of the City* (1948).

FAR LEFT: Dana Andrews (with gun) as a corrupt cop in *Where the Sidewalk Ends* (1950).

LEFT: Richard Widmark in another of the best Fox film noirs, *Pickup on South Street* (1953), with co-star Jean Peters on the floor .

RIGHT: Old New York Street dressed for *A Tree Grows in Brooklyn* (1945).

BOTTOM: This theatre façade was used in several films. Here it is in one of Maureen O'Hara's favorite films, *Sentimental Journey* (1946), advertising her character's play.

FAR LEFT: William Lundi-gan and Marilyn Monroe in *Love Nest* (1952).

LEFT: Jayne Mansfield gets some direction from director Frank Tashlin for her famous saunter down this street in *The Girl Can't Help It* (1956).

BOTTOM: Looking south down Old New York Street, the Cyclorama can be seen in the distance.

If film noir had not waned in the 1950s, Jayne Mansfield certainly would have chased the shadows away in her memorable walk down this street, aided by the ingenious satiric touch of director Frank Tashlin in *The Girl Can't Help It* (1956). Tashlin and Mansfield reached their career zenith the following year with *Will Success Spoil Rock Hunter?* (1957).

NEW ENGLAND STREET AND SQUARE

The prim houses looked real, well-kept, but deserted. It had the look of a pleasant town from which the populace has fled as if from some approaching horror. Such as television, maybe.
—Los Angeles Times, *January 1958*

Darryl Zanuck's penchant for celebrating Americana was never more apparent than in the films shot here, from Henry King's splendid tribute to the teaching profession *Remember the Day* (1942), to producer Sam Jaffe and Robert T. Kane's poignant *The Sullivans* (1944), and the charming family pictures starring Jeanne Crain. There was rarely trouble here, except when Zanuck's similar inclination toward pictures with a social conscience invaded the neighborhood. It could be said Miss Crain grew up here when she was able to take on the town and

ABOVE LEFT: Looking down from the church to the courthouse.

ABOVE RIGHT: A row of shops.

FAR LEFT: This street of homes were to the left of the church.

LEFT: This lovely Victorian was one of the more "lived-in" homes on the street—often the home of Jeanne Crain.

its virulent prejudice in *Pinky* (1949). That year the house at the top of the street that was usually hers was the scene of the violent climax between Richard Widmark, Sidney Poitier, and Linda Darnell in *No Way Out* (1950).

All that optimism peaked with *Good Morning, Miss Dove* (1955), a warm evocation of mid-twentieth-century America and its best values including a life well-lived. The set never looked better than when schoolteacher Miss Dove (Jennifer Jones) walks the length of it—as the town of Liberty Heights—from her home in the residential area (the same home Jeanne Crain frequently lived in) to the school across the square

in the opening sequence. The trend thereafter, exposing darker aspects of the American experience, showed up the very next year in the story of another teacher equally well-played by James Mason in Nicholas Ray's masterpiece *Bigger Than Life* (1956), and then in films like *Peyton Place* (1957), *The Young Lions* (1958), *Blue Denim* (1959) where Carol Lynley and Brandon de Wilde explored the ramifications of teen pregnancy decades before *Juno* (2006), and *Wild in the Country* (1961) where Elvis is arrested here. The set was allowed to show its age as Jefferson, Mississippi, for Jerry Wald's adaptation of William Faulkner's *The Sound and the Fury* (1959). A fire broke out in

ABOVE LEFT: Will Rogers on New England Street for *Doctor Bull* (1933).

ABOVE RIGHT: James Mason prepares for a scene for *Bigger Than Life* (1955). Director Nicholas Ray's first film (as dialogue director and a small role as a bakery clerk) was also made on the lot: *A Tree Grows in Brooklyn* (1945).

LEFT: Jennifer Jones on the set for *Good Morning, Miss Dove* (1955).

Although *Peyton Place* (1957) was mostly filmed on location some scenes, like this one where the boys go off to World War II, were filmed here.

the miniature set shop in September of 1959, adjacent to the blacksmith shop, destroying fourteen of the wood frame false front sets.

During the winter of 1960, Carol Lynley was back for one last glorious look at the set for a *Return to Peyton Place* (1961), peopled with Eleanor Parker, Mary Astor, Tuesday Weld, and Brett Halsey and Luciana Paluzzi, married in "reel" and real life.

LEFT: Carol Lynley runs through New England Street to share the news about her book getting published in *Return to Peyton Place* (1961).

BOTTOM LEFT: Lee Remick and Bradford Dillman exit the courthouse in *Sanctuary* (1961).

BOTTOM RIGHT: Who knew that in this winter scene from *Peyton Place* (1957), filmed in the height of summer, Terry Moore wore a bathing suit under her coat.

The filming of *The Song of Bernadette* (1943).

603.SPEC-1

BERNADETTE STREET

This is the story of Bernadette Soubirous who lived in Lourdes, a village in southern France close to the Spanish border. For those who believe in God, no explanation is necessary. For those who do not believe in God, no explanation is possible.

—Introduction to The Song of Bernadette *(1943), screenplay by George Seaton*

When financially troubled times forced Winfield Sheehan to abandon location shooting for *The Farmer Takes a Wife* (1935), he commissioned William Darling to design a system of canals and locks to simulate life on the Erie Canal in 1853 here. Gary Cooper and Joel McCrea and Spencer Tracy were considered before the star of Max Gordon's Broadway production Henry Fonda was brought west to make his film debut. His nine-year-old co-star Jane Withers, observing Fonda's nervousness on the set, took him aside to reassure him with a prayer.

"I said, 'God, he really needs help,'" she recalled. "He's new in the industry, but I think he's going to be awful good. So he just needs to have a little more confidence.' He gave me the most wonderful autographed picture. On it he wrote: 'To Jane, who helped me to break into this racket. With confidence and love.'"

Fonda's gratitude went further. He named his daughter after the young star, and when he died he left his favorite piece of movie memorabilia, his cap from *The Grapes of Wrath* (1940), to his old friend.

The Erie Canal set made way for "Bernadette Street;" the largest set yet constructed since the Welsh village was built out at the Century Ranch. Designed by William Darling and James Basevi for *The Song of Bernadette* (1943), the set was an early use of molded plaster in set construction, a necessary innovation because of World War II shortages. It proved to be so effective that it became an industry standard. Shot during the spring and summer of 1943, the film was based on war refugee Franz Werfel's account of the peasant girl in southern France whose visions of the Virgin Mary led to numerous miracles, the establishment of Lourdes as a religious shrine, and her own canonization in 1933. Werfel considered the work a heartfelt thank-you to the Virgin for his escape from the Nazis.

Jennifer Jones, cast as Bernadette, always felt that the particular success of the book and film—still accessible, and revered more than seventy years later—is its power to inspire. Of her performance Henry King recalled: "There's a scene where Bernadette sees the Blessed Virgin. Well, before I tested Jennifer Jones, twelve other actresses had tested for the part. All of them *looked* at the Blessed Virgin, but Jennifer *saw* Her."

ABOVE LEFT: On the other side of the bridge was the village's main plaza.

ABOVE RIGHT: Another view of the village

RIGHT: The model of Bernadette Street.

Jennifer Jones was back here as the beguiling *Cluny Brown* (1946) in another of Ernst Lubitsch's Fox classics, and then it was Whitecliff-by-the-Sea for *The Ghost and Mrs. Muir* (1947). Robert Wagner recalled it as an ultimate movie moment when he appeared here in a John Ford movie (*What Price Glory* (1952)), dying in no less than James Cagney's arms. The film also offers great views of both this and *The Keys of the Kingdom* set. This one was also memorably captured for posterity by Milton H. Greene, who shot playful poses of Marilyn Monroe on Sunday afternoons during the making of *Bus Stop* (1956).

The stars of *Snow White and the Three Stooges* (1961) have an interesting history on the lot. They made their film debut at Fox with *Soup to Nuts* in 1930, and eighty-two years later the Farrelly Brothers (Peter and Bobby) produced *The Three Stooges* (2012) as a tribute to them.

LEFT: A hazy morning in France recreated in Los Angeles on the backlot in *The Song of Bernadette* (1943).

BOTTOM LEFT: Director Henry King on the set of *The Song of Bernadette* (1943). As the top director at Fox, King usually asked for—and got—permission to film on location. This was impossible due to World War II. The alternative was to build this huge set.

BOTTOM RIGHT: Jennifer Jones asks Anne Revere a question about the script on the set of *The Song of Bernadette* (1943). Knitting was a popular hobby among many actresses to pass the many hours between scenes.

RIGHT: Tyrone Power asks for directions as he roams through Bernadette Street doubling as the French countryside in *The Razor's Edge* (1946). If he went to his left he would have run into the Los Angeles Country Club. Beverly Hills High School would have been straight ahead.

FAR RIGHT: Humphrey Bogart visits James Cagney on the set for *What Price Glory* (1952).

BOTTOM LEFT: Bernadette Street became Canadian for *The Iron Curtain* (1948), one of Hollywood's best early critical explorations of the Cold War. The film paired Gene Tierney and Dana Andrews (with back to camera) for the fourth time.

BOTTOM RIGHT: Michael Rennie and Debra Paget in *Les Miserables* (1952).

SUBURBAN STREET

Connected to New England Street was Suburban Street, whose best-known residents were the Jones family. Their series—Twentieth Century Fox's answer to MGM's popular Hardy family—began in 1936 with *Every Saturday Night,* and concluded with *On Their Own* in 1940, for sixteen feature "episodes." Of the eight homes on the street, Bldg. 506 was Sol Wurtzel's old bungalow from the Western Avenue studio that housed both the West Coast headquarters of Movietone News and the Studio

Club, founded in December of 1935 as a recreation spot for employees. There were Movietone News offices in New York, London, Paris, Berlin, and Sidney, Australia, issuing thirty-seven editions in nineteen languages with sixty field crews, offered in theaters twice a week. Ultimately more than four thousand newsreels and one thousand short films were made and distributed, until September 26, 1963. In March of 1980, Dennis Stanfill donated them to the University of South Carolina.

Suburban Street

ABOVE LEFT: Suburban Street circa 1959.

ABOVE RIGHT: Fred McMurray talks to daughters Natalie Wood and Betty Lynn in *Father was a Fullback* (1949).

RIGHT: Director John Ford demonstrates how to kick a can for *When Willie Comes Marching Home* (1950). The Sol Wurtzel Bungalow (behind him to the right) housed the Studio Club for employees.

FAR RIGHT: Cary Grant delightfully reverts to childhood tendencies in *Monkey Business* (1952).

Richard Widmark showed up on this set for *Red Skies of Montana* (1952), a tribute to the US Forestry Service. Trees were brought down from Lake Arrowhead, planted on the backlot, and rigged with gas jets to burn to greatest effect under controlled conditions. "We did it all here because the government takes a dim view of starting a fire in a national forest," noted cinematographer Charles G. Clarke.

ABOVE: Ethel Merman answers the door as the matriarch of the Dona-hues, the show-business family in *There's No Business Like Show Business* (1954).

FAR LEFT: Janet Gaynor (at door) reappeared on the backlot as Pat Boone's mother in *Bernardine* (1957). Boone is on her right and Dick Sargent is at her left.

LEFT: Robert Stack helps Jean Simmons into her mother's house in *Hilda Crane* (1956).

ABOVE: The cafeteria appearing as the Blue Grotto in *Bernardine* (1957).

RIGHT: The Cafeteria is dressed up as the border crossing for *Four Sons* (1940).

Bldg. 129: Cafeteria

Studio employees were always quick to point out that this cafeteria, was open to all, including extras, etc., while the Café de Paris was meant for stars and executives. It was transformed into an old mill in a tangle of gnarled trees for *Dr. Renault's Secret* (1942), advertised as "the first horror picture Twentieth Century Fox has ever made," starring J. Carrol Naish. Naish literally gave his blood for the company, donating blood when William Fox suffered injuries in that near-fatal automobile accident in 1929. He had worked at Fox ever since, beginning with his film debut in *Good Intentions* (1930).

When the Charlie Chan series was reprised for television as *The New Adventures of Charlie Chan* in 1956, Naish was cast as Chan. In this spooky spot, it is also worth noting that before they became Universal Studio's famed "monsters," Bela Lugosi, Boris Karloff, and Lon Chaney Jr. all lurked at Fox, and all three appeared in Chan films. After making his American film debut in Fox's *The Silent Command* (1923), Lugosi made *The Black Camel* (1931). Karloff appears in two of them: *Behind that Curtain* (1929) and *Charlie Chan at the Opera* (1936). Anna Leonowens, who was immortalized in Fox's *Anna and King of Siam* (1946), *The King and I* (1957), and *Anna and the King of Siam* (1999), was Karloff's great-aunt. Chaney Jr., who signed a two-year contract in 1937, appeared in *Charlie Chan on Broadway* (1937), *Mr. Moto's Gamble* (1938), and *Frontier Marshal* (1939).

BOTTOM LEFT: Interior of the cafeteria.

BOTTOM RIGHT: That's J. Carrol Naish on the roof for *Dr. Renault's Secret* (1942).

MIDWESTERN STREET

Designed by William Darling and his team for *The County Chairman* (1935)—starring Will Rogers and directed by John G. Blystone, who graduated from Sunshine comedies to this lot, where he made Fox films for a decade—this set is most famous as the one where Bill "Bojangles" Robinson and Shirley Temple danced in *The Littlest Rebel* (1935).

Of their dancing partnership in five classic films, Temple was proud that they were the first interracial dancing couple in movie history, while Robinson remained in awe of her talent: "That girl was so perfect it was embarrassing. I'd show her a step and the next day I come down and start to do the step and she'd say, 'Uncle Bill, yesterday you started on the other foot.' "

Tracks were laid so that trains could stop at the depot here, the station set running along "New" New York Street, the Train Shed where they were housed, and link up with tracks in Westwood to go anywhere in the country. Even the Shed was used for filming—most famously for housing the interior of the space ship that landed out there on the backlot from *The Day The Earth Stood Still* (1951) and the New York docks where Marilyn Monroe and Jane Russell board their ocean liner in *Gentlemen Prefer Blondes* (1953). The remarkable train yard—a fond memory for all who saw it—contained a European-style engine, multiple coaches, and an American caboose and historic cars from the Truckee Railroad that had been purchased in the company's earliest days. Our vote for the most sentimental, tear-inducing good-bye

ever staged here was for *Remember the Day* (1940). Claudette Colbert bids farewell to her favorite student (Douglas Croft), off to school, and to her husband (John Payne), off to war.

A study in contrasts: In 1948's *Road House* Ida Lupino arrives here to work in Jefty's (Richard Widmark) Roadhouse, only to fall in love with Cornel Wilde and cause what the *Los Angeles Times* described as "sordid slashing melodrama." The following year it was the Bethlehem, Connecticut, station for the inspiring *Come to the Stable,* where Loretta Young and Celeste Holm earned Academy Award nominations as nuns intent on building a children's hospital. Check out the station as part of the opening sequence to *The Girl Next Door* (1953) as proof of the sheer inventiveness of the

BOTTOM LEFT: The well-used train station on Midwestern Street.

BOTTOM RIGHT: Midwestern Street during the filming of *The County Chairman* (1935).

ABOVE: Midwestern Street during filming of an unidentified film in 1949 (and it's not an episode of *The Andy Griffith Show* despite being set in Mayberry!).

Fox musical. Speaking of the genre, Bing Crosby showed up before his stint at Fox at the station at Pine Tree, Vermont, with Danny Kaye, Rosemary Clooney, and Vera-Ellen for *White Christmas* (1954, Paramount).

Director/writer Philip Dunne recalled that the last sequence shot for *Wild in the Country* (1961)—in which Hope Lange and Tuesday Weld bid good-bye

to Elvis Presley—was also the last scene ever shot here, and Dunne's last work on the backlot.

"As we set up the railroad station set for our last scene, a Sherman tank was charging about in the background, knocking down the old sets. I remember thinking that not Attila the Hun, nor Genghis Khan, nor even Tecumseh Sherman himself on his march through Georgia, had cut such a wide geographical swath of destruction, as down went Caligula's Rome, Pinky's Southern mansion, Mrs. Muir's haunted house, George Apley's Boston, John O'Hara's Gibbsville, and Jesus's village of Cana. When we finished our scene, packed up, and were about to leave, I looked back to see the tank wheel, accelerate, and smash its way through our own set. I stood and watched as it ran back and forth through the rubble until the old railroad station was ground down to powder. Then my assistant director touched my shoulder and said, 'Come on, Phil, let's get the hell out of here.' He was in tears; I was long past them."

ABOVE: Shirley Temple and Bill Robinson in that classic dance routine down Midwestern Street for *The Littlest Rebel* (1935).

FAR LEFT: Claudette Colbert in the unforgettable *Remember the Day* (1941).

LEFT: Cornel Wilde and Gene Tierney share a fatal attraction that begins aboard this train in *Leave Her to Heaven* (1945).

RIGHT: Darryl Zanuck shows off one of the train cars parked on the set.

FAR RIGHT: Celeste Holm (in the jeep) chats with Ida Lupino on Midwestern Street during the filming of *Road House* (1948).

BOTTOM LEFT: Celeste Holm was back on the set with Loretta Young for *Come to the Stable* (1949). That's Dooley Wilson holding the wine crate.

BOTTOM RIGHT: Hope Lange is about to give Elvis a kiss goodbye in *Wild in the Country* (1962).

Sersen Lake

Named for the studio's remarkable head of special effects who created the underworld of *Dante's Inferno,* the sandstorm in *Suez,* the great fire of *In Old Chicago,* and the epic flood and earthquake in *The Rains Came,* this tank was two hundred feet wide and three hundred feet long and could hold 1,865,000 gallons. Although only three or four feet of water were necessary to fill the tank for filming, the center of the tank was thirty feet deep for the sinking of ships, etc. It was equipped with wave-makers that could be set at various speeds to create different types of waves; wind machines; and a special camera mounted on pontoons that could travel across the lake, pulled by cables attached to a power winch. The painted

View of Sersen Lake in the late 1950s. Old New York Harbor can be seen on the right and the newly constructed Beverly Hilton hotel can be seen in the distance on the left.

RIGHT: A view from the top of the Sersen Lake staircase looking southeast, late 1950s.

FAR RIGHT: View from the top of the Sersen Lake staircase looking south, late 1950s. Chicago Lake with Old New York Harbor structures is in the foreground; the backs of the New New York and Washington Square sets can be seen in the distance.

BOTTOM LEFT: View from the top of the Sersen Lake staircase looking northwest over Olympic Boulevard, late 1950s. The Keys of the Kingdom set can be seen.

BOTTOM RIGHT: View from the top of the Sersen Lake staircase looking north over Olympic Boulevard, late 1950s. Sligon Castle, the Slave Market (west side dressed as the palace for *The King and I* (1956)), and the Temple of Aton can be seen.

sky backing, facing south so that shooting could be done all day without shadows revealing what it was, ran 225 feet long and 73 feet high.

While existing studio documentation tells us that the tank had its name by the time *Tonight We Raid Calais* (1943) was made here in the fall of 1942, it does not note when the tank was built. Most likely it was built for *Crash Dive* (1943), but the backing may have been built earlier for *The Black Swan* (1942) which Darryl Zanuck intended to be the pirate film to end all pirate films.

Despite its success, Alfred Hitchcock's *Lifeboat* (1944) remains the most famous movie made out here. The primary set—a forty-foot boat—holds the record for the smallest set for a motion picture. The cast boarded the crowded, tiny vessel for the establishing scenes and then headed to the Cyclorama for the subsequent foggy ones.

The cast performed most of the movie, however, in an identical lifeboat raised off the floor of Stage Six with shots of the ocean captured in Florida. There was more work for the storm sequence in the Lower Moat. Chicago Lake was used for key scenes involving the tanker nearly capsizing the lifeboat, and the young Nazi sailor coming aboard. The opening and closing sequences were shot there last of all.

Zanuck and Hitchcock were always proud of the result, and as the film's reputation grew over the years, so did the tributes to a great filmmaker at the studio. Brian De Palma paid homage to *Psycho* (1960, Paramount) in *Phantom of the Paradise* (1974). Mel Brooks's tribute—with script contributions from Hitchcock—was *High Anxiety* (1977). He held a special screening on the lot for Hitchcock, who was pleased with his effort. Writer Larry Cohn credits his discussions with Hitchcock as

ABOVE LEFT: Sersen Lake may have been built for this set in *Crash Dive* (1943).

ABOVE RIGHT: Wide shot of Sersen Lake as seen in Alfred Hitchcock's *Lifeboat* (1944).

contributing to the success of *Phone Booth* (2003). Sacha Gervasi's *Hitchcock* (2012) pointed out his wife Alma's (played by Dame Helen Mirren) important contributions to his timeless work.

The backdrop made news when it suffered massive fire damage in October of 1947 that injured seven men. Scene docks and some miniatures were also destroyed. By 1952 it was head of special effects Ray Kellogg who had the lake filled once again, at the usual cost of $3,000, for *Titanic* (1953). He supervised the creation of the twenty-eight-foot miniature of the ship and the iceberg that rose to sink it in the opening sequence. He also facilitated

the film's dramatic conclusion, with a replica of the doomed ship swarming with an all-star cast on Stage Fourteen.

"It was bitter cold," recalled Barbara Stanwyck. "I was forty-seven feet in the air in a lifeboat . . . the water below was agitated. We were re-creating an actual tragedy and I burst into tears. I shook with great racking sobs and couldn't stop."

The success of Walt Disney's *20,000 Leagues under the Sea* (1954) launched a competitive golden age of sci-fi in Hollywood, on the lot, and in this tank. For his most ambitious film to date Walt Disney wanted the best, and that included Fox

pioneer Ralph Hammeras who was in charge of the studio's miniature and process department. His department shot Harper Goff's exquisite miniatures here for Disney's film. Sequences with the actors were also shot here, including those set on the island of the prison camp. Irwin Allen spent a quarter of a million dollars rivaling it all for *Voyage to the Bottom of the Sea* (1961). Although Al (David) Hedison turned down the role of Captain Crane, he accepted the role in the television series (1964–68) that ran longer than Paramount's *Star Trek* (1966–69), and was the longest running science-fiction show until *Star Trek: The Next Generation* (1987–94).

ABOVE LEFT: This is where the *Titanic* sank (in miniature) in the 1953 film.

ABOVE RIGHT: Filming The *Enemy Below* (1957) on Sersen Lake.

LEFT: More miniature ships on Sersen Lake used for *The Virgin Queen* (1955).

Filming the lake scene in *Journey to the Center of the Earth* (1959).

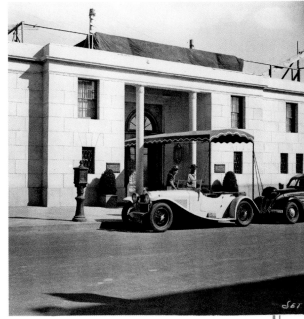

"NEW" NEW YORK STREET

This modern New York set (originally known as the "East Side") was designed by Richard Day and Albert Hogsett for *Chicken Wagon Family* (1939) starring Jane Withers, but *Elsa Maxwell's Hotel for Women* (1939), marking the film debut of Linda Darnell, was the first film actually shot here. The success of *Hotel* was in no small part due to the esteemed Miss Maxwell, who contributed to the script and produced a mini-franchise with *Free, Blonde and 21* (1940) and *Girl in 313* (1940). In years to come this set represented 5th Avenue with its chic night clubs (*Billy Rose's Diamond Horseshoe*, 1945), high end retail stores (Bullitt's department store in *Laura,* 1944), art galleries (Courbet Gallery in *An Affair to Remember,* 1957) and luxurious hotels and apartments (*Phone Call From A Stranger* (1951) and *From The Terrace* (1960)).

RIGHT: The brownstone on New New York Street.

FAR RIGHT: Bullitt's department store, based on the upscale Los Angeles department store Bullock's, was where Gene Tierney worked in *Laura* (1944). Here she is meeting up with Dana Andrews.

BOTTOM LEFT: The set was built to be Fifth Avenue in New York for *Chicken Wagon Family* (1939) starring Jane Withers (talking to the police officer).

BOTTOM RIGHT: "New" New York Street as seen in *The Dark Corner* (1947).

FAR LEFT: An awkward moment is had by all when Alfred Eaton (Paul Newman) and his wife (Joanne Woodward) run into his mistress (Ina Balin) in *From the Terrace* (1960).

LEFT: Cary Grant peeks through a shop window on "New" New York Street in *An Affair to Remember* (1957).

BOTTOM: Betty Grable (in black) during the opening scene in *My Blue Heaven* (1950). The townhouses of Washington Square can be seen on the right.

BELOW: Joseph Mankiewicz (with pipe) making *People Will Talk* (1951) and showing the less-used west facades.

ABOVE RIGHT: That's Mickey Hargitay jumping onto the car to make a statement in *Will Success Spoil Rock Hunter?* (1957). The townhouses of Washington Square are on the right.

RIGHT: Looking down "New" New York Street into Washington Square in the early 1960s.

View of the massive
Chicago Street set.
Washington Square,
"New" New York Street,
Adano Square, the Rail-
road Station, Chicago
Lake with Old New York
Harbor and Sersen Lake.
The nursery is at the
far right and Olympic
Boulevard curves along
the top.

RIGHT: No expense was spared in this extensive replica of nineteenth century Chicago built for *In Old Chicago* (1938) which included a miniature version of Lake Michigan.

BOTTOM LEFT and BOTTOM RIGHT: Views of the streets used *In Old Chicago* (1938).

THIS PAGE: More views of the expansive Chicago Street set.

ABOVE LEFT: Director Henry King (left) chats with Tyrone Power and Alice Faye during the filming of *In Old Chicago* (1938).

ABOVE RIGHT: Don Ameche, face forward in carriage, during filming for *In Old Chicago* (1938).

RIGHT: Tyrone Power makes sure his suit fits properly in this scene from *In Old Chicago* (1938).

LEFT: The recreation of the massive fire for *In Old Chicago* (1938) made many residents of nearby Beverly Hills fear that their city was on fire.

BOTTOM LEFT: Tyrone Power (right) found himself on Chicago Street again as the outlaw *Jesse James* (1939). Henry Fonda played his brother Frank.

BOTTOM RIGHT: Chicago Street became London in *The Little Princess* (1939) and this building became the hospital where Shirley Temple finds her father.

ABOVE LEFT: With some additions, part of Chicago Street became Springfield, Illinois for John Ford's *The Young Mr. Lincoln* (1939) with Henry Fonda. Here the two discuss a scene on set.

ABOVE RIGHT: This is part of the rural section of Springfield, Illinois built for *The Young Mr. Lincoln* (1939). John Ford and Henry Fonda are over by the covered wagons.

RIGHT: A year later, the Springfield section was altered to become Nauvoo, Illinois in *Brigham Young* (1940) complete with a partial recreation of the Mormon temple.

LEFT: Chicago Street served as San Francisco's Barbary Coast in *Hello, Frisco, Hello* (1943). The cast included (L-R) Jack Oakie, June Havoc, John Payne, and Alice Faye.

BOTTOM LEFT: Chicago Street got a British accent in *The Ghost and Mrs. Muir* (1947). That's Gene Tierney under the light fixture.

ABOVE LEFT: This movie theater façade popped up in several features such as in *Belles on Their Toes* (1952). The theater, of course, always showed Fox movies.

ABOVE RIGHT: The alley next to the theater was frequently used. Here Myrtle (Betty Grable) turns down Roy's (Michael Dunne) invitation to dinner after a show in *Mother Wore Tights* (1947).

RIGHT: This is how the alley appeared in *There's No Business Like Show Business* (1954).

Chicago Lake/Chicago Street/Old New York Harbor

"Of all the great bodies of water in the world and of all the mysterious water formations on earth, 20th Century Fox's studio lake is probably the strangest and most fascinating span of water in existence. It [is] the eighth wonder of the world."
—Henry Arnstein, The Movietone Mirror, June, 1941

Hyperbole aside, this body of water, originally three acres in area and six feet deep, was impressive. It was excavated in 1937 with steam shovel and spigot to serve as Lake Michigan for *In Old Chicago* (1938). On its western shore William Darling and Rudolph Sternad designed a five-city-block, six-acre set for the epic re-creation of that city's great fire of 1871, publicized as the longest disaster sequence in film history, utilizing 2,500 extras. Not publicized was the fact that when it was over, all the water drained right down to Beverly Hills.

Thereafter the lake bottom was kept asphalted, and a pumping system was devised that could fill the lake in twenty-four hours and empty it in eight into the Los Angeles storm sewers. Fish were added to prevent mosquitoes.

The eastern section of Chicago Street was extended to become Springfield, Illinois, for John Ford's *Young Mr. Lincoln* (1939) and Nauvoo, Illinois for *Brigham Young* (1940). In the final scene of *Lincoln,* when Henry Fonda as Lincoln walked portentously up a backlot hill, it started to rain, prompting John Ford to declare to his crew: "The tears of the multitudes." Fonda and Ford remembered the happy accident when they returned here years later for the documentary *The American West of John Ford* (1971). The backlot was gone by then—"homesteaded," as Fonda put it.

BOTTOM LEFT: Chicago Lake as it looked for most of its existence with the buildings of Old New York Harbor. The large backdrop screen of Sersen Lake can be seen on the left.

BOTTOM RIGHT: A picturesque photo of Old New York Harbor. Who would have guessed this was in Los Angeles?

For *The Black Swan* (1942) the lake was enlarged to twelve acres and four million gallons in order to hold four life-size ships, with the colorful Caribbean town of Maracaibo on its shore. The lake was temporarily dubbed "Lake Power" for Tyrone Power, by now an internationally renowned actor who made nine films here.

The father of the Fox horror film, John Brahm directed the stylish chillers, *The Undying Monster* (1942), *The Lodger* (1944), and *Hangover Square* (1945). A segment of the Chicago set was refurbished as London's Whitechapel district for *The Lodger* (1944). Set in the 1880s world of Jack the Ripper, *The Lodger* provided Laird Cregar with one of his finest roles. Costar Merle Oberon found her own reward: She fell in love with and married *The Lodger*'s cinematographer, Lucien Ballard, in 1945. Ballard designed the "obie" light to mask scars Oberon had received in an automobile accident.

"It is tragic, in a way, that visitors to Hollywood arrive with their eyes so fixed on the stars they miss the best of what the studios have to offer—their technical wizardry," wrote Frank S. Nugent. "Surely there is no star in Hollywood who could be compared in beauty with [Chicago Lake] when it was playing Little Old New York . . ." Rhapsodizing about this new set on the eastern shore of the lake, built for *Little Old New York* (1940), Nugent was another Darryl Zanuck acquisition. He had

ABOVE: The banks of Chicago Lake became a tropical isle for *The Son of Fury* (1941) with its stars Tyrone Power and Gene Tierney on the rocks.

RIGHT: Director Henry King, left, keeps the stars of *The Black Swan* (1942), Tyrone Power and Maureen O'Hara, amused. Old New York Harbor can be seen in the background.

been hired away from the *New York Times* because of his frequent panning of Fox films, into the undefined role of studio writer. Zanuck was only temporarily successful in doing the same with Walter Winchell, whom David Brown recalled could move

Old New York Harbor during the filming of its namesake *Little Old New York* (1940).

RIGHT: A large Chinese village was built on the banks of Chicago Lake for *The Keys of the Kingdom* (1944).

BOTTOM LEFT: Director Gregory Ratoff used Old New York Harbor for the globe-and-history trotting musical *Where Do We Go From Here?* starring Fred MacMurray (1945).

BOTTOM RIGHT: Though much of *Carousel* (1956) was filmed on location, Billy Bigelow's (Gordon MaCrae) death scene was filmed at Old New York Harbor. He is mourned by his wife Julie Jordan (Shirley Jones).

a stock up or down five or ten points by reporting a corporate rumor. In both cases Zanuck found it more profitable to have them critique his scripts instead of his movies.

Scenes from *Soldier of Fortune* (1955), starring Clark Gable and Susan Hayward, were shot on the lot because Hayward was involved in a divorce and custody battle for her twin sons and could not go to Hong Kong with Gable. *Love Is a Many-Splendored*

Thing (1955) was prepared at the same time, and is a fascinating companion piece from the thrifty studio-system days when productions shared interior and exterior sets on the lots, and in this case similar locations in Hong Kong. A Chinese junk from one or both of them—originating from *Destination Gobi* (1953)—was found at the bottom of the lake when it was finally drained.

BELOW: Betty Grable and Dale Robertson used the Harbor set for their remake of *The Farmer Takes a Wife* (1953).

866-S-4

THIS PAGE: The Whitechapel Street set, an extension of Chicago Street, was built for John Brahm's creepy *The Lodger* (1944) with Laird Cregar as Jack-the-Ripper.

ABOVE LEFT: The Palace of Varieties in *The Lodger* (1944) where Kitty Langley (Merle Oberon) performs.

ABOVE RIGHT: White-chapel Street was cast again as London in *Hangover Square* (1945), used here for the Guy Fawkes' bonfire scene.

FAR LEFT: Tyrone Power (right) talks to a young Lee Marvin in *Diplomatic Courier* (1952).

LEFT: Unbeknownst to Linda (Virginia Leith), Harry (Tommy Noonan) is a peeping Tom in *Violent Saturday* (1955).

WASHINGTON SQUARE

This impressive district, built for *Rose of Washington Square* (1939), had such equally impressive residents as Alexander Graham Bell (*The Story of Alexander Graham Bell,* 1939), Edgar Allan Poe (*The Loves of Edgar Allan Poe,* 1942), and Laura (*Laura,* 1944). Preparing for his role as a murderous composer in *Hangover Square* (1945), Laird Cregar dieted and lost over one hundred pounds. The drastic diet may have caused the heart attack that killed the gifted contract player shortly after filming, at the age of twenty-eight. On a lighter note, Dan Dailey stole a tree from the park for his family for Christmas (*Mother Wore Tights,* 1947), Rock Hunter (Tony Randall in the role of a lifetime) got famous when Jayne Mansfield drove up to meet him here in *Will Success Spoil Rock Hunter?* (1957), and Pat Boone partied here in *Mardi Gras* (1958). Its elegance had faded by the time it made its last appearance as Mary Astor's home in *Return to Peyton Place* (1961).

FAR LEFT: This corner of the set was a popular filming spot.

LEFT: Don Ameche lived here in *The Story of Alexander Graham Bell* (1939). Beloved character actor Gene Lockhart is in the carriage.

BOTTOM LEFT: Alice Faye sits on Tyrone Power's lap in between filming scenes for *Rose of Washington Square* (1939). Thirty years later the same story would make Barbra Streisand a star in *Funny Girl* (1968, Columbia).

BOTTOM RIGHT: Joan Crawford and Fonda in a scene from *Daisy Kenyon* (1947).

ABOVE: Washington Square in the John Brahm classic *Hangover Square* (1945).

ABOVE RIGHT: This is where Michael Rennie "boarded" in *The Day the Earth Stood Still* (1951). The buildings of Chicago Street can be seen in the distance.

RIGHT: Washington Square was the scene of the great fire in *Forever Amber* (1947). The Square's townhouses can be seen in the center of the picture.

Washington Square, viewed from the top of the townhouses, is dressed for winter, 1950. The large grip building can be seen just past the trees.

ABOVE: Roberta Carter (Mary Astor) is displeased when her son Ted Carter (Brett Halsey) shows up at her home here for *Return to Peyton Place* (1961) with new wife Raffaella (Luciana Paluzzi).

RIGHT: Movie star Rita Marlowe (Jayne Mansfield) arrives at the home of advertising executive Rockwell P. Hunter (Tony Randall) in *Will Success Spoil Rock Hunter?* (1957).

ADANO SQUARE

Designed for Louis D. Lighton and Lamar Trotti's memorable *A Bell For Adano* (1945) by Lyle Wheeler and Mark-Lee Kirk, this set also served as the Montmartre district of Paris for two legendary characters—Frank Sinatra and Maurice Chevalier—to bring up the curtain of *Can-Can* (1960).

LEFT: Adano Square.

BOTTOM LEFT: The main plaza built for *A Bell for Adano* (1945).

BOTTOM RIGHT: This bridge crossed over Chicago Lake to Adano Square.

RIGHT: *A Bell of Adano* (1945) star John Hodiak looks over a model of the set.

FAR RIGHT: Cary Grant and Ann Sheridan stopped at Adano Square when it doubled for Germany in *I Was a Male War Bride* (1949).

BOTTOM: Gene Tierney is stunning even as a blonde for her role in *A Bell for Adano* (1945).

FAR LEFT: James Mason ducked in and out of the funeral procession—and in and out of Adano Square—for the classic thriller *5 Fingers* (1952).

LEFT: Adano Square as the embassy for Ethel Merman in *Call Me Madam* (1953).

BOTTOM: Adano Square became Montmartre in *Can-Can* (1960). Frank Sinatra and Maurice Chevalier are at the café.

THE RAILROAD STATION

RIGHT: This larger backlot railroad station as dressed for *Thin Ice* (1937). Note the oil derrick in the background.

FAR RIGHT: Filming a scene for *Four Sons* (1940).

BOTTOM LEFT: As seen in *Orchestra Wives* (1941). Bandleader Glenn Miller is in the fedora on the right under the light.

BOTTOM RIGHT: Cesar Romero, left, greets Cornel Wilde, Sonja Henie, and S.Z. Sakall when the railroad station stood in for Canada in *Wintertime* (1943).

TOMBSTONE STREET

Kind of crazy, ain't they? The times . . . white men chasing gold, Indians chasing white men, Army chasing the Indians.

—River of No Return *(1954)*

Having worked on Ghost Town Street, Warner Baxter passed the mantle between the company's first generation of Western stars to a new one when he made *The Return of the Cisco Kid* (1939) here in the spring of 1939. Thereafter Cesar Romero would enjoy continuing the franchise with five more films here. That June and July he was also Doc Holliday and Randolph Scott was Wyatt Earp in Allan Dwan's *Frontier Marshal* (1939) that gave the set its name. It was actually the second filmization of a book Earp and author Stuart Lake had produced to present the legend as he wanted to be remembered. George O'Brien starred in the first version in 1934. Darryl Zanuck shared Dana Andrews's contract with Samuel Goldwyn, beginning with *Lucky Cisco Kid* (1940), and Andrews became one of the studio's best leading men for a decade.

"Westerns then were popular around the world," said Henry Fonda. "I didn't think of myself as Western. I didn't like horses and I didn't like to ride. You had to pay me a lot to get me on a horse."

There is irony, then, in the fact that Henry Fonda can lay claim to the longest career on this set, appearing in *Jesse James* (1939), Fox's top moneymaker of the year, its sequel *The Return of Frank James* (1940), *The Ox-Bow Incident* (1943), and as a marshal to the town of *Warlock* (1959). The street was only briefly used—for an exterior of Mrs. Nelson's Boarding House—for John Ford's *My Darling Clementine* (1946) in which Fonda delivered his most iconic performance in a Fox western. This third adaptation of Stuart Lake's book was shot in Monument Valley with the recreation of the street and interior sets over at the Western Avenue studio on Stages One, Six, and Seven.

Richard Zanuck remembered playing out here as a child. Fox employees like Philip Dunne recalled him fondly as "a young hellion in short pants."

Gregory Peck had a better time out here making two superior Westerns. This set became the gold-rich town of *Yellow Sky* (1949), that attracts Peck's outlaw gang, and Cayenne for Peck as the notorious Jimmy Ringo in *The Gunfighter* (1950). For the latter he received the "Silver Spur Award" as the outstanding Western star of 1950. Everyone was pleased except Spyros Skouras, who was enraged to see his star got away with a historically accurate look rather than a glamorous one. He claimed he lost a million dollars on the film because of "that goddamn mustache." He made up the difference and more by insisting that Peck's

Tombstone Street as it appeared in *Frontier Marshal* (1939).

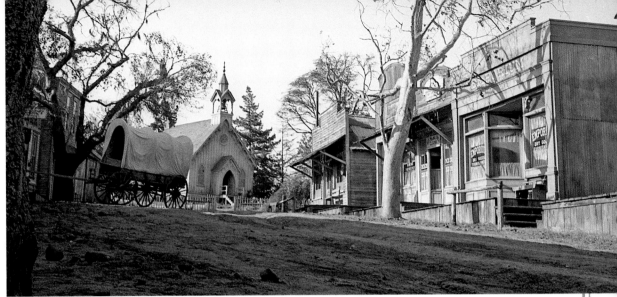

character live, not die, in Ernest Hemingway's *The Snows of Kilimanjaro (1952)*.

How fortunate Darryl Zanuck was to have James Stewart on the lot again and again from the time of his arrival well into the 1960s. *Broken Arrow* (1950) was among those great films Stewart made as a pioneering freelancer for Fox. The movie incorporated the stories of both Cochise (Jeff Chandler, in the performance of his career) and Geronimo, as well as one of contract player Debra Paget's best performances. The straight "A" graduate of the studio's schoolroom was nicknamed "Angel Face" by the crew. Her sister Lisa Gaye and brother Frank Griffin later appeared in Fox TV shows. Griffin was also a makeup artist on a number of the studio's films, making up Steve Martin for *Grand Canyon* (1993) and the 2003 remake of *Cheaper by the*

Dozen. Debra's niece Roxane Griffin was head of hairdressing for *Avatar* (2009).

Among another generation of Fox stars who moved in with the 1950s were Mitzi Gaynor and Dale Robertson, at their very best in the winning *Golden Girl* (1951). If Darryl Zanuck put George Montgomery under contract because he sounded like Clark Gable perhaps he did the same thing for this twice-wounded World War II veteran who talked like Bing Crosby and excelled playing Western gentlemen of the highest order first in Fox films and later on television including *Dynasty* (1981-89).

In 1956 this was the scene of two memorable gatherings. A cast of 450 of Hollywood's elite were invited to a luncheon to honor Prince Philip of Great Britain. Later, forty-three governors, from throughout the United States, were treated to a

TOP LEFT: Tombstone Street hotel.

TOP RIGHT: View of Tombstone Street in the 1950s.

ABOVE: Tombstone Street telegraph office.

RIGHT: Tombstone Street livery stable.

FAR RIGHT: Randolph Scott as the *Frontier Marshal* (1939).

BOTTOM: Tombstone Street became Towash, Arizona where Cesar Romero and Jean Rogers arrive on the overland stage for *Viva Cisco Kid* (1940).

Santa Maria steak barbecue while meeting in Los Angeles. In all, over one thousand were served while the US Marine Corps bands from Camp Pendleton and El Toro played for them. What goes around usually comes around in Hollywood. Nicholas Ray artfully directed Robert Wagner, Jeffrey Hunter, and Hope Lange here in *The True Story of Jesse James* (1957), a remake of the 1939 studio classic. It was in the late 1950s that a church with a bell in its tower showed up here that remained until the set was destroyed.

On January 7, 1958, Spyros Skouras, his assistant, John Healey, and director of property development for the studio, Edmond E. Herrscher, met nearly one hundred members of the press on the hotel set porch to make the official announcement of the backlot redevelopment. Skouras had hired

Herrscher, married to one of his nieces, in 1956 to explore better financial use of the property, and was encouraged by the word that came back from consultant Milton Meyer & Co. The new project's architect was Welton Becket, whose land-development projects included the UCLA campus, the Los Angeles International Airport, Bunker Hill, as well as the cities of Costa Mesa and San Leandro. The wrecking company began demolishing the backlot in April of 1961. Tombstone Street remained in use until it was finally burned to the ground for *The Comancheros* (1961).

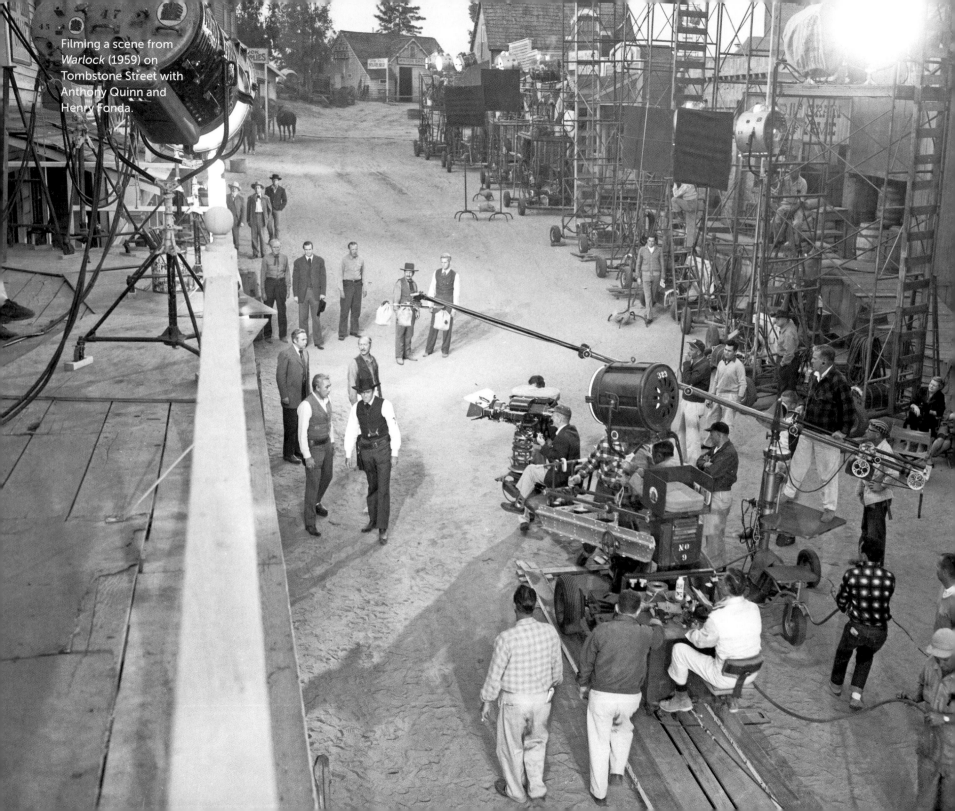

Filming a scene from *Warlock* (1959) on Tombstone Street with Anthony Quinn and Henry Fonda.

FAR LEFT: Mitzi Gaynor and Dale Robertson team up in the Gold Rush-era musical *Golden Girl* (1951). Una Merkel stands on the stairs.

LEFT: And what western street's history would be complete without a fight involving John Wayne? Here he is in *North to Alaska* (1960).

BOTTOM LEFT: Barbara Stanwyck, accosted by John Ericson, starred in *Forty Guns* (1957) here directed by Sam Fuller.

BOTTOM RIGHT: The presentation of the proposed layout of Century City was made on Tombstone Street on May 25, 1959.

ABOVE LEFT: The grotto built for *The Song of Bernadette* (1943).

ABOVE RIGHT: The Stockade.

THE GROTTO

A 450-foot-long section of the Gave River (thirty feet wide and three feet deep) was duplicated here as part of the grotto of Massabielle set for *The Song of Bernadette* (1943). It was here that Henry King filmed Jennifer Jones as young Bernadette, witnessing "a beautiful lady" and the miraculous appearance of water that made the actual site world-famous.

Debate raged as to whether the Virgin should be seen on screen or not. Ultimately she was portrayed by a pregnant Linda Darnell. The river was designed to be fed by one reservoir, drained into another, and then pumped back to flow down again. When the picture was finished, the pumps were stopped, but the "Gave River" kept right on flowing. A backlot miracle? No; it was soon discovered that the Chicago Lake's asphalt bottom had split open due to the air-pressure blasts from filming *A Yank in the R.A.F.* (1941), and water had drained into the "Gave River," half a mile away.

THE STOCKADE

This set, designed by Richard Day and Albert Hogsett, was used for Shirley Temple's *Susannah of the Mounties* (1939) and replicated in Utah for John Ford's *Drums Along the Mohawk* (1939). The latter captured Henry Fonda and Claudette Colbert at their best. Although well regarded for her sparkling comedic performances at other studios, Darryl Zanuck uniquely highlighted Colbert dramatic talents in a series of classic films. And Fonda came into his own as one of the studio's greatest talents under the eye of John Ford. If you had asked Henry Fonda what it took to be in the Ford stock company, the veteran of eight Ford films would probably have mentioned that it helped if you were a good "pitch" card player. The game was a common sight on the Fox lot when Ford was around. Players included Will Rogers, John Wayne, and Ward Bond, a fellow USC Trojan whom Wayne had brought to Fox, getting his career started with *Salute* (1929).

Other recreational activity on the backlot included, for a time, illuminated softball games between the actors, directors, producers, and writers at Fox and MGM. Nunnally Johnson remembered that once the games, played every Saturday, started causing injuries, Darryl Zanuck put a stop to them and plowed up the field. The area bordering Beverly Hills High School contained the Prop Wagon Shed, used as a storage area for every type of horse-drawn vehicle, stables for horses and mules, and the nursery.

ABOVE LEFT: Shirley Temple is wheeled to the set for *Susannah of the Mounties* (1939).

ABOVE RIGHT: The Stockade as a frontier fort in *The President's Lady* (1952) starring Charlton Heston and Susan Hayward.

LEFT: The stockade became a Nazi concentration camp in *Berlin Correspondent* (1943).

THE NURSERY

Culture? Ain't that what they put on flowers to make them grow?

—Doll Face *(1946)*

The original nursery was a greenhouse near the cafeteria. In the early 1940s a larger nursery of ten acres was built on the eastern side of the lot south of Olympic Boulevard. It consisted of a large and small lath house and a cloth house. These contained fragile flowers and plants as well as formal plants for use in hallways and hotel lobbies such as ferns, philedendrons, and potted palms. There were fifty beds of flowers and shrubs in various stages of bloom and growth all in gallon cans. Behind the cloth houses were more beds for larger and more mature trees in five-gallon tubs including hibiscus, oleander, myrtus, laurel, vibernum, and eucalyptus. Practicing botanist Glenn Harman was in charge. If he could not raise it here—fireproofed and able to "work" twenty-four hours a day, utilizing artificial daylight—he knew where to find it.

For example, when director Edmund Goulding wanted a few hundred begonias for *Down among the Sheltering Palms* (1953), Harman knew better than to mention that such exotics would not bloom for another six months. Instead he ordered an estimated 73,000 wild orchids, hibiscus, and bromeliads from the Hawaiian Islands. With the constant need for trees—and the unfortunate discovery that the heaviest of them could go right through the soundstage floor—one of the Fox nursery specialties was making their own. Harman kept a stock of dead trees on hand with the center core of the trunk and branches removed. Freshly cut branches were added on set. There was also a greenhouse west of Stage Sixteen that was replaced by a new guardhouse at the Pico gate.

SUEZ DESERT

Fred Sersen and Lou Witte provided twenty-four wind machines and laid down three thousand truckloads of sand to create a twenty-acre desert for the spectacular sandstorm sequence for *Suez* (1938), the epic Hollywood-ized story of Ferdinand de Lesseps (Tyrone Power) and his famous Canal. Before it could be filmed, however, much of the sand blew away. It cost the studio $30,000 to replace it.

The 20-acre desert set for *Suez* (1938). It was replaced by Tombstone Street.

The newly-constructed Train Shed served as a Parisian train station in this scene from *The Razor's Edge* (1946). Filming on the backlot was often a distraction to the students at Beverly Hills High School which is seen in the background.

ABOVE LEFT: The Train Shed included an interior set of an urban train station as seen here in *The House on Telegraph Hill* (1951).

ABOVE RIGHT: Train cars and a platform completed the set as seen here in *When My Baby Smiles at Me* (1948).

FAR LEFT: The Train Shed served as a busy New York terminal in this scene from *Miracle on 34th Street* (1947) with John Payne (in hat).

LEFT: Occasionally, other sets were built on the interior such as the Parisian café that Marilyn Monroe visits in *Gentlemen Prefer Blondes* (1953).

ABOVE LEFT: The flight deck for *Wing and a Prayer* (1944).

RIGHT MIDDLE: A view of the flight deck looking west.

ABOVE RIGHT: The view of the flight deck looking east. The tower of Beverly Hills City Hall can be seen at the far left while the Beverly Wilshire Hotel can be seen at the right.

RIGHT: Incredibly, the flight deck stood in for Jerusalem in *The Robe* (1953).

THE FLIGHT DECK

Director Henry Hathaway chose this spot for "Carrier X", designed by Lyle Wheeler and Lewis Creber, for his wartime classic *Wing and a Prayer* (1944) about the Battle of Midway, because it was on a high hill. A backdrop and six planes that flew into Clover Field were added to complete the illusion. The film featured contract player William Eythe; declared 4-F, he effectively filled roles at the studio throughout World War II.

THE KEYS OF THE KINGDOM SET

A brilliant career was launched from this set of a church and neighboring rectory, designed by James Basevi and William Darling for *The Keys of the Kingdom* (1944). David O. Selznick had purchased the book about an idealistic but unorthodox Catholic priest, who is sent to rebuild a mission in China. He then prepared a screen treatment and sold it to Fox with the proviso that they star Gregory Peck, his new discovery, and purchase half his contract.

Besides making the actor a star—he ultimately made fourteen esteemed pictures for the studio—this remarkable film was the first directed and written (with cowriter Nunnally Johnson) by Joseph L. Mankiewicz.

Mankiewicz's wife, actress Rose Stradner, made her final appearance in this film a memorable one as Mother Maria Veronica. Because of his talents evident on set, Peck encouraged Benson Fong, who played Father Chisholm's assistant, to open a Chinese restaurant. His success—it was on Vine Street in Hollywood—led to a chain of five more restaurants by 1971.

The lovely rock church and parish house of Tweedside, Scotland built for *The Keys of the Kingdom* (1944).

RIGHT: Father Francis Chisholm (Gregory Peck) walks past the church with Andrew (George Nokes) on his way to go fishing in *The Keys of the Kingdom* (1944).

FAR RIGHT: The set as the Cornish village for *My Cousin Rachel* (1952) where Philip Ashley (Richard Burton) causes quite a stir among the womenfolk. Director Henry Koster, in ball cap, has his back to the camera.

BOTTOM LEFT: Creating rain for a sad funeral scene in the Victorian thriller *Moss Rose* (1947).

BOTTOM RIGHT: The Chinese mission set also built for *The Keys of the Kingdom* (1944). In the foreground is the filming of the parachuting sequence in another Gregory Peck film *The Man in the Gray Flannel Suit* (1956).

SLIGON CASTLE

We'd go over there and play on the Prince Valiant castle. They had a lake. They had every kind of old car imaginable stored there. It was just an incredible playground to grow up in.
—Robby Wald, son of producer Jerry Wald

Rising from the highest hill on ye olde backlot was the evil Viking Sligon's Castle, in which Janet Leigh and Robert Wagner as *Prince Valiant* (1954) were imprisoned. Lyle Wheeler and Mark-Lee Kirk were its designers, Escapist fare at its best, with quite simply one of the most rousing scores ever composed—by Alfred Newman, of course—only Wagner had mixed feelings about the film. He had enjoyed Hal Foster's comic strip as a child, and the making of this lavish CinemaScope romp, until Dean Martin visited the set and mistook him for Jane Wyman with that black wig.

The set later became the royal residence of Bette Davis as *The Virgin Queen* (1955). Although intended as a Richard Todd vehicle entitled *Sir Walter Raleigh,* the production could not help but refocus on Bette Davis once she agreed to play Elizabeth I, reprising her favorite role of sixteen years earlier in *The Private Lives of Elizabeth and Essex* (1939, Warner Bros.).

Although her costar Joan Collins found Davis cold—believing jealousy of her youth was the cause, as portrayed by the aging star in Fox's *The*

ABOVE: A view of the massive Sligon Castle set built for *Prince Valiant* (1954).

LEFT: The interior courtyard of Sligon Castle during the filming of *Prince Valiant*. Note the borrowed MGM Klieg light.

Star (1952)—Davis considered hostilities inevitable, considering the roles they were playing. Certainly Collins was able to apply Davis's queenly antics to her role years later in *Dynasty*.

THE SLAVE MARKET

The historic opening sequence of *The Robe* (1953) was shot here. While effectively introducing audiences to the grandeur of CinemaScope, it also economically introduced all the main characters: Roman tribune Marcellus (Richard Burton), Greek slave Demetrius (Victor Mature), Diana (Jean Simmons), and soon-to-be emperor Caligula (Jay Robinson). The set, designed by Lyle Wheeler and George W. Davis, is also prominent in the sequel, *Demetrius and the Gladiators* (1954), where Susan Hayward bewitches and taunts the members of the gladiator school run by Ernest Borgnine. One of them is contract player Richard Egan, who showed up in another Fox epic, *The 300 Spartans* (1962).

The set would receive two major renovations. At a cost of $150,000, Egyptian columns and an adjacent four-columned portico and eighty-foot angled wall were added to transform it into the "Thebes of the 100 Gates" temple set for *The Egyptian* (1954). Then, when Darryl Zanuck decided the opening sequence of *The King and I* (1956) required more scope, another $400,000 was spent transforming it into a three-acre, twenty-five-building re-creation of nineteenth-century Siam.

ABOVE LEFT: The Slave Market as seen in *The Robe* (1953).

ABOVE RIGHT: The Slave Market as modified for *The King and I* (1956).

LEFT: Filming *The King and I* (1956).

THE WATERWAYS

This lovely area was designed by Lyle Wheeler and Addison Hehr for the remake of *Swamp Water* (1941) renamed *Lure of the Wilderness* (1952). Its star Jeffrey Hunter was discovered by a Fox talent scout during a performance of *All My Sons* at UCLA in 1950 where he was attending graduate school. He married Barbara Rush, recently signed at Paramount, the same year. One of Hollywood's most photogenic and classy couples, the stars were key to the success of a number of important films at Fox including Hunter's *Sailor of the King* (1953) and *The Proud Ones* (1956) and Rush's *Bigger Than Life* (1956) and *The Young Lions* (1958). They appeared together in *No Down Payment* (1957).

The following year the "Waterways" were expanded for the Betty Grable/Dale Robertson musical remake of *The Farmer Takes a Wife* (1953).

This set also enjoyed an expansion because of Darryl Zanuck's ambitions for *The King and I* (1956). He so enjoyed the "We Kiss in a Shadow/I Have Dreamed" musical sequence—originally performed on the "harem garden" set on Stage Fourteen—that he demanded the more-lavish outdoor setting stunningly accomplished here. The performers were Rita Moreno as Tuptim and Carlos Rivas in his American film debut as Lun Tha. Rivas recalled that Dorothy Dandridge was originally cast as his costar, but Moreno's performance in his screen test got her the part.

The set was perfect for another idyllic Rodgers and Hammerstein setting: the military camp and amphitheater for the musical numbers "This Nearly

Was Mine" and "You've Got to Be Carefully Taught" for *South Pacific* (1958). In later years the area was overrun with *The Alligator People* in 1959, and used for the TV series *Adventures in Paradise* (1959–62).

Tom Tryon and Elana Eden played lovers here in *The Story of Ruth* (1960). Tryon was so traumatized by working for Otto Preminger in *The Cardinal* (1960, Warner Bros.) and *In Harm's Way* (1965, Paramount) that he quit his acting career and turned novelist, successfully turning out *The Other*. He successfully adapted it for the screen, and it became one of Fox's best horror films.

After two years of production, once the Waterways were destroyed, the cast and crew of *Adventures in Paradise* moved down to the Permanent Gardens and the Lower Moat.

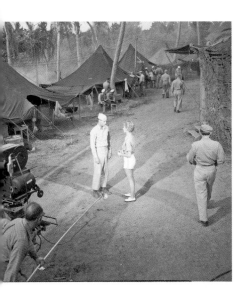

LEFT: Pensive Joanne Woodward stands ready for her cue in *The Long, Hot Summer* (1958).

BOTTOM LEFT: Lt. Joe Cable (John Kerr) and Nellie Forbush (Mitzi Gaynor) meet up on the Company Street, one of the few scenes from *South Pacific* (1958) shot on the backlot; most of the film was shot in Hawaii.

BOTTOM MIDDLE: Rossano Brazzi and John Kerr performing "You Have to Be Carefully Taught" on the Waterways set.

BOTTOM RIGHT: Israeli star Elana Eden makes her American film debut opposite Tom Tryon in *The Story of Ruth* (1960).

RIGHT: The Waterways became the swamps of Louisiana for the camp classic *The Alligator People* (1959).

BOTTOM LEFT: Gardner McKay, sitting in the chair at far right, with fellow cast members of the episode "Nightmare in the Sun." from *Adventures in Paradise*.

BOTTOM RIGHT: Though shot in many locales, the native village in *Adventures in Paradise* (1959–62) was here on the Waterways.

Additional Backlot Sets

FAR LEFT: This fort set was built for *Hudson's Bay* (1941). Publicity at the time noted that it took 60 tons of ice per day for the snow-making machine in the foreground to maintain that set covered in snow.

LEFT: Grandstand used in *It Happened in Flatbush* (1942). Stars Carole Landis and Lloyd Nolan take a break between scenes.

BOTTOM LEFT: The flying saucer from *The Day the Earth Stood Still* (1951) landed in the northeast corner of the backlot near Beverly Hills High School.

BOTTOM RIGHT: Loretta Young, readies herself for *Kentucky* (1938). This large horse estate set was built a few hundred yards east of Building 88.

ABOVE: This picturesque winter scene for *High Time* (1960), starring Bing Crosby, Fabian, Tuesday Weld, and Richard Beymer, was at Wheeler Park, named for Lyle Wheeler, on the backlot.

RIGHT: Laurel and Hardy on the set of *Great Guns* (1942). Building 88 can be seen in the background.

BLDG. 502: SANTA MONICA STUDIO GATE (1926)

There were actually two gates here of note known as the Santa Monica Gate. The first, the grand one designed by William Darling and built at a cost of $300,000, incorporated a gate, gatekeeper's lodge, and central tower known as "El Paredon," flanked by Spanish-Moorish walls. It was complete by September of 1926 for the grand opening of the backlot. The Mission Bell–shaped electric signs followed soon after. Although palms were planted inside so that this could be *the* grand thoroughfare through the backlot, the second gate to the east proved more practical, since it ran along the border of the lot and was a straight shot to the Olympic bridge.

Adjacent was the garage for the transportation department, including Jim Ruman's famed studio collection of vintage automobiles dating back to 1897. Impressive rows of trees ready for filming were also stored here, neatly boxed. David Brown recalled that employees—who either parked their car in lots along Santa Monica Boulevard or commuted on the city streetcar—could take a "jitney" across the backlot to their offices on the South Lot.

Sculptor Mahonri Young recorded his experience driving through here in his diary, dated June 9, 1929: "I rode out to Fox Hills, the new Fox lot. Before you arrive at the new buildings the road goes through a large village of old movie sets. It is fantastic and weird, something like the war zone, and something like the backstage of a theatre. As we came back, we discussed the place we had been and the suburb we were going through. The young actor [Charles Farrell] with me felt that the scenery was more real than this reality we were passing. I had much the same feeling . . . A fantastic, unbelievable place, this Los Angeles with all its suburbs."

ABOVE: Looking west from the guard house with the tower in the distance.

LEFT: The Santa Monica Gate with the guard house on the left. Entering here you would drive down the eastern side of the original lot, cross the Olympic Bridge and end up on Avenue D on the main lot.

Santa Monica Boulevard looking west at approximately where Avenue of the Stars now intersects. This photo was probably taken on dedication day in October 1928. The large Fox Hills Studio sign was neon and could reportedly be seen from miles around. An identical sign stood at the other end of the property at the current intersection of Santa Monica Boulevard and Century Park West.

FAR LEFT: The large ornamental tower gate was christened "El Paredon." It appears to have been used, at least briefly, as an entrance but was soon abandoned in favor of the one further east.

LEFT: Inside the Santa Monica Gate looking out. The Los Angeles Country Club can be seen across Santa Monica Boulevard.

BOTTOM: This is the Galaxy Way Parking Structure soon after its completion. For many years, this was the only sign on the lot with the studio's name visible to the public.

BLDG. 56: GALAXY WAY PARKING STRUCTURE (1996)

On the site of the canvas and grip building (Bldg. 310), the garage for the sound trucks, the studio coffee shop, and parking lot "D," a new studio gate off Century City's Galaxy Way was built, incorporating this employee and guest parking structure. Saving lot space—750 cars had traditionally filled the northwest section of the lot—this structure holds 1,372. The Sound Building (BLDG. 56) was replaced by the Fox Plaza parking structure.

After Earl Sponable laid out the lot's stages and equipment for sound in 1928, chief sound

RIGHT: The Galaxy Way Parking Structure as seen from Avenue of the Palms, 2007. Julie Andrews in *The Sound of Music* (1965) is the first thing you see when entering the Pico gate. The edge of Stage Twenty-one, with its mural from *Star Wars Episode V: The Empire Strikes Back* (1980), is at the right.

BOTTOM LEFT: The original "Sound Building."

BOTTOM RIGHT: The large Grip building that occupied the site for decades.

engineer Edmund H. Hansen made Bldg. 56, completed the following year with its own projection room, the proud heart of that technology at Movietone City, particularly when he was making history with it like he did in *In Old Arizona* (1929).

The first major sound feature—not to mention Western—made outdoors routed the skeptics, who thought "talkies" could not be made outside a soundstage. He helped to perfect the "dubbing" rerecording technique used to remove those extraneous outdoor noises, as well as indoor ones. Among other pioneers here were Thomas T. Moulton, who came with Zanuck from Twentieth Century Pictures, and Carl Faulkner, who subsequently ran the department. Among sound director Edmund Hansen's achievements was winning the department's first Oscar for *Wilson* (1944).

First, the "dailies" shot each day were reviewed, and if dubbing was required, the film editor was notified. He or she informed the continuity department, who developed typewritten dialogue sheets sent to the dubbed-dialogue department. The film was then prepared for the dubbing stage in loops for the actors. The recording was then sent to a dialogue editor to match it with the soundtrack. Since the recording and mixing of sound was this department's primary duty, the staff also facilitated recordings out on the backlot by running underground brass wiring to the permanent sets out there. The Wurlitzer organ from Stage One also ended up here in January of 1930, wired to all the soundstages so that music and sound effects could be piped through.

Through the 1950s and '60s an amazing array of talent continued to work here, including Fred Hynes, who worked with James P. Corcoran on *Cleopatra* (1963) and *The Sound of Music* (1965), Walter Rossi, and mixers like Murray Spivack (who had done *King Kong,* 1933, RKO), who truly mastered the art with films like *Hello, Dolly!* (1969).

With the downsizing of all departments in the 1960s, the sound department moved into the Darryl Zanuck Theatre. Among those who used the building afterwards were Richard Zanuck and David Brown, when they returned to the lot in August of 1980 as an independent production team. Leslie Moonves and Gregory Harrison—who appeared together in the TV movie *Enola Gay: The Men, the Mission, the Atomic Bomb* (1980)—had their production offices here, as well as Bruce Geller, creator of the *Mission: Impossible* TV show. Moonves became the president of Warner Bros., and then CBS.

Look for the building's exterior as a hospital for *Good Morning, Miss Dove* (1955) and *From the Terrace* (1960), and as the rear stage-door entrance where Pat Boone and Ann-Margret emerge for *State Fair* (1962).

"I think everyone on the lot had a crush on Ann-Margret," said publicist Alan Loeb. "I certainly

RIGHT: Interior shot of the Rehearsal Hall (also known as Stage Seven), during the filming of *Monkey Business* (1952). Cary Grant is teaching Marilyn Monroe how to roller-skate. Director Howard Hawks is sitting on the crate.

BOTTOM LEFT: Interior of the Coffee Shop that was located behind the Commissary.

BOTTOM RIGHT: The Rehearsal Hall was probably chosen as the site for the graduation dance for *Peyton Place* (1957) because it looked like a high school gym.

did. I'll never forget the time I was leading a tour and we stopped by the *Stagecoach* (1966) set and she gave me a hug. My entire department found out about it, and later my boss called me in to ask if there was anything going on between us!"

As improvements were made to the Pico gate in the 1990s, its street, which now ends here, was lined with palm trees and christened the "Avenue of the Palms" in 1998. It all visually culminates with a mural of Julie Andrews from *The Sound of Music* (1965) attached to this parking structure.

ABOVE LEFT: Many a musical had its genesis here on Stage Seven where routines were developed and practiced. Here *South Pacific* (1958) director Joshua Logan shows Mitzi Gaynor how he wants her to "wash that man right out of her hair."

ABOVE RIGHT: Robert Wagner tried his hand at musical-comedy in *Say One For Me* (1959). Here he practices his routine with wife Natalie Wood in the Rehearsal Hall.

LEFT: The most famous apes in the world practice capturing humans for *Planet of the Apes* (1968) behind Buildings 58 and 59 (at left).

For advertising purposes *The Sound of Music* (1965) was billed as "The Happiest Sound in All in the World" as the banner on Bldg. 89 at the Pico Gate announces. On the lot it was known as "The Sound of Money." It was the first blockbuster of the modern era.

THE FIFTIETH ANNIVERSARY
SOUND OF MUSIC PRODUCTION TOUR
"In The Last Golden Days of the Studio System" (1960–1965)

Seven months after Richard Rodgers and Oscar Hammerstein's last Broadway musical, *The Sound of Music*, opened on November 16, 1959, Spyros Skouras approved the lease of screen rights for 15 years at $1.25 million, the largest amount yet spent on a literary property. He is a firm believer in bringing such stories of faith, hope, and family — in this case a true one of the von Trapp family — to the screen.

When Darryl Zanuck takes back control of the beleaguered studio and Bldg. 88 he announces on December 10, 1962, that the *The Sound of Music* is finally under way with his signing of Ernest Lehman to prepare the screenplay and a budget of $5.5 million. It is a brave declaration that Twentieth Century Fox is not through, and in fact capable of producing a major musical. Lehman writes the screenplay in his suite in Bldg. 80. It is completed by March 20, 1964.

FAR LEFT: Child star Angela Cartwright tests for the role of Brigitta. Fox would be her home for the next few years as one of the stars of *Lost in Space* (1965-68) which was filmed on the lot.

LEFT: Rehearsing the choreography for "So Long, Farewell" by Dee Dee Wood (in white, back to camera) and Marc Breaux (at piano), with stand-ins for Julie Andrews and Christopher Plummer.

ABOVE LEFT: Rehearsing the choreography for the mountaintop portion of "Do-Re-Mi."

ABOVE MIDDLE and RIGHT: The cast practices their bicycling on the lot for the "Do- Re-Me" sequence. From left to right: Angela Cartwright, Nicholas Hammond, Charmian Carr, Marc Breaux, Duane Chase, and Debbie Turner. The Century City condominiums rising in the background are at the corner of the Avenue of the Stars and Pico Boulevard.

When he is assigned as director and producer in October of 1963, Robert Wise joins a production team already assembled in Bldg. 78, including supervising, including supervising production designer Boris Leven; Roger Edens, who blocks out the musical numbers, including the spectacular opening sequence; and Irwin Kostal (music director) and Saul Chaplin (associate producer), attending to the music. Although Darryl Zanuck champions Doris Day for the role of Maria von Trapp, director Robert Wise and screenwriter Ernest Lehman choose Julie Andrews in November of 1963, and sign her to a two-picture deal.

Christopher Plummer is cast as Captain von Trapp, Eleanor Parker as the Baroness, and Richard Haydn as Uncle Max.

Art director Boris Leven's team includes assistant art director Harry Kemm, L. B. Abbott, and Emil Kosa Jr. in charge of visual effects, and set decorators Ruby Levitt and Walter M. Scott. Maurice "Zuby" Zuberano is employed by Robert Wise to create the film's storyboards in ten weeks that can be used for reference throughout production.

On Wednesday, December 11, 1963, Julie Andrews makes her first appearance on the lot as the star of the picture when she is invited by

Robert Wise and studio executives to lunch in the commissary.

On February 10, 1964, Charmian Carr (Liesl), the last of the seven von Trapp children to be cast, meets her screen siblings: Nicholas Hammond (Friedrich), Heather Menzies (Louisa), Duane Chase (Kurt), Angela Cartwright (Brigitta), Debbie Turner (Marta), and Kym Karath (Gretl) for the first time on Maria's bedroom set on Stage Fifteen. for a regimen of photo tests and rehearsals, including dance lessons and biking around the lot in preparation for the "Do-Re-Mi" sequence.

ABOVE: The seven children's voices are augmented by others on Stage One.

FAR LEFT: Irwin Kostal directs the scoring on Stage One.

LEFT: View of Stage One during music rehearsals. The large brass bed on the left was used for practicing "My Favorite Things."

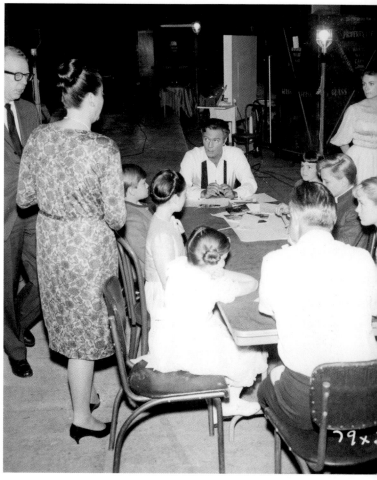

RIGHT: One of the costume fittings on stage. Angela Cartwright remembers "the amazing seamstresses that flitted around us shortening and adjusting each outfit like the fairy godmothers in Cinderella."

BOTTOM LEFT: Costume designer Dorothy Jeakins, left, has a wardrobe conference with Christopher Plummer, middle, and director Robert Wise, right, in Plummer's dressing room in Bldg. 86.

FAR RIGHT: Rehearsing the dining room sequence where Liesl sneaks out. Director Robert Wise is at the end of the table with his back to the camera.

The children (except Carr and Karath) are schooled in Bldg. 80 for three hours a day by Frances Klamt, followed by shooting for no more than five hours a day.

Julie Andrews went in for hair and makeup tests in Bldg. 38, and remembers coming out with orange hair when efforts to heighten her natural blonde highlights went awry. Instead it was completely bleached blonde. Dan Truhitte (Rolfe) and Nicholas Hammond both had their hair dyed blond and had similar bad experiences. Hammond remembers what a painful process it was, while Truhitte claims his hair never grew back correctly.

Helping the actors is dialect coach Pamela Danova (training each with a mid-Atlantic accent), vocal supervisor Bobby Tucker, and choreographers

Dee Dee Wood and Marc Breaux, whom Julie Andrews recommends after her happy experience with them on *Mary Poppins* (1964, Disney).

Marni Nixon, who dubbed other actresses for years, is finally cast onscreen as a singing nun. To strengthen the sound of the seven actors portraying the von Trapp children, four additional voices are used during the recordings on Stage One, including Charmian's little sister Darleen. Margery MacKay, wife of the rehearsal pianist, performs the singing on the soundtrack for Peggy Wood (Mother

LEFT: Even pajamas have to look perfect! Another costume test for "My Favorite Things."

BOTTOM LEFT: The filming of "My Favorite Things." Choreographer Marc Breaux stands at the foot of the bed.

BOTTOM RIGHT: Charmian Carr is wetted down for her entrance into Maria's (Julie Andrews) bedroom set. An amused director, Robert Wise, stands behind her.

ABOVE LEFT: The nuns rehearse with Julie Andrews' stand-in on the Nonnburg Abbey set..

ABOVE RIGHT: The nuns, in their street clothes, trying to figure out how to solve a problem like Maria.

RIGHT: The extraordinary graveyard set of Non-nburg Abbey during the final confrontation between Captain von Trapp and Rolfe.

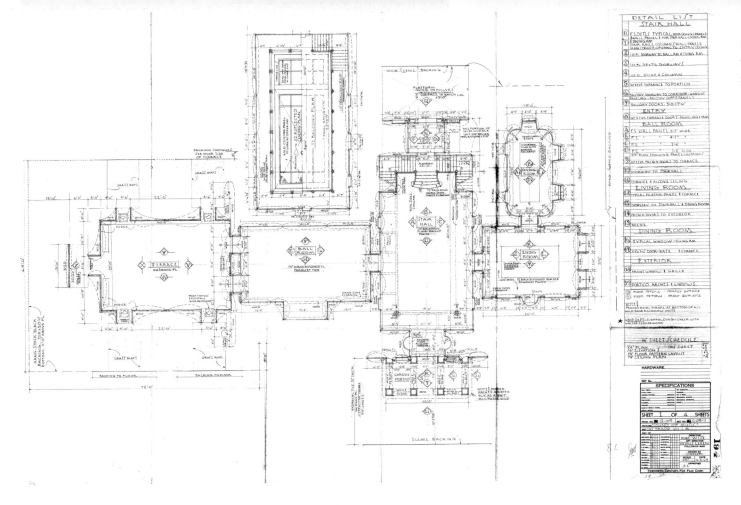

LEFT: The blueprints for the von Trapp villa interior set built on Stage Fifteen.

Abbess). The scoring is supervised by Saul Chaplin and Irwin Kostal, and Kostal conducts the studio orchestra here the first week of November. Whether Christopher Plummer's voice was going to be used on the soundtrack is debated.

Principal photography is green-lit in Bldg. 88 for Thursday, March 26, 1964. Richard Zanuck wires Robert Wise:

"Dear Bobby: Today we launch Sound of Music, which is the most important picture on our production schedule . . . I couldn't have more confidence in the team of technicians and actors that we have assembled on Stage Fifteen for this picture, but my greatest satisfaction is that you are at the helm, and I am secure in knowing that we will have a great and monumental achievement."

ABOVE: The von Trapp children prepare to introduce themselves to Fraulein Maria on Stage Fifteen.

RIGHT: Taking a lunch break. (From L-R) Duane Chase, Nicholas Hammond, Heather Menzies, Angela Cartwright, and Debbie Turner.

Principal photography begins at 10:36 a.m. on March 26, with Julie Andrews, Charmian Carr, and Norma Varden (Frau Schmidt) assembled here. The first scene shot was between Andrews and Varden. Then Carr made her film debut in the scene in which she climbs up to Maria's room in a rainstorm. "My Favorite Things" is shot the following day, marking the acting debut of many of the children.

The wardrobe is designed by studio veteran Dorothy Jeakins. This is her favorite picture.

Since the Mother Abbess of the actual Nonnberg Abbey had refused to let the film company shoot inside, its exterior courtyard and interior room off the cloister are are recreated on Stage Sixteen. Filming begins in the Abbey cloister on April 2 with the nuns walking to chapel, chanting "Dixit Dominus." Then "Maria" is filmed April 3–8, and the sequence where Julie Andrews and the nuns prepare for Maria's wedding, on April 9.

Filming in the Abbey entrance room, Maria's room, and outside hallway is done on April 9 on Stage Five, and in the graveyard set on Five on April 13–17.

Richard Zanuck writes Robert Wise on April 9, 1964:

"Dear Bobby: I can't tell you how absolutely thrilled I've been by the footage you have been getting. As you know, we have four pictures shooting on the lot, and I run

approximately forty minutes of dailies each day. Please don't tell the other producers or directors, but I can hardly wait each day to get to your film, which I always run at the end. Each day it makes me more happy."

Cast and crew depart for a planned six and a half weeks in Salzburg, Austria, for location filming that summer. Due to various problems—particularly the rainy weather—it takes eleven weeks.

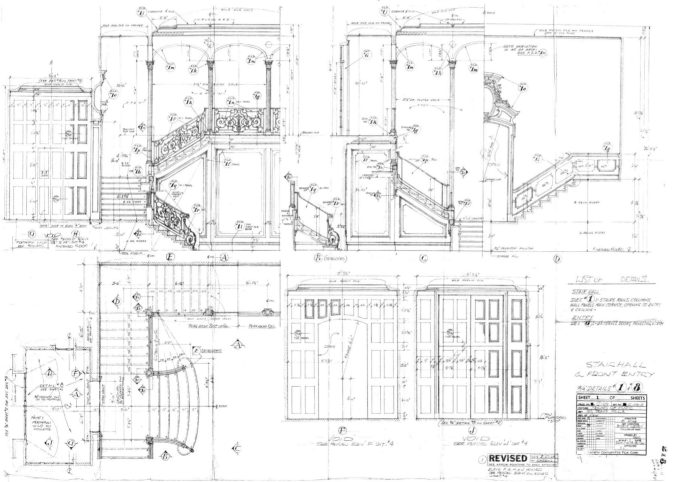

RIGHT: Art director Boris Leven stands in front of one of the most famous sets he ever designed in his long career in Hollywood.

FAR RIGHT: Richard Haydn, as Max, stands in front of the gilt wall paneling during the party scene.

BELOW: Blueprint of elevation of paneling in ballroom.

LEFT: The ballroom and terrace of the von Trapp home set were on Stage Fifteen.

ABOVE: There is always a lot of standing around and waiting on a movie set!

RIGHT: Light check on the elegant Eleanor Parker as the Baroness.

BOTTOM: "So Long, Farewell" is performed on Stage Fifteen.

Meanwhile, Saul Chaplin and script supervisor Betty Levin fall in love and marry four years later. The real Maria von Trapp gets into the act, appearing in the background while Julie Andrews sings "I Have Confidence." The sequence required thirty-seven takes, prompting her to declare: "Mr. Wise, I have just abandoned a lifelong ambition to work in the movies."

Filming on the lot begins again on Stage Fifteen on July 6, with the von Trapp family in the dining room of the new von Trapp villa sets, including the foyer and grand staircase set, and the ballroom, courtyard, terrace, dining room, and parlor. The party, "So Long, Farewell," and "Laend-ler" musical sequences are filmed from July 15–24. On July 27 Eleanor Parker and Christopher Plummer have their final scene in the terrace set. On July 30 work begins on "The Lonely Goatherd" puppet show. After work here with the cast, the real puppeteers Bil and Cora Baird go to work on Stage Three with a second unit.

On August 6–7 the children sing "The Sound of Music" to their father, and the intimate family version of "Edelweiss" is performed in the parlor. On August 10 the last piece of the emotional sequence in which the von Trapp children sing "The Sound of Music" for their father is filmed, marking the last day the children all work together. They receive their own wrap party with cider-filled champagne glasses. The children are reunited on the lot on March 10, 1965, to dress for the Los Angeles premiere in their party clothes from the movie.

Angela Cartwright remained on the lot to make *Lost in Space* (1966–68), and later appeared in *Room 222* (1969–74). Heather Menzies returned to guest star in *S.W.A.T.* (1975–76), starring Robert Urich. They dated for a year before Urich took her to a nearby restaurant and proposed. They were married until Urich's death from cancer in 2002.

Look for the von Trapp grand hall in *Do Not Disturb* (1964), *What a Way to Go!* (1964), *Way . . . Way Out* (1966), *Caprice* (1967), *The St. Valentine's Day Massacre* (1967), and *Valley of the Dolls* (1968).

Shooting resumes on Stage Eight on August 11–13 for Julie Andrews and Christopher Plummer on a "green" set, re-creating the von Trapps' garden and gazebo, shot at an estate in Salzburg called Schloss Leopoldskron, for the "Something Good" musical sequence. Robert Wise resorts to shooting them in silhouette when the couple cannot stop laughing over a noisy arc lamp.

The "Sixteen Going on Seventeen" musical sequence is filmed on Stage Eight on August 14–19.

BOTTOM LEFT: Filming "The Lonely Goatherd."

BOTTOM RIGHT: A publicity event on the steps of the Commissary to show off the marionettes created by Bill Baird (seen at far right). In true publicity style, the audience was contrived and consisted of the kids' parents and Fox publicists!

Cast and crew hold their breath when Charmian Carr goes crashing through a plate-glass wall of the gazebo during the dance because the wardrobe department failed to put rubber skids on the soles of her new shoes. She completes the sequence with a bandaged ankle. It is the last major scene filmed for the movie.

Julie Andrews completes the "I Have Confidence" sequence filmed on location on a bus in front of a process screen on Stage Six on August 13. Principal photography ends, with more process work with Richard Haydn, Eleanor Parker, and Christopher Plummer in the Captain's car, through September 1.

Automated Dialogue Replacement (ADR) takes place here in the basement of Bldg. 226 from August 25 to September 8, when post-sync dubbing begins. "You always hope to use the original track," said Wise, "but if there are interferences, you go back into the studio and you take a section, and you run it and run it, and then you redo the dialogue. It's very time-consuming, and you have to be careful about the sync." Christopher Plummer is allowed to sing his songs over two days after production-long efforts with voice coach Bobby Tucker. Everyone agrees his singing needs to be replaced, and Bill Lee is hired on October 1, 1964.

William Reynolds edits the film in Bldg. 32.

ABOVE LEFT: Christopher Plummer takes a break from a photo shoot outside of the Portrait Studio. The windows of the Commissary are seen on the left. The brick planter box still surrounds this tree in 2016.

ABOVE RIGHT: One of the photos from the shoot.

RIGHT: Nicholas Hammond, left, and Duane Chase, right, try skateboarding in front of Stage Eleven.

The first major musical number to be completed is the "Do-Re-Mi" sequence that thrills cast and crew when they see it for the first time at a screening on the lot in August. The "rough cut" up to the "Do-Re-Mi" sequence is screened on September 18 for Richard Rodgers and his wife. The final rough cut of the picture is ready by October 2, 1964. Final edits take place on January 21, 1965. The final "answer print" from Technicolor and soundtrack is approved for release on February 5, 1965, at two hours and fifty-six minutes.

On August 25–26, 1964, Julie Andrews, Christopher Plummer, Eleanor Parker, and the children had their formal portraits taken in Bldg. 58.

FAR LEFT: The entry hall remained on Stage Fifteen for many years, and was used again in films like *Do Not Disturb* (1965) as a Paris hotel lobby.

LEFT: As a Russian Embassy in *Way...Way Out* (1966).

BOTTOM LEFT: As Sir Jason's mansion in *Caprice* (1967).

BOTTOM RIGHT: As Al Capone's home in *The St. Valentine's Day Massacre* (1967).

ABOVE: As the main hall in the opening sequence of *What a Way to Go!* (1964).

RIGHT: As a fancy restaurant in *Valley of the Dolls* (1967).

Saul Chaplin and Irwin Kostal view the completed cut on October 5, 1964, and then prepare and supervise the scoring on Stage One. For two weeks—beginning October 16—Irwin Kostal arranges and orchestrates the background score. On November 2 scoring sessions begin. Veteran Buddy Cole passes away the day after completing his performance of the organ pieces for the score. Music editor Robert Mayer cuts and mixes the recordings. Murray Spivack is in charge of finalizing the six-track stereo magnetic master soundtrack, including sound effects. Chaplin supervised the creation of the soundtrack album. Released March 20, 1965, it reached Gold Record status and remains on the best-selling charts for 233 weeks. Combined with the sales and popularity of the original 1959 Broadway cast album, *The Sound of Music* remains the most popular musical score of all time.

In charge of the film's publicity in Bldg. 88 is Mike Kaplan, who readies the advertising campaign for *The Sound of Music* beginning in February 1964, coming up with "The Happiest Sound in All the World" as its slogan. From its inception, the film is planned as one of the studio's "road show" productions, treated like the opening of a major Broadway show. He also spearheads a campaign to win Academy Award recognition. The studio was free to release the film after the Broadway show ended its run after 1,443 performances, on June 15, 1963. The

final print is readied for two previews in mid-January 1965.

The Sound of Music, at a final cost of $8.2 million, premiered on March 2, 1965, in New York, and then in 131 American theaters and 261 theaters overseas, becoming a now-legendary smash hit. Domestic rentals for 1965 neared the $115 million level, a new record for the company.

Three years later the Zanucks proudly declare that the studio is debt-free from the dark days of *Cleopatra* (1963). Ultimately the film runs for nearly five years in its first run—a record still never equaled. Its enormous profits encourage a third expansion of the Westwood lot in the southwest corner and along the eastern boundary of the studio east of Avenues B and C, including four new soundstages in 1965, two more in 1966, and the building of a number of sets, including a new $250,000 Western Street for *Stagecoach*, and Dolly Street for *Hello, Dolly!* (1969). The movie continues to inspire. After numerous theatrical reissues, Fox got $21.5 million in July of 1978 for a phenomenal twenty-two-year run for the film on NBC. It has since been released, and never out of print, in all the various home video formats. Critic Charles Champlin wrote: "*The Sound of Music* works because we still, more often than not, ask the movies to give shape to our dreams rather than our nightmares, to spell out our wishes and fancies instead of our fears, and *The Sound of Music* says with a towering clarity

ABOVE: Kym Karath celebrates her sixth birthday in the schoolroom in Building 80 with the other cast members. Their teacher, Frances Klamt, and publicist Mike Kaplan also attend.

that there is still innocence in the world, that love conquers all and right will prevail."

Besides the five Academy Awards and five nominations bestowed upon *The Sound of Music* in 1966, The Academy of Motion Picture Arts and Sciences saluted the film's fiftieth anniversary at their 2015 Oscar show. Of the film's legacy Agathe, the eldest daughter of the von Trapp family, wrote in her 2004 memoir:

"The creators of *The Sound of Music* were true to the spirit of our family's story. After meeting so many people over the years who told me how they had derived such great enjoyment and inspiration from the musical and the movie...is it not easy to see the hand of God in all this?"

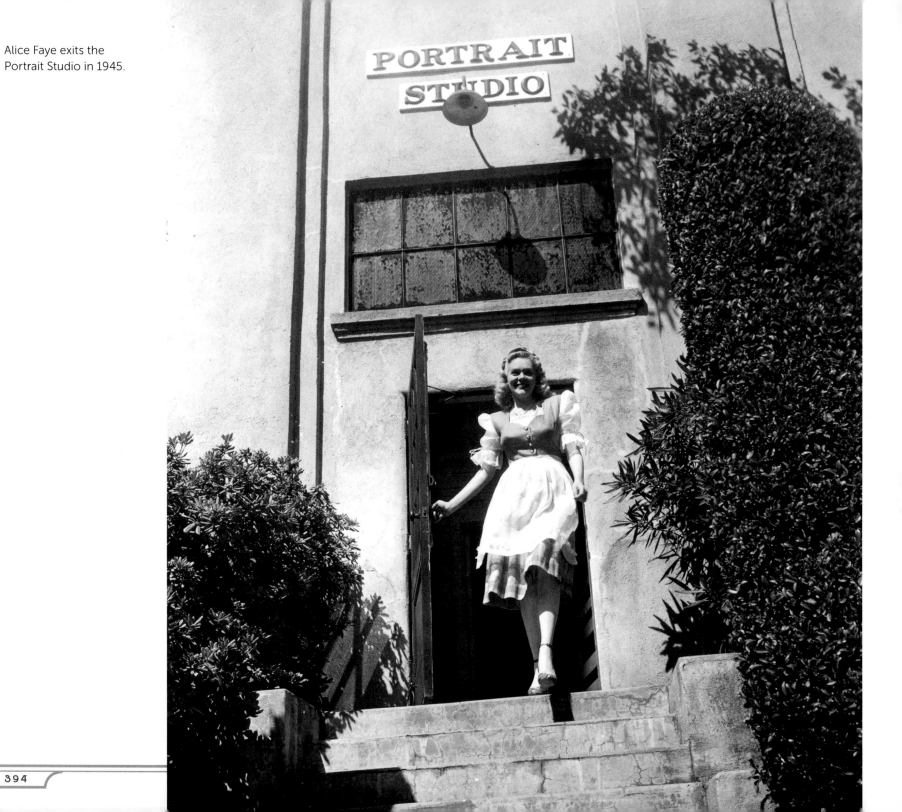

Alice Faye exits the Portrait Studio in 1945.

BLDG. 58: THE PORTRAIT STUDIO (1929)

First in operation at the Western Avenue lot, the portrait studio was transferred here, where it remained until 1971. Almost every major star in Hollywood sat for portrait sittings here, since for most of the twentieth century the motion picture industry relied on print media for advertising its films. Glamour portraits, candids, and amusing novelty, holiday-themed art were standard fare. Actors and actresses on contract at Fox received special attention, with a portrait file (called a "Starhead") dedicated solely to them.

Take Gene Tierney, for example: When she arrived on the lot she was introduced to publicist Peggy McNaught, who, in short order, had photographers like Gene Kornman and Frank Powolny taking pictures of her everywhere, both on and off the lot, while promoting her for fashion layouts in magazines and newspapers. Each photo would then be marked with her own studio publicity number to keep track of the voluminous photography. Tierney's Starhead file would ultimately reach 1,550 photographs—and that did not include any stills from her films.

BOTTOM LEFT: Linda Darnell, with golden tresses for her role in *Forever Amber* (1947), get ready for a photo shoot with Gene Kornman (at right with glasses).

BOTTOM RIGHT: Jeanne Crain strikes a glamorous pose in 1944.

Kornman, one of the leading still photographers in Hollywood, spent most of his career at Fox. He once estimated that he had taken over half a million photographs in the first twenty years of his career. Among his favorites was Shirley Temple, who came to Fox about the same time he did. She was primarily photographed (well over 7,500 portraits!) by Anthony Ugrin. Of course, the most famous photograph to originate from this lot, and this studio, was Betty Grable's pinup shot, taken here in early 1943.

"We were making a picture called *Sweet Rosie O'Grady* at the time," Grable recalled, "and in one scene an artist was to draw me for a cover on *Police Gazette*. He wanted the measurements and the figure just right, so I climbed into the tight bathing suit and posed for a bunch of pictures. Frank, as usual, wasn't quite satisfied. Then he got the idea for the pose with me looking back over my shoulder. It never was really intended for publication, but when the boys in the publicity department saw it they had a few thousand prints made. Thanks to the servicemen overseas it turned out to be a pinup sensation, and it did a lot for me. But back of the picture was Mr. Powolny and his camera genius."

At least ten million copies of the photo are estimated to have been distributed during World War II, and it remains the most reproduced movie still in history.

Powolny, who came to work at Fox in 1923, became a still photographer while working on John Ford's *The Three Bad Men* (1926), and then moved into the portrait gallery due to the insistence of much-impressed Loretta Young. In 1956, after the Labor Day holiday weekend, Powolny received Elvis Presley here for his first photo session for the movies, and was impressed enough to note: "If I'm any judge, he'll stay up there as long as Sinatra and Crosby have done."

Instead of a staffed portrait studio, photographers are now hired on a per-picture contract basis. This building currently houses special effects and dry-cleaning services for employees. Look for the exterior and doorway to the portrait studio in *Holiday for Lovers* (1959) and *Shock Treatment* (1964).

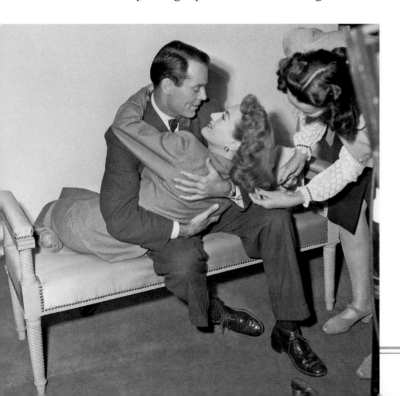

FAR LEFT: Joan Crawford poses in Henry Fonda's arms for *Daisy Kenyon* (1947).

LEFT: This was apparently a tiresome photo session for Maureen O'Hara, Clifton Webb, and Robert Young, stars of *Sitting Pretty* (1948).

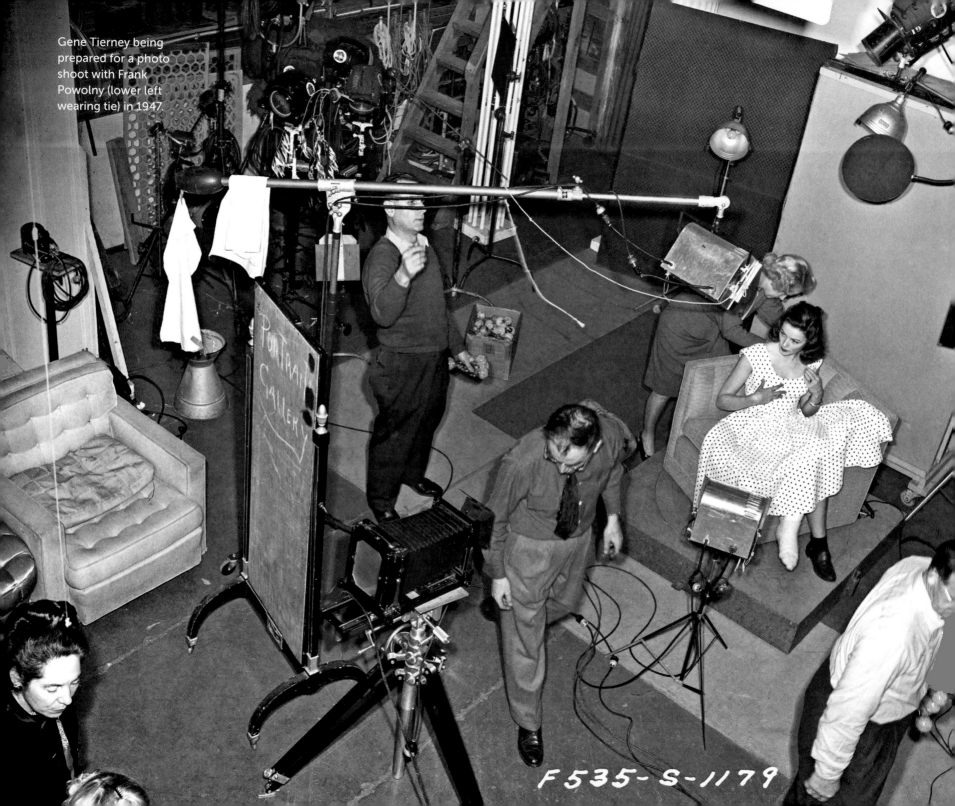

Gene Tierney being prepared for a photo shoot with Frank Powolny (lower left wearing tie) in 1947.

F535-S-1179

FAR LEFT: This is the earliest known print of the Betty Grable pin-up, the stamp on the back indicates that it was approved by the MPAA on February 17, 1943. Note the garter belt that has been retouched on Betty's left leg. The photo was taken on a whim by Frank Powolny as part of a photo shoot to create props for *Sweet Rosie O'Grady* (1943).

Some of the photos from the photo shoot that produced the famous pin-up and the resulting illustrated props for the film.

BOTTOM LEFT: Frank Powolny poses with an altered version of his most famous photograph at this retirement party in the Portrait Studio, 1966.

ABOVE LEFT: Sophia Loren made her English-speaking film debut in *Boy on a Dolphin* (1957) as a treasure-hunting sea diver. This photo got a lot of attention, and became one of the most popular pin-ups of the 1950s.

ABOVE RIGHT: Similarly, Raquel Welch's career got a huge boost after she appeared as Loana in this scrap leather bikini in *One Million Years B.C.* (1966).

RIGHT: Terry Moore's infamous ermine swim-suit ensemble designed by Edith Head.

Just a few of the many thousands of faces that were photographed in the Portrait Studio: (top row, L–R) Myrna Loy, Marguerite Churchill, Una Merkel. Neil Hamilton and Elissa Landi, taken for *The Woman in Room 13* (1932). (bottom row) Tyrone Power and Loretta Young, taken for *Love is News* (1937). Basil Rathbone, taken for *The Adventures of Sherlock Holmes* (1939), and Cesar Romero.

(Top row, L-R) Lena Horne, taken for *Stormy Weather* (1943), Laird Cregar, taken for *Heaven Can Wait* (1943), Anne Baxter, (bottom row) Dana Andrews, Carmen Miranda, taken for *Week-End in Havana* (1941), Bette Davis, taken for *All About Eve* (1950), and James Mason.

(Top row, L-R) Marilyn Monroe, Deborah Kerr, taken for *The King and I* (1956), Gregory Peck, taken for *The Man in the Gray Flannel Suit* (1956), (bottom row) Suzanne Pleshette, taken for *Fate is the Hunter* (1964), Diane Baker, Jeffrey Hunter, and Elvis Presley, taken for *Flaming Star* (1960).

Themed holiday photography was standard fare for decades. Here are a few examples from kitschy to lovely. (Top row, L-R) Natalie Wood, Janet Gaynor, John Wayne, Joan Collins, (bottom row) Shirley Jones, cast of *The Sound of Music*.

(Top row, L-R) Jayne Mansfield, Ann-Margret, Shirley Temple, Rita Moreno, (bottom row) Doris Day, Mitzi Gaynor, Debra Paget

BLDG. 58: MEN'S WARDROBE (1929)

ABOVE: Building 58 with the Commissary lawn in front. Building 59 is at the right. The rising staircase is part of the Galaxy Way parking structure.

RIGHT: Rossano Brazzi gets measured for a suit for his role in *South Pacific* (1958).

FAR RIGHT: "Does this hat go with this suit and shoes?" Men's Wardrobe was a one-stop-shop for all sartorial needs. Note the rows of police and military badges on the wall, 1949.

MS-1463

MS-1392

FAR LEFT: Boots, boots, and more boots in Bldg. 58, 1950.

LEFT: Marine, Army, Navy—you name it Fox had a uniform for it, 1949.

BOTTOM LEFT: Interior of Bldg. 58 when it was the Men's Wardrobe Department, 1936. When the building was converted to office space, the mezzanine was extended to create a full second floor, and the large windows on the left were replaced by smaller ones.

BOTTOM RIGHT: One challenging aspect of the wardrobe department is ensuring that the correct medals, badges, and insignias of anyone in uniform—from hotel bellhops to army generals—are correct.

RIGHT: Building 59 in 2007.

BELOW LEFT: Original 1932 caption: "Alfred Santell, himself, accompanied Marian Nixon to the large wardrobe at Movietone City where they spent all afternoon selecting the simple costumes Marian will wear in her forthcoming sound version of *Rebecca of Sunnybrook Farm* (1932).

BELOW RIGHT: Building 59 circa 1937.

BLDG. 59: WOMEN'S WARDROBE (1929)

This was another of the departments during the years of the studio system that was part of the assembly line, and an assembly line in and of itself. There were salons where costume designers' work was discussed, the back room constantly abuzz with sewing machines where the costumes were made, fitting rooms where the stars were dressed, and storage where costumes were carefully cataloged for reuse.

From the beginning Movietone City had the best under Rita Kaufman, including Earl Luick, Herschel McCoy, Rene Hubert, and Lewis Royer Hastings ("Royer"). The talented Sophie Wachner could create costumes from the most mundane, such as Irish peasants for *Song O' My Heart* (1930), to the fantastic, for *Just Imagine* (1930).

After the merger Royer became head of the wardrobe department, and Gwen Wakeling, from Twentieth Century Pictures, was the studio's head costume designer until 1942. Travis Banton succeeded as head of the department in 1940. Charles LeMaire, a veteran of the Broadway shows of Florenz Ziegfeld and George White, as well as the circus of John Ringling North, first showed up here at White's request to design the costumes for *George White's Scandals* (1934).

ABOVE LEFT: Charles LeMaire goes over sketches and fabric in his office, circa 1946.

ABOVE RIGHT: William Travilla stands with the mannequins for Sharon Tate, Judy Garland, Barbara Parkins, and Patty Duke for whom he created the wardrobe for *Valley of the Dolls* (1967).

FAR LEFT: Royer displays one of the studio's creations for *One in a Million* (1936) in his office that also served as a fitting room. When facing the building on the outside, the windows in the picture are on the right of the main entrance.

LEFT: Betty Grable tries out a new costume for *Tin Pan Alley* (1940) while costume designer Travis Banton sees how it compares to his original sketch.

LeMaire took over the department in 1943 upon his discharge from the army, agreeing to handle the additional work of designing for some of the studio's pictures each year. He began with *Billy Rose's Diamond Horseshoe* (1945), when producer Bill Perlberg heard he had worked with Rose. During his dazzling tenure he had Yvonne Wood and Helen Rose to design the trademark looks of Carmen Miranda; Bonnie Cashin, whose remarkable work began with *Laura* (1944); and Rene Hubert, for *Forever Amber* (1947), all of which showcased the department at its height.

Gene Tierney's husband, designer Oleg Cassini, made a name for himself here (*The Razor's Edge*, 1946, and *The Ghost and Mrs. Muir*, 1947), appearing as himself in *Where the Sidewalk Ends* (1950). In the 1950s—after Gregory Peck startled everyone by collapsing with a coronary during fittings for *David and Bathsheba* (1951)—LeMaire hired Edith Head to do *All About Eve* (1950). The notorious ermine bikini that got the Korean War's number-one pinup Terry Moore sent home amid a blaze of publicity was also Head's.

Dorothy Jeakins, who designed costumes for everything from *Niagara* (1953) and *Titanic* (1953) to *South Pacific* (1958) and *Young Frankenstein* (1974), had a particular gift for making rich-looking wardrobe out of inexpensive materials.

Although LeMaire's studio contract ended in March of 1959, he stayed on until the early 1960s, freelancing three features annually. A key

campaigner to have the Academy of Motion Picture Arts and Sciences recognize costume designers, his department won the first time they were nominated for *All About Eve* (1950). Another win for *Love Is a Many-Splendored Thing* (1955) created his greatest worldwide fashion stir: the Chinese-style sheath dress. His last work here was for David O. Selznick's *Tender Is the Night* (1961).

What an extraordinary curtain call this department had in those wild 1960s as the studio system drew to a close. Credit Edith Head for *What a Way to Go!* (1964) and *Butch Cassidy and the Sundance Kid* (1969), Ray Aghayan for the *Flint* films (1966-67), *Caprice* (1967), and *Doctor Dolittle* (1967), and Irene Sharaff for *Cleopatra* (1963) and *Hello, Dolly!* (1969). Not surprisingly *Cleopatra* set a new

ABOVE LEFT: Each movie star would have a mannequin with her measurements: at the far right is Gene Tierney's, followed by Vera Ellen's, and the sixth one down belonged to Lynn Bari, 1946.

ABOVE MIDDLE: The workroom on the south side of the building, circa 1936.

ABOVE RIGHT: Each rack contains costumes pulled for separate productions.

LEFT: The workroom circa 1965.

record, with 26,000 costumes utilized. Vittorio Nino Novarese designed for the men, and Renie Conley designed for the other actresses and extras.

"I used to disappear into the wardrobe department," recalled Darryl Zanuck's daughter, Darrylin. "When I got home, I'd draw clothes designs and show them to my father. He'd write on them 'great' or 'it stinks.'"

Darrylin later operated a dress shop in the Acapulco Hilton, where she designed the clothes sold and the fabrics they were made of, and ran a wholesale business.

The wardrobe department closed in October of 1977, and its glittering collection merged with Western Costume. The department reopened in the late 1980s and now resides on the fifth floor of Bldg. 99. This building currently houses Twentieth Century Fox's feature-film production offices. Head of production Emma Watts and her creative team are located in Bldg. 88. Meanwhile, a vestige of the building's glamorous past remains: Running along the east exterior wall you can still see the opening where wardrobe could be distributed.

CARMEN MIRANDA

ABOVE: Beau Bridges, Michelle Pfeiffer, and Jeff Bridges in *The Fabulous Baker Boys* (1989).

RIGHT: The entrance to Stage Twenty-two.

STAGE TWENTY-TWO (1966)

The prolific Bridges family has all appeared in Fox films and television shows. Beau Bridges, who starred in *Norma Rae* (1979) and *Max Payne* (2008), began making *The Goodwin Games* here in 2013. Beau's father's Lloyd appeared in *A Walk in the Sun* (1946), *The Loner* (1965–66), and the *Hot Shots!* films (1991-1993). Beau and younger brother Jeff appeared together in *The Fabulous Baker Boys* (1989). Jeff also composed some of the music for Fox's *John and Mary* (1969), starring Dustin Hoffman and Mia Farrow.

STAGE TWENTY-ONE (1966)

Peyton Place for the 1990s? Certainly David E. Kelley's Rome, Wisconsin, re-created on stages such as this one for the surreal *Picket Fences* (1992–96), was, in the creator's words, "about community, family, the workplace, and the town integrated into this community." Tom Skerritt (*Alien*), Kathy Baker (*Edward Scissorhands*), and *South Pacific*'s (1958) own Ray Walston were among its inhabitants.

Painted on its south wall, the stage has a mural depicting the light-saber battle between Darth Vader and Luke Skywalker from *Star Wars V: The Empire Strikes Back* (1980), completed in the spring of 1996. The film's director Irvin Kirshner once said of filmmaking: "You guess at everything. You guess the script will be good, and that the actors you chose will be right. You guess that you'll have enough money to finish the picture, and after every scene you guess that this will be the scene that will work. It's a helluva way to spend millions of dollars!"

BOTTOM: The mural of the climactic lightsaber duel between Luke Skywalker and Darth Vader for *Star Wars Episode V: The Empire Strikes Back* (1980) adorns the south exterior wall of Stage Twenty One. All six *Star Wars* films distributed by Fox were not made here, but various places overseas, including the Fox Studios Sydney.

A mural of *The Simpsons*
(1989 -) on the exterior
of Stage Twenty.

STAGE TWENTY (1966)

Who would have thought that when Rex Harrison was let go in disgrace in the 1940s, he would return in such triumph in the 1960s. It was impossible to ignore talent like his, as evidenced here on the set of *Doctor Dolittle*'s (1967) elegant study, where he performed "Reluctant Vegetarian" and "Talk to the Animals." Although the film's fans continue to consider it, in the words of one of its most memorable performers, Anthony Newley, "altogether marvelous," Harrison found the film more difficult than *Cleopatra* (1963). The bad weather in England, and, later, in the Caribbean, proved to be a secondary problem to working with so many animals that—in the case of a chimp, Pomeranian puppy, and duck—bit him. There was also the goat that ate Fleischer's script, and the parrot who yelled "Cut!" at inopportune moments.

A star on the rise when Joel Schumacher made *Dying Young* (1991) here, Julia Roberts got her start at Fox in Aaron Spelling's *Satisfaction* (1988). That same year she appeared in studio's sleeper hit, *Sleeping with the Enemy* (1991), and remains a major star at the company's century mark. Most recently she returned to work in Tarsem Singh Dhandwar's *Mirror Mirror* (2012, Relativity Media).

ABOVE: This is the set on Stage Twenty for *Dr. Dolittle* (1967) with Rex Harrison amongst the animals. That is the back of Anthony Newley's head.

LEFT: Julia Roberts had one of her best early roles in *Dying Young* (1991). Some of the interior shots were made on this stage. This photo from the opening scene was filmed on New York Street when it doubled for Oakland, California.

BLDG. 31: THE CAMERA BUILDING (1936)/BLDGS. 16-19 (1928)

As part of Darryl Zanuck's expansion of the lot, Building 31 was built to house the camera department on the first floor, the script department on the second floor, and the studio switchboard on the third floor. Adjoining it were earlier facilities for the studio generator (publicized as big enough for a city of fifty thousand) and camera repair and maintenance. As of 2015, one of these original Westinghouse generators is still providing the power to Stage Nine. For years the studio offered a shoeshine and repair service at the east end of Bldg. 19 that made regular rounds.

"According to Dad, the most important man on the lot, the one you wanted on your side, was not Darryl Zanuck but Henry the Bootblack," recalled Tom Mankiewicz. "He shined the shoes of every

ABOVE: The east side of the Camera Building. Among the department's breakthroughs was a camera that did not have to be immobilized inside a booth when sound motion pictures were introduced.

RIGHT: Northeast entrance sign, circa late 1940s.

FAR RIGHT: Loading dock for cameras on the west side of the building, 1940s.

executive on a daily basis. They were constantly on the phone and talked freely in front of him while he worked. As a result, he knew everything that was going on at Fox: whose contract was being dropped, what project was going to get a green light or be canceled, and who was currently in or out of favor."

It became "Joe's [Quattrochi] Shoppe" for the same service in 1982. The shoeshine service and barbershop exist still today in the basement of Bldg. 88. Bldg. 31 is the one that had "Think 20th" painted on the south side during the Richard Zanuck era, and was the first building restored under the studio's lot-wide preservation program, beginning in the spring of 1994. In 1998 the walkway from this building to the commissary was refurbished and landscaped at a cost that caused employees to dub it "the million-dollar walkway."

ABOVE LEFT: Workers from the script department exit the southeast entrance.

ABOVE: Avenue D as it appeared before the installation of "the Million Dollar Walkway" transforming it from a car thoroughfare to a pedestrian walkway, circa 1962.

LEFT: Studio head Richard Zanuck stands in front of Bldg 31 hoping everyone will "Think 20th" the studio's marketing campaign in the mid-1960s.

STAGE NINE (1928)

The oldest stage on the Fox lot, it once contained one of the most famous sets and key props in Fox history: Gene Tierney's elegant apartment and portrait for *Laura* (1944). In June of 1943 Otto Preminger convinced the studio to purchase Vera Caspary's popular novel, chose Rouben Mamoulian as director and his wife Azadia to paint the title character's portrait for this set, and cast Jennifer Jones as star. Jones turned him down because mentor David O. Selznick did not like the project, and Mamoulian and Azadia were fired when he saw their initial efforts. Preminger ended up taking a photo of Tierney by Frank Powolny and having it enlarged and lightly brushed with paint to create the effect he wanted.

John Hodiak was considered for the role of the detective who falls for Laura, until Dana Andrews convinced Virginia Zanuck that he was right for the role on the aircraft carrier set on the backlot while he was filming *Wing and a Prayer* (1944). Although Laird Cregar was considered for the acid-tongued critic, Waldo Lydecker, who becomes fatally obsessed with Laura while transforming her into a sophisticate, Broadway musical-comedy star Clifton Webb was cast instead. Preminger wanted to use Duke Ellington's "Sophisticated Lady" as the theme song, but Alfred Newman had other ideas, providing David Raksin to write the music.

"We were a mixture of second choices—me, Clifton, Dana, the song, the portrait," recalled Gene Tierney. "Otto held us together, pushed and lifted what might have been a good movie into one that became something special."

Tierney was back for *The Razor's Edge* (1946) and a justly famous romantic scene with Tyrone Power on a sweeping staircase here, reputedly involving eighty-one technicians. Costar Anne Baxter attributed their sizzling onscreen chemistry to an off-screen romance, but Tierney was actually involved in a short-lived romance with a naval hero named John F. Kennedy, whom she had met when he toured the lot and her farmhouse set for *Dragonwyck*, on Stage Five.

It can safely be said that Celeste Holm earned her Academy Award for *Gentleman's Agreement* (1948) on this stage. It contained the set of her character's apartment for the key sequences toward the end of the film with Gregory Peck.

She was certainly under pressure to do her best, because Darryl Zanuck—knowing her only as musical-comedy star Ado Annie, in Rodgers & Hammerstein's *Oklahoma!*—doubted she was up to the part. So he tested her by having her perform these most important scenes first. It had been a rough first year for the star, who remembered having the unfortunate timing of coming to Fox after another Broadway star, Tallulah Bankhead, arrived, and caused plenty of trouble. Of course she passed the mogul's test, and went on to enhance a number of Fox films, as much for her warm sense of humor as that impressive dramatic talent.

Here, Richard Todd as Scottish minister

ABOVE: The lab where an experiment goes awry in the sci-fi classic *The Fly* (1958). Helene DeLambre (Patricia Owens) is about to find out what really happened to her husband Andre (Al Hedison).

RIGHT: Anne Dettrey (Celeste Holm) consoles Philip Green (Gregory Peck) in *Gentleman's Agreement* (1947).

Peter Marshall delivered those stirring sermons in the recreated interiors of the Church of the Presidents in Washington, D.C. For the rest of his life Todd was proud to note that *A Man Called Peter* (1955), his Fox debut, surpassed the three most expensive Fox productions of the year: *Untamed*, *The Tall Men*, and *The Racers* at the box office. It is a reminder for us of Fox's unique legacy for releasing many of the most inspiring pictures about faith and hope from *The Song of Bernadette* (1943), and those extraordinary companion pieces *The Keys of the Kingdom* (1944) and *The Inn of the Sixth Happiness* (1958), to *I'd Climb the Highest Mountain* (1951), *The Robe* (1953), *Francis of Assisi* (1961), *The Gospel Road* (1973), and *Son of God* (2014).

Two sci-fi films shot here include *The Fly*, (1958) with its iconic lab set, and Jerry Lewis's *Way . . . Way Out* (1966), set in faraway 1994, in which he plays a space weatherman married to Connie Stevens.

The stage here was transformed by Walter Scott and interior designer Ted Graber into a royal garden party for noted film buff, Queen Elizabeth II, on February 27, 1983, with five hundred celebrities, business leaders, and government officials in attendance.

A record was set in American television history the very next day, when 106 million people tuned in to watch the two-and-a-half-hour series finale to *M*A*S*H*, made here. It was ironic that the studio's most popular attraction at the time was shot on

one of its least-desirable stages, since no one at the time had expected it to be such a hit. Not only was it one of the oldest sets, but it was also not invested with the same quality materials as the others. Cast and crew remember the stage as hot in summer, cold in winter, and infested with fleas and mice. With the end of the series' eleven-year run, the studio donated two boxcar loads of memorabilia to the Smithsonian Institution in Washington, D.C.

All in the Family: the television show *Bones*, shot here, stars Emily Deschanel, daughter of cinematographer Caleb Deschanel (*Hope Floats*, 1998; *Anna and the King*, 1999; *Abraham Lincoln: Vampire Hunter*, 2012) and sister of Emily—Zooey Deschanel (FOX's *New Girl*, 2011– , *[500] Days of Summer*, 2009).

A mural of the making of *The Ox-Bow Incident* (1943) is painted on the east side of the stage, as viewed from over the shoulder of director William Wellman.

BLDG. 41: TOM MIX BARN (1920S)

Tom Mix housed Tony the Wonder Horse here, a sorrel he purchased in 1917 and rode throughout his career. His heyday was over when he departed the lot in 1928 to make films elsewhere, before retiring in 1934. When Mix was killed in an automobile crash in 1940, a plaque was dedicated to him here:

Tom Mix
1880–1940
Thru You Posterity Shall Glimpse the
Glory of the West that Was.

Until Bldg. 89 was built, the property department was housed here, and then the mechanical effects and arsenal department, founded in 1923 by Louis J. Witte, moved in from the Western Avenue Studio's west lot. A graduate from the University in Washington in engineering and a former employee of the DuPont Chemical Company, Witte was in charge of movie explosions, fires, fogs and smokes, sound effects, and the operation of practically every kind of gimmick imaginable for thirty years. The arsenal's collection of weapons, ranging from pistols and rifles to crossbows and machine guns (valued at $135,000 in 1950) was considered one of the largest in the country.

Shortly after Pearl Harbor was bombed Witte received a call from Fort MacArthur, then Los Angeles's main military base, requesting the loan of studio

ABOVE LEFT: Tom Mix.

ABOVE RIGHT: The dedication of the Tom Mix Barn with producer Sol Wurtzel on the left of the plaque and Pauline Moore and Cesar Romero on the right.

RIGHT: The exterior of the Barn circa 1929.

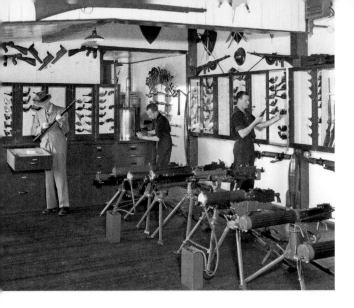

guns. By nightfall Witte and a studio crew had gathered fifteen Vickers, Thompson, Lewis, and Browning guns and four thousand rounds of ammunition. For a surprisingly long period of time this arsenal was the principal armament defending the city's main airport.

The building shows up as a train station in the first episode of *Peyton Place* and in *Hush . . . Hush, Sweet* *Charlotte* (1964), utilizing the corbels of the one that had been torn down, from Midwestern Street. Note that the studio street behind the building is named "Peyton Place Street." By then office services was housed within. More recently, the Barn housed the production offices for David Friendly Productions, Shawn Levy's 21 Laps Entertainment, and Fox Digital Studios.

ABOVE LEFT: The studio's armory was located here for many years.

ABOVE MIDDLE: Betty Grable poses with some of the armaments for *Footlight Serenade* (1942).

ABOVE RIGHT: For many years the Sound Effects department was also located in the Barn.

LEFT: The exterior of the Barn in 2007.

ABOVE: Bldg. 42 as it appeared in the 1930s as an Irish cottage with a thatched roof.

RIGHT: The original occupant of Bldg. 42, Irish tenor John McCormack, stands at right beside Charles Farrell.

FAR RIGHT: Bldg. 42 as it appeared in 2007.

Bldg. 42: The Janet Gaynor Bungalow (1929)/ Bldg. 44: The Will Rogers Bungalow (1929)

California, it's a great old state. We furnish the amusement to the world. Sometimes consciously. Sometimes unconsciously. Sometimes by our films. Sometimes by our politicians.

—Will Rogers

Among the monuments built and institutions named for that great American, Will Rogers, Bldg. 44, custom-built for the star, is entirely unique. It once faced the now-vanished formally landscaped Tennessee Park with its two World War I field guns at opposite corners. By the time he occupied it, the Oklahoma-born, part-Cherokee high school dropout had risen from Wild West trick roper and Ziegfeld Follies star to become the most popular draw in every form of media—newspaper, radio, and motion pictures—as a folksy humorist and a beloved humanitarian.

Appearing in films since 1918, Rogers signed his first contract with Fox on March 22, 1929, and then another in January 1935, making twenty films and becoming the highest-paid actor in Hollywood. Rogers's daily routine included waking in time to ride his horse from his ranch in the Santa Monica hills to the beach to watch the sunrise, return for breakfast, and then arrive on the lot earlier than anyone else for his latest film. After riding home for lunch or dining at the Café de Paris, Rogers would use the bungalow to type his articles, which he then read to the delight of the cast and crew of his pictures.

Others recall that he used his car more often than the bungalow, parked near whatever stage or backlot set he was working on. Jane Withers, who worked with him in *Doubting Thomas* (1935), looked forward to his phone call during her tutoring session. "Is it time for recess?" he would ask. She would put on her roller skates and skate over to his bungalow, where she knew he kept the key over the door. There he taught her to play chess.

Upon his death John Ford, who directed three of his best films, hosted a memorial. During Rogers's funeral at Forest Lawn, as fifty thousand mourners passed by the closed coffin, every studio in Hollywood stopped production. That evening the Hollywood Bowl was filled for another tribute. In movie theaters across the country two minutes of silence were observed.

"A smile has disappeared from the lips of America," said John McCormack, "and her eyes are now suffused with tears. He was a man, take this for all in all, we shall not look upon his like again."

McCormack's neighboring bungalow (Bldg. 42) resembled the thatched-roof Irish cottages of his

ABOVE: Charles Farrell and Janet Gaynor, Hollywood's most popular movie couple in the late 1920s and early 1930s.

Fox film debut, *Song O' My Heart* (1930), complete with shamrocks in the garden. When McCormack departed the lot, it was given to Janet Gaynor. She added a piano—when "talkies" came along and she began making musicals—and rose bushes along the fence. Winfield Sheehan made sure fresh flowers were delivered to her every day.

"Janet Gaynor was a gracious and lovely lady," recalled costar Ginger Rogers, "and Charlie Farrell was the handsome boyfriend every young girl coveted. I was surprised they weren't in love with each other. I got the feeling they might have had a thing for each other at one time, though now they were just friends."

"Janet and I were always receiving wedding anniversary presents in the mail care of the studio,"

said Farrell. "The fans didn't know what date our anniversary fell on, which is logical since we were never married."

When Gaynor departed in the fall of 1936, the studio loaned the bungalow out to visiting stars. Warner Baxter was known to use the Rogers bungalow and cook his famous chili con carne, to the delight of coworkers. Myrna Loy remembered staying in the Gaynor bungalow while she made *The Rains Came* (1939). Steve McQueen got to use it while making *The Sand Pebbles* (1966).

Joseph Mankiewicz occupied Will Rogers's bungalow during his studio tenure. In 1960 the bungalows were joined for the offices of Jerry Wald Productions. After his misadventures with *The Girl in Pink Tights* (1955)—a project Marilyn Monroe refused to make—and *Carousel* (1956)—that he refused to make—Frank Sinatra finally made a movie on the lot and settled the lawsuit against him for *Carousel* by starring in *Can-Can* (1960). He used this bungalow while appearing in *Von Ryan's Express* (1965), *Tony Rome* (1967), *The Detective* (1968), and *Lady in Cement* (1968).

Roderick Thorp, author of *The Detective*, wrote a sequel titled *Nothing Lasts Forever* in 1979, partially inspired by seeing *The Towering Inferno* (1974). Producer Lawrence Gordon saw no more than the cover of the book, with its fiery building and a helicopter, and impulsively purchased it and adapted it into *Die Hard* (1988). Interestingly, its star Bruce Willis had once passed Sinatra as an extra in *The First Deadly Sin* (Filmways, 1980).

The bungalow later served Aaron Spelling and Leonard Goldberg during their reign as the best television producers in Hollywood, utilizing eight of the studio's soundstages for their shows.

Although there are decorative bushes sculpted in various shapes throughout the lot, the one here of Bart Simpson—not to mention the Homer Simpson statue of his hand holding a doughnut—identifies the current residents. On the Rogers side is James L. Brooks. In the Gaynor side are *The Simpsons* writers. A worthy successor to the pioneering Paul Terry, Matt Groening's self-proclaimed "celebration of the American family at its wildest"

ABOVE LEFT: Janet Gaynor's dressing room.

ABOVE RIGHT: Janet Gaynor poses by the north window in the front room of her bungalow.

LEFT: Front room in the Janet Gaynor bungalow.

RIGHT: View looking east of the bungalow as it appeared in 2015. It's not hard to tell which production company now inhabits the space with a topiary of Bart at left and the standee of Homer's hand reaching for a donut. The Tom Mix Barn can be seen behind Bart.

BELOW LEFT: Will Rogers on the lot writing his famous newspaper column in his car.

BELOW RIGHT: Photo presumably submitted (and rejected—as the torn corner indicates) to Will Rogers with the publicist's comments at the bottom.

is the longest-running prime-time comedy series (animated or otherwise) in US television history. The show and movie have fun with its Fox connections, containing such town shops as The French Confection and Valley of the Dolls toy store, and guest appearances by Fox veterans Pat Boone, Donald Sutherland, Elizabeth Taylor, Susan Sarandon, Mark Hamill, Ben Stiller, Arnold Schwarzenegger, Anne Hathaway, and Rupert Murdoch. Groening's *Futurama* (presented by "30th Century Fox") likewise contains numerous spoofs on the studio's product over the years.

"All I know is what I (Do) (see) in the movies."

Let me know which you prefer see or do. Herman

LEFT: Will Rogers' bungalow dressing room at the time he occupied it. The exterior was specially designed in a desert style with a garden of rare cacti, century plants, mesquite and greasewood. The stone on the exterior is the same that was used on his home in what is now the Will Rogers State Park.

BOTTOM LEFT: Interior of Will Rogers' bungalow looking north.

BOTTOM MIDDLE: Interior of Will Rogers' bungalow looking south. The large fireplace was still extant in 2015.

BOTTOM RIGHT: The second room in Will Rogers' bungalow.

BLDG. 49: BUNGALOW 7 (1929)

This three-room bungalow was probably built for Buddy G. DeSylva, the prolific Broadway composer who joined up with Lew Brown and Ray Henderson in 1925 to form a songwriting and music publishing team, and then broke away in 1929 to produce films under contract to Fox for eight years. Years later Henry Ephron produced a Fox musical based on DeSylva's life called *The Best Things in Life Are Free* (1956).

In later years writer/producer Chris Carter had his office here. He developed two projects for Twentieth Century Fox Television, *The X-Files* (1993–2002) and *Millenium*. *The X-Files*, which inspired two feature films and a brief reboot in 2016.

BLDG. 69: THE SHIRLEY TEMPLE BUNGALOW (1930)

There is no country in the world, both civilized and uncivilized, where at some time or another her pictures have not been shown. In the Orient she is called 'Scharey,' in Central Europe it is 'Schirley,' but throughout the English-speaking world, 'Shirley Temple' stands as a universal symbol of childhood. No child in history has been so well known or universally beloved.

—Hollywood trade paper Cavalcade, *1939*

This cottage was built—painted blue and white—with a white picket fence for the arrival of European songbird Lilian Harvey in 1933. Her film *My Lips Betray* (1933) is notable for an early feature-film appearance by Walt Disney's Mickey Mouse. The following year Disney provided Janet Gaynor's nightmare sequence for Frank Lloyd's *Servants' Entrance* (1934).

When Harvey walked off the set of *George White Scandals* (1934), costar Rudy Vallee launched a new star by replacing her with protégée Alice Faye. Glamorous Gloria Swanson inherited Lilian's bungalow, "La Maison des Rêves" (House of Dreams), when she made *Music in the Air* (1934).

That December Gertrude Temple drove to the studio for an audition for her five-year-old daughter, who remembered that they were refused entry. Gertrude explained that Fox songwriter Jay Gorney (composer of the Depression-era classic, "Brother, Can You Spare a Dime?") had seen one of little Shirley's *Frolics of Youth* films, and had invited them to the studio to meet producer Lew Brown about a role in *Stand Up and Cheer!*.

LEFT: Shirley enjoyed this gift from frequent co-star Bill Robinson.

BOTTOM LEFT: Actress Lilian Harvey stands in front of the bungalow. Part of the Berkeley Square set can be seen in the distance.

BOTTOM MIDDLE: Glamour portrait of Gloria Swanson taken during the filming of *Music in the Air* (1934) when she inhabited the bungalow.

BOTTOM RIGHT: Shirley Temple on the swing in the front yard of the bungalow. The Tom Mix Barn, Bldg. 54 Dressing Rooms A, and the back of Stages Three and Four can be seen behind her.

TOP: Original 1930s caption: "Shirley Temple, imitating her favorite comedian Harold Lloyd, reads to her pet Chihuahua in her bungalow."

ABOVE: Shirley studying at her desk in the bedroom of her bungalow.

RIGHT: Shirley's bedroom in the bungalow.

FAE RIGHT: Shirley's dressing table in the bedroom of her bungalow.

They were eventually granted access to the lot, and Shirley Temple's subsequent success earned her this bungalow. From 1935 to 1938, she was the world's most popular movie star, receiving an all-time record of 60,000 fan letters monthly. There were 384 Shirley Temple fan clubs nationwide, with 3,800,000 members. At her seventh birthday party twenty thousand fans in Bali met to pray for her. She rivaled President Franklin Roosevelt and Edward VIII as the world's most photographed person at the time. The exceptionally popular doll fashioned in her image by the Ideal Novelty and Toy Company in 1934 (the most popular to date) saved them from bankruptcy. Meanwhile, Shirley worked six days a week on the lot for three hours a day, took her meals here, and then was tutored an additional three hours. She often made four films a year, requiring six or seven weeks each. Frances Klamt came to the studio as her private tutor in 1936. Fluent in several languages,

Klamt served as the studio translator, and in 1939 became dean of education, teaching all of the lot's children in the Old Writers' Building for decades.

As a goodwill ambassador herself, Shirley received President Roosevelt (twice), the Chilean Navy's chief of staff, the Australian prime minister, the son of Benito Mussolini, Prince Purachatra Jayakara of Siam, Amelia Earhart, Albert Einstein, H. G. Wells, and General John J. Pershing. In 1937 pilots of the first nonstop flight from Russia to the United States landed near the studio in order to meet Temple. Buddy DeSylva introduced her to Bill Robinson and his wife Fannie here before production on *The Little Colonel* (1935) commenced. One gift from "Uncle Billy" was a pint-sized, red-leather-seat racing car that she could gleefully buzz around the lot in, "once getting the knack of turning corners, pumping the clutch, and ignoring the brake!" Such antics and the unmuffled engine noise

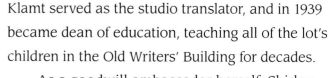

eventually relegated the car to her own driveway.

Despite the famous names that dwelled here after her departure, including John Barrymore, Ginger Rogers, George Cukor, Peggy Ann Garner, and Orson Welles, and its use as the studio dentists' office and dispensary in 1955 (run by the physician brother of murdered mobster, Bugsy Siegel), until it moved into the craft services building, the bungalow remains unique because of Shirley Temple Black.

In 1934—a career high-water mark, with nine phenomenally popular features completed—Temple received a special miniature Academy Award statuette. Presenter Irwin S. Cobb said, "When Santa Claus brought you down Creation's chimney, he brought the loveliest Christmas present that has ever been given to the world."

ABOVE LEFT: The living room of Shirley's bungalow.

ABOVE MIDDLE: Shirley got a small-scale piano in her bungalow.

ABOVE RIGHT: The bungalow came equipped with a full kitchen. Here she is practicing with her dance coach Jack Donohue.

LEFT: Shirley at her kitchen table in the bungalow with Nick Janios who is checking on whether she likes the food the Commissary is providing.

RIGHT: Child star Peggy Ann Garner inherits the bungalow in 1944.

FAR RIGHT: Peggy Ann Garner enters the gate of the bungalow. The Janet Gaynor bungalow can be seen behind her.

BOTTOM LEFT: Building 69 in 2015.

BOTTOM RIGHT: This building also served as the studio's hospital until it moved to Building 99 in 1997. This is how it appeared in circa 1967.

Bldg. 80: Old Writers' Building (1932)

When Sidney Kent and Will Rogers dedicated this building on December 9, 1932, with a cornerstone that still reads: "To the motion picture writers, the supreme storytellers of the 20th Century," it represented the importance of screenwriting with the advent of sound motion pictures. The thirty writers that could be housed within rose to further prominence—in fact, to a level of respect achieved at no other Hollywood studio—upon the arrival of Darryl Zanuck. By 1941, fifty-three writers were under contract to him. He set a tough standard—scripts were expected to be completed within ten weeks, and weekly reports were issued to check on their progress —but he allowed them more responsibility, and preferred to develop producers from within their ranks.

"The Old Writers' Building is something of a misnomer," recalled Elia Kazan, "an old building where Fox housed young writers whose tenure was of uncertain duration."

Indeed, the three-room writers' bungalows with bathrooms that originally nearly encircled the building were preferred to the offices within its forty rooms. Look for the now-vanished ones to the east torn down in 1975 (where Bldg. 310 is) in *The Lieutenant Wore Skirts* (1956).

Wherever they were housed, many of Hollywood's greatest have worked for Fox over the years, including Zanuck's "Big Three": Philip Dunne, a twenty-five-year veteran first hired in the spring of 1930 as a reader, who later wrote speeches for Adlai Stevenson and John F. Kennedy; Nunnally Johnson, known on the lot as "Robert Benchley with a Georgia accent," who quipped that he wrote scripts for CinemaScope by putting the paper in the typewriter sideways; and Lamar Trotti, who came to Fox in 1934 when his boss Colonel Jason Joy became head of the story department, and excelled in producing Americana for the next twenty years.

Other Fox writers included F. Scott Fitzgerald, whose difficulties during his Hollywood period are dramatized in *Beloved Infidel* (1959); Aldous Huxley, who adapted *Jane Eyre* (1944); Dudley Nichols, who weathered the Sheehan and Zanuck eras by sheer talent, a non-exclusive contract, and the support of John Ford (fifteen screenplays); Fritz Lang (*Man Hunt*, 1941); Jean Renoir (*Swamp Water*, 1941); and Elia Kazan (*Pinky*, 1949).

The lot's feel-good writer, Valentine Davies, got the idea for his Academy Award–winning *Miracle on 34th Street* (1947) while he was in the army

ABOVE LEFT: The south side of the Old Writers' Building. The large windows on the left of the first floor is where the studio's school was housed.

ABOVE RIGHT: Frances Klamt in her classroom with photos of her famous students on the wall, mid-1960s.

LEFT: The schoolroom in 1945 with (L-R) unidentified girl, June Haver, Peggy Ann Garner, Barbara Lawrence, Roddy McDowall, and Barbara Whiting.

during World War II and went into Macy's to buy a present for his wife. When Somerset Maugham refused to write a sequel to *The Razor's Edge* (1946), the property lay dormant until the screen rights were signed over to Columbia for their 1984 remake as a trade for those of *Romancing the Stone.* Zanuck also consulted with—and produced the works of—John Steinbeck, and produced more films from eating, drinking, and storytelling companion Ernest Hemingway than any other studio.

When Lamar Trotti died unexpectedly while writing *There's No Business Like Show Business* (1954), Broadway imports Henry and Phoebe Ephron took over. Henry wrote and produced *Carousel* (1956) and *Desk Set* (1957), and hoped to make a movie about Elvis and manager Colonel Parker (with Orson Welles as Parker), but Spyros Skouras nixed it. Their Broadway-turned-film-hit *Take Her, She's Mine* (1963) was based on letters their daughter Nora wrote from college.

Nora Ephron—writer (*Silkwood*, 1983; *This is My Life*, 1992) and director (*Sleepless in Seattle*, Tristar Pictures, 1993)—never forgot attending the studio screening of *An Affair to Remember* in 1957. When her music editor Nick Meyers sought out and made a copy of the original recording of the score for *Sleepless*, she found Newman's original far superior to a modern recording when they tried to replicate it.

Truman Capote contributed to *The Innocents* (1961), the definitive screen adaptation of Henry James's *The Turn of the Screw*. Husband-and-wife team Renee Taylor and Joseph Bologna uniquely developed an autobiographical screenplay (*Made For Each Other*, 1971) and starred in it. Loyal to Ring Lardner Jr. for his work at Fox (*Laura, Forever Amber, The Forbidden Street*), Darryl Zanuck boldly signed him to a new picture after the writer testified before the House Un-American Activities Committee (HUAC). He was ordered to fire him and complied. Zanuck was more successful in protecting directors like Lewis Milestone and Jules Dassin—who he sent overseas and was rewarded with the classic *Night and the City* (1950). Lardner was invited back to write the Oscar-winning script for *M*A*S*H* (1970).

"It was a real privilege to work at Fox in that [Zanuck] period," said Francis Ford Coppola. "I remember going to the [commissary] and seeing Ryan O'Neal and Mia Farrow, who were working on *Peyton Place*. It was a big traumatic moment when, allegedly in a huff, she cut off all her hair—and there she was in the lunchroom with no hair. And on my way back to my office to work on *Patton*, I'd pass the set for the television series *Voyage to the Bottom of the Sea*, and I'd go sit all by myself in the submarine. All of a sudden I'd stand up and say, 'Dive! Dive! Dive!' *Patton* had any number of

FAR LEFT: John Steinbeck prepares to introduce the collection of filmed short stories of *O. Henry's Full House*. (1952). Director Henry Hathaway is at the left.

LEFT: Henry and Phoebe Ephron.

BOTTOM: The original sign above the building's entrance.

stylized touches that made the screenplay unpopular ten years before and very popular years later. I believe to this day that if I hadn't won the Oscar for *Patton* I would have been fired off *The Godfather*."

Lonne Elder III was the first African American to win an Oscar for the screenplay for *Sounder* (1972). Among Neil Simon's works at Fox *I Ought to Be in Pictures* (1982) provides a memorable snapshot of Hollywood, and even a brief glimpse of the lot (with Ann-Margret as a hairdresser!) in the early 1980s.

The stock film library, one of the studio's oldest departments, is still in operation here. Established to supply stock footage for studio productions, its now-extensive library has been open to outside filmmakers since 1953. The script vault in the basement, the "steno pool" of twenty-five women, the fan mail department, and the studio schoolroom on the first floor on the southwest side of the building are gone. Frances Klamt's schoolroom had two rows of wooden desks with the names of the famous children who studied there carved into them. She dedicated one wall to autographed photographs of all her famous pupils. Angela Cartwright recalled that minors only went to school here when they were not working on the set. In either case, twenty minutes of study were required before they could be pulled out of class for moviemaking.

"Imagine studying and then being called to the makeup department," said Linda Darnell. "Next I will shoot a scene and then, with a few minutes to spare, rush back to class to split an infinitive. I would be kissing Tyrone Power and the school teacher would come and tell me it was time for my history lesson. I never before or since have been so embarrassed."

"I always felt guilty when the crew sat around waiting and I hadn't finished my three hours of schooling," said Natalie Wood. "I always remember running to the set when I was called."

"I finished high school here," recalled Fabian. "I was there when all the contract players were let go in 1964 except for Stuart Whitman, Carol Lynley, and myself. The [studio] system crumbled, and the roles you needed to build a career just weren't there."

The building has since housed production offices for film (director Richard Fleischer) and television (writer/producer David E. Kelley). Kelley lived the Hollywood dream. More interested in screenwriting than in being a lawyer, he came to Fox at the invitation of Steven Bochco, who was looking for writers who knew about law for *L.A. Law* (1986–94). Rising through the ranks, he helped Bochco develop *Doogie Howser, M.D.* (1989–93), starring Neil Patrick Harris, before leaving the show to create *Picket Fences* (1992–96). He enjoyed success with *Chicago Hope* (1994–2000), *The Practice* (1997–2004), *Ally McBeal* (1997–2002), *Boston Public* (2000–04), *Boston Legal* (2004–08), and *The Crazy Ones* (2013). He even married a movie star, Michelle Pfeiffer.

Although the words over the front archway ("A play ought to be an image of human nature for the delight and instruction of mankind") are long gone the original finial on the top of the building (a quill pen in an inkwell) was re-created by the studio's metal shop and restored there recently.

Bldg. 79: Jesse L. Lasky Building (1932)

After being ousted from Paramount during the Great Depression, Lasky, one of Hollywood's true pioneers, set up offices here in 1932 as an independent producer. He made fifteen films for the studio over three years, with a fifty-fifty split of profits. He had his own projection room that was torn down when the large satellites were installed next door. Today the building is used for postproduction.

ABOVE: Filming the musical *Redheads on Parade* (1935) produced by Jesse L. Lasky.

FAR LEFT: The exterior of the Jesse L. Lasky Building in 2015.

LEFT: Director Dorothy Arzner and screenwriter Sonya Levien (left), confer with Jesse L. Lasky about *The Captive Bride* that went unproduced. Levien wrote the screenplay for *Cavalcade* (1933) and *State Fair* (1933).

Bldg. 310: Grip Department/Production Offices (2007):

One of the newest buildings on the lot, the first floor contains the current offices of the grip department and storage for all of the grip and lighting equipment, including a huge canvas-cutting room. The upper three floors house offices of various production companies, thereby removing many of the trailers that used to clog the lot. Look for the old grip and canvas department building—in its original location, in the northeast corner of the lot—in the Jeanne Crain/Jean Peters film *Vicki* (1953) as the repair shop.

Mel Brooks attributes his making of *History of the World: Part I* (1981) to a studio grip who asked him what his next picture was going to be. Brooks answered that it would be his biggest yet . . . called "History of the World!"

ABOVE: The massive canvas room.

RIGHT: Grip equipment.

BOTTOM LEFT: South entrance of Grip Department.

BOTTOM RIGHT: Northeast corner of Building 310.

Stage Sixteen (1937)

Darryl Zanuck permitted John Ford, a member of the Naval Reserve since 1934, to use his soundstages to train filmmakers for World War II reconnaissance, training, and combat films for the Office of Strategic Services. Of course, escapist fare continued to flourish, including Ernst Lubitsch's *A Royal Scandal* (1945). The elaborate private quarters of Russia's Catherine the Great, played by Tallulah Bankhead, were built here.

"Grandfather [Frank Lloyd Wright] visited me on the set," costar Anne Baxter recalled, "and watched Tallulah Bankhead working. He said quite loudly, 'Not bad for an old dame,' and Tallulah, who was uneasy about her age, visibly bristled. The next take required her to lightly tap me, but she responded with an uppercut that sent me reeling. Then she smiled sweetly and retired to her dressing room."

Recovering from a heart attack, director Lubitsch asked Otto Preminger to finish the film. Preminger had special reason to be kind to Tallulah. She had enlisted the aid of her father (the Speaker of the House of Representatives) and uncle (a senator) to get his family, fleeing the Nazis, out of Europe.

The climactic courtroom scene in *Peyton Place* (1957), filmed here, reflects star Lana Turner's own family tragedy when, less than five months after the film's release, her fourteen-year-old daughter Cheryl stabbed Turner's abusive lover Johnny

ABOVE LEFT: Entrance to Stage Sixteen.

ABOVE RIGHT: William Eythe, standing next to Tallulah Bankhead, receives direction from Otto Preminger (hand in pocket by camera) during the filming of *A Royal Scandal* (1945).

ABOVE: Director Martin Ritt directs James Earl Jones in *The Great White Hope* (1970). Interiors for the film were shot on Stage Sixteen though it appears that this picture was taken during rehearsals on Stage Five or Six.

Stompanato to death. That courtroom drama resulted in Cheryl's acquittal and a 32 percent jump in ticket sales. Turner always had difficulty watching the film after that, since she is wearing jewelry Stompanato gave her.

James Earl Jones knew all about prizefighting when he made *The Great White Hope* (1970) here because of his prizefighter-turned-actor father Despite the Tony he earned on Broadway and the acclaim for this film his most famous work for Fox was yet to come, as the voice of Darth Vader in the *Star Wars* films.

After making his debut at the studio in the Fox 2000 romantic comedy *One Fine Day* (1996), which used this stage, George Clooney was featured in a cameo in Terrence Malick's *The Thin Red Line* (1998), and received praise for his performances in Fox Searchlight's *The Descendants* (2011) and Fox 2000's *The Monuments Men* (2014).

The studio added a permanent 500,000-gallon water tank for the flooded-kitchen set for the first sequences shot underwater here for *Alien Resurrection* (1997). It was the first *Alien* movie shot on the lot, at Sigourney Weaver's request. The tank was later used for reshoots for *Titanic* (1997), a tragic story the studio perpetuated like no other. Besides its role in *Cavalcade* (1933), the 1953 *Titanic*, and in a 1966 episode of Irwin Allen's *Time Tunnel*, there is *The Poseidon Adventure* (1972), inspired by the

disaster, and references to it in *The Rocky Horror Picture Show* (1975) and *Author! Author!* (1982).

For many, Brad Pitt's performance in *Fight Club* (1999) is his best. The interior scenes of Edward Norton / Brad Pitt's home were shot here. Rising to stardom from television shows like Fox's own *21 Jump Street,* Brad Pitt married Jennifer Aniston, who sparkled in *She's the One* (1996), *Picture Perfect* (1997), *The Object of My Affection* (1998), *The Good Girl* (2002), and *Marley and Me* (2008). Although he liked the script enough to send it to director Doug Liman, Pitt was initially not interested in starring in Regency's stylish spy-vs.-spy action film, *Mr. and Mrs. Smith* (2005). He changed his mind and ultimately fell in love with costar Angelina Jolie here on the lot, and on this stage. He also appeared in

Terrence Malick's *Tree of Life* (2011), and made possible, as coproducer, Steve McQueen's Oscar-winning *12 Years a Slave* (2013).

The spaceship *Serenity* in Joss Whedon's cult hit *Firefly* (2002) was built on two stages, to accommodate its two levels. With a CGI-generated exterior, the cargo area and sleeping quarters were here. The cockpit, galley, and engine were on Stage Fifteen. Star Nathan Fillion never forgot his first day on this stage: "The big cargo bay door was open, and I walked up into the cargo bay up this ramp. Someone [called out] 'Captain on deck!' And everybody turned and stopped and did, like, a little mock salute. A couple of people applauded. And I thought, 'Oh, my God. I just got on a spaceship.' The moment was not lost on me. Every kid wants it."

ABOVE LEFT: The set tank built for *Alien Resurrection* (1997) on Stage Sixteen. More horror: by 2015 FX's *American Horror Story* (2011 -) was being produced on the lot, and the extraordinary Art Deco Hotel Cortez lobby and mezzanine set was built here for Season Five.

ABOVE RIGHT: Edward Norton and Brad Pitt in *Fight Club* (1998).

Elizabeth Taylor as Cleopatra entering Rome.

CLEOPATRA AND THE LOT

Twentieth Century Fox's *Jane Eyre* (1944) featured an eleven-year-old World War II evacuee from England named Elizabeth Taylor. By 1958, when the studio wanted her again, she had rocketed to international fame. "She knocks Khrushchev off the front page!" observed Richard Burton. Spyros Skouras, Buddy Adler, and independent producer Walter Wanger were preparing a film they hoped would be a major cinematic event. They wanted a big important cast, and the best artisans for an epic to rival such recent blockbusters as Paramount's *The Ten Commandments* (1956) and MGM's *Ben-Hur* (1959). They wanted Alex North to compose a score that would be a masterpiece of the art form.

"We got what we wanted," admitted David Brown. All this, and the most notorious production history the company has ever known, and the only film to close down the lot.

CLEOPATRA TIMELINE

JANUARY 1958: Spyros Skouras announces that the Westwood studio backlot will be redeveloped. Legend has it that it was the crippling cost of *Cleopatra* that forced the company to sell off the backlot. Not true. In fact, *Cleopatra* had yet to be initiated when this announcement was made. Far more

pressing was the fact that the company's filmmaking plant was not turning out moneymakers, and the expansion of Greater Los Angeles was making the property extremely valuable and driving up taxes.

SEPTEMBER 30, 1958: Walter Wanger is invited to meet with Skouras about remaking *Cleopatra* (1918). Wanger is enthusiastic. Buddy Adler greenlights the production with a $2 million budget, including a sixty-four-day shooting schedule and Wanger's choice of contract stars.

OCTOBER 22, 1958: Adler meets at the Café de Paris with Wanger proposing Joan Collins, Joanne Woodward, or Suzy Parker for the title role. Joan Collins was the first to test. Her loss of the part was particularly bitter, since during these years on the lot she never reached the first tier

of stardom. Instead, she referred to herself as a "utility infielder" who got the parts Gene Tierney and Susan Hayward did not want, and even wore their old costumes. Susan Hayward was in fact the earliest strong contender for the role. She even had the vote of corporate headquarters in New York. But Wanger always wanted Elizabeth Taylor. He makes a transatlantic telephone call while she honeymoons with Eddie Fisher in Europe and offers her the part. She jokingly asks for $1 million, and gets it. Prior to that the studio had only considered paying that amount to Ingrid Bergman to be under contract in the late 1950s. She had turned it down.

OCTOBER 15, 1959: Elizabeth Taylor is "cast" before newsreel cameras in Buddy Adler's office, but does not actually sign until June 28, 1960, after months of negotiation. Director Rouben Mamoulian is signed that month for the picture, now budgeted for up to $4 million. He assigns five different writers to the script and is still unsatisfied. Wanger hires John DeCuir as art director. Skouras orders lavish sets to be built at London's Pinewood Studio. Peter Finch and Stephen Boyd are cast as Caesar and Marc Antony. The production leaves Los Angeles.

APRIL 4, 1961: Word reaches the lot that the English cold and damp is ruining the sets and making Taylor seriously ill. After an emergency tracheotomy and hospitalization, she requires a three-month recovery period. Marilyn Monroe is briefly considered to replace her, as production is moved back to the Westwood lot.

SPRING 1961: For six weeks surveyors and bull-dozers prepare and grade a site for sets on the back-lot, incorporating the Slave Market and Sligon Castle, as well as the huge columns from *The Big Fisherman* (1959), rented from Universal. The company returns with a new director and screenwriter, Joseph L. Mankiewicz, who brings along his sons Tom and Chris to help. Mankiewicz wants a new Antony. His first choice was Marlon Brando, who had played the part brilliantly for him at MGM in 1950. When he proved unavailable, second choice Richard Burton was very expensively extricated from the Lerner & Loewe Broadway hit, *Camelot*. Although Mankiewicz tried to get Laurence Oliver or Trevor Howard for Caesar, he is happy to work with Rex Harrison again.

BOTTOM LEFT: Elizabeth Taylor and Richard Burton share a quiet moment on the set of *Cleopatra* (1963) in Rome.

BOTTOM RIGHT: Richard Burton, left, Elizabeth Taylor and director Joseph Mankiewicz on the set of *Cleopatra* (1963) in Rome.

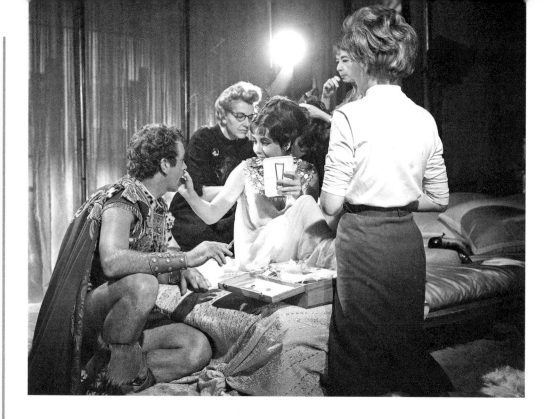

ABOVE LEFT: Elizabeth Taylor is distracted by Richard Burton while the hair and makeup team gets her ready.

ABOVE RIGHT: The most famous love affair in Fox, if not Hollywood, history.

SUMMER 1961: Forced to shoot by day and write by night—with assistance from Sidney Buchman and Ranald MacDougall, not to mention William Shakespeare and George Bernard Shaw, whose texts the scholarly Mankiewicz frequently referred to, and Wanger himself—Mankiewicz finally produces a 220-page script. "Most of the stage space here is taken up with television," complained Walter Wanger, "and what is left is needed for George Stevens's *Greatest Story Ever Told*, so it was suddenly decided to get us off the lot." Stevens's project, another costly Spyros Skouras effort, is canceled by the board of directors in August of 1961 when preproduction costs spiral to $2 million. *Cleopatra* will commence in Rome (at Benito Mussolini's famed Cinecitta studio), with location work in Egypt in the fall. While building Alexandria near Anzio, still-active land mines explode, killing a workman and injuring others. The extraordinary amount of construction materials needed for the Roman sets at Cinecitta cause a national shortage. Meanwhile, the incomplete backlot sets, including the Palace of Alexandria, would tower over Olympic Boulevard until they were destroyed with the rest of the backlot in 1961.

SEPTEMBER 1961: Spyros Skouras is pleased to hear from Mankiewicz that principal photography has begun. Then he looks at the costs and is horrified. "We didn't make an Italian picture. We made an American picture in Italy," Skouras said. "Ninety technicians we sent by jet, with hotel accommodations and living expenses for all of them." Walter Wanger recalled, "There was a continuing problem brought on by the fact that the studio had lost more than $60,000,000 in the past few years. Consequently, the jockeying for power among the incumbent board of directors and minority stockholders resulted in conflicting, expensive, on-again, off-again decisions from on-again, off-again groups in power."

NOVEMBER 16, 1961: Spyros Skouras and Peter Levathes leave the lot to fly to Italy for a six-hour conference regarding the budget. Skouras tells frustrated stockholders that *Cleopatra* will now cost $8 million, while Levathes is approving its rise to $15 million. Retaining the stubborn belief that the picture would save his studio, Skouras could not have imagined that by the time principal photography wrapped that summer, *Cleopatra* would cost more than twice that amount.

JANUARY 1962: News comes to Bldg. 88 that production has resumed after Christmas, and that Richard Burton and Elizabeth Taylor are performing for the first time together. A love affair is sparked that resounds around the world unlike any in Hollywood history, and places the spotlight more than ever on the troubled production, creating the paparazzi phenomenon. The couple is denounced on the floor of Congress and in Rome, by the Vatican. Spyros Skouras sends the order that Walter Wanger is to be fired mid-year for the continued mismanagement. "The making of the film was more dramatic than the movie itself," observed David Brown. "There was no way of separating the corporate drama from the on-screen drama . . . Forests must have been cut down to make paper for the scripts that followed . . . the production wandered all over the world . . . Only the Romans left more ruins in Europe. Rome's paparazzi have never recovered from what writer Brenda Maddox called 'the most public adultery in the world.' " writer Jess Walter noted, "This is where modern celebrity began—the Kardashians and the Lohans—you can trace it to this moment where a kind of Hollywood decadence reached a peak. It destroyed in one fell swoop the old studio system and brought in its place the kind of celebrity which doesn't distinguish between good and bad."

MAY 8, 1962: The day of days—Cleopatra's triumphant procession into Rome atop a twenty-eight-foot Sphinx is shot. "The only analogous situations I can think of would be staging a presidential

ABOVE: This statue of Rameses stood by the Pico Gate guardhouse to advertise the film in 1963.

inauguration combined with Macy's Thanksgiving Day parade," said star Hume Cronyn. "Once this huge procession got in motion, it had the forward momentum of a 200,000-ton oil tanker. The logistics were mind-boggling." The scene had been scheduled to be shot six months earlier, but when cinematographer Leon Shamroy saw the Roman forum set—more massive than the original—he declared, "There are not enough lights in Europe to light this!," and insisted the production wait until the sun could properly fill it with light to his satisfaction. Elizabeth Taylor never forgot that day: "During the take . . . I found there were no arms to the throne. There was nothing to hold onto except that little child. I thought I would tear his hair out I was so terrified of heights. There were ten thousand extras, and my life had been threatened because of the scandal, and all throughout the crowds were the equivalent of FBI guys packing guns! We came through the arch and the crowd broke loose—they broke through the barriers—and rushed toward me, and I thought, this is it. My children are up there watching all this. Good-bye, God, thank you. Then the crowds started yelling, 'Baci [Kisses], Liz! Baci, Liz!" I burst out crying, saying 'Thank you! Thank you!' "

JUNE 12, 1962: When Skouras and Levathes shut down *Something's Got to Give* (1962) with a

$3 million loss, *Cleopatra* becomes the only Fox film in production. "Since Fox was shooting only *Cleopatra* and nothing else, the entire worldwide expense of running the company was added to the film's budget," said Tom Mankiewicz. "If two Fox employees went out to lunch in, say, Paris, the cost of that meal was charged to *Cleopatra*. This meant that the announced budget was perceived as not only unforgivably profligate, but obscene." When his wedding in Rome goes awry, Mike Nichols befriends Richard Burton and Elizabeth Taylor, who later appear in his film debut as a director, *Who's Afraid of Virginia Woolf?* (1966, Warner Bros.). His Fox milestones are *Silkwood* (1983) and *Working Girl* (1988).

JULY 1962: Darryl Zanuck is back on the lot and closes it down to save expenses, all the while trying to salvage *Cleopatra* by canceling shooting on July 24, so that he could review the existing footage, reputedly over ninety hours of film shot over the past ten months.

During the fall and winter of 1962, a new battle rages, this time on the lot, over the final edit of the picture. Mankiewicz and his editor Dorothy Spencer cut a five-hour-and-twenty-minute version that he believes should be released as two pictures, like Shakespeare's *Caesar and Cleopatra*, and then

Antony and Cleopatra. Darryl Zanuck had other ideas: cutting the picture by nearly two hours, approving a further $2 million to complete it, with additional sequences to piece the remaining fragments together written by Mankiewicz, including the spectacular opening scene shot in Spain.

MARCH 4, 1963: Ironically the Pico gate is reopened on the day *Cleopatra* completes production and is prepared for a summer release. The $44 million final cost—adjusted for inflation to $400 million today—surpasses the cost of *Titanic* (1997). Mankiewicz disowns the Zanuck cut of four hours and six minutes.

JUNE 12, 1963: Sold out four months in advance, the most publicized picture of the year premieres in New York at the Rivoli Theatre., The film played as first-run for a year in Hollywood. Andy Warhol called it the most influential film of the 1960s where fashion was concerned. In 1981 Joan Collins returned to the lot to play Alexis Carrington Colby in Aaron Spelling's *Dynasty* (1981–89). She would be Queen of the Lot after all. In the 1990s the cut footage is restored, but Roddy McDowall, Martin Landau, and Tom Mankiewicz's attempts to restore the director's original vision—even with the help of Bill Mechanic—are unsuccessful. The film enjoys a fiftieth anniversary screening at the Croisette, as a Cannes Film Festival selection on May 21, 2013.

"There will always be movies, of course," said *Cleopatra* publicist Nathan Weiss, "and presumably better ones than there ever were before; and yet they won't quite be as grand, as foolish, as they used to be. How marvelous that *Cleopatra*, the last of them, transcends them all!"

ABOVE: Composer Alex North supervises the synching of the sound to the picture.

RIGHT: Exterior of Stage Fifteen in 2015.

Stage Fifteen (1936)

Although the studio produced a very good *Sherlock Holmes* in 1932 with Clive Brook, Basil Rathbone made the role forever his own when he starred here in *The Hound of the Baskervilles* (1939) and *The Adventures of Sherlock Holmes* (1939), on loan from MGM. To his coworkers he admitted that to play the hero of his childhood meant as much to him as playing "ten *Hamlets*." Decades later, David Shore's *House M.D.* (2004-12) continued this stage tradition with many Sherlock Holmes references.

If this stage were to be dedicated, however, certainly it would be to Sonja Henie. Her first Fox film was titled *One in a Million* (1936), and she truly was. The young Norwegian danced at the age of four and began ice-skating at six, won Norway's skating championship at fourteen, and became world champion at fifteen. She became the World Champion Women's Figure Skater ten times, and won gold medals and set world marks in three successive Winter Olympics—the first female athlete to do so—in 1928 (setting the record as the youngest athlete ever to do so for seventy years), 1932, and 1936.

In March 1936, she turned professional, toured with an ice show, and got what she wanted once again: a studio contract and an ice rink, on this stage. The underground facilities that produced it for her extraordinary musical fantasies were later

LEFT: Shooting *The Hound of the Baskervilles* (1939) with Basil Rathbone as Sherlock Holmes (in light coat) and Nigel Bruce as Dr. Watson.

ABOVE: The daily job of ice scraping was part of the job to prepare Sonja Henie's ice rink within Stage Fifteen.

RIGHT: Sonja Henie, with outstretched arms, stands ready to perform on the set of *Everything Happens at Night* (1939).

copied nationwide for ice shows (that she popularized) and hockey rinks. The rink measured 100 by 150 feet in length, and a special camera platform with metal sled runners attached to a metal stake in the center of the rink allowed cameramen to follow her onto the ice.

Publicized as the athlete who won more championships than any other in history, and certainly the first great sports celebrity in North America, by 1938 she was rated the third-biggest moneymaking star, and received the Cross of the Order of St. Olaf by the Norwegian government. Her uniqueness as the most dominant personality in the history of skating—particularly in Hollywood—remains unchallenged sixty years after she retired from the lot.

Star Dust (1940), shot here, loosely traced Linda Darnell's own success story: under contract as the fifteen-year-old winner of the Jesse L. Lasky Gateway to Hollywood contest, and introduced to the Fox star-making machine—Miss Enright, who worked to erase her Texas accent; hairdresser Gladys Witten, who developed her hairstyles; Olive Hughes, who fitted her for costumes in the wardrobe department; and Frances Klamt, who was her teacher at the studio school.

Jeanne Crain made two of her best films here.

This was "The Midway" for *State Fair* (1945), where Darryl Zanuck successfully launched the nineteen-year-old as a new "Janet Gaynor type" in her best-remembered role, as Margy Frake. Margy's bedroom set, where Crain performed the Oscar-winning "It Might as Well Be Spring" (voice-doubled by LouAnn Hogan), was also filmed here.

Phil Brown, playing her boyfriend, was later featured as Luke Skywalker's Uncle Owen, in *Star Wars Episode IV*. Costar Dana Andrews said he

BOTTOM LEFT: Linda Darnell as Carolyn Sayres takes instruction from her drama coach (Charlotte Greenwood) in *Star Dust* (1940).

BOTTOM RIGHT: The Oscar winning Rodgers and Hammerstein song "It Might as Well be Spring" from *State Fair* (1945) was introduced here by Jeanne Crain.

The midway in *State Fair* (1945).

could not sing and was dubbed. In fact, he was a wonderful singer, something he never let the studio know for fear he would be typecast in musicals. Fair barker Henry ("Harry") Morgan later gained fame for his role in the *M*A*S*H* television series. The colorful carnival wagons were stored for years in the southwest corner of the lot. *Margie*, like many of her films, was in Technicolor as a sign of her box office stature. Cast and crew of "the sweetheart of 1946" fondly remember drinking cocoa for a month while they shot the ice-skating sequence here.

"Jeanne was very much like she was in *Margie*," remembered screen boyfriend Alan Young, "wide-eyed but very intelligent, maybe a little sharper than she appeared. And she was so beautiful: you could dip a spoon into her skin like ice cream."

After appearing in Otto Preminger's elegant treat *The Fan* (1949), hitting a career high point with *Pinky* (1949), and being recognized as the biggest box-office draw of the year, she lost the role of Eve in *All About Eve* (1950) to Anne Baxter, due to pregnancy. She was unhappy to return to the role of another teenager in *Cheaper by the Dozen* (1950).

"Well, I accepted the role and the whole thing turned out to be a very joyful association," she recalled of the studio's number one hit that year. "I played Myrna Loy's daughter three times. It amuses me because Myrna, who never had children, was so perfect as a mother, while I, the mother of

ABOVE: The ice-skating sequence from *Margie* (1946) with Jeanne Crain.

seven, was never considered the motherly type."

Ironically, Anne Baxter's pregnancy allowed Crain to get another memorable part in *People Will Talk* (1951). She also appeared in another of Darryl Zanuck's social conscience pictures, *Take Care of My Little Girl* (1951), about sororities. Her Fox career ended with *Vicki* (1953), co-starring best friend Jean Peters.

Twentieth Century Fox has produced Hollywood's two greatest ghost stories: *The Ghost and Mrs. Muir* (1947) and *The Innocents* (1961). When Darryl Zanuck set about to make *Muir*, he hoped to have John Ford direct it and Katharine Hepburn to star in it. But by the time the key sets were completed here, Joseph Mankiewicz was director and Gene Tierney and Rex Harrison were its stars.

ABOVE LEFT: Gene Tierney and Rex Harrison during the filming of *The Ghost and Mrs. Muir* (1947).

ABOVE RIGHT: Hope Lange as the aspiring assistant to demanding Joan Crawford in *The Best of Everything* (1959).

With them was eight-year-old Natalie Wood, at the zenith of her childhood career, working in *Muir* and *Miracle on 34th Street* (1947) simultaneously.

"When I first met her, I asked her if she could read the script," said Mankiewicz, "and when she said 'Yes' with great authority, I then asked, 'Can you spell?' She nodded again. Then I really threw her a curve and asked her to spell Mankiewicz. She did, and I was converted to Natalie on the spot."

June Haver proved what a trouper she was during rehearsals here for the exhilarating title tune sequence with Dan Dailey for *The Girl Next Door* (1953). An accident put her in the hospital for months. She returned and completed the film, making it her best, and last. Like her character in

the film she was ready for something more—ultimately, a successful marriage to her *Where Do We Go from Here?* (1945) costar, Fred MacMurray.

Office politics were never so glamorous or entertainingly melodramatic as in *The Best of Everything* (1959). The title could easily have referred to the film's cast and lavish production values, including the huge "Fabian Offices" set, located here. Featured star Suzy Parker did not share her character's tragic fate. She married her *Circle of Deception* (1961) co-star Bradford Dillman and retired soon after.

After making *Rhinestone* (1984) here with Sylvester Stallone, Dolly Parton had better luck when her production company Sandollar optioned Joss Whedon's *Buffy the Vampire Slayer* (1992), to

be produced by Kaz Kuzui and Howard Rosenman, and directed by Kaz's wife, Fran Rubel Kuzui. It was submitted to Fox, and with the recommendation of script reader Jorge Saralegui, it was financed and distributed by the studio, starring Kristy Swanson (*Hot Shots!*, 1991), Donald Sutherland, and future stars Hilary Swank (*Boys Don't Cry*, 1999) and David Arquette.

When Saralegui became vice president of production, he had Joss work on the script for *Speed* (1994) and *Alien: Resurrection* (1997). Then Gail Berman of Sandollar proposed that Whedon make a television series out of *Buffy* that would be closer to his vision of the character. While Twentieth Century Fox Television would make it, the FOX network turned it down, deeming it too close to *Party of Five* (1994–2000, Columbia Television). The WB picked it up instead, launching a phenomenon in 1997 that was later picked up by FOX. The series starred Sarah Michelle Gellar and David Boreanaz, who played the 240-year-old vampire Angel, who eventually earned his own series, *Angel* (1999–2004), and came to the lot for *Bones* (2005–   ). Two young actors not cast in *Buffy* (Ryan Reynolds and Nathan Fillion) ended up in *Two Guys, A Girl and a Pizza Place* (1998–2001), shot on Stage Twenty. It was Gail Berman again, now running FOX, who green-lit and then cancelled Whedon's cult hit *Firefly* in 2001, starring Fillion.

LEFT: Life would imitate art when June Haver gave up her film successful film career just like her character did in the opening sequence of *The Girl Next Door* (1953).

BELOW LEFT: June Haver is helped up by Dan Dailey from her fall during "The Girl Next Door" dance sequence.

BLDG. 99: CRAFT SERVICES BUILDING (1996)

Talk about a historic site: this was once was the elegant London neighborhood of Noel Coward's Marryot family for the company's first Best Picture Academy Award-winner *Cavalcade* (1933). The set was also used in, among others, Jesse Lasky's *Berkeley Square* (1933), Darryl Zanuck's *The House of Rothschild* (1934), and *The Lottery Lover* (1935). After it was demolished to make way for Stages Ten and Eleven in the 1937–38 expansion project, sets for *Hollywood Cavalcade* (1939) were built here, including a prison set seen in *Within These Walls* (1945).

The area was transformed into a Western street for *Stagecoach* (1966), and later used for *Butch Cassidy and the Sundance Kid* (1969) and *Myra Breckinridge* (1970). A young Cloris Leachman, who appeared in the whorehouse sequence filmed here for *Cassidy*, later became a veteran of Fox films and television. *Cassidy* screenwriter William Goldman later wrote the script for *The Princess Bride* from his book of the same name. His efforts to get his favorite project off the ground as a film are legendary; even *Cassidy* star Robert Redford tried to get it made. Although Fox optioned the book when it was published in the early 1970s, it took a partnership with Rob Reiner to finally get the film made in 1987.

With the selling of the final piece of the backlot in 1978, and the demolition of its buildings and

ABOVE: Joss Whedon directs Nathan Fillion and cast on the set of *Firefly* (2002-03).

RIGHT: (L-R) Pete (Richard Ruccolo), Berg (Ryan Reynolds), and Johnny (Nathan Fillion) in the episode "Halloween 2: Mind Over Body" from the series *Two Guys, A Girl, and a Pizza Place* (1998-2001). Fifteen years later Reynolds would star in Fox's highest grossing R-rated picture, *Deadpool* (2016). The studio also helped distribute the top grossing R-rated film of all time: *The Passion of the Christ* (2004).

LEFT: The exterior of Bldg. 99 in 2007.

BOTTOM LEFT: The Berkeley Square set. The tall townhouses in the center are actually the back of Bldg. 12. The upper stories are trompe l'oeil paintings.

BOTTOM RIGHT: The back of Bldg. 12 where the Berkeley Square townhouses once stood.

RIGHT: The east side of Berkeley Square looking south.

FAR RIGHT: Una O'Connor and Herbert Mundin, right, meet on the set in this scene from *Cavalcade* (1933). The east side of Berkeley Square can be seen in the background.

BOTTOM LEFT: Looking southwest across Berkeley Square. This is now the site of Bldg. 99.

BOTTOM RIGHT: The "lower" London set built for *Cavalcade* (1933).

sets in June of 1979, the studio needed a new site for the services that had been located there. To this site temporarily came the electrical machine shop, sheet-metal shop, corporate records, and the carpet department, with the fixtures and grip departments established further to the west. A "Crafts Center" (Bldg. 631) was built in 1979 on the current site of Bldg. 103. It housed the mill, mechanical effects, the paint department, sign shop, prop and miniature departments, and stores and receiving. All of these buildings were torn down when they were consolidated here in Bldg. 99, which opened in April of 1996.

The first floor of the Craft Services Building contains library services (handling the motion picture library), the film preservation department, and the archives of the studio. In eight humidity-and-temperature-controlled vaults, motion picture film, photographs, posters, and props are kept, as well as a vault for digital storage. The origin of the Fox studio archive dates back to 1992, when studio archivists began to collect significant props, including "Wilson" from *Cast Away* (2000), the golden tablet from *Night at the Museum* (2006), and a life-size robot from *I, Robot* (2004). The studio's historic photograph collection has had quite a journey, beginning in Bldg. 1, moving to the basement of Bldg. 88 in the Zanuck era, and then to UCLA in in the 1970s, before all 6,500 boxes found a home in the photo archive here in 2003. The second floor contains the medical department, fire and safety department, staff shop, sign shop, paint shop, set lighting, and the film shipping and receiving dock.

Art Frantz, former head of the set lighting and grip department who retired in 2010, set up a display of historic photos and maps on the wall. The third floor is the studio's latest mill and studio supply. The fourth floor contains the security and production offices. The fifth floor contains the facilities department, which handles

the maintenance of the studio's physical facilities, and the design, planning, and construction department.

The wardrobe department, where thousands of costumes (petticoats, overcoats, evening formals, etc.) used in *Titanic* (1997) are stored, contains the largest collection of early-twentieth-century clothing in America. Even though most of the company's vintage costumes were sold off in the 1970s, under Mike Voght the department continues to reclaim historic pieces. Key costumes worn by major stars are kept in a separate vault. There are also workshops for custom-made costumes and fitting rooms.

BOTTOM LEFT: This set for *Hollywood Cavalcade* (1939) was built where the Berkeley Square set once stood. Building 22 is in the center, and Stage Sixteen can be seen at the left.

BOTTOM RIGHT: Filming another scene for *Hollywood Cavalcade* (1939). The Old Writers' Building can be seen in the center.

ABOVE LEFT: The Western street built for *Stagecoach* (1966), with Stage Sixteen and Bldg. 22 rising above it.

ABOVE RIGHT: The cast of *Stagecoach* (1966).

FAR LEFT: The eastern side of Western Street looking north. The Tom Mix Barn can be seen in the distance.

LEFT: Paul Newman stands on the balcony of the bordello on western street for *Butch Cassidy and the Sundance Kid* (1969).

ABOVE LEFT: Remnants of the western street lasted until the 1990s. This photo was taken in 1984.

ABOVE RIGHT: Samples of posters in the studio's permanent archive collection: *Cleopatra* (1918), *4 Devils* (1929), and a rare pre-release poster for *Revenge of the Jedi* (*Return of the Jedi*, 1983).

RIGHT: Film cans in Vault 8 of Building 99.

FAR RIGHT: The south entrance where the Medical Department is currently located.

Employees recount that it was during their fittings for *Mr. and Mrs. Smith* (2005) that Brad Pitt and Angelina Jolie got to know each other by going up to the roof to smoke. There is also a small display room with a rotating exhibit of current and past costumes from Fox films, including a stained undershirt and denim pants that Bruce Willis wore in *Die Hard 2* (1990), Mrs. Doubtfire's sweater with a prosthetic bosom, and Wolverine's jacket.

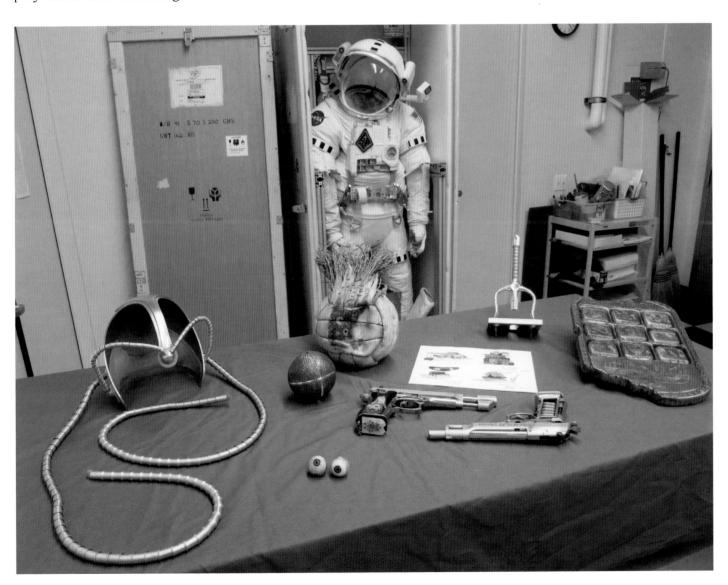

BELOW: Props preserved in the studio's permanent collection include: Cerebro's helmet from *X-Men 2* (2003), a "pup" from *Prometheus* (2012), a pair of eyeballs from *Minority Report* (2002), Wilson from *Cast Away* (2000), pistols and concept art from *William Shakespeare's Romeo + Juliet* (1996), Elektra's special effects sai from *Daredevil* (2003), and the golden tablet of Ahkmenrah from *Night at the Museum 2: Battle of the Smithsonian* (2009). One of the spacesuits from *The Martian* (2015) stands crated in the background.

ABOVE: Set lighting.

ABOVE RIGHT: The massive mill.

RIGHT: The Staff Shop.

FAR RIGHT: The Sign Shop.

MOULIN
ROUGE
CORSETS

RIGHT: Dressing Room A in the Wardrobe Dept. Brad Pitt and Angelina Jolie (*Mr. and Mrs. Smith*, 2005) are among the many stars who have had their costume fittings here.

MIDDLE RIGHT: A costume from *Planet of the Apes* (1968) on the left, and another made for a more recent film in the franchise on the right.

FAR RIGHT: A suit of armor from *Night at the Museum: Secret of the Tomb* (2014).

BOTTOM LEFT: Bruce Willis's costume from *Die Hard 2* (1989).

BOTTOM MIDDLE: Since only one side of the ship was built for *Titanic* (1997), actors had to wear sweaters with "White Star Line" printed backwards which, once the film was flopped, could be read.

BOTTOM RIGHT: One of Kate Winslet's dresses from *Titanic* (1997).

FAR LEFT: An extraordinary amount of Fox history converges in this display case. Tyrone Power's top hat from *Lloyd's of London* (1937) (top right), Betty Grable's dance outfit from *When My Baby Smiles at Me* (1948), Hugh Jackman's claws from *X-Men* (2001), Lana Turner's hat from *Peyton Place* (1957), and Klinger's hat from the *M*A*S*H* television series.

LEFT: In the same case is *Mrs. Doubtfire*'s (1991) sweater and Drew Barrymore's slippers from *Ever After* (1996).

BOTTOM LEFT: One of Hugh Jackman's jackets from the *X-Men* franchise.

BOTTOM MIDDLE: More costumes from the vintage collection: (L-R) Dress worn by Maureen O'Hara in The *Black Swan* (1942), coat worn by Tyrone Power in *Pony Soldier* (1953), and a dress worn by Anne Baxter in *A Royal Scandal* (1945).

BOTTOM RIGHT: Racks used by wardrobe designers to pull clothing for a movie or TV show. Each rack represents a different show.

RIGHT: The massive Art Department building still dominates the south end of the lot in 2015. The back portion that juts up is where the rigging was for painting backdrops. Bldg. 78 is at left.

BELOW LEFT: A view of the drafting tables on the first floor in the 1930s.

BELOW RIGHT: A view of the same room in the 1960s.

Bldg. 12: The Joseph Urban Art Department Building (1930)

The Art Department

The south end of this building was known since the studio's earliest days as the place where the painting of huge "backings" for films—and, later, television shows—was done, as well as their main titles and inserts. A dedication plaque to Joseph Urban is located at the western entrance to the building, denoting it as: "The Art Building designed by our friend and associate, Joseph Urban, born Vienna (1872), died New York, 1933." Considered to be one of the most famous designers of the twentieth century, including for his productions of Broadway's *Ziegfeld Follies*, Urban came west to work on *East Lynne* (1931) and *Doctors' Wives* (1931). He pioneered art direction for color films, with the short-lived Fox Nature Color process.

Another plaque should recognize the work of painter Emil Jean Kosa Jr. Coworkers recall that he never wished to remove the "Jr." from his name due to his great respect for his Czech father's skill at painting. Their work together, in numerous public and private buildings, reveals a unique appreciation of the California landscape. Paris-born, and schooled at the Prague Academy of Fine Arts, L'École des Beaux-Arts in Paris, and the California Art Institute in Los Angeles, Kosa's work here from 1932 to 1948 earned two Academy Awards.

Of course, his greatest contribution was creating the Twentieth Century Fox logo, painted on eight layers of glass and animated frame by frame. He was but one of some seventy members of this department—including art directors, sketch artists, stock custodians, model makers, blueprinters, and draftsmen—during Hollywood's Golden Age. At any given time, they could simultaneously be working on ten or fifteen movies, some before the cameras and some in prepreparation, with sixteen art directors and their four assistants, twenty-five set designers, seven set illustrators, six model makers, and assorted assistants.

William Darling, who signed a contract with Fox in 1922, headed the department until 1946. He designed key studio buildings and soundstages, as well as the Santa Monica Gate. Assisting him were supervising art director Richard Day and department manager James Basevi. With the release of each new first-draft continuity script, the department would get to work. Day and Basevi would assign an art director one to three months in advance of principal photography. On some films, however, the art department's responsibility was so massive that work began up to a year ahead, such as for *The Razor's Edge* (1946), under the personal supervision of Mr. Day, art director Nathan Jurand, and his assistant, Herman Blumenthal.

Day and Jurand would then besiege the research department with requests for photographs of the

ABOVE: Joseph Urban was considered the foremost authority on stage settings in the world in the early 1930s, inspiring the studio to hire and name the art department building after him. He is seen here in his office with one of his model stage sets.

film's locales in order to create set sketches. Keeping close tabs on rewrites and altered versions of the story, they eliminated sketches that would not appear in the final film. With final approval, four or five set illustrators then went to work translating the sketches into more-detailed "portraits of place." Model makers went to work building miniature sets. Final consultations between the art director, director, producer, photographer, and any others vitally concerned took place before the art director signed off on the completed plans. Then thirty-five prints of the final set drawings were sent out, usually one to each department involved. Some got more—the mill, usually six—depending on the complexity of the work.

There were two secretaries inside in separate offices to greet you—one for the head of the department, who had his office on the first floor along with many of the most important art directors, with an atrium to enjoy. The second was for the department in general. Draftsmen working at long tables could be found on the first floor and in a smaller room on the second floor, along with the offices of more art directors. The first floor also featured a blueprint room, model shop, and insert stage, where the miniatures and all those inserts (like a letter held before the camera for moviegoers to read) were filmed.

Early contributors to Fox's reputation for top-drawer production values were Ben Carre and Duncan Cramer; Gordon Wiles, who won the department's first Oscar for *Transatlantic* (1931); and set decorator Thomas Little, who worked on a record 430 productions over his eighteen-year career at Fox.

Walter Scott's fifty years with Twentieth Century Fox began in 1931, when Oliver Stratten, head of Fox's prop department, hired him on the swing gang (laborers who work for decorators). Scott worked for four years on "B" films on the Western Avenue lot, becoming a set decorator in 1933. He moved to the Pico lot and "A" pictures in 1935 when Darryl Zanuck joined the studio, and became supervising set decorator in 1952. Ultimately, he worked on 370 feature films and 400 episodes of television series and pilots. He earned

LEFT: This is the large room equipped with the rigging system so that the backdrop canvases could be raised or lowered for painting.

BELOW: Many a movie and television show has relied on a painted backdrop to create the illusion of being set somewhere else other than on a soundstage as this cityscape demonstrates. Here grips pull the massive backdrop out of Stage Sixteen, circa the early 1950s.

ABOVE LEFT: The Insert department was located in Bldg. 12.

ABOVE MIDDLE: Turning pages in a book, writing a letter, or signing one's name are all examples of insert work.

ABOVE RIGHT: Creating the title cards and screen credits.

RIGHT: Filming the title cards and credits.

twenty-one Oscar nominations for set decoration, winning the award for *The Robe*, *The King and I*, *The Diary of Anne Frank*, *Fantastic Voyage*, and *Hello, Dolly!* Scott's last credit was for *The Towering Inferno*. As a decorating consultant, he planned and furnished many of the offices at the studio; he also handled arrangements for receptions and special events, including the Carousel Ball, a gala benefit for the Children's Diabetes Foundation of Denver sponsored by Marvin Davis and his wife, Barbara.

In 1944 Lyle Wheeler was hired as supervising art director, and from 1947 to 1960 he was head of the art department. He received twenty-nine Oscar nominations during his career. Jack Martin Smith then took over the department.

Credit many of those incredibly designed musical numbers, from *Delicious* (1931) to *Gentlemen Prefer Blondes* (1953), to the able Joseph Wright. He began by working closely with the dance and musical directors and then submitting a working sketch to the cinematographer to see if it was practical. Then, especially when the film was in Technicolor, he consulted the appropriate expert in the wardrobe department to ensure a harmonious blending of wardrobe and set design. The giant, foot-tapping mechanical dummy in *The Dolly Sisters* (1945) and backgrounds for *Mother Wore Tights* (1947) were Wright creations.

Career highlights for art director and production designer John DeCuir, who came to Fox in 1949, include *Three Coins in the Fountain* (1954), *Daddy Long Legs* (1955), *The King and I* (shared with Wheeler in 1956), *Island in the Sun* (1957), *South Pacific* (1958), *Cleopatra* (1963), *The Agony*

and the Ecstasy (1965), and *The Other Side of Midnight* (1977). "My father called him the city planner," recalls Tom Mankiewicz, "because Johnny thought big. He was brilliant. For *Cleopatra* he built a Roman Forum that was three times the size of the original."

Boris Leven, a Russian immigrant, was a student at New York's Beaux Arts School of Design before he came to work here in 1937. Of Leven's work on location in Taiwan for *The Sand Pebbles* (1966), Richard Crenna recalled, "It was amazing! As far as the eye could see Boris Leven had recreated Shanghai in 1926. I turned to 'Dickie' Attenborough and said, 'Dickie, we're in a *movie*!'"

ABOVE LEFT: This distinctive courtroom set was witness to several important cinematic trials including the one in *The Black Swan* (1942) and in *Leave Her to Heaven* (1945).

ABOVE MIDDLE: This five-star hotel room with French boiserie paneling hosted many guests throughout the years including Cary Grant, Jayne Mansfield, Jane Wyman, and Clifton Webb. This is how it appeared when Tommy Sands stayed here in *Sing, Boy, Sing* (1958).

ABOVE RIGHT: The elegant staircase from the Borst home in D*rums Along the Mohawk* (1939) was incorporated into many other movie homes.

Special Effects Department

The sign on the door of the most secret department in any Hollywood studio reads "Special Effects." What goes on behind that door, where a corps of artists and cameramen work, is strictly hush-hush.

—Los Angeles Times, *1944*

For generations of Fox employees, the eastern end of this building was known as the "Sersen department" for its founder Fred Sersen, a veteran

of over 225 films. From a one-man operation at Western Avenue beginning in 1918, he built the special effects department that peaked at sixty staff members over his thirty-four-year career. Among that talent were artists of matte work (Emil Kosa, Emil Kosa Jr., Clyde Scott), glass shots (Chris Von Schneidau), miniatures (Ralph Hammeras, Lee Le Blanc), camerawork (Bill Albert, Bill Abbott, Al Irving), scenic backgrounds (George Hamilton, Lee Cox, Otto Schroeter, Bill Lobberegt), trick shots (Sy Bartlett), photo finishing (J. B. Allin), and cutting (Wally White). There was also his assistant Ray Kellogg and department electrician Jack McEvoy and grip Charlie Hoffman. A key developer of glass

and matte shots to replace actual locales, Sersen and E. H. Hansen won Oscars for best special effects the first year the category was introduced for *The Rains Came* (1939).

The process began with Sersen reviewing each script for necessary work, sketching it out in continuity, and then discussing it with the producer and director. If everyone agreed he set a prospective cost to be approved for the film's budget. Then the scenes were photographed, usually a combination of the actors on set, second unit, and/or miniatures. Then this department put it all together, utilizing a combination of matte shots, double-printing, and scenic background paintings.

ABOVE LEFT: Not all the Art Department's creations were necessarily beautiful.

ABOVE MIDDLE: A modern hotel lobby from *Charlie Chan's Murder Cruise* (1940).

ABOVE RIGHT: The interior of the spaceship for *The Day the Earth Stood Still* (1951).

Beginning in 1957, L. B. Abbott had an extraordinary run as head of the special effects department. Joe Musso, who started here doing conceptual artwork and storyboards for *The Blue Max* (1966), recalled a bit of building lore that took place on the insert stage and miniature tank. In an attempt to get the iguana to "act" properly with a lizard for their scenes in *Journey to the Center of the Earth* (1959)—when all they wanted to do was nap under the warm lights—one of the special effects men twisted its tail. The result was much more than anticipated. It jumped out of the tank, crawled through the doorway that led into the art department, and surprised the draftsmen with its hideous cinematic appendages.

Musso recalled that the department changed forever after their work on *Tora! Tora! Tora!* (1970), with the end of the Zanuck era. The lot had suffered through the transfer of power before when William Fox was forced out, but this time it was fatal to many of the studio's departments. Ed Hutson, who came into the art department in 1957 as a clerk in the scene dock section, and worked his way up to managing it in the 1970s, recalled that the special effects department was closed, and the art department—at the time, they were working on *Emperor of the North* (1973)—moved across Olympic Boulevard to Bldg. 38 on the North Lot, virtually demoted in stature. The department's ancillary bungalows between the Urban Building and Stage Nine were torn down. All the beautiful conceptual paintings artists had done through the years at the studio, once carefully cataloged in a room here, were stolen. Fortunately, the painted scenic backings from decades of Fox films were given to John Cokely, who worked in that division. He formed J. C. Backings to rent them out. Fox, of course, became a regular

customer. Eventually his company moved to the Sony Studios lot (the former MGM studio), where they continue to be used to this day.

The art department later moved into the fourth floor of Bldg. 99, specially designed for them, but were then demoted again to the west end of the Zanuck Theatre, and, finally, to the first floor of Bldg. 89, where it stayed until it was closed in 2006. After they left this building it was renovated into administrative offices. Then, in 2014, it was completely gutted, the backdrop rigging was finally removed, and windows were added to the south wall for new offices for the producers of *Glee* (2009–15). The building is also used by New Regency Productions, the feature-film arm of Regency Enterprises that, in combination with Regency Television (a joint venture with Fox Television), forms Regency Enterprises, founded by Arnon Milchan and Joseph P. Grace. Interestingly, Martin Scorsese's only Fox film, *The King of Comedy* (1982), shot in New York, was Arnon Milchan's first film as producer.

TOP RIGHT: Building 78 as it appeared in 2015.

MIDDLE RIGHT: For decades, the heads of every department on the lot would meet daily in this conference room to discuss each film in production. This photo was taken during the production of *Valley of the Dolls* (1967). The cameraman seen at right is taking footage for a Jacqueline Susann TV special.

BOTTOM: Ansel Elgort and Shailene Woodley recreate their on-screen kiss from *The Fault in Our Stars* (2014) on the bench installed behind Bldg 78 to commemorate the film.

BLDG. 78: THE PRODUCTION BUNGALOW (1920)

Few buildings on the lot are as historically important as this one. Beginning his Fox career as a clerk for the Box Office Attractions Company, Sol M. Wurtzel was promoted as stenographer to Charles Levin, secretary of Fox Theaters, and then as private secretary to William Fox in 1915. Two years later Fox entrusted him with the role of superintendent of West Coast production, headquartered at the Western Avenue Studio. He survived further company shakeups and thrived through the Twentieth Century Fox merger, for twenty-eight years. This, his original office at the Western Avenue Studio, was relocated to the lot in 1932 when he built another. The bungalow was moved here after Bldg. 88 was erected as the adjoining "production bungalow" during the Zanuck era. The heads of all studio departments (approximately thirty persons) met here to discuss current film—and, later, television—projects at 11:30 a.m. each morning, chaired by the assistant head of studio production.

The bungalow served another crucial purpose in 1962, when Richard Zanuck closed down the lot and operated from here for six months. Elizabeth Gabler, head of Fox 2000, currently has her offices here. Behind the bungalow is a trophy from one of her biggest successes, *The Fault in Our Stars* (2014). It is a bench, similar to the one used in Amsterdam for a key sequence with stars Shailene Woodley and Ansel Elgort. The actors showed up to replay that scene as part of a dedication ceremony. The plaque on the bench reads:

Some infinities are bigger than other infinities
The Fault in Our Stars
Dedicated to our Fault fanatics & their little infinities
September 16, 2014

STAGE TEN (1937)

A quick look at Bldg. 78 and the lot in its heyday can be seen as Deborah Kerr emerges from this stage as Hollywood columnist Sheilah Graham for *Beloved Infidel* (1959).

Among the starry passenger list for *The Love Boat* (1977–86), filmed here and on other stages on the lot, Gavin MacLeod (Captain Stubing) remembers Tom Hanks as the most promising of the young actors featured on the show. The forty-two-year-old *Pacific Princess* (one of two actual ships primarily featured in the show) was decommissioned in 2008, and finally scrapped in Turkey in 2013.

Bruce Willis and Cybill Shepherd made *Moonlighting* here, produced by Glenn Gordon Caron. Willis turned down *Die Hard* (1988) the first time because of his commitment to this show. Then when his costar got pregnant, he suddenly had eleven weeks in which to make it

Stages Ten and Seventeen remain in use as versatile "swing stages" for the use of any Fox TV show. A mural celebrating *The Seven Year Itch* (1955) is painted on the north side of this stage. These murals from classic Fox films, by billboard experts Eller Media Co., were first commissioned beginning in 1997.

BOTTOM LEFT: The north side of Stage Ten bears a mural of Marilyn Monroe and Tom Ewell from *The Seven Year Itch* (1955). "Dolly" Street can be seen at the left and Bldg. 12 and Bldg. 78 can be seen at right.

BOTTOM RIGHT: From left to right Herbert Rudley, Karin Booth, and Deborah Kerr as columnist Sheilah Graham in *Beloved Infidel* (1959).

RIGHT: Believed to be the earliest photo of Marilyn Monroe on the lot, it was approved by the MPAA on October 25, 1946 just two months after Marilyn's contract started. Here she is eating lunch in the Café de Paris with Jean Peters who is in costume for her role in *Captain from Castile* (1947).

Marilyn Monroe on the Lot

I wanted so much to do something right in my art when so much in my life was going bad . . .
My one desire is to do my best, the best that I can from the moment the camera starts until it stops.
That moment I want to be perfect, as perfect as I can make it . . . Lee [Strasberg] says I have to start
with myself, and I say, "With me?" Well, I'm not so important! Who does he think I am, Marilyn
Monroe or something?

—Marilyn Monroe

New England Street

"I used to think as I looked out on the Hollywood night, 'There must be thousands of girls sitting alone like me, dreaming of becoming a movie star. But I'm not going to worry about them. I'm dreaming the hardest.'" Those dreams and that drive got Norma Jeane Mortenson a six-month contract on August 24, 1946, as Marilyn Monroe—a name she put together with the studio's director of casting, Ben Lyon—and a role in *Scudda Hoo! Scudda Hay!* (1948). Her scene here, coming down the church steps and greeting June Haver, is all that survived the cutting-room floor.

Stage Eleven

Marilyn Monroe's first important performance in *All about Eve* (1950) on this stage earned her a seven-year contract.

Bldg. 58: The Portrait Studio

Harry Brand launched his largest publicity campaign to date to make Monroe a star by distributing more than three thousand black-and-white stills to newspapers that first year. Because the star had a special rapport with still photographers, displaying none of the anxieties that plagued her film career, this was a special haven for her.

Bldg. 57: The Commissary

Like all young stars proud to bring family to see the lot, Marilyn Monroe invited half sister Berniece Baker Miracle to see her screen test and eat here in 1946. Years later, on her way to the commissary, she met Elia Kazan and Arthur Miller standing by Stage Eight. When Miller, who married Monroe (1956–61), refused to name names to the House Un-American Activities Committee in June

ABOVE: Marilyn poses in front of the barn on the King Farm on the backlot.

ABOVE LEFT: Marilyn on Old French Street on the backlot.

ABOVE RIGHT: Marilyn with Chicago Lake behind her.

1956, Marilyn stood by him at great peril to her career. Miller returned the favor when Jerry Wald asked him to contribute to the screenplay of *Let's Make Love* (1960) as a supportive measure. Miller received an Oscar nomination in 1996 for the Fox adaptation of his masterpiece, *The Crucible* (1996).

BLDG. 52: THE HALL OF MUSIC

The building was used as a theater in the opening sequence of *As Young as You Feel* (1951), marking Monroe's first credit above the title. Studio publicists got her on the cover of *Life* magazine for the first time in the spring of 1952. *Time* dubbed her

"a saucy, hip-swinging, [five-foot-five-and-a-half-inch] personality who has brought back to the movies the kind of unbridled sex appeal that has been missing since the days of Clara Bow and Jean Harlow."

STAGE FIVE

The star-making scene in *Niagara* (1953), when Marilyn Monroe emerged from Cabin B of the Rainbow Cabins set in a hot pink dress designed by Dorothy Jeakins, was directed here by Henry Hathaway. She dazzles the crowd singing "Kiss" (recorded live on the set), written for her by Lionel Newman and Haven Gillespie. Hathaway was so impressed that he wanted to direct her in a new

RIGHT: Marilyn arrived late at this cocktail party for the Fox Salesmen Convention and succeeded in upstaging every other major star in attendance. It was held at the Café de Paris on June 14, 1951.

FAR RIGHT: Marilyn at the bottom of the staircase for *All About Eve* (1950), with George Sanders behind her, Gary Merrill on the left, and director Joseph Mankiewicz talking to Bette Davis at the top of the staircase.

BOTTOM: The hot pink dress Marilyn wore in *Niagara* (1953) photographed in the Women's Wardrobe building.

version of *Of Human Bondage*, costarring Montgomery Clift. Zanuck said no.

STAGE ONE

Marilyn Monroe got the career-defining role of Lorelei Lee in *Gentlemen Prefer Blondes* (1953) because of timing—Betty Grable, the star for whom the property was purchased, had slipped out of the top-ten after a decade—and the enthusiastic support of Jule Styne, the composer of the Broadway musical with Leo Robin. Her signature performance of "Diamonds Are a Girl's Best Friend," recorded here and filmed on Stage Sixteen, is a Hollywood classic. Frequent teacher, collaborator and friend Lionel Newman recalled that it took eleven takes before she was satisfied with the recording. Four days after completing the film Monroe began work on *How to Marry a Millionaire* (1953), offering movie buffs the rare opportunity to

Marilyn prepares to perform "Diamond's Are a Girl's Best Friend" for *Gentlemen Prefer Blondes* (1953).

Marilyn Monroe, Betty Grable and Lauren Bacall dream of millionaires on the balcony of their apartment on Stage Fourteen for *How to Marry a Millionaire* (1953).

view Alfred Newman conducting his signature piece, "Street Scene," with the augmented studio orchestra.

STAGE FOURTEEN

How to Marry a Millionaire (1953), refashioned by Nunnally Johnson from Betty Grable's *Moon Over Miami* (1941), is a great example of how much of a Fox film could be shot on one soundstage, including the penthouse set, where the characters played by Lauren Bacall, Betty Grable, and Marilyn Monroe live. Grable allayed fears that she and her intended replacement would not get along by shaking Monroe's hand that first day and saying: "Honey, I've had it. Go get yours. It's your turn now."

Monroe could certainly relate to playing a near-sighted model terrified of being seen wearing glasses. "She was so nearsighted that she could hardly see without them," recalled sister-in-law June DiMaggio. " 'I only wear them when I want to see,' she'd tell us laughingly. Her sunglasses were prescription lenses, too, so she could keep them on and maintain her image."

THE CYCLORAMA

For *River of No Return* (1954), Marilyn Monroe won praise from chief of special effects Paul Wurtzel as she rocked and rolled on the raft in front of a process screen here with Robert Mitchum and young Tommy Rettig. By now Monroe was the most

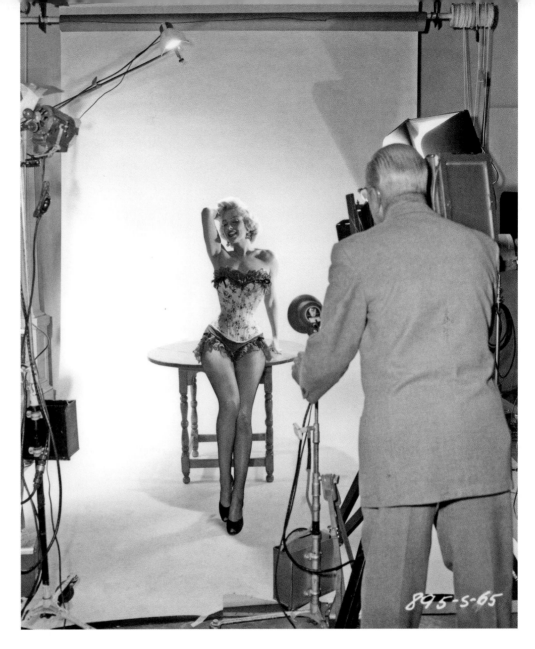

ABOVE: A photo shoot in the Portrait Studio (Bldg 58) for *River of No Return* (1954).

TOP: One of the hundreds of portraits taken of Marilyn, this one (#F999-S-364) became particularly famous when it was used by Andy Warhol for his silkscreen prints.

ABOVE: A wardrobe test for the famous dress in *The Seven Year Itch* (1955).

important star on the lot, earning more than any other actor. Taking advantage of a loophole in her contract, she left the lot to improve her acting skills at New York's Actors Studio, and came back to the studio with new coach Paula Strasberg.

Jane Fonda recalled that she was inspired to become an actress when the Strasbergs moved in next door and she befriended Paula's daughter Susan. Susan suggested that Jane enroll in her father's classes, and she did. In turn, Meryl Streep was grateful for Jane's support during the making of *Julia* (1977). "She took me by the hand into the world of movies!" she said.

BLDG. 86: STARS' DRESSING ROOMS

Terry Moore recalled that Marilyn Monroe and Jane Russell had suites here for *Gentlemen Prefer Blondes* (1953). She frequently heard Russell call down the hallway: "Come on, kid, let's go, we're late!" Monroe moved into the ground-floor suite M in the southeast corner of the building with the production of *There's No Business Like Show Business* (1954), when Betty Grable moved out. Friends knew Marilyn was in by the lingering scent of Chanel No. 5—including Grable, whose equanimity and ability to roll with the punches must have been a marvel to Monroe. Ironically, when Monroe turned down Nunnally Johnson's *How to Be Very, Very Popular* (1955)—a part Johnson had based on his own

experiences with her—Grable came back to make that one last film for Fox.

Like most Fox stars Marilyn Monroe was prepared for public events here, as with the premiere of *How to Marry a Millionaire*. Hairdresser Gladys Rasmussen and makeup man Alan Snyder met her early in the afternoon for what amounted to a six-hour star treatment, with select members of the press. Two ladies from the wardrobe department arrived with her gown, shoes, and furs, and a messenger boy delivered borrowed jewelry.

When Monroe returned to the lot in 1962 to make *Something's Got to Give*, she could frequently be found in dressing room M with Paula Strasberg, who coached her in her last five films.

STAGE NINE

When Monroe's agent Charles Feldman and director Billy Wilder partnered to purchase George Axelrod's play, *The Seven Year Itch*, Harry Brand unleashed one of his greatest publicity stunts. He informed the media that Marilyn Monroe was going to New York to shoot scenes for the movie in September of 1954. The Fox team shot fifteen takes of the iconic scene of Monroe's skirt flying up over a subway vent to roars of approval from the crowd gathered at the corner of Lexington Avenue and Fifty-First Street. Billy Wilder had the street and scene re-created here for the movie. Paul Wurtzel always considered it a career highlight that he was the

one who operated the fan beneath that subway grate.

Axelrod utilized his experience working with Marilyn Monroe to write another Broadway hit, *Will Success Spoil Rock Hunter?*—bringing Jayne Mansfield to prominence—before writing the screenplay for Monroe's next film, *Bus Stop. The Seven Year Itch* was the biggest hit of the year for Fox, ensuring that all of her demands for a new seven-year, four-picture contract were met, including recognition of her own Marilyn Monroe Productions. She signed it on December 31, 1955.

ABOVE LEFT: Tom Ewell and Marilyn Monroe walk out of the movie theatre in New York for the famous skirt-blowing sequence for *The Seven Year Itch* (1955).

ABOVE RIGHT: Here is a still taken in New York.

LEFT: And here is a still of the recreated set on Stage Nine. Note that the Fleurette Hats store has become Fleurette Jewelry.

BLDG. 59: WOMEN'S WARDROBE

By designing Marilyn Monroe's pink gown for *Gentlemen Prefer Blondes* (1953), her Western wardrobe for *River of No Return* (1954), and the white pleated halter dress for *The Seven Year Itch* (1955), William Travilla becomes another close friend of hers.

STAGE ELEVEN

On this stage Marilyn Monroe performed "My Heart Belongs to Daddy," "Incurably Romantic," "Let's Make Love," and "Specialization" for Jerry Wald's *Let's Make Love* (1960), directed by George Cukor.

"When she arrived, everybody smartened up, as if her presence was the light that fell on everyone," recalled costar Frankie Vaughan.

PICO BOULEVARD ENTRANCE:

The studio depended on the guard here to clock in stars like Marilyn Monroe as they entered the studio. In this way a record was made of her consistent tardiness. Exasperated studio lawyer Frank Ferguson complained: "[E]ach calendar year seems to end in a crisis which has been created by this girl."

"She is not malicious," observed Jerry Wald. "She is not temperamental. She is a star—a self-illuminating body, an original, a legend. You hire a legend and it's going to cost you dough."

ABOVE: Marilyn and her co-star Don Murray at the south end of the Stars' Dressing Rooms Building during the filming of *Bus Stop* (1956). The windows on the first floor belonged to Marilyn's suite.

STAGE FOURTEEN

Joshua Logan directed Marilyn Monroe's scenes in the Blue Dragon Café here, including her performance of "That Old Black Magic," for *Bus Stop* (1956).

The interior and exterior of the Arden home was built here for Monroe's thirtieth film, *Something's Got to Give*. It was her last film under contract. By the time it was set to begin, on April 23, 1962, she had become Fox's most bankable star since Shirley Temple, having earned over $200 million for the studio.

On May 17, 1962, there was a delay when Monroe boarded the helicopter that whisked her from the lot to LAX to fly to New York's Madison Square Garden to make a memorable appearance at President John F. Kennedy's birthday party. Upon her return she delighted the press by modeling and swimming nude poolside here on May 23. The resulting photos appeared on more than seventy magazine covers in thirty-two countries.

Cast and crew celebrated Monroe's thirty-sixth birthday after work on Friday, June 1. When she called out with illness for the seventeenth time on Monday, June 4, production shut down. On June 8 she was officially fired by the studio, and on June 11, the picture was officially suspended.

Monroe rallied, asked the cast back, requested that Jean Negulesco replace Cukor, and signed a new $1 million, two-picture contract on August 1.

ABOVE LEFT: The *Something's Got to Give* set on Stage Fourteen where Marilyn did her nude bathing scene was a recreation of director George Cukor's own home.

ABOVE RIGHT: Marilyn lounges in Dressing Room "M" in Building 86 with Paula Strasberg. The couch placed there when Joan Crawford used the room in the 1940s is still in evidence in 1962. The porthole window above Marilyn's head is no longer there: it was removed when the room was split into two offices.

On August 5 she was discovered dead at home from a drug overdose.

BLDG. 38: MAKEUP AND HAIRDRESSING DEPARTMENT

During the fifteen-year period when Allan "Whitey" Snyder applied her makeup here, Monroe had exacted a promise from him: If something ever happened to her, she wanted him to make her up that final time. Snyder fulfilled his promise at the Westwood Village Mortuary on Tuesday, August 7, 1962.

After her death Darryl Zanuck said, "I disagreed and fought with her on many occasions, but we were always personal friends. Hollywood suffered a genuine loss as, in spite of her temperament, which sometimes flared to conceal her basic shyness, she never let the public down."

The exterior of Stage Eleven which is connected to Stage Ten on the north side. That is Bldg. 12 in the distance, and Bldg. 99 is to the left.

STAGE
11

STAGE ELEVEN (1937)

When Alice Faye bowed out of *Roxie Hart* (1942), Darryl Zanuck brought old friend Ginger Rogers to Fox to make the film on various studio soundstages, including this one, initiating the first of several delightful collaborations between star and studio. The working title of the film—written and produced by Nunnally Johnson, based on Maurine Watkins's play—was *Chicago*. Choreographer and director Bob Fosse borrowed it for his Broadway musical version of the story that opened in the summer of 1975. Fosse made one of its songs, "All That Jazz," the title of his autobiographical Fox film in 1979.

A Letter to Three Wives (1948) and *All About Eve* (1950) remain classic examples of studio collaboration in the Zanuck era. When Mankiewicz floundered with his script for *A Letter to Four Wives*, Darryl Zanuck suggested he cut the fourth wife (to be played by Anne Baxter), eliminating sixty pages. Watch for the scene shot here during the summer of 1948, when Linda Darnell observes the portrait of Addie Ross (Celeste Holm) in a silver frame in Porter Hollingsway's (Paul Douglas) library. Her disgust is genuine. She is looking at a photograph of Otto Preminger. Director Joseph Mankiewicz placed it there on purpose to get just such a reaction, well aware of her troubles with the ill-fated *Forever Amber* (1947).

For *Eve*, this was Margo Channing's (Bette Davis) apartment, famous for the actress's

deathless line: "Fasten your seat belts; it's going to be a bumpy night!" Together Zanuck and Mankiewicz gathered the cast. Mankiewicz considered Susan Hayward and Broadway star Gertrude Lawrence for Margo. Lawrence chose to pursue Rodgers and Hammerstein instead, to write a musical version of Fox's own *Anna and the King of Siam* (1946) for her. They acquiesced with *The King and I* on Broadway. Lawrence would later be portrayed by Julie Andrews in *Star!* (1968). Zanuck preferred Claudette Colbert for the part and she was signed,

but bowed out only a few weeks before shooting when she injured her back on the lot, making *Three Came Home* (1950). Bette Davis then got the part. When Jeanne Crain's pregnancy ruled her out as Eve, Anne Baxter was chosen.

"We had so much fun," recalled Anne Baxter of *Eve*. "We were supposed to be at each other's throats. It was nothing like that, and Bette fell madly in love with [costar] Gary Merrill. On top of everything else, love was in bloom. It was marvelous." Again Zanuck provided the editing, both to the script and in the projection room, that made a great film even better.

After meeting at the amusement park on Stage Five as Billy Bigelow and Julie Jordan, Gordon MacRae and Shirley Jones performed the classic "If I Loved You" for *Carousel* (1956) here. The musical sequences during the clambake were on Stage Fifteen, the ballet on Stage Five, and Jones and Claramae Turner sang "You'll Never Walk Alone" at the harbor set on Chicago Lake. Cary Grant and Deborah Kerr drew further tears for that famous final scene made here for *An Affair to Remember* (1957), and Bette Midler delivered her powerhouse performance for *The Rose* (1979) here too. The film's title song was named one of top 100 movie songs by the American Film Institute, and earned songwriter Amanda McBroom a Golden Globe, and Midler a Grammy. Director Mark Rydell would work with Bette Midler again in their musical salute to World War II, *For the Boys* (1991).

BOTTOM LEFT: Director Leo McCarey gives some final instructions to Cary Grant and Deborah Kerr as they prepare for the classic ending for *An Affair to Remember* (1957).

BOTTOM RIGHT: Bette Midler in *The Rose* (1979).

An overhead shot of "The Lady In The Tutti Frutti Hat" sequence from *The Gang's All Here* (1943), choreographed by Busby Berkeley.

LEFT: A view of Stages Fourteen, Fifteen, and Sixteen looking west down First Street, circa 1962.

STAGE FOURTEEN (1936)

At Warner Bros. Darryl Zanuck had written a screenplay for Fanny Brice, entitled *My Man* (1928). When he had *Rose of Washington Square* (1939) produced here, Brice and Nicky Arnstein, who recognized the thinly veiled biography of their romance, sued the studio and settled out of court. Zanuck, however, got what he wanted: several months of great publicity for one of Alice Faye's best musicals.

Contributing to Darryl Zanuck's success in surpassing all prior Hollywood disaster films with *The Rains Came* (1939) was a rich screenplay by Philip Dunne, a cast of the rank of Tyrone Power and Myrna Loy, and the investment of a water tank here. The tank was also used to great effect in *The Black Swan* (1942), *Moontide* (1942), *The Snake Pit* (1948), and *Titanic* (1953). *Moontide* star Ida Lupino was back here, playing an aging actress, in an episode of *Charlie's Angels* ("I Will Be Remembered," 1977) that offers great views of the lot.

The tank was covered over for two of the most famous Fox film sets: the courtroom to decide whether Santa Claus existed for *Miracle on 34th Street* (1947) and the three-story building with its hidden attic for George Stevens' *The Diary of Anne*

ABOVE LEFT: The large tank as used in *Moontide* (1941).

ABOVE RIGHT: Fred Gailey (John Payne) defended Kris Kringle (Edmund Gwenn) on Stage Fourteen in *Miracle on 34th Street* (1947).

Frank (1959). Joseph Schildkraut, Shelley Winters, Gusti Huber, Ed Wynn, Lou Jacobi, Richard Beymer—and Millie Perkins and Diane Baker in their Fox debuts—were the inhabitants of that attic. Otto Frank, the sole survivor of those hidden away from Nazi persecution, visited the studio and the set. He had been an active collaborator in bringing the play and film to life from his daughter's diary. Nearly forty years after helping his father with the film, George Stevens Jr. returned to Fox as executive producer for *The Thin Red Line* (1998). The Frank home was later the setting for another Fox classic *The Fault in Our Stars* (2014).

Only the extraordinary box-office power of Doris Day could turn the lights of this stage back on after they were darkened over the sets of

Something's Got to Give with the tragic death of Marilyn Monroe. The re-vamped *Move Over, Darling* (1963) earned more than any recent Fox film save *The Longest Day* (1962). Interestingly, Day's last film for the studio, *Caprice* (1967), was its last in CinemaScope. The studio followed the rest of the industry and began using the superior Panavision process. Leon Shamroy, who shot the first (*The Robe*) and the last of them makes an appearance in the film.

The *Hello, Dolly!* (1969) company—including Barbra Streisand and Louis Armstrong (in his final film appearance)—spent a month perfecting the "Hello, Dolly" musical number on the magnificent $375,000 four-tiered Harmonia Gardens restaurant set, designed by John DeCuir, and featuring faux stained glass, marble fountains, and the grandest staircase of them all. It all went dramatically to ruin as the "cathedral interior" for *Beneath the Planet of the Apes* (1970) discovered by James Franciscus. By the time *Escape from the Planet of the Apes* (1971) was made, the apes were no longer restricted to soundstages, but roamed the lot in the opening sequence. They can be seen conquering Cenury City under the leadership of Roddy McDowall in *Conquest of the Planet of the Apes* (1972).

The grandson of J. Gordon Edwards, Blake Edwards appeared on these stages first as an actor in the early 1940s and then as director of films like *The Man Who Loved Women* (1983, Columbia) that he made here starring his wife Julie Andrews as Burt Reynolds's psychoanalyst.

Although the exterior and lobby of the Fox Plaza Tower was used as the Nakatomi Corporation Plaza in the opening scenes of *Die Hard* (1988), the enormous atrium on the thirtieth floor was a set here. The

This view of the massive set for *The Diary of Anne Frank* (1959) includes most of the principal cast members in the top left.

air-traffic control tower and miniature runways were also located here for the sequel, *Die Hard 2* (1990).

Sandra Bullock, who made her Fox debut in *Love Potion #9* (1992), became a star in the thrilling bus ride *Speed* (1994) that used this stage for its opening elevator-rescue sequence. Among those involved in casting her was Jan de Bont, who called upon his own eerie experience getting stuck in an elevator on the fortieth floor of the Fox Plaza building during the making of *Die Hard* to direct that scene. De Bont was later crucial in bringing Steven Spielberg's *Minority Report* (2002) to Fox, originally as director, and then as producer, which also used this stage.

The studio's tradition of showcasing action stars and their stunt work stretches all the way back to the uniquely elaborate thrills of Tom Mix's pictures, and pioneers like Harvey Perry and John Weld and even Mrs. Buck Jones. The triumph of the memorable moments has been tempered only by

ABOVE LEFT: Director George Stevens, left, and Millie Perkins meet Otto Frank on the set of *The Diary of Anne Frank* (1959).

ABOVE: Ellen (Doris Day) tries to reconnect with her children in *Move Over, Darling* (1963).

LEFT: Steve McQueen steps into his Corvette between Stages Fourteen and Fifteen, in front of his trailer, during the filming of *The Sand Pebbles* (1966). Many consider his performance the finest in his storied career.

RIGHT: Barbra Streisand sings the title song on the staircase of the Harmonia Gardens restaurant set for *Hello, Dolly!* (1969).

BOTTOM LEFT: That same staircase ended up as a set for *Beneath the Planet of the Apes* (1971).

BOTTOM RIGHT: Clint Ritchie, left, jokes with director Roger Corman during the filming of *The St. Valentine's Day Massacre* (1967). This picture was taken on Stage Fifteen on the set of Al Capone's home (the repurposed main foyer from *The Sound of Music* (1965).

the tragedies incurred, such as the death of stunt flier Lt. Ormer Locklear during the making of *The Skywayman* (1920). There is not likely to be a better Fox stunt man theme song summing it all up than the one in Glen A. Larson's tongue-in-cheek tribute to *The Fall Guy* (1981–1986).

Robin Williams returned to series television after thirty-one years to make David E. Kelley's television series *The Crazy Ones* (2013) here, with Sarah Michelle Gellar. It would be his last. Shortly after the show was canceled Williams took his own life in August of 2014. He left behind a legacy that includes the classic *Mrs. Doubtfire* (1993).

RIGHT: The extravaganza of "Before the Parade Passes By." This view is looking north along Avenue of the Palms. The New Executive Building (Bldg. 100) now stands where the elevated train and station are located.

FAR RIGHT: Paul Newman, Robert Redford, and Katharine Ross pose on New York Street during the filming of *Butch Cassidy and the Sundance Kid* (1969).

New York Street ("Dolly" Street)

When you came through the gate to your office, you were in your own kingdom. You were protected by your own police, and your needs were taken care of down to your home. In fact, the studio was your home. Your secretary brought her own coffeepot when she was assigned to you, and she worked on a seniority system. Dick and I planted the seeds for others. The bones are still at Fox. The Hello, Dolly! *set is still standing, being slowly replaced by office skyscrapers.*

—David Brown, production executive

By the spring of 1968 production designer John DeCuir—and practically every set decorator at the studio—had transformed fifteen acres of the lot into an elaborate recreation of 14th Street in 1890s New York for *Hello, Dolly!* (1969). There were sixty buildings in all—some ingeniously disguising eleven actual ones. For example, the Administration Building and its forecourt were transformed into the Harmonia Gardens and New York Public Library. Horse-drawn trolleys ran along the streets, while a steam engine train ran along 600 feet of elevated track. This kind of never-again-to-be-replicated spectacle resulted in breathtaking musical numbers like "Dancing" and the most lavish musical number in film history, "Before the Parade Passes By." But even as the fifth highest grossing film of the year *Hello, Dolly!* did not surmount its production costs, and the set was initially left standing simply

ABOVE: Panorama view of the Fifth Avenue set built for *Hello, Dolly!* (1969). This street is now known as Avenue of the Palms. Bldg. 89 is at the left and Bldg. 88 became the collonade entrance to the Harmonia Gardens at right. It was one of the most lavish sets ever built in Hollywood. Only the middle section, that was Mulberry Street, still exists.

ABOVE LEFT: New York and California merge at the corner of New York Street with Avenue of the Palms at the right.

ABOVE RIGHT: A trompe l'oeil mural obscures Stage 14 at the end of the street.

RIGHT: In the heart of Fox's version of the Big Apple.

because the studio could not afford to tear it down. Dennis Stanfill considered turning it into an amusement area, but it has become a much better cash cow as a rental. Eventually most of "Dolly Street" made way for studio development, and only Mulberry Street remains in use for television shows (*NYPD Blue, The X-Files, Bones, House, How I Met Your Mother, Weird Loners*), screen tests (*The Three Stooges*, 2012), promotional material (*Die Hard With a Vengeance*), occasional feature filming (*Water for Elephants*), and star-studded company celebrations.

ABOVE LEFT: The episode "Safe Home" with Rick Schroeder, left, Dennis Franz, and Austin Majors, is one of many shot here for *NYPD Blue* (1993-2005). The elephant door to Stage Ten can be seen at right.

ABOVE RIGHT: The Royal Diner where Seeley Booth (David Boreanaz) and Bones Brennan (Emily Deschanel) regularly hang out is not really in Washington, D.C. but here on New York Street as seen in the episode "Blue Line."

BOTTOM: This is the townhouse where Dr. Gregory House (Hugh Laurie) lived from 2004-2012 in *House*.

RIGHT: Darryl Zanuck strikes a formal pose in 1941. He is holding *Benjamin Blake* a novel by Edison Marshall that he would adapt into *Son of Fury* (1942) starring Tyrone Power and Gene Tierney.

DARRYL ZANUCK ON THE LOT

"[Darryl Zanuck's] Twentieth Century Fox pictures were an eloquent voice for morality—not in the narrowest sense of that word, but in the general sense that, unlike too many motion pictures today, they emphasized courage, self-reliance, honor, and integrity. These are the classic Victorian virtues, and Zanuck, in spire of the fact that he personally added the 'Twentieth Century' to his studio's name, was essentially a Victorian. The anti-hero, the pimp, the drug pusher, and the cheat found no place in Zanuck's world—or if they did, they got their comeuppance before the final fade-out."

—Philip Dunne, screenwriter

Darryl Zanuck's six-days-a-week schedule began with his arrival at Building 88 between 10:30am and 11am, usually speeding, in a Zanuck green Cadillac. The color, specially made by the studio, dominated his office, the building, the makeup department, studio equipment and trucks and even studio telephones. All morning he dictated studio memos to avoid unnecessary meetings. He wanted Dictaphones everywhere—at home and work—so that he could constantly let loose his creative thoughts and nervous energy. He always had an office boy stationed outside his office to carry his messages.

He took his role as supervisor of all production at Twentieth Century Fox literally. There were the studio's selected synopses of novels, magazine articles, plays and original stories to read. Those he favored—or original ideas of his own—were sent on to Will Hays office for Production Code approval, and if he got that he sent it to a studio writer for a treatment ("never over 25

ABOVE: A young Richard "Dickie" Zanuck at his father's desk in 1938.

pages!") or script outline. Critics who labeled the studio "Nineteenth Century Fox" for his penchant for period films missed the point. Moneymaking nostalgia allowed the mogul to slip in more daring fare like *The Grapes of Wrath* (1940). Then he assigned a producer, usually choosing a few films to make himself. He met with Lew

Schreiber to ensure casting of each picture was made three months in advance so adjustments could be made to the script. The rest of the cast must be gathered and approved six weeks in advance. The production department received a final script three weeks before shooting to break down each pictures' needs including sets, costumes, and special effects and to gather cost estimates for each to ensure it all matched the approved budget of each film. Only then was a director assigned. Zanuck's studio system worked, despite the creative restrictions placed on his artists, by the success and sheer loyalty he engendered."I admired him for his guts and the quality he had of grabbing a headline and generating the speed and enthusiasm all down the line to make a good picture quickly—at this, he was a master and the hardest-working little guy you have ever seen in all your life," offered William Wellman.

Certainly Zanuck's workaholic way-of-life was influenced by the frugal production methods at Warner Bros. He tested his filmmakers to ensure they were competent and working equally hard, and remained confident and enthusiastic about their projects.

"Every assignment would become the greatest picture ever made," recalled Philip Dunne, "and remain so until, in the drafty forecourt of some preview theatre, a subordinate would dejectedly remark: 'Well, we got a great woman's picture.'"

At 1:30pm Zanuck went to lunch at the commissary.

"Darryl swept out of his office, accompanied by the producer or director with whom he'd been conferring or a distinguished guest from 'outside,'" recalled Elia Kazan. "Following him came staff people…it was like the movement of a flotilla of warships. He'd receive the salute of those he passed; everyone he acknowledged with a greeting was proud of it."

"Zanuck had an aide who threw paper balls in the air for him to swing at with his polo mallet while he walked," recalled Ernest Lehman. "One day the man was fired, and the story circulated was that he had struck Darryl out!"

After lunch were story conferences to develop treatments or scripts or further develop an unsatisfactory script.

"Armed with notepads, a troupe of us—producer, director, head of casting, head of production, and others of that ilk—would file into Zanuck's office, a largish room with a huge desk cluttered with mementoes," recalled Richard Fleischer.

"He'd take a script," said Henry Hathaway, "and the first thing he'd do was put a big Z across the front. That's his script forever. And he'd really know it. He'd know a script from lines and scenes and everything and he'd make all his marks. Molly [Mandaville] was Zanuck's girl Friday. She sat in on every story conference that he ever had and made notes about what everybody said about everything and then typed it up.

FAR LEFT: Director Elia Kazan, Albert Dekker, and Gregory Peck meet in Zanuck's office to discuss the production of the controversial *Gentleman's Agreement* (1947). The film was among those that Zanuck made to champion social, religious, and racial tolerance in films like *The Grapes of Wrath* (1940), *Brigham Young* (1940), and *Pinky* (1949).

LEFT: Almost every day would end with Darryl Zanuck viewing the daily rushes.

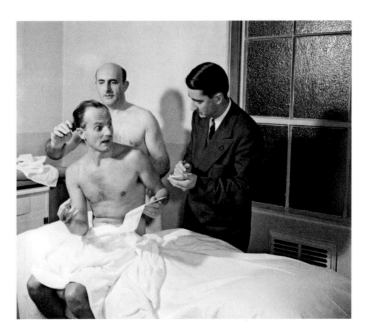

BOTTOM LEFT: Darryl Zanuck's reserved parking spot on Avenue D by Bldg. 88. His office suite was just left of the entrance door on the first floor.

BOTTOM RIGHT: Zanuck was always working even when relaxing in his private spa in the basement of Bldg. 88. Here he is with Sam Silver, the studio's barber and an assistant.

She was terrific. She knew everything."

"He would pace up in down between the interconnecting rooms of his office talking about what he liked," said screenwriter Ernest Lehman, "what he didn't like, and what he wanted you to do." "I had an assistant who complained when Zanuck got very enthusiastic when he'd think of a love scene," recalled Nunnally Johnson. "My assistant, who happened to be rather pretty, said, 'I wish he would stop casting me as the girl.'"

"The Zanuck story conferences are legendary, the source of anecdotes which are still told and retold," observed Philip Dunne. "The conference notes, which reached writer and producer a day or two after the conference, were our Holy Writ. They included almost everything that had been said at the conference and underlined the firm decisions which had been reached, but nothing was meant to be taken literally."

From these conferences would emerge the scripts that were sent along with many notes to the producers the next morning as well as memos to other departments about casting, the design of sets, and the final distribution of films. Known for his practical jokes Darryl once delighted in placing a trained ape into his executive chair, turning the lights down and summoning a new writer.

"Going to see Zanuck was always an experience," recalled Maureen O'Hara. "His office was an oddly shaped room, oblong, so that you had to walk quite a distance from the door to reach him. As I entered, I could see him, at the other end of the room, seated rigidly behind his expansive desk, position squarely on a raised platform."

At 5:00 pm, he descended to the basement to use his fully-equipped exercise room where he enjoyed four or five rounds with "Fidel," the U.S. bantamweight champion, and then a dip in the swimming pool followed by a massage by Sam Silver. Then he took a nap. He was awake by 7:30 pm for dinner, and then headed to the "Z" screening room to sit in his leather chair and begin screenings with another Dictaphone and a telephone to talk to the cutter in the projection booth. He attributed his editing skill to two mentors: Ralph Dietrich and Ray Enright.

"Once photography was finished on a film, Zanuck maintained a hands-off policy about the editing," recalled Richard Fleischer. "Hands off, that is, until he'd screened the version of the picture that the producer and the director felt was the best they could do. He had the uncanny knack after seeing a film for the first time, of immediately putting his finger on exactly what was wrong with it. Without hesitation he would order new scenes written and put into production. Virtually every movie made at Fox went back to the sound stages for additional scenes."

"He cut, cut, cut," recalled David Brown. "His film philosophy was much like Ernest Hemingway's writing philosophy. In the best of Hemingway's stories, the reader somehow understands what has been left out, and the stories race along with beautiful simplicity. So it was with Zanuck's better pictures."

"My nickname for him was 'Czar of all the rushes,'" recalled Joseph Mankiewicz.

"The seating arrangement for these viewings

was as follows: Zanuck sat in the first row with the director, in this case me...and the editor," recalled Otto Preminger. "Behind us were about a dozen of Zanuck's yes-men."

"After a screening he would stand up and he would pace back and forth talking about the film," recalled William Reynolds, "always with a cigar. He could go through it practically frame-by-frame after seeing it once. It was remarkable."

Examples of his skill proliferate. Although the contentious nature of Zanuck's relationship with John Ford is legend, the director ultimately remarked: "Darryl is a genius and I don't use the word lightly. He was head and shoulders above all the other producers."

ABOVE LEFT: Darryl Zanuck, right, goes over a script with his hand-picked successor Buddy Adler.

ABOVE RIGHT: Darryl Zanuck with his wife Virginia and their children Darrilyn, Richard, and Susan.

"He'd run the rushes," recalled Henry Hathaway, "and then he'd look at rough cuts, answer prints, everything, and then when he'd say, 'OK, that's all,' he'd say to me or somebody else that he was going to run a feature and did we want to stay?"

"Most things are decided around here at 3:00 am because Mr. Zanuck works so much at night," said Jeanne Crain. "Very few stars have any say."

"There was little need for him to be on the set," said David Brown, "because his work was done mostly at night, and extensive notes were sent to the director each shooting day, often with comments on every 'take.' Zanuck's philosophy of filmmaking can be summed up in a sentence, his, of course: 'They call them moving pictures because they're supposed to move!'"

"We worked a six-day week, there was no such thing as overtime," recalled Robert Wagner, "and the large board at the studio that contained the shooting schedule for each picture on the lot was rarely altered—if Darryl wanted a movie made in forty days and you fell a little behind, then you could confidently expect to be pulling an all-nighter on that fortieth day because it would, by God, be done in the allotted time."

"Of all the big-boss producers, Darryl was unquestionably the man with the greatest gifts," summed up Orson Welles. "True personal, professional, and artistic gifts for the filmmaking process itself. He began as a writer and in a sense he never stopped functioning as a writer."

Bldg. 88: Old Executive Building (1936)

On June 7, 1937, this three-story executive office building, commissioned by Darryl Zanuck, was officially dedicated. By then, Stages Ten, Eleven, Fourteen, Fifteen, and Sixteen and Bldgs. 31, 32, 86, and 89 were completed as well. The $2.5 million in improvements—including repaving the studio streets and installing lights along them—was a sign that the studio's fortunes were rising from the depths of the Depression. They were paid for largely from Shirley Temple's pictures. In fact, in its early days, fellow child star Dick Moore recalled this building became known as the Temple Building except when Zanuck was within earshot.

Among the traditions Zanuck started here was ordering rotating gold-framed photographs of the studio's ten key stars to be hung in the first-floor reception room. That continues into the twenty-first century, with framed posters and production stills from prominent movies on the walls. Watch for the exterior and reception area in *Dancing in the Dark* (1950).

Reflecting Zanuck's more "hands-on" approach as an executive his four-room connecting office suite (including bedroom and bathroom) was on the first floor in the middle of the west side of the building. Rival studio moguls preferred to be ensconced on upper floors. Although remodeled over the years, Zanuck's offices remain where the head of the studio resides. The private stairs are still there,

RIGHT: The site of Bldg. 88 was originally used to build a modern ocean liner set for the film *So This Is London* (1930).

FAR RIGHT: Original 1930 caption "NOTHING TOO BIG FOR THE FOX-MOVIETONE PRODUCTION *SO THIS IS LONDON,* starring Will Rogers. An exact reproduction of an ocean liner was built at Fox-Movietone City for this production. In the foreground may be seen Charles Clarke, chief cameraman and Director John G. Blystone." Note the oil derricks that can be seen rising on the left.

but Zanuck's basement "health club," including a private barbershop, massage room, steam room, and swimming pool (maintained at 52 degrees) run by friend Sam "the Barber" Silver has been replaced with an executive gym. Watch for Sam as the barber to a movie mogul in *You're My Everything* (1949). The 33-seat "Z" and 33-seat "S" executive screening rooms are still down there named for the two men who used them most: Zanuck and his second-in-command Lew Schreiber. Beginning as a casting director, studio manager Schreiber was well-respected on the lot for his negotiations with actors and labor unions.

The second floor held offices for the producers. Directors and the publicity and marketing departments were on the third floor. Harry Brand, Twentieth Century Fox's first head of publicity (1935–63), was hired by Joe Schenck at United Artists and remained with him at Twentieth Century Pictures Inc., and then here. Supervising as many as seventy movies annually, Brand and his staff also handled publicity for all the Fox stars. When publicist Nathan Dyches optioned *Pinky* (1949), he formed Pomeroy Enterprises, Inc., with Brand to help get it made. When asked who their favorite actor was on the lot, they answered "Victor Mature," who was named an honorary press agent. When Mature asked for his own office, his nameplate temporarily replaced the ladies' room sign. For years

afterwards the ladies using that particular facility fondly dubbed it "The Old Vic."

In 1968 a low-flying, single-engine airplane crashed into the west side of the building, between the second and third floors, killing the pilot. No Fox employees were injured, except for producer Sy Bartlett, who received bruises from being knocked to the ground by the blast. Roland Hill of the art department recalled that the plane hit the building in front of Richard Zanuck's parking space. Zanuck had just left the building for location shooting.

Besides regaining some financial stability for the company, Dennis Stanfill also made important upgrades to the lot, including computerizing the telephone service that had not been updated since its installation in the 1930s. Up until then eighteen female phone operators had manned the system in staggered shifts for fifteen hours a day.

At the northwest corner of the building, in front of the five old payroll windows where employees and extras could line up to get their paychecks, is a crepe myrtle tree commemorating the release of *Avatar* (2009), on the fortieth anniversary of Earth Day on April 22, 2010. At the end of the company's first century of filmmaking the film remains its biggest moneymaker, and re-popularized 3-D movies.

Before the Old Executive Building was built, this was the site of an enormous, full-size ocean liner set built for Will Rogers's *So This Is London*

LEFT: View of Bldg. 88 soon after completion. It was part of a large expansion project that included the construction of new soundstages (note Stage Fourteen has been completed and Stage Fifteen is under construction in the background).

BOTTOM LEFT: Closeup of one of the entrances on the east façade. This is one of the few places where the Twentieth Century Fox logo could actually be seen on the lot.

BOTTOM RIGHT: Bldg. 88 as the airport in *Berlin Correspondent* (1942) with Virginia Gilmore and Dana Andrews trying to escape the Nazis.

RIGHT: One of the job requirements of a contract player was assisting with VIP tours of the lot. Here Marilyn Monroe, exiting the north entrance on the west side of Bldg. 88, accompanies Spyros Skouras during the visit of King Paul and Queen Frederika of Greece in 1953.

FAR RIGHT: The Publicity Department has always been housed in Bldg. 88 where it fulfills requests for stills from Fox movies. All of those photos stored in the filing cabinets and boxes on the wall are now part of the Photo Archive and are safely stored in a huge vault in Bldg. 99.

BOTTOM LEFT: Former contract player Stepin Fetchit, right, is welcomed back to the lot in the lobby of Bldg. 88 on October 31, 1951. The lobby used to feature large portraits of the biggest contract players. From left to right on the wall are William Lundigan, Gene Tierney, and Gregory Peck.

BOTTOM RIGHT: Richard "Dickie" Zanuck got his start in the movie business by selling newspapers and magazines on the lot.

A photo taken looking south down Avenue D during the filming of *To the Shores of Tripoli* (1942). Stage Ten, Bldg. 12, and Bldg. 78 can all be seen. The silver stars on the flag represent Fox employees serving in the armed forces while a gold star represented those who had died in service during World War II.

903-5-7

ABOVE LEFT: Bldg. 88 has served as the set of a hospital in several films including *Shock Treatment* (1964) where it was a mental institution. Carol Lynley, at left, looks on as a scene is filmed with co-star Stuart Whitman, (in third wheelchair from right) in the east parking lot.

ABOVE RIGHT: Marlon Brando on the lot during the making of *Desiree* (1954). That is Bldg. 88 in the background.

(1930) and seen in *Transatlantic* (1932), and, spectacularly afire in *Dante's Inferno* (1935).

Of course the building has been used frequently for films and television. *Shock Treatment* (1964) offers a great look at the building, as well as the original configuration of the two Pico guard shacks. In the second season of *Charlie's Angels*, the Angels walk out the southwest door of this building as a police station while John Forsythe narrates, "But I took them away from all that, and now they work for me. My name is Charlie." During the Alan Ladd Jr. regime, Leonard Goldberg and Jerry Weintraub considered remaking *How to Marry a Millionaire* starring the Angels.

"Holy Cow, Batman! That's a huge umbrella." Many of the exteriors of the *Batman* (1966-68) TV show were shot on the lot. Here Bldg. 88 stood in for the Gotham Missile Corporation in the episode "Fine Feathered Finks."

GOTHAM MISSILE CORPORATION

RIGHT: The south end of Bldg. 88 as it appeared in the mid-1960s before the construction of the *Hello, Dolly!* (1969) street set in 1968 which now obscures this view. Stage Ten, left, can be seen with its mod color scheme. With the construction of Stages Seventeen, Eighteen, and Nineteen, seen at right, there was now enough stage space for film and television productions at the main lot which prompted the sale of the Western Avenue studio.

FAR RIGHT: Lee Grant poses for a wardrobe continuity shot for *Valley of the Dolls* (1967) in the east parking lot.

BOTTOM LEFT: Alan Ladd, Jr. in his office in Bldg. 88.

BOTTOM RIGHT: The main corridor on the first floor of Bldg. 88 decorated with posters and stills of Fox's most famous films. Though updated, the first floor retains its original 1930s configuration while the upper floors have been largely altered.

ABOVE LEFT: The "S" and "Z" screening rooms in the basement of Bldg. 88 in 2015. The lobby features photos of Fox Best Picture winners. Starting at the far end, *Cavalcade* (1933), *How Green Was My Valley* (1941), *Gentleman's Agreement* (1947), *All About Eve* (1950), *The Sound of Music* (1965), *Patton* (1970), and *Chariots of Fire* (1981). More recent winners are on the facing wall.

ABOVE RIGHT: Logo on one of the main doors. Bldg. 100 can be seen in the reflection.

LEFT: Interior of the "Z" screening room.

William Goetz, Darryl Zanuck, and Lew Schreiber stroll in front of Stages Five and Six in 1938.

THE CORPORATE HISTORY PART TWO: THE ZANUCK YEARS (1935-1971)

Show business isn't just scenery, lights, greasepaint and glitter, it's heart. Because, if your show hasn't got a heart, you haven't got a show. That's what I tried to convey when I wrote the song "There's No Business Like Show Business."

—Irving Berlin, songwriter, unused introduction to There's No Business Like Show Business *(1954)*

Not long after it was announced that Twentieth Century Fox would be run by Joseph Schenck as chairman of the board, Sidney Kent as president, and Sol Wurtzel in charge of the "B" unit at the Western Avenue Studio, Winfield Sheehan resigned, refusing to share responsibilities with Darryl Zanuck.

After using a cramped lot that was not their own for eighteen months, and eighteen productions for Twentieth Century Pictures, Inc., Schenck and Zanuck were overjoyed with the vast resources of Movietone City when they arrived in July of 1935. Its employees soon got to know Zanuck's family: his wife Virginia ("The ultimate praise Darryl could pay any film was: 'Virginia [Zanuck] cried,' " recalled Elia Kazan) and three children, Darrylin, Susan, and Richard.

After clearing the deck—halting twelve of Winfield Sheehan's projects in preproduction and six already shooting and replacing them with ones he was already preparing for Twentieth Century Pictures—Zanuck set in motion his own way of doing things. Together with Edward Eberle, the studio production manager he brought from Warner Bros., they dropped the average shooting schedule from sixty days to forty days. Also on Zanuck's team was executive assistant Lew Schreiber, publicity director Harry Brand, and story editor Julian Johnson. The Twentieth Century Pictures Inc. logo was modified by Emil Kosa Jr., and Alfred Newman likewise rerecorded the fanfare for what employees affectionately called "the monument."

Among Darryl Zanuck's most immediate concerns was developing stars. In 1935 it was a depleted collection indeed. Charles Farrell and Janet Gaynor were on the wane, and that very summer he lost his greatest star and the world's greatest box-office attraction. Will Rogers was killed at the age of fifty when his plane crashed in fog near Point Barrow, Alaska. His last two films released were—to no one's surprise—his greatest box-office winners: *Steamboat Round the Bend* (1935) and *In Old Kentucky* (1935). Now seven-year-old Shirley Temple was more valuable to him than ever. Hers was a career to maximize, and he did just that.

Zanuck's first star-making success was Alice Faye, a recent Winfield Sheehan acquisition. Behind the Jean Harlow–like makeup and platinum blonde hair he uncovered a beautiful woman with an extraordinary voice and warm personality. Under contract for twelve years, and starring in twenty-two musicals, she became Twentieth Century Fox's first Queen of the Lot, until she voluntarily retired in 1945 as Mrs. Phil Harris.

Assisting with Faye's career was producer Kenneth Macgowan, who Zanuck brought from RKO in 1935. For a decade Macgowan's productions would be among the best on the lot, and help make more stars like Tyrone Power (*Lloyd's of London* (1937), *In Old Chicago* (1938)), Richard Greene (*Four Men and a Prayer* (1938)), Don Ameche (*The Story of Alexander Graham Bell* (1939)), and Linda Darnell (*Star Dust*, 1940). In November 1935 the first Twentieth Century Fox film, *Metropolitan*, was released, starring Lawrence Tibbett, a New York Metropolitan Opera star since 1923, and one of the world's finest baritones. Many of the studio's releases that first year were more critical successes than box-office ones, but it was a profitable beginning, perfectly timed as the country moved out of the Depression. The formula for success that Zanuck had developed at Warner Bros. and then Twentieth Century Pictures—a potent combination of films celebrating Americana, prestige pictures, and musicals, often with a social conscience—would continue to flourish at the new company, as well. By the end of the 1936, Zanuck's team had doubled the studio's profits from the prior year by increasing production to fifty features, six series of short subjects with one two-reeler every week, and over thirty one-reelers. The following year Robert T. Kane's *Wings of the Morning* (1937) marked the impressive debut of the Fox British subsidiary New World Pictures, Ltd.

For *Ramona* (1936), the studio's very first all-Technicolor effort, Darryl Zanuck cast Loretta

Young. Seeing greater possibilities for her when they worked together at Warner Bros., he had put her under contract in June 1933 at Twentieth Century Pictures. There he raised her stature in *The House of Rothschild* (1934) with George Arliss, *Call of the Wild* (1935) with Clark Gable, and *Clive of India* (1935) with Ronald Colman. *Ramona* solidified Young's stardom and position, supplanting Janet Gaynor, and setting a classy tradition for future stars to emulate. Darryl Zanuck subsequently paired Loretta Young with Tyrone Power, and their three romantic comedies in 1937 made them household names as the best-looking couple

in the movies. Fox quickly became the premier Technicolor dream factory of Hollywood, using it more often and more vibrantly than any other studio.

Meanwhile the studio launched more stars, including the three Ritz Brothers in *Sing, Baby, Sing* (1936), and Sonja Henie in *One in a Million* (1936). Darryl Zanuck lured Henry Fonda into a studio contract with the promise of the lead role in *The Grapes of Wrath* (1940).

By the end of 1940 Fox was second only to MGM in profits, proving it could attract the talent of America's most popular composer, Irving Berlin

(*Alexander's Ragtime Band*, 1938); stage an epic on the scale of any company in Hollywood (*The Rains Came*, 1939); celebrate Americana as well as anyone (*Drums Along the Mohawk*, 1939; *Jesse James*, 1939); and master the screen biography (*Young Mr. Lincoln*, 1939; *Stanley and Livingstone*, 1939). Significantly, Tyrone Power was featured in many of these films. Zanuck's gamble of investing in Power's pictures during his first five years—more than he had ever spent before—paid off. With exceptional good looks, and underrated acting abilities that allowed him to move with ease from serious drama to action film to comedy to musical, he was the heartthrob of the nation and king of the box office by 1939. Director and mentor Henry King recalled that he never saw an actor work harder at his craft than Power. Of King, who worked on the lot for more than three decades and made many of the studio's best films, Alice Faye said, "he simply *was* Twentieth Century Fox."

The end of the 1930s also meant the end of an era, with the departure of Shirley Temple. The world's biggest box-office attraction from 1935 to 1938 had "sparkled" unwaveringly throughout the decade, but her popularity had waned as she matured, and misfires like *The Blue Bird* (1940) damaged her career. Darryl Zanuck intended that a biography of President Woodrow Wilson would be the masterpiece of mid-1940s film production.

It was a particularly tall order after two John Ford Academy Award winners, *The Grapes of Wrath* (1940) and *How Green Was My Valley* (1941), had launched the extraordinary careers of Maureen O'Hara and Roddy McDowall. His plans were curtailed by America's entry into World War II with the bombing of Pearl Harbor—caught of course by a Fox Movietone cameraman (Al Brick). He retooled the factory for service pictures; many of which became Hollywood's finest including *Man Hunt* (1941), *This Above All* (1942), *Crash Dive* (1943), *Guadalcanal Diary* (1943), *The Moon is Down* (1943), *The Sullivans* (1944), *Winged Victory* (1944), *A Bell for Adano* (1945), and *A Walk in the Sun* (1945). For a world that would also need diversion from war's tragedies, Zanuck signed Ernst Lubitsch as a producer/director in 1942 that resulted in a sparkling series of films beginning with *Heaven Can Wait* (1943). Attaining a commission as a lieutenant colonel in the Army Signal Corps to supervise the making of training and combat films only intensified Zanuck's interest in *Wilson* as a postwar argument for a world police force.

William Goetz, left in charge for nine months, dealt with the loss of foreign revenue and many of his stars and technicians to the service. He found an ideal ally in brother-in-law David O. Selznick. Hollywood's most successful independent producer and first-rate creator of stars was always in need of cash and ready to make a deal. These negotiations resulted in *Lifeboat* (1944), *Jane Eyre* (1944), *The Keys of the Kingdom* (1944), *Titanic* (1953), *A Farewell to Arms* (1957), *Tender is the Night* (1962), and a cavalcade of truly remarkable stars including Joan Fontaine, Gregory Peck, Dorothy McGuire, Vivien Leigh, Rory Calhoun, David Wayne, Louis Jourdan, Ingrid Bergman, and Robert Mitchum. Most precious to Selznick was Jennifer Jones who was carefully and spectacularly launched in the studio's highest grossing movie to date, *The Song of Bernadette* (1943).

There were power shifts at Fox upon Darryl Zanuck's return in May of 1943. Sidney Kent had died on March 19, 1942, and was replaced by Spyros Skouras, head of National Theatres. After an unsuccessful attempt to keep Zanuck from returning William Goetz left to found International Pictures that later merged with Universal. That same year Joseph Schenck was jailed for income tax evasion because of his involvement in the George Browne-Willie Bioff bribery scandal. Wendell L. Willkie, the 1940 Republican nominee for President of the United States, temporarily succeeded him. Schenck returned after four months as executive production head and later co-founded the Magna Corporation with Michael Todd to exploit the visual splendors of Todd-AO. He retired in 1953.

When *Wilson* finally emerged in 1944, the passion that went into it drew critical acclaim and ten Academy Award nominations, but its flaws made it financially the greatest disappointment of Zanuck's career. The box-office receipts for that year actually flowed from an unlikely source. Otto Preminger, whom Zanuck fired over his direction of *Kidnapped* (1938), had reappeared with a new studio contract under Bill Goetz. After appearing in *The Pied Piper* (1942) and *Margin for Error* (1943), and directing the latter as well, Preminger convinced Goetz to purchase Vera Caspary's novel, *Laura* (1944). The film was a major box-office hit that erased Darryl Zanuck's enmity, and Preminger went on to make a number of remarkable films at the studio.

Laura made stars of Dana Andrews, Clifton Webb, and, particularly, Gene Tierney, who became the studio's prestige star and the new Queen of the Lot when she earned an Academy Award nomination the following year for her performance in *Leave Her to Heaven* (1945). The film, released during Christmas of 1945, was the biggest hit in the industry to date, earning $8.2 million. Her costar was Cornel Wilde, an athletic new Fox leading man who had come to Hollywood as a fencing instructor after representing the American team in fencing during the 1936 Olympics. *Dragonwyck* (1946) was an even bigger-budgeted showcase for Tierney. Starring in all three films was another Broadway acquisition, Vincent Price.

ABOVE: Spyros Skouras

Meanwhile, the Fox musical thrived in the 1940s. *Variety* once raved: "New superlatives need to be invented to describe properly the lavish, lush splendor of production in Technicolor that Darryl F. Zanuck made available to the staff of fine craftsmen whose talents have been deftly blended in a great hit show." The review was for *That Night in Rio* (1941), but it could have been penned for any of the studio's sparkling output that decade under the leadership of producers like William LeBaron, Milton Sperling, George Jessel, William Perlberg, Lamar Trotti, Mack Gordon, and the performances of some significant new stars.

Down Argentine Way (1940) launched the careers of Betty Grable and Brazilian bombshell, Carmen Miranda. Miranda's beloved outrageousness belied the hardworking, consummate professional that employees remember on the lot. And Grable's contributions to Twentieth Century Fox, like Shirley Temple's, cannot be underestimated. Her films were remarkably consistent moneymakers for a record thirteen years, and she became the most popular pinup during World War II, renowned and insured by the studio for those million-dollar legs. June Haver, groomed as a successor for Grable, also surpassed expectations. Memorably paired with all of them for romantic interest was Juilliard-trained singer John Payne.

Jeanne Crain, one of Fox's loveliest stars, shot to stardom, and the studio achieved a new plateau of musical excellence with Richard Rodgers and Oscar Hammerstein's *State Fair* (1945). Darryl Zanuck had invited the Broadway composers of *Oklahoma!* to remake the studio's 1933 hit, *State Fair*, as a musical. They agreed, but only if they could remain on the East Coast. Rodgers would recall with amusement the creation process: "The story, which was set in Iowa, would be filmed in California, while the music and lyrics would be written in Fairfield, Connecticut, and Doylestown, Pennsylvania." *State Fair* also made stars of Vivian Blaine, with her rich contralto, and popular '40s crooner Dick Haymes.

Knowing that his queen Betty Grable needed a king as he prepared *Mother Wore Tights* (1947), Darryl Zanuck borrowed Dan Dailey from MGM. Incredibly, that musical-minded studio had never taken advantage of his talent as a song-and-dance man. Zanuck did, and *Mother Wore Tights* was a major success, and Grable's favorite and best musical. The pair encored memorably in *When My Baby Smiles at Me* (1948), earning Dailey an Oscar nomination as Best Actor, the first musical-comedy actor ever to be so honored.

The return of important talents to Fox after World War II resulted in a pair of studio masterpieces. John Ford made *My Darling Clementine* (1946) and Darryl Zanuck re-introduced Tyrone Power in an appropriately prestigious personal production of *The Razor's Edge* (1946). Linda Darnell, who had risen to fame co-starring with Power in Rouben Mamoulian's celebrated *The Mark of Zorro* (1940) and *Blood and Sand* (1941), was reaching the height of her career performing memorably in *Clementine* and Otto Preminger's *Forever Amber* (1947).

Darnell also appeared in *Anna and the King of Siam* (1946), starring Darryl Zanuck's latest British acquisition Rex Harrison. Harrison had come to prominence in *Night Train* (1941), produced by the British arm of Twentieth Century Fox. Zanuck also scored a coup by acquiring Irene Dunne as his costar. One of the great ladies of the silver screen, Dunne would be back as another memorable and formidable English lady, Queen Victoria in *The Mudlark* (1950). Harrison, meanwhile, was even better in Preston Sturges's *Unfaithfully Yours*, but with the tragic suicide of Fox comedienne Carole Landis on July 4, 1948, for which the media and public blamed him, his contract was canceled and the movie was put into limited release.

Nightmare Alley (1947) remains the most unique of Tyrone Power's post–World War II films, if only for the opportunity to see his versatility as an antihero. The film was not a popular success, and Power spent the rest of his career back in heroic roles and comedies, including *Captain from Castile*

(1947), with new star Jean Peters, *The Luck of the Irish* (1948), and *Prince of Foxes* (1949).

By now the studio was expert at turning out family films. From Zanuck's penchant for Americana came a new studio subgenre: equestrian films that moved from state to state. Launched with *Kentucky* (1938) and *Maryland* (1940), the beautifully produced Technicolor productions continued with *My Friend Flicka* (1943), starring Roddy McDowall. McDowall was featured in the sequels *Thunderhead, Son of Flicka* (1946) and *Green Grass of Wyoming* (1948), which featured Peggy Cummins. *Home in Indiana* (1944) followed the pattern, introducing another youngster named Lon McCallister. *Smoky* (1946) and *The Homestretch* (1947) wrapped up the series.

Meanwhile, newcomers Anne Baxter and John Hodiak fell in love in reel (and real) life in *Sunday Dinner for a Soldier* (1944), while other juvenile finds included Peggy Ann Garner, playing the mischievous *Junior Miss* (1945), and Connie Marshall in the classic weepie, *Sentimental Journey* (1946). Best of all was the evergreen *Miracle on 34th Street* (1947), starring Maureen O'Hara and young Natalie Wood, and *Sitting Pretty* (1948), starring Clifton Webb, which inspired numerous Mr. Belvedere follow-ups.

Darryl Zanuck's successful diversification was necessary as he faced new challenges in the late 1940s. Box-office receipts dropped as the American audience's interest in a growing number of

ABOVE: Richard Rodgers and Oscar Hammerstein II first teamed up with Fox for *State Fair* (1945). The relationship was an enduring one that created some of the finest screen musicals ever produced.

alternative leisure activities—including television—increased. The Supreme Court divorced Hollywood studios from their theater chains and that ready cash flow. While the Skouras brothers took on the television problem, Zanuck increased film production in Great Britain to unlock Fox funds frozen by a country devastated by war. *The Mudlark* (1950), *No Highway in the Sky* (1951), *Sailor of the King* (1953), and *The Deep Blue Sea* (1955) were among the best of these.

To avoid the rising costs of making movies in Southern California, Zanuck looked to the East Coast and overseas. And what better to film on the streets of New York than the kind of realistic fare that was coming out of Italy? Zanuck hired Louis de Rochemont of *The March of Time* newsreels to pioneer "docudrama" with the cooperation of the FBI in a small-budget feature named *The House on 92nd Street* (1945), directed by Henry Hathaway.

With the success of the docudrama genre and increasingly popular film noir—or a unique mixture of both—Zanuck had a new recipe for success, particularly with *The Dark Corner* (1946), *Somewhere in the Night* (1946), *Kiss of Death* (1947), *13 Rue Madeleine* (1947), *Call Northside 777* (1948), *Cry of the City* (1948), *The Street with No Name* (1948), *Road House* (1948), *Thieves' Highway* (1949), *Night and the City* (1950), *No Way Out* (1950), *Fourteen Hours* (1951), and *The Steel Trap* (1952).

The realism seeped into Fox dramas, including such masterpieces as *The Snake Pit* (1948), *Twelve O'Clock High* (1950), and *Deadline—U.S.A.* (1952). Perfectly in line with Zanuck's preference for bolder, tougher, even controversial subject matter were Elia Kazan's *A Tree Grows in Brooklyn* (1945), *Boomerang* (1947), *Gentleman's Agreement* (1947), *Pinky* (1949), and *Panic in the Streets* (1950). All of these films brought along a rich new vein of studio talent, including Richard Widmark, Sidney Poitier, Celeste Holm, Richard Conte, Paul Douglas, Richard Basehart, Gary Merrill, Hugh Marlowe, Lynn Bari, and Mark Stevens.

These efforts contributed to make Darryl Zanuck's Twentieth Century Fox the best in the industry at the end of the 1940s, by verdict of both the box office and the critics. His dream factory could produce the greatest variety of entertainment, including television. Although that division was founded in 1949, the enterprising Skouras brothers had in fact been exploring the potential of the new medium since 1945. While National Theatres president Charles Skouras set up an exploratory television department, Spyros invested $10 million in the European Eidophor system that promised to transmit images onto National Theatres' screens to rival home television, from studios in San Francisco and Oakland. Although the system ultimately proved unsatisfactory, and a purchase of ABC went awry, TCF Television Productions, Inc. (1949–55) began production in New York under Peter Levathes, with *Crusade in Europe* (1949) on ABC and *Fox News Reel* on NBC, and then at the Fox Western Avenue Studio under the leadership of Sid Rogell.

Another man key to Darryl Zanuck's success was celebrated at the twenty-second annual Academy Award ceremony on March 23, 1950. Of the five Oscars that the studio earned for its 1949 films, Joseph L. Mankiewicz received the Best Director and Best Screenplay awards for *A Letter to Three Wives* (1949). It was the seventh and most successful to date of his Fox efforts, including *The Keys of the Kingdom* (1944), *Dragonwyck* (1945), *Somewhere in the Night* (1946), *The Late George Apley* (1947), *The Ghost and Mrs. Muir* (1947), and *Escape* (1948).

Mankiewicz's *House of Strangers* (1949) showcased Susan Hayward, who had arrived unceremoniously at Twentieth Century Fox when producer Walter Wanger—suffering financial troubles from an ill-fated version of *Joan of Arc* (1948)—sold her contract to the studio. Zanuck struck box-office gold when he matched her with Gregory Peck in *David and Bathsheba* (1951) and then *The Snows of Kilimanjaro* (1952).

"On the basis of our investment alone," said Zanuck at the time, "Susan Hayward is our most valuable player. We've tied up nearly one-quarter of our studio budget on her."

Unbelievably, Mankiewicz scored Oscar gold again in 1950 with *All About Eve* . The film not only won Oscars for his direction and script, but also received twelve other nominations and a total of six wins—a new industry record. It rejuvenated Bette Davis's career, and she would gratefully reward the company with four more box-office hits in the years to come. George Sanders's Oscar-winning performance was the culmination of thirty-three years of superlative work in Fox films, from being plucked out of a group of British tourists on the lot by Henry King for *Lloyd's of London* (1937) through *The Kremlin Letter* (1970).

Thelma Ritter, one of Mankiewicz's favorite actresses, certainly attributed her career as one of the best-loved character actors of all time to the producer. Although an attention-getter in her very first Fox film (an uncredited role as the exhausted Christmas shopper in *Miracle on 34th Street*), her role in her follow-up, *Call Northside 777* (1948), was cut. It was not until *A Letter to Three Wives* and then *Eve* that her career really took off.

All About Eve also launched Marilyn Monroe's career. Her one-year 1946 studio contract had produced nothing but bit roles, as disappointing for her as it was for the studio. She drifted around Hollywood until her star-making role in *Eve* earned her a new contract, after which she progressively climbed to stardom in eight small-budget but entertaining

ABOVE: Louis de Rochemont

ABOVE: Celeste Holm won Best Supporting Actress and Elia Kazan won Best Director for *Gentleman's Agreement* (1947). The film also won Best Picture.

black-and-white films, including *Love Nest* (1951), *Don't Bother to Knock* (1952), and *Monkey Business* (1952). Her performance in the smash Technicolor hit *Niagara* (1953) solidified her fame.

Mankiewicz's *No Way Out* (1950) introduced Sidney Poitier to movie audiences, and marked the zenith of Linda Darnell's career. As always, if Darryl Zanuck was convinced a story was worth telling, risks were taken. *The Day the Earth Stood Still* (1951) was such a risk both as science fiction before the genre took off, and particularly as a picture with a message of peace to a nation submerged in the Cold War and the Korean War. Director Robert Wise came through with an enormous, influential hit, earning a Golden Globe as the "Best Film Promoting International Understanding," and launching the studio's reputation as a leader in science-fiction filmmaking.

In 1952, newcomers David Brown and Audrey Dalton saw this Twentieth Century Fox at its zenith. Brown was hired by Darryl Zanuck to head the story department, and Paramount star Dalton was loaned for two of the studio's best films: *My Cousin Rachel* (1952) and *Titanic* (1953).

"At that time Fox had twenty-eight producers under contract," recalled Brown, "almost as many directors, a full roster of stars, contract players, a full symphony orchestra under Alfred Newman, and writers who were guaranteed forty weeks' work and twelve weeks' vacation."

"My first impression of the Fox lot was that it was huge," said Dalton. "I would go to work through the little Santa Monica gate. One had to drive for what seemed to me like miles on a narrow two-lane road south to reach the offices and soundstages, which were situated closer to the Pico Boulevard gate. At that time, the contract and working producers and directors had individual bungalows on different little streets around the lot, so this is where one went to be interviewed or to audition.

"The backlot as I remember had acres of just fields, trees, and wild grass, crisscrossed by narrow roads. Appropriate other additions could be done by the art director to dress the scene for specific scenes and eras, adding bushes and rocks, etc., as needed. When you were out there it was so quiet, no traffic noises at all. It was like being out in the country, and of course no tall buildings in sight. It was years before even the Mormon temple was built on little Santa Monica Boulevard, with the angel Moroni on top—the tallest building on the west side for years."

It would take all these impressive assets—and even more nerve—for Spyros Skouras's next venture. Aware of still-declining box-office receipts and the ever-growing threat of television, he had been impressed with the wide-screen and sonic wonders of *This Is Cinerama* (1952), but was keenly aware of its limitations. He turned to Earl Sponable, head of the studio's research and development unit, for a successful compromise. They found it, ironically, while searching for a solution to properly project the Eidophor system.

It was the work of Professor Henri Chretien in France who had created the wide-screen "Anamorphoscope" in the 1920s, utilizing standard 35mm film. His anamorphic lenses compressed an image shot during filming and then projected it onto a screen two and a half times as wide as it was high to form a 2:55:1 aspect ratio as opposed to the industry standard of 1:33:1. Skouras made a deal and subsequently copyrighted it as CinemaScope. The name was purchased for $50,000 from Don Fetter, who had developed a process for recording TV broadcasts onto film and coined it "CinemaScope." Zanuck announced ambitious plans to release the bulk of his films in the new format. The risks were enormous. Besides the $4.1 million investment in *The Robe* (1953), the most prestigious of the upcoming CinemaScope releases, Spyros Skouras had to convince exhibitors to spend $20,000 to upgrade their theaters, and then persuade rival Hollywood studios that CinemaScope should be the industry standard, with a $25,000 price tag per film. He was successful on both counts.

"It was spectacular," recalled Darryl Zanuck. "He led the crusade, as he called it. 'This will save the movies!' he told them. The whole Bible-thumping bit. I think the fact that he was able to mastermind the exhibitors of the country to switch to CinemaScope was Skouras's greatest moment of triumph."

By the time *The Robe* premiered, 1,500 theaters were equipped for CinemaScope, and rival studios were signing up for it. The film was a spectacular hit, and made CinemaScope's accompanying "stereophonic sound" another industry standard. Significantly, Hollywood's effort to use 3-D as another way to bring in audiences was not quite as successful. Spyros Skouras, like the other studios, experimented with it in *Inferno* (1953) and *Gorilla at Large* (1954), and found it wanting.

Skouras and Zanuck had continued the William Fox tradition of coming out first in the scramble to reinvigorate the industry in a big way. Although *The Robe* starred one of Zanuck's greatest discoveries, Richard Burton, it is costar Victor Mature's career that would benefit the most from wide-screen epics. But there was a price: The studio's resident hunk had earned a reputation as a good actor—particularly in film noir, beginning with his film debut in *I Wake up Screaming* (1941)—but all that was lost to this bigger-than-life persona holding together *The Robe*'s sequel, *Demetrius and the Gladiators* (1954), and *The Egyptian* (1954).

With him in *Demetrius* was Susan Hayward, continuing her string of hits even as Marilyn

TOP: David Brown

ABOVE: Oscar winners for *All About Eve* (1950): director Joseph Mankiewicz, producer Darryl Zanuck and Best Supporting Actor George Sanders.

Monroe ascended the throne as the new Queen of the Lot, with her own CinemaScope debut in *How to Marry a Millionaire.*

In an era when the Hollywood studio system was fighting for its life, such 1954 CinemaScope offerings as *Prince Valiant, Three Coins in the Fountain, River of No Return, Broken Lance, Carmen Jones, Desiree,* and *There's No Business Like Show Business*—raised Fox profits by an incredible 400 percent.

Also key to Zanuck's success in the 1950s was tapping the youth market that was emerging for the first time by successfully developing Robert Wagner, Joan Collins, Jeffrey Hunter, Terry Moore, Barry Coe, Debra Paget, Mitzi Gaynor, and Jayne Mansfield. He brought Marlon Brando to Fox and Elvis Presley into the movies. There were also UK imports like Michael Rennie, Richard Todd, and Stephen Boyd. And he caught the best of the stars now freelancing, including James Stewart, Olivia de Havilland, James Cagney, Clark Gable, Cary Grant, Humphrey Bogart, Errol Flynn, Lana Turner, Lauren Bacall, Fred Astaire, and Gary Cooper.

Combining this talent with state-of-the-art CinemaScope visuals and sound—and the studio's traditions for well-written stories and superb music scores—provided a potent box-office mix in *The Seven Year Itch* (1955), *Prince of Players* (1955), *Violent Saturday* (1955), *A Man Called Peter* (1955), *Daddy Long Legs* (1955), *The Virgin Queen* (1955),

Good Morning, Miss Dove (1955), and *The Rains of Ranchipur* (1955).

Further profits—and prestige—were guaranteed when Darryl Zanuck produced wide-screen incarnations of Rodgers and Hammerstein Broadway hits *Carousel* (1956) and *The King and I* (1956). Although the Broadway team made *Oklahoma!* (1955) as an independent venture in Mike Todd's Todd-AO wide-screen process, Zanuck convinced them to distribute a CinemaScope version too. The deal included the film rights to *Carousel* and *The King and I.* To compete with Todd-AO's visual superiority, Zanuck encouraged the development of the improved CinemaScope 55 for both films. Among the cast of schoolchildren singing "You'll Never Walk Alone" at the conclusion of *Carousel* was Fox starlet Lili Gentle, who became the wife of his son Richard Zanuck. Among the fortuitous outcomes of *The King and I* was bringing genteel favorite Deborah Kerr to Fox, who graced a number of the studio's films with impressive performances well into the 1960s.

Another far-reaching effect of *The Robe* for Darryl Zanuck was more personal. Increasingly tired of running the entire studio, his desire to supervise a smaller collection of pictures was piqued when he discovered that independent *Robe* producer Frank Ross earned more than he did. Zanuck's last personal production at the studio, *The*

Man in the Gray Flannel Suit (1956), was one of his best. By the time it premiered he had worked out an agreement to independently produce films in Europe, and by February of 1957, he had appointed Buddy Adler as his successor and made his son his venture's West Coast contact.

Adler, Columbia's former head of production, had impressed Zanuck with *Violent Saturday* (1955) by proving a CinemaScope movie could be made inexpensively. He impressed him again with a remarkable series of films about love and war set in exotic Asian locales including *Soldier of Fortune* (1955), *Love Is A Many-Splendored Thing* (1955), *House of Bamboo* (1955), and *The Left Hand of God* (1955). He did it again with *Bus Stop* (1956), starring Marilyn Monroe and new stars Hope Lange and Don Murray, and even more spectacularly with *Anastasia* (1956). For the latter he took the risk no one else in Hollywood wanted to take by signing Ingrid Bergman, ostracized from Hollywood and the United States for having an extramarital affair. Bolstered by a cast of the highest order, including Yul Brynner and Helen Hayes, the radiant star rewarded him with an extraordinary box office success and won a Best Actress Oscar for herself.

From Columbia Adler brought Jerry Wald, whose first release, *An Affair to Remember* (1957), remains the studio's most enduring romantic comedy, while *Peyton Place* (1957) revealed his skill at transforming controversial subjects into box-office gold, as he had done with *From Here to Eternity* (1953, Columbia). *Peyton Place* earned nine Academy Award nominations and a substantial studio legacy, including a sequel and a long-running television series that made stars of Mia Farrow and Ryan O'Neal.

That year at the Oscars Adler's Fox had two of its leading ladies up for Best Actress: Lana Turner for *Peyton Place* and Joanne Woodward for *The Three Faces of Eve* (1957). Woodward was another Adler discovery signed in 1955, despite Darryl Zanuck's protestations. That evening Adler cabled Zanuck: "You remember my mistake? She won the Oscar last night!"Her next role, in Jerry Wald's classic *The Long, Hot Summer* (1958), was equally significant. Anthony Franciosa, a recent New York import who had scored an Oscar nomination for his Broadway-to-Hollywood role in Buddy Adler's *A Hatful of Rain* (1957), was considered for the lead opposite his *Rain* costar, Eva Marie Saint. Then Saint got pregnant and Joanne Woodward was up for the part. Wald thought Paul Newman, under contract to Warner Bros., would be better for her and asked her if she knew him. In fact, they had known each other since they had worked on Broadway in *Picnic* in 1952. Their romance during the making of *The Long, Hot Summer* led to marriage, and decades of great work for Fox. Franciosa

ABOVE: Jerry Wald

ABOVE: Buddy Adler

remained in the film as Woodward's brother married to Lee Remick; another star making memorable her Fox debut and the subsequent films to follow.

Despite more excellent choices from Adler, including David Weisbart's *April Love* (1957), *Desk Set* (1957) starring Spencer Tracy and Katharine Hepburn, Frank Tashlin's *Will Success Spoil Rock Hunter?* (1957), Eugene Frenke's *Heaven Knows, Mr. Allison* (1957); Kurt Neumann's *The Fly* (1958); Rodgers and Hammerstein's *South Pacific* (1958), a second Ingrid Bergman masterpiece *The Inn of the Sixth Happiness* (1958), Richard's Zanuck's first film *Compulsion* (1959), and George Stevens's *The Diary of Anne Frank* (1959), CinemaScope turned out to be only temporary life support for the studio system.

In fact it worsened the problem because these widescreen pictures required bigger budgets and costly location work that led to fewer pictures being made and less need of the Fox lots, whose real estate value was going up. These spectacles had obliterated the edgy yet sophisticated black-and-white dramas and comedies that the studio had produced so well in the late 1940s and early 1950s. Directors like Elia Kazan, who wanted to continue to make films like that, took *A Streetcar Named Desire* (1951) and *On the Waterfront* (1954) elsewhere.

The lack of Darryl Zanuck's guiding hand, so skilled at selecting, casting, and editing Fox films, also began to show, and the studio's star system and product and box office suffered. It struggled further when, for budgetary reasons, the studio's family—its departments of creative personnel—were broken up and let go affecting the quality of the movies. This despite Spyros Skouras's revenue-seeking efforts. To avoid the US Justice Department's recent edict that studios could not own American theaters, he had purchased theaters in South Africa, Europe, and England. The studio began releasing "B" pictures from a Fox studio in South Africa and from Regal Pictures, but by that time the deteriorating state of the company was public knowledge.

Even with a new roundup, including Tuesday Weld, Dana Wynter, Sheree North, France Nuyen, Bradford Dillman, Tommy Sands, Millie Perkins, Diane Baker, Carol Lynley, Barbara Eden, Fabian, and Stuart Whitman, newspaper reports circulated that the company was exploring possible mergers or sharing of real estate with Warner Bros. or MGM.

Then Skouras made an announcement: Twentieth Century Fox would direct the development of that Westwood backlot into a $400,000,000 residential and business area known as the "Radio City of the West." It was the end of an era. From Madrid, Spain, came word that fall that Tyrone Power was dead of a heart attack on the set of the United Artists film, *Solomon and Sheba* (1959).

Another death—that of Buddy Adler during the summer of 1960, from a brain tumor—and the choice of Robert Goldstein and then Peter Levathes as his successors, gave Spyros Skouras much cause for regret. Their ambitious remake of *Cleopatra*—an attempt at joining the high-stakes world of epic filmmaking—was hemorrhaging money. Desperate for cash, he threw out plans to develop the backlot himself and sought to sell the entire studio property of 265 acres to the combined Aluminum Corp. of America and William Zeckendorf's Webb & Knapp, for $56 million.

Even as he accepted the $2.5 million down payment, this deal went awry. Zeckendorf informed him that his company was in financial difficulty and might default. Not until Skouras slashed the price to $43 million did Alcoa agree to pay for the parcel in April of 1961. They also agreed to lease back 75.7 acres to Fox with an option to purchase it back. Meanwhile Alan Williams, the public relations director of the new real estate project, christened it "Century City, the City of Tomorrow," the "biggest land deal in the West," to include eighty-eight buildings covering twelve million square feet, including the 750-room Century Plaza Hotel, office buildings, apartment buildings, and a 500,000-square-foot regional shopping center. Within the remaining acreage of the lot, rife with "political infighting, backstabbing, [and] whispering down the corridors," as Richard Zanuck remembered it, seeds of hope were planted. With Spyros Skouras's stamp of approval, Henry Klinger,

BOTTOM LEFT: Robert Goldstein with a chart of upcoming productions.

BOTTOM MIDDLE: Peter Levathes

BELOW: Irwin Allen

BOTTOM RIGHT: Mark Robson stands at the south end of Bldg. 88. Stage Ten can be seen in the background.

Charles Brackett's production of Jules Verne's *Journey to the Center of the Earth* (1959) with *The Lost World* (1960), *Voyage to the Bottom of the Sea* (1961), and *Five Weeks in a Balloon* (1962).

Meanwhile, Darryl Zanuck's independent unit was planning to top such ambitious efforts as *The Sun Also Rises* (1957), *Island in the Sun* (1957), and *The Roots of Heaven* (1958) with *The Longest Day* (1962), an epic retelling of the D-Day invasion of Normandy based on war correspondent Cornelius Ryan's book. The project featured, incredibly, forty-three international stars. It took four secretaries keeping track of all Hollywood filmmaking activity—and a producer like Darryl Zanuck—to incorporate them all.

When the cash-strapped studio offered Zanuck only $8 million for the budget, he put up an additional $2 million himself. Associate producer Elmo Williams helped manage the enormous project, working with four governments for the use of military personnel and equipment, and coordinating the now-famous battle sequences. Increasingly concerned that Spyros Skouras, in his desperation for funds, would scrap his road-show release plans, and infuriated at the state of the company, Darryl Zanuck returned to the United States during the summer of 1962 to confront the board of directors in New York.

"It was one of the most amazing performances

a New York story editor since the days of William Fox, purchased a fifteen-year lease of the screen rights of Rodgers and Hammerstein's *The Sound of Music*. As part of the deal, Rodgers provided new songs for a remake of *State Fair* (1962), starring the studio's best crooner, Pat Boone, and new Fox star Ann-Margret.

Other bright spots were the release of Jerry Wald's *Sons and Lovers* (1960), Robert Rossen's *The Hustler* (1961), Jack Clayton's horror masterpiece, *The Innocents* (1961), and Mark Robson's *Lisa* (1962). Writer, director, and producer Irwin Allen found his niche following up on the success of

I've ever seen in my life," recalled Richard Zanuck. "He went to the Board. He was a large stockholder, but minuscule to all the others. He hit them on an emotional level as the founder of the company, and absolutely attacked them one by one, and after a couple of hours of this tirade they were totally wiped out. By the time it was over he had taken over the company. It was as simple as that."

The Zanucks were in—and the Spyros Skouras regime was out. Assigning Elmo Williams to head European production, Darryl then asked his twenty-seven-year-old son who should be the new head of production. Richard handed him a piece of paper on which he had written: "Me." His father agreed.

"It was one of his gutsiest moves," said Richard. "He had great confidence in me. I knew the studio operations better than anybody."

Father and son then systematically began to turn the company around. Closing down both studios, Richard Zanuck let most of the employees go save the cast and crew of the *The Many Loves of Dobie Gillis* TV show, while his father salvaged *Cleopatra* (1963). Among the casualties that summer was Jerry Wald and his plans for making Robert Kennedy's *The Enemy Within*. Issuing the last films of the Skouras regime, including *The Condemned of Altona* (1963), *Sodom and Gomorrah* (1962), and *The Leopard* (1963), all co-productions with Titanus Films in Rome, the Zanucks celebrated

the new one with the grandest premiere the studio had ever known in Paris on September 25, for *The Longest Day*. The title was emblazoned in lights on the Eiffel Tower where Edith Piaf sang "La Marseillaise." The film that Cornelius Ryan dubbed "the most accurate wartime movie ever made [and] a brilliant example of the final work of the last of the angry moguls" was indeed the last Darryl Zanuck would personally produce, and a happy worldwide hit.

The reopening of the Century City studio's Pico gate on Monday, March 4, 1963, was symbolic of renewed activity on both lots. Fourteen productions by the father-son team were announced as under way, for $50 million. The parameters of the new partnership were set: Richard was in Southern California developing projects, and his father was in Paris or New York to grant final approval. Of the fourteen, ten were shot on the lots, including agent-turned-producer Arthur P. Jacobs's *What a Way to Go!* (1964). The studio's first releases, *Take Her, She's Mine* (1963) starring James Stewart and *Move Over, Darling* (1963) starring Doris Day, made a healthy profit, and even *Cleopatra* (1963) was one of the top grossing films of the year.

To take advantage of the postwar filmmaking renaissance in Europe, Darryl Zanuck set up a new division, International Classics, to distribute films like Michael Cacoyannis's *Zorba the Greek*

TOP: Producer Saul Chaplin accepts the Oscars for *The Sound of Music* (1965).

ABOVE: Robert Wise holds the novel of *The Sand Pebbles* (1966), the pet project he was allowed to make following his blockbuster *The Sound of Music* (1965).

TOP: The team that made *Planet of the Apes* (1968): director Franklin Schaffner, writer Rod Serling, producer Arthur P. Jacobs, and star Charlton Heston.

ABOVE: George C. Scott in *Patton* (1970).

(1965). This one was at the request of former contract player Anthony Quinn when support from United Artists faltered. The move paid off richly for Zanuck: Quinn received a Best Actor nomination for his signature film role, and the world was inspired by Cacoyannis's message that life is worth living despite the horrors along the way.

So everyone at Twentieth Century Fox learned with *The Sound of Music* (1965). The release of the most successful movie musical of all time allowed for a third Zanuck-era renaissance. In the 1930s Darryl Zanuck had brought the company back to prominence. In the 1950s the studio's CinemaScope output was the wonder of the industry. Now, in an era when Hollywood wondered if it was going to survive at all, another array of ambitious productions came forth with all the dazzling artistry of the studio system in its last golden days.

There was *Rapture* (1965), *Those Magnificent Men in Their Flying Machines* (1965), *The Agony and the Ecstasy* (1965), *The Blue Max* (1966), *How to Steal a Million* (1966), *Fantastic Voyage* (1966), *The Sand Pebbles* (1966), *Doctor Dolittle* (1967), *Two For The Road* (1967), *The Planet of the Apes* (1968), *Star!* (1968), *Justine* (1969), *The Prime of Miss Jean Brodie* (1969), *Butch Cassidy and the Sundance Kid* (1969), *Hello, Dolly!* (1969), *M*A*S*H* (1970), *Patton* (1970), *The Sicilian Clan* (1970), *Tora! Tora! Tora!* (1970), *The Great White Hope* (1970), and *The French Connection* (1971). In all, it was a period that would reap 159 Oscar nominations. Arthur P. Jacobs's *Planet of the Apes*—entirely unique as a cultural phenomenon, and for relaunching the Fox franchise as major "A" productions—starred Linda Harrison, the former Miss Maryland, who became Richard Zanuck's second wife in 1969.

The company's television division was also reinvigorated by former actor William Self (*The Thing from Another World*, RKO, 1953), who joined the company in 1958 as a producer. Over the next fifteen years he rose to president of TCF-TV by producing *The Many Loves of Dobie Gillis* (1959–63), *Peyton Place* (1964–69), the first hit prime-time soap opera in the history of the medium, and Irwin Allen's popular science-fiction series *Voyage to the Bottom of the Sea* (1964–68), *Lost in Space* (1965–68), *The Time Tunnel* (1966–67), and *Land of the Giants* (1968–70). Then there were the phenomena of *Batman* (1966–68) and *M*A*S*H* (1972-83).

From 1965 through 1968 the studio took over American distribution of films from the celebrated British Hammer Studio. Among them was *One Million Years B.C.* (1966) starring Raquel Welch who was put under contract. The Zanucks only became interested in launching her as the studio's next sex symbol when producer James Broccoli wanted her as the girl in his next James Bond adventure. Ironically, that phenomenally popular series released by United Artists originally starred Sean Connery, whose talents had been wasted under contract to Fox.

The studio benefited from the resulting spy-film craze. *Our Man Flint* (1966), starring James Coburn in his signature role as Derek Flint, led to a sequel, *In Like Flint* (1967), and *Our Man Flint: Dead on Target*, a television movie that aired on ABC in 1975. Coburn was slated for—and turned down—the leading role in John Huston's excellent Cold War spy thriller, *The Kremlin Letter* (1970). Max von Sydow, who starred in the film, was also featured in *The Quiller Memorandum* (1966).

As his father had developed teen stars in the 1950s for the growing youth market, Richard Zanuck was aware that by the late 1960s they accounted for more than half the box office. It was an audience in social upheaval that he believed wanted the same cutting-edge, uninhibited entertainment that was flowing out of Europe. So although he green-lit big-budget, family-friendly films in the hope of repeating *The Sound of Music*'s success, he also produced films that were increasingly graphic in their depiction of sex, violence, and drug use. The success of Mark Weisbart's *Valley of the Dolls* (1967) encouraged him to bring in sexploitation producer Russ Meyer (*Beyond the Valley of the Dolls*, 1970; *The Seven Minutes*, 1971), and to go for a first-time

X rating with Robert Fryer's *Myra Breckinridge* (1970).

At the August 29, 1969, meeting of the board of directors in New York, Darryl Zanuck was elected chairman and chief executive officer, and Richard was made president. The younger Zanuck's plan to rename the company Twenty-First Century Fox was not implemented, nor was his idea of selling the Westwood studio and transplanting offices and production facilities to Beverly Hills, their Century Ranch, or even Las Vegas.

He did make cutbacks by closing the Paris and London offices, and he hired Dennis Stanfill, a US Naval Academy–trained treasurer of the Times-Mirror Corporation that October to strengthen the studio's financial state. It needed it. After six profitable years, the company's theatrical film rentals dropped into the red: -$27,502,000 in 1969, and in 1970, down further to a record low of -$76,388,000. He had heavily invested in *Doctor Dolittle* (1967), *Star!* (1968), *Hello, Dolly!* (1969), and *Tora! Tora! Tora!* (1970), all of which did not perform at the box office as hoped. Darryl Zanuck was equally disturbed at the direction his son was taking the company with films like *Myra Breckinridge*.

"After making a string of incredibly successful pictures we made some colossal failures," said Richard Zanuck. "There was a lot of friction

ABOVE: Gene Hackman accepting the Oscar for Best Actor in *The French Connection* (1971).

between my father and me, and the Board decided to call it a day."

That day was December 29, 1970. Richard Zanuck and David Brown resigned, essentially fired by Darryl, who continued as the company's chairman and chief executive officer. Dennis Stanfill was designated executive vice president of finance and operations control, to rescue the company. Before their departure they completed *The French Connection* (1971), produced by Philip D'Antoni and directed by William Friedkin. Based on the true story of the largest international narcotics smuggling bust in New York City history in the 1960s, the film was a box office hit, and earned five Academy Awards, including Best Picture. *The French Connection* was the last great success of the Zanuck era at Twentieth Century Fox. The year it was released Spyros Skouras died—two years after he had resigned his honorary chairmanship.

Darryl Zanuck remained an influence at the studio until his and Elmo Williams's departure in 1973, but it was never the same as when father and son had ruled the empire. He died on December 22, 1979. At his funeral at Westwood's United Methodist Church, strains from *The Longest Day* could be heard. Richard Zanuck and David Brown, however, would figure prominently again in the future of Hollywood—and Twentieth Century Fox.

BLDG. 102: SHIRLEY TEMPLE BLACK CHILD DEVELOPMENT CENTER (2002)

Shirley Temple Black remains an integral part of Twentieth Century Fox's heritage, and the bronze sculpture of her that flanks the Shirley Temple Black Development Center on the Fox lot serves as a reminder of her enduring legacy and her ability to unite and entertain both young and old.

—Jim Gianopulos, chairman and CEO, Twentieth Century Fox

In May of 2002 Shirley Temple Black returned to the lot to dedicate this Center, accommodating children of Fox employees for day care. Since her film career ended she had held office as the first female White House chief of protocol, and had served as ambassador to Ghana and Czechoslovakia and as a US delegate to the United Nations. A bronze statue by Nijel Binns depicts Shirley from *Baby Take a Bow* (1934). She died in 2014.

"Few people had as many personal assets to represent the United States as Shirley Temple Black," said President Gerald Ford, who also served on the Fox board of directors. "This country owes her a great deal."

STAGE SEVENTEEN (1966)

Beginning on January 11, 1967, Barry Coe initiated a short-lived $2 daily tour—or a $50-per-head VIP tour of the studio, which included a chauffeur-driven limousine, champagne, and visits to working sets—from tour headquarters above Stage Seventeen. During the summer of 1982, Gray Line Tours offered a short-lived ninety-minute, last-chance walking tour when it looked like Marvin Davis was going to develop the lot into condominiums. Robert Wagner continued the tradition as celebrity spokesman, including offering glimpses of the studio on Fox Movie Channel programming.

The Star Chamber (1983), made here, brought Michael Douglas to Fox for the first time. The son of screen legend Kirk Douglas, who had one of his finest early roles in *A Letter to Three Wives* (1949), Michael Douglas would continue the family legacy at Fox by appearing in a half-dozen notable Fox films.

Twenty-six-year-old actor Jon-Erik Hexum of *Cover Up* (1984–85) accidentally killed himself with a blank-loaded .44 caliber prop Magnum pistol as weeklong shooting on *Cover Up* was wrapping on Friday, October 12, 1984. Upon completing a scene, he loaded three harmless empty cartridges and two gunpowder-filled blanks and spun the cylinder before saying, "Let's see if I've got one for me," and firing.

Steven Bochco's landmark *NYPD Blue* (1993–2005) focused on the detectives of the New York Police Department's 15th Precinct, but filmed primarily in LA and on the lot, including on stages such as this one. Produced by MTM Enterprises, and inspired by shows like *M*A*S*H* and *Fort Apache the Bronx* (1981), the show revolutionized television. Relishing controversy and breaking down television taboos—and virtually creating the contemporary ensemble drama—Bochco adopted a gritty look, incorporating handheld cameras and more-realistic sets and dialogue. When Bochco was fired by MTM, Fox happily signed him up, and he developed *L.A. Law* (1986–94), partially inspired by studio classic, *The Verdict* (1982).

Neil Patrick Harris (*Gone Girl*, 2014) must consider this stage his home away from home. He starred in his signature role here as *Doogie Howser, M.D.* (1989–93), and then returned for *How I Met Your Mother* (2005–14).

Beginning in 2005 this stage was home to one of FX's highest-rated shows, *It's Always Sunny in Philadelphia*, created by and starring Rob McElhenney. He married costar Kaitlin Olson in 2008. To boost its initial low ratings, Danny DeVito was added to the cast and happily stayed there. DeVito's career at the studio stretched back to an appearance in *Starsky & Hutch* (1975–79), costarring with Michael Douglas and Kathleen Turner in the *Romancing the Stone* films, and later directing them in *The War of the Roses* (1989) across the lot on Stages Fourteen, Fifteen, and Sixteen.

Stage Eighteen (1966)

This stage contained the operating room, nurses' station, and patient rooms for David E. Kelley's *Chicago Hope* (1994–2000). The hospital's "staff," including Hector Elizondo, E. G. Marshall (who made his film debut in *The House on 92nd Street*, 1945), Adam Arkin (*Made for Each Other*, 1971), Mark Harmon, and Peter MacNicol *(Ally McBeal)* also used the emergency and waiting room, ambulance pull-up area, and treatment rooms on Stage Seventeen. The hospital executive suites were on Stage Nineteen. The stages were joined by common walls with large doors so that it was possible to

A view of Stages Seventeen, Eighteen and Nineteen with some of the sets from *New Girl* (2011–) out front. The Century City Intercontinental Hotel and Fox Plaza rise in the distance.

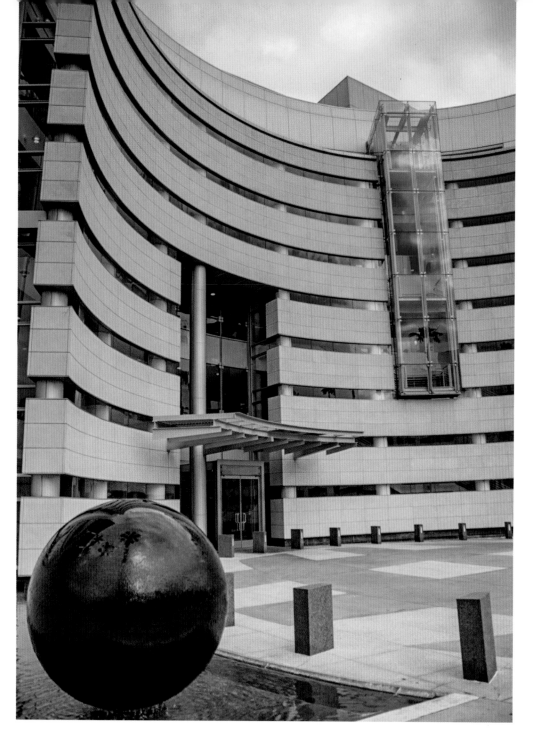

shoot a scene starting in one part of the hospital and continue into other stages.

Another *Chicago Hope* staff member, Mandy Patinkin, is also well known for his appearance in *The Princess Bride* (1987). The writer, director, cast, and crew credit the perennial appeal of the Act III production (a company headed by Norman Lear) to their personal connection to the classic fairytale. None more than Patinkin, who utters the film's most remembered lines: "My name is Inigo Montoya. You killed my father. Prepare to die."

"I'd lost my father in 1972," he said. "It just hit a chord with me, that I want my father back just like my character does. In my mind when I killed that six-fingered man I killed the cancer that killed my father. For a moment he was alive, and my fairytale came true."

BLDG. 100: NEW EXECUTIVE BUILDING (1998)

On the subject of high finance Deborah Kerr explains to Cary Grant in *An Affair to Remember* (1957) that: "The big secret seems to be to merge a sick corporation with a healthy one and everyone gets well." Such was the success of Rupert Murdoch's News Corp. and Twentieth Century Fox, and that extraordinary legacy is rather dramatically marked for all time on the lot with the New Executive Building and Fox Network Center, both designed by Richard Meier. They reflect Murdoch's

era with the company much as the original administration buildings reflect Winfield Sheehan and Darryl Zanuck.

Besides housing his office on the top floor, and those of News Corp. and Fox Broadcasting Company, this building features a semicircular courtyard carved out of the west face. The News Corp. logo is imprinted in the pavement, incorporating a fountain. Upon entering the "The News Café," at the south end of the first floor, you are greeted by Marilyn Monroe, Lauren Bacall, and Betty Grable and their boyfriends eating lunch in a blow-up from *How to Marry A Millionaire* (1953). Similar food-themed photos from Fox films are hung in the semiprivate booths along the east wall. Near the cash registers for this primary studio eatery—with its blond wood paneling, square tables with polished-rock tops, and a mix of Charles Eames plywood and Harry Bertoia chairs—is a mounted display of a prop table setting from *Titanic* (1997).

OPPOSITE: The main entrance of Bldg. 100 in 2015.

ABOVE LEFT: This bust of Homer Simpson is outside of The News Café with "Dolly Street" in the background.

ABOVE RIGHT: Interior of The News Café.

LEFT: Props from *Titanic* (1997).

RIGHT: Martin Ritt stands in front of the western street built for *Stagecoach* (1966)

FAR RIGHT: Mel Brooks

BELOW: Alan Ladd, Jr. stands in front of the elevated train set from *Hello, Dolly!* (1969) on what is now the Avenue of the Palms. At left is Bldg. 88 with its Harmonia Gardens façade.

THE CORPORATE HISTORY PART THREE: A NEW HOPE (1971-2015)

You always have to keep changing in this business—attitudes, methods, everything.

—Alan Ladd Jr., president, Twentieth Century Fox

By 1971 Twentieth Century Fox typified the Hollywood film factory of that era, painfully transitioning away from the old studio system toward a future that was uncertain. Adolph Zukor's Paramount—once William Fox's chief rival—was the first to be swallowed up by a corporate conglomerate, Gulf + Western, in 1966. Transamerica bought United Artists in 1967. Jack Warner sold his studio away to Kinney National Services.

Like others, Fox, crippled by debt, sold off its history, including the company's New York headquarters, the Western Avenue Studio, the Century Ranch, and studio props and costumes. Leading the company forward were Dennis Stanfill as chairman, and former Columbia executive Gordon Stulberg as president in charge of production. The titles were the same but the industry was different. Producers, directors, and stars—no longer under long-term exclusive contract—were the ones in power now, and Stulberg tried to court them into signing deals despite a spirit of retrenchment and cautious creativity.

When Irwin Allen sought to dispel the fear by renewing filmmaking on a grand scale with *The Poseidon Adventure*, Stulberg would only pay half of it. Gathering friends, Allen got a loan and the film became the greatest moneymaking hit of 1973, earning him an industry reputation as the "Master of Disaster." Although he discussed with *Poseidon* star Carol Lynley his idea to make an epic avalanche film as a follow-up, he ultimately coordinated a historic partnership with Warner Bros. to make *The Towering Inferno* (1974). The box office bonanza was the first time two major studios shared an expensive production, a trendsetting move that the studio would

TOP: Dennis Stanfill

ABOVE: Gordon Stulberg

repeat in the years to come. Ironically Dennis Stanfill removed Gordon Stulberg in December of 1975 for low-key, low-performing films reflecting a budget-consciousness that he enforced. Most reflected a shattered world—like Hollywood—and celebrated the nonconformity and politics of the decade. Some of the best were from studio veterans: Paul Newman and Joanne Woodward's *The Effect of Gamma Rays on Man-In-The-Moon Marigolds* (1972), Joseph Mankiewicz's final film, *Sleuth* (1972), Philip D'Antoni's *The Seven Ups* (1973), and Arthur P. Jacobs's *Planet of the Apes* sequels. Martin Ritt produced a stunning trio of films about race relations: *The Great White Hope* (1970), *Sounder* (1972), and *Conrack* (1974). Among a new generation, Charles Grodin and Cybill Shepherd had memorable career boosts in Neil Simon's *The Heartbreak Kid* (1972), as did James Caan in *Cinderella Liberty* (1973), and Timothy Bottoms in *The Paper Chase* (1973) and *The Crazy World of Julius Vrooder* (1974). *The Last American Hero* (1973), produced by Joe Wizan and starring Jeff Bridges, and *Dirty Mary, Crazy Larry* (1974) with Peter Fonda, explored the world of car racing. John Hough, who directed the latter, also made one of the decade's best horror films, *The Legend of Hell House* (1973); Robert Mulligan's *The Other* (1972) was another.

Inspired by the glam rock era the horror movie musical is a unique niche within the studio's musical legacy. The company released its take on *The Phantom of the Opera* legend with Brian De Palma's cult favorite *Phantom of the Paradise* (1974), and never was a Twentieth Century Fox trailer more true to its source than the one that declared: "You've seen all kinds of movies. But you've never seen anything like *The Rocky Horror Picture Show*...A different set of jaws!" Referring ironically to the enormous hit at Universal, produced by Richard Zanuck and David Brown, *Rocky* lost money even with its modest budget. It was not until it was discovered by midnight movie theatre audiences that the cult developed and net the film more than $50,000,000.

Now Dennis Stanfill looked to Alan Ladd Jr., who he promoted to vice president of production in 1975. Like Irwin Allen, Ladd did not believe Hollywood was through, and key to his success was his enthusiastic embracing of a new era of filmmaking and its filmmakers. He reawakened the company's activity abroad by supporting Richard Lester's all-star hit, *The Three Musketeers* (1974), Werner Herzog's *Nosferatu the Vampyre* (1979), and Bernardo Bertolucci's *Luna* (1979). He brought Mel Brooks to the lot to make *Young Frankenstein* (1974), launching a twenty-year collaboration with the studio. He allowed Brooks's protégé Gene Wilder to direct comedies of his own, including *Silver Streak* (1976), initiating a popular screen partnership with Richard

Pryor. This successful pattern—taking risks with people he trusted—earned him the presidency within a year, and the affectionate nickname of "Laddie" on the lot.

Sensing a hit franchise, he accepted a failing production from Warner Bros., entrusted it to neophyte director Richard Donner, cast studio veterans Gregory Peck and Lee Remick, and suggested that the satanic main character survive rather than be killed. *The Omen* (1976) was a smash hit, with the highest-grossing opening in the studio's history: $4.3 million in three days. There were sequels (*Omen II*, *Omen III*), a television movie *Omen IV: The Awakening*, a failed television series, and a remake in 2006.

Then there was writer/director George Lucas who came to him to finance his homage to the Saturday-matinee serials of his youth when Universal—where he made *American Graffiti* (1973)—said no. With the studio still in a cash-strapped state, Laddie took the profits from *The Omen* and said yes.

Star Wars Episode IV: A New Hope was released on May 25, 1977. Not since *The Robe* had a single film thrust the studio—and the rest of the industry— into a new era of filmmaking, relying on special effects, improved sound, and the increasing value of merchandising and the foreign market. It even bumped the traditional summer release date from the middle of June to the end of May. The studio that had

helped to pioneer wide-screen movies with stereo sound in the 1950s reintroduced it in *Star Wars*. Ray Dolby's noise-reduction and stereo system received national attention when used on release prints of *Star Wars*, and became an industry standard.

George Lucas's THX (named after his film *THX 1138*, 1971) was likewise developed to create better theater sound, just as his Industrial Light and Magic (ILM) was founded in 1975 in a warehouse in Van Nuys to create better visual effects. With the success of *Star Wars* and its sequels, ILM was reopened in San Rafael and is, like THX, a division of Lucasfilm Ltd. Both would continue to be utilized by Twentieth Century Fox. The film also inspired another generation of Fox filmmakers.

"I saw *Star Wars* [on its] opening day at Grauman's Chinese Theatre in Hollywood when I was fourteen," recalled Dean Devlin. "I was ninth in line. It redefined the way I think about science fiction and fantasy. After that I knew what I wanted to do for the rest of my life!"

"I really got energized by *Star Wars*," recalled James Cameron, "and in fact I quit my job as a truck driver and decided if I wanted to be a film-maker, I had better get going!"

"George Lucas's *Star Wars* lifted us out of our depression in the 1970s and into an awareness and focus on space and its possible future," noted broadcast journalist Walter Cronkite. "It stood by itself."

TOP: Richard Donner

ABOVE: George Lucas

ABOVE: Ridley Scott

By the end of 1977 the Ladd regime had reason to celebrate—not only the $150 million that George Lucas's *Star Wars* reaped for Twentieth Century Fox (the final tally for Lucasfilm was $430 million worldwide by 1979), but also because of the acclaim generated for Fred Zinnemann's *Julia*, and Herbert Ross's *The Turning Point*. Together they garnered thirty-three Oscar nominations. Laddie had taken the studio's feature-film division from $195 million to $301 million, and from three Oscar nominations to thirty-three. He had also saved the lot. That Alcoa lease on the studio property would have gotten prohibitively expensive had not *Star Wars IV* come along and allowed Dennis Stanfill to buy back the studio's acreage and provide necessary upgrades and renovations.

The success of *Star Wars IV* also allowed Dennis Stanfill to further diversify the company. By now Fox owned three television stations under the subsidiary United Television Inc.: KMSP (Minneapolis), KMOL (San Antonio), and KTVX (Salt Lake City). To these he added resorts in California and Colorado, including the Pebble Beach Company and Aspen Skiing Company, as well as Coca-Cola Bottling Midwest. He formed a joint cable company with United Artists called Hollywood Home Theater, and embraced the home-video market by leasing an assortment of pre-1972 films to Magnetic Video Corp. and RCA. In 1979 he purchased Magnetic, which was reorganized into Twentieth Century Fox Video in 1982.

Laddie's Midas touch continued. There were concerns that the story of a Southern textile mill union organizer was not box office, particularly when Jane Fonda, the star of the project, dropped out. *Norma Rae* (1979) provided a triumphant $11 million for the studio and a delightful new movie star named Sally Field. The tiny $2.3 million seminal coming-of-age story, *Breaking Away* (1979), made $10 million. Although the downward spiral of a late-1960s rock star seemed a depressing prospect, *The Rose* (1979) featured an impressive film debut for Bette Midler.

Laddie's second important contribution to the studio's science-fiction canon was approving *Alien* (1979) and its two key elements: Sigourney Weaver for the lead instead of the traditional male hero, and the unique vision of director Ridley Scott, who had likewise been inspired by *Star Wars* and stepped in after Richard Donner had turned it down. The new Fox franchise made Weaver a Fox star and brought James Cameron and David Fincher into the fold as directors of its sequels.

When Laddie began negotiations with Dennis Stanfill for a larger share of Fox's profits, with his three-year contract ending in December 1979, the differences between the men came to a head. Stanfill wanted to continue to keep a tight rein on studio spending—too tight for Laddie, who departed in July.

In August Stanfill promoted vice president of European production Sandy Lieberson to president in charge of studio production, and Ashley Boone, whose seven years in sales and marketing included the promotion of *Star Wars IV*, to head distribution. That fall he made Alan Hirschfield, who had recently guided Columbia through its own troubled times in the 1970s, their boss as vice chairman of the board and chief operating officer.

Hirschfield brought with him his team in production (Daniel Melnick and protégée Sherry Lansing), marketing and distribution (Norman Levy), and television (Harris Katleman). Inevitably Sandy Lieberson and Ashley Boone departed. Hirschfield moved Norm Levy into distribution, and asked Daniel Melnick to head production. Wanting instead to make films independently at the studio, he suggested Sherry Lansing. She had recently developed *The China Syndrome* (1979), a Zanuck-like exploration of a controversial issue that broke Columbia's opening-day box-office record, and the Oscar-rich *Kramer vs. Kramer* (1979) with Stanley R. Jaffe. The schoolteacher-turned-model-turned-actress-turned-studio-executive was now the first woman to head a major Hollywood studio. *Variety* issued the headline: "20th Century Gets a First Lady."

Excitement rose in Century City with the release of the team's first success, *All That Jazz* (1979). Bob Fosse's outrageous autobiographical musical made money as one of the most honored films of the year. This enthusiasm carried into the new decade with the release of the last of Laddie's productions, including *Nine to Five* (1980), and the distribution of *Star Wars V: The Empire Strikes Back* (1980).

While Sherry Lansing developed her own slate of films, Norman Levy sought "pickups" from independent filmmakers, forging successful distribution deals with Melvin Simon Productions (*My Bodyguard*, 1980; *The Stunt Man*, 1980), Albert S. Ruddy (*Cannonball Run*, 1981), and ABC Motion Pictures (*Silkwood*, 1983; *Prizzi's Honor*, 1985). Profits and prestige were lost, however, when Norm Levy turned down Sherry Lansing's request to distribute *Chariots of Fire* (1981). Growing antagonism led to fear of takeover when Herb Siegel's Chris-Craft Industries, Inc., began to buy Fox stock in an effort to acquire those television stations.

Allied with them was one of the most powerful oil and real estate billionaires in the country. Marvin Harold Davis from Denver, Colorado, wanted to make a "fun" investment in Twentieth Century Fox, with Aetna Insurance and Casualty Company and commodities broker Marc Rich as partners. He assured Stanfill and the board of directors that he was not a looter and would be hands-off with studio management.

TOP: Alan Hirschfield

ABOVE: Sherry Lansing strikes a pose on New York Street.

ABOVE: Joe Wizan

Aware that they were vulnerable to a more-hostile takeover—and certainly, with no better offers in sight—the formal merger agreement was presented to stockholders on June 8, 1981. With the $722 million purchase the studio was folded into the Davis family's TCF Holdings. Chris-Craft got what it wanted, too: a key position on the board of directors of Fox's United Television stations.

Almost immediately Stanfill had reason to regret the sale, as Davis's true intentions were revealed. To pay back his debt Davis sold off a large portion of that protective layer that Stanfill had recently built up for the company. Then he showed interest in the studio's valuable real estate. He wanted to sell it and redevelop it, with 2,200 condominiums and offices including the Fox Plaza Tower. In negotiations for a partnership with CBS—who would distribute Fox movies on cable TV and home video—he reasoned that production could resume at the forty-acre CBS Television City property.

This was not the act of an absentee landlord, and the hostilities led to Stanfill's resignation on June 29, 1981. Although it reached the point where blueprints of the redevelopment were drawn up,, Marvin Davis decided that, due to the weak real estate market, the studio would remain in Century City for at least five years. In the meantime, he found that he enjoyed the status of Hollywood mogul, and promoted Alan Hirschfield to chairman and chief executive officer. He was not pleased with Sherry Lansing's 1981–1982 offerings that posted a loss. For Christmas there were two hits: *Modern Problems* (1981) starring Chevy Chase, and Stanley R. Jaffe's antiwar *Taps* (1981), featuring up-and-comers Tom Cruise and Sean Penn. The rest were ambitious but too often missed the mark. A lack of support—leaving her unable to make or protect movies she wanted to produce—was short-circuiting Lansing's success.

Harris Katleman was more successful in revitalizing the television division by bringing Glen A. Larson to the studio to create *The Fall Guy* (1981–86), transforming *Nine to Five* into a popular series, and reintroducing *Mr. Belvedere* (Christopher Hewett instead of Clifton Webb) to audiences from 1985 to 1990.

Before he left, Laddie brought Richard Zanuck and David Brown back to the lot in 1979. At Universal they had re-teamed Paul Newman and Robert Redford in the Academy Award–winning hit, *The Sting* (1973), and they had launched Steven Spielberg's career with *Jaws* (1975). Now they made *The Verdict*, directed by Sidney Lumet and starring Paul Newman, as the studio's prestige Christmas release of 1982. That the producers—as well as Daniel Melnick and Sherry Lansing—left the lot by the end of that year exposed the management troubles within

Davis's regime. Melnick and Lansing and Stanley R. Jaffe made deals at Barry Diller's Paramount, where Melnick had a hit with *Footloose* (1984), and Jaffe-Lansing Productions produced the monster hit, *Fatal Attraction* (1988).

As Hirschfield brought producer Joe Wizan back to Fox to replace Lansing in December of 1982, the last of her films were released, including Martin Scorcese's *King of Comedy* (1983) and more Neil Simon with Herbert Ross's *Max Dugan Returns* (1983). Norman Levy distributed *Star Wars VI: Return of the Jedi* (1983); Frank Yablans's *The Star Chamber* (1983), beginning Michael Douglas's career at the studio; the surprise hit, *Mr. Mom* (1983), with first-time producer Lauren Shuler; and Melvin Simon's $100 million hit, *Porky's* (1983). Fox Classics brought such films from abroad as *Eating Raoul* (1982), *Betrayal* (1983), the sleeper hit *The Man from Snowy River* (1982), and the Academy Award–winning *To Begin Again* (1982). *The Gods Must Be Crazy*, made in Botswana, became a distribution sensation in America in 1984.

Besides Joe Wizan's success with *Bachelor Party* (1984) that brought Tom Hanks to Fox, and *Revenge of the Nerds* (1984), the studio finally had a major hit of its own with *Romancing the Stone* (1984). Sherry Lansing, who had green-lit the film in late 1982, had supported the career of its producer, Michael Douglas, since their days together

at Columbia. Douglas in turn had faith in the script he had purchased in true Hollywood fashion from a Malibu waitress, and a director named Robert Zemeckis, who had only two minor movies to his credit.

When Paul Newman turned down the leading role, Douglas stepped in front of the camera, too, with costar Kathleen Turner, chosen by Joe Wizan. The film earned $80 million, launching Zemeckis's career, and the sequel, *Jewel of the Nile* (1985), earned $100 million.

But for hits like that, Marvin Davis suffered the embarrassment of *Two of a Kind* (1983) and *Rhinestone* (1984). He replaced Wizan in August of 1984

TOP: Rupert Murdoch.

ABOVE: Barry Diller.

with Lawrence Gordon who produced the hit *48 Hours* (1982) at Paramount. Hirschfield was out as well. Having made back his personal investment in Fox, and with partner Marc Rich mired in the largest tax-evasion case in US history, Davis was no longer finding it "fun" to run a Hollywood studio—especially after he had hired Barry Diller away from Paramount as the new chairman and chief executive officer in October of 1984. Almost immediately the relationship went bad, as Diller discovered the studio was sinking in $89 million worth of debt.

"The status of the company was not as promised," said Diller. "I had to struggle financially just to keep it going. Aside from its financial status, the worst discovery was [that] there was very little of a real company with any kind of thoughtful rationale and any kind of integration working for it. Wisely or unwisely, Mr. Davis did not want to invest further in the company. That's what brought Rupert Murdoch into the situation. I wanted him to come in very badly and worked to make it happen."

Like William Fox, the Australian-born newspaper mogul Rupert Murdoch was an empire-builder. Ready to move into electronic media, he had already tried to purchase Warner Bros. Instead, he purchased 50 percent of TCF Holdings, for $250 million in March of 1985. Six months later, he paid an additional $325 million to complete his purchase from Marvin Davis. With his News Corporation (the third largest in the world), Murdoch had the capital to spend on Fox: $1.55 billion went to acquire the Metromedia group of six major-market independent television stations in 1985 that attracted other satellites, to realize his and Diller's dream of a fourth American network. With founding members Jamie Kellner (president), David Johnson (advertising), Scott Sassa (publicity), and Garth Ancier (head of programming) they made television history on October 9, 1986 with the live debut of *The Late Show Starring Joan Rivers* (1986-87).

The Fox Broadcasting Company (stylized as FOX by consultant Chiat Day) successfully challenged the three major networks with the same kind of edgy, even controversial, entertainment and bold business practices that had built Murdoch's newspaper business. There was *Married...with Children* (1987-97), *The Tracey Ullman Show* (1987-90) and from it *The Simpsons* (1989–), *21 Jump Street* (1987-91), *America's Most Wanted* (1988–), and *COPS* (1989–). Counterprogramming measures like adding weekend prime-time line-ups then swiping eight affiliates and the NFL from CBS prompted the *Los Angeles Times* to remark: "Like him or loathe him, Rupert Murdoch is the last of the great media swashbucklers, a throwback to the pirates, cutthroats and visionaries who used to run the business before it was engulfed and devoured by giant risk-averse corporate behemoths."

"We had a very tentative start," recalled Murdoch, "but without Barry Diller and his application and his genius—he's a magnificent negotiator and a salesman—I don't think we'd have FOX today."

FOX or the Fox studio either. To save the studio, Diller instituted a 15 percent pay cut across-the-board, slashed department budgets, and laid off three hundred of its fifteen hundred employees.

"Barry was right. We were fat. We had too much overhead," said Harris Katleman, who credited Diller with allowing him to bring Steven Bochco to Fox: "I would have spent six months justifying it, and I would have lost Bochco in the meantime." Bochco became a long-term resident of the lot, in Irwin Allen's old quarters, producing *L.A. Law* (1986–94), *Hooperman* (1987–89), and *NYPD Blue* (1993–2005).

Money—as well as a badly needed dose of nostalgic pride—was also provided with the release of *Cocoon* (1985). It was the brainchild of Lili Fini, whom Richard Zanuck married in 1977 after five years of marriage to Linda Harrison. The science-fiction fantasy was the couple's first project as producers, with David Brown. But it took Barry Diller to get it green-lit, directed by Ron Howard, and starring a cluster of Fox legends, including Don Ameche, Hume Cronyn, and Jessica Tandy. Tyrone Power's son even made an appearance. The media

was inspired to sum up Ameche's Academy Award–winning comeback this way: "Don Ameche: A Class Act—Again!"

For a year and a half Lawrence Gordon produced films like *Jumpin' Jack Flash* (1986) with Whoopi Goldberg and *Lucas* (1986), bringing Charlie Sheen and Winona Ryder into the Fox fold before resigning due to illness. Embassy Communications chairman Alan Horn replaced him, but resigned after eight months, citing Diller's micromanagement. The joke around the lot was that working for Diller was akin to extinguishing a fire on the Alaska oil pipeline. If you were too close, you burned to death; if you moved too far away, you froze.

Diller promoted twenty-eight-year-old Scott Rudin—executive vice president under Gordon—to head production and hired his former ABC boss, Leonard Goldberg, as the new president and chief operating officer. Goldberg's projects—*Wall Street* (1987), *The Princess Bride* (1987), *Black Widow* (1987), and James L. Brooks's *Broadcast News* (1987)—had the confident sheen and social conscience that had been missing from the studio for years. Brooks, who had developed *Room 222* (1969–72) for the studio and then branched out to make movies at Paramount, was drawn back to the lot as much by his respect for Larry Gordon as for Barry Diller. Both soon had reason to be grateful for his return, with *The Tracey Ullman Show* (1987–90) and

TOP: James L. Brooks

ABOVE: John Davis

The Simpsons (1989–), and the founding of Gracie Films on the lot that would result in *Big* (1988), *Say Anything* (1989), *War of the Roses* (1989), and *The Simpsons Movie* (2007).

"I was there when Fox was a minute and a half from going under," Brooks said. "But Barry Diller brought it off. It was sheer force of will."

With Sylvester Stallone rampaging through Hollywood with box-office success in the 1980s as a former Green Beret named Rambo, Lawrence Gordon and Joel Silver saw to it that Arnold Schwarzenegger held his own at Fox with *Commando* (1985) and then *Predator* (1987). The latter brought director John McTiernan and producer John Davis (son of Marvin Davis) into the fold, initiated another franchise (including a merger with the *Alien* films), and is unique in Hollywood history for featuring two future California governors.

What a summer the assembled team had in 1988: *Big* in June, helmed by Scott Rudin and James L. Brooks, *Die Hard* in July, with the action-movie team of Lawrence Gordon, Joel Silver, and John McTiernan, and the distribution of *Young Guns* in August (with its inordinate amount of actors with famous fathers), produced by James G. Robertson and Joe Roth. *Big* forever catapulted Tom Hanks into the first rank of movie stardom as a comic and dramatic actor. *Die Hard* made Bruce Willis a movie star and initiated another franchise. The year did not end badly, either, with the winter release of Mike Nichols's *Working Girl* (1988).

In 1989 Murdoch split Twentieth Century Fox Film Corporation into two separate entities known as Twentieth Century Fox and Twentieth Television, and hired Peter Chernin, the former head of production at Lorimar, to replace Garth Ancier. Chernin expanded FOX from two nights of programming a week to seven making it the number one network among the coveted eighteen-to-forty-nine-year-old audience and second in profitability to ABC beginning in the 1991–1992 TV season.

That summer James Cameron's *The Abyss* (1989) was expected to continue the studio's blockbuster winning streak. The filmmaker boldly announced: "If I can't do what *2001: A Space Odyssey* did for science-fiction films in space in the underwater arena, then I don't want to make the movie." Although the film set the ambitious pattern for Cameron's later work at Fox—outdoing himself with special effects—and receiving critical acclaim (Peter Travers in *Rolling Stone* dubbed it "the greatest underwater adventure ever filmed"), editorial problems plagued the final result. The film was Fox's biggest earner that year at $50 million, but it cost $60 million. The 40 percent box-office drop from the previous year cost Leonard Goldberg his job. Inspired by the success of *Young Guns*,

Barry Diller hired Joe Roth to replace him, effective August 1, with the mandate to triple the studio's output of feature films.

Joe Roth assembled a new team—Harvard-trained lawyer Strauss Zelnick as president and chief operating officer and Tom Jacobson as head of production - that created two instant classics for the 1990 holiday season. *Home Alone* (1990) was rescued from turnaround at Warner Bros. launching the career of Chris Columbus as the premier director of family films in Hollywood, and another Fox child star Macauley Culkin. It was Roth who recognized the promotional possibilities of Culkin's iconic face shot ("the face that launched a thousand posters," as Columbus referred to it). Roth also brought Tim Burton to the lot who cast Johnny Depp, who got his career start in FOX's *21 Jump Street*, Winona Ryder, and Fox veteran Vincent Price in *Edward Scissorhands* (1990).

With the turn of a new decade, Twentieth Century Fox's home in Century City was once again in question. For necessary growth and access to the latest filmmaking technologies, Barry Diller had two options: build a new studio in Burbank, Santa Clarita, or Valencia, or undergo a $200 million redevelopment plan entailing an expansion of lot facilities from 1.1 million square feet to 1.9 million square feet. He chose the latter, which included plans for a new television broadcast facility, a new executive building, and studio postproduction upgrades.

Diller then shocked the industry on February 24, 1992, when he announced his resignation. Having made television history and reinvigorating Fox's film division, he wanted more of the company than Rupert Murdoch was willing to give. Just as suddenly Murdoch was no longer a distant figure on the Century City lot for a rearrangement of the Fox executive team. Fox's film and TV operations were now the fastest-growing part of his forty-year-old, $8 billion global empire, yet the studio was still only turning out fifteen pictures a year, and Joe Roth's box office clout, after more hits like *Die Hard 2* (1990) and *Sleeping with the Enemy* (1991) and *The Last of the Mohicans* (1992), was slipping with the release of *For the Boys* (1991), *Shining Through* (1992), *Hoffa* (1992), and *Toys* (1992).

Chase Carey, a former Columbia executive who had been with Fox since 1988, became Murdoch's right-hand man as chief operating officer of News Corp. Peter Chernin was put in charge of feature and television production as chairman, and Sandy Grushow was promoted into his old position. Under Grushow FOX became a full seven-nights-a-week network in 1993 enjoying success with *In Living Color* (1990–94), *Beverly Hills 90210* (1990–2000), *Picket Fences* (1992–96), *Melrose Place* (1992-99) and *Party of Five* (1994-2000) and aggressively acquired

ABOVE: Chase Carey

sports programming. The Fox Children's Network, launched in 1990, merged with Saban Entertainment to became Fox Kids Worldwide in 1995, based on the success of *The Mighty Morphin Power Rangers* (1993-96) and *X-Men* (1992-1997), and then the Fox Family Channel in 1997 with its acquisition of International Family Entertainment. It was sold to The Walt Disney Company in 2001.

At the studio Chernin brought in Bill Mechanic as the new president of Twentieth Century Fox in September of 1994, hoping Mechanic's skill at running home video and the international distribution of films at The Walt Disney Company could cushion them from bad theatrical film seasons as well. Meanwhile, vice president of production Elizabeth Gabler had an answer to the box-office doldrums. She had championed Anne Fine's *Madame Doubtfire* until she and producer Roger Birnbaum found the right team in Chris Columbus and actor Robin Williams. It was a six-year process that produced that extraordinary hit *Mrs. Doubtfire* (1993).

Bill Mechanic hired James Gianopulos, formerly a senior executive at Carolco Pictures and Paramount Pictures, to expand overseas profits. He was so successful at it he was made president of the division—taking Twentieth Century Fox International from $298 million in annual revenue in 1993 to $1 billion by 2004.

Chernin's studio restructure, unveiled in 1994, introduced new studio brands: Fox Searchlight Pictures, Fox Family, and Fox 2000, to ideally double production to thirty pictures a year. Tom Rothman was brought on board in July of 1994 to head Searchlight Pictures. It was hoped that he could create the same kind of sophisticated, art-house films he had produced at Samuel Goldwyn. Ed Burns's *The Brothers McMullen* (1995) was the first release, but it was first-time director Peter Cattaneo's *The Full Monty* (1997), the highest-grossing film made in the UK, which launched it in a big way.

Chris Meledandri's Fox Family Films was expected to cash in on the resurgence of interest in animated films in the 1990s, thanks to The Walt Disney Studio. Fox had periodically dabbled in animated feature releases, such as Richard Horner and Lester Osterman's *Raggedy Ann and Andy* (1977); Ralph Bakshi's *Wizards* (1977) and *Fire and Ice* (1983); Wayne Young and Peter Faiman's *FernGully: The Last Rainforest* (1992); David Kirschner and Jerry Mills's *Once Upon a Forest* (1993); and Maurice Hunt's *Pagemaster* (1994). Now, Bill Mechanic invested $100 million to convert a 60,000-square-foot building in Phoenix, Arizona, into Fox Animation Studios Inc., and hired veteran animators Don Bluth and Gary Goldman to run it with a planned slate of one full-length feature film every eighteen months. The magical *Anastasia* (1997) was the first.

Laura Ziskin, who had produced *Pretty Woman* (1990) for Touchstone Pictures, was chosen to head Fox 2000. Besides producing films ranging from *Volcano* (1997) to *Inventing the Abbotts* (1997), she also brought Richard Zanuck back to the lot with a three-year production deal. He re-imagined his own classic with Tim Burton's *Planet of the Apes* (2000). It was Tom Rothman who introduced the two men, igniting a famed partnership that proved fruitful elsewhere, with *Charlie and the Chocolate Factory* (2005, Warner Bros.), *Alice in Wonderland* (2010, Walt Disney Pictures), and *Dark Shadows* (2012, Warner Bros.). Besides the new studio brands, The FX Channel (FOX "Extended"), The Fox Movie Channel, and Fox Sports also launched in 1994. Fox News began airing in 1996. Two years later Rupert Murdoch, to make FOX a full-fledged network, purchased the New World Communications television chain becoming the largest television station owner in the United States.

"Building Fox Sports from the ground up was something which will always live with me," recalled David Hill, "but more particularly all the incredible men and women in front of, and behind the cameras who made Rupert's dream become a reality. But, my proudest moment was running FOX in the late '90s. Working with Peter Roth, Mike Darnell, and a group of fearless television warriors, we took it to #2 behind NBC by 1999."

Tom Jacobson ensured that the company's traditional "monument" held its own with an impressive digital facelift, featuring a sweeping new panoramic view of the logo against the Hollywood sky specially timed for the release of James Cameron's *True Lies* (1994). He had Jorge Saralegui as a new vice president of production—the first that had risen on the lot from script reader—responsible for Mark Gordon and writer Graham Yost's action-thriller hit, *Speed* (1994). Contributing to its success was cinematographer-turned-director Jan de Bont—who had excelled in shooting action sequences for *The Jewel of the Nile* (1985), *Die Hard* (1988), and *Shining Through* (1992)—and new Fox star Sandra Bullock. She appeared in the sequel and a project closer to her heart, *Hope Floats* (1998).

When Jacobson announced plans to depart the studio to create his own independent production company in September of 1995, Peter Chernin replaced him with Tom Rothman. Rothman's executive vice president Peter Rice and Saralegui approved more Gordon-Yost pictures (*Broken Arrow*, 1996; *Hard Rain*, 1998), and were responsible for bringing in talent like Baz Luhrmann (*William Shakespeare's Romeo + Juliet*, 1996; *Moulin Rouge*, 2001), Danny Boyle (*A Life Less Ordinary*, 1997), and Bryan Singer (*X-Men*).

Dean Devlin and Roland Emmerich's gloriously

TOP: Chris Meledandri

ABOVE: Peter Rice standing on Avenue of the Palms

old-fashioned summer blockbuster *Independence Day* (1996) contributed mightily to the rising reputation and morale of Bill Mechanic's Twentieth Century Fox. His team negotiated a record $1 billion film-financing package with Citicorp, and rebuilt the international, home video, music, and finance departments. It earned him the title of chairman and chief executive of Fox Filmed Entertainment. Chernin was promoted to president and chief operating officer of News Corp.

"After knocks, Fox rocks," proclaimed John Brodie in *Variety*.

Sandy Grushow's FOX then unleashed hits like David E. Kelley's *The Practice* (1997–2004) and *Ally McBeal* (1997–2002). A third-generation writer for television, Joss Whedon transformed his 1992 feature film *Buffy the Vampire Slayer* into a television series phenomenon, produced by Twentieth Century Fox Television for the WB Network as a mid-season replacement in 1997. By 1999 Twentieth Century Fox Television was the leading supplier of primetime programming with a record thirty prime-time series. Of its kids and sports programming, "they are ten steps ahead of everyone," observed Merrill Lynch media analyst Jessica Reif-Cohen. Inspired by the success of *The Simpsons*, FOX's "Animation Domination," included Mike Judge's *King of the Hill* (1997–2009), Seth MacFarlane's *Family Guy* (1999–2002, 2004–), and Loren Bouchard and Jim Dauterive's *Bob's Burgers* (2011–).

Forty-eight years after Darryl Zanuck had produced *Kangaroo* (1952), the first major American feature film made in Australia, Fox Studios Sydney opened there on May 2, 1998, as part of Rupert Murdoch's plan to increase production on an international scale. The reasons were simple: Films were cheaper to make outside America, and now had to appeal to a worldwide audience. In the 1960s, the United States had accounted for approximately 65 percent of the world movie box office. Now that had dropped to 41 percent. Kim Williams was hired as chief executive of the studio, with Murdoch's son Lachlan in charge of the company's Australian operations.

James Cameron's epic, Academy Award–winning *Titanic* (1997) certainly appealed to that international audience, contributing to the company's top-grossing summer to date. The film required the construction of the Fox Studios Baja near the Mexican resort community of Rosarito Beach. It covered forty acres and featured the world's largest water tank to date (holding 17 million gallons) for the 775-foot-long, 100-foot-tall, near-full-size, starboard-side re-creation of the *Titanic*. As costs escalated—and Cameron's budget reports ballooned from $120 million to $200 million—the industry began to wonder if the studio had embarked on another *Cleopatra* (1963) debacle.

Only by partnering with Paramount (who released the picture domestically in theaters and home video) did this *Titanic* arrive safely after 160 days of production at its premiere in Tokyo, on December 15, 1997. The film opened at number one, and remained there for a record-breaking fifteen weeks, finding success overseas in fifty-six countries.

Other hits that summer included Chris Carter's *The X-Files: Fight the Future* (1998), a big-screen adaptation of his TV phenomenon, family treats like Mirelle Soria and Tracey Trench's *Ever After* (1998), starring Drew Barrymore, and John Davis's *Dr. Dolittle* (1998), starring Eddie Murphy. Peter and Bobby Farrelly's *There's Something About Mary* (1998) surpassed the $100 million mark as the third-highest-grossing film of the year, and launched Cameron Diaz as a Fox star.

Thanks to the negotiations of Peter Chernin and Domestic Film Group's Tom Sherak, Fox was in the enviable position of releasing Hollywood's most-talked-about summer film the following year. After sixteen years George Lucas was ready to release the first of three *Star Wars* prequels: *Episode I: The Phantom Menace* (1999). To promote the prequels Lucas had restored and revised his original trilogy, which Fox was happy to redistribute (they had by now made $1.8 billion on the three films. A further record-breaking 22 million copies were sold on home video. A further benefit to the studio were

LEFT: Leonardo DiCaprio and Kate Winslet as Jack and Rose in the Best Picture winner *Titanic* (1997).

BELOW: Aerial view of the Fox Baja Studios where the massive ship for *Titanic* (1997) was built.

ABOVE LEFT: Shawn Levy

ABOVE MIDDLE: David Fincher

ABOVE RIGHT: Darren Aronofsky

Natalie Portman and Ewan McGregor, stars of the prequels, who became Fox stars.

Meanwhile, Lindsay Law, who replaced Tom Rothman at Fox Searchlight, distributed Julie Taymor's *Titus* (1999), Rothman's team offered Mike Judge's *Office Space* (1999), and Laura Ziskin finished off her career at the studio with Terrence Malick's first film in twenty years, *The Thin Red Line* (1998), David Fincher's *Fight Club* (1999), and a nod to the past, *Anna and the King* (1999). The question arose: Would Twentieth Century Fox change its name to reflect a new millennium? Years earlier Richard Zanuck had proposed that they do. The current administration said no..

"The Twentieth Century Fox logo stands for something," explained Tom Sherak. "When that logo goes on the screen, people know it as something. It has a history to it, and that history is very

important as to why we are a major studio."

For that new millenium Peter Chernin oversaw the creation of a new production team: Tom Rothman, as the newly created president of the Twentieth Century Fox Film Group, overseeing the films of the studio and Elizabeth Gabler's Fox 2000, Hutch Parker, the new president of production, and Peter Rice running Fox Searchlight. Together they forged new partnerships with Regency Enterprises (including the Academy Award–winning *12 Years A Slave*), Dune Entertainment/Color Force (*The X-Files: I Want to Believe, Marley and Me, The Diary of a Wimpy Kid*), DreamWorks (*Cast Away, Minority Report, Road to Perdition*), and TSG Entertainment (*The Maze Runner* franchise), while maintaining others with George Lucas (*Star Wars II: Attack of the Clones, Star Wars III: Revenge of the Sith*), Ridley Scott (*Kingdom of Heaven, Prometheus, The Counselor, The Martian*), James

Cameron (*Avatar*), and Shawn Levy (*Night at the Museum*).

Inspired by the success of the Warner Bros./DC Comics' *Superman* and *Batman* films, a collaboration with Marvel yielded two new franchises: *X-Men* (2000–14) and *Fantastic Four* (2005–15). Helping to make the *X-Men* films so successful was co-producer Richard Donner, twenty-four years after he launched the *Omen* series, and more importantly his wife Lauren Shuler Donner. All of these partnerships created a new array of Fox stars, including Colin Farrell, Ashley Judd, Hugh Jackman, Ben Stiller, and Michael Fassbender.

After a near-merger with MGM seventy years before, and decades of various partnership discussions, Fox signed an agreement in November of 2000 to take over foreign distribution of that studio's films. The following year they added the international distribution of their home video releases.

Elizabeth Gabler's Fox 2000 produced thoughtful thrillers like Joel Schumacher's *Phone Booth* (2003), a smash hit biography of Johnny Cash, *Walk the Line* (2005), and the company's two biggest hits of 2008 (*Alvin and the Chipmunks* and *Marley and Me*). Yet it remains unique for its celebration of books including *The Devil Wears Prada* (2006), *Ramona and Beezus* (2010), *The Chronicles of Narnia: The Voyage of the Dawn Treader* (2010), *Water for Elephants* (2011), *The Book Thief* (2013),

The Monuments Men (2014), *The Fault in Our Stars* (2014), *The Longest Ride* (2015), *Paper Towns* (2015), *Bridge of Spies* (2015) as well as the *Percy Jackson* franchise. Gabler's tenaciousness—it took seven years to make Robert Zemeckis's *Cast Away* (2000), and ten for Ang Lee's *Life of Pi* (2012)—paid off.

Under Peter Rice—with a team including Nancy Utley and Steve Gilula that would take over in 2009—the Fox Searchlight tradition of unfiltered, very personal slices of everyday life continued. There was Gurinder Chadha's inspirational 2003 hit, *Bend It Like Beckham*, Zach Braff's *Garden State* (2004), and Alexander Payne's acclaimed *Sideways* (2004) and *The Descendants* (2011). Jared Hess's *Napoleon Dynamite* (2005) was the studio's biggest grosser of the year, at $45 million.

Jason Reitman entrusted first-time screenwriter Diablo Cody with *Juno* (2006), and the film earned her an Oscar and the film, a gross of $230 million worldwide. Michael Arndt's *Little Miss Sunshine* (2007) produced another Oscar for screenplay and two new stars in Steve Carell and Abigail Breslin. Besides Adrienne Shelly's *Waitress* (2007) and Marc Webb's *(500) Days of Summer* (2009), director Darren Aronofsky inspired career-defining performances from Mickey Rourke as *The Wrestler* (2008) and Natalie Portman as *The Black Swan* (2010).

Terrence Malick was back to provide *The Tree of Life* (2013). Wes Anderson provided *Fantastic Mr.*

TOP: Nancy Utley

ABOVE: Steve Gilula

ABOVE: The cast and crew of *Slumdog Millionaire* (2009) celebrate on Oscar night.

RIGHT: *12 Years a Slave* (2013) also won the Academy Award for Best Picture.

FAR RIGHT: Hutch Parker

Fox (2009) and *The Grand Budapest Hotel* (2014). John Madden provided *The Best Exotic Marigold Hotel* (2011) and a sequel in 2015. John Crowley's *Brooklyn* (2015) and Davis Guggenheim's *He Named Me Malala* (2015) upheld the Zanuck storytelling traditions. There were even two multi-Oscar Best Picture Academy Award winners: Danny Boyle's *Slumdog Millionaire* (2008) and Alejandro Iñárritu's *Birdman* (2014).

When the disappointing box-office returns of Fox Animation Studios' second feature, *Titan A.E.* (2000), forced the closure of the six-year-old animation studio in Phoenix, Arizona, Fox Animation president Chris Meledandri oversaw the transformation of Blue Sky Studios from special effects

(*Alien Resurrection*, 1997; *Fight Club*, 1999; *Titan A.E.*, 2000) to an animated-feature division that produced the *Ice Age* franchise, *Robots* (2005), *Dr. Seuss's Horton Hears a Who* (2008), *Rio* (2011), *Epic* (2013), *Rio 2* (2014), and *The Peanuts Movie* (2015).

In 2000 Sandy Grushow, now heading FOX and Twentieth Century Fox Television, positioned Gail Berman to run FOX. The former head of Sandollar Productions, and founding president of Regency Television, took the network to the number one spot for the first time. Although FOX hit the target as the highest rated among eighteen to thirty-four-year-olds for the first time in 1998, Berman captured the even greater 18-49 demographic beginning in 2004 with one of the networks "reality" shows that were redefining the television game show. It was Rupert Murdoch's daughter Elisabeth who had urged the creation of an American version of Simon Fuller's popular British hit, *Pop Idol* (2001). It became *American Idol* (2002–16).

Gail Berman's counterparts at Twentieth Century Fox Television, which continued as the leading supplier of primetime programming in the industry, were Dana Walden and Gary Newman. Their shows were: *Judging Amy* (1999–2005), *Stark Raving Mad* (1999–2000), *24* (2001–10), *Firefly* (2002), *Arrested Development* (2003–13), *How I Met Your Mother* (2005–14), *Burn Notice* (2007–13), *Dollhouse* (2009–10) and *Modern Family* (2009–   ).

Hutch Parker topped a record-breaking 2003 (with hits like *X2: X-Men United*, *Cheaper by the Dozen*, *Master and Commander: The Far Side of the World*) with Roland Emmerich's *The Day After Tomorrow*, and *Dodgeball: A True Underdog Story* in 2004. Helping him by bringing his *Predator* and *Dr. Dolittle* franchises into the twenty-first century was John Davis, who produced *I, Robot* (2004) and *Garfield* (2004). There was also a a new family classic, *Because of Winn-Dixie* (2005). By 2006 Fox brought in over $5.8 billion—nearly twice what it had earned at the beginning of the new century. That year was a particularly good one, with *Night at the Museum*, *The Last King of Scotland*, *Borat*, and *Notes on a Scandal*. In 2008 a new division was launched: Fox International Productions, to develop relationships with overseas filmmakers in key markets, including India and Russia.

On June 30, 2009, Peter Chernin resigned and created his own Fox-based company, Chernin Entertainment, to release films and TV shows, and The Chernin Group to continue his media strategies that had brought Fox into the digital age. Chase Carey, who had served as co-chief operating officer with Chernin from 1996 until 2002, returned to the lot as his successor. The media noted that among Murdoch's subsequent promotions—Tom Rothman and Jim Gianopulos, as co-chairmen of Fox Filmed Entertainment, running television now as well, and

Nancy Utley and Steve Gilula, as chief operating officers of Fox Searchlight—Peter Rice was emerging as his protégé as chairman and CEO of the Fox Networks Group. Murdoch also split his empire into two publicly traded businesses to separate the valuable Fox entities from the less-successful newspaper division, now plagued with scandal. The allegations of phone hacking and police bribery had shut down the British *News of the World* in 2011. Thereafter, News Corp. would incorporate all of the print, digital and information services in the United States while Twenty-First Century Fox incorporated all the filmed entertainment, television, cable and satellite assets.

The final shakeup occurred at the end of the year when, amid a slate of films including John Madden's *The Best Exotic Marigold Hotel* (2012),

Ridley Scott's *Prometheus* (2012), Sacha Gervasi's *Hitchcock* (2012), and Benh Zeitlin's *Beasts of the Southern Wild* (2012), Tom Rothman stepped down.

The FX Channel came into its own under Peter Liguori, earning acclaim and notereity for pushing the creative envelope with its edgy programming even further than FOX. Its shows included *It's Always Sunny in Philadelphia* (2005–), *Damages* (2007–12), *Justified* (2010–15), and *American Horror Story* (2011–).

Liguori took Gail Berman's place at FOX in 2005 when she departed to run Paramount. In the tradition of Sherry Lansing, Berman was the first woman to run a television and motion picture studio. In 2014 FOX was combined with Twentieth Century Fox Television into the Fox Television Group headed by Dana Walden and Gary Newman because of their continued success with shows like *How I Met Your Mother* (2005–14), *Glee* (2009–15), *Modern Family* (2009–), *White Collar* (2009–14), *New Girl* (2011–), *Homeland* (2011–), *Sleepy Hollow* (2013–), and *Empire* (2015–). That same year Gail Berman was back launching The Jackal Group in partnership with the Fox Networks Group to produce television shows and feature films.

In November of 2014 Rupert Murdoch got Jim Gianopulos a new creative partner in DreamWorks former CEO, Stacey Snider. By then, determined as ever to grow his empire against the threat of new digital superpowers like Google, Comcast, and Time Warner Cable, he made news trying unsuccessfully to purchase Time Warner. Meanwhile, head of production Emma Watts engineered a resurgence of Twentieth Century Fox pictures—overshadowed by the success of Searchlight and Fox 2000—with the release of David Finscher's *Gone Girl* (2014), and by repackaging the *X-Men*, *Night at the Museum*, and *Planet of the Apes* franchises. The *Apes* films were produced by Peter Chernin, who also gave her another Ridley Scott spectacle, *Exodus: Gods and Kings* (2014). It all helped make Twentieth Century Fox the number-one studio in Hollywood once again, with a record $5.5 billion in global ticket sales, breaking the record previously held by Paramount Pictures in 2011. That was a proud feat for a company going into its hundredth year. Interestingly, it began (*Life's Shop Window*, 1914) and ended (*Joy*, 2015) its millennia producing stories about survivors.

BOTTOM LEFT: In March of 2014 Rupert Murdoch promoted his sons. Lachlan took charge of both divisions of News Corp. as non-executive co-chairman with his father.

BOTTOM MIDDLE: Younger son James was named co-chief operating officer with Chase Carey.

BOTTOM RIGHT: Stacey Snider.

BLDG. 101: THE FOX NETWORK CENTER (1999)

After its birth at the Fox/Metromedia Square, the old KTTV studio at 5746 Sunset Boulevard in Hollywood, the FOX network moved—along with KTTV, KCOP and Fox Sports— to the Fox Television Center at 1999 South Bundy Drive in West Los Angeles in 1996. FOX and Fox Sports then moved into this building specially designed for them with two sound stages for live broadcasts. It was Rupert Murdoch's second wife Anna who commissioned a California artist to create the hard-to-miss, thirty-six-foot-tall, ten-panel, tin and wood mural of his right index finger in the lobby.

ABOVE: The Fox Network Center.

RIGHT: Moe's neon sign.

BLDG. 103 (2006)

For most of the twentieth century this was the site of the major parking lot "B"for the studio. Then it became the temporary site for a crafts building in the 1970s, before this building was built in 2006. Besides housing offices for Fox 21 and the studio gym, *The Simpsons*-themed Moe's Café on the first floor—the smallest and most casual of the three studio eateries—is the only one to offer all three meals at the urging of Fox News and Fox Sports personnel, who work late into the night. The large patio hosts lot-wide events, including launches for new TV shows, health fairs, Food Truck Friday, and a barbecue once a week during the summer months.

ABOVE LEFT: The large plaza in front of Bldg 103.

ABOVE RIGHT: Dining room at Moe's.

FAR LEFT: Moe greets you as you enter.

LEFT: A bench commemorating *Modern Family* (2009–).

ABOVE LEFT: View of Bldg. 89 in the 1930s when it was the Prop Building. The north end of the building has been covered by the *Hello, Dolly!* (1969) set since 1968.

ABOVE RIGHT: The old docks where props would be loaded onto trucks and the massive freight elevator were still extant in 2015.

BLDG. 89: THE WILLIAM FOX BUILDING (THE PROPERTY BUILDING) (1936)

"They got so used to seeing me around Fox that they counted me in the annual inventory of props."

- Tyrone Power, star of 40 Fox films

This building's name is something of a misnomer, as founder William Fox had nothing to do with it. He made two known visits to the lot: once, in 1923, to purchase the property, and another in 1936 as part of a West Coast visit. He walked around that time and was recognized by no one.

By 1981 the building just needed a name, and in July of that year it officially got one in an employee contest. Howard Van Amstel (corporate supervisor of purchasing) and Roy Mazza (accounting clerk for feature-film production) both turned in the name suggestion on the same day. The building's three stories—100,000 square feet, plus basement—were in fact designed by Thomas K. Little to hold enormous amounts of weight for his property department, as well as the upholstering and furniture-making plant.

Darryl Zanuck chose his desk from this collection, an imposing one built to resemble George Washington's. Among rugs worth $75,000 and Gobelin tapestries could be found bed headboards you can trace back decades, from the twin oval ones from Shirley Temple's *Stowaway* (1936) that became Sharon Tate's deathbed in *Valley of the Dolls* (1967)

FAR LEFT: This lovely gilt mirror, as seen here in *Laura* (1944), hung around for years. It later decorated the office of the Charles Townsend detective agency in *Charlie's Angels* (1976-81).

TOP MIDDLE: These twin headboards had a long life as well: they were used by Shirley Temple's character in *Stowaway* (1936) and thirty years later were used in the death scene of Sharon Tate's character in *Valley of the Dolls* (1967).

TOP RIGHT: Interior of Bldg. 89 with its massive octagonal columns to support the weight of the props, 1939.

LEFT: Part of the Victorian furniture collection, 1939.

MIDDLE LEFT: 18th and 19th century European antiques.

to Loretta Young's fancy one in *Café Metropole* (1937) that became James Garner and Polly Bergen's in the honeymoon suite for *Move Over, Darling* (1963).

Even Gene Tierney's portrait from *Laura* (1944), stored here, was used again in *On the Riviera* (1951) and *Woman's World* (1954). Over a million items were cataloged for *The Egyptian* (1954), and many were sold to Paramount for Cecil B. DeMille's *The Ten Commandments* (1956). The USS *San Pablo* gunboat used in *The Sand Pebbles* (1966)—constructed in Hong Kong under the direction of Boris Leven—was the studio's largest prop

built to date. Actually defined as a hand prop, it was built flat-bottomed like a raft, with a motor to navigate the rivers of Taiwan.

The assistant propmaster for *The Sand Pebbles* was Dennis Parrish, who recalled that Frank Brown ran the prop department then, and Walter Scott ran set dressing. Parrish, who was the first propmaster to get screen credit at Fox for *The Flim-Flam Man* (1967), also worked on *Hello, Dolly!* (1969), and literally rounded up an army for *Patton* (1970). He recalled that the studio was at such a low point when he worked on his favorite Fox project, *The*

TOP LEFT: Part of the 1930s modern furniture collection. Look for the modern zebra chairs in the movie nightclubs of the 1930s and 1940s.

TOP RIGHT: More of the Fox prop department. Furniture from every era and every style was collected to fit the needs of Fox productions.

MIDDLE LEFT: Part of the extensive collection of French antiques that were acquired in Europe.

MIDDLE RIGHT: The hand prop department.

BOTTOM LEFT: Telephones and other electronic equipment. Note the FBC prop microphone—a prophetic prop in that this was decades before Fox created the real Fox Broadcasting Company.

BOTTOM RIGHT: Signs are always important props.

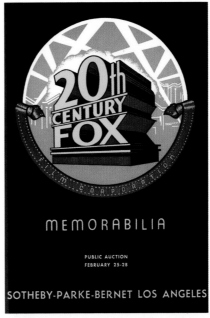

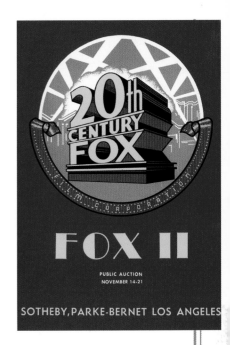

Vanishing Point (1971), that it was the only film shooting on the lot. Once again, as during the days of *Cleopatra*, the commissary was closed and only a coffee wagon in front of the administration building offered refreshments.

The cash-strapped studio auctioned off most of its props—valued at $3.5 million—at Sotheby, Parke-Bernet in 1971. Jane Withers, who had enjoyed playing in the prop house as a child, once spotting a big carved bear and promising to bring him home, bought and stored and therefore rescued much of the memorabilia.

Although the property department continued to operate for another ten years, much of the space here was renovated into offices. The only vestige of

ABOVE LEFT In the days before credit cards, it was necessary to have legitimate foreign currency on hand for movies with international locales, 1938.

ABOVE MIDDLE The first Fox auction took place on February 25-28, 1971.

ABOVE RIGHT: The second Fox auction took place on November 14-21, 1971.

LEFT: The Drapery Department is still located in the south end of Bldg. 89 where it has been since the 1930s. Here it is as it appeared in the 1960s.

ABOVE LEFT: Upholstering (and frequent re-upholstering) has always been a major function of the Drapery Department.

ABOVE MIDDLE: Maria's curtains in *The Sound of Music,* one of the most famous sets of curtains in movie history, originated here in the Drapery Department.

ABOVE RIGHT: Fox still has a set of those curtains.

RIGHT: Fox also still has such items as the fabric used for the couch in *The Seven Year Itch* (1955).

FAR RIGHT: The couch used in *The Seven Year Itch* (1955), now depicted on Stage Ten, was upholstered here.

the building's original use are the cement pylons visible inside, built to hold the weight of the props, as well as the huge freight elevator and loading dock. Look for that elevator in *Thank You, Mr. Moto* (1937). Although the drapery department is still located at the south end of the building, providing custom work for new productions, it got out of the rental business in 2006 and sold off its inventory of draperies, upholstery, and bed linens. Remainders of original fabric used for the couch in *The Seven Year Itch* (1955) and an original set of curtains from *The Sound of Music* (1965) are now safely housed in the wardrobe vaults.

FAR LEFT: Peter Lorre (no hat) stands on the west side of Bldg. 89 by the truck docks for his scene in *Mr. Moto Takes a Vacation* (1939).

LEFT: Three quarters of a century later, Seeley Booth (David Boreanaz), left, stands in the same spot as Peter Lorre in the *Bones* episode "The Friend in Need."

BOTTOM LEFT: Henry Fonda takes a bicycle ride down Avenue D with Bldg. 89 on the right and Stage Fourteen on the left during the filming of *The Ox-Bow Incident* (1943).

BOTTOM MIDDLE: Marilyn Monroe and a friend take a stroll north of Bldg. 89, 1954.

BOTTOM RIGHT: When Robert Ryan ran to the top of a department store roof in Tokyo in *House of Bamboo* (1954) he was actually running up the stairs of Bldg. 89. One of the buildings signature octagonal columns can be seen on the right.

RIGHT: The large neon sign on the southwest corner of the lot on Pico Boulevard near Fox Hills Drive, which was the original access road to the studio's main entrances on Orton and Tennessee Avenues. The star bungalows (including Will Rogers' with the chimney) can be seen in the mid-distance with Stages Three, Four and Five rising behind. This is now the site of the Pico West parking structure.

BOTTOM LEFT: The lovely Spanish Colonial wall was more restrained than the one on Santa Monica Boulevard because this was not built as an official entrance. The water tower on the right belonged to the Hillcrest Country Club.

BOTTOM RIGHT: Detail of the Pico Boulevard wall.

PICO BOULEVARD ENTRANCE

The guard at the gate checked my drive-on [pass], and then he asked, "Have you been on the lot before?" I introduced myself properly; I said I was the former president of the studio. Seriously, whenever I drive on the lot, I can't help thinking about the great times I had here. We had a lot of fun, which was important.

—Richard Zanuck, 2005

When the studio opened as Movietone City, there was a Spanish Colonial stucco wall here with a decorative tower less elaborate than the one on Santa Monica Boulevard. The wall stretched along Pico Boulevard, just like its counterpart on the north side of the studio. There was a large electric neon sign on the west end of the wall advertising "Fox Hills Studio" that was removed after the merger.

In April of 1936 Joseph Schenck authorized the purchase of 0.79 acre to create a new main entrance to the studio, moving the administrative headquarters from the west side of the lot to the east side with the construction of Bldg. 88. Gate 8 at 10201 Pico Boulevard has been the main entrance ever since. Guard shacks were created: one on the south end of Bldg. 88, and one on the north end. The Pico time office (for employees to punch their cards) was on the north end. The north gate was for employees, while the south gate was for visitors. "Twentieth Century Fox Film Corporation" signage was installed on the east side of Bldg. 89, while the "Twentieth Century Fox" neon sign resembling the famous logo was installed on the roof.

"How far you drove your car into a movie studio was a matter of considerable importance and something that was closely watched by those you worked with," recalled child star Dick Moore. "At Fox, the main parking area was inside the front gate, tended by guards. To reach the studio, you had to pass through a second gate. If you could drive past the second guard right onto the lot, you knew your option was going to get picked up, or that they liked you at the studio."

While many movie stars showed up here looking the part—Betty Grable and Marilyn Monroe in red and black Cadillacs respectively—Ann-Margret preferred her motorcycle, and producer Saul David remembered Raquel Welch arriving her first day in a Volkswagen that barely made it.

"Elvis loved going to the studio," recalled friend Jerry Schilling. "We all loved going to the studio. These poor kids from Memphis who a lot of times did not have enough money to get into a movie theater were now being driven onto the lot in limousines. It was exciting!"

Other than the addition of a large billboard just east of Bldg. 89 that had appeared by

BOTTOM: After the successful merger of Fox and Twentieth Century Pictures, the financially robust studio launched a major expansion project that turned the south end of the main lot, previously used for sets, into a site for permanent structures. The plans included a new administration building built on the opposite side of the lot from the original one (Bldg. 1) near Pico Boulevard and, hence, it was decided to make an official entrance here as well. Down came the Spanish wall to make room for Stages 14, 15, and 16 and the new Prop Building (Bldg. 89) with its signage and a new neon sign bearing the new company name.

the 1960s, Gate 8 remained unchanged until the construction of the *Hello, Dolly!* set in 1968. The south guardhouse was removed, and once filming was completed, a new, smaller guardhouse was installed. The north guardhouse and Pico time office remained in place, though disguised during filming. Check out the pilot episode of *The Fall Guy* (1981–86) for a great look at the entrance, still dominated by the *Hello, Dolly!* (1969) set.

By the early 1970s, the neon sign on Bldg. 89 had been removed. Stage Fourteen got "Twentieth Century Fox Film Corporation" inscribed on its south end, along with a new 1970s "glass dome" logo. That logo was replaced in 1984 with a new

one. Toward the end of the decade Gate Eight got a facelift to complement the new Bldg. 100. More of the *Dolly* street made way for a new guardhouse; a massive, beveled, seventeen-foot-high billboard completed in June 1996, filling the gap between Bldg. 89 and Stage Fourteen, and designed to feature current productions; and a long, low 210-foot cascading fountain along Pico, and four new drive-through portals opened in 1999. The billboard was completed in time to advertise the July 4 release of *Independence Day* (1996). Since then it has alternated between films and TV shows.

Of course, there are many stories from guards about gatecrashers. Irving "Gibby" Gibbs remembers

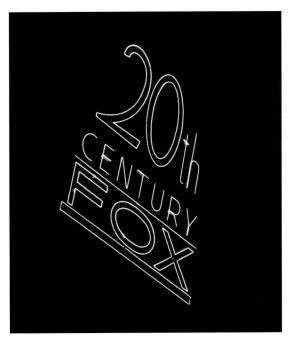

FAR LEFT: Closeup of the neon sign on Bldg. 89.

LEFT: And at night.

BOTTOM LEFT: The Pico Gate had a long approach with two entrances—one at the south end of Bldg. 88 and one at the north end. Here actor John Payne arrives at the north guardhouse, 1944.

BOTTOM RIGHT: The guardhouse at the south end of Bldg. 88 as it appeared in circa 1962. The north guardhouse is just out of the picture on the right.

RIGHT: View of the south guardhouse and Stages 10 and 11 behind. This view has not been seen since 1968 when the *Hello, Dolly!* (1969) street was built in front of these stages. The large statue of Rameses greeted visitors to promote *Cleopatra* (1963).

FAR RIGHT: Ann-Margret, in between Bldg. 89 and Stage 14, gets ready to exit the Pico Gate on her motorcycle during the filming of *The Pleasure Seekers* (1964). The parked "honey wagons" were used as trailers for movie stars on set for decades.

BOTTOM LEFT: The north guardhouse (left) and the Pico Time Office (right) where employees clocked in and out.

BOTTOM RIGHT: Frank Sinatra gets some real-life experience in law enforcement while filming *The Detective* (1968). The Pico Time Office is at right, the north guardhouse at left, and Stage 21 is behind.

some who offered money; the would-be actress who insisted that she was late on the set of *Greenwich Village* (1943) that had already finished shooting; and an ambitious stripper who wanted to work there, since Gypsy Rose Lee did, and even started to perform to prove her point. Ed Conlon recalled a strange fellow who prowled the perimeter of the studio, issuing death threats in a vain attempt to play the lead in *The Boston Strangler* (1968).

During the Los Angeles riots in 1992, Rupert Murdoch coolly lunched in the commissary with TV agents despite threats to the studio and vandalism

to this gate. At five the next morning, Murdoch showed up at Fox's KTTV-TV studios with coffee and bagels for the beleaguered news crews.

When one of the decades-old ficus trees lining Pico Boulevard dropped a branch into the street one morning in 2013, the decision was made to replace them with palms. With the south ends of Stages Fourteen, Fifteen, and Sixteen now visible, the studio resurrected the practice of advertising upcoming films and televisions shows on them in late December. Another significant change was the installation of the "Fox Studios" signage above the drive-in entrance. Although "Fox Studios" was chosen to reflect all the current divisions of the company, it certainly acts as a throwback to the days before the Twentieth Century Fox merger, and a reminder of the founder who started it all.

ABOVE LEFT: The neon sign on Bldg. 89 was altered to advertise *Hello, Dolly!* (1969) (glimpses of the set can be seen).

ABOVE RIGHT: A new logo and a new pylon on Pico Boulevard.

LEFT: Down with the old and up with the new Fox logo in 1984.

RIGHT: The Pico entrance advertising *Aliens* (1986). The large fountain is a remnant of the *Hello, Dolly!* (1969) set while the new Fox Plaza tower rises in the distance.

BOTTOM LEFT: A new beveled billboard was installed between Bldg. 89 and Stage 14 to advertise the summer blockbuster *Independence Day* (1996).

BOTTOM RIGHT: Large ficus trees had grown for decades along the north side of Pico Boulevard matching those on the south side of the street. In 2013 a large branch fell off one of the massive trees into the road but luckily no one was harmed. This prompted the studio to replace the decaying trees with palm trees. With new visibility, the studio revived the century-old tradition of advertising movies on the sides of soundstages.

Signage had been absent from the Pico Gate for decades. That situation was remedied at the beginning of 2014 with "FOX STUDIOS" being installed above the entrance.

RIGHT: Gene Tierney takes a call during the filming of *China Girl* (1942). This "phone call on set" shot was standard publicity fare for years—almost every movie star had a similar shot taken at one point or another while working at Fox. This one stands out because it actually appears to be a candid.

Society mavens who used to be showgirls is the premise of *Stepping Sisters* (1932). What else can we say?"

FE. 2.-2

The combination of Cinemascope, color photography, romance, and Italy made *Three Coins in the Fountain* (1954) a huge success. Most of the exterior scenes were shot on locaton; this one, however, was not. (L-R) Jean Peters, Maggie McNamara, and Dorothy McGuire.

898-X-143

FOX BY THE NUMBERS PART ONE:
THE AWARDS

Part One of Fox by the Numbers offers a chronological listing of Twentieth Century Fox's Academy Award-winning movies and Emmy-award-winning television shows by their release date. Part Two is a chronological listing of the movies and television shows produced at least in part on the Fox sound stages, backlot, and the Century Ranch since at least the Zanuck era. Since Stage One at the Westwood lot was used primarily for recording the scores and songs for Twentieth Century Fox films (see the Studio Tour) in the self-contained days of the Hollywood studio system, that list begins after that period to show the variety of studios that continue to use it. Part Three is the studio filmography.

1927

May 6:
7th Heaven premieres as a silent film at the Carthay Circle Theater in Los Angeles. The film earns Academy Awards for Director (**Frank Borzage**), Writing/Adaptation (**Benjamin Glazer**), and nominations for Best Picture and Art Direction (**Harry Oliver**). **Janet Gaynor** wins for Best Actress (for her combination of roles in *7th Heaven, Street Angel and Sunrise*). A Movietone soundtrack version with a music score by Erno Rappe including non-synchronized voices and sound effects is released on September 10.

September 23:
Sunrise premieres in New York with a Movietone soundtrack of music and effects and earns Academy Awards for Unique and Artistic Picture, Cinematography (**Charles Rosher, Karl Struss**), and a nomination for Art Direction (**Rochus Gliese**).

1928

April 9:
Street Angel is released, and is nominated for an Academy Award for Art Direction (**Harry Oliver**). **Ernest Palmer** is also nominated for Cinematography for *Street Angel* and *4 Devils* (1929).

1929

January 20:
In Old Arizona opens as the first all-talking sound-on-film feature, and earns **Warner Baxter** an Academy Award for Best Actor. The movie is nominated for Best Picture, Directing (**Irving Cummings**), Writing (**Tom Barry),** and Cinematography (**Arthur Edeson**).

May 29:
The Valiant is released, and is nominated for Academy Awards for Best Actor (**Paul Muni** in his film debut) and **Tom Barry** for Best Writing.

1930

November 23:
Just Imagine is released as the first film to utilize the Teague Back Projector that popularizes the use of back projection in Hollywood. **Stephen Goosson** and **Ralph Hammeras** are nominated for Best Art Direction.

1931

March 8:
This third studio version of *East Lynne* is released, and nominated for an Academy Award for Best Picture.

August 13:
Bad Girl is released, and earns Academy Awards for Directing (**Frank Borzage**) and Writing (**Edwin Burke**). It is nominated for Best Picture.

August 30:
Transatlantic is released, and earns **Gordon Wiles** the Academy Award for Art Direction.

The Fox Film Corp. wins a Class II Technical Academy Award "for effective use of synchro-projection composite photography."

1933

February 10:
State Fair is released, and is nominated for Academy Awards for Best Picture and Adapted Screenplay (**Paul Green, Sonya Levien**).

April 15:
Cavalcade is released, and wins Academy Awards for Best Picture, Directing (**Frank Lloyd),** Assistant Director (**William Tummel),** and Art Direction (**William S. Darling**). **Diana Wynyard** is nominated for Best Actress.

October 1:
Berkeley Square is released, and **Leslie Howard** is nominated for an Academy Award for Best Actor.

Percy Ikerd is nominated for an Assistant Director Academy Award for his work in the 1932-33 period including such Fox work as *Rackety Rax* (1932), *Best of Enemies* (1933), *Charlie Chan's Greatest Case* (1933), *Dangerously Yours* (1933), *The Last Trail* (1933), and *Pleasure Cruise* (1933).

The Fox Film Corp. and **Fred Jackman** and Warner Bros. Pictures Inc. and **Sidney Sanders** of RKO Studios, Inc. earn Academy Award Class III scientific or technical honorable mention for their development and effective use of the translucent cellulose screen in composite photography.

1934

April 7:
Twentieth Century Pictures' *The House of Rothschild* is released and receives an Academy Award nomination for Best Picture (**Darryl Zanuck**).

August 24:
Twentieth Century Pictures' *The Affairs of Cellini* is released and receives Academy Award nominations for Actor (**Frank Morgan**), Cinematography (**Charles Rosher**), Art Direction (**Richard Day**), and Sound (**Thomas T. Moulton**).

November 16:
The White Parade is released and earns Academy Award nominations for Best Picture (**Jesse L. Lasky**) and Sound (**E.H. Hansen**).

1935

January 1:
King of Burlesque is released and receives an Academy Award nomination for Dance Direction (**Sammy Lee)** for the "Lovely Lady" and "Too Good to Be True" sequences.

April 20:
Twentieth Century Pictures' *Les Miserables* premieres, and is nominated for Academy Awards for Best Picture (**Darryl Zanuck**), Cinematography (**Gregg Toland**), Film Editing (**Barbara McLean**), and Assistant Director (**Eric Stacey**).

September 13:
The Gay Deception is released. **Don Hartman** and **Stephen Avery** are nominated for an Academy Award for Best Writing (Original Story).

October 25:
Thanks a Million is released and receives an Academy Award nomination for Sound (**E.H. Hanson).**

1936

August 21:
Sing Baby, Sing is released. **Richard A. Whiting** and **Walter Bullock** receive an Academy Award nomination for Best Song "When Did You Leave Heaven."

October 23:
Pigskin Parade is released, and **Stuart Erwin** is nominated for an Academy Award for Best Supporting Actor.

December 11:
Banjo on My Knee is released, and is nominated for an Academy Award for Best Sound (**E.H. Hansen**).

December 31:
One in a Million opens, and **Jack Haskell** is nominated for an Academy Award for Best Dance Direction for "Skating Ensemble."

1937

January 29:
Lloyd's of London premieres in New York and Los Angeles and receives

Academy Award nominations for Art Direction (**William S. Darling**) and Film Editing (**Barbara McLean**).

July 30:
Wee Willie Winkie opens and **William S. Darling** and **David Hall** are nominated for an Academy Award for Art Direction.

September 3:
Thin Ice is released. **Harry Losee** is nominated for an Academy Award for Dance Direction for the "Prince Igor Suite."

October 29:
Ali Baba Goes to Town is released. **Sammy Lee** is nominated for an Academy Award for Dance Direction for "Swing is Here to Stay."

1938

April 15:
In Old Chicago is released and earns Academy Awards for Supporting Actress (**Alice Brady**), Assistant Director (**Robert Webb**) and nominations for Best Picture (**Darryl Zanuck**), Original Story (**Niven Busch**), Scoring (**Louis Silvers**) and Sound (**E.H. Hansen**).

March 10:
Darryl Zanuck wins his first Irving G. Thalberg Memorial Award.

August 19:
Alexander's Ragtime Band is released and receives an Academy Award for Scoring (**Alfred Newman**) and nominations for Best Picture (**Darryl Zanuck**), Original Story (**Irving Berlin**), Art Direction (**Bernard Herzbrun, Boris Leven**), Film Editing (**Barbara McLean**), and Song "Now It Can Be Told" (**Irving Berlin**).

October 28:
Suez is released and receives Academy Award nominations for Cinematography (**Peverell Marley),** Score (**Louis Silvers**) and Sound (**E.H. Hansen**).

December 30:
Kentucky is released and receives an Academy Award for Supporting Actor (**Walter Brennan**).

Timber Toppers (**Ed Thorgensen** Sports Series) is nominated for an Academy Award as one-reel short subject.

1939

May 30:
Young Mr. Lincoln is released and receives an Academy Award nomination for Writing (**Lamar Trotti**).

June 30:
Second Fiddle is released and is nominated for an Academy Award for Best Song "I Poured My Heart into a Song" (**Irving Berlin**).

September 15:
The Rains Came opens and **Fred Sersen and E.H. Hansen** win the first Academy Award for special effects. The film is nominated for Editing (**Barbara McLean**), Art Direction (**William S. Darling, George Dudley**), Sound (**E.H. Hansen**), and Score (**Alfred Newman**).

November 3:
Drums Along the Mohawk is released and **Edna May Oliver** is nominated for an Academy Award for Best Supporting Actress.

1940

January 5:
Swanee River is released and receives an Academy Award nomination for Scoring (**Louis Silvers**).

January 19:
The Blue Bird is released, and is nominated for Academy Awards for Special Effects (**Fred Sersen; E.H. Hanson**) and Cinematography (**Arthur Miller, Ray Rennahan**).

March 15:
The Grapes of Wrath premieres, and receives Academy Awards for Directing (**John Ford**) and Supporting Actress (**Jane Darwell**). The film is nominated for Best Picture (**Darryl Zanuck**), Actor (**Henry Fonda**), Screenplay (**Nunnally Johnson**), Film Editing (**Robert Simpson)** and Sound (**E.H. Hanson**).

May 24:
Lillian Russell is released and is nominated for an Academy Award for Art Direction (**Richard Day, Joseph C. Wright**).

October 11:
Down Argentine Way is released and is nominated for Academy Awards for Cinematography (**Leon Shamroy, Ray Rennahan**), Art Direction (**Richard Day, Joseph C. Wright**), and Song "Down Argentine Way" (**Harry Warren, Mack Gordon**).

November 8:
The Mark of Zorro is released and is nominated for an Academy Award for Best Score (**Alfred Newman**).

November 29:
Tin Pan Alley is released and wins an Academy Award for Scoring (**Alfred Newman**).

December 29:
Night Train is released, and receives an Academy Award nomination for Original Story (**Gordon Wellesley**).

The 20th Century-Fox Camera Department (**Daniel Clark, Grover Laube, Charles Miller, Robert W. Stevens**) wins a special Academy Award for technical development: "for the design and construction of the 20th Century Silenced Camera.

1941

January 24:
Tall, Dark and Handsome is released and is nominated for an Academy Award for Screenplay (**Karl Tunberg, Darrell Ware**).

May 30:
Blood and Sand is released and receives an Academy Award for Cinematography (**Ernest Palmer, Ray Rennahan**) and a nomination for Art Direction—Interior Decoration (**Richard Day, Joseph C. Wright; Thomas Little**).

August 15:
Sagebrush and Silver (Magic Carpet series) is released and nominated for an Academy Award for Best Short Subject.

August 29:
Sun Valley Serenade is released and receives Academy Award nominations for Cinematography (**Edward Cronjager**), Score (**Emil Newman**) and Song "Chattanooga Choo Choo" (**Harry Warren, Mack Gordon**). For the song RCA Victor presented **Glenn Miller** with

a solid gold record of the song. It was the first time a gold record was issued.

September 26:
A Yank in the R.A.F. is released and receives an Academy Award nomination for Special Effects (**Fred Sersen, E.H. Hansen**).

October 28:
How Green Was My Valley is released and wins Academy Awards for Best Picture, Directing (**John Ford**), Supporting Actor (**Donald Crisp**), Cinematography (**Arthur Miller**), Art Direction—Interior Decoration (**Richard Day, Nathan Juran; Thomas Little**) and is nominated for Writing (**Philip Dunne**), Supporting Actress (**Sara Allgood**), Screenplay (**Philip Dunne**), Score (**Alfred Newman**), Film Editing (**James B. Clarke**), and Sound (**E.H. Hansen**).

Life of a Thoroughbred is nominated for an Academy Award for Short Subject Documentary (**Truman Talley**).

Soldiers of the Sky is nominated for an Academy Award for Best Short Subject Documentary (**Truman Talley**).

1942

March 11:
To the Shores of Tripoli opens and receives an Academy Award nomination for Cinematography (**Edward Cronjager, William V. Skall**).

April 30:
My Gal Sal is released and wins an Academy Award for Art Direction—Interior Decoration (**Richard Day, Joseph Wright; Thomas Little**) and a nomination for Scoring (**Alfred Newman**).

May 12:
This Above All is released, and wins an Academy Award for Art Direction—Interior Decoration (**Richard Day, Joseph Wright; Thomas Little**) and receives nominations for Cinematography (**Arthur Miller**), Sound (**E.H. Hansen**) and Film Editing (**Walter Thompson**).

May 29:
Moontide is released and receives an Academy Award nomination for Cinematography (**Charles Clarke**).

June 26:
Ten Gentlemen from West Point is released and **Leon Shamroy** receives an Academy Award nomination for Cinematography.

August 12:
The Pied Piper premieres in Rochester, New York (due to an in-joke in the film about whether Rochester is a city or state), and receives Academy Award nominations for Best Picture, Actor (**Monty Woolley**), and Cinematography (**Edward Cronjager**).

September 4:
Orchestra Wives is released, and receives an Academy Award nomination for Best Song "I've Got a Gal in Kalamazoo" (**Harry Warren, Mack Gordon). Glenn Miller** disbanded his orchestra to enter the military after completing the movie. During a 1944 tour entertaining the troops his Paris-bound plane was officially declared missing.

September 14:
The Battle of Midway (United States Navy) is released and receives a special Academy Award for ""the historical value of its achievement in offering a camera record of one of the decisive battles of the world - a record unique both for the courage of those who made it under fire, and for its magnificent portrayal of the gallantry of our armed forces in battle."

November 6:
It's Everybody's War (United States Office of War Information) is released and is nominated for an Academy Award for Best Short Subject Documentary.

December 4:
The Black Swan is released and receives an Academy Award for Cinematography (**Leon Shamroy**) and nominations for Special Effects (**Fred Sersen, Roger Herman, George Leverett**) and Score (**Alfred Newman**).

Africa, Prelude to Victory (March of Time) is nominated for an Academy Award for Best Short Subject Documentary.

All Out for "V" (Terrytoons series) is nominated for an Academy Award for Best Cartoon

Desert Wonderland (Magic Carpet series) is nominated for an Academy Award for Best Short Subject.

Daniel B. Clark and 20th Century Fox Camera Department receives an Academy Award Honorable Mention for technical developments

1943

March 26:
Hello, Frisco, Hello premieres in San Francisco. **Harry Warren** and **Mack Gordon** win the Academy Award for their song, "You'll Never Know." **Charles G. Clarke** and **Allen Davey** are nominated for Best Cinematography.

April 13:
Desert Victory (British Ministry of Information) is released and wins an Academy Award for Best Documentary.

April 22:
Crash Dive is released and **Fred Sersen** and **Roger Heman** win an Academy Award for special effects.

May 21:
The Ox-Bow Incident is released and is nominated for an Academy Award for Best Picture.

June 18:
Coney Island is released, and **Alfred Newman** is nominated for an Academy Award for Scoring.

August 11:
Heaven Can Wait premieres in New York and the film receives Academy Award nominations for Best Picture, Directing (**Lubitsch),** and Cinematography (**Edward Cronjager**).

August 27:
Holy Matrimony is released and is nominated for an Academy Award for Screenplay (**Nunnally Johnson**).

November 5:
Youth in Crisis (March of Time series) is released and nominated for an Academy Award for Best Short Subject Documentary.

November 11:
The Battle of Russia (United States Department of War Special Service Division) is released and nominated for an Academy Award for Best Documentary

December 24:
The Gang's All Here is released, and is nominated for an Academy Award for Art Direction—Interior Decoration (**James Basevi, Joseph C. Wright; Thomas Little**).

December 25:
The Song of Bernadette is released, and wins Academy Awards for Best Actress (**Jennifer Jones**), Art Direction (**James Basevi, William Darling, Thomas Little**), Cinematography (**Arthur Miller**), and Scoring (**Alfred Newman**). The film is nominated for Best Picture (**Darryl Zanuck**), Supporting Actress (**Anne Revere,** a descendant of **Paul Revere**), Supporting Actress (**Gladys Cooper**), Supporting Actor (**Charles Bickford**), Editing (**Barbara McLean**), Sound (**E.H. Hansen**), Screenplay (**George Seaton**), and Directing (**Henry King**).

Charles Galloway Clarke and **20th Century-Fox Camera Department** get an Academy Award Honorable Mention for technical developments

Champions Carry On (**Ed Thorgerson's** Sports Reviews series) is nominated for an Academy Award for Best Short Subject (**Edmund Reek**).

1944

January 12:
Lifeboat premieres and is nominated for Academy Awards for Directing (**Alfred Hitchcock**), Screenplay (**John Steinbeck**), and Cinematography (**Glen MacWilliams**).

February 3:
The Sullivans opens, and receives an Academy Award nomination for Screenplay (**Edward Doherty, Jules Schermer**). **Mr.** and **Mrs. Sullivan** attend this tribute to their sons in New York.

May 12:
My Boy Johnny (Terrytoons Series) is nominated for an Academy Award for Best Cartoon (**Paul Terry**).

July 3:
Home in Indiana opens and receives an Academy Award for Cinematography (**Edward Cronjager**).

August 1:
Widow **Edith Wilson** attends the New York premiere of *Wilson*. The film receives Academy Awards for Screenplay (**Lamar Trotti**), Art Direction—Interior Decoration (**Wiard Ihnen, Thomas Little**), Cinematography (**Leon Shamroy**), Sound (**E. H. Hansen**) and Editing (**Barbara McLean**). The film is nominated for Best Picture, Actor (**Alexander Knox**), Directing (**Henry King**), Score (**Alfred Newman**), and Special Effects (**Fred Sersen, Roger Heman**).

July 24:
A Wing and a Prayer opens in Los Angeles and receives an Academy Award for Screenplay (**Jerome Cady**).

September 5:
Sweet and Low-Down is released, earning an Academy Award nomination for the song "I'm Making Believe" by **James V. Monaco** and **Mack Gordon**.

October 19:
Irish Eyes Are Smiling is released and receives an Academy Award nomination for Score (**Alfred Newman**).

November 1:
Laura premieres and receives an Academy Award for Cinematography (**Joseph LaShelle**) and nominations for Supporting Actor (**Clifton Webb** for his Fox debut), Directing (**Otto Preminger**), Art Direction—Set Decoration (**Lyle Wheeler, Leland Fuller; Thomas Little**), and Screenplay (**Jay Dratler, Samuel Hoffenstein, Betty Reinhardt**).

December 15:
The Keys of the Kingdom premieres, and receives Academy Award nominations for Actor (**Gregory Peck** in his Fox debut), **Arthur Miller** (Cinematography), Art Direction—Set Decoration (**James Basevi, William Darling; Thomas Little, Frank E. Hughes**), and Score (**Alfred Newman**).

Blue Grass Gentlemen (**Ed Thorgerson's** Sports Reviews series) is nominated for an Academy Award for Best Short Subject (**Edmund Reek**).

Grover Laube and **20ᵗʰ Century-Fox Camera Department** receives an Academy Award honorable mention for technical achievement

1945

January 17:
The Fighting Lady (United States Navy) is released and wins an Academy Award for Best Short Subject Documentary. The award brings its creator **Louis de Rochemont**, producer of Time Inc.'s "March of Time" newsreel series, to **Darryl Zanuck's** attention who brings him on board to make "docu-dramas."

February 28:
A Tree Grows in Brooklyn is released, and receives an Academy Award for Supporting Actor (**James Dunn**) a special award for "the most promising juvenile performer of 1945" (**Peggy Ann Garner**) and a nomination for Screenplay (**Frank Davis, Tess Slesinger). Kazan** mentors

March 15:
Darryl F. Zanuck receives his second Irving G. Thalberg Award.

June 19:
Producer **Winfield Sheehan** dies before *Captain Eddie*, his last film, is released. The film is nominated for Special Effects (**Fred Sersen, Sol Haprin, Roger Heman, Harry Leonard**).

August 3:
Mighty Mouse in Gypsy Life (Terrytoon Series) is released and **Paul Terry** (producer) is nominated for an Academy Award.

August 30:
State Fair premieres in Des Moines, Iowa and receives an Academy Award for Song "It Might As Well Be Spring" and nomination for Scoring (**Alfred Newman, Charles Henderson**).

September 10:
The House on 92ⁿᵈ Street is released and wins an Academy Award for Story (**Charles G. Booth**).

October 5:
The Dolly Sisters premieres in Chicago, and **James Monaco** and **Mack Gordon** are nominated for an Academy Award for Song "I Can't Begin To Tell You."

December 20:
Leave Her to Heaven premieres and receives an Academy Award for Cinematography (**Leon Shamroy**), and nominations for Actress (**Gene Tierney**), Art Direction—Set Decoration (**Lyle Wheeler, Maurice Ransford; Thomas Little**) and Sound (**Thomas T. Moulton**).

Michael S. Leshing, Benjamin C. Robinson, Arthur B. Chatelain, and **Robert C. Stevens** are nominated for a Class III Academy Award citation.

1946

February 15:
Along The Rainbow Trail is released and receives an Academy Award nomination for one-reel short subject (**Edmund Reek**).

June 20:
Anna and the King of Siam premieres in New York, and receives Academy Awards for Cinematography (**Arthur Miller**) and Art Direction—Set Decoration (**Lyle Wheeler, William Darling; Thomas Little, Frank E. Hughes**) and nominations for Supporting Actress (**Gale Sondergaard**), Screenplay (**Sally Benson, Talbot Jennings**), and Score (**Bernard Herrmann**).

August 1:
Centennial Summer opens and receives Academy Award nominations for Song "All Through the Day" (**Jerome Kern, Oscar Hammerstein II**) and Scoring (**Alfred Newman**).

December 1:
The Razor's Edge premieres and **Anne Baxter** earns the Academy Award for Supporting Actress. The film is nominated for Best Picture, Supporting Actor (**Clifton Webb**), and Art Direction- Set Decoration (**Richard Day, Nathan Juran; Thomas Little, Paul S. Fox**).

Edmund Reek is nominated for an Academy Award for the one-reel short subject *Golden Horses* (**Ed Thorgerson's** Sports Review Series)

Atomic Power (March of Time Series) is nominated for an Academy Award as best short subject documentary.

Carl Faulkner receives an Academy Award honorable mention for technical developments.

1947

January 1:
Miracle on 34th Street premieres and receives Academy Awards for Supporting Actor (**Edmund Gwenn**), Screenplay (**George Seaton**) and Story (**Valentine Davies**). The film is nominated for Best Picture.

January 1:
Boomerang! opens and receives an Academy Award nomination for Screenplay (**Richard Murphy**).

June 26:
The Ghost and Mrs. Muir is released, receives an Academy Award nomination for Cinematography (**Charles Lang, Jr.)**, and spawns a TV series (1968-70).

August 15:
Symphony of a City is released and **Edmund H. Reek** wins the Academy Award for Best Short Subject (One reel Movietone Specialty).

August 27:
Kiss of Death opens in Los Angeles and receives Academy Awards nominations for Supporting Actor (**Richard Widmark** in his film debut) and screenplay (**Eleazar Lipsky**).

September 1:
Mother Wore Tights premieres in New York, and wins an Academy Award for Scoring (**Alfred Newman**) and nominations for Cinematography (**Harry Jackson**) and Song "You Do" (**Josef Myrow, Mack Gordon**).

September 24:
The Foxes of Harrow is released and receives an Academy Award nomination for Art Direction—Set Decoration (**Lyle Wheeler, Maurice Ransford; Thomas Little, Paul S. Fox**).

October 10:
Forever Amber is released, and **David Raksin** is nominated for an Academy Award for his score.

November 11:
Gentleman's Agreement opens, and among the staggering 51 awards the film earns were Academy Awards for Best Picture, Direction (**Elia Kazan**), and Supporting Actress (**Celeste Holm**). The film received nominations for Actor (**Gregory Peck**), Actress (**Dorothy McGuire**), Supporting Actress (**Anne Revere**), Screenplay (**Moss Hart**), and Film Editing (**Harmon Jones**)

December 25:
Captain from Castile premieres and receives an Academy Award nomination for Score (**Alfred Newman**).

1948

January 1:
That Lady in Ermine is released and receives an Academy Award nomination for Song "This is the Moment" (**Frederick Hollander, Leo Robin**).

January 1:
Deep Waters is released and receives an Academy Award nomination for Special Effects (**Ralph Hammeras, Fred Sersen, Edward Snyder, Roger Herman**).

April 1:
Sitting Pretty premieres in New York and receives an Academy Award nomination for Best Actor (**Clifton Webb**).

June 9:
Green Grass of Wyoming opens and receives an Academy Award nomination for Cinematography (**Charles G. Clarke**).

September 15:
Luck of the Irish is released and receives an Academy Award nomination for Supporting Actor (**Cecil Kellaway**).

November 10:
When My Baby Smiles at Me premieres in San Francisco and receives Academy Award nominations for Actor (**Dailey**) and Scoring (**Alfred Newman).**

November 13:
The Snake Pit premieres in New York and wins an Academy Award for Sound (**Thomas T. Moulton**), and nominations for Best Picture, Actress (**Olivia de Havilland**), Directing (**Anatole Litvak**), Screenplay (**Frank Partos, Millen Brand**) and Score (**Alfred Newman**).

Nick Kalten, **Louis J. Witte** (20th Century Fox Studio Mechanical Effects Department) win (Scientific or Technical Class II) Academy Awards for a process of preserving and flame-proofing foliage.

1949

January 20:
A Letter to Three Wives is released and **Joseph L. Mankiewicz** wins Academy Awards for Director and Screenplay. The film is nominated for Best Picture

March 12:
Mother is a Freshman is released and receives an Academy Award nomination for Costume Design (**Kay Nelson**).

June 10:
It Happens Every Spring is released and receives an Academy Award nomination for Screenplay (**Shirley W. Smith, Valentine Davies**).

August 4:
Sand premieres and receives an Academy Award nomination for Cinematography (**Charles G. Clarke).**

September 1:
Come to the Stable opens and receives Academy Award nominations for Actress (**Loretta Young**),, Supporting Actress (**Celeste Holm** and **Elsa Lanchester**), Art Direction—Set Decoration (**Lyle Wheeler, Joseph C. Wright; Thomas Little, Paul S. Fox**), Screenplay (**Clare Boothe Luce**), Cinematography (**Joseph LaShelle**), and Song "Through A Long and Sleepless Night" (**Alfred Newman, Mack Gordon**).

November 1:
Pinky premieres in New York and receives Academy Award nominations for Actress (**Jeanne Crain**), and Supporting Actress (**Ethel Barrymore** and **Ethel Waters**).

November 9:
Prince of Foxes opens and receives Academy Award nominations for Cinematography (**Leon Shamroy**) and Costume Design (**Vittorio Nino Novarese**).

December 21:
Twelve O'Clock High opens and receives an Academy Award for Supporting Actor (**Dean Jagger**) and nominations for Best Picture, Actor (**Gregory Peck**), and Sound (**Thomas Moulton**).

A Chance to Live (The March of Time series) wins an Academy Award for best documentary short subject (**Richard de Rochemont**, producer).

1950

January 22:
The Titan: Story of Michelangelo is released and wins the Academy Award for Best Short Subject feature.

January 27:
During the second annual Emmy Award ceremony Fox earns its first Emmy for its first show *Crusade in Europe* based on **General Dwight Eisenhower's** book. It is the first documentary series produced for television.

February 1:
When Willie Comes Marching Home is released and receives an Academy Award nomination for Screenplay (**Sy Gomberg**).

May 24:
Wabash Avenue is released and receives an Academy Award nomination for Song "Wilhelmina" (**Josef Myrow, Mack Gordon**).

June 12:
Panic in the Streets is released and receives an Academy Award for Screenplay (**Edna** and **Edward Anhalt**).

June 23:
The Gunfighter opens and receives an Academy Award nomination for Screenplay (**William Bowers, Andre de Toth**).

August 1:
Broken Arrow premieres in Broken Arrow and Tulsa, Oklahoma and receives Academy Award nominations for Supporting Actor (**Jeff Chandler**) and Screenplay (**Albert Maltz**) and Cinematography (**Ernest Palmer**). It spawns a TV series (1956-60).

August 16:
No Way Out opens and **Joseph L. Mankiewicz** is nominated for an Academy Award for Screenplay.

September 1:
The Black Rose is released and receives an Academy Award nomination for Costume Design (**Michael Whittaker**).

September 29:
Mister 880 is released and receives an Academy Award nomination for Supporting Actor (**Edmund Gwenn**).

October 2:
I'll Get By is released and receives an Academy Award nomination for Scoring (**Lionel Newman**).

October 13:
All About Eve opens and is nominated for a record fourteen Academy Awards and wins six: Best Picture, Supporting Actor (**George Sanders**), Director (**Joseph L. Mankiewicz**), Screenplay (**Joseph L. Mankiewicz**), Costume Design (**Edith Head, Charles LeMaire)**, and Sound (**Thomas T. Moulton).** Other nominations are Actress (**Bette Davis** and **Anne Baxter**), Supporting Actress (**Celeste Holm** and **Thelma Ritter**), Cinematography (**Milton Krasner**), Art Direction—Set Decoration (**Lyle Wheeler, George W. Davis; Thomas Little, Walter M. Scott**), Film Editing (**Barbara McLean**), and Score (**Alfred Newman**).

November 28:
The Mudlark opens, is feted with a Royal Film Performance in London, and receives an Academy Award nomination for Costume Design (**Edward Stevenson, Margaret Furse**).

James B. Gordon and the 20th **Century-Fox Camera Department** wins Class II Academy Award for the design and development of Multiple Image Film Viewer

1951

January:
Why Korea? is released and wins the Academy Award for Short Subject Documentary (**Edmund Reek**, producer).

January 1:
The Frogmen opens and receives Academy Award nominations for Writing (**Oscar Millard**), and Cinematography (**Norbert Brodine).**

March 29:
Darryl Zanuck receives his record third Irving G. Thalberg Award.

April 1:
Fourteen Hours opens, and is nominated for an Academy Award for Art Direction—Set Decoration (**Lyle Wheeler, Leland Fuller; Thomas Little, Fred J. Rode**

April 20:
On The Riviera opens and receives Academy Award nominations for Art Direction—Set Decoration (**Lyle Wheeler, Leland Fuller; Thomas Little, Walter M. Scott),** (Musical Settings by **Joseph C. Wright**) and Score (**Alfred Newman**).

May 13:
The House on Telegraph Hill is released and receives an Academy Award for Art Direction—Set Decoration (**Lyle Wheeler, John DeCuir; Thomas Little, Paul S. Fox**).

August 10:
David and Bathsheba opens and is nominated for Academy Awards for Screenplay (**Philip Dunne**), Cinematography (**Leon Shamroy**), Art Direction—Set Decoration (**Lyle Wheeler, George Davis; Thomas Little, Paul S. Fox**), Costume Design (**Charles LeMaire, Edward Stevenson**), and Score (**Alfred Newman**).

November 1:
Golden Girl is released and receives an Academy Award nomination for Song "Never" (**Lionel Newman, Eliot Daniel**).

November 1:
The Model and the Marriage Broker is released and receives an Academy Award nomination for Costume Design (**Charles LeMaire, Renie**).

December 21:
Decision before Dawn premieres, and is nominated for Academy Awards for Best Picture (**Anatole Litvak, Frank McCarthy**) and Film Editing (**Dorothy Spencer).**

1952

February 1:
Viva Zapata! opens and **Anthony Quinn** wins an Academy Award for Best Supporting Actor. The nominees were **Marlon Brando** (Best Actor), **Lyle Wheeler, Leland Fuller; Thomas Little, Claude Carpenter** (Art Direction—Set Decoration), **Alex North** (Score), and **John Steinbeck** (Writing).

February 22:
Five Fingers is released and is nominated for an Academy Award for Directing (**Joseph L. Mankiewicz**), and Writing (**Michael Wilson**). The acclaimed film later becomes a television series that runs 1959-60.

April 4:
With a Song in My Heart opens and receives an Academy Award for Scoring (**Alfred Newman**) and nominations for Actress (**Susan Hayward**), Supporting Actress (**Thelma Ritter**), Costume Design (**Charles LeMaire**), and Sound (**Thomas T. Moulton**).

May 2:
Pride of St. Louis opens and is nominated for an Academy Award for Writing (**Guy Trosper**).

September:
A Light in the Window (Art Film Series) is released and wins an Academy Award for Best Short Subject (**Boris Vermont**, producer).

September 17:
The Snows of Kilimanjaro premieres in New York and is nominated for Academy Awards for Art Direction—Set Decoration (**Lyle Wheeler, John DeCuir; Thomas Little, Paul S. Fox**) and Cinematography (**Leon Shamroy**).

October:
Joy of Living (Art Film Series) is released produced by **Boris Vermont** and is nominated for an Academy Award for best one-reel short subject.

December 11:
The Star is released and **Bette Davis** is nominated for an Academy Award for Best Actress.

December 24:
My Cousin Rachel opens and receives Academy Award nominations for Supporting Actor (**Richard Burton** in his American film debut), Art Direction—Set Decoration (**Lyle Wheeler, John DeCuir; Walter M. Scott**), Cinematography (**Joseph LaShelle**), and Costume Design (**Charles LeMaire, Dorothy Jeakins**).

1953

February 12:
Beneath the 12-Mile Reef opens, and receives an Academy Award nomination for Cinematography (**Edward Cronjager**). The first Fox film released in CinemaScope was also the first to include a CinemaScope short subject (*Vesuvius Express*) that is nominated for an Academy Award for best two-reel short subject produced by **Otto Lang**.

April 1:
Call Me Madam is released and wins an Academy Award for Scoring (**Alfred Newman**) and a nomination for Costume Design (**Irene Sharaff**).

April 16:
Titanic opens on the anniversary of the luxury liner's tragic sinking, and receives an Academy Award for Writing (**Charles Brackett, Walter Reisch, Richard Breen**) and nomination for Art Direction—Set Decoration (Lyle Wheeler, Maurice Ransford; Stuart Reiss).

May 20:
The Desert Rats is released, and **Richard Murphy** is nominated for an Academy Award for Screenplay.

May 21:
The President's Lady premieres in Nashville, Tennessee and receives nominations for Art Direction—Set Decoration (**Lyle Wheeler, Leland Fuller; Paul S. Fox**) and Costume Design (**Charles LeMaire, Renie**).

June 17:
Pickup on South Street is released. **Thelma Ritter** is nominated for an Academy Award for best Supporting Actress.

September 16:
The Robe premieres in New York at the Roxy in CinemaScope, and then on September 24 a four day festival culminates in the West Coast

premiere at Grauman's Chinese Theater in Hollywood. **Jean Simmons** places her footprints in the famous forecourt, and a special plaque commemorating the premiere is placed beside it. The film wins Academy Awards for Art Direction - Set Decoration (**Lyle Wheeler, George W. Davis; Walter M. Scott, Paul S. Fox**), and Costume Design (**Charles LeMaire, Emile Santiago**) and nominations for Best Picture (**Frank Ross**), Actor (**Richard Burton**), and Cinematography (**Leon Shamroy**). Pacific Title's artist **Rocky Longo** recreates the company's logo for CinemaScope.

November 5:
How to Marry a Millionaire opens, and is nominated for an Academy Award for Costume Design (**Charles LeMaire, Travilla**).

The Word is released, produced by **John Healy** and **John Adams**, and receives an Academy Award nomination for best documentary short subject.

Twentieth Century-Fox wins a special Academy Award for the development of CinemaScope

Earl Sponable, Sol Halprin, Lorin Grignon, Professor Henri Chretien, Herbert Bragg, and **Carl Faulkner** win a Class I Scientific and Technical Academy award

1954

February 6:
Hell and High Water is released and is nominated for an Academy Award for best Special Effects (**Ray Kellogg**).

May 4:
The First Piano Quartette (Music Series) is released and **Otto Lang** is nominated for an Academy Award for best one-reel short subject.

May 14
Night People opens, and receives an Academy Award nomination for Screenplay (**Jed Harris, Tom Reed**).

June 2:
Three Coins in the Fountain premieres in New York and is nominated for an Academy Award for Best Picture (**Sol C. Siegel**), Cinematography (**Milton Krasner**), and Song "Three Coins in the Fountain." by **Jule Styne** and **Sammy Cahn**.

August 1:
Jet Carrier is released and is nominated for best two-reel short subject and short subject documentary produced by **Otto Lang.**

August 24:
The Egyptian opens, and receives an Academy Award nomination for Cinematography (**Leon Shamroy**).

September 25:
Broken Lance opens in New York and wins an Academy award for Writing (**Philip Yordan**) and a nomination for Supporting Actress (**Katy Jurado**).

October 28:
Carmen Jones opens and received Academy Award nominations for Actress (**Dorothy Dandridge**) and Scoring (**Herschel Burke Gilbert**).

November 17:
Desiree premieres in San Francisco and receives Academy Award nominations for Art Decoration—Set Decoration (**Lyle Wheeler, Leland Fuller; Walter M. Scott, Paul S. Fox**) and Costume Design (**Charles LeMaire, Rene Hubert**).

December 16:
There's No Business like Show Business premieres in New York and receives Academy Award nominations for Writing (**Lamar Trotti**), Costume Design (**Charles LeMaire, Travilla, Miles White**) and Scoring (**Alfred Newman, Lionel Newman**).

1955

April 1:
A Man Called Peter premieres simultaneously in New York, London, and Glasgow, Scotland. **Harold Lipstein** is nominated for an Academy Award for Best Cinematography.

May 5:
Daddy Long Legs opens as the first Fox film advertised extensively on television. The film is nominated for Art Direction—Set Decoration (**Lyle Wheeler, John DeCuir; Walter Scott, Paul S. Fox**), Song "Something's Gotta Give" by **Johnny Mercer,** and Scoring (**Alfred Newman).**

July 22:
The Virgin Queen is released, and **Charles LeMaire** and **Mary Wills** are nominated for an Academy Award for Costume Design.

August 18:
Love is a Many-Splendored Thing opens, and wins Academy Awards for the title song by **Sammy Fain** and **Paul Francis Webster,** Scoring (**Alfred Newman),** and Costume Design (**Charles LeMaire**). The film is nominated for Best Picture (**Buddy Adler**), Actress (**Jennifer Jones**), Cinematography (**Leon Shamroy**), Art Direction—Set Decoration (**Lyle Wheeler, George W. Davis; Walter M. Scott, Jack Stubbs**) and Sound (**Carl W. Faulkner**).

December 14:
The Rains of Ranchipur opens in New York and is nominated for Special Effects (**Ray Kellogg**).

Edmund Reek wins an Academy Award for best one-reel short subject, *Survival City* (Movietone CinemaScope Series).

Class III Scientific and Technical Academy Award for combination lens for CinemaScope photography

Class III Scientific and Technical Academy Award for spraying process creating simulated metallic surfaces

Class III Scientific and Technical Academy Award for improved spotlight to maintain fixed light over varied distance

1956

June 1:
The Dark Wave is released and is nominated for two Academy Awards for two-reel Short Subject and Documentary (**John Healy**)

June 29:
The King and I is released, and receives an Academy Award for Best Actor (**Yul Brynner**), Art Direction—Set Decoration (**Lyle Wheeler, John DeCuir; Walter M. Scott, Paul S. Fox**), Costume Design (**Irene Sharaff**), Scoring (**Alfred Newman, Ken Darby**), and Sound (**Carl Faulkner**). The film is nominated for Best Picture (**Charles Brackett**), Actress (**Deborah Kerr**), Directing (**Walter Lang**), and Cinematography (**Leon Shamroy**).

August 31:
Bus Stop opens, **Don Murray** is nominated for an Academy Award for Best Supporting Actor for his film debut, and the movie spawns a TV series (1961-62).

September 28:
The Best Things in Life Are Free premieres in New York. **Lionel Newman** is nominated for an Academy Award for Scoring.

October 1:
Between Heaven and Hell opens, and receives an Academy Award nomination for Score (**Hugo Friedhofer**).

November 1:
Teenage Rebel is released and receives Academy Award nominations for Art Decoration—Set Decoration (**Lyle R. Wheeler, Jack Martin Smith; Walter M. Scott, Stuart A. Reiss**) and Costume Design (**Charles LeMaire, Mary Wills**).

December 13:
Stagecoach to Fury is released; the first film produced by Regal Films contracted by Darryl Zanuck to expand production of CinemaScope films with "B's" in "RegalScope." It was the same widescreen process but Zanuck wanted to keep the name CinemaScope for his "A" pictures. **Walter Strenge** is nominated for an Academy Award for Cinematography.

December 13:
Anastasia premieres and **Ingrid Bergman** wins the Academy Award for Best Actress. The film is also nominated for Best Score (**Alfred Newman**).

Maurice E. (Buddy) Adler receives the Irving G. Thalberg Memorial Award.

1957

April 10:
Boy on a Dolphin opens, and **Hugo Friedhofer** is nominated for an Academy Award for Scoring.

July 11:
An Affair to Remember is released, and receives Academy Award nominations for Cinematography (**Milton Krasner**), Song "An Affair

to Remember" (**Harry Warren, Harold Adamson, Leo McCarey**), Scoring (**Hugo Friedhofer**), and Costume Design (**Charles LeMaire**).The film marks **Jerry Wald's** Fox debut as a producer.

July 17:
A Hatful of Rain opens, marking the Fox debut of **Anthony Franciosa** who earns an Academy Award nomination as Best Actor.

September 23:
The Three Faces of Eve is released marking the Fox debut of **Joanne Woodward** who wins a Best Actress Academy Award.

November 7:
Heaven Knows, Mr. Allison is released, and receives Academy Award nominations for Best Actress (**Deborah Kerr**) and Best Adapted Screenplay (**John Lee Mahin, John Huston**).

November 27:
April Love is released. **Sammy Fain** and **Paul Francis Webster** are nominated for an Academy Award for their mega-hit title song.

December 13:
Peyton Place opens, and is nominated for Best Picture (**Jerry Wald**), Actress (**Lana Turner**), Supporting Actor (**Arthur Kennedy, Russ Tamblyn**), Supporting Actress (**Hope Lange, Diane Varsi**), Supporting Actor (**Russ Tamblyn**), Directing (**Mark Robson**), Writing (**John Michael Hayes**), and Cinematography (**William Mellor**).

December 14:
A Farewell to Arms premieres in Los Angeles. **Vittorio De Sica** is nominated for an Academy Award for Supporting Actor.

December 25:
The Enemy Below is released, and **Walter Rossi** wins a Best Special Effects Academy Award for audible effects. The film is in CinemaScope which hits its peak year as the most popular widescreen format with 64 films released throughout Hollywood.

1958

March 19:
South Pacific premieres in New York. It is the first Fox Todd-AO film (developed by producer **Mike Todd** and the American Optical Company). The film wins an Academy Award for Sound (**Fred Hynes**)

and nominations for Cinematography (**Leon Shamroy**) and Scoring (**Alfred Newman, Ken Darby**)..

April 2:
The Young Lions opens, and is nominated for Academy Awards for Cinematography (**Joe MacDonald**), Sound (**Carl Faulkner**) and Scoring (**Hugo Friedhofer**).

July 31:
A Certain Smile opens, and is nominated for Academy Awards for Art Decoration—Set Decoration (**Lyle Wheeler, John DeCuir; Walter M. Scott, Paul S. Fox**), Costume Design (**Charles LeMaire, Mary Wills**) and Song "A Certain Smile" (**Sammy Fain, Paul Francis Webster**).

November 18:
Mardi Gras opens, and **Lionel Newman** is nominated for an Academy Award for Scoring.

December:
Sidney's Family Tree (Terrytoons) is released and is nominated for an Academy Award as Short Subject (**William M. Weiss**).

December 31:
The Inn of the Sixth Happiness premieres and receives an Academy Award nomination for Director (**Mark Robson**).

1959

March 18:
The Diary of Anne Frank opens, and wins Academy Awards for Supporting Actress (**Shelley Winters**), Art Direction—Set Decoration (**Lyle R. Wheeler, George Davis; Walter M. Scott, Stuart A, Reiss**), and Cinematography (**William C. Mellor**) and nominations for Best Picture (**George Stevens**), Supporting Actor (**Ed Wynn**), Directing (**George Stevens**), Costume Design (**Charles LeMaire, Mary Wills**), and Score (**Alfred Newman**).

June 19:
Say One for Me is released. **Lionel Newman** is nominated for an Academy Award for Scoring.

October 9:
The Best of Everything premieres in New York. **Adele Palmer** is nominated for an Academy Award for Costume Design and **Alfred Newman** and **Sammy Cahn** are nominated for Best Song "The Best of Everything."

December 16:
Journey to the Center of the Earth opens, and is nominated for Academy Awards for Art Direction—Set Decoration (**Lyle Wheeler, Franz Bachelin, Herman A. Blumenthal; Walter M. Scott, Joseph Kish**), Sound (**Carl Faulkner**) and Special Effects (**L.B. Abbott, James B. Gordon, Carl Faulkner**).

1960

March 9:
Can-Can opens in New York and is nominated for Academy Awards for Costume Design (**Irene Sharaff**) and Scoring (**Nelson Riddle**).

March 12:
Seven Thieves is released. **Bill Thomas** is nominated for an Academy Award for Costume Design.

June 28:
Murder, Inc. is released and receives an Academy Award nomination for Supporting Actor (**Peter Falk**).

August 2:
Sons and Lovers opens in New York and wins an Academy Award for Cinematography (**Freddie Francis**). The film is nominated for Best Picture (**Jerry Wald**), Actor (**Trevor Howard**), Supporting Actress (**Mary Ure**), Directing (**Jack Cardiff**), Writing (**Gavin Lambert, T.E.B. Clarke**), and Art Direction—Set Decoration (**Tom Morahan; Lionel Couch**).

September 8:
Let's Make Love is released. **Lionel Newman** and **Earle H. Hagen** are nominated for an Academy Award for Scoring.

September 16:
High Time is released and **James Van Heusen** and **Sammy Cahn** are nominated for an Academy Award for "The Second Time Around." A Class III Scientific and Technical Award is given to **Anthony Paglia** and the 20th Century Fox Studio Mechanical Effects Dept.

1961

September 25:
The Hustler opens and receives an Academy Award for Cinematography (**Eugen Shuftan**) and Art Direction—Set Decoration (**Harry Horner, Gene Callahan**), and nominations for Best Picture (**Robert Rossen**), Actor (**Paul Newman**), Actress (**Piper Laurie**), Supporting Actor (**Jackie Gleason** & **George C. Scott**), Directing (**Robert Rossen**), and Writing (**Sidney Carroll, Robert Rossen**).

George Seaton receives the Jean Hersholt Humanitarian Award.

The 20th Century Fox Research Department receives a Class II Scientific and Technical Academy Award for a system of decompressing and recomposing CinemaScope pictures for conventional aspect ratios (**E.I. Sponable, Herbert E. Bragg** and Deluxe Laboratories)

1962

January 19:
Tender is the Night premieres and **Sammy Fain** and **Paul Francis Webster** are nominated for an Academy Award for their song "Tender is the Night."

September 25:
The Longest Day opens, and receives Academy Awards for Cinematography (**Jean Bourgoin, Walter Wottitz**) and Special Effects (**Robert MacDonald, Jacques Maumont**), and nominations for Best Picture (**Darryl Zanuck**), Art Direction-Set Decoration (**Ted Haworth, Leon Barsacq, Vincent Korda; Gabriel Bechir**), Film Editing (**Samuel E. Beetley**).

November 1:
Gigot is released in New York, and **Michel Magne** is nominated for an Academy Award for Scoring.

1963

June 1:
The Stripper is released in New York and **Travilla** is nominated for an Academy Award for Costume Design.

June 12:
Cleopatra premieres as the longest commercially-made American film released in America at 4 hours and 3 minutes. The film wins Academy Awards for Cinematography (**Leon Shamroy**), Art Direction—Set

Direction (**John DeCuir, Jack Martin Smith, Hilyard Brown, Herman Blumenthal, Elven Webb, Maurice Pelling, Boris Juraga; Walter M. Scott, Paul S. Fox, Ray Moyer**), Costume Design (**Irene Sharaff, Vittorio Nino Novarese, Renie**), and Special Effects (**Emil Kosa, Jr.**) and is nominated for Best Picture (**Walter Wanger**), Actor (**Rex Harrison**), Sound (**James P. Corcoran, Fred Hynes**), Film Editing (**Dorothy Spencer**), and Score (**Alex North**).

July 15:
The Leopard is released, and **Piero Tosi** is nominated for an Academy Award for Costume Design.

1964

May 12:
What a Way to Go is released, and receives Academy Award nominations for Art Direction—Set Decoration **Jack Martin Smith, Ted Haworth; Walter M. Scott, Stuart A. Reiss**) and Costume Design (**Edith Head, Moss Mabry**).

September 14:
Voyage to the Bottom of the Sea debuts on TV and runs through 1968. It wins 4 Emmys.

September 15:
Peyton Place debuts, and runs through 1969 winning one Emmy.

September 30:
Fate is the Hunter is released. **Milton Krasner** is nominated for an Academy Award for Best Cinematography.

September 11:
The Visit is released. **Rene Hubert** is nominated for an Academy Award for Costume Design.

December 17:
Zorba the Greek is released and earns three Academy Awards: Supporting Actress (**Lila Kedrova),** Cinematography (**Walter Lassally**), and Art Direction—Set Decoration (**Vassilis Fotopoulos**). The film is nominated for Best Picture (**Michael Cacoyannis**), Actor (**Anthony Quinn**), Directing (**Michael Cacoyannis**), and Writing (**Michael Cacoyannis**).

December 24:
Hush...Hush, Sweet Charlotte is released and receives Academy Award nominations for Supporting Actress (**Agnes Moorehead**), Cinematography (**Joseph Biroc),** Art Direction—Set Decoration (**William Glasgow, Raphael Bretton**), Costume Design (**Norma Koch),** Film Editing (**Michael Luciano**), Song "Hush...Hush, Sweet Charlotte" (**Frank DeVol, Mack David),** and Score (**Frank DeVol).**

December 25:
The Pleasure Seekers is released and is nominated for an Academy Award for Best Scoring (**Lionel Newman, Alexander Courage**).

The 20th Century Fox Studio Mechanical Effects Dept. earns a Class III Scientific and Technical Academy Award for mechanical effects (**Anthony Paglia**).

1965

March 2:
The Sound of Music premieres in New York; winning Academy Awards for Best Picture (**Robert Wise**), Directing (**Robert Wise**), Sound (**James P. Corcoran, Fred Hynes**), Film Editing (**William Reynolds**), Scoring (**Irwin Kostal**) and nominations for Best Actress (**Julie Andrews**), Supporting Actress (**Peggy Wood**), Cinematography (**Ted McCord**), Art Direction—Set Decoration (**Boris Leven; Walter M. Scott, Ruby Levitt**), and Costume Design (**Dorothy Jeakins**),

June 16:
Those Magnificent Men in Their Flying Machines—Or How I Flew from London to Paris in 25 hours and 11 minutes debuts, and director **Ken Annakin** and **Jack Davies** are nominated for an Academy Award for their screenplay.

June 23:
Von Ryan's Express is released and is nominated for an Academy Award for Best Sound Effects (**Walter A. Rossi**).
September 1:
Morituri is released and receives Academy Award nominations for Best Cinematography (**Conrad Hall**) and Costume Design (**Moss Mabry).**.

October 7:
The Agony and the Ecstasy is released and receives Academy Award nominations for Cinematography (**Leon Shamroy**), Art Direction—Set Decoration (**John DeCuir, Jack Martin Smith; Dario Simoni),**

Costume Design (**Vittorio Nino Novarese**) Score (**Alex North**), and Sound (**James P. Corcoran**).

December 15:
Flight of the Phoenix is released and receives Academy Award nominations for Best Supporting Actor (**Ian Bannen**) and Film Editing (**Michael Luciano)**.

1966

August 24:
Fantastic Voyage premieres in Los Angeles and wins Academy Awards for Art Direction - Set Decoration (**Jack Martin Smith, Dale Hennesy, Walter M. Scott, Stuart A. Reiss**), and Special Effects (**Art Cruickshank**), and is nominated for Cinematography (**Ernest Laszlo**), Film Editing (**William B. Murphy**), and Sound Effects (**Walter Rossi**)

September 9:
The Time Tunnel debuts on TV and runs through 1967. It wins one Emmy.

September 28:
The Bible...In The Beginning is released, and is nominated for an Academy Award for Best Score (**Toshiro Mayuzumi**).

December 20:
The Sand Pebbles is released, and receives Academy Award nominations for Best Picture (**Robert Wise**), Actor (**Steve McQueen**), Supporting Actor (**Mako**), Cinematography (**Joseph MacDonald**), Art Direction—Set Decoration (**Boris Leven; Walter M. Scott, John Sturtevant, William Kiernan**), Sound (**James P. Corcoran**), Film Editing (**William Reynolds**), and Score (**Jerry Goldsmith**).

1967

April 27:
Two for the Road is released and **Frederic Raphael** is nominated for an Academy Award for Best Screenplay.

December 15:
Valley of the Dolls premieres aboard the Italian cruise ship Princess Italia. **John Williams** is nominated for an Academy Award for Best Scoring.

December 19:
Doctor Dolittle opens, and wins Academy Awards for Best Song "Talk To The Animals" by **Leslie Bricusse** and Best Special Effects (**L.B. Abbott**) and is nominated for Best Picture (**Arthur P. Jacobs**), Cinematography (**Robert Surtees**), Art Direction—Set Decoration (**Mario Chiari, Jack Martin Smith, Ed Graves; Walter M. Scott, Stuart A. Reiss**), Sound (Twentieth Century Fox Studio Sound Department), Film Editing (**Samuel E. Beetley, Marjorie Fowler**), and Scoring (**Lionel Newman, Alexander Courage**).

1968

February 8:
Planet of the Apes opens, and is nominated for Academy Awards for Best Costume Design (**Morton Haack**) and Original Score (**Jerry Goldsmith**). **John Chambers** receives an honorary Academy Award for his makeup. The franchise includes: *Beneath the Planet of the Apes* (1970), *Escape from the Planet of the Apes* (1971), *Conquest of the Battle of the Apes* (1972), *Battle for the Planet of the Apes* (1973), *Planet of the Apes* (2001), and *Rise of the Planet of the Apes* (2011). *Dawn of the Planet of the Apes* (2014) is nominated for an Academy Award for Sound Editing (**Joe Letteri, Dan Lemmon, Daniel Barrett, Erik Winquist**). *War for the Planet of the Apes* is released in 2017. There were also television series: *Planet of the Apes* (1974) and *Return to the Planet of the Apes* (1975).

October 22:
Star! opens, and is nominated for Best Supporting Actor (**Daniel Massey**), Cinematography (**Ernest Laszlo**), Art Direction—Set Decoration (**Boris Leven; Walter M. Scott, Howard Bristol**), Costume Design (**Donald Brooks**), Best Song "Star" (**James Van Heusen, Sammy Cahn**), Score (**Lennie Hayton**), and Sound (Twentieth Century Fox Studio Sound Dept.)

1969

February 24:
The Prime of Miss Jean Brodie is screened as a Royal Command Performance for the **Queen Mother** and **Princess Margaret**. The film stars **Maggie Smith** (who wins a Best Actress Academy Award)**,** and husband **Robert Stephens**. The film is nominated for Best Song "Jean" (**Rod McKuen**).

September 17:
Room 222 debuts on TV, runs through 1974, and wins 3 Emmys.

October 10:

Butch Cassidy and the Sundance Kid opens and spawns three television movies, and a prequel, *Butch and Sundance: The Early Days* (1979). **Redford** dedicates his non-profit Sundance Institute in Provo, Utah, and its annual film festival, to encourage and develop independent filmmakers in 1981. **Paul Newman** co-founds "The Hole in the Wall Gang Camps" for children with serious illnesses in 1986. The film wins Academy Awards for Screenplay (**William Goldman**), Cinematography (**Conrad Hall**), Best Song "Raindrops Are Falling On My Head" (**Burt Bacharach, Hal David**), Score (**Burt Bacharach**) and is nominated for Best Picture (**John Foreman**), Directing (**George Roy Hill**), and Sound (**William Edmondson, David Dockendorf**). The film holds the record for winning the most (9) BAFTA Awards.

December 16:

Hello, Dolly! premieres, and wins Academy Awards for Best Art Decoration—Set Decoration (**John DeCuir, Jack Martin Smith, Herman Blumenthal; Walter M. Scott, George James Hopkins, Raphael Bretton**), Score (**Lennie Hayton, Lionel Newman**), and Sound (**Jack Solomon, Murray Spivack**). It is nominated for Best Picture (**Ernest Lehman**), Cinematography (**Harry Stradling**), Costume Design (**Irene Sharaff**), and Film Editing (**William Reynolds**).

1970

January 25:

M*A*S*H premieres, and the film wins an Academy Award for Screenplay (**Ring Lardner, Jr.**) and nominations for Best Picture (**Ingo Preminger**), Directing (**Robert Altman** in his Fox debut) and Supporting Actress (**Sally Kellerman**), and Film Editing (**Danford B. Greene**). **Robert Duvall**, who makes his Fox debut in the film, later stars and co-produces *Crazy Heart* (2009) and stars in **Billy Bob Thornton's** *Jayne Mansfield's Car* (2012).

February 1:

Patton opens, and wins Academy Awards for Best Picture (**Frank McCarthy**), Screenplay (**Francis Ford Coppola, Edmund H. North**), Best Actor (**George C. Scott**, who declined the award), Directing (**Franklin J. Schaffner**), Art Direction—Set Direction (**Urie McCleary, Gil Parrando; Antonio Mateos, Pierre-Louis Thevenet**), Sound (**Douglas Williams, Don Bassman**), and Film Editing (**Hugh S. Fowler**). The film received nominations for Best Cinematography (**Fred Koenekamp**), Visual Effects (**Alex Weldon**), and Score (**Jerry Goldsmith**).

September 23:

Tora! Tora! Tora! is released. The film receives Academy Award nominations for Cinematography (**Charles F. Wheeler, Osami Furuya, Sinsaku Himeda, Masamichi Satoh**), Art Direction-Set Direction (**Jack Martin Smith, Yoshiro Muraki, Richard Day, Taizoh Kawashima; Walter M. Scott, Norman Rockett, Carl Biddiscombe**), Sound (**Murray Spivak, Herman Lewis**), Film Editing (**James E. Newcom, Pembroke J. Herring, Inoue Chikaya**) and Visual Effects (**A. D. Flowers, L. B. Abbott**).

October 16:

The Great White Hope is released and receives Academy Award nominations for Best Actor (**James Earl Jones**) and Actress (**Jane Alexander**). The film marked **Alexander's** film debut.

1971

October 9:

The French Connection premieres in New York, inspires a sequel *The French Connection II* (1975), and wins Academy Awards for Best Picture (**Philip D'Antoni**), Directing (**William Friedkin**), Actor (**Gene Hackman**), Writing (**Ernest Tidyman**), and Film Editing (**Jerry Greenberg**). The film is nominated for Best Supporting Actor (**Roy Scheider**), Sound (**Theodore Soderberg, Christopher Newman**), and Cinematography (**Owen Roizman**).

1972

April 21:

The Hot Rock opens, and is nominated for an Academy Award for Film Editing (**Frank P. Keller, Fred W. Berger**).

May 23:

The Poseidon Adventure is released, and receives Academy Awards for Best Song "The Morning After" (**Al Kasha, Joel Hirschhorn**) and a Special Achievement Award for visual effects (**L.B. Abbott, A.D. Flowers**). The film is nominated for Supporting Actress (**Shelley Winters**), Cinematography (**Harold E. Stine**), Art Direction—Set Direction (**William Creber, Raphael Bretton**), Costume Design (**Paul Zastupnevich**), Sound (**Theodore Soderberg, Herman Lewis**), Score (**John Williams**), and Film Editing (**Harold F. Kress**).

September 24:
Sounder opens, and earns Academy Award nominations for Best Picture (**Robert B. Radnitz**), Actor (**Paul Winfield**), Actress (**Cicely Tyson**), and Screenplay (**Lonne Elder, III**). *Sounder, Part 2* was released in 1976.

September 17:
M*A*S*H debuts on TV and runs 11 seasons. It is the first show to earn $100 million in domestic syndication, and wins 14 Emmys.

October 22:
The Discreet Charm of the Bourgeoisie is released, and wins the Academy Award for Best Foreign Language Film (France) as well as a nomination for Screenplay (**Luis Buñuel;, Jean-Claude Carrière**).

December 10:
Sleuth opens, and receives Academy Award nominations for Best Actor (**Laurence Olivier**), Actor (**Michael Caine**), Directing (**Joseph L. Mankiewicz**), and Score (**John Addison**).

December 17:
The Heartbreak Kid opens in Los Angeles. **Eddie Albert** is nominated for Best Supporting Actor and **Jeannie Berlin** is nominated for Supporting Actress. The film contains the iconic song "I'd Like to Buy the World a Coke" with music and lyrics by **Bill Backer, Billy Davis, Roger Cook** and **Roger Greenaway**.

1973

October 16:
The Paper Chase opens in New York. **John Houseman**, at 71, wins the Academy Award for Best Supporting Actor. **Houseman** would reprise the part as the dictatorial Harvard professor Kingsfield in a Fox television series (1978-1986). The film is nominated for Screenplay (**James Bridges**) and Sound (**O. Mitchell, Lawrence O. Jost**).

December 18:
Cinderella Liberty opens, and is nominated for Best Actress (**Marsha Mason**), Best Song "Nice To Be Around" (**John Williams, Andy Williams**) and Score (**John Williams**).

1974

April 22:
Claudine is released starring **Diahann Carroll** who is nominated for an Academy Award for Best Actress. **Carroll** was the first African American to star in a television series: Fox's *Julia* (1968-1971).

August 12:
Harry and Tonto opens in New York and wins an Academy Award for Best Actor (**Art Carney**) and a nomination for Original Screenplay (**Paul Mazursky, Josh Greenfeld**).

August 31:
Phantom of the Paradise is released, and is nominated for an Academy Award for Score (**Paul Williams, George Aliceson Tipton**).

December 14:
The Towering Inferno is released and wins Academy Awards for Cinematography (**Fred Koenekamp, Joseph Biroc**), Editing (**Harold F. Cress, Carl Kress**) and Song "We May Never Love Like This Again" (**Al Kasha, Joel Hirschhorn**). The film is nominated for Best Picture (**Irwin Allen**), Supporting Actor (**Fred Astaire**), Art Direction—Set Direction (**William Creber, Ward Preston; Raphael Bretton**), Sound (**Theodore Soderberg, Herman Lewis**), and Score (**John Williams**).

December 15:
Young Frankenstein premieres in New York marking the Fox debut of **Gene Wilder** and **Mel Brooks** as a director. It is nominated for Academy Awards for Screenplay (**Gene Wilder, Mel Brooks**) and Sound (**Richard Portman, Gene S. Cantamessa**).

1975

February 26:
The Four Musketeers opens in New York. **Yvonne Blake** and **Ron Talsky** are nominated for an Academy Award for Costume Design.

October 15:
Whiffs is released. **George Barrie** and **Sammy Cahn** are nominated for an Academy Award for Best Song "Now That We're in Love."

December 25:
Scent of a Woman is released in Italy and then distributed in the U.S. by Fox. The film is nominated for Best Foreign Language Film and Screenplay (**Ruggiero Maccari, Dino Risi**).

1976

June 25:
The Omen is released, and **Jerry Goldsmith** wins an Academy Award for Original Score and is nominated for Original Song "Ave Satani."

The film spawns sequels: *Damien - Omen II* (1978), *The Final Conflict* (1981) that also marks composer **Lionel Newman's** last work at Fox and *The Omen* (2006). A television movie *The Omen IV: The Awakening* aired in 1991.

December 3:
Silver Streak opens, and **Donald Mitchell, Douglas Williams, Richard Tyler,** and **Hal Etherington** are nominated for the Academy Award for Best Sound.

1977

May 25:
Star Wars Episode IV: A New Hope is released and wins Academy Awards for Film Editing (**Paul Hirsch, Marcia Lucas, Richard Chew**), Art Direction—Set Decoration (**John Barry, Norman Reynolds, Leslie Dilley; Robert Christian**), Costume Design (**John Mollo**), Sound (**Don MacDougall, Ray West, Bob Minkler, Derek Ball**), Visual Effects (**John Stears, John Dykstra, Richard Edlund, Grant McCune, Robert Blalack**), Special award for Sound Effects (**Benjamin Burtt, Jr.**), Score (**John Williams**). The film is nominated for Best Picture (**Gary Kurtz**), Supporting Actor (**Alec Guinness**), Directing (**George Lucas**), and Writing (**George Lucas**).

June 8:
The Other Side of Midnight opens in New York. **Irene Sharaff** is nominated for an Academy Award for Costume Design.

October 2:
Julia premieres, and marks the film debut of **Meryl Streep**. The movie earned Academy Awards for Supporting Actor (**Jason Robards**), Supporting Actress (**Vanessa Redgrave**), and Adapted Screenplay (**Alvin Sargent**) and nominations for Best Picture (**Richard Roth**), Actress (**Jane Fonda**), Supporting Actor (**Maximilian Schell**), Directing (**Fred Zinnemann**), Cinematography (**Douglas Slocombe**), Costume Design (**Anthea Sylbert**), Film Editing (**Walter Murch**), and Score (**Georges Delerue**).

November 14:
The Turning Point is released, and is nominated for Best Picture, Actress (**Anne Bancroft**), Actress (**Shirley MacLaine**), Supporting Actor (**Mikhail Baryshnikov**), Supporting Actress (**Leslie Browne**), Directing (**Herbert Ross**), Original Screenplay (**Arthur Laurents**), Cinematography (**Robert Surtees**), Art Direction—Set Decoration

(**Albert Brenner; Marvin March**), Sound (**Theodore Soderberg, Paul Wells, Douglas O. Williams, Jerry Jost**), and Film Editing (**William Reynolds**).

1978

March 1:
An Unmarried Woman opens in New York and receives Academy Award nominations for Best Picture (**Paul Mazursky, Tony Ray**), Original Screenplay (**Paul Mazursky**), and Actress (**Jill Clayburgh**).

October 5:
The Boys from Brazil is released starring **Gregory Peck** and **Sir Laurence Olivier** who is nominated for an Academy Award for Best Actor. Other nominations include Film Editing (**Robert E. Swink**) and Original Score (**Jerry Goldsmith**).

1979

March 2:
Norma Rae opens, and wins Academy Awards for Best Actress (**Sally Field**), Original Song "It Goes Like It Goes" (**David Shire, Norman Gimbel**) and nominations for Best Picture (**Tamara Asseyev, Alex Rose**) and Adapted Screenplay (**Irving Ravetch, Harriet Frank, Jr.**).

May 25:
Alien premieres, and **H. R. Giger, Carlo Rambaldi, Brian Johnson, Nick Allder,** and **Denys Ayling** win the Academy Award for Visual Effects. **Michael Seymour, Les Dilley Roger Christian** and **Ian Whittaker** are nominated for Art Direction—Set Decoration. The franchise includes: *Aliens* (1986), *Alien 3* (1992), *Alien: Resurrection* (1997), and *Prometheus* (2012). See also the *Predator* franchise.

June 21:
Butch and Sundance: The Early Days is released and receives an Academy Award nomination for Costume Design (**William Ware Theiss**).

July 20:
Breaking Away opens in Los Angeles and wins an Academy Award for Original Screenplay (**Steve Tesich**) and nominations for Best Picture (**Peter Yates**), Directing (**Peter Yates**), Supporting Actress (**Barbara Barrie**), and Score (**Patrick Williams**).

November 7:
The Rose opens and receives Academy Award nominations for Actress (**Bette Midler** in her Fox debut), Supporting Actor (**Frederic Forrest**), Sound (**Theodore Soderberg, Douglas Williams, Paul Wells, Jim Webb**), and Film Editing (**Robert L. Wolfe, C. Timothy O'Meara**).

December 20:
All That Jazz premieres, and brings Fox four Academy Awards: Art Direction—Set Decoration (**Philip Rosenberg, Tony Walton; Edward Stewart, Gary Brink**),Costume Design (**Albert Wolsky**), Film Editing (**Alan Heim**), Original Score (**Ralph Burns**)) and five nominations: Best Picture (**Robert Alan Aurthur**), Actor (**Roy Scheider**), Directing (**Bob Fosse**), Writing (**Robert Alan Aurthur, Bob Fosse**), Cinematography (**Giuseppe Rotunno**).

1980

May 21:
Star Wars Episode V: The Empire Strikes Back is released, and wins an Academy Award for Sound (**Bill Varney, Steve Maslow, Gregg Landaker, Peter Sutton**) and a special achievement award for Visual Effects (**Brian Johnson, Richard Edlund, Dennis Muren, Bruce Nicholson**). The film is also nominated for Score (**John Williams**), and Art Direction—Set Decoration (**Norman Reynolds, Leslie Dilley, Harry Lange, Alan Tomkins; Michael Ford**).

June 20:
Brubaker is released starring **Robert Redford. W.D. Richter** and **Arthur Ross** are nominated for an Academy Award for Screenplay.

June 27:
The Stunt Man is released, and receives Academy Award nominations for Best Actor (**Peter O'Toole**), Directing (**Richard Rush**) and Adapted Screenplay (**Lawrence B. Marcus, Richard Rush**).

October 6:
Kagemusha (The Shadow Warrior) is released and earns Academy Award nominations for Best Foreign Language Film (Japan) and Art Direction (**Yoshiro Muraki**).

December 14:
Tribute opens in New York. **Jack Lemmon** is nominated for an Academy Award for Best Actor.

December 19:
9 to 5 opens featuring the film debut of **Dolly Parton**, who is nominated for an Academy Award for writing the title song. Two series were created in 1982-1983 and from 1986-1988.

1982

February 12:
Quest for Fire premieres, and earns French Cesar Awards for best foreign film and director and an Academy Award for Makeup (**Sarah Monzani, Michèle Burke**). Director **Jean-Jacques Annaud** would be back in 1986 with **Sean Connery** in *The Name of the Rose* that earned another Cesar.

December 17:
The Verdict opens, and is nominated for Academy Awards for Best Picture (**Richard Zanuck, David Brown**), Actor (**Paul Newman**), Supporting Actor (**James Mason**), Directing (**Sidney Lumet**), and Adapted Screenplay (**David Mamet**).

1983

February 19:
Betrayal is released, and nominated for an Academy Award for Writing (**Harold Pinter**).

April 1:
Heart like a Wheel is released and is nominated for an Academy Award for Best Costume Design (**William Ware Theiss**).

May 25:
Star Wars Episode VI: Return of the Jedi opens and earns a special Academy Award for Visual Effects (**Richard Edlund, Dennis Muren, Ken Ralston, Phil Tippett**) and nominations for Art Direction—Set Decoration (**Norman Reynolds, Fred Hole, James Schoppe; Michael Ford**), Score (**John Williams**), Sound (**Ben Burtt, Gary Summers, Randy Thom, Tony Dawe**), Sound Effects Editing (**Ben Burtt**).

December 14:
Silkwood opens and receives Academy Award nominations for Best Actress (**Meryl Streep**), Supporting Actress (**Cher**), Directing (**Mike Nichols**), Film Editing (**Sam O'Steen**), and Writing (**Nora Ephron, Alice Arlen**).

December 20:
To Be or Not to Be opens, and **Charles Durning** receives an Academy Award nomination for Best Supporting Actor.

1984

March 30:
Romancing the Stone premieres and is nominated for an Academy Award for Film Editing (**Donn Cambern, Frank Morriss**).

December 19:
Reuben, Reuben is released, and nominated for Academy Awards for Actor (**Tom Conti**) and Adapted Screenplay (**Julius J. Epstein**).

1985

March 15:
Mr. Belvedere debuts on TV and runs through 1990. It wins one Emmy.

June 14:
Prizzi's Honor is released, and **Anjelica Huston** wins the Academy Award for Supporting Actress. The film is nominated for Best Picture (**John Foreman**), Actor (**Jack Nicholson**), Supporting Actor (**William Hickey**), Writing (**Richard Condon, Janet Roach**), Costume Design (**Donfeld**), Directing (**John Huston**), and Film Editing (**Rudi Fehr, Kaja Fehr**),

June 21:
Cocoon is released, starring **Don Ameche** (who wins an Academy Award for Best Supporting Actor). The film is nominated for Academy Awards for Visual Effects (**Ken Ralston, Ralph McQuarrie, Scott Farrar, David Berry**). A sequel *Cocoon: The Return* is released in 1988.

1986

July 18:
Aliens is released, and wins Academy Awards for Sound Effects Editing (Don Sharpe) and Visual Effects (**Robert Skotak, Stan Winston, John Richardson, Suzanne Benson**) and nominations for Best Actress (**Sigourney Weaver**), Art Direction—Set Decoration (**Peter Lamont; Crispian Sallis**), Film Editing (**Ray Lovejoy**), Score (**James Horner**), and Sound (**Graham V. Hartstone, Nicolas Le Messurier, Michael A. Carter, Roy Charman**).

August 15:
The Fly is released, and earns an Academy Award for Makeup (**Chris Walas, Stephan Dupuis**) and sequel *Fly II* in 1989.

October 3:
L.A. Law debuts on TV, runs through 1994, and wins 15 Emmys.

December 25:
The Morning After is released and is nominated for an Academy Award for Best Actress (**Jane Fonda**).

1987

February 13:
Mannequin is released. **Albert Hammond** and **Diane Warren** are nominated for an Academy Award for Best Original Song "Nothing's Gonna Stop Us Now."

April 5:
Married with Children (running through 1997) and *The Tracey Ullman Show* (running through 1990) debut on TV. Among the guest stars in *Married*, in 1995, is **Keri Russell** who would star in *Arrested Development* (2003 -), *Waitress* (2007), *The Americans* (2013 -) and *Dawn of the Planet of the Apes* (2014). *The Tracey Ullman Show* was FOX's first show to win an Emmy—8 in fact.

June 12:
Predator is released. **Joel Hynek, Robert M. Greenberg, Richard Greenberg** and **Stan Winston** are nominated for an Academy Award for Best Visual Effects. Subsequent films include *Predator 2* (1990), *AVP: Alien vs. Predator* (2004), *Aliens vs. Predator—Requiem* (2007), and *Predators* (2010).

September 23:
Hooperman debuts on TV, runs through 1989, and wins one Emmy.

September 25:
The Princess Bride premieres. **Willy DeVille** is nominated for an Academy Award for Best Original Song "Storybook Love."

December 11:
Wall Street opens and finds a ready audience with real-life corporate scandals breaking open and the stock market plunging 500 points just two months before the premiere. **Michael Douglas** wins an Academy Award for Best Actor. Equally effective is **Charlie Sheen** who returned to Fox for the film spoofs *Hot Shots!* (1991) and *Hot Shots Part Deux!* (1993), and stars in 20th Television's *Anger Management* (2012-14).

December 16:

Broadcast News premieres. It is nominated for Best Picture (**James L. Brooks**), Actor (**William Hurt**), Actress (**Holly Hunter**), Supporting Actor (**Albert Brooks**), Writing (**James L. Brooks**), Cinematography (**Michael Ballhaus**), and Film Editing (**Richard Marks**).

1988

April:
America's Most Wanted debuts becoming FOX's first breakout ratings hit popularizing tabloid TV and has won one Emmy to date.

June 3:
Big is released to theaters. As *Miracle on 34th Street* had enshrined New York's Macy's as a magical screen landmark, *Big* made the FAO Schwarz Toy Store on Fifth Avenue famous for the classic piano duet of **Tom Hanks** and **Robert Loggia**. There is a further connection here: **Elizabeth Perkins**, the object of Tom Hanks' romantic attentions, would reprise **Maureen O'Hara's** role in **John Hughes** remake of *Miracle* in 1994. *Big* receives Academy Award nominations for Actor (**Tom Hanks**) and Writing (**Gary Ross, Anne Spielberg**).

July 15:
Die Hard premieres and is nominated for Academy Awards for Sound (**Don Bassman, Kevin F. Cleary, Richard Overton, Al Overton**), Film Editing (**Frank J. Urioste, John F. Link**), Sound Effects Editing (**Stephen H. Flick, Richard Shorr**), and Visual Effects (**Richard Edlund, Al DiSarro, Brent Boates, Thaine Morris**). Sequels include *Die Hard 2: Die Harder* (1990), *Die Hard With a Vengeance* (1995), *Live Free Or Die Hard* (2007), and *A Good Day to Die Hard* (2013).

December 21:
Working Girl premieres and is nominated for Best Picture (**Douglas Wick**), Directing (**Mike Nichols**), and Supporting Actress (**Joan Cusack** and **Sigourney Weaver**). It makes **Melanie Griffith** a star; earning her an Academy Award nomination and Golden Globe. **Carly Simon** wins an Academy Award for the *Working Girl* song: "Let the River Run." The film spawned a television show and **Griffith's** daughter **Dakota Johnson** starred in *Ben and Kate* (2012-2013) and *A Bigger Splash* (2015).

1989

August 9:
The Abyss opens, and wins an Academy Award for Visual Effects (**John Bruno, Dennis Muren, Hoyt Yeatman, Dennis Skotak**) and nominations for Art Direction—Set Direction (**Leslie Dilley, Anne Kuljian**), Sound (**Kevin F. Cleary, Richard Overton, Lee Orloff**), and Cinematography (**Mikael Salomon**). A 1993 release of **James Cameron's** preferred edit adding 28 minutes of footage popularizes "Director's Cuts" on home video.

October 13:
The Fabulous Baker Boys is released and receives Academy Award nominations for Best Actress (**Michelle Pfeiffer),** Cinematography (**Michael Ballhaus**), Best Film Editing (**William Steinkamp**), and Original Score (**David Grusin**).

December 13:
Enemies, A Love Story is released and receives Academy Award nominations for two Supporting Actresses (**Anjelica Houston, Lena Olin**) and Screenplay (**Roger L. Simon, Paul Mazursky**).

December 17:
The Simpsons (1989 -) debuts and has won 32 Emmys to date.

1990

April 15:
In Living Color debuts and runs through 1994. It features new stars (**Jim Carrey, David Alan Grier, Kim Wayans, Shawn Wayans, Damon Wayans, Jamie Foxx),** and wins 1 Emmy.

August 1:
Young Guns II opens, and **Jon Bon Jovi** is nominated for an Academy Award for Song "Blaze of Glory."

November 16:
Home Alone opens, and is nominated for Academy Awards for Original Song "Somewhere in My Memory" (**John Williams, Leslie Bricusse**) and Score (**John Williams**). *Home Alone 2: Lost in New York* is released in 1992.

December 7:
Edward Scissorhands premieres and **Ve Neill** and **Stan Winston** are nominated for an Academy Award for Best Makeup.

Richard D. Zanuck and **David Brown** win the Irving G. Thalberg Memorial Award.

1991

August 14:
The Commitments is nominated for an Academy Award for Film Editing (**Gerry Hambling**).

August 21:
Barton Fink is released, and nominated for Academy Awards for Supporting Actor (**Michael Lerner**), Art Direction—Set Direction (**Dennis Gassner, Nancy Haigh**) and Costume Design (**Richard Hornung**).

November 27:
For the Boys opens, and **Bette Midler** is nominated for an Academy Award for Best Actress.

December 25:
Grand Canyon opens in Los Angeles. **Lawrence Kasdan** and **Meg Kasdan** are nominated for an Academy Award for Best Original Screenplay.

1992

March 13:
My Cousin Vinny opens in Los Angeles. **Marisa Tomei** wins the Academy Award for Best Supporting Actress.

May 22:
Alien 3 is released, and **George Gibbs** is nominated for an Academy Award for Visual Effects.

September 18:
Picket Fences (1992–1996) debuts on TV and wins 14 Emmys.

September 25:
The Last of the Mohicans is released and nominated for an Academy Award for Best Sound (**Chris Jenkins, Doug Hemphill, Mark Smith, Simon Kaye).**

December 18:
Toys opens in Los Angeles starring **Robin Williams** and is nominated for Academy Awards for Art Direction—Set Decoration (**Ferdinando Scarfiotti, Linda DeScenna**) and Costume Design (**Albert Wolsky**).

December 25:

Hoffa starring **Jack Nicholson** opens and receives Academy Award nominations for Cinematography (**Stephen H. Burum**) and Makeup (**Ve Neill, Greg Cannom, John Blake**).

1993

September 10:
The X-Files debuts on TV, and runs through 2002. The show wins 13 Creative Arts Emmys and 3 Emmys, and spawns *The X-Files* (1998), *The X-Files: I Want to Believe* (2008), and *The X-Files Re-Opened* (2015 TV special)

September 21:
NYPD Blue debuts on TV and runs through 2005 winning 20 Emmys.

November 24:
Mrs. Doubtfire is released and **Greg Cannom** and **Ve Neill** and **Yolanda Toussieng** are nominated for an Academy Award for Makeup.

1994

June 10:
Speed premieres, and earns two Academy Awards (**Gregg Landaker, Steve Maslow, Bob Beemer** and **David R. B. MacMillan** for Best Sound and **Stephen Hunter Flick** for Sound Effects Editing) and one nomination for Film Editing (**John Wright**).

July 15:
True Lies opens and is nominated for an Academy Award for Visual Effects (**John Bruno, Thomas L. Fisher, Jacques Stroweis, Patrick McClung**).

September 18:
Chicago Hope debuts on TV and runs through 2000. The show wins 7 Emmys.

December 14:
Nell is released and **Jodie Foster** is nominated for an Academy Award for Best Actress.

1996

July 3:
Independence Day premieres, and earns an Academy Award for Best Visual Effects (**Volker Engel** who appears briefly in the movie as a

victim of one of his own fiery explosions) - **Douglas Smith, Clay Pinney**, and **Joseph Viskocil**). The film is nominated for Best Sound (**Chris Carpenter, Bill W. Benton, Bob Beemer, Jeff Wexler**).

October 4:
That Thing You Do is released, and **Adam Schlesinger** is nominated for an Academy Award for Best Original Song "That Thing You Do."

November 1:
Baz Luhrmann's *William Shakespeare's Romeo & Juliet* is released. **Catherine Martin** and **Brigitte Broch** are nominated for an Academy Award for Art Direction-Set Decoration.

November 27:
The Crucible premieres and is nominated for Academy Awards for Best Supporting Actress (**Joan Allen**) and Best Adapted Screenplay (**Arthur Miller**).

December 20:
One Fine Day is released, and nominated for an Academy Award for Original Song "For the First Time" (**James Newton Howard** and **Jud J. Friedman** and **Allan Dennis Rich**)..

1997

March 4:
The Practice debuts on TV and runs through 2004. It wins 15 Emmys.

March 10:
Buffy the Vampire Slayer debuts on TV, runs through 2003, and wins 2 Emmys.

August 13:
The Full Monty opens in Los Angeles and earns an Academy Award for Original Score (**Anne Dudley**) as well as nominations for Best Picture (**Uberto Pasolini**), Directing (**Peter Cattaneo**), and Original Screenplay (**Simon Beaufoy**).

September 8:
Ally McBeal debuts on TV, runs through 2002, and wins 7 Emmys.

November 14:
Anastasia premieres; it is the first film of new division Fox Family Films and Fox Animation Studios Inc. The film is nominated for Academy

Awards for Best Original Song "Journey to the Past" (**Stephen Flaherty, Lynn Ahrens**) and Score (**Stephen Flaherty, Lynn Ahrens**; orchestral Score by **David Newman**).

December 19:
Titanic is released, and wins Academy Awards for Best Picture (**James Cameron**), Directing (**James Cameron**), Cinematography (**Russell Carpenter**), Art Direction-Set Decoration (**Peter Lamont, Michael Ford**), Costume Design (**Deborah L. Scott**), Sound (**Gary Rydstrom, Tom Johnson, Gary Summers, Mark Ulano**), Film Editing (**Conrad Buff, James Cameron, Richard A. Harris**), Sound Effects Editing (**Tom Bellfort, Christopher Boyes**), Original Song "My Heart Will Go On" (**James Horner, Will Jennings**), Score (**James Horner**), Visual Effects (**Robert Legato, Mark Lasoff, Thomas L. Fisher, Michael Kanfer**). The film is nominated for Actress (**Kate Winslet**), Supporting Actress (**Gloria Stuart**), and Makeup (**Tina Earnshaw, Greg Cannom, Simon Thompson**).

December 31:
Oscar and Lucinda is released, and **Janet Patterson** is nominated for an Academy Award for Best Costume Design.

1998

May 15:
Bulworth starring **Warren Beatty** and **Halle Berry** is released and receives an Academy award nomination for Original Screenplay (**Warren Beatty, Jeremy Pikser**).

December 25:
The Thin Red Line is released and is nominated for Academy Awards for Best Picture (**Robert Michael Geisler, John Roberdeau and Grant Hill**), Directing (**Terrence Malick),** Writing (**Terrence Malick**), Cinematography (**John Toll**), Film Editing (**Billy Weber, Leslie Jones, Saar Klein**), Music (**Hans Zimmer**), and Sound (**Andy Nelson, Anna Behlmer, Paul Brincat**).

1999

January 31:
The Family Guy debuts on TV and to date has won 5 Emmys

March 28:
Futurama debuts on TV, and is the winner of 6 Emmys.
May 19:

Star Wars Episode I: The Phantom Menace is released and is nominated for Academy Awards for Sound (**Gary Rydstrom, Tom Johnson, Shawn Murphy, John Midgley),** Sound Effects Editing (**Ben Burtt, Tom Bellfort**), and Visual Effects (**John Knoll, Dennis Muren, Scott Squires, Rob Coleman**).

September 19:
Judging Amy debuts and wins one Emmy.

October 8:
Boys Don't Cry is screened at the New York Film Festival and **Hilary Swank** becomes an international star and Academy Award-winner for Best Actress. **Chloe Sevigny** is nominated for Best Supporting Actress.

October 15:
Fight Club premieres in Los Angeles. **Ren Klyce** and **Richard Hymns** were nominated for an Academy Award for Sound Effects Editing.

December 17:
Anna and the King premieres and earns Academy Award nominations for Art Direction—Set Decoration (**Luciana Arrighi, Ian Whittake**r) and Costume Design (**Jenny Beavan).**

December 24:
Titus is released based on the play *Titus Andronicus* by **William Shakespeare** starring Anthony Hopkins. **Milena Canonero** is nominated for an Academy Award for Best Costume Design.

2000

January 9:
Malcolm in the Middle debuts on TV and runs through 2006 winning 7 Emmys.

July 14:
X-Men premieres and a new franchise is born: *X2* (2003), *X-Men: The Last Stand* (2006), *X-Men Origins: Wolverine* (2008), *X-Men: First Class* (2011), *The Wolverine* (2013), and *X-Men: Days of Future Past* (2014). *Deadpool* and *X-Men: Apocalypse* were released in 2016. There were also television series: *X-Men* (1992-97), *X-Men: Evolution* (2000-03), *Wolverine and the X-Men* (2008-09), *Wolverine* (2011 -), and *X-Men* (2011 -).

December 15:

Quills is released and **Geoffrey Rush** is nominated for an Academy Award for Best Actor as the Marquis de Sade. The film is also nominated for Art Direction-Set Decoration (**Martin Childs, Jill Quertier**), and Costume Design (**Jacqueline West**).

December 22:
Cast Away is released. The film is the first in an ongoing partnership with DreamWorks, and receives Academy Award nominations for Best Actor (**Tom Hanks)** and Best Sound (**Randy Thom, Tom Johnson, Dennis Sands, William B. Kaplan**).

2001

May 18:
Moulin Rouge is released and receives Academy Awards for Art Direction (**Catherine Martin, Brigitte Broch)** and Costume Design (**Catherine Martin, Angus Strathie)** and is nominated for Best Picture (**Martin Brown, Baz Luhrmann, Fred Baron**), Best Actress (**Nicole Kidman**), Cinematography (**Donald M. McAlpine**), Film Editing (**Jill Bilcock**), Makeup (**Maurizio Silvi, Aldo Signoretti**), Sound (**Andy Nelson, Anna Behlmer, Roger Savage, Guntis Sics**).

June 13:
Sexy Beast is released, and **Ben Kingsley** is nominated for an Academy Award for Best Supporting Actor.

November 21:
24 (2001-2010) debuts on TV, wins 20 Emmys, and spawns *24* (2008 TV movie), *24: Live Another Day* (2014 TV miniseries), and *24: Legacy* (2017 TV series).

2002

March 15:
After Fox purchased them in 1999, Blue Sky Studios releases its first animated feature. The sequels include *Ice Age: The Meltdown* (2006), *Ice Age: Dawn of the Dinosaurs* (2009), *Ice Age: Continental Drift* (2012), and *Ice Age: Collision Course* (2016). **Chris Wedge** is nominated for Best Animated Feature Film.

May 8:
Unfaithful (Fox 2000 Pictures) is released. **Diane Lane** is nominated for an Academy Award for Best Actress.

May 16:

Star Wars Episode II: Attack of the Clones premieres. **Rob Coleman, Pablo Helman, John Knoll** and **Ben Snow** are nominated for an Academy Award for Visual Effects.

June 11:
American Idol debuts on FOX and runs through 2016. The season finales were ranked number one an unprecedented eight times in a row between 2003 and 2011. The show has won 8 Emmys.

June 21:
Minority Report is released and receives an Academy Award nomination for Sound Editing (**Richard Hymns, Gary Rydstrom).** The movie becomes a 2015 TV series.

July 12:
Road to Perdition; the story of a father (**Tom Hanks**) and son (**Tyler Hoechlin**) made by a father (**Richard Zanuck**) and son (**Dean Zanuck**). **Conrad L. Hall** wins the Academy Award for Best Director and **Paul Newman** is nominated for Best Supporting Actor. The film receives nominations for Art Direction (**Dennis Gassner; Nancy Haigh**), Original Score (**Thomas Newman**), Sound Editing (**Scott A. Hecker**), and Sound (**Scott Millan, Bob Beemer, John Patrick Pritchett**).

September 20:
Firefly debuts on FOX and is canceled by December 12. The show wins 1 Emmy.

2003
August 20:
Thirteen (Fox Searchlight) is released. **Holly Hunter** is nominated for an Academy Award for Best Supporting Actress.

November 2:
Arrested Development debuts on TV, and to date had won 6 Emmys.

November 14:
Master and Commander: The Far Side of the World is released by Twentieth Century Fox, Universal, and Miramax. The film receives Academy Awards for Sound Editing (**Richard King),** and Cinematography (**Russell Boyd**) and nominations for Best Picture (**Samuel Goldwyn Jr., Peter Weir, Duncan Henderson**), Directing (**Peter Weir)**, Art Direction-Set Direction (**William Sandell, Robert Gould**),

Costume Design (**Wendy Stites). Editing (Lee Smith),** Makeup (**Edouard Henriques III, Yolanda Toussieng**), Sound Mixing (**Paul Massey, D.M. Hemphill, Arthur Rochester**), and Visual Effects (**Dan Sudick, Stefen Fangmeier, Nathan McGuinness, Robert Stromberg**).

November 26:
In America opens in Los Angeles and is nominated for Academy Awards for Best Actress (**Samantha Morton**), Supporting Actor (**Djimon Hounsou**) and Original Screenplay (**Jim Sheridan, Naomi Sheridan, Kirsten Sheridan).**

November 26:
Gone Nutty is released and **Carlos Saldanha** and **John C. Donkin** are nominated for Best Animated Short Film (Blue Sky Studios).

2004
July 16:
I, Robot opens in Los Angeles starring **Will Smith** and **Bridget Moynahan** and is nominated for an Academy Award for Visual Effects (**John Nelson, Andrew R. Jones, Erik Nash, Joe Letteri**).

October 20:
Sideways opens and wins an Academy Award for Adapted Screenplay (**Alexander Payne, Jim Taylor),** and is nominated for Best Picture (**Michael London**), Supporting Actor (**Thomas Haden Church**), Supporting Actress (**Virginia Madsen**), and Directing (**Alexander Payne**).

November 12:
Kinsey premieres at the Telluride Film Festival. **Laura Linney** is nominated for Best Supporting Actress.

2005
May 19:
Star Wars Episode III: Revenge of the Sith is released and receives an Academy Award nomination for Makeup (**Dave Elsey, Nikki Gooley**). On October 30, 2012 **George Lucas** sells Lucasfilm to The Walt Disney Company for $4 billion including the *Star Wars* franchise. While Disney now owns and can release future films in the series Fox retains distribution rights to *Star Wars* IV in perpetuity worldwide and theatrical, nontheatrical and home video rights worldwide for the other five through May 2020.
November 18:

Walk the Line is released and **Reese Witherspoon** wins the Academy Award for Best Actress (and does her own signing as country-western singer **June Carter**). The film receives nominations for Best Actor (**Joaquin Phoenix**, who also did his own singing as **Johnny Cash**), Costume Design (**Arianne Phillips**), Editing (**Michael McCusker**), and Sound Mixing (**Paul Massey, D.M. Hemphill, Peter F. Kurland**). **Johnny Cash** and **June Carter** appeared in *The Gospel Road* (1973).

Robert Altman receives an Honorary Academy Award "in recognition of a career that has repeatedly reinvented the art form and inspired filmmakers and audiences alike."

2006

September 27:
The Last King of Scotland opens. **Forest Whitaker** wins the Academy Award for Best Actor as real-life Ugandan dictator Idi Amin.

June 30:
The Devil Wears Prada puts Fox back in the glamour business with Academy Award-nominated costume designer **Patricia Field** and **Meryl Streep** earning her 14th nomination for Best Actress.

July 26:
Little Miss Sunshine is released, and wins Academy Awards for Original Screenplay (**Michael Arndt**) and Supporting Actor (**Alan Arkin**). The film is nominated for Best Picture (**David T. Friendly, Peter Saraf, Marc Turtletaub**), and Supporting Actress (**Abigail Breslin**).

November 3:
Borat: Cultural Learnings of America for Make Benefit Glorious Nation of Kazakhstan is released and is nominated for an Academy Award for Best Adapted Screenplay (**Sacha Baron Cohen, Anthony Hines, Peter Baynham, Dan Mazer, Todd Phillips**).

November 21:
No Time For Nuts (Blue Sky Studios) is released and nominated for an Academy Award for Best Animated Short Film (**Chris Renaud, Michael Thurmeier**).

December 27:
Notes on a Scandal opens in New York and Los Angeles and is nominated for Academy Awards for Best Actress (**Judi Dench),** Supporting Actress **(Cate Blanchett),** Adapted Screenplay (**Patrick Marber**), and Original Score (**Philip Glass).**

Sherry Lansing receives the 2006 Jean Hersholt Humanitarian Award.

2007

May 16:
Once makes its American debut at the Sundance Film Festival**. Glen Hansard** and **Marketa Irglova** win the Academy Award for Best Original Song for "Falling Slowly."

July 24:
Damages debuts and runs through 2012 winning 9 Emmys.

November 28:
The Savages is released and earns Academy Award nominations for Best Actress (**Laura Linney**) and Original Screenplay (**Tamara Jenkins**).

December 5:
Juno is released and earns an Academy Award for **Diablo Cody** for Original Screenplay. The film is also nominated for Best Picture (**Lianne Halfon, Mason Novick, Russell Smith**), Actress (**Ellen Page**), and Directing (**Jason Reitman**).

2008

April 18:
The Russian documentary *Water* is released in America by Fox and receives an Academy Award nomination as Best Foreign Language Film.

November 12:
Slumdog Millionaire wins Academy Awards for Best Picture (**Christian Colson**), Directing (**Danny Boyle**), Cinematography (**Anthony Dod Mantle**), Editing (**Chris Dickens**), Original Score (**A.R. Rahman**), Original Song "Jai Ho" (**A.R. Rahman** and **Gulzar**), Sound Mixing (**Ian Tapp, Richard Pryke, Resul Pookutty**), and Adapted Screenplay (**Simon Beaufoy**). The film is nominated for Best Song "O Saya" (**A.R. Rahman, Maya Arulpragasam**).

November 26:
Australia opens in Los Angeles. **Catherine Martin** is nominated for an Academy Award for Best Costume Design.
December 17:

The *Wrestler* is released and earns Academy Award nominations for Best Actor (**Mickey Rourke**), and Supporting Actress (**Marisa Tomei**).

2009

May 19:
Glee debuts on TV, ran through 2015, and won 4 Emmys and 2 Creative Arts Emmys.

September 23:
Modern Family debuts and has won 17 Emmys and 4 Creative Arts Emmys to date.

November 13:
Fantastic Mr. Fox is released and nominated for Academy Awards for Best Animated Feature Film (**Wes Anderson**) and Original Score (**Alexandre Desplat**).

December 16:
Crazy Heart opens and earns Academy Awards for Actor (**Jeff Bridges**), and Song "The Weary Kind" (**Ryan Bingham, T Bone Burnett**). **Maggie Gyllenhaal** is nominated for Best Supporting Actress.

December 18:
Avatar opens and receives Academy Awards for Cinematography (**Mauro Fiore),** Visual Effects (**Joe Letteri, Stephen Rosenbaum, Richard Baneham, Andrew R. Jones)** and Art Direction (**Rick Carter, Robert Stromberg; Kim Sinclair**). The film is nominated for Best Picture (**James Cameron, Jon Landau**), Directing (**James Cameron**), Editing (**Stephen Rivkin, John Refoua, James Cameron**), Score (**James Horner**), Sound Editing (**Christopher Boyes, Gwendolyn Yates Whittle**), and Sound Mixing (**Christopher Boyes, Gary Summers, Andy Nelson, Tony Johnson**). Four sequels are planned for release beginning in 2018.

2010

March 16:
Justified debuts on TV, runs through 2015, and wins 2 Emmys.

June 29:
Louie debuts on the FX Network and has won 3 Emmys.
November 5:

127 Hours is released. **James Franco** - who made his film debut in *Never Been Kissed* (1999) - is nominated for an Academy Award for Best Actor. The film is also nominated for Best Picture (**Christian Colson, Danny Boyle, John Smithson**), Editing (**Jon Harris**), Score (**A.R. Rahman**), Song "If I Rise" (**A.R. Rahman, Dido** and **Rollo Armstrong**), and Adapted Screenplay (**Danny Boyle, Simon Beaufoy**).

November 12:
Unstoppable is released and receives an Academy Award nomination for Sound Editing (**Mark P. Stoeckinger**).

December 3:
The Black Swan is released and **Natalie Portman** wins the Academy Award for Best Actress. The film is nominated for Best Picture (**Mike Medavoy, Brian Oliver, Scott Franklin**), Cinematography (**Matthew Libatique**), Directing (**Darren Aronofsky**), and Film Editing (**Andrew Weisblum**).

2011

April 15:
Twentieth Century Fox Animation/Blue Sky's *Rio* receives an Academy Award nomination for Best Song "Real in Rio" (**Sergio Mendes, Carlinhos Brown, Siedah Garrett**). *Rio 2* is released in 2014.

May 27:
Tree of Life is released and is nominated for Academy Awards for Best Picture (**Sarah Green, Bill Pohlad, Dede Gardner, Grant Hill**), Directing (**Terrence Malick**), and for best Cinematography (**Emmanuel Lubezki).**

August 5:
The Chernin Group's first feature film *The Rise of the Planet of the Apes* is released. **Joe Letteri, Dan Lemmon, R. Christopher White,** and **Daniel Barrett** are nominated for an Academy Award for Visual Effects.

October 2:
Homeland debuts and wins 6 Emmys and 2 Creative Arts Emmys.

2011

October 5:
American Horror Story debuts and has won 4 Emmys and 4 Creative Arts Emmys to date. The show features new Fox stars **Evan Peters** (*X-Men: Days of Future Past* (2011), *X-Men: Apocalypse* (2016)) and **Matt Bomer** (*White Collar* (2009-14), *In Time* (2011)).

November 16:
The Descendants premieres earning an Academy Award for Best Adapted Screenplay (**Alexander Payne, Nat Faxon, Jim Rash**) and nominations for Best Picture (**Jim Burke, Alexander Payne, Jim Taylor**), Actor (**George Clooney**), Directing (**Alexander Payne**), Editing (**Kevin Tent**).

2012

June 8:
Prometheus is nominated for an Academy Award for Visual Effects (**Richard Stammers, Trevor Wood, Charley Henley, Martin Hill**).

June 27:
Beasts of the Southern Wild opens and receives Academy Award nominations for Best Picture (**Dan Janvey, Josh Penn, Michael Gottwald**), Directing (**Benh Zeitlin**), Adapted Screenplay (**Lucy Alibar, Benh Zeitlin**), and Actress (**Quvenzhane Wallis**).

July 13:
Twentieth Century Fox Animation's *Maggie Simpson in The Longest Daycare* is released, and nominated for an Academy Award for Best Short Film (**David Silverman**).

October 19:
The Sessions opens and **Helen Hunt** is nominated for an Academy Award for Best Supporting Actress.

November 21:
Life of Pi premieres and wins Academy Awards for Directing (**Ang Lee**), Cinematography (**Claudio Miranda**), Score (**Mychael Danna**), and Visual Effects (**Bill Westenhofer, Guillaume Rocheron, Erik-Jan De Boer, Donald R. Elliott**). The film is nominated for Best Picture (**Gil Netter, Ang Lee, David Womark**), Adapted Screenplay (**David Magee**), Editing (**Tim Squyres**), Original Song "Pi's Lullaby" (**Mychael Danna, Bombay Jayashri**), Production Design (**David Gropman, Anna Pinnock**), Sound Editing (**Eugene Gearty, Philip Stockton**), and Sound Mixing (**Ron Bartlett, D.M. Hemphill, Drew Kunin**). The world's largest wave-making water tank was built for the film in Taiwan holding 1.7 million gallons.

November 23:
The release of *Hitchcock* marks the seventh decade of studio involvement from the prolific **Huston** family with **Danny Huston, John's** son, in the cast. The film received an Academy Award nomination for Makeup and Hairstyling (**Howard Berger, Peter Montagna, Martin Samuel**).

2013

January 30:
The Americans debuts, and to date has won 1 Emmy.

March 22:
Under an agreement signed in August of 2012, Fox starts distributing DreamWorks animated product beginning with the release of The Croods. The film is nominated for an Academy Award for Best Animated Feature (Chris Sanders, Kirk DeMicco, Kristine Belson).

October 18:
12 Years a Slave is released and wins Academy Awards for Best Picture (**Brad Pitt, Dede Gardner, Jeremy Kleiner, Steve McQueen, Anthony Katagas**), Supporting Actress (**Lupita Nyong'o**) and Adapted Screenplay (**John Ridley**) and nominations for Actor (**Chiwetel Ejiofor**), Supporting Actor (**Michael Fassbender**), Costume Design (**Patricia Norris**), Directing (**Steve McQueen**), Film Editing (**Joe Walker**), Production Design (**Adam Stockhausen, Alice Baker**).

November 8:
The Book Thief is released and **John Williams** is nominated for his 49th Academy Award for Best Original Score.

November 27:
Philomena is released and is nominated for Best Picture (**Gabrielle Tana, Steve Coogan, Tracey Seaward**), Actress (**Judi Dench**), Original Score (**Alexandre Desplat**), and Adapted Screenplay (**Steve Coogan, Jeff Pope**).

2014

March 7:
Grand Budapest Hotel is released and wins Academy Awards for Costume Design (**Milena Canonero**), Makeup (**Frances Hannon, Mark**

Coulier), Score (**Alexandre Desplat**), Art Direction (**Adam Stockhausen; Anna Pinnock**) and nominations for Best Picture, Directing (**Wes Anderson**), Screenplay (**Wes Anderson, Hugo Guinness**), Cinematography (**Robert Yoeman**), and Film Editing (**Barney Pilling**).

May 23:
X-Men: Days of Future Past (2014) is released, and nominated for an Academy Award for Sound Editing (**Richard Stammers, Lou Pecora, Tim Crosbie, Cameron Waldbauer**).

June 13:
DreamWorks Animation's *How to Train Your Dragon 2* is distributed by Fox and is nominated for an Academy Award for Best Animated Feature Film.

October 3:
Gone Girl is released and is nominated for an Academy Award for Best Actress (**Rosamund Pike**).

October 17:
Birdman: (Or The Unexpected Virtue of Ignorance) is released and wins Academy Awards for Best Picture, Director (**Alejandro G. Iñárritu**), Screenplay (**Alejandro G. Iñárritu, Nicolás Giacobone, Alexander Dinelaris, Jr., Armando Bo**), Actor, (**Michael Keaton**), Cinematography (**Emmanuel Lubezki**) and nominations for Supporting Actor (**Edward Norton**), Supporting Actress (**Emma Stone**), and Sound Editing (**Martin Hernández, Aaron Glascock**)

December 5:
Wild is released and is nominated for an Academy Award for Best Actress (**Reese Witherspoon**).

2015

January 26:
Brooklyn premieres at the Sundance Film Festival and is nominated for Academy Awards for Best Picture (**Finola Dwyer, Amanda Posey**), Actress (**Saoirse Ronan**), and Adapted Screenplay (**Nick Hornby**).

October 2:
The Martian is released and is nominated for Academy Awards for Best Picture (**Simon Kinberg, Ridley Scott, Michael Schaefer,**

Mark Huffam), Actor (**Matt Damon**), Adapted Screenplay (**Drew Goddard**), Production Design (**Arthur Max, Celia Bobak**), Sound

(**Paul Massey, Mark Taylor, Mac Ruth**), Sound Editing (**Oliver Tarney**), and Visual Effects (**Richard Stammers, Anders Langlands, Chris Lawrence, Steven Warner**).

October 16:
Bridge of Spies is released and wins an Academy Award for Best Supporting Actor (**Mark Rylance**), and nominations for Best Picture (**Steven Spielberg, Marc Platt, Kristie Macosko Krieger**), Scoring (**Thomas Newman**), Production Design (**Adam Stockhausen, Rena DeAngelo, Bernhard Henrich**), Sound (**Andy Nelson, Gary Rydstrom, Drew Kunin**), and Screenplay (**Matt Charman, Ethan Coen, Joel Coen**).

December 4:
Youth is released and is nominated for an Academy Award for Best Song "Simple Song #3" (**David Lang**).

December 16:
The Revenant is released and wins Academy Awards for Best Actor (**Leonardo DiCaprio**), Cinematography (**Emmanuel Lubezki**), and Directing (**Alejandro G. Iñárritu**), and nominations for Best Picture (**Arnon Milchan, Steve Golin, Alejandro G. Iñárritu, Mary Parent, Keith Redmon**), Supporting Actor (**Tom Hardy**), Costume Design (**Jacqueline West**), Editing (**Stephen Mirrione**), Makeup (Siân **Grigg, Duncan Jarman, Robert A. Pandini**), Production Design (**Jack Fisk, Hamish Purdy**), Sound Editing (**Martin Hernandez, Lon Bender**), Sound Mixing (**Jon Taylor, Frank A.** Montaño, **Randy Thom, Chris Duesterdiek**), and Visual Effects (**Richard McBride, Matthew Shumway, Jason Smith, Cameron Waldbauer**).

December 25:
Joy is released and nominated for an Academy Award for Best Actress (**Jennifer Lawrence**).

STAGE ONE:
Second Honeymoon, Hot Water, Wife, Doctor and Nurse, Charlie Chan

FOX BY THE NUMBERS PART TWO:
WHERE THE MOVIES WERE MADE
THE WESTERN AVENUE STUDIO

On Broadway, Dangerously Yours, Big Town Girl, Love and Hisses, International Settlement, Checkers, City Girl, Walking Down Broadway, Alexander's Ragtime Band, Battle of Broadway, A Trip to Paris, Keep Smiling, Always Goodbye, One Wild Night, Gateway, Passport Husband, Mr. Moto's Last Warning, Five of a Kind, Meet the Girls, Road Demon, Safety in Numbers, While New York Sleeps, A Very Practical Joke, Down on the Farm, Mr. Moto Takes a Vacation, Up The River, Pardon Our Nerve, Everybody's Baby, Wife Husband and Friend, Charlie Chan in Honolulu, Jones Family in Hollywood, News Is Made at Night, The Boyfriend, The Escape, Quick Millions, Chicken Wagon Family, Heaven With A Barbed Wire Fence, 20,000 Men A Year, Too Busy To Work, The Honeymoon Is Over, City of Chance, The Man Who Wouldn't Talk, Young As You Feel, Free, Blonde and 21, Lillian Russell, Sailor's Lady, Charlie Chan's Murder Cruise, Charlie Chan at the Wax Museum, The Great Profile, Murder Over New York, Charter Pilot, Jennie, Golden Hoofs, Ride Kelly Ride, Michael Shayne, Private Detective, Murder Among Friends, Sleepers West, Scotland Yard, Dead Men Tell, Great American Broadcast, Man Hunt, Dressed to Kill, Dance Hall, Marry The Boss's Daughter, We Go Fast, Man At Large, Cadet Girl, Small Town Deb, I Wake Up Screaming, Blue, White, and Perfect, A Gentleman At Heart, The Mad Martindale, Night Before the Divorce, Who Is Hope Schuyler?, Whispering Ghosts, The Man Who Wouldn't Die, It Happened in Flatbush, Footlight Serenade, A-Haunting We Will Go, Just Off Broadway, The Man in the Trunk, That Other Woman, He Hired His Boss, Over My Dead Body, Time to Kill, Quiet Please, Murder, Tonight We Raid Calais, Margin for Error, The Moon is Down, They Came to Blow Up America, Bomber's Moon, Roger Touhy, Gangster, Guadalcanal Diary, The Night Is Ending, Tampico, The Eve of St. Mark, Four Jills in a Jeep, The Keys of the Kingdom, Ladies of Washington, Take it Or Leave It, Laura, Sweet and Low-Down, Diamond Horseshoe, Bon Voyage, Colonel Effingham's Raid, Molly and Me, Circumstantial Evidence, The Dolly Sisters, Don Juan Quilligan, The Embezzler, Strange Triangle, Fallen Angel, Doll Face, Sentimental Journey, Behind Green Lights, Shock, The Shocking Miss Pilgrim, Dark Corner, My Darling Clementine, I Wonder Who's Kissing Her Now, Mother Wore Tights, Moss Rose, Nightmare Alley, Call Northside 777, You Were

Meant For Me, Fury of Furnace Creek, Sitting Pretty, The Street With No Name, The Iron Curtain, Luck of the Irish, That Wonderful Urge, Mr. Belvedere Goes to College, Slattery's Hurricane, Oh, You Beautiful Doll, Pinky, Father Was A Fullback, Dancing in the Dark, Three Came Home, When Willie Comes Marching Home, Ticket to Tomahawk, Cheaper By the Dozen, Where the Sidewalk Ends, I'll Get By, Stella, All About Eve, Fourteen Hours, Follow the Sun, You're In The Navy Now, As Young As You Feel, The Secret of Convict Lake, Love Nest, Lydia Bailey, People Will Talk, Let's Make It Legal, With A Song In My Heart, The Model and the Marriage Broker, Pride of St. Louis, Return of the Texan, The I Don't Care Girl, Lure of the Wilderness, What Price Glory?, We're Not Married, My Wife's Best Friend, My Pal Gus, Titanic, Gentlemen Prefer Blondes, Dangerous Crossing, Blueprint For Murder, Woman's World, Desiree, Black Widow, The Racers, Prince of Players, A Man Called Peter, Violent Saturday, The Many Loves of Dobie Gillis (TV), Bus Stop (TV)

STAGE TWO:

Wife, Doctor and Nurse, Stanley and Livingstone, 45 Fathers, Borrowing Trouble, Sally, Irene and Mary, Checkers, Walking Down Broadway, Alexander's Ragtime Band, Trip to Paris, Always Goodbye, One Wild Night, Passport Husband, Time Out For Murder, Mr. Moto's Last Warning, Five of a Kind, Road Demon, A Very Practical Joke, Up The River, Wife Husband and Friend, Winner Take All, Rose of Washington Square, The Boyfriend, Second Fiddle, Charlie Chan at Treasure Island, Stop - Look and Love, Hollywood Cavalcade, Swanee River, Too Busy To Work, The Man Who Wouldn't Talk, Young As You Feel, I Was An Adventuress, Free, Blonde and 21, Star Dust, Earthbound, Lillian Russell, On Their Own, Young People, Girl in 313, Manhattan Heartbeat, Pier 13, Street of Memories, The Bride Wore Crutches, Charlie Chan at the Wax Museum, The Great Profile, For Beauty's Sake, Murder Over New York, Tin Pan Alley, Ride Kelly Ride, Michael Shayne, Private Detective, Tall, Dark and Handsome, Sleepers West, The Great American Broadcast, Man Hunt, Accent on Love, Dressed to Kill, Charlie Chan in Rio, Man At Large, Confirm or Deny, Cadet Girl, Small Town Deb, Moon Over Her Shoulder, Young America, The Perfect Snob, Blue, White, and Perfect, My Gal Sal,

Right to the Heart, The Mad Martindales, The Night Before the Divorce, Footlight Serenade, A-Haunting We Will Go, Just Off Broadway, Careful, Soft Shoulder, The Man in the Trunk, China Girl, Springtime in the Rockies, That Other Woman, Life Begins At 8:30, Crash Dive, Immortal Sergeant, Claudia, Coney Island, Stormy Weather, Jitterbugs, Sweet Rosie O'Grady, The Lodger, Roger Touhy, Gangster, Four Jills in a Jeep, Wilson, Greenwich Village, Sweet and Low-Down, Irish Eyes Are Smiling, Take It Or Leave It, Thunderhead, Son of Flicka, Hangover Square, Molly and Me, The Dolly Sisters, Don Juan Quilligan, Canadian War Bond Rally, Strange Triangle, The Spider, Doll Face, Sentimental Journey, Shock, Somewhere in the Night, Dark Corner, It Shouldn't Happen To a Dog, If I'm Lucky, I Wonder Who's Kissing Her Now, Mother Wore Tights, Moss Rose, Nightmare Alley, Give My Regards to Broadway, Call Northside 777, You Were Meant For Me, Fury of Furnace Creek, The Street With No Name, The Iron Curtain, Unfaithfully Yours, When My Baby Smiles At Me, Everybody Does It, You're My Everything, Oh, You Beautiful Doll, Dancing in the Dark, Three Came Home, Wabash Avenue, When Willie Comes Marching Home, Under My Skin, My Blue Heaven, I'll Get By, Call Me Mister, For Heaven's Sake, Half Angel, Meet Me After The Show, As Young As You Feel, The Secret of Convict Lake, Love Nest, People Will Talk, Golden Girl, Let's Make It Legal, With a Song in My Heart, Wait Till The Sun Shines Nellie, The I Don't Care Girl, Girl Next Door, Stars and Stripes Forever, Tonight We Sing, Night Without Sleep, Pickup on South Street, The Kid From Left Field, Mr. Scoutmaster, There's No Business Like Show Business, Black Widow, The Racers, Prince of Players, The Girl in the Red Velvet Swing, The Last Rookie, My Friend Flicka (TV), The Many Loves of Dobie Gillis (TV), Bus Stop (TV)

STAGE THREE:

Hot Water, Charlie Chan on Broadway, Life Begins in College, Dangerously Yours, Borrowing Trouble, Big Town Girl, Island in the Sky, Love and Hisses, Sally, Irene and Mary, Love On A Budget, Walking Down Broadway, Rascals, Battle of Broadway, A Trip to Paris, Speed to Burn, Keep Smiling, Mysterious Mr. Moto, One Wild Night, Gateway, Passport Husband, Mr. Moto's Last Warning, Meet The Girls, Safety in Numbers, While New York Sleeps, A Very Practical Joke, Pardon Our Nerve, Everybody's Baby, Chasing Danger, Charlie Chan in Honolulu, Mr. Moto in Danger Island, News is Made At Night, The Boyfriend, Quick Millions, Stop - Look and Love, Chicken Wagon Family, Heaven With A Barbed Wire Fence, Pack Up Your Troubles, The Honeymoon is Over, City of Chance, Charlie Chan in Panama, Young As You Feel, Free, Blonde and 21, Star Dust, Charlie Chan's Murder Cruise, Girl in 313, Manhattan Heartbeat, Street of Memories, The Bride Wore Crutches, The

Great Profile, For Beauty's Sake, Murder of New York, Jennie, Michael Shayne, Private Detective, Murder Among Friends, Scotland Yard, Dead Men Tell, Great American Broadcast, Sun Valley Serenade, Man Hunt, Dressed to Kill, Dance Hall, Charlie Chan in Rio, Weekend in Havana, Marry the Boss's Daughter, We Go Fast, Man At Large, Confirm or Deny, Cadet Girl, Moon Over Her Shoulder, Remember the Day, Blue, White, and Perfect, Right to the Heart, Rings on Her Fingers, The Mad Martindales, Night Before the Divorce, Who Is Hope Schuyler?, Whispering Ghosts, The Magnificent Dope, Footlight Serenade, The Postman Didn't Ring, The Loves of Edgar Allan Poe, A Haunting We Will Go, Orchestra Wives, Thru Different Eyes, Careful, Soft Shoulder, Girl Trouble, The Man in the Trunk, That Other Woman, He Hired His Boss, The Meanest Man in the World, Life Begins at 8:30, Crash Dive, The Undying Monster, Over My Dead Body, Time To Kill, Tonight We Raid Calais, Margin for Error, They Came to Blow Up America, Stormy Weather, Jitterbugs, Holy Matrimony, The Dancing Masters, Tampico, The Lodger, Home in Indiana, Four Jills in a Jeep, Wilson, In The Meantime, Darling, Bermuda Mystery, Laura, Hangover Square, Colonel Effingham's Raid, Molly and Me, The Caribbean Mystery, The Bullfighters, Dragonwyck, Junior Miss, Within These Walls, Strange Triangle, The Spider, Sentimental Journey, Cluny Brown, Behind Green Lights, Somewhere in the Night, Johnny Comes Flying Home, It Shouldn't Happen to a Dog, Home Sweet Homicide, I Wonder Who's Kissing Her Now, Moss Rose, Nightmare Alley, You Were Meant For Me, The Street With No Name, The Iron Curtain, Road House, A Letter to Three Wives, You're My Everything, Slattery's Hurricane, House of Strangers, Pinky, Three Came Home, Whirlpool, Love That Brute, When Willie Comes Marching Home, Ticket to Tomahawk, Under My Skin, No Way Out, My Blue Heaven, I'll Get By, For Heaven's Sake, On The Riviera, Follow the Sun, I Can Get It For You Wholesale, You're in the Navy Now, The Guy Who Came Back, The Secret of Convict Lake, Love Nest, The Model and the Marriage Broker, Pride of St. Louis, Phone Call From A Stranger, The I Don't Care Girl, The Girl Next Door, Don't Bother to Knock, Dream Boat, Monkey Business, Stars and Stripes Forever, Tonight We Sing, Night Without Sleep, Something For The Birds, The Robe, Gentlemen Prefer Blondes, Dangerous Crossing, The Kid From Left Field, Mr. Scoutmaster, Demetrius and the Gladiators, The Egyptian, Woman's World, There's No Business Like Show Business, Black Widow, The Racers, Prince of Players, A Man Called Peter, Violent Saturday, Man Without a Gun (TV), The Third Man (TV), Young Jesse James, Margie (TV), The Time Tunnel (TV)

STAGE FOUR:

Change of Heart (1938), Alexander's Ragtime Band, Safety in Numbers,

The Escape, Footlight Serenade, The Dancing Masters, The Best Things in Life Are Free, The Last Rookie, The Third Voice, The Many Loves of Dobie Gillis (TV), *Bus Stop* (TV), *The Time Tunnel* (TV)

STAGE FIVE:

Champagne Charlie, Charlie Chan on Broadway, Dangerously Yours, 45 Fathers, Walking Down Broadway, Four Men and a Prayer, Speed to Burn, Always Goodbye, Mysterious Mr. Moto, Passport Husband, Mr. Moto's Last Warning, Meet the Girls, Everybody's Baby, Chasing Danger, Mr. Moto in Danger Island, High School, The Escape, Charlie Chan at Treasure Island, Chicken Wagon Family, I Was An Adventuress, Charlie Chan's Murder Cruise, Pier 13, The Man I Married, Tin Pan Alley, Murder Among Friends, Dead Men Tell, Man Hunt, A Yank in the R.A.F., Marry the Boss's Daughter, Cadet Girl, Blue, White, and Perfect, To The Shores of Tripoli, Rings on Her Fingers, Whispering Ghosts, The Postman Didn't Ring, Little Tokyo U.S.A., The Man in the Trunk, He Hired His Boss, Margin for Error, They Came To Blow Up America, Bomber's Moon, Sweet Rosie O'Grady, Tampico, The Eve of St. Mark, Nob Hill, The Dolly Sisters, Canadian War Bond Rally, Strange Triangle, It Shouldn't Happen To A Dog, The Brasher Doubloon, With A Song in My Heart, The Many Loves of Dobie Gillis (TV), *Bus Stop* (TV)

STAGE SIX:

Hot Water, Charlie Chan on Broadway, Life Begins in College, Dangerously Yours, Borrowing Trouble, Big Town Girl, Island in the Sky, Love and Hisses, Checkers, City Girl, Love On A Budget, Walking Down Broadway, A Trip To Paris, Speed to Burn, Keep Smiling, One Wild Night, Passport Husband, Time Out For Murder, Five of a Kind, Meet the Girls, Safety in Numbers, While New York Sleeps, A Very Practical Joke, Down On The Farm, Pardon Our Nerve, Everybody's Baby, The Jones Family in Hollywood, News is Made At Night, The Boyfriend, Stop - Look and Love, 20,000 Men A Year, Too Busy To Work, City of Chance, The Man Who Wouldn't Talk, Charlie Chan in Panama, Young As You Feel, Viva Cisco Kid, On Their Own, Manhattan Heartbeat, Street of Memories, The Bride Wore Crutches, Charlie Chan at the Wax Museum, Golden Hoofs, Scotland Yard, Ride Kelly Ride, Man Hunt, A Yank in the R.A.F., Marry the Boss's Daughter, Confirm or Deny, Blue, White, and Perfect, Night Before The Divorce, Whispering Ghosts, It Happened in Flatbush, Footlight Serenade, The Loves of Edgar Allan Poe, A Haunting We Will Go, Orchestra Wives, Little Tokyo U.S.A., The Man in the Trunk, Dr. Renault's Secret, Crash Dive, The Undying Monster, Chetniks, Tonight We Raid Calais, Jitterbugs, Roger Touhy, Gangster, The Night is Ending, The Dancing Masters, Tampico, The Eve of St. Mark, Four Jills in a Jeep, Bermuda Mystery,

The Big Noise, Something for the Boys, Nob Hill, Hangover Square, Molly and Me, The Caribbean Mystery, Canadian War Bond Rally, Strange Triangle, Doll Face, Sentimental Journey, Behind Green Lights, Shock, Somewhere in the Night, My Darling Clementine, The Brasher Doubloon, Moss Rose, Green Grass of Wyoming, Fury of Furnace Creek, The Street With No Name, Thieves' Highway, Slattery's Hurricane, Dancing in the Dark, Bloodhounds of Broadway, My Wife's Best Friend, Bus Stop (TV)

STAGE SEVEN:

The Man Who Wouldn't Talk, Charlie Chan in Panama, Viva Cisco Kid, On Their Own, Dance Hall, Charlie Chan in Rio, Marry the Boss's Daughter, We Go Fast, Cadet Girl, Moon Over Her Shoulder, Young America, Blue, White, and Perfect, On The Sunny Side, The Mad Martindales, Night Before the Divorce, Secret Agent of Japan, The Loves of Edgar Allan Poe, A Haunting We Will Go, Little Tokyo, U.S.A., The Man in the Trunk, Chetniks, Tonight We Raid Calais, They Came To Blow Up America, Bomber's Moon, Jitterbugs, Roger Touhy, Gangster, Guadalcanal Diary, Tampico, Bermuda Mystery, Ladies of Washington, Take it Or Leave It, Thunderhead Son of Flicka, Nob Hill, Circumstantial Evidence, Don Juan Quilligan, Within These Walls, The Embezzler, Strange Triangle, Behind Green Lights, Johnny Comes Flying Home, It Shouldn't Happen To A Dog, Home Sweet Homicide, My Darling Clementine, The Brasher Doubloon, Green Grass of Wyoming, What Price Glory?, My Friend Flicka (TV), *The Fiend Who Walked the West, Man Without a Gun* (TV), *The Many Loves of Dobie Gillis* (TV), *Young Jesse James, The Time Tunnel* (TV), *Anderson and Co.* (TV), *The Kowboys* (TV)

STAGE EIGHT:

Passport Husband, City of Chance, Street of Memories, Little Tokyo U.S.A., Dragonwyck, My Friend Flicka (TV), *Man Without a Gun* (TV), *The Many Loves of Dobie Gillis* (TV), *Bus Stop* (TV)

EXTERIORS OF THE WESTERN AVENUE STUDIO LOT:

Safety in Numbers, The Escape, 20,000 Men A Year, Charlie Chan's Murder Cruise, Pier 13, Murder Among Friends, Tampico, Strange Triangle, Just Off Broadway, The Many Loves of Dobie Gillis (TV), *Bus Stop* (TV)

THE WESTWOOD STUDIO

**BERKELEY SQUARE
(site of BLDG. 99)**
Cavalcade
Berkeley Square
The House of Rothschild
Olsen's Big Moment
Springtime for Henry
Lottery Lover
King of Burlesque
Bad Boy

**CAFE DE PARIS (BLDG. 57
Commissary)**
To the Shores of Tripoli
My Pal Gus
The Racers
Beloved Infidel
Bachelor Flat
The Loved One (MGM)
Judd for the Defense (TV)
The Sweet Ride
Silent Movie

**CAMERA BUILDING
(BLDG. 31)**
The Lieutenant Wore Skirts

FRENCH ALLEY
The Holy Terror (1937)
One Mile From Heaven
Charlie Chan in Panama
Johnny Apollo
Murder Among Friends
Tonight We Raid Calais
Say One for Me
Let's Make Love

Bachelor Flat
Take Her, She's Mine
What A Way to Go!
Peyton Place (TV)
Do Not Disturb
Morituri
The Time Tunnel (TV)
Our Man Flint
Green Hornet (TV)
Caprice
A Guide for the Married Man
Land of the Giants (TV)
Julia (TV)
The Detective
The Sweet Ride
Valley of the Dolls
Beyond the Valley of the Dolls
Fireball Forward (TV)

**HALL OF MUSIC, THE
(BLDG. 52)**
20,000 Men a Year
To the Shores of Tripoli
As Young As You Feel
My Cousin Rachel
Perry Mason (TV)
Beloved Infidel
The Rookie
Move Over, Darling
Hush . . . Hush Sweet Charlotte
Room 222 (TV)
Paper Man (TV)
Charlie's Angels (TV)
The Fall Guy (TV)
Hart to Hart (TV)

**JANET GAYNOR/WILL
ROGERS BUNGALOWS
(BLDGS. 42 & 44)**
Bachelor Flat
Escape From the Planet of the Apes
The Seven Minutes

**LITTLE THEATER, THE
(BLDG. 2)**
Dreamboat
Vicki
The Three Faces of Eve
Star!

MACHINE SHOP
Johnny Apollo
A Man Called Peter
The Fly (1958)
From the Terrace

**MAKEUP AND HAIRDRESS-
ING DEPARTMENT (BLDG. 38)**
To the Shores of Tripoli

**NEW WRITER'S BUILDING,
THE (BLDG. 203)**
To The Shores of Tripoli
The Three Faces of Eve
Perry Mason (TV)
Swingin' Along
The Time Tunnel (TV)
Charlie's Angels (TV)

**NEW YORK STREET
("Dolly" Street)**
Hello, Dolly!

Felony Squad (TV)
Land of the Giants (TV)
Myra Breckinridge
The Great White Hope
Nanny and the Professor (TV)
Beyond the Valley of the Dolls
The Seven Minutes
Class of '55 (TV)
The Rookies (TV)
At Long Last Love
Starsky and Hutch (TV)
Charlie's Angels (TV)
Trapper John M.D. (TV)
Fatso
Modern Problems
The Fall Guy (TV)
Johnny Dangerously
Moonlighting (TV)
Jumping Jack Flash
Hooperman (TV)
Downtown
Dying Young
NYPD Blue (TV)
The X-Files (TV)
NYPD Blue (TV)
The Practice (TV)
Chicago Hope (TV)
The Underground Comedy Movie
Phone Booth
Reno 911! (TV)
House M.D. (TV)
Paparazzi
Kitchen Confidential (TV)
Bones (TV)
How I Met Your Mother (TV)
Arrested Development (TV)

Date Movie
The Loop (TV)
Rules for Starting Over (TV)
Journeyman (TV)
Underdog
Unhitched (TV)
Prison Break (TV)
Back to You (TV)
Shark (TV)
24 (TV)
Notorious
Dollhouse (TV)
So You Think You Can Dance (TV)
It's Always Sunny in Philadelphia (TV)
Lie to Me (TV)
Underground Comedy
The A-Team
Friends with Benefits (TV)
Traffic Light (TV)
Love Lives
Water for Elephants
Love Lives
Don't Trust the B---- in Apartment 23 (TV)
New Girl (TV)
X-Men: First Class
Awake (TV)
The Amazing Spiderman
Victor
The Big Lug
Ben & Kate (TV)
Goodwin Games (TV)
1600 Penn (TV)
How to Live With Your Parents (TV)
Back in the Game (TV)
The Crazy Ones (TV)
Gang Related (TV)
Enlisted (TV)
Dads (TV)
Let's Be Cops
Fresh Off the Boat (TV)
Murder in the First (TV)

Agent X (TV)
Weird Loners (TV)
The Grinder (TV)
American Horror Story (TV)

OCEAN LINER (site of BLDG. 88)
So This Is London (1930)
Transatlantic
Business and Pleasure
Cheaters at Play
Week Ends Only
Infernal Machine
Pilgrimage
Pleasure Cruise
Shanghai Madness
Call It Luck
Grand Canary
She Was a Lady
The World Moves On
The Daring Young Man
The Gay Deception
Dante's Inferno

OLD EXECUTIVE BUILDING (BLDG. 88) (see also OCEAN LINER)
Island in the Sky
Rascals
Speed to Burn
High School
It Could Happen to You
Hollywood Cavalcade
Johnny Apollo
Public Deb No. 1
The Man I Married
The Bride Wore Crutches
Private Nurse
We Go Fast
Moon Over Her Shoulder
To the Shores of Tripoli
Berlin Correspondent
Little Tokyo, U.S.A.

Holy Matrimony
The Night is Ending
The Dancing Masters
Ladies of Washington
Pinky
Dancing in the Dark
Mother Didn't Tell Me
Whirlpool
I'll Get By
For Heaven's Sake
Half Angel
The I Don't Care Girl
Deadline - U.S.A.
Monkey Business
Mr. Scoutmaster
A Man Called Peter
The Rains of Ranchipur
The Lieutenant Wore Skirts
Bigger Than Life
Teenage Rebel
The Alligator People
The Man Who Understood Women
The Best of Everything
Beloved Infidel
High Time
Seven Thieves
Swingin' Along
Madison Avenue
Bachelor Flat
Peyton Place (TV)
Batman (TV)
Judd for the Defense (TV)
Valley of the Dolls
The Boston Strangler
Tora! Tora! Tora!
Charlie's Angels (TV)
Johnny Dangerously
Stuck on You

OLD PARK ROW
Perry Mason (TV)
Kiss Them for Me
The Young Lions

A Private's Affair
Wild in the Country

OLD WRITERS' BUILDING (BLDG. 80)
Professional Soldier
Sharpshooters
Scotland Yard
The Lieutenant Wore Skirts
Kiss Them for Me
Perry Mason (TV)
The Third Man (TV)
Five Fingers (TV)
Swingin' Along
Peyton Place (TV)
The Ghost and Mrs. Muir (TV)
The Sweet Ride
Land of the Giants (TV)
Judd for the Defense (TV)
Julia (TV)
Myra Breckinridge

ORIGINAL ADMINISTRATION BUILDING (BLDG. 1)
The Cowboy and the Blonde
To the Shores of Tripoli
The Dancing Masters
Belles on Their Toes
Destination Gobi
Blueprint for Murder
The Lieutenant Wore Skirts
Batman (TV)
Time Tunnel (TV)
Felony Squad (TV)
Land of the Giants (TV)
They Call It Murder (TV)
Paper Man (TV)

PICO GATE
Second Fiddle
The Cowboy and the Blonde
Berlin Correspondent
Dancing Masters

Nob Hill
I'll Get By
Dancing in the Dark
As Young as You Feel
Stars and Stripes Forever
The I Don't Care Girl
Destination Gobi
Monkey Business
The Racers
The Man in the Gray Flannel Suit
The Lieutenant Wore Skirts
High Time
Adventures in Paradise (TV)
Five Fingers (TV)
The Third Man (TV)
Charlie's Angels (TV)
The Fall Guy (TV)

PRODUCTION BUNGALOW, THE (BLDG. 78)

For Beauty's Sake
A Yank in the R.A.F.
Hush . . . Hush Sweet Charlotte

RESEARCH LIBRARY (BLDG. 3)

Rise and Shine
Green Hornet (TV)

SOUND BUILDING, THE

The Bullfighters
I'll Get By
How to be Very, Very Popular
Good Morning, Miss Dove
The Lieutenant Wore Skirts
Bernardine
From the Terrace
State Fair (1962)
Bachelor Flat
Hush . . . Hush, Sweet Charlotte
Peyton Place (TV)

STARS' DRESSING ROOMS BUILDING (BLDG. 86)

Mother Didn't Tell Me
The Girl Can't Help It
Perry Mason (TV)
Beloved Infidel
Mardi Gras
The Right Approach
Peyton Place (TV)

TENNESSEE AVENUE GATE ENTRANCE

The Jones Family in Hollywood
The Cowboy and the Blonde
To the Shores of Tripoli
I'll Get By
O, Henry's Full House
The Rookie
Myra Breckinridge
Silent Movie
The World's Greatest Lover
Charlie's Angels (TV)
L.A. Law (TV)
Doogie Howser, M.D. (TV)

TOM MIX BARN (BLDG. 41)

Peyton Place (TV)
Hush. . . Hush, Sweet Charlotte

WESTERN STREET (site of BLDG. 99)

Stagecoach (1966)
The Time Tunnel (TV)
Butch Cassidy and the Sundance Kid
Myra Breckinridge

WILLIAM FOX (PROP) BUILDING (BLDG. 89)

Thank You Mr. Moto
Time Out for Murder
While New York Sleeps
Mr. Moto Takes a Vacation
Everybody's Baby
Charlie Chan at Treasure Island
Brigham Young
Public Deb No. 1
Ride Kelly Ride
Sun Valley Serenade
The Model and the Marriage Broker
House of Bamboo
In Love and War
Bones (TV)

ZANUCK THEATRE

Bernardine
Beloved Infidel
All Hands on Deck
Madison Avenue
The Stripper

STAGE ONE:

Bandolero, Escape from the Planet of the Apes, The Towering Inferno, Jaws (Universal), *The Love Boat* (TV), *The Paper Chase* (TV), *Dallas* (TV), *Knots Landing* (TV), *Star Trek The Motion Picture* (Paramount), *Dance Fever* (TV), *Trapper John, M.D.* (TV), *Dynasty* (TV), *Hill Street Blues* (TV), *The Fall Guy* (TV), *Falcon Crest* (TV), *9 to 5* (TV), *Matt Houston* (TV), *The Man Who Loved Women, Two of a Kind, All The Right Moves, Trauma Center* (TV), *Manimal* (TV), *It's Not Easy* (TV), *Hunter* (TV), *Mr. Mom, Hardcastle and McCormick* (TV), *Masquerade* (TV), *Automan* (TV), *Hotel* (TV), *Emerald Point, N.A.S.* (TV), *After M*A*S*H* (TV), *Unfaithfully Yours, Cover Up* (TV), *The Sun Also Rises* (TV), *Johnny Dangerously, Dark Mirror* (TV), *Sentimental Journey* (TV), *Velvet* (TV), *W*A*L*T*E*R* (TV), *Love Thy Neighbor* (TV), *Scorned and Swindled* (TV), *Indiana Jones and the Temple of Doom* (Paramount), *Violated* (Cinematronics), *Micki + Maude* (Columbia), *Rhinestone, Revenge of the Nerds, The River Rat* (Cinema Group Ventures), *Body Rock* (New World Pictures), *Cocoon, The Man With One Red Shoe, Mr. Belvedere* (TV), *Half Nelson* (TV), *MacGyver* (TV), *Our Family Honor* (TV), *Moonlighting* (TV), *Secret Weapons* (TV), *Hollywood Wives* (TV), *In Like Flynn* (TV), *The Colbys* (TV), *Peyton Place: The Next Generation* (TV), *Covenant* (TV), *A Letter to Three Wives* (TV), *Porky's Revenge, Turk 182!, Prizzi's Honor* (ABC Motion Pictures), *Mischief, Silverado* (Columbia), *Enemy Mine, Bad Medicine, The Jewel of the Nile, Murphy's Law* (TV), *The Boy Who Could Fly, SpaceCamp* (ABC Motion Pictures), *Lucas, Big Trouble in Little China, The Fly, The Girl Who Spelled Freedom* (TV), *Rockabye* (TV), *The Sin of Innocence* (TV), *A Masterpiece of Murder* (TV), *Captain Eo* (Musical Short for Disneyland), *Popeye Doyle* (TV), *Dark Mansions* (TV), *Christmas Eve* (TV), *Aliens, Goodnight Mother* (Universal), *Jumpin' Jack*

Flash, Howard the Duck (Universal), *Half Moon Street* (RKO), *The Name of the Rose, L.A. Law* (TV), *Our House* (TV), *Heart of the City* (TV), *Sledge Hammer!* (TV), *Perfect Strangers* (TV), *Matlock* (TV), *Three Amigos!, Square Dance* (NBC Productions), *Project X, Star Trek: The Next Generation* (TV), *Harry and the Hendersons* (Universal), *Harry's Hong Kong* (TV), *The Tracey Ullman Show* (TV), *The Highwayman* (TV), *J.J. Starbuck* (TV), *Leg Work* (TV), *Jake and the Fat Man* (TV), *Beauty and the Beast* (TV), *Wiseguy* (TV), *The Room Upstairs* (TV), *I'll Take Manhattan* (TV), *Casanova* (TV), *Cracked Up* (TV), *Kids Like These* (TV), *The Three Kings* (TV), *Black Widow (1987), Cold Steel* (Cinetel Films), *Police Academy 4* (Warner Bros.), *Spaceballs* (MGM), *In The Heat of the Night* (TV), *Dirty Dozen: The Series* (TV), *Predator, Revenge of the Nerds II, Less Than Zero, Wall Street, Can't Buy Me Love* (Touchstone Pictures), *The Monster Squad* (HBO), *The Pick-Up Artist, Weeds* (Kingsgate Films), *The Witches of Eastwick* (Warner Bros.), *Ironweed* (HBO), *The Sicilian, Broadcast News, Beaches* (Touchstone Pictures), *Off Limits, Big, The Presidio* (Paramount), *License to Drive, Die Hard, Nightmare at Bitter Creek* (TV), *Bring Me The Head of Dobie Gillis* (TV), *Blue Grass* (TV), *State of Fear* (TV), *Favorite Son* (TV), *Where the Hell's That Gold* (TV), *Quiet Victory: The Charlie Wedemeyer Story* (TV), *The Rescue* (Touchstone Pictures), *Ernest Saves Christmas* (Touchstone Pictures), *War and Remembrance* (TV), *Last Rites* (MGM), *Cocoon: The Return, Bad Dreams, A Night in the Life of Jimmy Reardon* (Island Pictures), *Young Guns, Alien Nation, Father Dowling Mysteries* (TV), *Baywatch* (TV), *Nightingales* (TV), *Doogie Howser, M.D.* (TV), *Young Riders* (TV), *The Simpsons* (TV), *Quantum Leap* (TV), *Say Anything, Working Girl, Big Man On Campus* (Regency), *The Fly II, Worth Winning, Gleaming the Cube* (David Foster Productions), *The Abyss, Jacknife* (Kings Road Entertainment), *Born on the Fourth of July* (Universal), *Look Who's Talking* (Tri-Star Pictures), *Skin Deep* (Morgan Creek), *The Fabulous Baker Boys, The War of the Roses, Going Places* (TV), *Tiny Toon Adventures* (TV), *Weekend at Bernie's, Home Fires Burning* (TV), *She Knows Too Much* (TV), *Terror On Highway 91* (TV), *Fire and Rain* (TV), *How I Got Into College, Narrow Margin* (Carolco Pictures), *Die Hard 2, Cop Rock* (TV), *TaleSpin* (TV), *The Trials of Rosie O'Neill* (TV), *Downtown, The Rescuers Down Under* (Disney), *Betsy's Wedding* (Touchstone Pictures), *Presumed Innocent* (Warner Bros.), *Short Time* (Gladden Entertainment), *Vital Signs, Come See The Paradise, The Kissing Place* (TV), *Murder in Mississippi* (TV), *Gunsmoke: The Last Apache* (TV), *Roller Coaster Rabbit, Web of Deceit* (TV), *Nightmare on the 13th Floor* (TV), *Kaleidoscope* (TV), *Look Who's Talking Too* (Tri-Star Pictures), *Misery* (Castle Rock), *Strawberry Road* (Japan), *Crazy People* (Paramount), *Home Alone, Grand Canyon, The Adventures of Ford Fairlane,*

Miller's Crossing, Predator 2, Edward Scissorhands, F/X 2. Regarding Henry (Paramount), *Lies Before Kisses* (TV), *Child of Darkness, Child of Light* (TV), *Backfield in Motion* (TV), *Daddy* (TV), *Mannequin: On The Move, Sleeping with the Enemy, Class Action, The Five Heartbeats, Only the Lonely, Dying Young, Dutch, Dark Shadows* (TV), *Sisters* (TV), *Step by Step* (TV), *Brooklyn Bridge* (TV), *Picket Fences* (TV), *Barton Fink* (Circle Films), *29th Street* (JVC Entertainment), *For the Boys, Hook* (Tri-Star Pictures), *Suburban Commando* (New Line Cinema), *The Doctor* (Touchstone Pictures), *Mobsters* (Universal), *Prince of Tides* (Columbia), *Paradise* (Touchstone Pictures), *JFK* (Warner Bros.), *All I Want For Christmas* (Paramount), *The Addams Family* (Orion), *My Girl, Hot Shots!, The Butcher's Wife* (Paramount), *True Colors* (Paramount), *The Hand That Rocks the Cradle* (Hollywood Pictures), *Capitol Critters* (TV), *Love Potion No. 9, Rapid Fire, This My Life, Shining Through, White Men Can't Jump, My Cousin Vinny, Home Alone 2, Passed Away* (Hollywood Pictures), *Patriot Games* (Paramount), *Alien 3, Prelude to a Kiss, Night and the City* (Penta Films), *Man Trouble* (Penta Films), *Honey I Blew Up The Kid* (Disney), *The Last of the Mohicans, A League of Their Own* (Columbia), *This is My Life, Buffy the Vampire Slayer, Forever Young* (Warner Bros.), *Stay Tuned* (Warner Bros.), *Hoffa, Dracula* (American Zoetrope), *Toys, Wind* (American Zoetrope), *Leap of Faith* (Paramount), *Newsies* (Disney), *Krippendorf's Tribe* (Touchstone Pictures), *Jurassic Park* (Universal), *Homeward Bound: The Incredible Journey* (Disney), *Hot Shots! Part Deux, For Love Or Money* (Universal), *The Pickle* (Columbia), *The Vanishing, Hear No Evil, Once Upon a Forest, Robin Hood: Men in Tights, Rookie of the Year, Rising Sun, Only the Strong, The Good Son, Freaked, The Beverly Hillbillies, Mrs. Doubtfire, Ghost in the Machine, Teenage Mutant Ninja Turtles III* (Golden Harvest), *The Saint of Fort Washington* (Carrie Productions), *Aspen Extreme* (Hollywood Pictures), *The Meteor Man* (MGM), *Schindler's List* (Universal), *Jack the Bear, The Sandlot, The Chase, Bad Girls, PCU, Speed, Baby's Day Out, Airheads, The Scout, Miracle on 34th Street, Trapped in Paradise, The Pagemaster, Nell, Far From Home: Adventures of Yellow Dog, Bye, Bye Love, Kiss of Death, Die Hard: With a Vengeance, Braveheart* (Paramount), *Mighty Morphin Power Rangers: The Movie, Nine Months, Bushwacked, A Walk in the Clouds, The Brothers McMullen, Waiting to Exhale, Dunstan Checks In, Broken Arrow, The Truth About Cats and Dogs, Down Periscope, Independence Day, The Great White Hype, Courage Under Fire, Chain Reaction, She's the One, That Thing You Do!, William Shakespeare's Romeo + Juliet, Jingle All The Way, The Crucible, Millennium* (TV), *The Van, One Fine Day, Blood and Wine, Inventing the Abbotts, Paradise Road, Volcano, Speed 2: Cruise Control, Out to Sea, Picture Perfect, The Full Monty, King of the Hill* (TV), *Soul*

Food, The Edge, The Ice Storm, Oscar and Lucinda, Anastasia, Alien Resurrection, Home Alone 3, Titanic, Firestorm, Great Expectations, The Horse Whisperer (Touchstone Pictures), Six Days Seven Nights (Touchstone Pictures), The Newton Boys, The Object of My Affection, Hope Floats, Bulworth, Small Soldiers (Universal), Rush Hour (New Line Cinema), Blade (New Line Cinema), The X-Files: The Movie, Dr. Dolittle, How Stella Got Her Groove Back, The Imposters, The Siege, Cousin Bette, There's Something About Mary, Ever After: A Cinderella Story, Slums of Beverly Hills, A Cool, Dry Place, Thin Red Line, Blast From the Past (New Line Cinema), The Deep End of the Ocean (Columbia), Mod Squad (MGM), Austin Powers: The Spy Who Shagged Me (New Line Cinema), The Haunting (DreamWorks), Dudley Do-Right (Universal), The Hurricane (Beacon), The Story of Us (Castle Rock), Family Guy (TV), Bartok the Magnificent, Galaxy Quest (DreamWorks), The Matrix (Warner Bros.), The Sixth Sense (Hollywood Pictures), Office Space, Never Been Kissed, Pushing Tin, Entrapment, Brokedown Palace, Simply Irresistible, Drive Me Crazy, Anna and the King, A Midsummer's Night Dream, Ravenous, Lake Placid, Best Laid Plans, Fight Club, Anywhere But Here, Light It Up, Dreaming of Joseph Lees, The Beach, The Closer You Get, Supernova (MGM), Here On Earth, Where The Heart Is, Frequency (New Line Cinema), Duets (Hollywood Pictures), Meet the Parents (Universal), Big Momma's House, Titan A.E., Me, Myself, and Irene, X-Men, Bedazzled, Men of Honor, Dude Where's My Car, What Lies Beneath (DreamWorks), Woman On Top, Bootmen, The Legend of Bagger Vance (DreamWorks), Quills, Castaway, Tigerland, Antitrust (MGM), Someone Like You, Jurassic Park III (Universal), Invincible (Werner Herzog), Life As A House (New Line), Joy Ride, Black Knight, Behind Enemy Lines, Freddy Got Fingered (Regency), Glitter, Don't Say A Word, The Affair of the Necklace, Monkeybone (Universal), Kingdom Come, Pearl Harbor (Touchstone Pictures), From Hell, Moulin Rouge, Dr. Dolittle 2, Planet of the Apes, Joe Somebody, Say It Isn't So, Cinderella 2: Dreams Come True (Disney), High Crimes, Life Or Something Like It (Regency), Austin Powers in Goldmember (New Line Cinema), The Tuxedo (DreamWorks), In America , Phone Booth, The Banger Sisters, Garage Days, Ice Age, Red Dragon (Universal), One Hour Photo, Like Mike, Tears of the Sun (Columbia), The Bourne Identity (Universal), The First $20 Million Is Always the Hardest, Minority Report, Unfaithful, Solaris, Drumline, Kung Pow: Enter the Fist, Brown Sugar, Road to Perdition, Antwone Fisher, Bringing Down the House (Touchstone Pictures), The Order, The Lizzie McGuire Movie (Disney), Runaway Jury, The Matrix Reloaded (Warner Bros.), Hulk (Universal), Pirates of the Caribbean: The Curse of the Black Pearl (Disney), Seabiscuit (Universal), When Zachary Beaver Came to Town (Revere Pictures), The Matrix Revolutions (Warner Bros.), Chasing Papi, The Last Samurai (Warner Bros.), Just Married, Daredevil, The League of Extraordinary Gentlemen, X2, Down With Love, Le Divorce, Master and Commander: The Far Side of the World, Cheaper By The Dozen, Welcome to Mooseport, Miracle (Disney), Winnie the Pooh: Springtime With Roo (Disney), Dawn of the Dead (Universal), Anchorman: The Legend of Ron Burgandy (DreamWorks), Steamboy (Sony), Collateral (DreamWorks), Man on Fire, Ladder 49 (Touchstone), Taxi , The Bourne Supremacy (Universal), Surviving Christmas (DreamWorks), Flight of the Phoenix, Catch That Kid, The Clearing, Sideways, Johnson Family Vacation, Garfield, Dodgeball: A True Underdog Story, I, Robot, Club Dread, The Girl Next Door (Regency), The Chronicles of Riddick (Universal), Alien Vs. Predator, Garden State, The Phantom of the Opera (Warner Bros.), Fat Albert, Elektra, Hide and Seek, Robots, Guess Who, Just Like Heaven (DreamWorks), Cinderella Man (Universal), Fantastic Four, The Island, The Honeymooners (Paramount), The Skeleton Key (Universal), Jarhead (Universal), The Family Stone, The Perfect Man (Universal), Trust the Man, King Kong (Universal), The Sandlot 2, Bewitched (Columbia), Fever Pitch, Walk the Line, Little Manhattan (Regency), Red Eye (DreamWorks), The Day After Tomorrow, First Daughter, Kingdom of Heaven, The Ringer, The Longest Yard (Paramount), Stay, Zathura: A Space Adventure (Sony), Serenity (Universal), Mr. & Mrs. Smith, Rebound, Because of Winn-Dixie, Bee Season, Are We There Yet? (Sony), Roll Bounce, Supercross, In Her Shoes, Cheaper by the Dozen 2, American Dad! (TV), Final Destination 3 (New Line Cinema), You, Me, and Dupree (Universal), A Good Year, Pirates of the Caribbean: Dead Men's Chest (Disney), The Fountain (Warner Bros.), Notes On A Scandal, Behind Enemy Lines II: Axis of Evil, My Super Ex-Girlfriend (Regency), Little Children (New Line Cinema), Miami Vice (Universal), Idiocracy, No Time For Nuts, Rocky Balboa (MGM), American Dreamz (Universal), Big Momma's House 2, Ice Age: The Meltdown, The Sentinel, Dr. Dolittle 3, X-Men: The Last Stand, Like Mike 2, Garfield: A Tail of Two Kitties, The Devil Wears Prada, The Omen, John Tucker Must Die, ATL (Warner Bros.), Just My Luck, Flicka, Blood Diamond (Warner Bros.), Tristan + Isolde, Eragon, The Last King of Scotland, The Namesake, Little Miss Sunshine, Borat, Night at the Museum, The Pursuit of Happyness (Sony), Aquamarine, Phat Girlz, Everyone's Hero, Date Movie, The Good German (Warner Bros.), Charlotte's Web (Paramount), World Trade Center (Paramount), Reno 911!: Miami (Paramount), Disturbia (DreamWorks), The Air I Breathe (NALA Films), Rush Hour 3 (New Line Cinema), Hairspray (New Line Cinema), Transformers (DreamWorks), The Comebacks, Dr. Dolittle 3, Deck the Halls, Turistas, Fantastic Four: Rise of the Silver Surfer, Live Free and Die Hard, The Simpsons Movie, The Seeker: The Dark is Rising, The Invasion (Warner Bros.), Cinderella

III: A Twist in Time (Disney), I Think I Love My Wife, September Dawn (Sony), Are We Done Yet? (Sony), Alvin and the Chipmunks, The Darjeeling Limited, Michael Clayton (Castle Rock), Hitman, Aliens Vs. Predator – Requiem, Lucifer (RG Entertainment), Wrong Turn 2, Epic Movie, The Savages, Pathfinder, Firehouse Dog (Regency), Sunshine, Under the Same Moon, National Treasure 2: Book of Secrets (Disney), Juno, Pirates of the Caribbean: At World's End (Disney), The Mummy: Tomb of the Dragon Emperor (Universal), Max Payne, Leatherheads (Universal), Revolutionary Road (DreamWorks), Bolt (Disney), Bedtime Stories (Disney), Jumper, Seven Pounds (Columbia), Dr. Seuss' Horton Hears A Who, Surviving Sid, Tinker Bell (Disney), What Happens in Vegas, Meet Dave, The Day the Earth Stood Still, Street Kings, Dr. Dolittle 4: Tail to the Chief, The X-Files: I Want To Believe, The Happening, The Tale of Despereaux (Universal), I Am Legend (Warner Bros.), The Onion Movie, Australia, Rocker, WALL-E (Disney), The Secret Life of Bees, Mirrors (Regency), Meet the Spartans, Shutter, Deception, Wanted (Universal), Sex and the City (New Line Cinema), Marley & Me, Bachelor Party 2, The Rebound (Weinstein), Madea Goes To Jail (Lionsgate), Imagine That (Paramount), He's Just Not That Into You (New Line Cinema), Fast & Furious (Universal), My Life in Ruins, Public Enemies (Universal), I Love You, Beth Cooper, Post Grad, The Ugly Truth (Columbia), (500) Days of Summer, Jennifer's Body, Land of the Lost (Universal), The Cleveland Show (TV), Surrogates (Touchstone Pictures), Cirque Du Freak: The Vampire's Assistant (Universal), Bride Wars, Dragonball: Evolution, G-Force (Disney), Amelia, Fantastic Mr. Fox, X-Men Origins: Wolverine, Night at the Museum: Battle of the Smithsonian, Adam, G.I. Joe: The Rise of Cobra (Paramount), Ice Age: Dawn of the Dinosaurs, Aliens in the Attic, Gentlemen Broncos, All About Steve, Miss March, Avatar, Alvin and the Chipmunks: The Squeakquel, Temple Grandin (HBO), Dinner for Schmucks (Paramount), 127 Hours, The Debt (Miramax), How Do You Know (Columbia), Tooth Fairy, Burlesque (Sony), Percy Jackson and the Olympians: The Lightning Thief, Diary of a Wimpy Kid, Sex and the City 2 (New Line Cinema), Date Night, Just Wright, Knight and Day, Despicable Me (Universal), Marmaduke, The A-Team, Predators, Ramona and Beezus, Why Did I Get Married Too? (Lionsgate), Never Let Me Go, The Alien Girl, Wall Street: Money Never Sleeps, Our Family Wedding, 27 Dresses, Cyrus, Vampires Suck, Black Swan, Gulliver's Travels, Love & Other Drugs, Repo Men (Universal), Unstoppable, The Town (Warner Bros.), The Wolfman (Universal), Little Fockers (Universal), Diary of a Wimpy Kid 2: Rodrick Rules, Cedar Rapids, A Little Bit of Heaven (Davis Entertainment), The Best Exotic Marigold Hotel, Salmon Fishing in the Yemen (Lionsgate), Battle Los Angeles (Columbia), The Adjustment Bureau (Universal), Shame, Martha Marcy May Marlene, What's Your Number? (Regency), The Sitter, The Darkest Hour (Regency), Terra Nova (TV), Revenge (TV), Your Highness (Universal), Fast Five (Universal), Rio, Snow Flower and the Secret Fan, Mr. Popper's Penguins, Water for Elephants, X-Men: First Class, Rise of the Planet of the Apes, The Big Year, The Descendants, Ice Age: A Mammoth Christmas, Alvin and the Chipmunks: Chipwrecked!, We Bought a Zoo, Another Earth, The Hidden Face, Glee: The 3D Concert Movie, Big Mommas: Like Father, Like Son, This Means War, Monte Carlo, The Help (DreamWorks), Win Win, Mission Impossible: Ghost Protocol (Paramount), In Time, Rango (Paramount), The Art of Getting By , Super 8 (Paramount), Margaret, Joyful Noise (Alcon Entertainment), Battleship (Universal), Wreck-It-Ralph (Disney), The News Room (TV), Revolution (TV), Halo 4(343 Industries), The Three Stooges, Ice Age: Continental Drift, The Watch, Chronicle, Madea's Witness Protection (Lionsgate), G.I. Joe: Retaliation (Paramount), Diary of a Wimpy Kid: Dog Days, Life of Pi. Parental Guidance, Lincoln (DreamWorks), A Good Day to Die Hard, Ted (Universal), The Lorax (Universal), The Incredible Burt Wonderstone (New Line Cinema), Oblivion (Universal), Star Trek Into Darkness (Paramount), Man of Steel (Warner Bros.), Epic, After Earth (Columbia), Captain Phillips (Columbia), Despicable Me 2 (Universal), Saving Mr. Banks (Disney), The Internship, White House Down (Columbia), The Smurfs 2 (Columbia), The Wolverine, The Lone Ranger (Disney), Percy Jackson: Sea of Monsters, Winter's Tale (Warner Bros.), The Book Thief, Rio 2, The Maze Runner, A Million Ways to Die in the West (Bluegrass Films), X-Men: Days of Future Past, Dawn of the Planet of the Apes, The Judge (Warner Bros.), Jupiter Ascending (Warner Bros.), Get On Up (Imagine Entertainment), Gone Girl, Tomorrowland (Disney), Tinkerbell: The Pirate Fairy (Disney), Night at the Museum 3: Secret of the Tomb, Big Hero 6 (Disney), Spy, Bridge of Spies, Minions (Columbia), Ride Along 2 (Universal), Fantastic Four, Ted 2 (Universal), The Peanuts Movie

STAGE TWO:
Danger – Love at Work, Wife, Doctor and Nurse, Rebecca of Sunnybrook Farm, Love and Hisses, International Settlement, Sally, Irene and Mary, Josette, Kidnapped, Alexander's Ragtime Band, Four Men and a Prayer, Little Miss Broadway, Always Goodbye, My Lucky Star, Kentucky, Straight, Place and Show, Time Out For Murder, Five of a Kind, Sharpshooters, Tail Spin, Up The River, Thanks For Everything, Wife, Husband and Friend, The Jones Family in Hollywood, Rose of Washington Square, The Story of Alexander Graham Bell, Second Fiddle, Everything Happens At Night, Hollywood Cavalcade, Here I Am A Stranger, The Adventures of Sherlock Holmes, Swanee River, The Man Who Wouldn't Talk, Brigham Young, I Was an Adventuress, Earthbound, The Gay Caballero, The Great

American Broadcast, Man Hunt, Charlie Chan in Rio, Wild Geese Calling, We Go Fast, Cadet Girl, Song of the Islands, This Above All, Moontide, Secret Agent of Japan, The Man Who Wouldn't Die, The Magnificent Dope, A-Haunting We Will Go, Thru Different Eyes, Berlin Correspondent, Careful, Soft Shoulder, Little Tokyo U.S.A., He Hired The Boss, The Meanest Man in the World, Quiet Please, Murder, Dixie Dugan, The Moon is Down, Jane Eyre, Stormy Weather, Jitterbugs, The Gang's All Here, No Exceptions, The Lodger, Home in Indiana, The Purple Heart, A Wing and a Prayer, Irish Eyes are Smiling, Something for the Boys. A Tree Grows in Brooklyn, Nob Hill, Col. Effingham's Raid, Dragonwyck, Jungle Marines, Anna and the King of Siam, Centennial Summer, Behind Green Lights, Carnival in Costa Rica, Margie, The Homestretch, The Ghost and Mrs. Muir, Give My Regards To Broadway, Daisy Kenyon, Cry of the City, Second Chance, The Snake Pit, The Walls of Jericho, Yellow Sky, Sand, Everybody Does It, Mother is a Freshman, You're My Everything, Thieves' Highway, Oh, You Beautiful Doll, Wabash Avenue, Whirlpool, Night and the City, My Blue Heaven, Where The Sidewalk Ends, Two Flags West, Call Me Mister, The Jackpot, Half Angel, The 13th Letter, David and Bathsheba, The Frogmen, Down Among the Sheltering Palms, Mr. Belvedere Rings the Bell, The Desert Fox, People Will Talk, 5 Fingers, The I Don't Care Girl, O. Henry's Full House, Dream Boat, Bloodhounds of Broadway, Tonight We Sing, Night Without Sleep, Destination Gobi, Pickup on South Street, The Robe, The Desert Rats, Ten North Frederick, Fraulein, The Bravados, Rally 'Round The Flag, Boys!, Compulsion, The Man Who Understood Women, Adventures in Paradise (TV), Five Fingers (TV), The Third Man (TV), Hong Kong (TV), Take Her, She's Mine, What A Way To Go, Shock Treatment, Peyton Place (TV), Fate is the Hunter, Goodbye, Charlie, Dear Brigitte, John Goldfarb, Please Come Home, Our Man Flint, The Time Tunnel (TV), Batman (TV), In Like Flint, The Ghost and Mrs. Muir (TV), The St. Valentine's Day Massacre, Marriage of a Young Stockbroker, James at 16 (TV), The Paper Chase (TV), Dynasty (TV), The Buddy System, Johnny Dangerously

STAGE THREE:

Second Honeymoon, The Baroness and the Butler, Danger - Love at Work, Wife, Doctor and Nurse, Dangerously Yours, 45 Fathers, Charlie Chan at Monte Carlo, Sally, Irene and Mary, Happy Landing, Josette, Rascals, Kidnapped, Alexander's Ragtime Band, Four Men and a Prayer, Mr. Moto's Gamble, Little Miss Broadway, Three Blind Mice, Just Around The Corner, My Lucky Star, Hold That Co-Ed, Tail Spin, Thanks for Everything, The Story of Alexander Graham Bell, Return of the Cisco Kid, Young Mr. Lincoln, It Could Happen To You, Here I Am A Stranger, Heaven With a Barbed-Wire Fence, Pack Up Your Troubles, Swanee

River, Johnny Apollo, The Honeymoon's Over, City of Chance, The Man Who Wouldn't Talk, Brigham Young, I Was an Adventuress, Sailor's Lady, The Return of Frank James, The Mark of Zorro, Hudson's Bay Company, Michael Shayne, Private Detective, Tall, Dark and Handsome, Scotland Yard, A Very Young Lady, The Great American Broadcast, The Last of the Duanes, Wild Geese Calling, Riders of the Purple Sage, Confirm or Deny, I Wake Up Screaming, Song of the Islands, My Gal Sal, To The Shores of Tripoli, Rings on Her Fingers, The Pied Piper, The Postman Didn't Ring, Little Tokyo U.S.A., Manila Calling, The Meanest Man in the World, Dixie Dugan, Immortal Sergeant, Coney Island, Jane Eyre, Heaven Can Wait, Sweet Rosie O'Grady, Holy Matrimony, Claudia and David, Buffalo Bill, Home in Indiana, The Purple Heart, Greenwich Village, A Wing and a Prayer, Something for the Boys, Sunday Dinner for a Soldier, Nob Hill, A Royal Scandal, The Dolly Sisters, Don Juan Quilligan, Do You Love Me?, Within These Walls, The Spider, Doll Face, Shock, The Dark Corner, Claudia and David, The Razor's Edge, Thunder in the Valley, The Homestretch, Forever Amber, Mother Wore Tights, Moss Rose, Miracle on 34th Street, Nightmare Alley, The Snake Pit, You Were Meant For Me, The Walls of Jericho, Sitting Pretty, The Iron Curtain, The Luck of the Irish, Unfaithfully Yours, Road House, That Wonderful Urge, Sand, I Was A Male War Bride, The Beautiful Blonde From Bashful Bend, You're My Everything, Thieves' Highway, House of Strangers, It Happens Every Spring, Twelve O'Clock High, Mother Didn't Tell Me, When Willie Comes Marching Home, Cheaper By The Dozen, My Blue Heaven, Rawhide, Stella, Call Me Mister, Bird of Paradise, Follow the Sun, Take Care of My Little Girl, Meet Me After the Show, The Guy Who Came Back, Mr. Belvedere Rings the Bell, The Day The Earth Stood Still, People Will Talk, The Pride of St. Louis, Phone Call From A Stranger, Belles On Their Toes, The I Don't Care Girl, Lure of the Wilderness, The Outcasts of Poker Flat, O. Henry's Full House, We're Not Married, Night Without Sleep, Niagara. The President's Lady, Titanic, Gentlemen Prefer Blondes, Dangerous Crossing, A Blueprint for Murder, Vicki, Mr. Scoutmaster, The Egyptian, Desiree, There's No Business Like Show Business, The Racers, The Seven Year Itch, A Man Called Peter, Violent Saturday, The Virgin Queen, Love is a Many-Splendored Thing, The Tall Men, G.E. "Cavalcade" (TV), The View From Pompey's Head, Hilda Crane, The Best Things in Life Are Free, The True Story of Jesse James, Love Me Tender, Bernardine, Kiss Them For Me, April Love, Fraulein, The Bravados, The Fiend Who Walked The West, Rally 'Round The Flag, Boys!, The Remarkable Mr. Pennypacker, Adventures in Paradise (TV), Five Fingers (TV), The Third Man (TV), Compulsion, Can-Can, North to Alaska, Misty, Voyage to the Bottom of the Sea, Bachelor Flat, Rio Conchos, Peyton Place (TV), John Goldfarb, Please Come Home, Felony Squad (TV), The Ghost and Mrs. Muir (TV),

The Young Prosecutors (TV), *Nanny and the Professor* (TV), *Paper Man* (TV), *They Call It Murder, Class of '55* (TV), *I Ought To Be In Pictures, Vital Signs*

STAGE FOUR:

In Old Chicago, Love and Hisses, Wild and Woolly, International Settlement, Happy Landing, Thank You, Mr. Moto, City Girl, Mr. Moto's Gamble, Little Miss Broadway, Keep Smiling, Always Goodbye, Mysterious Mr. Moto, Suez, Five of a Kind, Sharpshooters, Mr. Moto Takes a Vacation, The Arizona Wildcat, Thanks for Everything, High School, Rose of Washington Square, Second Fiddle, Elsa Maxwell's Hotel For Women, City in Darkness, 20,000 Men a Year, Swanee River, Johnny Apollo, Day-Time Wife, He Married His Wife, Brigham Young, Star Dust, Maryland, The Return of Frank James, The Mark of Zorro, Hudson's Bay Company, Chad Hanna, Tall, Dark and Handsome, A Very Young Lady, Blood and Sand, Man Hunt, A Yank in the R.A.F., Charley's Aunt, Son of Fury, Castle in the Desert, To The Shores of Tripoli, Rings on Her Fingers, The Man Who Wouldn't Die, The Postman Didn't Ring, Little Tokyo U.S.A., The Meanest Man in the World, Life Begins at 8:30, Chetniks, Tonight We Raid Calais, Coney Island, The Song of Bernadette, Jane Eyre, Heaven Can Wait, Holy Matrimony, Claudia, Happy Land, No Exceptions, The Lodger, The Eve of St. Mark, Home in Indiana, Wilson, Sweet and Low Down, Laura, Thunderhead, Something for the Boys, Winged Victory, Sunday Dinner for a Soldier, A Royal Scandal, Where Do We Go From Here, Colonel Effingham's Raid, The Dolly Sisters, Dragonwyck, Anna and the King of Siam, Carnival in Costa Rica, Margie, Claudia and David, The Razor's Edge, If I'm Lucky, The Late George Apley, The Homestretch, Forever Amber, Mother Wore Tights, Moss Rose, The Foxes of Harrow, Give My Regards to Broadway, Daisy Kenyon, The Snake Pit, The Walls of Jericho, The Iron Curtain, The Luck of the Irish, Apartment for Peggy, Road House, Sand, Mother is a Freshman, The Beautiful Blonde From Bashful Bend, You're My Everything, Thieves' Highway, Come to the Stable, Oh, You Beautiful Doll, Three Came Home, When Willie Comes Marching Home, My Blue Heaven, Stella, Halls of Montezuma, Bird of Paradise, The 13th Letter, Meet Me After The Show, Anne of the Indies, Mr. Belvedere Rings The Bell, The Desert Fox, You're In The Navy Now, People Will Talk, Let's Make it Legal, The Model and the Marriage Broker, 5 Fingers, The Pride of St. Louis, The I Don't Care Girl, Deadline - U.S.A., Les Miserables, Dream Boat, Pony Soldier, Bloodhounds of Broadway, Big Man, Powder River, Treasure of the Golden Condor, Titanic, The Silver Whip, Dangerous Crossing, A Blueprint for Murder, Woman's World, Desiree, Black Widow (1954), A Man Called Peter, How to Be Very, Very Popular, The Tall Men, The Rains of Ranchipur, On The Threshold

Of Space, The Revolt of Mamie Stover, 23 Paces to Baker Street, D-Day, The Sixth of June, Between Heaven and Hell, The Best Things in Life Are Free, The Girl Can't Help It, Love Me Tender, Bernardine, Three Brave Men, The True Story of Jesse James, April Love, Perry Mason (TV), *A Certain Smile, Fraulein, From Hell To Texas, Ten North Frederick, Adventures in Paradise* (TV), *Five Fingers* (TV), *The Sound and the Fury, Beloved Infidel, Hound-Dog Man, Can-Can, Return to Peyton Place, Wild in the Country, The Second Time Around, The Marriage Go-Round, Madison Avenue, Move Over, Darling, Shock Treatment, Fate is the Hunter, Peyton Place* (TV), *Dear Brigitte, John Goldfarb, Please Come Home, The Time Tunnel* (TV), *Felony Squad* (TV), *Judd for the Defense* (TV), *Southern Fried* (TV.), *Arnie* (TV), *Myra Breckinridge, Beyond the Valley of the Dolls, Along Came A Spider* (TV), *They Call It Murder* (TV), *The Bear and I* (Disney), *The Paper Chase* (TV), *Vital Signs, Picket Fences* (TV)

STAGE FIVE:

Second Honeymoon, Danger - Love at Work, Wife, Doctor and Nurse, Stanley and Livingstone, 45 Fathers, Charlie Chan at Monte Carlo, Sally, Irene and Mary, Happy Landing, Thank You, Mr. Moto, Change of Heart, Josette, Rascals, Kidnapped, Alexander's Ragtime Band, Four Men and a Payer, Little Miss Broadway, Keep Smiling, Always Goodbye, Three Blind Mice, Just Around The Corner, Suez, Barricade, Submarine Patrol, Jesse James, Sharpshooters, While New York Sleeps, Arizona Wildcat, Tail Spin, The Three Musketeers, The Hound of the Baskervilles, Rose of Washington Square, The Story of Alexander Graham Bell, Return of the Cisco Kid, Second Fiddle, Elsa Maxwell's Hotel For Women, Everything Happens At Night, Hollywood Cavalcade, Drums Along the Mohawk, City of Darkness, The Blue Bird, The Grapes of Wrath, Brigham Young, I Was An Adventuress, Viva Cisco Kid, Lillian Russell, Young People, Public Deb No. 1, The Return of Frank James, Youth Will Be Served, Hudson's Bay Company, Chad Hanna, Tin Pan Alley, Tobacco Road, Blood and Sand, Moon Over Miami, Sun Valley Serenade, Man Hunt, The Last of the Duanes, Charley's Aunt, How Green Was My Valley, Week-End in Havana, We Go Fast, Swamp Water, Song of the Islands, Son of Fury, Castle in the Desert, Tales of Manhattan, A Gentleman at Heart, Rings on Her Fingers, Ten Gentlemen From West Point, The Man Who Wouldn't Die, Thunder Birds, The Magnificent Dope, Orchestra Wives, Twelve Men in a Box, Girl Trouble, That Other Woman, Dr. Renault's Secret, Crash Dive, The Undying Monster, Over My Dead Body, Dixie Dugan, Immortal Sergeant, Tonight We Raid Calais, Time to Kill, Coney Island, The Song of Bernadette, Hello, Frisco, Hello, The Moon is Down, Jane Eyre, Claudia, Pin-Up Girl, Wilson, Irish Eyes Are Smiling, The Big Noise, A Tree Grows in Brooklyn, Winged Victory, Sunday Dinner for a Soldier, Nob Hill,

Diamond Horseshoe, Where Do We Go From Here?, A Bell for Adano, Hangover Square, Junior Miss, Do You Love Me?, Within These Walls, Fallen Angel, The Enchanted Voyage, The Spider, Smoky, Doll Face, Sentimental Journey, Shock, Dragonwyck, The Razor's Edge, Behind Green Lights, Three Little Girls in Blue, Somewhere in the Night, Margie, The Late George Apley, I Wonder Who's Kissing Her Now, Captain From Castile, The Brasher Doubloon, The Shocking Miss Pilgrim, Moss Rose, Nightmare Alley, Daisy Kenyon, Gentleman's Agreement, The Lady in Ermine, The Iron Curtain, Unfaithfully Yours, Down to the Sea in Ships, Letter to Three Wives, The Fan, Come to the Stable, Pinky, Broken Arrow, Whirlpool, A Ticket to Tomahawk, Under My Skin, My Blue Heaven, Rawhide, All About Eve, I'll Get By, For Heaven's Sake, Half Angel, On The Riviera, Take Care of My Little Girl, David and Bathsheba, Meet Me After The Show, Down Among The Sheltering Palms, Mr. Belvedere Rings The Bell, Golden Girl, With A Song In My Heart, The Pride of St. Louis, Belles On Their Toes, The I Don't Care Girl, Deadline - U.S.A., We're Not Married, Monkey Business, The Farmer Takes a Wife, Stars and Stripes Forever, Treasure of the Golden Condor, My Pal Gus, Niagara, Taxi, Big Man, Something For The Birds, Destination Gobi, Call Me Madam, The Robe, Hell and High Water, City of Bad Men, Prince Valiant, Demetrius and the Gladiators, Garden of Evil, Three Coins in the Fountain, The Egyptian, Desiree, The Racers, Daddy Long Legs, Soldier of Fortune, House of Bamboo, How To Be Very, Very Popular, Seven Cities of Gold, The Tall Men, The Girl in the Red Velvet Swing, Good Morning, Miss Dove, Carousel, The Proud Ones, Between Heaven and Hell, Hilda Crane, Bigger Than Life, The Last Wagon, Three Brave Men, Desk Set, Will Success Ruin Rock Hunter, Peyton Place, Kiss Them For Me, Ten North Frederick, A Certain Smile, Mardi Gras, The Gift of Love, Sing Boy Sing, The Remarkable Mr. Pennypacker, The Sound and the Fury, The Story On Page One, Holiday for Lovers, Compulsion, Say One For Me, Journey To The Center Of The Earth, Adventures in Paradise (TV), Five Fingers (TV), The Third Man (TV), Blue Denim, A Private's Affair, From The Terrace, The Story of Ruth, The Lost World, Wake Me When It's Over, The Right Approach, The Comancheros, The Second Time Around, Voyage to the Bottom of the Sea, Sanctuary, The Marriage-Go-Round, Mr. Hobbs Takes A Vacation, Tender is the Night, Hemingway's Adventures of a Young Man, Something's Got To Give (unfinished)/Move Over Darling, Take Her, She's Mine, What A Way To Go, Shock Treatment, The Pleasure Seekers, Dear Brigitte, John Goldfarb, Please Come Home, The Reward, The Sound of Music, Von Ryan's Express, Lost in Space (TV), Fantastic Voyage, Way...Way Out, A Guide For The Married Man, Caprice, The Time Tunnel (TV), In Like Flint, Valley of the Dolls, The Secret Life of an American Wife, The Sweet Ride, The Detective, The Mod Squad (TV), The Boston

Strangler, Star!, Hello, Dolly!, Justine, Tora! Tora! Tora!, The Great White Hope, Move, Beneath the Planet of the Apes, The Only Game in Town, The Challenge (TV), The Mephisto Waltz, Mr. and Mrs. Bo Jo Jones (TV), The Seven Minutes, Conquest of the Planet of the Apes, Oh, Nurse! (TV), Class of '55 (TV), Young Frankenstein, At Long Last Love, Silent Movie, The Other Side of Midnight, The World's Greatest Lover, Damien Omen II, The Fury, Trapper John, M.D. (TV), L.A. Law (TV), The X-Files (TV), Murder One (TV), Jingle All The Way, My Stepmother is an Alien (Columbia), Bulworth, Arrested Development (TV), Daddy Day Care, Prison Break (TV), Modern Family (TV)

STAGE SIX:
Second Honeymoon, The Baroness and the Butler, Ali Baba Goes To Town, Danger – Love At Work, Hot Water, Wife, Doctor and Nurse, Stanley and Livingstone, Rebecca of Sunnybrook Farm, Love and Hisses, Sally, Irene and Mary, Happy Landing, Change of Heart, Josette, Kentucky Moonshine, Kidnapped, Alexander's Ragtime Band, Four Men and a Prayer, Mysterious Mr. Moto, I'll Give A Million, Just Around The Corner, My Lucky Star, Gateway, Suez, Kentucky, Straight, Place and Show, Hold that Co-Ed, Submarine Patrol, Sharpshooters, Tail Spin, The Little Princess, The Hound of the Baskervilles, The Story of Alexander Graham Bell, The Three Musketeers, Wife, Husband and Friend, Charlie Chan in Honolulu, Second Fiddle, Elsa Maxwell's Hotel For Women, The Rains Came, Hollywood Cavalcade, Frontier Marshal, Drums Along The Mohawk, Swanee River, Little Old New York, The Blue Bird, Johnny Apollo, Day-Time Wife, He Married His Wife, Charlie Chan in Panama, Young As You Feel, Star Dust, Maryland, Lucky Cisco Kid, Young People, Manhattan Heartbeat, Public Deb No. 1, Street of Memories, The Man I Married, Down Argentine Way, The Return of Frank James, The Bride Wore Crutches, Yesterday's Heroes, The Mark of Zorro, Charter Pilot, Chad Hanna, Tin Pan Alley, Western Union, That Night in Rio, The Cowboy and the Blonde, I Wake Up Screaming, Remember the Day, Who Is Hope Schuyler?, Thunder Birds, Moon Over Miami, The Black Swan, Springtime in the Rockies, The Moon Is Down, Crash Dive, Jane Eyre, The Gang's All Here, The Dancing Masters, Lifeboat, Wilson, Laura, The Keys of the Kingdom, A Wing and a Prayer, The Big Noise, Thunderhead, Son of Flicka, Something for the Boys, Sunday Dinner for a Soldier, Where Do We Go From Here?, The Dolly Sisters, Fallen Angel, The Enchanted Voyage, The Spider, Centennial Summer, Johnny Comes Flying Home, The Dark Corner, The Razor's Edge, If I'm Lucky, The Homestretch, Mother Wore Tights, Miracle on 34th Street, The Foxes of Harrow, Daisy Kenyon, Call Northside 777, Gentleman's Agreement, You Were Meant For Me, The Walls of Jericho, Sitting Pretty, The Snake Pit,

Apartment For Peggy, Road House, This Wonderful Urge, Down to the Sea in Ships, Chicken Every Sunday, Everybody Does It, I Was A Male War Bride, Twelve O'Clock High, The Beautiful Blonde From Bashful Bend, Come To The Stable, A House of Strangers, Father Was A Fullback, Broken Arrow, When Willie Comes Marching Home, Under My Skin, The Gunfighter, Ticket to Tomahawk, You're In The Navy Now, The Jackpot, On The Riviera, The House on Telegraph Hill, Follow the Sun, I Can Get It For You Wholesale, The Guy Who Came Back, The Frogmen, Down Among the Sheltering Palms, Anne of the Indies, The Desert Fox, The Day The Earth Stood Still, My Cousin Rachel, Lydia Bailey, Viva Zapata!, With A Song In My Heart, The Model and the Marriage Broker, 5 Fingers, Way Of A Gaucho, Diplomatic Courier, The I Don't Care Girl, Lure of the Wilderness, Deadline – U.S.A., We're Not Married, The Snows of Kilimanjaro, Dream Boat, Stars and Stripes Forever, Tonight We Sing, My Wife's Best Friend, Night Without Sleep, Something For The Birds, White Witch Doctor, Call Me Madam, Inferno, Vicki, Mr. Scoutmaster, Hell and High Water, Prince Valiant, The Egyptian, There's No Business Like Show Business, Soldier of Fortune, The House of Bamboo, River of No Return, The Rains of Ranchipur, The Girl in the Red Velvet Swing, Love is a Many-Splendored Thing, Daddy Long Legs, Bus Stop, The King and I, Teenage Rebel, Fraulein, Desk Set, Will Success Spoil Rock Hunter?, From Hell To Texas, The Girl Can't Help It, An Affair to Remember, Peyton Place, The Long. Hot Summer, In Love and War, Mardi Gras, A Certain Smile, The Young Lions, The Hunters, The Fiend Who Walked The West, The Barbarian and the Geisha, The Gift of Love, Sing Boy Sing, Rally 'Round The Flag, Boys, The Man Who Understood Women, Compulsion, Say One For Me, Journey To The Center of the Earth, Adventures in Paradise (TV), The Third Man (TV), Can-Can, Blue Denim, The Story of Ruth, Sanctuary, The Second Time Around, The Fiercest Heart, Snow White and the Three Stooges, Wild in the Country, The Marriage-Go-Round, Hemingway's Adventures of a Young Man, Five Weeks in a Balloon, The Wizard of Baghdad, The Comancheros, Bus Stop (TV), The Stripper, Something's Got To Give (unfinished)/Move Over Darling, Mr. Hobbs Takes A Vacation, Shock Treatment, Hush...Hush, Sweet Charlotte, The Time Tunnel (TV), Rio Conchos, Lost in Space (TV), Do Not Disturb, Morituri, Our Man Flint, John Goldfarb, Please Come Home, The Flight of the Phoenix, The Boston Strangler, Star!, The Detective, Hello, Dolly!, Justine, Che!, Beneath the Planet of the Apes, Nanny and the Professor (TV), The Challenge (TV), Myra Breckinridge, Beyond the Valley of the Dolls, Move, Mephisto Waltz, Paper Man (TV), Mr. and Mrs. Bo Jo Jones (TV), The Seven Minutes, The Poseidon Adventure, Class of '55 (TV), The Towering Inferno, Starsky & Hutch (TV), At Long Last Love, The Turning Point, Nine to Five, Big Trouble in Little China, Predator 2, The X-Files (TV), Bones (TV)

STAGE EIGHT:

Prisoner of Shark Island, Captain January, Wife, Doctor and Nurse, Stanley and Livingston, Dangerously Yours, 45 Fathers, Island in the Sky, Love and Hisses, International Settlement, Sally, Irene and Mary, City Girl, Josette, Rascals, Kentucky Moonshine, Alexander's Ragtime Band, Four Men and a Prayer, Battle of Broadway, Little Miss Broadway, Always Goodbye, One Wild Night, Three Blind Mice, Just Around The Corner, My Lucky Star, Gateway, Passport Husband, Straight, Place and Show, Time Out For Murder, Mr. Moto's Last Warning, Five of a Kind, Sharpshooters, A Very Practical Joke, Down on the Farm, Up The River, The Little Princess, Susannah of the Mounties, Young Mr. Lincoln, The Rains Came, Stop – Look and Love, Drums Along The Mohawk, Swanee River, Johnny Apollo, He Married His Wife, Brigham Young, I Was An Adventuress, Lillian Russell, Maryland, Four Sons, The Man I Married, Down Argentine Way, The Return of Frank James, The Mark of Zorro Hudson's Bay Company, Western Union, Golden Hoofs, Romance of the Rio Grande, Ride On, Vaquero, Tall, Dark and Handsome, Sleepers West, Blood and Sand, Dressed to Kill, How Green Was My Valley, Swamp Water, Moon Over Miami, I Wake Up Screaming, Young America, Remember the Day, Song of the Islands, Son of Fury, Castle in the Desert, Roxie Hart, A Gentleman at Heart, To The Shores of Tripoli, Ten Gentlemen From West Point, Secret Agent of Japan, Orchestra Wives, Little Tokyo U.S.A., Girl Trouble, China Girl, Springtime in the Rockies, Crash Dive, Coney Island, Hello, Frisco, Hello, They Came To Blow Up America, The Song of Bernadette, Heaven Can Wait, Pin-Up Girl, No Exceptions, Buffalo Bill, The Purple Heart, The Keys of the Kingdom, A Wing and a Prayer, Laura, Wilson, Leave Her To Heaven, Nob Hill, Circumstantial Evidence, Captain Eddie, Dragonwyck, Fallen Angel, Doll Face, Sentimental Journey, Cluny Brown, Behind Green Lights, The Late George Apley, Thunder in the Valley, The Homestretch, I Wonder Who's Kissing Her Now, Forever Amber, Mother Wore Tights, Nightmare Alley, The Foxes of Harrow, Give My Regards to Broadway, Daisy Kenyon, The Snake Pit, Call Northside 777, You Were Meant For Me, The Walls of Jericho, Sitting Pretty, Apartment For Peggy, Cry of the City, Unfaithfully Yours, That Wonderful Urge, Chicken Every Sunday, Mother is a Freshman, Mr. Belvedere Goes to College, House of Strangers, It Happens Every Spring, Pinky, Dancing in the Dark, Love That Brute, When Willie Comes Marching Home, The Gunfighter, No Way Out, Stella, Mr. 880, Fourteen Hours, Bird of Paradise, The House On Telegraph Hill, You're in the Navy Now, Anne of the Indies, The Desert Fox, Lydia Bailey, Fixed Bayonets, Way Of A Gaucho, The Outcasts of Poker Flat, O. Henry's Full House, We're Not Married, The Snows of Kilimanjaro, Pony Soldier, My Pal Gus, Niagara, Big Man, White Witch Doctor, Powder River, Destination Gobi, The President's Lady, The Robe,

Sailor of the King, City of Bad Men, Inferno, How To Marry A Millionaire, Prince Valiant, Three Coins in the Fountain, Woman's World, Broken Lance, There's No Business Like Show Business, Untamed, Daddy Long Legs, Soldier of Fortune, The Virgin Queen, How To Be Very, Very Popular, Love Is A Many-Splendored Thing, The Left Hand of God, The View From Pompey's Head, The Rains of Ranchipur, Good Morning, Miss Dove, The Lieutenant Wore Skirts, G.E. "Cavalcade," The Bottom of the Bottle, The Man in the Gray Flannel Suit, The Revolt of Mamie Stover, 23 Paces to Baker Street, D-Day, The Sixth of June, Between Heaven and Hell, Hilda Crane, Bus Stop, The Best Things in Life Are Free, Teenage Rebel, The Girl Can't Help It, The Three Faces of Eve, Will Success Spoil Rock Hunter?, Bernardine, An Affair to Remember, Ten North Frederick, The Young Lions, A Certain Smile, From Hell To Texas, The Bravados, Mardi Gras, The Hunters, From Hell to Texas, South Pacific, Warlock, Say One For Me, The Man Who Understood Women, The Sound and the Fury, A Private's Affair, The Blue Angel, Holiday For Lovers, Adventures in Paradise (TV), Five Fingers (TV), The Third Man (TV), Compulsion, We Pointed Them North, The Best of Everything, North To Alaska, High Time, Let's Make Love, Can-Can, Hong Kong (TV), From The Terrace, The Marriage-Go-Round, Wild in the Country, The Little Shepherd of Kingdom Come, Return to Peyton Place, Pirates of Tortuga, The Second Time Around, Sanctuary, Madison Avenue, Tender is the Night, Bachelor Flat, Mr. Hobbs Takes A Vacation, State Fair, Take Her, She's Mine, The Stripper, What A Way To Go, The Pleasure Seekers, Peyton Place (TV), Fate is the Hunter, Dear Brigitte, The Sound of Music, The Reward, Morituri, John Goldfarb, Please Come Home, Do Not Disturb, The Flight of the Phoenix, Batman (TV), Our Man Flint, Stagecoach, Fantastic Voyage, The Time Tunnel (TV), Valley of the Dolls, Caprice, Judd for the Defense (TV), The St. Valentine's Day Massacre, Star!, Bandolero, The Boston Strangler, The Sweet Ride, Julia (TV), Room 222 (TV), The Detective, Justine, M*A*S*H, Myra Breckinridge, The Great White Hope, Beyond the Valley of the Dolls, The Mephisto Waltz, Paper Man (TV), The Marriage of a Young Stockbroker, The Seven Minutes, Escape From The Planet of the Apes, The Paper Chase, The Towering Inferno, Charlie's Angels (TV), Hart to Hart (TV), Dynasty (TV), To Be Or Not To Be, The Buddy System, Johnny Dangerously, Rhinestone, L.A. Law (TV), Big Trouble in Little China, Murder One (TV), Total Security (TV), Shark (TV), Lie to Me (TV), 1600 Penn (TV), Enlisted (TV), Ted 2, Life in Pieces (TV)

STAGE NINE:

Second Honeymoon, Wife, Doctor and Nurse, Charlie Chan on Broadway, Dangerously Yours, 45 Fathers, Love and Hisses, International Settlement, Sally, Irene and Mary, Happy Landing, Change of Heart, Josette,

Walking Down Broadway, Alexander's Ragtime Band, Four Men and a Prayer, Mr. Moto's Gamble, Battle of Broadway, Always Goodbye, Mysterious Mr. Moto, Three Blind Mice, Just Around The Corner, My Lucky Star, Suez, Kentucky, Passport Husband, Straight, Place and Show, Barricade, Hold That Co-Ed, Road Demon, Sharpshooters, A Very Practical Joke, A Very Practical Joke, Up The River, Tail Spin, Thanks For Everything, Wife, Husband and Friend, Charlie Chan in Honolulu, Mr. Moto in Danger Island, High School, Rose of Washington Square, The Gorilla, News is Made At Night , Young Mr. Lincoln, The Rains Came, Charlie Chan at Treasure Island, Hollywood Cavalcade, The Adventures of Sherlock Holmes, Pack Up Your Troubles, Charlie Chan in the City of Darkness, Little Old New York, Johnny Apollo, The Honeymoon's Over, Day-Time Wife, Blonde and 21, Lillian Russell, Maryland, Girl in 313, Manhattan Heartbeat, Public Deb No. 1, The Man I Married, Down Argentine Way, The Bride Word Crutches, The Great Profile, For Beauty's Sake, Tin Pan Alley, Michael Shayne, Private Detective, That Night in Rio, Tall, Dark and Handsome, Blood and Sand, The Cowboy and the Blonde, Sun Valley Serenade, Belle Starr, A Yank in the R,A,F., Accent on Love , Dressed to Kill, Private Nurse, Charlie Chan in Rio, Wild Geese Calling, Weekend in Havana, We Go Fast, Small Town Deb, Rise and Shine, Roxie Hart, The Perfect Snob, On The Sunny Side, Tales of Manhattan, Right to the Heart, Rings on Her Fingers, This Above All, Who Is Hope Schuyler?, Sundown Jim, Thunder Birds, The Magnificent Dope, The Loves of Edgar Allan Poe, The Black Swan, Iceland, China Girl, Springtime in the Rockies, Manila Calling, My Friend Flicka, The Meanest Man in the World, Crash Dive, The Undying Monster, Dixie Dugan, Coney Island, The Moon is Down, Jane Eyre, Holy Matrimony, The Gang's All Here, The Night is Ending, Happy Land, The Lodger, The Eve of St. Mark, Home in Indiana, The Keys of the Kingdom, Laura, Wilson, Something for the Boys, Winged Victory, Diamond Horseshoe, A Royal Scandal, Captain Eddie, The Story With Two Endings - O.W.I. Short, The Dolly Sisters, Dragonwyck, Don Juan Quilligan, Do You Love Me?, The Spider, Smoky, Margie, The Shocking Miss Pilgrim, Johnny Comes Flying Home, The Dark Corner, The Razor's Edge, My Darling Clementine, Thunder in the Valley, The Ghost and Mrs. Muir, The Foxes of Harrow, Daisy Kenyon, Gentleman's Agreement, Scudda Hoo, Scudda Hay!, The Snake Pit, Call Northside 777, You Were Meant For Me, Sitting Pretty, The Street With No Name, The Iron Curtain, Apartment for Peggy, Cry of the City, Unfaithfully Yours, Road House, That Wonderful Urge, Down to the Sea in Ships, Yellow Sky, Chicken Every Sunday, Everybody Does It, Mother Was A Freshman, The Beautiful Blonde From Bashful Bend, You're My Everything, Thieves' Highway, Come to the Stable, Father Was A Fullback, Mother Didn't Tell Me, Under My Skin, No Way Out, My Blue Heaven, Stella, Mister 880,

For Heaven's Sake, The House On Telegraph Hill, Follow The Sun, Take Care of My Little Girl, The Frogmen, As Young As You Feel, The Guy Who Came Back, Meet Me After The Show, The Desert Fox, Anne of the Indies, Let's Make It Legal, The Model and the Marriage Broker, Elopement, Pride Of St. Louis, Belles On Their Toes, Phone Call From A Stranger, With A Song in My Heart, Return of the Texan, Lure of the Wilderness, The Girl Next Door, O. Henry's Full House, What Price Glory?, We're Not Married, Monkey Business, Night Without Sleep, Something For The Birds, Powder River, The Farmer Takes a Wife, Taxi, Destination Gobi, The Silver Whip, Pickup on South Street, The Robe, Man on a Tightrope, Gentlemen Prefer Blondes, City of Bad Men, Mr. Scoutmaster, River of No Return, Hell and High Water, The Egyptian, Desiree, There's No Business Like Show Business, Prince of Players, The Seven Year Itch, A Man Called Peter, Violent Saturday, The Virgin Queen, Love is a Many-Splendored Thing, The Girl in the Red Velvet Swing, Good Morning, Miss Dove, The Lieutenant Wore Skirts, G.E. "Cavalcade," On The Threshold of Space, The Man in the Gray Flannel Suit, The Girl Can't Help It, The Dark Wave, Bigger Than Life, The Best Things in Life Are Free, Teenage Rebel, Three Brave Men, Oh, Men! Oh, Women!, A Hatful of Rain, The Way To The Gold, Bernardine, An Affair to Remember, No Down Payment, Mardi Gras, Ten North Frederick, The Young Lions, The Gift of Love, From Hell to Texas, The Fiend Who Walked The West, Rally 'Round The Flag, Boys!, The Man Who Understood Women, The Fly, Adventures in Paradise (TV), The Third Man (TV), A Private's Affair, Here Come The Jets, The Return of the Fly, The Best of Everything, The Blue Angel, The Stripper, Move Over, Darling, What A Way To Go, Peyton Place (TV), Shock Treatment, Fate is the Hunter, John Goldfarb, Come Home, Felony Squad (TV), Julia (TV), Che!, Move, Cover Me Babe, Tora! Tora! Tora!, Cover Me Babe, Arnie (TV), M*A*S*H (TV), After M*A*S*H (TV), Jumpin' Jack Flash, The Wizard (TV), Hooperman (TV), Cop Rock (TV), Civil Wars (TV), Toys, Hot Shots Part Deux, NYPD Blue (TV), Bones (TV)

STAGE TEN:

Danger - Love at Work, Wife, Doctor and Nurse, Life Begins in College, Rebecca of Sunnybrook Farm, Big Town Girl, Love and Hisses, Sally, Irene and Mary, Happy Landing, City Girl, Change of Heart, Alexander's Ragtime Band, Four Men and a Prayer, Mr. Moto's Gamble, Always Goodbye, Three Blind Mice, Just Around The Corner, Hold That Co-Ed, Sharpshooters, While New York Sleeps, A Very Practical Joke, Down on the Farm, Mr. Moto Takes a Vacation, Up The River, The Little Princess, Thanks for Everything, Mr. Moto in Danger Island, Charlie Chan in Rio, Return of the Cisco Kid, Young Mr. Lincoln, Second Fiddle, Everything Happens at Night, The Rains Came, Hollywood Cavalcade, Here I Am A Stranger, The Adventures of Sherlock Holmes, Pack Up Your Troubles, Charlie Chan in the City of Darkness, Little Old New York, The Blue Bird, Johnny Apollo, Earthbound, Maryland, Public Deb No. 1, I Married A Nazi, The Gay Caballero, For Beauty's Sake, Yesterday's Heroes, Charter Pilot, Chad Hanna, Ride on Vaquero, Tall, Dark and Handsome, The Cowboy and the Blonde, Sun Valley Serenade, Man Hunt, A Yank in the R.A.F., Week-End in Havana, Marry the Boss's Daughter, We Go Fast, Confirm or Deny, Dangerous But Passable, Small Town Deb, Moon Over Her Shoulder, I Wake Up Screaming, Young America, Remember the Day, Highway to Hell, Song of the Islands, Rise and Shine, Castle in the Desert, My Gal Sal, Roxie Hart, Tales of Manhattan, A Gentleman At Heart, This Above All, Moontide, Not For Children, Ten Gentleman From West Point, Thunder Birds, The Pied Piper, The Loves of Edgar Allan Poe, Orchestra Wives, Girl Trouble, That Other Woman, The Meanest Man in the World, They'll Live Again, Over My Dead Body, Quiet Please, Murder, Dixie Dugan, Margin for Error, Hello, Frisco, Hello, The Song of Bernadette, Heaven Can Wait, Wintertime, Sweet Rosie O'Grady, Holy Matrimony, The Gang's All Here, Three Sisters of the Moors, The Night is Ending, The Dancing Masters, Buffalo Bill, The Sullivans, In the Meantime, Darling, The Keys of the Kingdom, A Wing and a Prayer, Irish Eyes are Smiling, Winged Victory, Nob Hill, Diamond Horseshoe, A Bell For Adano, Dragonwyck, Within These Walls, The Enchanted Voyage, Sentimental Journey, Cluny Brown, Claudia and David, The Razor's Edge, If I'm Lucky, The Late George Apley, Who's Kissing Her Now, Forever Amber, Captain From Castile, Give My Regards to Broadway, Daisy Kenyon, Gentleman's Agreement, That Lady in Ermine, The Street With No Name, The Snake Pit, Cry of the City, When My Baby Smiles at Me, A Letter to Three Wives, The Fan, The Beautiful Blonde From Bashful Bend, Slattery's Hurricane, Oh, You Beautiful Doll, Three Came Home, Whirlpool, No Way Out, I'll Get By, Two Flags West, For Heaven's Sake, Half Angel, On The Riviera, The House on Telegraph Hill, I Can Get It For You Wholesale, You're In The Navy Now, David and Bathsheba, The Guy Who Came Back, As Young As You Feel, The Secret of Convict Lake, Down Among the Sheltering Palms, The Desert Fox, With a Song in My Heart, 5 Fingers, Wait Till The Sun Shines Nellie, Lure of the Wilderness, The I Don't Care Girl, The Girl Next Door, Deadline—U.S.A., O. Henry's Full House, Dream Boat, Stars and Stripes Forever, Bloodhounds Of Broadway, Tonight We Sing, Night Without Sleep, Something For The Birds, Call Me Madam, The Silver Whip, The Robe, The Desert Rats, Inferno, Demetrius and the Gladiators, Three Coins in the Fountain, Broken Lance, There's No Business Like Show Business, The Seven Year Itch, Daddy Long Legs, The Girl in the Red Velvet Swing, Love is a Many-Splendored Thing, The View From Pompey's Head, Good Morning,

Miss Dove, The Lieutenant Wore Skirts, G.E. "Laura" (TV), The Bottom of the Bottle, The Man in the Gray Flannel Suit, 23 Paces to Baker Street, Bus Stop, The Best Things in Life Are Free, Three Brave Men, The Girl Can't Help It, Oh, Men! Oh, Women!, Kiss Them For Me, Peyton Place, The Three Faces of Eve, Ten North Frederick, The Young Lions, The Gift of Love, The Barbarian and the Geisha, Sing Boy Sing, A Nice Little Bank That Should Be Robbed, The Hunters, Rally 'Round the Flag, Boys, Adventures in Paradise (TV), The Remarkable Mr. Pennypacker, The Best of Everything, Beloved Infidel, Miracle of the Hills, The Man Who Understood Women, Blue Denim, Can-Can, Wake Me When It's Over, One Foot in Hell, The Story of Ruth, North to Alaska, All Hands on Deck, Bus Stop (TV), Sanctuary, Wild in the Country, The Chapman Report, Return to Peyton Place, Tender is the Night, Bachelor Flat, State Fair, Take Her, She's Mine, The Stripper, The Pleasure Seekers, Goodbye, Charlie, Dear Brigitte, Batman (TV), Our Man Flint, Judd for the Defense (TV), Julia (TV), M*A*S*H, Young Frankenstein, Love Boat (TV), Moonlighting (TV), Baby Boom, NYPD Blue (TV), House M.D. (TV), Touch (TV), Ted 2, American Horror Story (TV)

STAGE ELEVEN:

In Old Chicago, The Baroness and the Butler, Wife, Doctor and Nurse, 45 Fathers, Rebecca of Sunnybrook Farm, Love and Hisses, Sally, Irene and Mary, Happy Landing, Kidnapped, Alexander's Ragtime Band, Four Men and a Prayer, Three Blind Mice, Just Around The Corner, My Lucky Star, Suez, Kentucky, Mr. Moto Takes A Vacation, Barricade, Hold That Co-Ed, Submarine Patrol, Tail Spin, Pardon Our Nerve, Thanks For Everything, Wife, Husband and Friend, Mr. Moto in Danger Island, The Jones Family in Hollywood, The Hound of the Baskervilles, The Story of Alexander Graham Bell, The Gorilla, Young Mr. Lincoln, Second Fiddle, Elsa Maxwell's Hotel For Women, Everything Happens at Night, Hollywood Cavalcade, Charlie Chan in the City of Darkness, The Blue Bird, Johnny Apollo, The Grapes of Wrath, I Was an Adventuress, Free, Blonde and 21, Lillian Russell, Young People, Four Sons, Public Deb No. 1, Street of Memories, The Man I Married, The Return of Frank James, The Great Profile, For Beauty's Sake, Yesterday's Heroes, Jennie, Tin Pan Alley, Golden Hoofs, Tall, Dark and Handsome, A Very Young Lady, The Cowboy and the Blonde, Man Hunt, Belle Starr, Week-End in Havana, Swamp Water, I Wake Up Screaming, Remember The Day, Rise and Shine, The Perfect Snob, Roxie Hart, A Gentleman At Heart, Rings on Her Fingers, This Above All, Moontide, Ten Gentlemen From West Point, Secret Agent of Japan, Thunder Birds, The Magnificent Dope, The Pied Piper, The Postman Didn't Ring, The Loves of Edgar Allan Poe, That Other Woman, The Black Swan, Little Tokyo U.S.A., Springtime in the Rockies, My Friend

Flicka, Life Begins at 8:30, Quiet Please, Murder, Chetniks, Hello, Frisco, Hello, The Song of Bernadette, Sweet Rosie O'Grady, The Gang's All Here, Happy Land, The Sullivans, The Eve of St. Mark, Home in Indiana, The Purple Heart, Greenwich Village, The Keys of the Kingdom, Bermuda Mystery, Sunday Dinner for a Soldier, A Tree Grows in Brooklyn, Nob Hill, A Bell For Adano, State Fair, The Dolly Sisters, Dragonwyck, Do You Love Me?, The Enchanted Voyage, Smoky, Anna and the King of Siam, Claudia and David, The Razor's Edge, Carnival in Costa Rica, If I'm Lucky, The Homestretch, Forever Amber, Captain From Castile, Nightmare Alley, The Foxes of Harrow, The Snake Pit, You Were Meant For Me, The Walls of Jericho, That Lady in Ermine, Apartment For Peggy, When My Baby Smiles At Me, A Letter to Three Wives, Mother is a Freshman, Mr. Belvedere Goes to College, I Was A Male War Bride, You're My Everything, Thieves' Highway, Come To The Stable, Oh, You Beautiful Doll, All About Eve, Whirlpool, The Gunfighter, No Way Out, Where The Sidewalk Ends, I'll Get By, American Guerilla in the Philippines, Half Angel, The House on Telegraph Hill, I Can Get It For You Wholesale, Take Care of My Little Girl, Meet Me After The Show, The Guy Who Came Back, As Young As You Feel, The Day The Earth Stood Still, Love Nest, With A Song In My Heart, The Model and the Marriage Broker, The Pride of St. Louis, Phone Call From A Stranger, The I Don't Care Girl, Lure of the Wilderness, The Girl Next Door, Deadline - U.S.A., O. Henry's Full House, Les Miserables, We're Not Married, Stars and Stripes Forever, Tonight We Sing, White Witch Doctor, Powder River, Destination Gobi, The President's Lady, The Silver Whip, The Robe, City of Bad Men, Demetrius and the Gladiators, Three Coins in the Fountain, Desiree, The Seven Year Itch, Soldier of Fortune, Violent Saturday, The Virgin Queen, The Left Hand of God, The Girl in the Red Velvet Swing, The Lieutenant Wore Skirts, Good Morning, Miss Dove, Carousel, The Revolt of Mamie Stover, D-Day, The Sixth of June, Between Heaven and Hell, Bigger Than Life, The Dark Wave, The Best Things in Life Are Free, Teenage Rebel, Three Brave Men, Oh, Men! Oh, Women!, The Three Faces of Eve, Bernardine, An Affair to Remember, Peyton Place, Mardi Gras, Ten North Frederick, The Young Lions, The Gift of Love, Sing Boy Sing, A Nice Little Bank That Should Be Robbed, From Hell to Texas, In Love and War, Rally 'Round The Flag, Boys!, The Fly, The Remarkable Mr. Pennypacker, Five Fingers (TV), The Third Man (TV), The Best of Everything, The Story On Page One, Warlock, Compulsion, Here Come The Jets, The Man Who Understood Women, Holiday For Lovers, Let's Make Love, Wake Me When It's Over, The Wizard of Baghdad, The Right Approach, The Comancheros, Take Her, She's Mine, The Stripper, What A Way To Go, The Pleasure Seekers, Peyton Place (TV), Goodbye, Charlie, Fantastic Voyage, Way...Way Out, Doctor Dolittle , The Ghost and Mrs. Muir (TV), Nanny and the Professor

(TV), *Class of '55* (TV), *Going Places* (Universal), *The Towering Inferno*, *Damnation Alley*, *The Love Boat* (TV), *Trapper John M.D.* (TV), *The Rose*, *Emerald Point N.A.S.* (TV), *Moonlighting* (TV), *Toys*, *Airheads*, *Alien Resurrection*, *Martial Law* (TV), *Anywhere But Here*, *Dr. Dolittle II*, *House M.D.* (TV), *Don't Trust the B- in Apartment 23* (TV), *Gang Related* (TV), *American Crime Story* (TV)

STAGE FOURTEEN:
In Old Chicago, *Stanley and Livingstone*, *Rebecca of Sunnybrook Farm*, *Big Town Girl*, *Love and Hisses*, *Happy Landing*, *Charlie Chan at Monte Carlo*, *International Settlement*, *Thank You, Mr. Moto*, *City Girl*, *Change of Heart*, *Rascals*, *Kentucky Moonshine*, *Alexander's Ragtime Band*, *Four Men and A Prayer*, *Mr. Moto's Gamble*, *Little Miss Broadway*, *Keep Smiling*, *Always Goodbye*, *One Wild Night*, *Three Blind Mice*, *Suez*, *Time Out For Murder*, *Barricade*, *Always in Trouble*, *The Three Musketeers*, *Chasing Danger*, *Rose of Washington Square*, *The Story of Alexander Graham Bell*, *The Gorilla*, *The Return of the Cisco Kid*, *Young Mr. Lincoln*, *Second Fiddle*, *The Rains Came*, *Hollywood Cavalcade*, *Pack Up Your Troubles*, *The Blue Bird*, *I Was an Adventuress*, *Free, Blonde and 21*, *Lillian Russell*, *Young People*, *Four Sons*, *Public Deb No. 1*, *Street of Memories*, *The Man I Married*, *The Return of Frank James*, *The Great Profile*, *For Beauty's Sake*, *Yesterday's Heroes*, *Jennie*, *Tin Pan Alley*, *Golden Hoofs*, *That Night in Rio*, *Tall, Dark and Handsome*, *A Very Young Lady*, *The Great American Broadcast*, *Sun Valley Serenade*, *Man Hunt*, *Belle Starr*, *Private Nurse*, *Charley's Aunt*, *How Green Was My Valley*, *Lone Star Ranger*, *Marry The Boss's Daughter*, *We Go Fast*, *Confirm Or Deny*, *Swamp Water*, *Great Guns*, *I Wake Up Screaming*, *Song of the Islands*, *Rise and Shine*, *Tales of Manhattan*, *To The Shores of Tripoli*, *This Above All*, *Moontide*, *Ten Gentlemen From West Point*, *The Pied Piper*, *The Black Swan*, *That Other Woman*, *Girl Trouble*, *The Ox-Bow Incident*, *My Friend Flicka*, *The Undying Monster*, *Immortal Sergeant*, *Tonight We Raid Calais*, *Hello, Frisco, Hello*, *The Moon Is Down*, *Jane Eyre*, *Stormy Weather*, *Wintertime*, *Sweet Rosie O'Grady*, *The Gang's All Here*, *Buffalo Bill*, *Pin-Up Girl*, *Wilson*, *Greenwich Village*, *The Keys of the Kingdom*, *Sweet and Low-Down*, *Irish Eyes Are Smiling*, *Diamond Horseshoe*, *Colonel Effingham's Raid*, *A Bell For Adano*, *Circumstantial Evidence*, *State Fair*, *The Dolly Sisters*, *Dragonwyck*, *Do You Love Me?*, *Leave Her To Heaven*, *The Enchanted Voyage*, *The Spider*, *Centennial Summer*, *Three Little Girls in Blue*, *Carnival in Costa Rica*, *The Dark Corner*, *The Homestretch*, *Forever Amber*, *Captain From Castile*, *Miracle on 34th Street*, *Nightmare Alley*, *The Foxes of Harrow*, *The Snake Pit*, *Fury at Furnace Creek*, *The Walls of Jericho*, *That Lady in Ermine*, *The Luck of the Irish*, *That Wonderful Urge*, *Yellow Sky*, *The Fan*, *The Beautiful Blonde From Bashful Bend*,

You're My Everything, *Slattery's Hurricane*, *Come to the Stable*, *Dancing in the Dark*, *Wabash Avenue*, *Love That Brute*, *When Willie Comes Marching Home*, *A Ticket to Tomahawk*, *Under My Skin*, *Cheaper By The Dozen*, *My Blue Heaven*, *Where The Sidewalk Ends*, *I'll Get By*, *Mister 880*, *Call Me Mister*, *Half Angel*, *The House On Telegraph Hill*, *Follow the Sun*, *I Can Get It For You Wholesale*, *Take Care of My Little Girl*, *Down Among the Sheltering Palms*, *With A Song In My Heart*, *Fixed Bayonets*, *David and Bathsheba*, *People Will Talk*, *Golden Girl*, *Viva Zapata!*, *Red Skies of Montana*, *Wait Till The Sun Shines Nellie*, *Belles On Their Toes*, *The Girl Next Door*, *We're Not Married*, *The Snows of Kilimanjaro*, *Dreamboat*, *Stars and Stripes Forever*, *My Cousin Rachel*, *Tonight We Sing*, *Titanic*, *Gentlemen Prefer Blondes*, *The Desert Rats*, *Dangerous Crossing*, *How to Marry a Millionaire*, *Prince Valiant*, *Three Coins in a Fountain*, *The Egyptian*, *There's No Business Like Show Business*, *Black Widow (1954)*, *Prince of Players*, *A Man Called Peter*, *Soldier of Fortune*, *House of Bamboo*, *The Tall Men*, *The View From Pompey's Head*, *Love is a Many-Splendored Thing*, *The Lieutenant Wore Skirts*, *The Revolt of Mamie Stover*, *Hilda Crane*, *Bus Stop*, *The King and I*, *Love Me Tender*, *The Bottom of the Bottle*, *D-Day, The Sixth of June*, *Fraulein*, *The True Story of Jesse James*, *Will Success Spoil Rock Hunter?*, *Three Faces of Eve*, *An Affair to Remember*, *Boy On A Dolphin*, *Oh, Men! Oh, Women!*, *Kiss Them For Me*, *The Long, Hot Summer*, *Ten North Frederick*, *Stopover Tokyo*, *The Young Lions*, *The Fiend Who Walked The West*, *The Diary of Anne Frank*, *The Blue Angel*, *Woman Obsessed*, *Beloved Infidel*, *Adventures in Paradise* (TV), *Five Fingers* (TV), *The Third Man* (TV), *Let's Make Love*, *Can-Can*, *Seven Thieves*, *Madison Avenue*, *Wild in the Country*, *Swingin' Along*, *Bus Stop* (TV), *Sanctuary*, *Return to Peyton Place*, *Pirates of Tortuga*, *Hemingway's Adventures of a Young Man*, *All Hands On Deck*, *Tender is the Night*, *Bachelor Flat*, *Mr. Hobbs Takes A Vacation*, *Something's Got To Give (unfinished)/Move Over Darling*, *Take Her, She's Mine*, *What A Way To Go*, *Goodbye, Charlie*, *The Pleasure Seekers*, *Shock Treatment*, *Fate is the Hunter*, *Morituri*, *Do Not Disturb*, *Fantastic Voyage*, *Our Man Flint*, *The Sand Pebbles*, *A Guide For The Married Man*, *Doctor Dolittle*, *In Like Flint*, *Valley of the Dolls*, *The St. Valentine's Day Massacre*, *Justine*, *The Sweet Ride*, *Star!*, *Hello, Dolly!*, *Beneath the Planet of the Apes*, *Southern Fried* (TV), *Move*, *The Great White Hope*, *The Seven Minutes*, *The Marriage of a Young Stockbroker*, *Class of '55* (TV), *Going Places* (Universal), *Swiss Family Robinson* (TV), *High Anxiety*, *The Fury*, *9 to 5*, *Modern Problems*, *9 to 5* (TV), *Emerald Point N.A.S.* (TV), *The Man Who Loved Women* (Columbia), *Commando*, *Jumpin' Jack Flash*, *Black Widow (1954)*, *Die Hard*, *War of the Roses*, *Edward Scissorhands*, *Die Hard II*, *Downtown*, *Hot Shots*, *Toys*, *Hot Shots Part Deux*, *Jack the Bear*, *Speed*, *Airheads*, *Broken Arrow*, *Alien*

Resurrection, Martial Law (TV), Anywhere But Here, Cast Away, Dr. Dolittle II, Minority Report, House M.D. (TV), Mr. and Mrs. Smith, How to Live With Your Parents (For The Rest of Your Life) (TV), The Crazy Ones (TV), Fresh Off the Boat (TV)

STAGE FIFTEEN:

Life Begins in College, Happy Landing, Kentucky Moonshine, Kidnapped, Always Goodbye, Mysterious Mr. Moto, One Wild Night, My Lucky Star, Barricade, Submarine Patrol, Jesse James, Tail Spin, Wife, Husband and Friend, The Jones Family in Hollywood, High School, The Hound of the Baskervilles, Rose of Washington Square, Second Fiddle, Everything Happens At Night, Hollywood Cavalcade, Here I Am A Stranger, The Adventures of Sherlock Holmes, Drums Along The Mohawk, Pack Up Your Troubles, Charlie Chan in the City of Darkness, The Honeymoon's Over, I Was An Adventuress, Star Dust, Earthbound, Lillian Russell, Maryland, The Brat, The Man I Married, Down Argentine Way, The Return of Frank James, The Bride Wore Crutches, Yesterday's Heroes, Hudson's Bay Company, Tin Pan Alley, Western Union, Ride On Vaquero, Tobacco Road, A Very Young Lady, Blood and Sand, Great American Broadcast, Sun Valley Serenade, Belle Starr, How Green Was My Valley, Weekend in Havana, I Wake Up Screaming, Son of Fury, Tales of Manhattan, To The Shores of Tripoli, This Above All, China Girl, My Friend Flicka, The Meanest Man in the World, Chetniks, Immortal Sergeant, Coney Island, Hello, Frisco, Hello, Heaven Can Wait, Wintertime, Guadalcanal Diary, No Exceptions, Buffalo Bill, The Sullivans, The Eve of St. Mark, Home in Indiana, Greenwich Village, A Wing and a Prayer, Bermuda Mystery, Ladies of Washington, Sweet and Low-Down, Irish Eyes Are Smiling, Something for the Boys, Winged Victory, Diamond Horseshoe, Where Do We Go From Here?, The Bullfighters, A Bell for Adano, State Fair, Don Juan Quilligan, Junior Miss, Leave Her to Heaven, Fallen Angel, It's A Pleasure, Doll Face, Anna and the King of Siam, Dragonwyck, Margie, The Razor's Edge, The Late George Apley, Carnival in Costa Rica, The Homestretch, I Wonder Who's Kissing Her Now, Second Chance, The Ghost and Mrs. Muir, The Foxes of Harrow, Gentleman's Agreement, The Snake Pit, Scudda Hoo! Scudda Hay!, Fury at Furnace Creek, Deep Waters, The Street With No Name, The Luck of the Irish, Cry of the City, Unfaithfully Yours, When My Baby Smiles At Me, That Wonderful Urge, Letter to Three Wives, The Fan, Everybody Does It, Mother Is A Freshman, I Was A Male War Bride, The Beautiful Blonde From Bashful Bend, You're My Everything, Oh, You Beautiful Doll, Dancing in the Dark, Wabash Avenue, Love That Brute, A Ticket To Tomahawk, No Way Out, My Blue Heaven, I'll Get By, All About Eve, Call Me Mister, For Heaven's Sake, The House on Telegraph Hill, Follow The Sun, I Can Get It For You

Wholesale, David and Bathsheba, Down Among the Sheltering Palms, Golden Girl, Elopement, 5 Fingers, Phone Call From A Stranger, The Girl Next Door, Deadline – U.S.A., Les Miserables, Dreamboat, Stars and Stripes Forever, Bloodhounds of Broadway, My Cousin Rachel, The Robe, Gentlemen Prefer Blondes, Dangerous Crossing, Prince Valiant, Demetrius and the Gladiators, Desiree, Untamed, The Racers, The Seven Year Itch, Daddy Long Legs, A Man Called Peter, Soldier of Fortune, Violent Saturday, House of Bamboo, Love is a Many-Splendored Thing, The View From Pompey's Head, G.E. "Cavalcade," Carousel, The King and I, D-Day, The Sixth of June, Hilda Crane, The Best Things in Life Are Free, The Girl Can't Help It, The Way To The Gold, The Three Faces of Eve, April Love, The Long, Hot Summer, No Down Payment, In Love And War, A Certain Smile, The Young Lions, The Fly, The Man Who Understood Women, Five Fingers (TV), The Sound and the Fury, The Alligator People, The Return of the Fly, The Best of Everything, Holiday For Lovers, Beloved Infidel, The Third Man (TV), Seven Thieves, The Fiercest Heart, From The Terrace, High Time, The Lost World, Wake Me When It's Over, Snow White and the Three Stooges, The Marriage-Go-Round, Tender is the Night, State Fair, Bachelor Flat, Hemingway's Adventures of a Young Man, Five Weeks in a Balloon, The Stripper, Take Her, She's Mine, What A Way To Go, Do Not Disturb, Rio Conchos, Shock Treatment, Fate is the Hunter, Peyton Place (TV), Morituri, Flight of the Phoenix, The Sound of Music, Our Man Flint, Way...Way Out, Batman (TV), In Like Flint, A Guide For The Married Man, Valley of the Dolls, Judd for the Defense (TV), Caprice, The Secret Life of an American Wife, The St. Valentine's Day Massacre, Star!, The Sweet Ride, The Detective, Hard Contract, Justine, Daughter of the Mind (TV), Che!, Hello, Dolly!, Tora! Tora! Tora!, The Only Game in Town, Anderson and Co. (TV), Julia (TV), Bracken's World, Myra Breckinridge, The Great White Hope, Move, The Challenge, Beyond the Valley of the Dolls, Along Came A Spider (TV), The Seven Minutes, Paper Man (TV), Escape From The Planet of the Apes, Conquest of the Planet of the Apes, At Long Last Love, Silent Movie, Silver Streak, The World's Greatest Lover, The Turning Point, The Other Side of Midnight, Kiss Me Goodbye, Unfaithfully Yours, Rhinestone, Big Trouble in Little China, Black Widow (1954), Project X, Die Hard, War of the Roses, Edward Scissorhands, Die Hard 2, Ghost in the Machine, Broken Arrow, Alien Resurrection, Dr. Dolittle, Martial Law (TV), One Fine Day, The Siege, The Fight Club, Bedazzled, Dr. Dolittle II, Minority Report, Firefly (TV), House M.D. (TV), Mr. & Mrs. Smith, Ben and Kate (TV), Back in the Game (TV), American Crime Story (TV)

STAGE SIXTEEN:

Second Honeymoon, In Old Chicago, The Baroness and the Butler, Danger – Love at Work, Life Begins In College, Happy Landing, Kentucky

Moonshine, Kidnapped, Alexander's Ragtime Band, Little Miss Broadway, Mysterious Mr. Moto, I'll Give A Million, Suez, Barricade, Hold That Co-Ed, Submarine Patrol, Tail Spin, Mr. Moto in Danger Island, High School, Rose of Washington Square, Second Fiddle, The Rains Came, Chicken Wagon Family, Hollywood Cavalcade, The Adventures of Sherlock Holmes, The Blue Bird, I Was an Adventuress, Lillian Russell, Maryland, Girl in 313, The Brat, The Man I Married, Down Argentine Way, The Return of Frank James, Yesterday's Heroes, Hudson's Bay Company, Tin Pan Alley, Maryland, I Married A Nazi, Down Argentine Way, The Return of Frank James, Yesterday's Heroes, That Night in Rio, Tall, Dark and Handsome, Dead Men Tell, Belle Starr, A Yank in the R.A.F., Accent on Love, Private Nurse, Wild Geese Calling, Week-End in Havana, Lone Star Ranger, I Wake Up Screaming, Rise and Shine, The Perfect Snob, My Gal Sal, Tales of Manhattan, To The Shores of Tripoli, Moontide, Thunder Birds, The Magnificent Dope, It Happened in Flatbush, Footlight Serenade, Iceland, Just Off Broadway, Berlin Correspondent, Careful, Soft Shoulder, Springtime in the Rockies, The Meanest Man in the World, Life Begins at 8:30, Crash Dive, Girl Trouble, Tonight We Raid Calais, Quiet Please, Murder, Immortal Sergeant, Hello, Frisco, Hello, The Moon Is Down, The Song of Bernadette, Stormy Weather, Wintertime, Holy Matrimony, Sweet Rosie O'Grady, The Gang's All Here, Three Sisters of the Moors, Pin-Up Girl, The Sullivans, The Night is Ending, Wilson, Sweet and Low-Down, Irish Eyes Are Smiling, Something for the Boys, Nob Hill, A Royal Scandal, A Bell For Adano, Colonel Effingham's Raid, The Dolly Sisters, Leave Her To Heaven, Shock, Sentimental Journey, Three Little Girls in Blue, The Shocking Miss Pilgrim, The Razor's Edge, If I'm Lucky, The Late George Apley, The Brasher Doubloon, Who's Kissing Her Now, Second Chance, Forever Amber, Gentleman's Agreement, The Snake Pit, Call Northside 777, You Were Meant For Me, Sitting Pretty, The Luck of the Irish, Cry of the City, Road House, That Wonderful Urge, Everybody Does It, Mother is a Freshman, Mr. Belvedere Goes to College, House of Strangers, It Happens Every Spring, Dancing in the Dark, Mother Didn't Tell Me, Cheaper By The Dozen, My Blue Heaven, I'll Get By, All About Eve, I'd Climb the Highest Mountain, Mister 880, Call Me Mister, On The Riviera, Meet Me After The Show, Down Among the Sheltering Palms, The Day The Earth Stood Still, Love Nest, Lydia Bailey, With a Song in My Heart, 5 Fingers, Elopement, The Pride of St. Louis, Way of a Gaucho, Phone Call From A Stranger, Diplomatic Courier, The Girl Next Door, The Farmer Takes a Wife, Stars and Stripes Forever, Les Miserables, Something For The Birds, My Pal Gus, Call Me Madam, The President's Lady, The Robe, Gentlemen Prefer Blondes, Sailor of the King, The Desert Rats, Desiree, King of the Khyber Rifles, There's No Business Like Show Business, Demetrius and the Gladiators, The Racers, Prince of Players, The Seven Year Itch, A Man

Called Peter, Soldier of Fortune, Violent Saturday, How To Be Very, Very Popular, Love is a Many-Splendored Thing, The Left Hand of God, The Tall Men, The Girl in the Red Velvet Swing, The Rains of Ranchipur, The King and I, The Bottom of the Bottle, The Man in the Gray Flannel Suit, 23 Paces To Baker Street, D-Day, The Sixth of June, Fraulein, Desk Set, Between Heaven and Hell, The Girl Can't Help It, A Hatful of Rain, Peyton Place, The Long, Hot Summer, In Love and War, The Barbarian and the Geisha, The Hunters, Ten North Frederick, The Young Lions, A Certain Smile, A Nice Little Bank That Should Be Robbed, These Thousand Hills, Warlock, The Man Who Understood Women, Woman Obsessed, A Private's Affair, Blue Denim, Beloved Infidel, The Third Man (TV), Can-Can, Hong Kong (TV), High Time, From The Terrace, Wake Me When It's Over, The Marriage-Go-Round, Pirates of Tortuga, Return to Peyton Place, Bus Stop (TV), Sanctuary, State Fair, Madison Avenue, Five Weeks in a Balloon, Take Her, She's Mine, Goodbye, Charlie, The Stripper, Move Over, Darling, What A Way To Go, Fate is the Hunter, Dear Brigitte, The Reward, The Sound of Music, Von Ryan's Express, The Sand Pebbles, Stagecoach, Fantastic Voyage, Our Man Flint, Batman (TV), Doctor Dolittle, In Like Flint, The Valentine's Day Massacre, The Detective, Star!, The Ghost and Mrs. Muir (TV), Daughter of the Mind (TV), Butch Cassidy and the Sundance Kid, Hello, Dolly!, The Flim Flam Man (TV), The Great White Hope, Myra Breckinridge, Beneath the Planet of the Apes, Beyond the Valley of the Dolls, Along Came A Spider (TV), The Mephisto Waltz, The Seven Minutes, The Marriage of a Young Stockbroker, Mr. and Mrs. Bo Jo Jones (TV), Fireball Forward (TV), The Towering Inferno, Making Love, Kiss Me Goodbye, Unfaithfully Yours, Rhinestone, Romancing The Stone, The Man With One Red Shoe, Project X, Die Hard, War of the Roses, Edward Scissorhands, Die Hard II, Rising Sun, Down Periscope, One Fine Day, Alien: Resurrection, Fight Club, Bedazzled, Dr. Dolittle 2, Firefly (TV), House M.D. (TV), Flightplan, War of the Worlds (Paramount), Shark (TV), Lie To Me (TV), Gang Related (TV), Ted 2, American Horror Story (TV)

STAGE SEVENTEEN:

The Time Tunnel (TV), The Sand Pebbles, Caprice, Doctor Dolittle, Judd for the Defense (TV), Julia (TV), A Guide for the Married Man, Land of the Giants (TV), The Flim Flam Man (TV), Bracken's World (TV), Escape From The Planet of the Apes, Cade's County, Topper Returns (TV), Going Places (Universal), Love Boat (TV), The Star Chamber, Trauma Center (TV), Cover Up (TV), Big Trouble in Little China, The Tracey Ullman Show (TV), True Colors (TV), Chicago Hope (TV) Doogie Howser, M.D. (TV), Picket Fences (TV), Judging Amy (TV), NYPD Blue (TV), How I Met Your Mother (TV), It's Always Sunny in Philadelphia (TV), Diary of a Wimpy Kid, The New Girl (TV), Cooper Barrett's Guide to Surviving Life (TV)

STAGE EIGHTEEN:

Way...Way Out, The Time Tunnel (TV), *Felony Squad* (TV), *Valley of the Dolls, Judd for the Defense* (TV), *The Sweet Ride, Land of the Giants* (TV), *Justine, M*A*S*H, Escape From The Planet of the Apes, The Star Chamber, Cover Up* (TV), *Big Trouble in Little China, Chicago Hope* (TV), *Doogie Howser, M.D.* (TV), *Picket Fences* (TV), *NYPD Blue* (TV), *Judging Amy* (TV), *The New Girl* (TV)

STAGE NINETEEN:

Way...Way Out, The Time Tunnel (TV), *Felony Squad* (TV), *Land of the Giants* (TV), *Julia* (TV), *Bracken's World* (TV), *Valley of the Dolls, Caprice, The Sweet Ride, Escape From The Planet of the Apes, The Star Chamber, Big Trouble in Little China, Black Widow (1954), Worth Winning, Chicago Hope* (TV), *Doogie Howser, M.D.* (TV), *Picket Fences* (TV), *NYPD Blue* (TV), *Judging Amy* (TV), *X-Men: First Class, New Girl* (TV).

STAGE TWENTY:

Doctor Dolittle, Bandolero, Planet of the Apes, The Sweet Ride, The Secret Life of an American Wife, Julia (TV), *Valley of the Dolls, Mr. and Mrs., Bo Jo Jones* (TV), *The Bears and I* (Disney), *Fatso, Dynasty* (TV), *The Star Chamber, The Buddy System, Predator 2, Civil Wars* (TV), *Dying Young, The Great White Hype, Two Guys, A Girl and a Pizza Place* (TV), *Reba* (TV), *Dads* (TV)

STAGE TWENTY-ONE:

The Time Tunnel (TV), *Doctor Dolittle, In Like Flint, The Secret Life of an American Wife, Star!, The Boston Strangler, The Planet of the Apes, Escape from the Planet of the Apes, Land of the Giants* (TV), *City Beneath The Sea* (TV), *Topper Returns* (TV), *At Long Last Love, Damnation Alley, The Other Side of Midnight, The Rose, The Star Chamber, Predator II, Dying Young, Picket Fences* (TV), *Jack the Bear, Rising Sun, South Central* (TV), *Anything But Love* (TV), *Dharma & Greg* (TV), *Knight and Day, Friends With Better Lives* (TV), *Ted 2, The Grinder* (TV)

STAGE TWENTY-TWO:

In Like Flint, Dr. Dolittle, Planet of the Apes, Star!, The Detective, Che!, Land of the Giants (TV), *City Beneath the Sea* (TV), *Conquest of the Planet of the Apes, At Long Last Love, Silent Movie, Damnation Alley, The Other Side of Midnight, 9 to 5, The Fall Guy* (TV), *Making Love, Have Faith* (TV), *Anything But Love* (TV), *South Central* (TV), *Dharma & Greg* (TV), *How I Met Your Mother* (TV), *The Goodwin Games* (TV), *The Grinder (TV)*

THE WESTWOOD STUDIO BACKLOT

ADANO SQUARE

A Bell for Adano
Carnival in Costa Rica
The Foxes of Harrow
I Was a Male War Bride
Wabash Avenue
The Day the Earth Stood Still
Lydia Bailey
With a Song in My Heart
5 Fingers
Diplomatic Courier
Les Miserables

Tonight We Sing
My Cousin Rachel
Destination Gobi
Call Me Madam
The Desert Rats
The Racers
Daddy Long Legs
House of Bamboo
The Rains of Ranchipur
The Man in the Gray Flannel Suit
Between Heaven and Hell
Boy on a Dolphin

The Young Lions
Fraulein
The Third Man (TV)
The Man Who Understood Women
Holiday for Lovers
Blue Angel
Adventures in Paradise (TV)
Five Fingers (TV)
Can-Can
Pirates of Tortuga

ALGERIAN STREET

Under Two Flags
Wee Willie Winkie
Ali Baba Goes to Town
Four Men and a Prayer
Suez
Mr. Moto's Last Warning
Submarine Patrol
Chasing Danger
The Jones Family in Hollywood
The Rains Came
Charlie Chan in Panama

Viva Cisco Kid
Chetniks!
Bomber's Moon
No Exceptions
Four Jills in a Jeep
The Keys of the Kingdom
Anna and the King of Siam
David and Bathsheba
Dreamboat
Destination Gobi
The Robe
Demetrius and the Gladiators
King of the Khyber Rifles
The Egyptian
Desiree
Soldier of Fortune
The Left Hand of God
The Rains of Ranchipur
D-Day the Sixth of June
Five Gates to Hell
Adventures in Paradise (TV)
Five Fingers (TV)
The Story of Ruth
One Foot in Hell
The Wizard of Baghdad

BERNADETTE STREET
The Song of Bernadette
The Keys of the Kingdom
Moss Rose
Forever Amber
Thunder in the Valley
The Ghost and Mrs. Muir
Dragonwyck
Cluny Brown
The Razor's Edge
That Lady in Ermine
The Iron Curtain
Thieves' Highway
When Willie Comes Marching Home
The Day the Earth Stood Still
Lydia Bailey

With a Song in My Heart
Les Miserables (1952)
What Price Glory (1952)
Treasure of the Golden Condor
Tonight We Sing
My Cousin Rachel
Prince Valiant
Desiree
The Man in the Gray Flannel Suit
D-Day the Sixth of June
Adventures in Paradise (TV)
Five Fingers (TV)
The Rookie
Snow White and the Three Stooges

CAFETERIA
International Settlement
Mr. Moto's Gamble
It Should Happen to You
Here I am a Stranger
The Honeymoon is Over
Free, Blonde, and 21
Four Sons (1940)
Youth Will Be Served
Scotland Yard
On the Sunny Side
A-Haunting We Will Go
Dr. Renault's Secret
Tonight We Raid Calais
Bomber's Moon
Laura
Johnny Comes Flying Home
Nightmare Alley
My Blue Heaven
Bernardine
The Marriage-Go-Round

CANAL, THE
The Farmer Takes a Wife (1935)
International Settlement
Thank You Mr. Moto
Mysterious Mr. Moto
Mr. Moto's Last Warning

Mr. Moto in Danger Island
The Rains Came

CHICAGO LAKE (including Old New York Harbor)
In Old Chicago
The Gorilla
Little Old New York
Chad Hanna
The Blue Bird
Johnny Apollo
Sailor's Lady
Hudson's Bay
Son of Fury
Scotland Yard
Dead Men Tell
The Cowboy and the Blonde
Man Hunt
To the Shores of Tripoli
The Loves of Edgar Allan Poe
Hello, Frisco, Hello
The Moon is Down
They Came to Blow Up America
Tampico
Lifeboat
Greenwich Village
The Keys of the Kingdom
Wing and a Prayer
Where Do We Go From Here?
A Bell for Adano
Captain from Castile
Nightmare Alley
Forever Amber
Deep Waters
Down to the Sea in Ships
Will James' Sand
Lydia Bailey
The Farmer Takes a Wife (1953)
Destination Gobi
The President's Lady
Pickup on South Street
Hell and High Water
Prince Valiant

Prince of Players
Soldier of Fortune
The Rains of Ranchipur
The Bottom of the Bottle
Between Heaven and Hell
Carousel
South Pacific
Adventures in Paradise (TV)
Pirates of Tortuga

CHICAGO STREET
In Old Chicago
Suez
Stanley and Livingstone
Island in the Sky
International Settlement
Thank You Mr. Moto
Change of Heart
Love on a Budget
Rascals
Kentucky Moonshine
Alexander's Ragtime Band
Mr. Moto's Gamble
Little Miss Broadway
Mysterious Mr. Moto
I'll Give a Million
Straight, Place, and Show
Submarine Patrol
Jesse James
The Little Princess
Pardon Our Nerve
Everybody's Baby
The Hound of the Baskervilles
Boy Friend
Young Mr. Lincoln
The Adventures of Sherlock Holmes
Swanee River
Johnny Apollo
Brigham Young
Lillian Russell
The Sailor's Lady
Public Deb No. 1
The Bride Wore Crutches

Michael Shayne, Private Detective
Tin Pan Alley
Western Union
Tall, Dark, and Handsome
Scotland Yard
Man Hunt
Belle Starr
A Yank in the R.A.F.
Lone Star Ranger
Marry the Boss's Daughter
Confirm or Deny
This Above All
Secret Agent of Japan
Hello, Frisco, Hello
Sweet Rosie O'Grady
Holy Matrimony
Paris After Dark
The Dancing Masters
Buffalo Bill
Pin-Up Girl
The Lodger
Wilson
Greenwich Village
In the Meantime, Darling
Irish Eyes are Smiling
Take It or Leave It
Laura
Something for the Boys
A Tree Grows in Brooklyn
Nob Hill
Billy Rose's Diamond Horseshoe
Somewhere in the Night
The Shocking Miss Pilgrim
The Dark Corner
I Wonder Who's Kissing Her Now
Mother Wore Tights
Moss Rose
The Ghost and Mrs. Muir
Give My Regards to Broadway
Call Northside 777
The Iron Curtain
When My Baby Smiles at Me
Chicken Every Sunday

You're My Everything
Where the Sidewalk Ends
Mister 880
With a Song in My Heart
Belles on Their Toes
Tonight We Sing
Stars and Stripes Forever
Night Without Sleep
Mr. Scoutmaster
There's No Business Like Show Business
Black Widow (1954)
Prince of Players
The Tall Men
Three Brave Men
The True Story of Jesse James
Will Success Spoil Rock Hunter?
The Third Man (TV)
Holiday for Lovers
The Young Jesse James

COLONIAL HOME, THE
Carolina
The Little Colonel
The Littlest Rebel
Battle of Broadway
Kentucky
Josette
Hold That Co-ed
Swanee River
Johnny Apollo
He Married His Wife
Rise and Shine
Michael Shayne, Private Detective
The Man Who Wouldn't Die
My Gal Sal
The Gang's All Here
The Loves of Edgar Allan Poe
The Dancing Masters
Roger Touhy, Gangster
Something for the Boys
Colonel Effingham's Raid
Shock

Three Little Girls in Blue
Somewhere in the Night
The Foxes of Harrow
Mother Wore Tights
Gentleman's Agreement
The Street With No Name
That Wonderful Urge
You're My Everything
Pinky
The Model and the Marriage Broker
Something for the Birds
Stars and Stripes Forever
The President's Lady
Inferno
Broken Lance
The Gambler from Natchez
Prince of Players
Daddy Long Legs
How to Be Very, Very Popular
The Girl in the Red Velvet Swing
The View from Pompey's Head
Between Heaven and Hell
Teenage Rebel
The Girl Can't Help It
Will Success Spoil Rock Hunter?
Perry Mason (TV)
Sing, Boy, Sing
The Sound and the Fury
Return of the Fly
The Alligator People
The Best of Everything
The Rookie
The Story on Page One
North to Alaska
Twelve Hours to Kill
High Time
Sanctuary
The Little Shepherd of Kingdom Come
Pirates of Tortuga

CYCLORAMA, THE
Second Honeymoon
Stanley and Livingston
Life Begins in College
International Settlement
Sally, Irene, and Mary
Kidnapped (1938)
Four Men and a Prayer
I'll Give a Million
Three Blind Mice
Gateway
The Hound of the Baskervilles
Susannah of the Mounties
Return of the Cisco Kid
The Rains Came
Pack Up Your Troubles
Little Old New York
The Grapes of Wrath
Brigham Young
Hudson's Bay
Western Union
Belle Starr
Wild Geese Calling
How Green Was My Valley
Swamp Water
Rise and Shine
My Gal Sal
Tales of Manhattan
Whispering Ghosts
The Pied Piper
The Black Swan
The Ox-Bow Incident
Crash Dive
The Undying Monster
Tonight We Raid Calais
They Came to Blow Up America
Bomber's Moon
Wintertime
Guadalcanal Diary
Buffalo Bill
Lifeboat
The Purple Heart
The Keys of the Kingdom

A Tree Grows in Brooklyn
Sunday Dinner for a Soldier
The Caribbean Mystery
Jungle Marines
Doll Face
Somewhere in the Night
The Homestretch
Daisy Kenyon
Road House
Down to the Sea in Ships
Slattery's Hurricane
Three Came Home
Wabash Avenue
Follow the Sun
David and Bathsheba
Down Among the Sheltering Palms
With a Song in My Heart
Fixed Bayonets
Les Miserables (1952)
Niagara
My Cousin Rachel
Mr. Scoutmaster
River of No Return
The Enemy Below
Journey to the Center of the Earth
(1959)

DUTCH MOAT, THE
Little Old New York
I Was an Adventuress
Tin Pan Alley
To the Shores of Tripoli
This Above All
Thunder Birds
China Girl
Manila Calling
Crash Dive
Tonight We Raid Calais
The Moon is Down
Tampico
The Sullivans
The Keys of the Kingdom
Wing and a Prayer

Three Little Girls in Blue
Deep Waters
Down to the Sea in Ships
Slattery's Hurricane
The Frogmen
The Desert Fox
Red Skies of Montana
Fixed Bayonets!
Diplomatic Courier
Deadline U.S.A.
Destination Gobi
Titanic (1953)
The Rains of Ranchipur
Stopover Tokyo
The Enemy Below
South Pacific
Adventures in Paradise (TV)
Journey to the Center of the Earth
(1959)
Wake Me When It's Over
The True Story of Jesse James
High Time
Snow White and the Three Stooges

FLIGHT DECK, THE
Wing and a Prayer
Dragonwyck
Three Little Girls in Blue
The Dark Corner
When Willie Comes Marching
Home
David and Bathsheba
Viva Zapata!
Diplomatic Courier
Dreamboat
Titanic (1953)
The Robe
Hell and High Water
Prince Valiant
The Left Hand of God
South Pacific
Fraulein

GREEN TANK
Hell and High Water
Prince Valiant
The Enemy Below

JUNGLE, THE
Passport to Hell
Danger—Love at Work
Mr. Moto Takes a Chance
Big Town Girl
City Girl (1938)
Change of Heart (1938)
Rascals
Mr. Moto's Gamble
Mysterious Mr. Moto
One Wild Night
Always in Trouble
Thanks for Everything
Mr. Moto in Danger Island
The Rains Came
Pack Up Your Troubles
Charlie Chan in Panama
Young People
Youth Will Be Served
Charter Pilot
Western Union
Ride Kelly Ride
Michael Shayne, Private Detective
Tall, Dark, and Handsome
Blood and Sand
Man Hunt
Man at Large
Swamp Water
Great Guns
Song of the Islands
Son of Fury
The Perfect Snob
Ten Gentlemen From West Point
Manila Calling
They'll Live Again
Bomber's Moon
Guadalcanal Diary
The Eve of St. Mark

The Caribbean Mystery
Jungle Marines
Wake Up and Dream
Anna and the King of Siam
The Foxes of Harrow
Three Came Home
I'll Get By
Lydia Bailey
Treasure of the Golden Condor
White Witch Doctor

KEYS OF THE KINGDOM SET
The Keys of the Kingdom
Thunder in the Valley
Forever Amber
Moss Rose
When Willie Comes Marching
Home
What Price Glory (1952)
My Cousin Rachel

KING FARM, THE
Way Down East (1935)
Rebecca of Sunnybrook Farm
(1938)
One Wild Night
Kentucky
Time Out for Murder
Down on the Farm
Winner Takes All
The Honeymoon is Over
The Man Who Wouldn't Talk
Maryland
Young People
The Brat
The Return of Frank James
Jennie
Golden Hoofs
Sleepers West
Young America (1942)
Remember the Day
Rise and Shine
Roxie Hart

Right to the Heart
Who is Hope Schuyler?
The Postman Didn't Ring
The Ox-Bow Incident
They'll Live Again
Bomber's Moon
Roger Touhy, Gangster
No Exceptions
The Eve of St. Mark
Ladies of Washington
Colonel Effingham's Raid
Captain Eddie
The Bullfighters
State Fair (1945)
Smoky (1946)
Three Little Girls in Blue
You're My Everything
Elopement
Return of the Texan
Lure of the Wilderness
O. Henry's Full House
The Farmer Takes a Wife (1953)
The President's Lady
City of Bad Men
The Prince of Players
Violent Saturday
The Tall Men
The Proud Ones
The True Story of Jesse James
Love Me Tender
The Wayward Bus
The Three Faces of Eve
Will Success Spoil Rock Hunter?
The Long, Hot Summer
The Fiend Who Walked the West
The Fiercest Heart
Sanctuary
The Little Shepherd from Kingdom Come

LOWER MOAT, THE
The River
The Sea Wolf

A Devil with Women
The Man Who Came Back
Shanghai Madness
She Learned About Sailors
Jesse James
Inside Story
The Rains Came
Moontide
He Hired His Boss
Lifeboat
The Lodger
Winged Victory
Where Do We Go From Here?
Captain Eddie
Do You Love Me
Sentimental Journey
Three Little Girls in Blue
Home Sweet Homicide
The Homestretch
The Foxes of Harrow
That Lady in Ermine
The Luck of the Irish
Road House
Down to the Sea in Ships
Three Came Home
Love That Brute
The Halls of Montezuma
The Frogmen
Titanic (1953)
Beneath the 12-Mile Reef
Hell and High Water
Miracle of the Hills
South Pacific
Journey to the Center of the Earth
(1959)
Adventures in Paradise (TV)
The Story of Ruth
The Wizard of Baghdad
Voyage to the Bottom of the Sea
Hemingway's Adventures of a
Young Man
The Time Tunnel (TV)
Caprice

Land of the Giants (TV)
The Towering Inferno

MIDWESTERN STREET
The County Chairman
One Wild Night
The Littlest Rebel
In Old Chicago
Wild and Woolly
Big Town Girl
International Settlement
Love on a Budget
Speed to Burn
Mysterious Mr. Moto
Submarine Patrol
Arizona Wildcat
Thanks for Everything
Jones Family in Hollywood
High School
The Story of Alexander Graham
Bell
Second Fiddle
Hollywood Cavalcade
Here I am a Stranger
Swanee River
The Grapes of Wrath
Young as You Feel
Shooting High
Star Dust
Lillian Russell
Public Deb No. 1
Street of Memories
The Return of Frank James
The Bride Wore Crutches
Youth Will Be Served
Chad Hanna
Tobacco Road
The Great American Broadcast
A Yank in the R.A.F.
Young America
Roxie Hart
This Above All
Moontide

Iceland
Berlin Correspondent
Little Tokyo, U.S.A.
The Meanest Man in the World
Holy Matrimony
The Dancing Masters
No Exceptions
The Lodger
The Sullivans
Wilson
Irish Eyes are Smiling
Sunday Dinner for a Soldier
Colonel Effingham's Raid
Circumstantial Evidence
Captain Eddie
The Dolly Sisters
Within These Walls
Canadian War Bond Rally
Strange Triangle
Leave Her to Heaven
Wake Up and Dream
Smoky (1946)
The Shocking Miss Pilgrim
Johnny Comes Flying Home
If I'm Lucky
Give My Regards to Broadway
You Were Meant for Me
The Walls of Jericho (1948)
Apartment for Peggy
Road House
Will James' Sand
Mother is a Freshman
Come to the Stable
Oh, You Beautiful Doll
It Happens Every Spring
Father was a Fullback
Dancing in the Dark
Love That Brute
When Willie Comes Marching
Home
The 13th Letter
Follow the Sun
Take Care of My Little Girl

The Guy Who Came Back
Mr. Belvedere Rings the Bell
The Pride of St. Louis
Wait Till the Sun Shines, Nellie
Belles On Their Toes
Return of the Texan
The Girl Next Door
O. Henry's Full House
We're Not Married
Stars and Stripes Forever
White Christmas (Paramount)
Broken Lance
Prince of Players
A Man Called Peter
Soldier of Fortune
Violent Saturday
House of Bamboo
Love is a Many-Splendored Thing
The View from Pompey's Head
The Rains of Ranchipur
The Lieutenant Wore Skirts
The Revolt of Mamie Stover
The True Story of Jesse James
Love Me Tender
The Wayward Bus
Bernardine
Ten North Frederick
Fraulein
The Hunters
The Remarkable Mr. Pennypacker
Rally 'Round the Flag, Boys!
Mardi Gras
Blue Denim
The Alligator People
Beloved Infidel
Adventures in Paradise (TV)
The 3rd Voice
From the Terrace
Twelve Hours to Kill
Sanctuary
Wild in the Country

NEW ENGLAND STREET AND SQUARE

Doctor Bull
Sailor's Luck
David Harum
Judge Priest
The County Chairman
Wild and Woolly
Danger - Love at Work
Life Begins in College
Rascals
Speed to Burn
My Lucky Star
Kentucky
Five of a Kind
Inside Story
Up the River (1938)
Thanks for Everything
The Story of Alexander Graham Bell
Second Fiddle
The Rains Came
Here I am a Stranger
Swanee River
The Man Who Wouldn't Talk
He Married His Wife
Young People
Public Deb No. 1
The Return of Frank James
Jennie
Golden Hoofs
Tobacco Road
A Very Young Lady
How Green Was My Valley
Remember the Day
Rise and Shine
Right to the Heart
Who is Hope Schuyler?
The Loves of Edgar Allan Poe
A-Haunting We Will Go
Orchestra Wives
The Man in the Trunk
That Other Woman

They'll Live Again
Jitterbugs
The Sullivans
Wilson
A Tree Grows in Brooklyn
Winged Victory
Colonel Effingham's Raid
Circumstantial Evidence
Captain Eddie
Don Juan Quilligan
Canadian War Bond Rally
Strange Triangle
Wake Up and Dream
Centennial Summer
The Shocking Miss Pilgrim
Johnny Comes Flying Home
Claudia and David
The Late George Apley
Scudda Hoo! Scudda Hay!
Give My Regards to Broadway
You Were Meant for Me
Fury at Furnace Creek
The Walls of Jericho (1948)
Sitting Pretty
The Iron Curtain
Apartment for Peggy
Down to the Sea in Ships
A Letter to Three Wives
Mr. Belvedere Goes to College
Thieves' Highway
Pinky
When Willie Comes Marching Home
Cheaper by the Dozen
No Way Out
Stella
Follow the Sun
Take Care of My Little Girl
The Guy Who Came Back
As Young as You Feel
Mr. Belvedere Rings the Bell
Elopement
Wait Till the Sun Shines, Nellie

Belles On Their Toes
O. Henry's Full House
We're Not Married
The Farmer Takes a Wife (1953)
My Wife's Best Friend
The President's Lady
Prince of Players
The View from Pompey's Head
Good Morning, Miss Dove
On the Threshold of Space
Hilda Crane
Bigger Than Life
Three Brave Men
The Way to the Gold
The Three Faces of Eve
Bernardine
Will Success Spoil Rock Hunter?
Peyton Place
The Young Lions
Fraulein
Sing, Boy, Sing
A Nice Little Bank That Should Be Robbed
The Remarkable Mr. Pennypacker
Rally 'Round the Flag, Boys!
The Sound and the Fury
Five Fingers (TV)
A Private's Affair
Compulsion
Blue Denim
High Time
Twelve Hours to Kill
Sanctuary
Return to Peyton Place
The Little Shepherd of Kingdom Come
Wild in the Country
Hemingway's Adventures of a Young Man

"NEW" NEW YORK STREET

Chicken Wagon Family
Hotel for Women

Here I Am a Stranger
Charlie Chan in City of Darkness
Tall, Dark, and Handsome
I Wake Up Screaming
Rise and Shine
Who is Hope Schuyler?
Just Off Broadway
The Meanest Man in the World
Take It or Leave It
Laura
Billy Rose's Diamond Horseshoe
Where Do We Go From Here?
Don Juan Quilligan
Junior Miss
Do You Love Me
Sentimental Journey
Shock
The Dark Corner
It Shouldn't Happen to a Dog
Claudia and David
Daisy Kenyon
Call Northside 777
The Snake Pit
Cry of the City
When My Baby Smiles at Me
That Wonderful Urge
You're My Everything
Oh, You Beautiful Doll
House of Strangers
It Happens Every Spring
Mother Didn't Tell Me
Cheaper by the Dozen
My Blue Heaven
I'll Get By
Stella
Call Me Mister
Meet Me After the Show
The Day the Earth Stood Still
People Will Talk
Phone Call from a Stranger
Dreamboat
Bloodhounds of Broadway
My Wife's Best Friend

Night Without Sleep
Taxi
Pickup on South Street
Mr. Scoutmaster
The Girl Can't Help It
Oh, Men! Oh, Women!
Desk Set
An Affair to Remember
Will Success Spoil Rock Hunter?
Perry Mason (TV)
Sing, Boy, Sing
A Nice Little Bank That Should Be
Robbed
The Best of Everything
Five Fingers (TV)
The Third Man (TV)
From the Terrace
Twelve Hours to Kill
Swingin' Along
Madison Avenue

NURSERY, THE
Will Success Spoil Rock Hunter?
Twelve Hours to Kill

OLD FRENCH STREET AND SQUARE
6 Hours to Live
Zoo in Budapest
Thunder in the Night
Seventh Heaven (1937)
Charlie Chan at Monte Carlo
International Settlement
Thank You Mr. Moto
Josette
Kidnapped (1938)
Four Men and a Prayer
A Trip to Paris
Always Goodbye
Mysterious Mr. Moto
I'll Give a Million
Suez
Sharpshooters

Mr. Moto Takes a Vacation
The Three Musketeers
Chasing Danger
The Adventures of Sherlock Holmes
Pack Up Your Troubles
Charlie Chan in City of Darkness
Johnny Apollo
The Man Who Wouldn't Talk
I was an Adventuress
Earthbound
Four Sons (1940)
The Man I Married
Tin Pan Alley
Scotland Yard
Man Hunt
Son of Fury
Secret Agent of Japan
The Pied Piper
China Girl
Dr. Renault's Secret
Chetniks!
Tonight We Raid Calais
They Came to Blow Up America
Jane Eyre
Heaven Can Wait
Bomber's Moon
Paris After Dark
The Dancing Masters
Wilson
Sweet and Low-Down
The Caribbean Mystery
The Dolly Sisters
Forever Amber
A Man Called Peter
The Virgin Queen
The Story of Ruth
Snow White and the Three Stooges

OLD NEW YORK STREET
Bad Girl
Skyline
Disorderly Conduct
Down to Earth

Handle with Care
Week Ends Only
Face in the Sky
Hello, Sister!
Hold Me Tight
Bad Boy
Ginger
Paddy O'Day
One Mile From Heaven
This is My Affair
Danger - Love at Work
Charlie Chan on Broadway
45 Fathers
Big Town Girl
Island in the Sky
Love and Hisses
Sally, Irene, and Mary
Thank You Mr. Moto
City Girl (1938)
Walking Down Broadway
Kentucky Moonshine
Mr. Moto's Gamble
Battle of Broadway
Speed to Burn
Always Goodbye
One Wild Night
Passport Husband
Straight, Place and Show
Time Out for Murder
Five of a Kind
Road Demon
While New York Sleeps
Inside Story
Mr. Moto Takes a Vacation
Up the River
Pardon Our Nerve
Thanks for Everything
The Jones Family in Hollywood
The Rose of Washington Square
Chicken Wagon Family
Hollywood Cavalcade
Here I am a Stranger
Swanee River

Lillian Russell
Marriage in Transit
Public Deb No. 1
The Brat
Street of Memories
Jennie
Tin Pan Alley
Tall, Dark, and Handsome
Murder Among Friends
The Great American Broadcast
Man Hunt
Accent on Love
Private Nurse
Marry the Boss's Daughter
I Wake Up Screaming
My Gal Sal
Roxie Hart
Tales of Manhattan
A Gentleman at Heart
Rings on Her Fingers
Thunder Birds
The Magnificent Dope
It Happened in Flatbush
Footlight Serenade
Orchestra Wives
Just Off Broadway
Berlin Correspondent
Careful, Soft Shoulders
Little Tokyo, U.S.A
He Hired His Boss
The Meanest Man in the World
Life Begins at 8:30
They'll Live Again
Time to Kill
Dixie Dugan
They Came to Blow Up America
Coney Island
Stormy Weather
Heaven Can Wait (1943)
Sweet Rosie O'Grady
Roger Touhy, Gangster
The Gang's All Here
Paris After Dark

The Dancing Masters
The Eve of St. Mark
Wilson
Greenwich Village
Sweet and Low-Down
Irish Eyes are Smiling
Take It or Leave It
A Tree Grows in Brooklyn
Nob Hill
Circumstantial Evidence
Captain Eddie
The Dolly Sisters
Dragonwyck
Don Juan Quilligan
Fallen Angel
Smoky (1946)
Doll Face
Sentimental Journey
Behind Green Lights
Somewhere in the Night
The Shocking Miss Pilgrim
The Dark Corner
It Shouldn't Happen to a Dog
Claudia and David
If I'm Lucky
The Late George Apley
The Home Stretch
The Brasher Doubloon
I Wonder Who's Kissing Her Now
Call Northside 777
The Street With No Name
The Luck of the Irish
Cry of the City
When My Baby Smiles at Me
Oh, You Beautiful Doll
House of Strangers
Wabash Avenue
Love That Brute
Cheaper by the Dozen
No Way Out
Where the Sidewalk Ends
I'll Get By
Mister 880

I Can Get It for You Wholesale
The Guy Who Came Back
The Day the Earth Stood Still
Love Nest
The Model and the Marriage Broker
The Pride of St. Louis
Belles on Their Toes
The I Don't Care Girl
O. Henry's Full House
The Snows of Kilimanjaro
Dreamboat
Bloodhounds of Broadway
Tonight We Sing
Pickup on South Street
Vicki
The Kid from Left Field
Mr. Scoutmaster
Black Widow (1954)
Prince of Players
How to be Very, Very Popular
The Girl in the Red Velvet Swing
The Lieutenant Wore Skirts
The Best Things in Life are Free
The Girl Can't Help It
An Affair to Remember
The Young Lions
Fraulein
A Private's Affair
Journey to the Center of the Earth (1959)
Beloved Infidel
The Many Loves of Dobie Gillis (TV)
The Third Man (TV)
Wake Me When It's Over
Let's Make Love
North to Alaska
Swingin' Along
The Right Approach
The Second Time Around
Bus Stop (TV)
Hemingway's Adventures of a Young Man

PERMANENT GARDENS, THE
Down to Earth
6 Hours to Live
Sherlock Holmes (1932)
Second Hand Wife
Zoo in Budapest
She Was a Lady
Walls of Gold
Servants' Entrance
The Lottery Lover
Professional Soldier
One Mile From Heaven
Girls' Dormitory
Wild and Woolly
The Baroness and the Butler
Danger—Love at Work
45 Fathers
Charlie Chan at Monte Carlo
Walking Down Broadway
One Wild Night
Straight, Place and Show
Mr. Moto's Last Warning
Sharpshooters
Mr. Moto Takes a Vacation
Pardon Our Nerve
Mr. Moto in Danger Island
The Jones Family in Hollywood
The Rains Came
Hollywood Cavalcade
Here I am a Stranger
He Married His Wife
I was an Adventuress
Maryland
The Brat
Charley's Aunt
Swamp Water
I Wake Up Screaming
Son of Fury
Tales of Manhattan
Moontide
The Mad Martindales
Ten Gentlemen from West Point
Who is Hope Schuyler?

Springtime in the Rockies
That Other Woman
The Meanest Man in the World
Crash Dive
Dr. Renault's Secret
Bomber's Moon
The Gang's All Here
The Dancing Masters
No Exceptions
Home in Indiana
Wilson
The Big Noise
Nob Hill
Billy Rose's Diamond Horseshoe
The Caribbean Mystery
Do You Love Me
Anna and the King of Siam
Three Little Girls in Blue
The Homestretch
Forever Amber
Mother Wore Tights
Moss Rose
The Foxes of Harrow
Apartment for Peggy
Will James' Sand
The Fan
Oh, You Beautiful Doll
Call Me Mister
Half Angel (1951)
Bird of Paradise (1951)
House on Telegraph Hill
Take Care of My Little Girl
Lydia Bailey
Phone Call From a Stranger
Lure of the Wilderness
The Girl Next Door
Les Miserables (1952)
Stars and Stripes Forever
My Wife's Best Friend
My Cousin Rachel
Prince Valiant
Desiree
Untamed

The Racers
A Man Called Peter
The Girl in the Red Velvet Swing
The View from Pompey's Head
Between Heaven and Hell
Teenage Rebel
The True Story of Jesse James
The Way to the Gold
Peyton Place
The Hunters
The Fly (1958)
The Remarkable Mr. Pennypacker
The Sound and the Fury
Say One for Me
The Return of the Fly
The Alligator People
The Best of Everything
Journey to the Center of the Earth
(1959)
Adventures in Paradise (TV)
Five Fingers (TV)
The Third Man (TV)
Twelve Hours to Kill
High Time
The Marriage-Go-Round
Swingin' Along
Sanctuary
The Right Approach
Wild in the Country

RAILROAD STATION, THE
One in a Million
Thin Ice
Four Men and a Prayer
Everything Happens at Night
Four Sons (1940)
This Above All
Orchestra Wives
Immortal Sergeant
In the Meantime, Darling
Wintertime
The Keys of the Kingdom
Buffalo Bill

SERSEN LAKE
Crash Dive
Tonight We Raid Calais
Tampico
Lifeboat
Wing and a Prayer
The Big Noise
Winged Victory
Billy Rose's Diamond Horseshoe
Where Do We Go From Here?
Captain Eddie
Dragonwyck
Anna and the King of Siam
Three Little Girls in Blue
The Razor's Edge (1946)
The Foxes of Harrow
Deep Waters
Down to the Sea in Ships
Slattery's Hurricane
Dancing in the Dark
Cheaper by the Dozen (1950)
Meet Me After the Show
Down Among the Sheltering Palms
Anne of the Indies
The Desert Fox
Red Skies of Montana
Elopement
Phone Call from a Stranger
Niagara
Destination Gobi
Titanic (1953)
The Robe
Gentlemen Prefer Blondes
Sailor of the King
Hell and High Water
River of No Return
Desiree
Untamed
The Racers
The Virgin Queen
Love is a Many-Splendored Thing
The Seven Cities of Gold
The Rains of Ranchipur

The King and I
The Man in the Gray Flannel Suit
The Revolt of Mamie Stover
Kiss Them for Me
D-Day the Sixth of June
A Hatful of Rain
The Enemy Below
Rally 'Round the Flag, Boys!
South Pacific
Journey to the Center of the Earth
(1959)
Adventures in Paradise (TV)
High Time
The Wizard of Baghdad
The Voyage to the Bottom of the
Sea
Snow White and the Three Stooges

SLAVE MARKET AND TEMPLE SET
The Robe
The Egyptian
Desiree
The Rains of Ranchipur
The King and I
The Fiend Who Walked the West
Five Fingers (TV)
The Fiercest Heart
The Fiercest Heart

SLIGON CASTLE
Prince Valiant
The Egyptian
The Virgin Queen
The Left Hand of God
Peyton Place
Adventures in Paradise (TV)
The Wizard of Baghdad
Francis of Assisi
Snow White and the Three Stooges

SPANISH STREET
Four Men and a Prayer

Mr. Moto's Last Warning
Submarine Patrol
Chasing Danger
Mr. Moto in Danger Island

Charlie Chan in Panama
Charter Pilot
Blood and Sand
Secret Agent of Japan

The Black Swan
China Girl
Tampico
The Robe

The Rains of Ranchipur

STAGE A:

Wild and Woolly, Ali Baba Goes to Town, Rebecca of Sunnybrook Farm, Big Town Girl, Charlie Chan at Monte Carlo, Happy Landing, Thank You, Mr. Moto, City Girl, Rascals, Kentucky Moonshine, Kidnapped, Four Men and a Prayer, Speed to Burn, Always Goodbye, Mysterious Mr. Moto, One Wild Night, I'll Give A Million, Just Around The Corner, My Lucky Star, Gateway, Straight Place and Show, Mr. Moto's Last Warning, Hold That Co-Ed, Sharpshooters, A Very Practical Joke, Mr. Moto Takes A Vacation, Pardon Our Nerve, Thanks For Everything, Winner Take All, The Hound of the Baskervilles, The Story of Alexander Graham Bell, Charlie Chan In Reno, News Is Made At Night, It Could Happen to You, Stop, Look and Love, Hollywood Cavalcade, Here I Am A Stranger, Pack Up Your Troubles, Charlie Chan in City of Darkness, The Honeymoon is Over, The Man Who Wouldn't Talk, The Cisco Kid and the Lady, Brigham Young, Shooting High, Earthbound, Sailor's Lady, On Their Own, Lucky Cisco Kid, Four Sons, For Beauty's Sake, Charter Pilot, Tin Pan Alley, Michael Shayne: Private Detective, Murder Among Friends, Scotland Yard, Great American Broadcast, Accent on Love, Dressed to Kill, Private Nurse, Wild Geese Calling, Lone Star Ranger, Great Guns, Young America, On The Sunny Side, Right to the Heart, Rings on Her Fingers, Moontide, It Happened in Flatbush, Thru Different Eyes, Berlin Correspondent, The Ox-Bow Incident, My Friend Flicka, Over My Dead Body, Tonight We Raid Calais, Time to Kill, Dixie Dugan, Coney Island, Jane Eyre, Stormy Weather, Immortal Sergeant, Heaven Can Wait, Bomber's Moon, The Gang's All Here, Guadalcanal Diary, The Dancing Masters, Buffalo Bill, The Sullivans, The Eve of St. Mark, Home in Indiana, Greenwich Village, In The Meantime, Darling, Bermuda Mystery, Irish Eyes Are Smiling, The Big Noise, O.W.I Gasoline Short Subject, Something for the Boys, Where Do We Go From Here?, Circumstantial Evidence, Captain Eddie, State Fair, Don Juan Quilligan, Sentimental Journey, Shock, Three Little Girls in Blue, Carnival in Costa Rica, The Razor's Edge, Home Sweet Homicide, The Brasher Doubloon, Captain From Castile, Give My Regards to Broadway, Deep Waters, Cry of the City, Slattery's Hurricane, Dancing in the Dark, Halls of Montezuma, Half Angel, Bird of Paradise, You're in the Navy Now, The Frogmen, The Day The Earth Stood Still, Fixed Bayonets, Les Miserables, The Snows of Kilimanjaro, Treasure of the Golden Condor, Pony Soldier, Niagara, White Witch Doctor, The Glory Brigade, Titanic, Pickup on South Street, The Desert Rats, Hell and High Water,

Desiree, Untamed, A Man Called Peter, Soldier of Fortune, The Virgin Queen, The Left Hand of God, The Girl in the Red Velvet Swing, On The Threshold of Space, The King and I, The Revolt of Mamie Stover, Boy on a Dolphin, The Gift of Love, The Roots of Heaven, Journey To The Center Of The Earth, The Third Man (TV)

STAGE B:

In Old Chicago, Danger—Love at Work, Life Begins in College, Big Town Girl, Island in the Sky, Love and Hisses, Sally, Irene and Mary, Thank You, Mr. Moto, Checkers, City Girl, Change of Heart, Rascals, Kentucky Moonshine, Kidnapped, Mr. Moto's Gamble, Speed to Burn, One Wild Night, My Lucky Star, Gateway, Suez, Passport Husband, Straight Place and Show, Mr. Moto's Last Warning, Five of a Kind, Always in Trouble, Sharpshooters, Up The River, Pardon Our Nerve, Thanks For Everything, Chasing Danger, Mr. Moto in Danger Island, Winner Take All, The Hound of the Baskervilles, News Is Made At Night, It Could Happen To You, Hollywood Cavalcade, Pack Up Your Troubles, Charlie Chan in City of Darkness, The Cisco Kid and the Lady, Charlie Chan in Panama, Shooting High, I Was An Adventuress, Viva Cisco Kid, Maryland, Lucky Cisco Kid, Street of Memories, The Man I Married, The Gay Caballero, Charter Pilot, Jennie, Scotland Yard, Romance on the Rio Grande, Ride Kelly Ride, Great American Broadcast, Sun Valley Serenade, Private Nurse, Wild Geese Calling, Lone Star Ranger, Man At Large, Cadet Girl, Great Guns, The Perfect Snob, Right to the Heart, To The Shores of Tripoli, Moontide, Thunder Birds, The Loves of Edgar Allan Poe, Berlin Correspondent, China Girl, That Other Woman, The Ox-Bow Incident, Dr. Renault's Secret, Over My Dead Body, Tonight We Raid Calais, Chetniks, Immortal Sergeant, They Came To Blow Up America, Jane Eyre, Stormy Weather, Bomber's Moon, Jitterbugs, Roger Touhy, Gangster, Guadalcanal Diary, Pin-Up Girl, Happy Land, The Eve of St. Mark, The Night Is Ending, Home in Indiana , Four Jills in A Jeep, In the Meantime, Darling, A Wing and a Prayer, The Big Noise, Something for the Boys, Circumstantial Evidence, The Caribbean Mystery, The Bullfighters, Strange Triangle, Doll Face, Behind Green Lights, Somewhere in the Night, Johnny Comes Flying Home, The Dark Corner, It Shouldn't Happen to A Dog, Home Sweet Homicide, If I'm Lucky, 13 Rue Madeleine, The Homestretch, Moss Rose, Miracle on 34th Street, Scudda Hoo! Scudda Hay!, Give My Regards To Broadway, Green Grass of Wyoming, The Walls of Jericho, Apartment For

Peggy, That Wonderful Urge, Chicken Every Sunday, Wabash Avenue, Halls of Montezuma, Follow the Sun, The Day the Earth Stood Still, Lydia Bailey, Red Skies of Montana, Wait Till the Sun Shines Nellie, Phone Call from A Stranger, Diplomatic Courier, The I Don't Care Girl, What Price Glory?, Treasure of the Golden Condor, Stars and Stripes Forever, Bloodhounds Of Broadway, My Wife's Best Friend, Night Without Sleep, Something For the Birds, My Pal Gus, Powder River, The President's Lady, The Glory Brigade, The Robe, Desert Rats, Hell and High Water, Three Coins In The Fountain, The Egyptian, Broken Lance, Black Widow (1954), Violent Saturday, How To Be Very, Very Popular, The Girl in the Red Velvet Swing, Rains of Ranchipur, The Man In The Gray Flannel Suit, The Proud Ones, Hilda Crane, The Last Wagon, Fraulein, The True Story of Jesse James, The Wayward Bus, An Affair to Remember, The Enemy Below, Sing Boy Sing, From Hell to Texas, The Bravados, A Nice Little Bank That Should Be Robbed, The Fiend Who Walked The West, These Thousand Hills, One Foot in Hell, Flaming Star, The Sad Horse, Adventures in Paradise (TV), The Many Loves of Dobie Gillis (TV), Five Fingers (TV), Return of the Fly, Twelve Hours to Kill, Story on Page One, Wild in the Country, Wake Me When It's Over, All Hands on Deck, Voyage to the Bottom of the Sea (TV), Our Man Flint, The Time Tunnel (TV), Land of the Giants (TV), Arnie (TV), Tora! Tora! Tora!, City Beneath the Sea (TV), They Call It Murder (TV), The Towering Inferno

STOCKADE, THE
Susannah of the Mounties
Hudson's Bay
Berlin Correspondent
I Was a Male War Bride
On the Riviera
Pony Soldier
The President's Lady
The Oregon Trail

SUBURBAN STREET
High School
It Could Happen to You
Quick Millions
Stop, Look, and Love
Too Busy to Work
The Honeymoon is Over
The Man Who Wouldn't Talk
Young as You Feel
Sailor's Lady
On Their Own
Small Town Deb
Great Guns
Remember the Day
Rise and Shine
The Perfect Snob
Roxie Hart
On the Sunny Side
A-Haunting We Will Go
Thru Different Eyes
The Man in the Trunk

They'll Live Again
Over My Dead Body
Time to Kill
Dixie Dugan
The Dancing Masters
Circumstantial Evidence
No Exceptions
Jungle Marines
The Embezzler
Strange Triangle
Somewhere in the Night
Johnny Comes Flying Home
Margie
Give My Regards to Broadway
Sitting Pretty
Mother is a Freshman
Father was a Fullback
Mother Didn't Tell Me
Whirlpool
When Willie Comes Marching Home
The Jackpot
Half Angel (1951)
Follow the Sun
As Young as You Feel
Red Skies of Montana
Elopement
The Pride of St. Louis
Phone Call from a Stranger
The Girl Next Door
Dreamboat
Monkey Business

My Pal Gus
Mr. Scoutmaster
There's No Business Like Show Business
A Man Called Peter
Good Morning, Miss Dove
The Man in the Gray Flannel Suit
Hilda Crane
Bigger than Life
The Way to the Gold
Bernardine
Will Success Spoil Rock Hunter?
The Gift of Love
A Nice Little Bank That Should Be Robbed
A Private's Affair
Twelve Hours to Kill
Rally 'Round The Flag, Boys!
High Time
All Hand's on Deck
Return to Peyton Place

TOMBSTONE STREET
Return of the Cisco Kid
Frontier Marshall
Heaven with a Barbed Wire Fence
The Cisco Kid and the Lady
Viva Cisco Kid
Lucky Cisco Kid
The Return of Frank James
The Gay Caballero

Western Union
Castle in the Desert
Sundown Jim
The Ox-Bow Incident
My Darling Clementine
Yellow Sky
Fury at Furnace Creek
Broken Arrow
The Gunfighter
Golden Girl
The Outcasts of Poker Flat
Powder River
The Silver Whip
City of Bad Men
River of No Return
The Tall Men
The Proud Ones
Man Without a Gun (TV)
The True Story of Jesse James
The Gift of Love
The Fiend Who Walked the West
These Thousand Hills
Warlock
Miracle of the Hills
The Oregon Trail
Young Jesse James
One Foot in Hell
North to Alaska
The Second Time Around
Bachelor Flat
The Comancheros

TRAIN SHED, THE

The Razor's Edge (1946)
If I'm Lucky
The Brasher Doubloon
I Wonder Who's Kissing Her Now
Mother Wore Tights
Nightmare Alley
Miracle on 34th Street (1947)
The Walls of Jericho (1948)
The Iron Curtain
The Luck of the Irish
Cry of the City
When My Baby Smiles at Me
That Wonderful Urge
Will James' Sand
Slattery's Hurricane
It Happens Every Spring
Three Came Home
Twelve O'Clock High
Wabash Avenue
Love That Brute
When Willie Comes Marching Home
A Ticket to Tomahawk
Under My Skin
Where the Sidewalk Ends
Stella
The Jackpot
Half Angel (1951)
On the Riviera
House on Telegraph Hill
I Can Get It for You Wholesale
The Frogmen
As Young As You Feel
Anne of the Indies
The Desert Fox
The Day the Earth Stood Still
Lydia Bailey
Viva Zapata!
With A Song in My Heart
Red Skies of Montana
5 Fingers
Diplomatic Courier

The Girl Next Door
Deadline U.S.A.
O. Henry's Full House
We're Not Married
Dreamboat
Pony Soldier
Stars and Stripes Forever
Something for the Birds
Powder River
My Cousin Rachel
Pickup on South Street
The Robe
Gentlemen Prefer Blondes
Dangerous Crossing
Beneath the 12-Mile Reef
Inferno
How to Marry a Millionaire
Vicki
The Kid from Left Field
Hell and High Water
Demetrius and the Gladiators
Desiree
There's No Business Like Show Business
The Racers
A Man Called Peter
Violent Saturday
How to Be Very, Very Popular
Love is a Many-Splendored Thing
The Rains of Ranchipur
The Man in the Gray Flannel Suit
The Revolt of Mamie Stover
D-Day the Sixth of June
Between Heaven and Hell
The True Story of Jesse James
Love Me Tender
The Wayward Bus
Bernardine
Will Success Spoil Rock Hunter?
Kiss Them for Me
The Enemy Below
South Pacific
Fraulein

Sing, Boy, Sing
The Remarkable Mr. Pennypacker
A Woman Obsessed
The Oregon Trail
Beloved Infidel
Hound-Dog Man
Adventures in Paradise (TV)
Five Fingers (TV)
Seven Thieves
From the Terrace
Twelve Hours to Kill
Swingin' Along
Voyage to the Bottom of the Sea
The Second Time Around
Wild in the Country

TYROLEAN STREET

Caravan
Music in the Air
Heidi
Happy Landing
Keep Smiling
The Three Musketeers (1938)
Everything Happens at Night
Pack Up Your Troubles
The Blue Bird
Four Sons
Chetniks!
Bomber's Moon

WASHINGTON SQUARE

Rose of Washington Square
The Story of Alexander Graham Bell
The Adventures of Sherlock Holmes
Little Old New York
Lillian Russell
Elsa Maxwell's Public Deb No. 1
The Man I Married
A Yank in the R.A.F.
I Wake Up Screaming
The Magnificent Dope
The Meanest Man in the World

That Other Woman
The Loves of Edgar Allan Poe
Holy Matrimony
Roger Touhy, Gangster
Immortal Sergeant
Ladies of Washington
The Lodger
Hangover Square
Laura
Molly and Me
The Shocking Miss Pilgrim
Cluny Brown
The Late George Apley
Forever Amber
Mother Wore Tights
The Ghost and Mrs. Muir
Daisy Kenyon
Cry of the City
That Wonderful Urge
You're My Everything
The Fan
Love That Brute
My Blue Heaven
Take Care of My Little Girl
The Day the Earth Stood Still
Love Nest
Stars and Stripes Forever
Something for the Birds
Prince of Players
The Girl in the Red Velvet Swing
23 Paces to Baker Street
D-Day the Sixth of June
The Best Things in Life are Free
Desk Set
Will Success Spoil Rock Hunter?
The Young Lions
Ten North Frederick
The Remarkable Mr. Pennypacker
Mardi Gras
Compulsion
The Man Who Understood Women
Holiday for Lovers
A Private's Affair

Twelve Hours to Kill
The Little Shepherd of Kingdom
Come
Madison Avenue
Return to Peyton Place

WATERWAYS, THE
The Lure of the Wilderness
The Farmer Takes a Wife (1953)
Stars and Stripes Forever
White Witch Doctor
The President's Lady
Prince Valiant
River of No Return
The Egyptian
The Racers
Prince of Players
The Seven Year Itch
Daddy Long Legs
House of Bamboo
The Virgin Queen
The Left Hand of God
The Tall Men
The View from Pompey's Head
The Rains of Ranchipur
Carousel
The Lieutenant Wore Skirts
The King and I
The Bottom of the Bottle
The Revolt of Mamie Stover
Between Heaven and Hell
Love Me Tender
The True Story of Jesse James
The Way to the Gold
The Wayward Bus
The Three Faces of Eve
Bernardine
Will Success Spoil Rock Hunter?
Three Brave Men
Peyton Place
The Young Lions
The Gift of Love
South Pacific

The Long, Hot Summer
The Fiend Who Walked the West
Rally 'Round the Flag, Boys!
The Alligator People
Compulsion
The Rookie
The Sound and the Fury
Adventures in Paradise (TV)
The Third Man (TV)
The Remarkable Mr. Pennypacker
The Man Who Understood Women
Woman Obsessed
A Private's Affair
Holiday for Lovers
The Oregon Trail
Five Gates to Hell
From the Terrace
Wake Me When It's Over
Wild River
The Story of Ruth
One Foot in Hell
The Wizard of Baghdad
Flaming Star
High Time
The Marriage-Go-Round
The Fiercest Heart
Wild in the Country
Sanctuary
The Right Approach
The Little Shepherd from Kingdom
Come
The Pirates of Tortuga
Madison Avenue

WHEELER PARK
The Remarkable Mr. Pennypacker
Woman Obsessed
A Private's Affair
The Oregon Trail
The Rookie
The Young Jesse James
From the Terrace
High Time

The Fiercest Heart
Snow White and the Three Stooges

WHITECHAPEL STREET
The Lodger
Irish Eyes are Smiling
Nob Hill
The Dolly Sisters
Do You Love Me?
Fallen Angel
Give Me the Simple Life
The Spider
Three Little Girls in Blue
The Shocking Miss Pilgrim
The Dark Corner
The Razor's Edge
The Brasher Doubloon
I Wonder Who's Kissing Her Now
Moss Rose
That Lady in Ermine
Diplomatic Courier
Violent Saturday
How to be Very, Very, Popular
The Girl in the Red Velvet Swing
D-Day the Sixth of June
Fraulein
Compulsion
Five Fingers (TV)
The Third Man (TV)
The Pirates of Tortuga

THE CENTURY RANCH
Chicken Wagon Family
Chad Hanna
How Green Was My Valley
The Moon is Down
The Keys of the Kingdom
Thunderhead, Son of Flicka
Claudia and David
Thunder in the Valley
Scudda Hoo! Scudda Hay!
The Luck of the Irish
Come to the Stable

The Gunfighter
My Blue Heaven
Stella
Two Flags West
The Secret of Convict Lake
Lydia Bailey
People Will Talk
Golden Girl
Viva Zapata!
The Pride of St. Louis
Return of the Texan
The Outcasts of Poker Flat
What Price Glory?
The Farmer Takes a Wife
Bloodhounds of Broadway
White Witch Doctor
General Electric Theater (TV)
The President's Lady
The Silver Whip
The Robe
Mr. Scoutmaster
Prince Valiant
Broken Lance
Untamed
Prince of Players
The Seven Year Itch
My Friend Flicka (TV)
Violent Saturday
The Virgin Queen
Love is a Many-Splendored Thing
The Left Hand of God
The Tall Men
The Seven Cities of Gold
The Rains of Ranchipur
Carousel
The Bottom of the Bottle
The Man in the Gray Flannel Suit
D-Day, the Sixth of June
The Proud Ones
Between Heaven and Hell
Love Me Tender
Perry Mason (TV)
Man Without A Gun (TV)

The True Story of Jesse James
The Way to the Gold
The Wayward Bus
April Love
The Bravados
The Hunters
South Pacific
In Love and War
The Remarkable Mr. Pennypacker
The Man Who Understood Women
Blue Denim
These Thousand Hills
Five Gates to Hell
Adventures in Paradise (TV)
Hound-Dog Man

From the Terrace
Hong Kong (TV)
Flaming Star
Wake Me When It's Over
Young Jesse James
Snow White and the Three Stooges
Sanctuary
Wild in the Country
The Second Time Around
Five Weeks in a Balloon
Mr. Hobbs Takes a Vacation
Hemingway's Adventures of a
Young Man
Voyage to the Bottom of the Sea
(TV)

Daniel Boone (TV)
Valentine's Day (TV)
Rio Conchos
The Sand Pebbles
Stagecoach
Batman (TV)
Our Man Flint
The Time Tunnel (TV)
The Monroes (TV)
Judd for the Defense (TV)
Custer (TV)
The Planet of the Apes
Lancer (TV)
Butch Cassidy and the Sundance
Kid

Che
M*A*S*H
Tora! Tora! Tora!
The Challenge (TV)
Beneath the Planet of the Apes
M*A*S*H (TV)
The Rookies (TV)
The Towering Inferno
The Planet of the Apes (TV)
The Swiss Family Robinson (TV)
Charlie's Angels (TV)
Dynasty (TV)
Beverly Hills 90210 (TV)

FOX BY THE NUMBERS PART THREE:
THE STUDIO FILMOGRAPHY

FILM	STUDIO	RELEASE YEAR
LIFE'S SHOP WINDOW	WF	1914
WALLS OF JERICHO, THE	WF	1914
THIEF, THE	WF	1914
IDLER, THE	WF	1914
SAMSON	WF	1915
FOOL THERE WAS, A	WF	1915
GIRL I LEFT BEHIND ME , THE	WF	1915
GILDED FOOL, A	WF	1915
CELEBRATED SCANDAL, THE	WF	1915
CHILDREN OF THE GHETTO	WF	1915
KREUTZER SONATA	WF	1915
NIGGER, THE	WF	1915
FROM THE VALLEY OF THE MISSING	WF	1915
ANNA KARENINA	WF	1915
CLEMENCEAU CASE, THE	WF	1915
PRINCESS ROMANOFF	WF	1915

FILM	STUDIO	RELEASE YEAR
WOMAN'S RESURRECTION, A	WF	1915
PLUNDERER, THE	WF	1915
WORMWOOD	WF	1915
DEVIL'S DAUGHTER, THE	WF	1915
SHOULD A MOTHER TELL?	WF	1915
DR. RAMEAU	WF	1915
TWO ORPHANS, THE	WF	1915
SONG OF HATE, THE	WF	1915
REGENERATION	WF	1915
WONDERFUL ADVENTURE, A	WF	1915
SIN	WF	1915
LITTLE GYPSY, THE	WF	1915
SOUL OF BROADWAY, THE	WF	1915
FAMILY STAIN, THE	WF	1915
CARMEN	WF	1915
BLINDNESS OF DEVOTION	WF	1915

FILM	STUDIO	RELEASE YEAR
WOMAN'S PAST, A	WF	1915
BROKEN LAW, THE	WF	1915
GALLEY SLAVE, THE	WF	1915
UNFAITHFUL WIFE, THE	WF	1915
HER MOTHER'S SECRET	WF	1915
SOLDIER'S OATH, A	WF	1915
DESTRUCTION	WF	1915
GREEN-EYED MONSTER, THE	WF	1916
PARISIAN ROMANCE, A	WF	1916
FOURTH ESTATE, THE	WF	1916
SERPENT, THE	WF	1916
RULING PASSION, THE	WF	1916
FOOL'S REVENGE, THE	WF	1916
MERELY MARY ANN	WF	1916
FIGHTING BLOOD	WF	1916
WITCH, THE	WF	1916
MARBLE HEART, THE	WF	1916
GOLD AND THE WOMAN	WF	1916
WIFE'S SACRIFICE, A	WF	1916
BONDMAN, THE	WF	1916
BLUE BLOOD AND RED	WF	1916
SLANDER	WF	1916
MODERN THELMA, A	WF	1916
MAN OF SORROW, A	WF	1916
BLAZING LOVE	WF	1916
ETERNAL SAPPHO	WF	1916
SINS OF MEN	WF	1916
BATTLE OF HEARTS, A	WF	1916
SPIDER AND THE FLY	WF	1916
HYPOCRISY	WF	1916
WOMAN'S HONOR, A	WF	1916
EAST LYNNE	WF	1916
AMBITION	WF	1916
MAN FROM BITTER ROOTS, THE	WF	1916
CAPRICE OF THE MOUNTAINS	WF	1916
TORTURED HEART, A	WF	1916
BEAST, THE	WF	1916
UNDER TWO FLAGS	WF	1916
END OF THE TRAIL, THE	WF	1916
SPORTING BLOOD	WF	1916
DAREDEVIL KATE	WF	1916
LITTLE MISS HAPPINESS	WF	1916
STRAIGHT WAY, THE	WF	1916
UNWELCOME MOTHER, THE	WF	1916
HER DOUBLE LIFE	WF	1916
WHERE LOVE LEADS	WF	1916
FIRES OF CONSCIENCE	WF	1916
WAR BRIDE'S SECRET, THE	WF	1916
RAGGED PRINCESS, THE	WF	1916
DAUGHTER OF THE GODS, A	WF	1916
ROMEO AND JULIET	WF	1916
LOVE AND HATE	WF	1916
SINS OF HER PARENT	WF	1916
MEDIATOR, THE	WF	1916
JEALOUSY	WF	1916
MISCHIEF MAKER, THE	WF	1916
VIXEN, THE	WF	1916
BATTLE OF LIFE	WF	1916
LOVE THIEF, THE	WF	1916
VICTIM, THE	WF	1916
ISLAND OF DESIRE, THE	WF	1917
MODERN CINDERELLA, A	WF	1917
PRICE OF SILENCE, THE	WF	1917
BITTER TRUTH, THE	WF	1917
DARLING OF PARIS, THE	WF	1917
PRIMITIVE CALL, THE	WF	1917
ONE TOUCH OF SIN	WF	1917
NEW YORK PEACOCK, THE	WF	1917
SCARLET LETTER, THE	WF	1917
MELTING MILLIONS	WF	1917
TIGER WOMAN, THE	WF	1917
CHILD OF THE WILD, A	WF	1917
SISTER AGAINST SISTER	WF	1917
LOVE'S LAW	WF	1917
TALE OF TWO CITIES, A	WF	1917
BLUE STREAK, THE	WF	1917
HIGH FINANCE	WF	1917
HER GREATEST LOVE	WF	1917
TANGLED LIVES	WF	1917
HER TEMPTATION	WF	1917

FILM	STUDIO	RELEASE YEAR	FILM	STUDIO	RELEASE YEAR
SHE	WF	1917	ALL FOR A HUSBAND	WF	1917
DERELICT, THE	WF	1917	BRANDED SOUL, A	WF	1917
PRICE OF HER SOUL, THE	WF	1917	SCARLET PIMPERNEL, THE	WF	1917
ROYAL ROMANCE	WF	1917	BABES IN THE WOODS	WF	1917
AMERICAN METHODS	WF	1917	TROUBLE MAKERS	WF	1917
SMALL TOWN GIRL, THE	WF	1917	PRIDE OF NEW YORK, THE	WF	1917
BOOK AGENT, THE	WF	1917	UNKNOWN 274	WF	1917
HEART AND SOUL	WF	1917	HEART OF A LION, THE	WF	1917
FINAL PAYMENT, THE	WF	1917	KINGDOM OF LOVE, THE	WF	1917
SILENT LIE, THE	WF	1917	FOR LIBERTY	WF	1917
SLAVE, THE	WF	1917	MADAME DU BARRY	WF	1917
BROADWAY SPORT, THE	WF	1917	STOLEN HONOR	WF	1918
SOME BOY	WF	1917	UNDER THE YOKE	WF	1918
SIREN, THE	WF	1917	CUPID'S ROUND-UP	WF	1918
PATSY	WF	1917	HEART'S REVENGE, A	WF	1918
TWO LITTLE IMPS	WF	1917	CHEATING THE PUBLIC	WF	1918
TO HONOR AND OBEY	WF	1917	TREASURE ISLAND	WF	1918
INNOCENT SINNER, THE	WF	1917	FORBIDDEN PATH, THE	WF	1918
WIFE NUMBER TWO	WF	1917	HEART OF ROMANCE, THE	WF	1918
JACK AND THE BEANSTALK	WF	1917	JACK SPURLOCK, PRODIGAL	WF	1918
DURAND OF THE BAD LANDS	WF	1917	LES MISERABLES	WF	1918
SPY, THE	WF	1917	MORAL LAW, THE	WF	1918
SOUL OF SATAN, THE	WF	1917	SIX SHOOTER ANDY	WF	1918
EVERY GIRL'S DREAM	WF	1917	GIRL WITH THE CHAMPAGE EYES, THE	WF	1918
HONOR SYSTEM	WF	1917	BLINDNESS OF DIVORCE, THE	WF	1918
BETRAYED	WF	1917	DEBT OF HONOR, THE	WF	1918
WHEN FALSE TONGUES SPEAK	WF	1917	DEVIL'S WHEEL, THE	WF	1918
YANKEE WAY, THE	WF	1917	WOMAN AND THE LAW	WF	1918
CONQUEROR, THE	WF	1917	DAUGHTER OF FRANCE, A	WF	1918
NORTH OF FIFTY-THREE	WF	1917	ROUGH AND READY	WF	1918
RICH MAN'S PLAYTHING, A	Wf	1917	CAMOUFLAGE KISS	WF	1918
CAMILLE	WF	1917	BRIDGE OF FEAR, THE	WF	1918
CONSCIENCE	WF	1917	WESTERN BLOOD	WF	1918
ALADDIN AND THE WONDERFUL LAMP	WF	1917	SOUL OF BUDDHA	WF	1918
THOU SHALT NOT STEAL	WF	1917	AMERICAN BUDS	WF	1918
THIS IS THE LIFE	WF	1917	HER ONE MISTAKE	WF	1918
WHEN A MAN SEES RED	WF	1917	TRUE BLUE	WF	1918
ROSE OF BLOOD, THE	WF	1917	BRAVE AND BOLD	WF	1918
MISS U.S.A.	WF	1917	PEG OF THE PIRATES	WF	1918
PAINTED MADONNA, THE	WF	1917	CONFESSION	WF	1918

FILM	STUDIO	RELEASE YEAR
FIREBRAND, THE	WF	1918
BLUE-EYED MARY	WF	1918
ACE HIGH	WF	1918
WE SHOULD WORRY	WF	1918
SCARLET ROAD, THE	WF	1918
KID IS CLEVER, THE	WF	1918
OTHER MEN'S DAUGHTERS	WF	1918
HER PRICE	WF	1918
MISS INNOCENCE	WF	1918
FALLEN ANGEL	WF	1918
DOING THEIR BIT	WF	1918
BIRD OF PREY	WF	1918
CLEOPATRA	WF	1918
LIAR, THE	WF	1918
LAWLESS LOVE	WF	1918
PRUSSIAN CUR, THE	WF	1918
RIDERS OF THE PURPLE SAGE	WF	1918
BONNIE ANNIE LAURIE	WF	1918
QUEEN OF THE SEA	WF	1918
WHY AMERICA WILL WIN	WF	1918
MR. LOGAN, U.S.A.	WF	1918
QUEEN OF HEARTS, THE	WF	1918
CAILLAUX CASE, THE	WF	1918
KULTUR	WF	1918
SWAT THE SPY	WF	1918
WHEN A WOMAN SINS	WF	1918
ON THE JUMP	WF	1918
MARRIAGES ARE MADE	WF	1918
RAINBOW TRAIL, THE	WF	1918
FAN FAN	WF	1918
TELL IT TO THE MARINES	WF	1918
WOMAN WHO GAVE, THE	WF	1918
ALI BABA AND THE FORTY THIEVES	WF	1918
FAME AND FORTUNE	WF	1918
WHY I WOULD NOT MARRY	WF	1918
BUCHANAN'S WIFE	WF	1918
EVERY MOTHER'S SON	WF	1918
SHE DEVIL, THE	WF	1918
STRANGE WOMAN, THE	WF	1918
CAUGHT IN THE ACT	WF	1918

FILM	STUDIO	RELEASE YEAR
I WANT TO FORGET	WF	1918
I'LL SAY SO	WF	1918
FOR FREEDOM	WF	1918
TREAT 'EM ROUGH	WF	1919
LIGHT, THE	WF	1919
CALL OF THE SOUL	WF	1919
GIRL WITH NO REGRETS, THE	WF	1919
WOMAN, WOMAN!	WF	1919
LUCK AND PLUCK	WF	1919
SALOME	WF	1919
LOVE AUCTION, THE	WF	1919
HELL ROARIN' REFORM	WF	1919
SMILES	WF	1919
FORBIDDEN ROOM, THE	WF	1919
MAN HUNTER, THE	WF	1919
GAMBLING IN SOULS	WF	1919
WHEN MEN DESIRE	WF	1919
NEVER SAY QUIT	WF	1919
REBELLIOUS BRIDE, THE	WF	1919
THOU SHALT NOT	WF	1919
FIGHTING FOR GOLD	WF	1919
MARRIED IN HASTE	WF	1919
PITFALLS OF A BIG CITY	WF	1919
JUNGLE TRAIL, THE	WF	1919
LOVE THAT DARES, THE	WF	1919
HELP! HELP! POLICE!	WF	1919
MISS ADVENTURE	WF	1919
SIREN'S SONG, THE	WF	1919
COMING OF THE LAW	WF	1919
FALLEN IDOL, A	WF	1919
DIVORCE TRAP, THE	WF	1919
WHEN FATE DECIDES	WF	1919
WOMAN THERE WAS, A	WF	1919
COWARDICE COURT	WF	1919
MY LITTLE SISTER	WF	1919
PUTTING ONE OVER	WF	1919
BE A LITTLE SPORT	WF	1919
LONE STAR RANGER	WF	1919
WILDERNESS TRAIL, THE	WF	1919
ROSE OF THE WEST	WF	1919

FILM	STUDIO	RELEASE YEAR
SNEAK, THE	WF	1919
CHEATING HERSELF	WF	1919
WOLVES OF THE NIGHT	WF	1919
LOVE IS LOVE	WF	1919
KATHLEEN MAVOURNEEN	WF	1919
EVANGELINE	WF	1919
CHECKERS	WF	1919
ROUGH RIDING ROMANCE	WF	1919
WINNING STROKE, THE	WF	1919
BROKEN COMMANDMENTS	WF	1919
SPLENDID SIN, THE	WF	1919
LAST OF THE DUANES, THE	WF	1919
LA BELLE RUSSE	WF	1919
MERRY-GO-ROUND, THE	WF	1919
SACRED SILENCE	WF	1919
SNARES OF PARIS	WF	1919
LOST PRINCESS, THE	WF	1919
SPEED MANIAC, THE	WF	1919
CHASING RAINBOWS	WF	1919
EASTWARD HO!	WF	1919
LURE OF AMBITION, THE	WF	1919
SHOULD A HUSBAND FORGIVE?	WF	1919
GIRL IN BOHEMIA, A	WF	1919
VAGABOND LUCK	WF	1919
THIEVES	WF	1919
WINGS OF THE MORNING, THE	WF	1919
LOST MONEY	WF	1919
FEUD, THE	WF	1919
WEB OF CHANCE, THE	WF	1919
DANGER ZONE, THE	WF	1919
LINCOLN HIGHWAYMAN	WF	1919
TIN PAN ALLEY	WF	1919
FLAMES OF THE FLESH	WF	1920
PLUNGER, THE	WF	1920
WHAT WOULD YOU DO?	WF	1920
HEART STRINGS	WF	1920
SHARK, THE	WF	1920
CYCLONE, THE	WF	1920
FAITH	WF	1920
HER ELEPHANT MAN	WF	1920
LAST STRAW, THE	WF	1920
SHOD WITH FIRE	WF	1920
STRONGEST, THE	WF	1920
HELL SHIP, THE	WF	1920
DEVIL'S RIDDLE, THE	WF	1920
BLACK SHADOWS	WF	1920
DAREDEVIL, THE	WF	1920
ADVENTURER, THE	WF	1920
MANHATTAN KNIGHT, THE	WF	1920
MOLLY AND I	WF	1920
WOULD YOU FORGIVE?	WF	1920
FANTOMAS	WF	1920
NUMBER 17	WF	1920
TATTLERS, THE	WF	1920
MOTHER OF HIS CHILDREN	WF	1920
ORPHAN, THE	WF	1920
DESERT LOVE	WF	1920
LEAVE IT TO ME	WF	1920
DEAD LINE, THE	WF	1920
FORBIDDEN TRAILS	WF	1920
LOVE'S HARVEST	WF	1920
TERROR, THE	WF	1920
IRON HEART	WF	1920
WHITE LIES	WF	1920
WORLD OF FOLLY, A	WF	1920
TWINS OF SUFFERING CREEK, THE	WF	1920
SISTER TO SALOME	WF	1920
THREE GOLD COINS	WF	1920
WHITE MOLL, THE	WF	1920
SPIRIT OF GOOD, THE	WF	1920
JOYOUS TROUBLEMAKER, THE	WF	1920
ROSE OF NOME, THE	WF	1920
SQUARE SHOOTER	WF	1920
OVER THE HILL TO THE POORHOUSE	WF	1921
LITTLE WANDERER, THE	WF	1920
HER HONOR THE MAYOR	WF	1920
IF I WERE KING	WF	1920
MAN WHO DARED, THE	WF	1920
BRIDE 13	WF	1920
FIREBRAND TREVISON	WF	1920

FILM	STUDIO	RELEASE YEAR
SKYWAYMAN, THE	WF	1920
UNTAMED, THE	WF	1920
MERELY MARY ANN	WF	1920
WHILE NEW YORK SLEEPS	WF	1920
HUSBAND HUNTER, THE	WF	1920
FROM NOW ON	WF	1920
SUNSET SPRAGUE	WF	1920
CHALLENGE OF THE LAW, THE	WF	1920
TIGER'S CUB, THE	WF	1920
BEWARE OF THE BRIDE	WF	1920
DRAG HARLAN	WF	1920
GIRL OF MY HEART	WF	1920
FACE AT YOUR WINDOW, THE	WF	1920
LITTLE GREY MOUSE	WF	1920
TEXAN, THE	WF	1920
JUST PALS	WF	1920
IRON RIDER, THE	WF	1920
LAND OF JAZZ, THE	WF	1920
THIEF, THE	WF	1920
FLAME OF YOUTH, THE	WF	1920
SCUTTLERS, THE	WF	1920
BLIND WIVES	WF	1920
TWO MOONS	WF	1920
PRAIRIE TRAILS	WF	1920
PARTNERS OF FATE	WF	1921
CHEATER REFORMED, A	WF	1921
WHY TRUST YOUR HUSBAND	WF	1921
MOUNTAIN WOMAN, THE	WF	1921
WING TOY	WF	1921
BIG PUNCH, THE	WF	1921
WHILE THE DEVIL LAUGHS	WF	1921
DYNAMITE ALLEN	WF	1921
ROAD DEMON	WF	1921
BLUSHING BRIDE, THE	WF	1921
OLIVER TWIST JR.	WF	1921
KNOW YOUR MEN	WF	1921
BARE KNUCKLES	WF	1921
ONE-MAN TRAIL	WF	1921
HANDS OFF	WF	1921
LAMPLIGHTER, THE	WF	1921

FILM	STUDIO	RELEASE YEAR
TOMBOY, THE	WF	1921
SKIRTS	WF	1921
HIS GREATEST SACRIFICE	WF	1921
HEARTS OF YOUTH, THE	WF	1921
BEYOND PRICE	WF	1921
GET YOUR MAN	WF	1921
RIDIN' ROMEO, A	WF	1921
MOTHER HEART, THE	WF	1921
BIG TOWN IDEAS	WF	1921
STRAIGHT FROM THE SHOULDER	WF	1921
BIG TOWN ROUND-UP, THE	WF	1921
CHILDREN OF THE NIGHT	WF	1921
MAID OF THE WEST	WF	1921
LIVE WIRES	WF	1921
LOVETIME	WF	1921
SHAME	WF	1921
AFTER YOUR OWN HEART	WF	1921
PERJURY	WF	1921
PLAY SQUARE	WF	1921
SINGING RIVER	WF	1921
TO A FINISH	WF	1921
LITTLE MISS HAWKSHAW	WF	1921
EVER SINCE EVE	WF	1921
HICKVILLE TO BROADWAY	WF	1921
VIRGIN PARADISE, A	WF	1921
FOOTFALLS	WF	1921
CONNECTICUT YANKEE IN KING ARTHUR'S COURT, A	WF	1921
PRIMAL LAW, THE	WF	1921
WHAT LOVE WILL DO	WF	1921
NIGHT HORSEMAN, THE	WF	1921
BAR NOTHIN'	WF	1921
LADY FROM LONGACRE	WF	1921
THUNDERCLAP	WF	1921
QUEENIE	WF	1921
CINDERELLA OF THE HILLS	WF	1921
ROUGH DIAMOND, THE	WF	1921
BUCKING THE LINE	WF	1921
DESERT BLOSSOMS	WF	1921
RIDING WITH DEATH	WF	1921

FILM	STUDIO	RELEASE YEAR	FILM	STUDIO	RELEASE YEAR
DEVIL WITHIN, THE	WF	1921	FOR BIG STAKES	WF	1922
JOLT, THE	WF	1921	SELF-MADE MAN, A	WF	1922
JACKIE	WF	1921	TROOPER O'NEILL	WF	1922
LAST TRAIL, THE	WF	1921	OATH-BOUND	WF	1922
QUEEN OF SHEBA	WF	1921	FAST MAIL, THE	WF	1922
TRAILIN'	WF	1921	JUST TONY	WF	1922
WHATEVER SHE WANTS	WF	1921	NEW TEACHER, THE	WF	1922
ROOF TREE, THE	WF	1921	HONOR FIRST	WF	1922
ANY WIFE	WF	1922	MOONSHINE VALLEY	WF	1922
GLEAM O' DAWN	WF	1922	MONTE CRISTO	WF	1922
LITTLE MISS SMILES	WF	1922	WEST OF CHICAGO	WF	1922
WINNING WITH WITS	WF	1922	CRUSADER, THE	WF	1922
SKY HIGH	WF	1922	YOSEMITE TRAIL, THE	WF	1922
SMILES ARE TRUMPS	WF	1922	DO AND DARE	WF	1922
STRENGTH OF THE PINES	WF	1922	YOUTH MUST HAVE LOVE	WF	1922
BROADWAY PEACOCK	WF	1922	CALVERT'S VALLEY	WF	1922
CHASING THE MOON	WF	1922	BELLS OF SAN JUAN, THE	WF	1922
EXTRA! EXTRA!	WF	1922	MIXED FACES	WF	1922
PARDON MY NERVE	WF	1922	WITHOUT COMPROMISE	WF	1922
STAGE ROMANCE, A	WF	1922	VILLAGE BLACKSMITH, THE	WF	1922
IRON TO GOLD	WF	1922	ARABIA	WF	1922
RAGGED HEIRESS	WF	1922	SHIRLEY OF THE CIRCUS	WF	1922
ELOPE IF YOU MUST	WF	1922	LIGHTS OF NEW YORK, THE	WF	1922
UP AND GOING	WF	1922	LOVE GAMBLER, THE	WF	1922
ARABIAN LOVE	WF	1922	MY FRIEND THE DEVIL	WF	1922
WITHOUT FEAR	WF	1922	WHILE JUSTICE WAITS	WF	1922
MONEY TO BURN	WF	1922	BOSS OF CAMP FOUR, THE	WF	1922
WESTERN SPEED	WF	1922	WHO ARE MY PARENTS?	WF	1922
SHACKLES OF GOLD	WF	1922	GREAT NIGHT, THE	WF	1922
VERY TRULY YOURS	WF	1922	CALIFORNIA ROMANCE, A	WF	1922
FIGHTING STREAK, THE	WF	1922	PAWN TICKET 210	WF	1922
MEN OF ZANZIBAR, THE	WF	1922	CATCH MY SMOKE	WF	1922
YELLOW STAIN, THE	WF	1922	CUSTARD CUP, THE	WF	1923
NERO	WF	1922	FACE ON THE BARROOM FLOOR, THE	WF	1923
SILVER WINGS	WF	1922	FRIENDLY HUSBAND, A	WF	1923
STRANGE IDOLS	WF	1922	MAN, A	WF	1923
ROUGHSHOD	WF	1922	THREE WHO PAID	WF	1923
LIGHTS OF THE DESERT	WF	1922	FOOTLIGHT RANGER, THE	WF	1923
NANOOK OF THE NORTH	WF	1922	MAN'S SIZE, A	WF	1923
FOOL THERE WAS, A	WF	1922	BRASS COMMANDMENTS	WF	1923

FILM	STUDIO	RELEASE YEAR
ROMANCE LAND	WF	1923
TOWN THAT GOD FORGOT, THE	WF	1923
BUSTER, THE	WF	1923
TRUXTON KING	WF	1923
GOODBYE GIRLS	WF	1923
THREE JUMPS AHEAD	WF	1923
BUCKING THE BARRIER	WF	1923
MADNESS OF YOUTH	WF	1923
LOVEBOUND	WF	1923
SNOWDRIFT	WF	1923
BOSTON BLACKIE	WF	1923
STEPPING FAST	WF	1923
RED RUSSIA REVEALED	WF	1923
ELEVENTH HOUR, THE	WF	1923
SKID PROOF	WF	1923
ALIAS THE NIGHT WIND	WF	1923
IF WINTER COMES	WF	1923
SILENT COMMAND, THE	WF	1923
MAN WHO WON, THE	WF	1923
SECOND HAND LOVE	WF	1923
SOFT BOILED	WF	1923
GUNFIGHTER, THE	WF	1923
LONE STAR RANGER, THE	WF	1923
MONNA VANNA	WF	1923
HELL'S HOLE	WF	1923
ST. ELMO	WF	1923
DOES IT PAY?	WF	1923
TIMES HAVE CHANGED	WF	1923
BIG DAN	WF	1923
EXILES, THE	WF	1923
NO MOTHER TO GUIDE HER	WF	1923
CAMEO KIRBY	WF	1923
GOVERNOR'S LADY, THE	WF	1923
GRAIL, THE	WF	1923
SIX CYLINDER LOVE	WF	1923
TEMPLE OF VENUS, THE	WF	1923
MILE A MINUTE ROMEO	WF	1923
NORTH OF HUDSON BAY	WF	1923
SHEPHERD KING, THE	WF	1923
SOUTH SEA LOVE	WF	1923

FILM	STUDIO	RELEASE YEAR
WHEN ODDS ARE EVEN	WF	1923
KENTUCKY DAYS	WF	1923
NET, THE	WF	1923
YOU CAN'T GET AWAY WITH IT	WF	1923
CUPID'S FIREMAN	WF	1923
HOODMAN BLIND	WF	1923
GENTLE JULIA	WF	1923
EYES OF THE FOREST, THE	WF	1923
THIS FREEDOM	WF	1923
JUST OFF BROADWAY	WF	1924
NOT A DRUM WAS HEARD	WF	1924
SHADOW OF THE EAST, THE	WF	1924
BLIZZARD, THE	WF	1924
LADIES TO BOARD	WF	1924
LOVE LETTERS	WF	1924
WOLF MAN, THE	WF	1924
VAGABOND TRAIL, THE	WF	1924
MAN'S MATE, A	WF	1924
ARIZONA EXPRESS, THE	WF	1924
PLUNDERER, THE	WF	1924
TROUBLE SHOOTER, THE	WF	1924
CIRCUS COWBOY	WF	1924
LONE CHANCE, THE	WF	1924
WESTERN LUCK	WF	1924
ROMANCE RANCH	WF	1924
HEART BUSTER, THE	WF	1924
AGAINST ALL ODDS	WF	1924
MAN WHO CAME BACK, THE	WF	1924
THAT FRENCH LADY	WF	1924
DESERT OUTLAW, THE	WF	1924
FIGHT, THE	WF	1924
LAST OF THE DUANES, THE	WF	1924
IT IS THE LAW	WF	1924
DANTE'S INFERNO	WF	1924
HONOR AMONG MEN	WF	1924
CYCLONE RIDER, THE	WF	1924
HUNT, THE	WF	1924
OH YOU TONY	WF	1924
PAINTED LADY, THE	WF	1924
HEARTS OF OAK	WF	1924

FILM	STUDIO	RELEASE YEAR	FILM	STUDIO	RELEASE YEAR
GREAT DIAMOND MYSTERY, THE	WF	1924	KISS BARRIER, THE	WF	1925
RACE, THE	WF	1924	EVERY MAN'S WIFE	WF	1925
WARRENS OF VIRGINIA, THE	WF	1924	HEARTS AND SPURS	WF	1925
WINNER TAKE ALL	WF	1924	GREATER THAN A CROWN	WF	1925
GERALD CRANSTON'S LADY	WF	1924	BIG GAME HUNTER, THE	WF	1925
DARWIN WAS RIGHT	WF	1924	TIMBER WOLF	WF	1925
LAST MAN ON EARTH, THE	WF	1924	LIGHTNIN'	WF	1925
TEETH	WF	1924	BUSINESS ENGAGEMENT	WF	1925
DAUGHTERS OF THE NIGHT	WF	1924	LUCKY HORSESHOE, THE	WF	1925
PAUL JONES, JR.	WF	1924	KENTUCKY PRIDE	WF	1925
BRASS BOWL, THE	WF	1924	WHEEL, THE	WF	1925
MY HUSBANDS'S WIVES	WF	1924	HAVOC	WF	1925
MAN WHO PLAYED SQUARE,THE	WF	1924	IRON HORSE, THE	WF	1925
FLAMES OF DESIRE	WF	1924	EVERLASTING WHISPER, THE	WF	1925
TROUBLES OF A BRIDE, THE	WF	1924	THUNDER MOUNTAIN	WF	1925
ROUGHNECK, THE	WF	1924	FIGHTING HEART, THE	WF	1925
GOLD HEELS	WF	1924	TRANSIENTS IN ARCADIA	WF	1925
BURGLAR, THE	WF	1924	WINDING STAIR, THE	WF	1925
DEADWOOD COACH, THE	WF	1924	DURAND OF THE BADLANDS	WF	1925
FOLLY OF VANITY	WF	1924	THANK YOU	WF	1925
CURLYTOP	WF	1924	WRESTLER, THE	WF	1925
IN LOVE WITH LOVE	WF	1924	LAZYBONES	WF	1925
STAR DUST TRAIL, THE	WF	1924	FOOL, THE	WF	1925
ARIZONA ROMEO, THE	WF	1925	EAST LYNNE	WF	1925
DANCERS, THE	WF	1925	BEST BAD MAN, THE	WF	1925
PORTS OF CALL	WF	1925	FAILURE	WF	1925
CHAMPION OF LOST CAUSES	WF	1925	WHEN THE DOOR OPENED	WF	1925
DICK TURPIN	WF	1925	DESERT'S PRICE, THE	WF	1925
MAN WITHOUT A COUNTRY	WF	1925	PARISIAN KNIGHT, A	WF	1925
SPANISH ROMEO, A	WF	1925	WAGES FOR WIVES	WF	1925
TRAIL RIDER, THE	WF	1925	ANCIENT MARINER, THE	WF	1925
RIDERS OF THE PURPLE SAGE	WF	1925	GOLDEN STRAIN, THE	WF	1925
SCARLET HONEYMOON, THE	WF	1925	CUPID A LA CARTE	WF	1926
HUNTED WOMAN, THE	WF	1925	GILDED BUTTERFLY, THE	WF	1926
MARRIAGE IN TRANSIT	WF	1925	HIS OWN LAWYER	WF	1926
GOLD AND THE GIRL	WF	1925	PALACE OF PLEASURE	WF	1926
SHE WOLVES	WF	1925	YANKEE SENOR	WF	1926
WINGS OF YOUTH	WF	1925	OUTSIDER, THE	WF	1926
SCANDAL PROOF	WF	1925	FIRST YEAR, THE	WF	1926
RAINBOW TRAIL, THE	WF	1925	COWBOY AND THE COUNTESS	WF	1926

FILM	STUDIO	RELEASE YEAR
FEUD, THE	WF	1926
ROAD TO GLORY	WF	1926
ELSIE IN NEW YORK	WF	1926
JOHNSTOWN FLOOD, THE	WF	1926
MY OWN PAL	WF	1926
DIXIE MERCHANT, THE	WF	1926
HELL'S 400	WF	1926
YELLOW FINGERS	WF	1926
SIBERIA	WF	1926
FIGHTING BUCKAROO, THE	WF	1926
RUSTLING FOR CUPID	WF	1926
SANDY	WF	1926
TONY RUNS WILD	WF	1926
EARLY TO WED	WF	1926
SHAMROCK HANDICAP, THE	WF	1926
MAN FOUR-SQUARE, A	WF	1926
SOCIAL TRIANGLE	WF	1926
BLACK PARADISE	WF	1926
HARD BOILED	WF	1926
TRIP TO CHINATOWN, A	WF	1926
SILVER TREASURE, THE	WF	1926
GENTLE CYCLONE, THE	WF	1926
MORE PAY - LESS WORK	WF	1926
HONESTY -THE BEST POLICY	WF	1926
FIG LEAVES	WF	1926
THREE BAD MEN	WF	1926
FAMILY UPSTAIRS, THE	WF	1926
NO MAN'S GOLD	WF	1926
FLYING HORSEMAN	WF	1926
MARRIAGE LICENSE ?	WF	1926
SHOES	WF	1926
BLUE EAGLE, THE	WF	1926
WOMANPOWER	WF	1926
LILY, THE	WF	1926
MIDNIGHT KISS, THE	WF	1926
COUNTRY BEYOND, THE	WF	1926
GREAT K AND A TRAIN ROBBERY, THE	WF	1926
WHISPERING WIRES	WF	1926
30 BELOW ZERO	WF	1926
RETURN OF PETER GRIMM	WF	1926

FILM	STUDIO	RELEASE YEAR
CITY, THE	WF	1926
WHAT PRICE GLORY	WF	1926
WINGS OF THE STORM	WF	1926
CANYON OF LIGHT	WF	1926
GOING CROOKED	WF	1926
SUMMER BACHELORS	WF	1926
BERTHA THE SEWING MACHING GIRL	WF	1926
DESERT VALLEY	WF	1926
ONE INCREASING PURPOSE	WF	1927
STAGE MADNESS	WF	1927
AUCTIONEER, THE	WF	1927
MUSIC MASTER, THE	WF	1927
LAST TRAIL, THE	WF	1927
UPSTREAM	WF	1927
WAR HORSE, THE	WF	1927
MARRIAGE	WF	1927
MONKEY TALKS, THE	WF	1927
ANKLES PREFERRED	WF	1927
LOVE MAKES 'EM WILD	WF	1927
BRONCHO TWISTER	WF	1927
WHISPERING SAGE	WF	1927
HILLS OF PERIL	WF	1927
OUTLAWS OF RED RIVER	WF	1927
HEART OF SALOME	WF	1927
IS ZAT SO?	WF	1927
RICH BUT HONEST	WF	1927
CRADLE SNATCHERS	WF	1927
SLAVES OF BEAUTY	WF	1927
GOOD AS GOLD	WF	1927
SECRET STUDIO, THE	WF	1927
MADAM WANTS NO CHILDREN	WF	1927
CIRCUS ACE, THE	WF	1927
COLLEEN	WF	1927
MARRIED ALIVE	WF	1927
PAID TO LOVE	WF	1927
CHAIN LIGHTNING	WF	1927
TUMBLING RIVER	WF	1927
SINGED	WF	1927
LOVES OF CARMEN	WF	1927
TWO GIRLS WANTED	WF	1927

FILM	STUDIO	RELEASE YEAR
JOY GIRL, THE	WF	1927
GAY RETREAT, THE	WF	1927
SILVER VALLEY	WF	1927
EAST SIDE, WEST SIDE	WF	1927
PUBLICITY MADNESS	WF	1927
HIGH SCHOOL HERO	WF	1927
PAJAMAS	WF	1927
7TH HEAVEN	WF	1927
VERY CONFIDENTIAL	WF	1927
BLOOD WILL TELL	WF	1927
ARIZONA WILDCAT, THE	WF	1927
LADIES MUST DRESS	WF	1927
WOLF FANGS	WF	1927
WIZARD, THE	WF	1927
SILK LEGS	WF	1927
COME TO MY HOUSE	WF	1927
DRIVING LESSON, THE	WF	1928
GATEWAY OF THE MOON, THE	WF	1928
UNEASY MONEY	WF	1928
BRANDED SOMBRERO	WF	1928
WOMAN WISE	WF	1928
DAREDEVIL'S REWARD	WF	1928
SHARP SHOOTERS	WF	1928
SOFT LIVING	WF	1928
GIRL IN EVERY PORT	WF	1928
SQUARE CROOKS	WF	1928
HORSEMAN OF THE PLAINS, A	WF	1928
DRESSED TO KILL	WF	1928
WHY SAILORS GO WRONG	WF	1928
LOVE HUNGRY	WF	1928
STREET ANGEL	WF	1928
PLAY GIRL, THE	WF	1928
ESCAPE, THE	WF	1928
HONOR BOUND	WF	1928
HANGMAN'S HOUSE	WF	1928
HELLO CHEYENNE	WF	1928
THIEF IN THE DARK	WF	1928
NEWS PARADE, THE	WF	1928
INTERVIEW, THE	WF	1928
CHICKEN A LA KING	WF	1928

FILM	STUDIO	RELEASE YEAR
NO OTHER WOMAN	WF	1928
WILD WEST ROMANCE	WF	1928
DON'T MARRY	WF	1928
FLEETWING	WF	1928
FAMILY PICNIC, THE	WF	1928
PAINTED POST	WF	1928
ROAD HOUSE	WF	1928
COWBOY KID, THE	WF	1928
HONOR SYSTEM, THE	WF	1928
LOST IN THE ARTIC	WF	1928
GIRL-SHY COWBOY, THE	WF	1928
RIVER PIRATE, THE	WF	1928
FOUR SONS	WF	1928
FAZIL	WF	1928
WIN THAT GIRL	WF	1928
PLASTERED IN PARIS	WF	1928
BLACK JACK	WF	1928
AIR CIRCUS	WF	1928
DRY MARTINI	WF	1928
FARMER'S DAUGHTER, THE	WF	1928
ME GANGSTER	WF	1928
MOTHER MACHREE	WF	1928
MOTHER KNOWS BEST	WF	1928
SUNRISE	WF	1928
ROMANCE OF THE UNDERWORLD	WF	1928
PREP AND PEP	WF	1928
TAKING A CHANCE	WF	1928
NAPOLEON'S BARBER	WF	1928
RILEY THE COP	WF	1928
RED DANCE, THE	WF	1928
BLINDFOLD	WF	1928
HOMESICK	WF	1928
RED WINE	WF	1928
BATH BETWEEN, THE	WF	1928
LADIES MAN, THE	WF	1928
CAPTAIN LASH	WF	1929
IN OLD ARIZONA	WF	1929
FUGITIVES, THE	WF	1929
IN HOLLAND	WF	1929
SIN SISTER	WF	1929

FILM	STUDIO	RELEASE YEAR
DIPLOMATS, THE	WF	1929
MAKING THE GRADE	WF	1929
TRUE HEAVEN	WF	1929
HAPPY BIRTHDAY	WF	1929
FRIENDSHIP	WF	1929
GHOST TALKS, THE	WF	1929
NEW YEAR'S EVE	WF	1929
BELLE OF SAMOA	WF	1929
SOUND YOUR "A"	WF	1929
STRONG BOY	WF	1929
BENEATH THE LAW	WF	1929
SPEAKEASY	WF	1929
BLUE SKIES	WF	1929
STEWED, FRIED AND BOILED	WF	1929
GIRLS GONE WILD	WF	1929
TRENT'S LAST CASE	WF	1929
MEDICINE MEN, THE	WF	1929
MUSIC FIENDS	WF	1929
THRU DIFFERENT EYES	WF	1929
VEILED WOMAN, THE	WF	1929
WOMAN FROM HELL, THE	WF	1929
FAR CALL, THE	WF	1929
HEARTS IN DIXIE	WF	1929
KNIGHTS OUT	WF	1929
PROTECTION	WF	1929
JOY STREET	WF	1929
WALTZING AROUND	WF	1929
FOX MOVIETONE FOLLIES OF 1929	WF	1929
VALIANT, THE	WF	1929
HIRED AND FIRED	WF	1929
BLACK WATCH, THE	WF	1929
ONE-WOMAN IDEA, THE	WF	1929
ALL STEAMED UP	WF	1929
MASKED EMOTIONS	WF	1929
BEHIND THAT CURTAIN	WF	1929
NOT QUITE DECENT	WF	1929
BLACK MAGIC	WF	1929
PLEASURE CRAZED	WF	1929
MASQUERADE	WF	1929
DETECTIVES WANTED	WF	1929

FILM	STUDIO	RELEASE YEAR
CHASING THROUGH EUROPE	WF	1929
EXALTED FLAPPER, THE	WF	1929
LUCKY STAR	WF	1929
WORDS AND MUSIC	WF	1929
WHY LEAVE HOME?	WF	1929
SALUTE	WF	1929
BIG TIME	WF	1929
4 DEVILS	WF	1929
THEY HAD TO SEE PARIS	WF	1929
GIRL FROM HAVANA	WF	1929
DOLL SHOP, THE	WF	1929
RIVER, THE	WF	1929
FROZEN JUSTICE	WF	1929
COCK EYED WORLD, THE	WF	1929
MARRIED IN HOLLYWOOD	WF	1929
LOVE, LIVE AND LAUGH	WF	1929
SONG OF KENTUCKY, A	WF	1929
ROMANCE OF THE RIO GRANDE	WF	1929
NIX ON DAMES	WF	1929
MARCHING ON	WF	1929
SEVEN FACES	WF	1929
SOUTH SEA ROSE	WF	1929
CHRISTINA	WF	1929
HOT FOR PARIS	WF	1929
SUNNY SIDE UP	WF	1929
CUPIDO CHAUFFEUR	WF	1930
EN NOMBRE DE LA AMISTAD	WF	1930
DESCONCIERTO MATRIMONIAL	WF	1930
ENTRE PLATOS Y NOTAS	WF	1930
MEDIA NOCHE, A	WF	1930
LONE STAR RANGER, THE	WF	1930
CAMEO KIRBY	WF	1930
HARMONY AT HOME	WF	1930
SKY HAWK, THE	WF	1930
LET'S GO PLACES	WF	1930
MEN WITHOUT WOMEN	WF	1930
HAPPY DAYS	WF	1930
CITY GIRL	WF	1930
BIG PARTY, THE	WF	1930
SUCH MEN ARE DANGEROUS	WF	1930

FILM	STUDIO	RELEASE YEAR
GOLDEN CALF, THE	WF	1930
HIGH SOCIETY BLUES	WF	1930
CRAZY THAT WAY	WF	1930
TEMPLE TOWER	WF	1930
THREE SISTERS	WF	1930
DOUBLE CROSS ROADS	WF	1930
ARIZONA KID, THE	WF	1930
NEW MOVIETONE FOLLIES OF 1930	WF	1930
BORN RECKLESS	WF	1930
ON THE LEVEL	WF	1930
NOT DAMAGED	WF	1930
WOMEN EVERYWHERE	WF	1930
SO THIS IS LONDON	WF	1930
ROUGH ROMANCE	WF	1930
CHEER UP AND SMILE	WF	1930
GOOD INTENTIONS	WF	1930
WILD COMPANY	WF	1930
ONE MAD KISS	WF	1930
COMMON CLAY	WF	1930
DEL MISMO BARRO (SPANISH VERSION OF COMMON CLAY)	WF	1930
MAN TROUBLE	WF	1930
LAST OF THE DUANES, THE	WF	1930
SONG O' MY HEART	WF	1930
ON YOUR BACK	WF	1930
EL ULTIMO DE LOS VARGAS (SPANISH VERSION OF THE LAST OF THE DUANES)	WF	1930
SEA WOLF, THE	WF	1930
SOUP TO NUTS	WF	1930
LILIOM	WF	1930
UP THE RIVER	WF	1930
DEVIL WITH WOMEN, A	WF	1930
SCOTLAND YARD	WF	1930
EL VALIENTE	WF	1930
RENEGADES	WF	1930
BIG TRAIL, THE	WF	1930
DANCERS, THE	WF	1930
JUST IMAGINE	WF	1930
ARE YOU THERE?	WF	1930
LIGHTNIN'	WF	1930
OH, FOR A MAN	WF	1930

FILM	STUDIO	RELEASE YEAR
PRINCESS AND THE PLUMBER, THE	WF	1930
PART TIME WIFE	WF	1930
UNDER SUSPICION	WF	1930
TRANSATLANTIC	WF	1931
ORO LIQUIDO	WF	1931
IL GRANDE SENTIERO (ITALIAN VERSION OF THE BIG TRAIL)	WF	1931
LA PISTE DES GEANTS (FRENCH VERSION OF THE BIG TRAIL)	WF	1931
MAN WHO CAME BACK, THE	WF	1931
MEN ON CALL	WF	1931
ONCE A SINNER	WF	1931
FAIR WARNING	WF	1931
GIRLS DEMAND EXCITEMENT	WF	1931
LA GRAN JORNADA (SPANISH VERSION OF (THE BIG TRAIL)	WF	1931
DON'T BET ON WOMEN	WF	1931
BODY AND SOUL	WF	1931
DEL INFIERNO AL CIELO (SPANISH VERSION OF THE MAN WHO CAME BACK)	WF	1931
EAST LYNNE	WF	1931
THREE ROGUES	WF	1931
DOCTORS' WIVES	WF	1931
EL IMPOSTER (SPANISH VERSION OF SCOTLAND YARD)	WF	1931
MR. LEMON OF ORANGE	WF	1931
SEAS BENEATH, THE	WF	1931
CONNECTICUT YANKEE, A	WF	1931
UN YANQUI EN LA CORTE DEL REY ARTURO (SPANISH VERSION OF A CONNECTICUT YANKEE)	WF	1931
CHARLIE CHAN CARRIES ON	WF	1931
THREE GIRLS LOST	WF	1931
SPY, THE	WF	1931
QUICK MILLIONS	WF	1931
SIX CYLINDER LOVE	WF	1931
YOUNG SINNERS	WF	1931
ALWAYS GOODBYE	WF	1931
WOMEN OF ALL NATIONS	WF	1931
CUERPO Y ALMA (SPANISH VERSION OF BODY AND SOUL)	WF	1931
DADDY LONG LEGS	WF	1931

FILM	STUDIO	RELEASE YEAR
ANNABELLE'S AFFAIRS	WF	1931
BLACK CAMEL, THE	WF	1931
GOLDIE	WF	1931
ESCLAVAS DE LA MODA (SPANISH VERSION OF ON YOUR BACK)	WF	1931
HUSH MONEY	WF	1931
THEIR MAD MOMENT	WF	1931
HOLY TERROR, A	WF	1931
HAY QUE CASAR AL PRINCIPE (SPANISH VERSION OF PAID TO LOVE)	WF	1931
BAD GIRL	WF	1931
YOUNG AS YOU FEEL	WF	1931
TRANSATLANTIC	WF	1931
MERELY MARY ANN	WF	1931
BRAT, THE	WF	1931
CONOCES A TU MUJER? (SPANISH VERSION OF DON'T BET ON WOMEN)	WF	1931
MAMA	WF	1931
SPIDER, THE	WF	1931
LA LEY DEL HAREM (SPANISH VERSION OF FAZIL)	WF	1931
SKYLINE	WF	1931
WICKED	WF	1931
SOB SISTER	WF	1931
RIDERS OF THE PURPLE SAGE	WF	1931
YELLOW TICKET, THE	WF	1931
HEARTBREAK	WF	1931
CISCO KID, THE	WF	1931
AMBASSADOR BILL	WF	1931
MI ULTIMO AMOR (SPANISH VERSION OF THEIR MAD MOMENT)	WF	1931
OVER THE HILL	WF	1931
CHARLIE CHAN CARRIES ON)	WF	1931
SURRENDER	WF	1931
GOOD SPORT	WF	1931
DELICIOUS	WF	1931
CHICA BIEN	WF	1932
PASSPORT TO HELL, A (SPANISH)	WF	1932
RAINBOW TRAIL, THE	WF	1932
STEPPING SISTERS	WF	1932

FILM	STUDIO	RELEASE YEAR
DANCE TEAM	WF	1932
CHARLIE CHAN'S CHANCE	WF	1932
SILENT WITNESS, THE	WF	1932
CHEATERS AT PLAY	WF	1932
GAY CABALLERO, THE	WF	1932
SHE WANTED A MILLIONAIRE	WF	1932
MARIDO Y MUJER (SPANISH VERSION OF BAD GIRL)	WF	1932
AFTER TOMORROW	WF	1932
BUSINESS AND PLEASURE	WF	1932
DISORDERLY CONDUCT	WF	1932
DEVIL'S LOTTERY, THE	WF	1932
CARELESS LADY	WF	1932
AMATEUR DADDY	WF	1932
YOUNG AMERICA	WF	1932
TRIAL OF VIVIENNE WARE, THE	WF	1932
WHILE PARIS SLEEPS	WF	1932
WOMAN IN ROOM 13, THE	WF	1932
MAN ABOUT TOWN	WF	1932
SOCIETY GIRL	WF	1932
DIE GROSSE FAHRT (GERMAN VERSION OF THE BIG TRAIL)	WF	1932
WEEK ENDS ONLY	WF	1932
BACHELOR'S AFFAIRS	WF	1932
MYSTERY RANCH	WF	1932
REBECCA OF SUNNYBROOK FARM	WF	1932
ALMOST MARRIED	WF	1932
CRY OF THE WORLD, THE	WF	1932
FIRST YEAR, THE	WF	1932
CONGORILLA	WF	1932
PAINTED WOMAN, THE	WF	1932
PASSPORT TO HELL, A	WF	1932
DOWN TO EARTH	WF	1932
CHANDU -THE MAGICIAN	WF	1932
HAT CHECK GIRL	WF	1932
EL BESO REDENTOR	WF	1932
WILD GIRL	WF	1932
SIX HOURS TO LIVE	WF	1932
RACKETY RAX	WF	1932
GOLDEN WEST, THE	WF	1932

FILM	STUDIO	RELEASE YEAR	FILM	STUDIO	RELEASE YEAR
SHERLOCK HOLMES	WF	1932	DEVIL'S IN LOVE, THE	WF	1933
EL CABALLERO DE LA NOCHE (SPANISH VERSION OF DICK TURPIN)	WF	1932	ARIZONA TO BROADWAY	WF	1933
TOO BUSY TO WORK	WF	1932	F. P. ONE	WF	1933
TESS OF THE STORM COUNTRY	WF	1932	SHANGHAI MADNESS	WF	1933
CALL HER SAVAGE	WF	1932	EL PRECIO DE UN BESO (SPANISH VERSION OF ONE MAD KISS)	WF	1933
ME AND MY GAL	WF	1932	PILGRIMAGE	WF	1933
HANDLE WITH CARE	WF	1932	LAST TRAIL, THE	WF	1933
SEIS HORAS DE VIDA	WF	1933	PADDY, THE NEXT BEST THING	WF	1933
SECOND HAND WIFE	WF	1933	UNA VIUDA ROMANTICA	WF	1933
ROBBERS' ROOST	WF	1933	GOOD COMPANIONS, THE	WF	1933
FACE IN THE SKY, THE	WF	1933	CHARLIE CHAN'S GREATEST CASE	WF	1933
HOT PEPPER	WF	1933	DOCTOR BULL	WF	1933
EL ULTIMO VARON SOBRE LA TIERRA (SPANISH VERSION OF IT'S GREAT TO BE ALIVE)	WF	1933	MY WEAKNESS	WF	1933
INFERNAL MACHINE, THE	WF	1933	BERKELEY SQUARE	WF	1933
STATE FAIR	WF	1933	POWER AND THE GLORY, THE	WF	1933
SMOKE LIGHTNING	WF	1933	BOWERY, THE	TCP	1933
BROADWAY BAD	WF	1933	LADRON DE AMOR	WF	1933
DANGEROUSLY YOURS	WF	1933	WALLS OF GOLD	WF	1933
SAILOR'S LUCK	WF	1933	BROADWAY THRU A KEYHOLE	TCP	1933
AFTER THE BALL	WF	1933	MAD GAME, THE	WF	1933
HUMANITY	WF	1933	NO DEJES LA PUERTA ABIERTA (SPANISH VERSION OF PLEASURE CRUISE)	WF	1933
PLEASURE CRUISE	WF	1933	MY LIPS BETRAY	WF	1933
HELLO, SISTER	WF	1933	BLOOD MONEY	TCP	1933
CAVALCADE	WF	1933	OLSEN'S BIG MOMENT	WF	1933
TRICK FOR TRICK	WF	1933	JIMMY AND SALLY	WF	1933
BONDAGE	WF	1933	HOOPLA	WF	1933
WARRIOR'S HUSBAND, THE	WF	1933	ADVICE TO THE LOVELORN	TCP	1933
ZOO IN BUDAPEST	WF	1933	WORST WOMAN IN PARIS?, THE	WF	1933
PRIMAVERA EN OTONO	WF	1933	YO, TU Y ELLA	WF	1933
ADORABLE	WF	1933	SMOKY	WF	1933
HOLD ME TIGHT	WF	1933	I WAS A SPY	WF	1933
EL REY LOS GITANOS	WF	1933	MR. SKITCH	WF	1933
IT'S GREAT TO BE ALIVE	WF	1933	AS HUSBANDS GO	WF	1933
I LOVED YOU WEDNESDAY	WF	1933	UN CAPITAN DE COSACOS	WF	1934
BEST OF ENEMIES	WF	1933	GALLANT LADY	TCP	1934
LIFE IN THE RAW	WF	1933	I AM SUZANNE	WF	1934
MAN WHO DARED, THE	WF	1933	ORIENT EXPRESS	WF	1934
LA MELODIA PROHIBIDA	WF	1933	FRONTIER MARSHAL	WF	1934

FILM	STUDIO	RELEASE YEAR
MOULIN ROUGE	TCP	1934
SLEEPERS EAST	WF	1934
CAROLINA	WF	1934
LA CRUZ Y LA ESPADA	WF	1934
DEVIL TIGER	WF	1934
EVER SINCE EVE	WF	1934
LA CIUDAD DE CARTON	WF	1934
HOLD THAT GIRL	WF	1934
I BELIEVED IN YOU	WF	1934
DAVID HARUM	WF	1934
COMING OUT PARTY, THE	WF	1934
GEORGE WHITE'S SCANDALS	WF	1934
THREE ON A HONEYMOON	WF	1934
LOOKING FOR TROUBLE	TCP	1934
BOTTOMS UP	WF	1934
MURDER IN TRINIDAD	WF	1934
CONSTANT NYMPH, THE	WF	1934
HOUSE OF ROTHSCHILD, THE	TCP	1934
ALL MEN ARE ENEMIES	WF	1934
HEART SONG	WF	1934
LAST GENTLEMAN, THE	TCP	1934
STAND UP AND CHEER	WF	1934
SUCH WOMEN ARE DANGEROUS	WF	1934
NOW I'LL TELL	WF	1934
LILIOM	WF	1934
GRANADEROS DEL AMOR	WF	1934
BORN TO BE BAD	TCP	1934
CHANGE OF HEART	WF	1934
SPRINGTIME FOR HENRY	WF	1934
CALL IT LUCK	WF	1934
WILD GOLD	WF	1934
SHE LEARNED ABOUT SAILORS	WF	1934
BABY TAKE A BOW	WF	1934
CHARLIE CHAN'S COURAGE	WF	1934
BULLDOG DRUMMOND STRIKES BACK	TCP	1934
GRAND CANARY	WF	1934
HANDY ANDY	WF	1934
CAT'S PAW, THE	WF	1934
SHE WAS A LADY	WF	1934
AFFAIRS OF CELLINI	TCP	1934

FILM	STUDIO	RELEASE YEAR
PURSUED	WF	1934
WORLD MOVES ON, THE	WF	1934
CHARLIE CHAN IN LONDON	WF	1934
DUDE RANGER, THE	WF	1934
LOVE TIME	WF	1934
SERVANTS' ENTRANCE	WF	1934
JUDGE PRIEST	WF	1934
CARAVAN (ENGLISH & FRENCH VERSIONS)	WF	1934
365 NIGHTS IN HOLLYWOOD	WF	1934
PECK'S BAD BOY	WF	1934
DOS MAS UNO DOS	WF	1934
MARIE GALANTE	WF	1934
GAMBLING	WF	1934
ELINOR NORTON	WF	1934
FIRST WORLD WAR, THE	WF	1934
HELL IN THE HEAVENS	WF	1934
WHITE PARADE, THE	WF	1934
NADA MAS QUE UNA MUJER (SPANISH VERSION OF ONLY A WOMAN)	WF	1934
LAS FRONTERAS DEL AMOR	WF	1934
MUSIC IN THE AIR	WF	1934
HELLDORADO	WF	1934
MIGHTY BARNUM, THE	TCP	1934
BRIGHT EYES	WF	1934
BACHELOR OF ARTS	WF	1934
LOTTERY LOVER, THE	WF	1935
CLIVE OF INDIA	TCP	1935
MYSTERY WOMAN	WF	1935
COUNTY CHAIRMAN, THE	WF	1935
CHARLIE CHAN IN PARIS	WF	1935
UNDER PRESSURE	WF	1935
BABOONA	WF	1935
SENORA CASADA NECESITA MARIDO	WF	1935
WHEN A MAN'S A MAN	WF	1935
ONE MORE SPRING	WF	1935
LITTLE COLONEL, THE	WF	1935
FOLIES BERGERE OF PARIS (ENGLISH & FRENCH VERSIONS)	TCP	1935
GREAT HOTEL MURDER, THE	WF	1935
ASEGURE A SU MUJER	WF	1935

FILM	STUDIO	RELEASE YEAR	FILM	STUDIO	RELEASE YEAR
GEORGE WHITE'S 1935 SCANDALS	WF	1935	ROSA DE FRANCIA	TCF	1935
LIFE BEGINS AT FORTY	WF	1935	WAY DOWN EAST	TCF	1935
JULIETA COMPRA UN HIJO	WF	1935	PADDY O'DAY	TCF	1935
$10 RAISE	WF	1935	MUSIC IS MAGIC	TCF	1935
IT'S A SMALL WORLD	WF	1935	TE QUIERO CON LOCURA	TCF	1935
PECHMARIE	WF	1935	YOUR UNCLE DUDLEY	TCF	1935
LES MISERABLES	TCP	1935	MAN WHO BROKE THE BANK AT MONTE CARLO, THE	TCF	1935
HARD LUCK MARY	WF	1935	MY MARRIAGE	TCF	1935
CARDINAL RICHELIEU	TCP	1935	LITTLEST REBEL, THE	TCF	1935
LADIES LOVE DANGER	WF	1935	IN OLD KENTUCKY	TCF	1935
COWBOY MILLIONAIRE	WF	1935	NAVY WIFE	TCF	1935
OUR LITTLE GIRL	WF	1935	SHOW THEM NO MERCY	TCF	1935
DARING YOUNG MAN, THE	WF	1935	WHISPERING SMITH SPEAKS	TCF	1935
UNDER THE PAMPAS MOON	WF	1935	PROFESSIONAL SOLDIER	TCF	1935
BLACK SHEEP	WF	1935	KING OF BURLESQUE	TCF	1936
CHARLIE CHAN IN EGYPT	WF	1935	CHARLIE CHAN'S SECRET	TCF	1936
HARD ROCK HARRIGAN	WF	1935	IT HAD TO HAPPEN	TCF	1936
GINGER	WF	1935	HERE COMES TROUBLE	TCF	1936
DOUBTING THOMAS	WF	1935	PRISONER OF SHARK ISLAND	TCF	1936
ORCHIDS TO YOU	WF	1935	SONG AND DANCE MAN	TCF	1936
SILK HAT KID	WF	1935	COUNTRY DOCTOR	TCF	1936
CURLY TOP	WF	1935	EVERY SATURDAY NIGHT	TCF	1936
FARMER TAKES A WIFE, THE	WF	1935	EVERYBODY'S OLD MAN	TCF	1936
CALL OF THE WILD	TCP	1935	CHARLIE CHAN AT THE CIRCUS	TCF	1936
WELCOME HOME	WF	1935	O'MALLEY OF THE MOUNTED	TCF	1936
DRESSED TO THRILL	WF	1935	FIRST BABY, THE	TCF	1936
DANTE'S INFERNO	WF	1935	ROAD TO GLORY	TCF	1936
ANGELINA	WF	1935	GENTLE JULIA	TCF	1936
STEAMBOAT ROUND THE BEND	WF	1935	MESSAGE TO GARCIA	TCF	1936
REDHEADS ON PARADE	WF	1935	CAPTAIN JANUARY	TCF	1936
GAY DECEPTION, THE	WF	1935	FOLIES-BERGERE	TCF	1936
THUNDER IN THE NIGHT	WF	1935	COUNTRY BEYOND, THE	TCF	1936
THUNDER MOUNTAIN	WF	1935	UNDER TWO FLAGS	TCF	1936
HERE'S TO ROMANCE	WF	1935	CHAMPAGNE CHARLIE	TCF	1936
PIERNAS DE SEDA	WF	1935	HALF ANGEL	TCF	1936
CHARLIE CHAN IN SHANGHAI	WF	1935	EDUCATING FATHER	TCF	1936
METROPOLITAN	TCF	1935	LITTLE MISS NOBODY	TCF	1936
THIS IS THE LIFE	TCF	1935	HUMAN CARGO	TCF	1936
THANKS A MILLION	TCF	1935	SINS OF MAN	TCF	1936
BAD BOY	TCF	1935			

FILM	STUDIO	RELEASE YEAR
CRIME OF DR. FORBES, THE	TCF	1936
BORDER PATROLMAN, THE	TCF	1936
HIGH TENSION	TCF	1936
WHITE FANG	TCF	1936
POOR LITTLE RICH GIRL	TCF	1936
TO MARY - WITH LOVE	TCF	1936
GIRLS' DORMITORY	TCF	1936
PEPPER	TCF	1936
36 HOURS TO KILL	TCF	1936
BACK TO NATURE	TCF	1936
CHARLIE CHAN AT THE OPERA	TCF	1936
CHARLIE CHAN AT THE RACE TRACK	TCF	1936
SING BABY, SING!	TCF	1936
STAR FOR A NIGHT	TCF	1936
KING OF THE ROYAL MOUNTED	TCF	1936
RAMONA	TCF	1936
DIMPLES	TCF	1936
PIGSKIN PARADE	TCF	1936
THANK YOU, JEEVES!	TCF	1936
LADIES IN LOVE	TCF	1936
FIFTEEN MAIDEN LANE	TCF	1936
UNDER YOUR SPELL	TCF	1936
WILD BRIAN KENT	TCF	1936
CAN THIS BE DIXIE?	TCF	1936
PRIVATE NUMBER	TCF	1936
REUNION	TCF	1936
WHITE HUNTER	TCF	1936
LAUGHING AT TROUBLE	TCF	1936
BANJO ON MY KNEE	TCF	1936
CRACK-UP	TCF	1936
CAREER WOMAN	TCF	1936
STOWAWAY	TCF	1936
ONE IN A MILLION	TCF	1936
AS YOU LIKE IT	TCF	1937
SECRET VALLEY	TCF	1937
WOMAN WISE	TCF	1937
LLOYD'S OF LONDON	TCF	1937
HOLY TERROR, THE	TCF	1937
OFF TO THE RACES	TCF	1937
TIME OUT FOR ROMANCE	TCF	1937

FILM	STUDIO	RELEASE YEAR
ON THE AVENUE	TCF	1937
WINGS OF THE MORNING	TCF	1937
FAIR WARNING	TCF	1937
LOVE IS NEWS	TCF	1937
NANCY STEELE IS MISSING	TCF	1937
SEVENTH HEAVEN	TCF	1937
STEP LIVELY, JEEVES	TCF	1937
MIDNIGHT TAXI	TCF	1937
THAT I MAY LIVE	TCF	1937
IT HAPPENED OUT WEST	TCF	1937
CAFE METROPOLE	TCF	1937
GREAT HOSPITAL MYSTERY, THE	TCF	1937
CHARLIE CHAN AT THE OLYMPICS	TCF	1937
THIS IS MY AFFAIR	TCF	1937
BIG BUSINESS	TCF	1937
UNDER THE RED ROBE	TCF	1937
FIFTY ROADS TO TOWN	TCF	1937
ANGEL'S HOLIDAY	TCF	1937
BORN RECKLESS	TCF	1937
SING AND BE HAPPY	TCF	1937
SHE HAD TO EAT	TCF	1937
SLAVE SHIP	TCF	1937
CALIFORNIAN, THE	TCF	1937
WILD AND WOOLLY	TCF	1937
LADY ESCAPES, THE	TCF	1937
THINK FAST, MR. MOTO	TCF	1937
WEE WILLIE WINKIE	TCF	1937
LOVE UNDER FIRE	TCF	1937
YOU CAN'T HAVE EVERYTHING	TCF	1937
ONE MILE FROM HEAVEN	TCF	1937
WAKE UP AND LIVE	TCF	1937
WESTERN GOLD	TCF	1937
BORNEO	TCF	1937
THIN ICE	TCF	1937
DANGEROUSLY YOURS	TCF	1937
HOT WATER	TCF	1937
DANGER-LOVE AT WORK	TCF	1937
LIFE BEGINS IN COLLEGE	TCF	1937
LANCER SPY	TCF	1937
WIFE, DOCTOR AND NURSE	TCF	1937

FILM	STUDIO	RELEASE YEAR	FILM	STUDIO	RELEASE YEAR
HEIDI	TCF	1937	THREE BLIND MICE	TCF	1938
ROLL ALONG COWBOY	TCF	1937	MR. MOTO TAKES A CHANCE	TCF	1938
CHARLIE CHAN ON BROADWAY	TCF	1937	ALWAYS GOODBYE	TCF	1938
ALI BABA GOES TO TOWN	TCF	1937	WE'RE GOING TO BE RICH	TCF	1938
SECOND HONEYMOON	TCF	1937	PANAMINT'S BAD MAN	TCF	1938
45 FATHERS	TCF	1937	PASSPORT HUSBAND	TCF	1938
DINNER AT THE RITZ	TCF	1937	I'LL GIVE A MILLION	TCF	1938
BIG TOWN GIRL	TCF	1937	GATEWAY	TCF	1938
CHECKERS	TCF	1937	KEEP SMILING	TCF	1938
BORROWING TROUBLE	TCF	1937	ALEXANDER'S RAGTIME BAND	TCF	1938
LOVE AND HISSES	TCF	1937	MY LUCKY STAR	TCF	1938
THANK YOU, MR. MOTO	TCF	1937	HOLD THAT CO-ED	TCF	1938
CITY GIRL	TCF	1938	LITTLE MISS BROADWAY	TCF	1938
TARZAN'S REVENGE	TCF	1938	TIME OUT FOR MURDER	TCF	1938
CHANGE OF HEART	TCF	1938	STRAIGHT, PLACE AND SHOW	TCF	1938
HAWAIIAN BUCKAROO	TCF	1938	MEET THE GIRLS	TCF	1938
CHARLIE CHAN AT MONTE CARLO	TCF	1938	DOWN ON THE FARM	TCF	1938
HAPPY LANDING	TCF	1938	FIVE OF A KIND	TCF	1938
INTERNATIONAL SETTLEMENT	TCF	1938	MYSTERIOUS MR. MOTO	TCF	1938
BARONESS AND THE BUTLER, THE	TCF	1938	ALWAYS IN TROUBLE	TCF	1938
SMILING ALONG	TCF	1939	SUEZ	TCF	1938
WHO GOES NEXT?	TCF	1938	JUST AROUND THE CORNER	TCF	1938
LOVE ON A BUDGET	TCF	1938	SHARPSHOOTERS	TCF	1938
SALLY, IRENE AND MARY	TCF	1938	SUBMARINE PATROL	TCF	1938
WALKING DOWN BROADWAY	TCF	1938	CLIMBING HIGH	TCF	1938
REBECCA OF SUNNYBROOK FARM	TCF	1938	ROAD DEMON	TCF	1938
ISLAND IN THE SKY	TCF	1938	UP THE RIVER	TCF	1938
RAWHIDE	TCF	1938	THANKS FOR EVERYTHING	TCF	1938
MR. MOTO'S GAMBLE	TCF	1938	KENTUCKY	TCF	1938
IN OLD CHICAGO	TCF	1938	WHILE NEW YORK SLEEPS	TCF	1939
BATTLE OF BROADWAY, THE	TCF	1938	CHARLIE CHAN IN HONOLULU	TCF	1939
FOUR MEN AND A PRAYER	TCF	1938	MR. MOTO'S LAST WARNING	TCF	1939
TRIP TO PARIS, A	TCF	1938	JESSE JAMES	TCF	1939
KENTUCKY MOONSHINE	TCF	1938	ARIZONA WILDCAT, THE	TCF	1939
RASCALS	TCF	1938	THREE MUSKETEERS, THE	TCF	1939
KIDNAPPED	TCF	1938	TAIL SPIN	TCF	1939
SAFETY IN NUMBERS	TCF	1938	PARDON OUR NERVE	TCF	1939
JOSETTE	TCF	1938	WIFE, HUSBAND AND FRIEND	TCF	1939
SPEED TO BURN	TCF	1938	LITTLE PRINCESS, THE	TCF	1939
ONE WILD NIGHT	TCF	1938	INSIDE STORY	TCF	1939

FILM	STUDIO	RELEASE YEAR
EVERYBODY'S BABY	TCF	1939
WINNER TAKE ALL	TCF	1939
HOUND OF THE BASKERVILLES, THE	TCF	1939
MR. MOTO IN DANGER ISLAND	TCF	1939
STORY OF ALEXANDER GRAHAM BELL	TCF	1939
RETURN OF THE CISCO KID	TCF	1939
ROSE OF WASHINGTON SQUARE	TCF	1939
CHASING DANGER	TCF	1939
BOY FRIEND	TCF	1939
GORILLA, THE	TCF	1939
YOUNG MR. LINCOLN	TCF	1939
JONES FAMILY IN HOLLYWOOD, THE	TCF	1939
IT COULD HAPPEN TO YOU	TCF	1939
SUSANNAH OF THE MOUNTIES	TCF	1939
INSPECTOR HORNLEIGH	TCF	1939
CHARLIE CHAN IN RENO	TCF	1939
SECOND FIDDLE	TCF	1939
MR. MOTO TAKES A VACATION	TCF	1939
NEWS IS MADE AT NIGHT	TCF	1939
FRONTIER MARSHAL	TCF	1939
HOTEL FOR WOMEN	TCF	1939
CHICKEN WAGON FAMILY	TCF	1939
STANLEY AND LIVINGSTONE	TCF	1939
QUICK MILLIONS	TCF	1939
ADVENTURES OF SHERLOCK HOLMES	TCF	1939
CHARLIE CHAN AT TREASURE ISLAND	TCF	1939
RAINS CAME, THE	TCF	1939
STOP, LOOK AND LOVE	TCF	1939
HERE I AM A STRANGER	TCF	1939
GREAT COMMANDMENT, THE	TCF	1939
ESCAPE, THE	TCF	1939
HOLLYWOOD CAVALCADE	TCF	1939
PACK UP YOUR TROUBLES	TCF	1939
SHIPYARD SALLY	TCF	1939
20,000 MEN A YEAR	TCF	1939
DRUMS ALONG THE MOHAWK	TCF	1939
HEAVEN WITH A BARBED WIRE FENCE	TCF	1939
CHARLIE CHAN IN CITY IN DARKNESS	TCF	1939
TOO BUSY TO WORK	TCF	1939
DAYTIME WIFE	TCF	1939

FILM	STUDIO	RELEASE YEAR
CISCO KID AND THE LADY, THE	TCF	1939
INSPECTOR HORNLEIGH ON HOLIDAY	TCF	1939
BARRICADE	TCF	1939
HONEYMOON'S OVER, THE	TCF	1939
EVERYTHING HAPPENS AT NIGHT	TCF	1939
SWANEE RIVER	TCF	1939
BLUE BIRD, THE	TCF	1940
CITY OF CHANCE	TCF	1940
HE MARRIED HIS WIFE	TCF	1940
MAN WHO WOULDN'T TALK, THE	TCF	1940
HIGH SCHOOL	TCF	1940
LITTLE OLD NEW YORK	TCF	1940
YOUNG AS YOU FEEL	TCF	1940
CHARLIE CHAN IN PANAMA	TCF	1940
THEY CAME BY NIGHT	TCF	1940
GRAPES OF WRATH, THE	TCF	1940
FREE, BLONDE, AND 21	TCF	1940
STAR DUST	TCF	1940
JOHNNY APOLLO	TCF	1940
VIVA CISCO KID	TCF	1940
SHOOTING HIGH	TCF	1940
SO THIS IS LONDON	TCF	1940
I WAS AN ADVENTURESS	TCF	1940
ON THEIR OWN	TCF	1940
LILLIAN RUSSELL	TCF	1940
GIRL IN 313	TCF	1940
EARTHBOUND	TCF	1940
FOUR SONS	TCF	1940
CHARLIE CHAN'S MURDER CRUISE	TCF	1940
LUCKY CISCO KID	TCF	1940
SAILOR'S LADY	TCF	1940
MANHATTAN HEARTBEAT	TCF	1940
MARYLAND	TCF	1940
GIRL FROM AVENUE A, THE	TCF	1940
MAN I MARRIED, THE	TCF	1940
RETURN OF FRANK JAMES	TCF	1940
PIER 13	TCF	1940
GIRL IN THE NEWS, THE	TCF	1940
GREAT PROFILE	TCF	1940
YOUNG PEOPLE	TCF	1940

FILM	STUDIO	RELEASE YEAR
CHARLIE CHAN AT THE WAX MUSEUM	TCF	1940
ELSA MAXWELL'S PUBLIC DEB. NO. 1	TCF	1940
YESTERDAY'S HEROES	TCF	1940
BRIGHAM YOUNG	TCF	1940
GAY CABALLERO, THE	TCF	1940
DOWN ARGENTINE WAY	TCF	1940
MARK OF ZORRO, THE	TCF	1940
STREET OF MEMORIES	TCF	1940
YOUTH WILL BE SERVED	TCF	1940
TIN PAN ALLEY	TCF	1940
CHARTER PILOT	TCF	1940
MURDER OVER NEW YORK	TCF	1940
JENNIE	TCF	1940
CHAD HANNA	TCF	1940
NIGHT TRAIN	TCF	1940
HUDSON'S BAY	TCF	1941
MICHAEL SHAYNE PRIVATE DETECTIVE	TCF	1941
ROMANCE OF THE RIO GRANDE	TCF	1941
TALL, DARK AND HANDSOME	TCF	1941
RIDE KELLY RIDE	TCF	1941
GOLDEN HOOFS	TCF	1941
WESTERN UNION	TCF	1941
MURDER AMONG FRIENDS	TCF	1941
TOBACCO ROAD	TCF	1941
SLEEPERS WEST	TCF	1941
DEAD MEN TELL	TCF	1941
SCOTLAND YARD	TCF	1941
THAT NIGHT IN RIO	TCF	1941
RIDE ON VAQUERO	TCF	1941
MAIL TRAIN	TCF	1941
GREAT AMERICAN BROADCAST, THE	TCF	1941
COWBOY AND THE BLONDE, THE	TCF	1941
BLOOD AND SAND	TCF	1941
FOR BEAUTY'S SAKE	TCF	1941
MAN HUNT	TCF	1941
BRIDE WORE CRUTCHES	TCF	1941
VERY YOUNG LADY, A	TCF	1941
REMARKABLE MR. KIPPS, THE	TCF	1941
MOON OVER MIAMI	TCF	1941
ACCENT ON LOVE	TCF	1941

FILM	STUDIO	RELEASE YEAR
DANCE HALL	TCF	1941
CHARLEY'S AUNT	TCF	1941
DRESSED TO KILL	TCF	1941
WILD GEESE CALLING	TCF	1941
PRIVATE NURSE	TCF	1941
SUN VALLEY SERENADE	TCF	1941
CHARLIE CHAN IN RIO	TCF	1941
BELLE STARR	TCF	1941
WE GO FAST	TCF	1941
LAST OF THE DUANES, THE	TCF	1941
MAN AT LARGE	TCF	1941
YANK IN THE R.A.F., A	TCF	1941
GREAT GUNS	TCF	1941
RIDERS OF THE PURPLE SAGE	TCF	1941
WEEKEND IN HAVANA	TCF	1941
MOON OVER HER SHOULDER	TCF	1941
HOW GREEN WAS MY VALLEY	TCF	1941
SMALL TOWN DEB	TCF	1941
I WAKE UP SCREAMING	TCF	1941
SWAMP WATER	TCF	1941
RISE AND SHINE	TCF	1941
CADET GIRL	TCF	1941
MARRY THE BOSS'S DAUGHTER	TCF	1941
CONFIRM OR DENY	TCF	1941
PERFECT SNOB, THE	TCF	1941
REMEMBER THE DAY	TCF	1941
SON OF FURY	TCF	1941
BLUE, WHITE, AND PERFECT	TCF	1941
GENTLEMAN AT HEART, A	TCF	1942
RIGHT TO THE HEART	TCF	1942
YOUNG AMERICA	TCF	1942
ON THE SUNNY SIDE	TCF	1942
CASTLE IN THE DESERT	TCF	1942
NIGHT BEFORE THE DIVORCE	TCF	1942
TO THE SHORES OF TRIPOLI	TCF	1942
SONG OF THE ISLANDS	TCF	1942
LONE STAR RANGER	TCF	1942
RINGS ON HER FINGERS	TCF	1942
SUNDOWN JIM	TCF	1942
SECRET AGENT OF JAPAN	TCF	1942

FILM	STUDIO	RELEASE YEAR
WHO IS HOPE SCHUYLER?	TCF	1942
MY GAL SAL	TCF	1942
MAN WHO WOULDN'T DIE, THE	TCF	1942
THIS ABOVE ALL	TCF	1942
MAD MARTINDALES, THE	TCF	1942
WHISPERING GHOSTS	TCF	1942
IT HAPPENED IN FLATBUSH	TCF	1942
MOONTIDE	TCF	1942
MAGNIFICENT DOPE, THE	TCF	1942
THRU DIFFERENT EYES	TCF	1942
TEN GENTLEMEN FROM WEST POINT	TCF	1942
POSTMAN DIDN'T RING, THE	TCF	1942
LITTLE TOKYO U. S. A.	TCF	1942
UNITED WE STAND	TCF	1942
FOOTLIGHT SERENADE	TCF	1942
A-HAUNTING WE WILL GO	TCF	1942
ICELAND	TCF	1942
PIED PIPER, THE	TCF	1942
LOVES OF EDGAR ALLAN POE, THE	TCF	1942
ORCHESTRA WIVES	TCF	1942
BERLIN CORRESPONDENT	TCF	1942
CAREFUL, SOFT SHOULDERS	TCF	1942
MAN IN THE TRUNK, THE	TCF	1942
YOUNG MR. PITT, THE	TCF	1942
TALES OF MANHATTAN	TCF	1942
JUST OFF BROADWAY	TCF	1942
GIRL TROUBLE	TCF	1942
MANILA CALLING	TCF	1942
DR. RENAULT'S SECRET	TCF	1942
THUNDER BIRDS	TCF	1942
IT'S EVERYBODY'S WAR	TCF	1942
SPRINGTIME IN THE ROCKIES	TCF	1942
THAT OTHER WOMAN	TCF	1942
UNDYING MONSTER	TCF	1942
BLACK SWAN, THE	TCF	1942
CHINA GIRL	TCF	1942
WE ARE THE MARINES	TCF	1942
TIME TO KILL	TCF	1942
LIFE BEGINS AT 8:30	TCF	1942
OVER MY DEAD BODY	TCF	1943
STORMY WEATHER	TCF	1943
MEANEST MAN IN THE WORLD, THE	TCF	1943
DEATH AND TAXES	TCF	1943
IMMORTAL SERGEANT	TCF	1943
MY FRIEND FLICKA	TCF	1943
CLAUDIA	TCF	1943
MOON IS DOWN, THE	TCF	1943
CHETNIKS!	TCF	1943
MARGIN FOR ERROR	TCF	1943
ROXIE HART	TCF	1943
DIXIE DUGAN	TCF	1943
QUIET PLEASE, MURDER	TCF	1943
HELLO, FRISCO, HELLO	TCF	1943
HE HIRED THE BOSS	TCF	1943
DESERT VICTORY	TCF	1943
CRASH DIVE	TCF	1943
TONIGHT WE RAID CALAIS	TCF	1943
THEY CAME TO BLOW UP AMERICA	TCF	1943
OX-BOW INCIDENT, THE	TCF	1943
CONEY ISLAND	TCF	1943
JITTERBUGS	TCF	1943
BOMBER'S MOON	TCF	1943
HEAVEN CAN WAIT	TCF	1943
HOLY MATRIMONY	TCF	1943
WINTERTIME	TCF	1943
SWEET ROSIE O'GRADY	TCF	1943
PARIS AFTER DARK	TCF	1943
GUADALCANAL DIARY	TCF	1943
HAPPY LAND	TCF	1943
BATTLE OF RUSSIA, THE	TCF	1943
DANCING MASTERS, THE	TCF	1943
GANG'S ALL HERE, THE	TCF	1943
SONG OF BERNADETTE, THE	TCF	1943
ATTACK IN THE PACIFIC	TCF	1944
UNCENSORED	TCF	1944
LIFEBOAT	TCF	1944
LODGER, THE	TCF	1944
SULLIVANS, THE	TCF	1944
SAN DEMETRIO, LONDON	TCF	1944
PURPLE HEART, THE	TCF	1944

FILM	STUDIO	RELEASE YEAR	FILM	STUDIO	RELEASE YEAR
FOUR JILLS IN A JEEP	TCF	1944	CAPTAIN EDDIE	TCF	1945
BUFFALO BILL	TCF	1944	BELL FOR ADANO, A	TCF	1945
JANE EYRE	TCF	1944	NOB HILL	TCF	1945
TAMPICO	TCF	1944	WITHIN THESE WALLS	TCF	1945
PIN-UP GIRL	TCF	1944	STATE FAIR	TCF	1945
BERMUDA MYSTERY	TCF	1944	HOUSE ON 92ND STREET, THE	TCF	1945
EVE OF ST. MARK, THE	TCF	1944	DOLLY SISTERS, THE	TCF	1945
LADIES OF WASHINGTON	TCF	1944	AND THEN THERE WERE NONE	TCF	1945
ROGER TOUHY, GANGSTER	TCF	1944	SPIDER, THE	TCF	1945
HOME IN INDIANA	TCF	1944	FALLEN ANGEL	TCF	1945
TAKE IT OR LEAVE IT	TCF	1944	LEAVE HER TO HEAVEN	TCF	1945
WING AND A PRAYER	TCF	1944	WALK IN THE SUN, A	TCF	1945
CANDLELIGHT IN ALGERIA	TCF	1944	DOLL FACE	TCF	1945
SWEET AND LOW-DOWN	TCF	1944	SOMEWHERE IN THE NIGHT	TCF	1946
THREE SISTERS OF THE MOORS	TCF	1944	SHOCK	TCF	1946
IN THE MEANTIME, DARLING	TCF	1944	BEHIND GREEN LIGHTS	TCF	1946
BIG NOISE, THE	TCF	1944	CLAUDIA AND DAVID	TCF	1946
GREENWICH VILLAGE	TCF	1944	COLONEL EFFINGHAM'S RAID	TCF	1946
LAURA	TCF	1944	SENTIMENTAL JOURNEY	TCF	1946
SOMETHING FOR THE BOYS	TCF	1944	YANK IN LONDON, A	TCF	1946
IRISH EYES ARE SMILING	TCF	1944	JOHNNY COMES FLYING HOME	TCF	1946
SUNDAY DINNER FOR A SOLDIER	TCF	1944	DARK CORNER, THE	TCF	1946
KEYS OF THE KINGDOM, THE	TCF	1944	DRAGONWYCK	TCF	1946
WINGED VICTORY	TCF	1944	CLUNY BROWN	TCF	1946
FIGHTING LADY, THE	TCF	1944	DO YOU LOVE ME	TCF	1946
WILSON	TCF	1944	RENDEZVOUS 24	TCF	1946
TREE GROWS IN BROOKLYN, A	TCF	1945	STRANGE TRIANGLE	TCF	1946
HANGOVER SQUARE	TCF	1945	WANTED FOR MURDER	TCF	1946
THUNDERHEAD - SON OF FLICKA	TCF	1945	ANNA AND THE KING OF SIAM	TCF	1946
MOLLY AND ME	TCF	1945	IT SHOULDN'T HAPPEN TO A DOG	TCF	1946
ROYAL SCANDAL, A	TCF	1945	SMOKY	TCF	1946
CIRCUMSTANTIAL EVIDENCE	TCF	1945	CENTENNIAL SUMMER	TCF	1946
BULLFIGHTERS, THE	TCF	1945	DEADLINE FOR MURDER	TCF	1946
BILLY ROSE'S DIAMOND HORSESHOE	TCF	1945	BLACK BEAUTY	TCF	1946
ALL STAR BOND RALLY	TCF	1945	IF I'M LUCKY	TCF	1946
WHERE DO WE GO FROM HERE?	TCF	1945	THREE LITTLE GIRLS IN BLUE	TCF	1946
CARIBBEAN MYSTERY, THE	TCF	1945	HOME SWEET HOMICIDE	TCF	1946
DON JUAN QUILLIGAN	TCF	1945	STRANGE JOURNEY	TCF	1946
WAY AHEAD, THE	TCF	1945	MARGIE	TCF	1946
JUNIOR MISS	TCF	1945	DANGEROUS MILLIONS	TCF	1946

FILM	STUDIO	RELEASE YEAR	FILM	STUDIO	RELEASE YEAR
RAZOR'S EDGE, THE	TCF	1946	COUNTERFEITERS, THE	TCF	1948
WAKE UP AND DREAM	TCF	1946	IRON CURTAIN, THE	TCF	1948
MY DARLING CLEMENTINE	TCF	1946	ARTHUR TAKES OVER	TCF	1948
SHOCKING MISS PILGRIM, THE	TCF	1946	ANNA KARENINA	TCF	1948
BACKLASH	TCF	1946	WINNER'S CIRCLE, THE	TCF	1948
MIRACLE ON 34TH STREET	TCF	1947	GREEN GRASS OF WYOMING	TCF	1948
MEET ME AT DAWN	TCF	1947	GIVE MY REGARDS TO BROADWAY	TCF	1948
13 RUE MADELEINE	TCF	1947	THIS WAS A WOMAN	TCF	1948
BRASHER DOUBLOON, THE	TCF	1947	STREET WITH NO NAME, THE	TCF	1948
BOOMERANG	TCF	1947	CHECKERED COAT, THE	TCF	1948
LATE GEORGE APLEY, THE	TCF	1947	DEEP WATERS	TCF	1948
HOMESTRETCH, THE	TCF	1947	FIGHTING BACK	TCF	1948
CARNIVAL IN COSTA RICA	TCF	1947	ESCAPE	TCF	1948
JEWELS OF BRANDENBURG	TCF	1947	WALLS OF JERICHO, THE	TCF	1948
MOSS ROSE	TCF	1947	THAT LADY IN ERMINE	TCF	1948
GHOST AND MRS. MUIR, THE	TCF	1947	JUNGLE PATROL	TCF	1948
CRIMSON KEY, THE	TCF	1947	CREEPER, THE	TCF	1948
SECOND CHANCE	TCF	1947	NIGHT WIND	TCF	1948
I WONDER WHO'S KISSING HER NOW	TCF	1947	GAY INTRUDERS, THE	TCF	1948
KISS OF DEATH	TCF	1947	LUCK OF THE IRISH, THE	TCF	1948
MOTHER WORE TIGHTS	TCF	1947	ROAD HOUSE	TCF	1948
FOXES OF HARROW, THE	TCF	1947	CRY OF THE CITY	TCF	1948
FOREVER AMBER	TCF	1947	APARTMENT FOR PEGGY	TCF	1948
INVISIBLE WALL, THE	TCF	1947	CHALLENGE, THE	TCF	1948
NIGHTMARE ALLEY	TCF	1947	WHEN MY BABY SMILES AT ME	TCF	1948
THUNDER IN THE VALLEY	TCF	1947	SNAKE PIT, THE	TCF	1948
ROSES ARE RED	TCF	1947	BELLE STARR'S DAUGHTER	TCF	1948
GENTLEMAN'S AGREEMENT	TCF	1947	BUNGALOW 13	TCF	1948
DANGEROUS YEARS	TCF	1947	THAT WONDERFUL URGE	TCF	1948
CAPTAIN FROM CASTILE	TCF	1947	UNFAITHFULLY YOURS	TCF	1948
DAISY KENYON	TCF	1947	YELLOW SKY	TCF	1949
TENDER YEARS, THE	TCF	1948	TROUBLE PREFERRED	TCF	1949
CALL NORTHSIDE 777	TCF	1948	MINE OWN EXCUTIONER	TCF	1949
YOU WERE MEANT FOR ME	TCF	1948	CHICKEN EVERY SUNDAY	TCF	1949
LET'S LIVE AGAIN	TCF	1948	LETTER TO THREE WIVES	TCF	1949
HALF PAST MIDNIGHT	TCF	1948	MISS MINK OF 1949	TCF	1949
SITTING PRETTY	TCF	1948	DOWN TO THE SEA IN SHIPS	TCF	1949
SCUDDA HOO! SCUDDA HAY!	TCF	1948	CANADIAN PACIFIC	TCF	1949
FURY AT FURNACE CREEK	TCF	1948	MAN ABOUT THE HOUSE	TCF	1949
13 LEAD SOLDIERS	TCF	1948	MOTHER IS A FRESHMAN	TCF	1949

FILM	STUDIO	RELEASE YEAR
I CHEATED THE LAW	TCF	1949
TUCSON	TCF	1949
FAN, THE	TCF	1949
MR. BELVEDERE GOES TO COLLEGE	TCF	1949
FORBIDDEN STREET, THE	TCF	1949
BEAUTIFUL BLONDE FROM BASHFUL BEND, THE	TCF	1949
IT HAPPENS EVERY SPRING	TCF	1949
HOUSE OF STRANGERS	TCF	1949
YOU'RE MY EVERYTHING	TCF	1949
WILL JAMES' SAND	TCF	1949
SLATTERY'S HURRICANE	TCF	1949
I WAS A MALE WAR BRIDE	TCF	1949
COME TO THE STABLE	TCF	1949
THIEVES' HIGHWAY	TCF	1949
FATHER WAS A FULLBACK	TCF	1949
EVERYBODY DOES IT	TCF	1949
OH, YOU BEAUTIFUL DOLL	TCF	1949
PINKY	TCF	1949
PRINCE OF FOXES	TCF	1949
FIGHTING MAN OF THE PLAINS, THE	TCF	1949
WHIRLPOOL	TCF	1949
DANCING IN THE DARK	TCF	1949
TWELVE O'CLOCK HIGH	TCF	1949
ARTHUR RUBINSTEIN #101	TCF	1950
ARTHUR RUBENSTEIN #102	TCF	1950
JAN PEERCE AND NADINE CONNER	TCF	1950
JASCHA HEIFETZ #103	TCF	1950
JASCHA HEIFETZ #104	TCF	1950
WHEN WILLIE COMES MARCHING HOME	TCF	1950
DAKOTA LIL	TCF	1950
THREE CAME HOME	TCF	1950
MOTHER DIDN'T TELL ME	TCF	1950
UNDER MY SKIN	TCF	1950
CHEAPER BY THE DOZEN	TCF	1950
BIG LIFT, THE	TCF	1950
TICKET TO TOMAHAWK, A	TCF	1950
WABASH AVENUE	TCF	1950
LOVE THAT BRUTE	TCF	1950
NIGHT AND THE CITY	TCF	1950

FILM	STUDIO	RELEASE YEAR
PANIC IN THE STREETS	TCF	1950
GUNFIGHTER, THE	TCF	1950
WHERE THE SIDEWALK ENDS	TCF	1950
BROKEN ARROW	TCF	1950
CARIBOO TRAIL, THE	TCF	1950
STELLA	TCF	1950
NO WAY OUT	TCF	1950
BLACK ROSE, THE	TCF	1950
MY BLUE HEAVEN	TCF	1950
FAREWELL TO YESTERDAY	TCF	1950
MISTER 880	TCF	1950
I'LL GET BY	TCF	1950
TWO FLAGS WEST	TCF	1950
ALL ABOUT EVE	TCF	1950
JACKPOT, THE	TCF	1950
AMERICAN GUERRILLA IN THE PHILIPPINES	TCF	1950
FIREBALL, THE	TCF	1950
MUDLARK, THE	TCF	1950
FOR HEAVEN'S SAKE	TCF	1950
MAN WHO CHEATED HIMSELF, THE	TCF	1950
ANDRES SEGOVIA	TCF	1951
ELLEN DOSIA & EUGENE CONLEY	TCF	1951
MARIAN ANDERSON	TCF	1951
PIATIGORSKY	TCF	1951
HALLS OF MONTEZUMA	TCF	1951
TRIO	TCF	1951
CALL ME MISTER	TCF	1951
OF MEN AND MUSIC	TCF	1951
I'D CLIMB THE HIGHEST MOUNTAIN	TCF	1951
13TH LETTER , THE	TCF	1951
YOU'RE IN THE NAVY NOW	TCF	1951
LUCKY NICK CAIN	TCF	1951
SWORD OF MONTE CRISTO, THE	TCF	1951
BIRD OF PARADISE	TCF	1951
RAWHIDE	TCF	1951
FOURTEEN HOURS	TCF	1951
I CAN GET IT FOR YOU WHOLESALE	TCF	1951
ON THE RIVIERA	TCF	1951
FOLLOW THE SUN	TCF	1951
HALF ANGEL	TCF	1951

FILM	STUDIO	RELEASE YEAR
HOUSE ON TELEGRAPH HILL, THE	TCF	1951
FROGMEN, THE	TCF	1951
TAKE CARE OF MY LITTLE GIRL	TCF	1951
NO HIGHWAY IN THE SKY	TCF	1951
MR. BELVEDERE RINGS THE BELL	TCF	1951
AS YOUNG AS YOU FEEL	TCF	1951
SECRET OF CONVICT LAKE, THE	TCF	1951
DAVID AND BATHSHEBA	TCF	1951
MEET ME AFTER THE SHOW	TCF	1951
GUY WHO CAME BACK, THE	TCF	1951
PEOPLE WILL TALK	TCF	1951
MILLIONAIRE FOR CHRISTY, A	TCF	1951
DAY THE EARTH STOOD STILL, THE	TCF	1951
JOURNEY INTO LIGHT	TCF	1951
LOVE NEST	TCF	1951
DESERT FOX, THE	TCF	1951
ANNE OF THE INDIES	TCF	1951
GOLDEN GIRL	TCF	1951
MODEL AND THE MARRIAGE BROKER, THE	TCF	1951
LET'S MAKE IT LEGAL	TCF	1951
ELOPEMENT	TCF	1951
FIXED BAYONETS!	TCF	1951
GIRL ON THE BRIDGE, THE	TCF	1951
GUEST, THE	TCF	1951
I'LL NEVER FORGET YOU	TCF	1951
DECISION BEFORE DAWN	TCF	1951
JAPANESE WAR BRIDE	TCF	1952
PHONE CALL FROM A STRANGER	TCF	1952
RED SKIES OF MONTANA	TCF	1952
VIVA ZAPATA!	TCF	1952
RETURN OF THE TEXAN	TCF	1952
5 FINGERS	TCF	1952
DEADLINE-U.S.A.	TCF	1952
ROSE OF CIMARRON	TCF	1952
WITH A SONG IN MY HEART	TCF	1952
BELLES ON THEIR TOES	TCF	1952
PRIDE OF ST. LOUIS, THE	TCF	1952
OUTCASTS OF POKER FLAT, THE	TCF	1952
KANGAROO	TCF	1952
LYDIA BAILEY	TCF	1952

FILM	STUDIO	RELEASE YEAR
DIPLOMATIC COURIER	TCF	1952
WAIT TILL THE SUN SHINES, NELLIE	TCF	1952
LADY IN THE IRON MASK	TCF	1952
WE'RE NOT MARRIED	TCF	1952
DON'T BOTHER TO KNOCK	TCF	1952
DREAMBOAT	TCF	1952
LURE OF THE WILDERNESS	TCF	1952
WHAT PRICE GLORY	TCF	1952
LES MISERABLES	TCF	1952
MONKEY BUSINESS	TCF	1952
SNOWS OF KILIMANJARO, THE	TCF	1952
SOMETHING FOR THE BIRDS	TCF	1952
MY WIFE'S BEST FRIEND	TCF	1952
WAY OF A GAUCHO	TCF	1952
O. HENRY'S FULL HOUSE	TCF	1952
NIGHT WITHOUT SLEEP	TCF	1952
STEEL TRAP, THE	TCF	1952
BLOODHOUNDS OF BROADWAY	TCF	1952
THIEF OF VENICE, THE	TCF	1952
MY PAL GUS	TCF	1952
STAR, THE	TCF	1952
PONY SOLDIER	TCF	1952
STARS AND STRIPES FOREVER	TCF	1952
MY COUSIN RACHEL	TCF	1952
RUBY GENTRY	TCF	1952
I DON'T CARE GIRL, THE	TCF	1953
NIAGARA	TCF	1953
TAXI	TCF	1953
TONIGHT WE SING	TCF	1953
SILVER WHIP, THE	TCF	1953
TREASURE OF THE GOLDEN CONDOR	TCF	1953
BENEATH THE 12-MILE REEF	TCF	1953
DOWN AMONG THE SHELTERING PALMS	TCF	1953
CALL ME MADAM	TCF	1953
MAN ON A TIGHTROPE	TCF	1953
TITANIC	TCF	1953
INVADERS FROM MARS	TCF	1953
DESTINATION GOBI	TCF	1953
DESERT RATS, THE	TCF	1953
GIRL NEXT DOOR, THE	TCF	1953

FILM	STUDIO	RELEASE YEAR
GLORY BRIGADE, THE	TCF	1953
PRESIDENT'S LADY, THE	TCF	1953
POWDER RIVER	TCF	1953
PICKUP ON SOUTH STREET	TCF	1953
FARMER TAKES A WIFE, THE	TCF	1953
KID FROM LEFT FIELD, THE	TCF	1953
SAILOR OF THE KING	TCF	1953
WHITE WITCH DOCTOR	TCF	1953
INFERNO	TCF	1953
GENTLEMEN PREFER BLONDES	TCF	1953
DANGEROUS CROSSING	TCF	1953
BLUEPRINT FOR MURDER, A	TCF	1953
CITY OF BAD MEN	TCF	1953
MR. SCOUTMASTER	TCF	1953
THY NEIGHBOR'S WIFE	TCF	1953
VICKI	TCF	1953
MISS ROBIN CRUSOE	TCF	1953
HOW TO MARRY A MILLIONAIRE	TCF	1953
MAN CRAZY	TCF	1953
VESUVIUS EXPRESS	TCF	1953
KING OF THE KHYBER RIFLES	TCF	1953
MAN IN THE ATTIC	TCF	1953
CALYPSO CRUISE	TCF	1954
CORONATION PARADE, THE	TCF	1954
FABULOUS LAS VEGAS	TCF	1954
FAREWELL SYMPHONY	TCF	1954
LAND OF LEGEND	TCF	1954
NEW HORIZONS	TCF	1954
NEW VENEZUELA, THE	TCF	1954
THREE YOUNG TEXANS	TCF	1954
POLOVETZKIAN DANCES FROM PRINCE IGOR	TCF	1954
HELL AND HIGH WATER	TCF	1954
TOURNAMENT OF ROSES	TCF	1954
NEW FACES	TCF	1954
RACING BLOOD	TCF	1954
ROCKET MAN, THE	TCF	1954
PRINCE VALIANT	TCF	1954
RIVER OF NO RETURN	TCF	1954
GORILLA AT LARGE	TCF	1954
SIEGE AT RED RIVER	TCF	1954

FILM	STUDIO	RELEASE YEAR
MOTION PICTURE STUNT PILOT, THE	TCF	1954
NIGHT PEOPLE	TCF	1954
THREE COINS IN THE FOUNTAIN	TCF	1954
DEMETRIUS AND THE GLADIATORS	TCF	1954
PRINCESS OF THE NILE	TCF	1954
ROYAL TOUR OF QUEEN ELIZABETH AND PHILIP, THE	TCF	1954
GARDEN OF EVIL	TCF	1954
JET CARRIER	TCF	1954
GAMBLER FROM NATCHEZ, THE	TCF	1954
RAID, THE	TCF	1954
MIRACLE OF STEREOPHONIC SOUND, THE	TCF	1954
EGYPTIAN, THE	TCF	1954
BROKEN LANCE	TCF	1954
ADVENTURES OF HAJJI BABA, THE	TCF	1954
WOMAN'S WORLD	TCF	1954
CARMEN JONES	TCF	1954
BLACK WIDOW	TCF	1954
CINEMASCOPE PARADE, THE	TCF	1954
OUTLAW'S DAUGHTER, THE	TCF	1954
SUPERMAN AND THE JUNGLE DEVIL	TCF	1954
SUPERMAN IN EXILE	TCF	1954
SUPERMAN'S PERIL	TCF	1954
SUPERMAN AND SCOTLAND YARD	TCF	1954
BLACK 13	TCF	1954
DESIREE	TCF	1954
OTHER WOMAN,THE	TCF	1954
DEVIL'S HARBOR	TCF	1954
HUNTERS OF THE DEEP	TCF	1954
LONG JOHN SILVER	TCF	1954
THERE'S NO BUSINESS LIKE SHOW BUSINESS	TCF	1954
BIRTHDAY PARADE	TCF	1955
CHILDREN OF THE SUN	TCF	1955
DESERT FANTASY	TCF	1955
FAR EAST BASTIONS	TCF	1955
FLYING TO FISH	TCF	1955
FIFTH AVENUE TO FUJIYAMA	TCF	1955
GODS OF THE ROAD	TCF	1955
ISLES OF LORE	TCF	1955
LAND OF THE NILE	TCF	1955

FILM	STUDIO	RELEASE YEAR
PAGEANTS AND PASTIMES	TCF	1955
THIS SUPERSONIC AGE	TCF	1955
WINTER JAMBOREE	TCF	1955
PRINCE OF PLAYERS	TCF	1955
STAMPEDE CITY	TCF	1955
RACERS, THE	TCF	1955
WHITE FEATHER	TCF	1955
UNTAMED	TCF	1955
COLORADO HOLIDAY	TCF	1955
MAN CALLED PETER, A	TCF	1955
VIOLENT SATURDAY	TCF	1955
PUNTS AND STUNTS	TCF	1955
SORCERER'S APPRENTICE, THE	TCF	1955
DADDY LONG LEGS	TCF	1955
THAT LADY	TCF	1955
ADVENTURES OF SADIE, THE	TCF	1955
MAGNIFICENT MATADOR, THE	TCF	1955
SOLDIER OF FORTUNE	TCF	1955
ANGELA	TCF	1955
SEVEN YEAR ITCH, THE	TCF	1955
HOUSE OF BAMBOO	TCF	1955
LIFE IN THE BALANCE, A	TCF	1955
LIVING SWAMP, THE	TCF	1955
HOW TO BE VERY, VERY POPULAR	TCF	1955
VIRGIN QUEEN, THE	TCF	1955
LOVE IS A MANY-SPLENDORED THING	TCF	1955
SEVEN CITIES OF GOLD	TCF	1955
ABDULLAH'S HAREM	TCF	1955
LEFT HAND OF GOD, THE	TCF	1955
LOVER BOY	TCF	1955
GIRL IN THE RED VELVET SWING, THE	TCF	1955
PEPE EL TORO	TCF	1955
TALL MEN, THE	TCF	1955
DEEP BLUE SEA, THE	TCF	1955
VIEW FROM POMPEY'S HEAD, THE	TCF	1955
WARRIORS, THE	TCF	1955
GOOD MORNING MISS DOVE	TCF	1955
RAINS OF RANCHIPUR, THE	TCF	1955
LIEUTENANT WORE SKIRTS, THE	TCF	1956
BOTTOM OF THE BOTTLE, THE	TCF	1956

FILM	STUDIO	RELEASE YEAR
CAROUSEL	TCF	1956
ON THE THRESHOLD OF SPACE	TCF	1956
MOHAWK	TCF	1956
REVOLT OF MAMIE STOVER, THE	TCF	1956
PROUD ONES, THE	TCF	1956
HILDA CRANE	TCF	1956
MAN IN THE GRAY FLANNEL SUIT, THE	TCF	1956
23 PACES TO BAKER STREET	TCF	1956
MAN WHO NEVER WAS, THE	TCF	1956
D-DAY THE SIXTH OF JUNE	TCF	1956
DARK WAVE, THE	TCF	1956
MASSACRE	TCF	1956
KING AND I, THE	TCF	1956
BIGGER THAN LIFE	TCF	1956
QUEEN OF BABYLON	TCF	1956
BUS STOP	TCF	1956
LAST WAGON, THE	TCF	1956
BEST THINGS IN LIFE ARE FREE, THE	TCF	1956
BETWEEN HEAVEN AND HELL	TCF	1956
DESPERADOS ARE IN TOWN, THE	TCF	1956
TEENAGE REBEL	TCF	1956
LOVE ME TENDER	TCF	1956
BLACK WHIP, THE	TCF	1956
GIRL CAN'T HELP IT, THE	TCF	1956
OKLAHOMA!	TCF	1956
THREE BRAVE MEN	TCF	1956
ANASTASIA	TCF	1956
STAGECOACH TO FURY	TCF	1956
WOMEN OF PITCAIRN ISLAND, THE	TCF	1957
ENEMY BELOW, THE	TCF	1957
APRIL LOVE	TCF	1957
OH, MEN! OH, WOMEN!	TCF	1957
QUIET GUN, THE	TCF	1957
STORM RIDER, THE	TCF	1957
TRUE STORY OF JESSE JAMES, THE	TCF	1957
KRONOS	TCF	1957
SHE DEVIL, THE	TCF	1957
BREAK IN THE CIRCLE	TCF	1957
BOY ON A DOLPHIN	TCF	1957
RIVER'S EDGE, THE	TCF	1957

FILM	STUDIO	RELEASE YEAR
OASIS	TCF	1957
BADLANDS OF MONTANA	TCF	1957
DESK SET	TCF	1957
LURE OF THE SWAMP	TCF	1957
RESTLESS BREED, THE	TCF	1957
BIG SHOW, THE	TCF	1957
CHINA GATE	TCF	1957
WAY TO THE GOLD, THE	TCF	1957
WAYWARD BUS, THE	TCF	1957
ISLAND IN THE SUN	TCF	1957
SMILEY	TCF	1957
ABDUCTORS, THE	TCF	1957
APACHE WARRIOR	TCF	1957
GOD IS MY PARTNER	TCF	1957
AFFAIR TO REMEMBER, AN	TCF	1957
HATFUL OF RAIN, A	TCF	1957
WILL SUCCESS SPOIL ROCK HUNTER?	TCF	1957
HELL ON DEVIL'S ISLAND	TCF	1957
BACK FROM THE DEAD	TCF	1957
UNKNOWN TERROR	TCF	1957
SUN ALSO RISES, THE	TCF	1957
COPPER SKY, THE	TCF	1957
COURAGE OF BLACK BEAUTY	TCF	1957
DEERSLAYER, THE	TCF	1957
THREE FACES OF EVE, THE	TCF	1957
UNDER FIRE	TCF	1957
FORTY GUNS	TCF	1957
GHOST DIVER	TCF	1957
NO DOWN PAYMENT	TCF	1957
ROCKABILLY BABY	TCF	1957
YOUNG AND DANGEROUS	TCF	1957
RIDE A VIOLENT MILE	TCF	1957
STOPOVER TOKYO	TCF	1957
HEAVEN KNOWS MR. ALLISON	TCF	1957
BERNARDINE	TCF	1957
ABOMINABLE SNOWMAN	TCF	1957
ESCAPE FROM RED ROCK	TCF	1957
SEA WIFE	TCF	1957
PLUNDER ROAD	TCF	1957
KISS THEM FOR ME	TCF	1957

FILM	STUDIO	RELEASE YEAR
PEYTON PLACE	TCF	1957
FAREWELL TO ARMS, A	TCF	1957
CATTLE EMPIRE	TCF	1958
SING BOY SING	TCF	1958
DIAMOND SAFARI	TCF	1958
GIFT OF LOVE, THE	TCF	1958
AMBUSH AT CIMARRON PASS	TCF	1958
COUNT FIVE AND DIE	TCF	1958
SOUTH PACIFIC	TCF	1958
BLOOD ARROW	TCF	1958
BRAVADOS, THE	TCF	1958
GANG WAR	TCF	1958
YOUNG LIONS, THE	TCF	1958
LONG, HOT SUMMER, THE	TCF	1958
SHOWDOWN AT BOOT HILL	TCF	1958
TEN NORTH FREDERICK	TCF	1958
THUNDERING JETS	TCF	1958
SMILEY GETS A GUN	TCF	1958
FROM HELL TO TEXAS	TCF	1958
NAKED EARTH, THE	TCF	1958
SPACE MASTER X-7	TCF	1958
FRAULEIN	TCF	1958
DESERT HELL	TCF	1958
SIERRA BARON	TCF	1958
WOLF DOG	TCF	1958
CERTAIN SMILE, A	TCF	1958
FIEND WHO WALKED THE WEST, THE	TCF	1958
FLY, THE	TCF	1958
HUNTERS, THE	TCF	1958
HARRY BLACK AND THE TIGER	TCF	1958
BARBARIAN AND THE GEISHA, THE	TCF	1958
VILLA!	TCF	1958
ROOTS OF HEAVEN, THE	TCF	1958
IN LOVE AND WAR	TCF	1958
INTENT TO KILL	TCF	1958
RX FOR MURDER	TCF	1958
MARDI GRAS	TCF	1958
FRONTIER GUN	TCF	1958
NICE LITTLE BANK THAT SHOULD BE ROBBED, A	TCF	1958

FILM	STUDIO	RELEASE YEAR
INN OF THE SIXTH HAPPINESS, THE	TCF	1958
NAVY LARK, THE	TCF	1959
PROPHET OF TOMORROW	TCF	1959
I, MOBSTER	TCF	1959
'RALLY ROUND THE FLAG, BOYS!	TCF	1959
REMARKABLE MR. PENNYPACKER, THE	TCF	1959
ALASKA PASSAGE	TCF	1959
LITTLE SAVAGE, THE	TCF	1959
LONE TEXAN	TCF	1959
SAD HORSE,THE	TCF	1959
SOUND AND THE FURY, THE	TCF	1959
DIARY OF ANNE FRANK, THE	TCF	1959
WARLOCK	TCF	1959
COMPULSION	TCF	1959
THESE THOUSAND HILLS	TCF	1959
WOMAN OBSESSED	TCF	1959
HERE COME THE JETS	TCF	1959
SAY ONE FOR ME	TCF	1959
RETURN OF THE FLY	TCF	1959
SON OF ROBIN HOOD	TCF	1959
HOLIDAY FOR LOVERS	TCF	1959
MIRACLE OF THE HILLS	TCF	1959
BOBBIKINS	TCF	1959
ALLIGATOR PEOPLE	TCF	1959
BLUE ANGEL, THE	TCF	1959
OREGON TRAIL, THE	TCF	1959
PRIVATE'S AFFAIR, A	TCF	1959
BLUE DENIM	TCF	1959
FIVE GATES TO HELL	TCF	1959
BEST OF EVERYTHING, THE	TCF	1959
HOUND-DOG MAN	TCF	1959
SHERIFF OF FRACTURED JAW, THE	TCF	1958
MAN WHO UNDERSTOOD WOMEN, THE	TCF	1959
BELOVED INFIDEL	TCF	1959
BLOOD AND STEEL	TCF	1959
STORY ON PAGE ONE, THE	TCF	1959
JOURNEY TO THE CENTER OF THE EARTH	TCF	1959
SPACE ATTACK	TCF	1960
3rd VOICE, THE	TCF	1960
SINK THE BISMARCK	TCF	1960

FILM	STUDIO	RELEASE YEAR
CAN-CAN	TCF	1960
WIND CANNOT READ, THE	TCF	1960
MASTERS OF THE CONGO JUNGLE	TCF	1960
SEVEN THIEVES	TCF	1960
ROOKIE, THE	TCF	1960
DOG OF FLANDERS, A	TCF	1960
WILD RIVER	TCF	1960
WHEN COMEDY WAS KING	TCF	1960
13 FIGHTING MEN	TCF	1960
TWELVE HOURS TO KILL	TCF	1960
FLAME OVER INDIA	TCF	1960
VALLEY OF THE REDWOODS	TCF	1960
CRACK IN THE MIRROR	TCF	1960
THREE MURDERESSES	TCF	1959
WAKE ME WHEN IT'S OVER	TCF	1960
STORY OF RUTH, THE	TCF	1960
MURDER, INC.	TCF	1960
FROM THE TERRACE	TCF	1960
OPERATION AMSTERDAM	TCF	1960
LOST WORLD, THE	TCF	1960
IDIOT, THE	TCF	1960
YOUNG JESSE JAMES	TCF	1960
SONS AND LOVERS	TCF	1960
FOR THE LOVE OF MIKE	TCF	1960
HIGH-POWERED RIFLE	TCF	1960
SQUAD CAR	TCF	1960
WALK TALL	TCF	1960
LET'S MAKE LOVE	TCF	1960
SEPTEMBER STORM	TCF	1960
ONE FOOT IN HELL	TCF	1960
HIGH TIME	TCF	1960
CAPTAIN'S TABLE, THE	TCF	1960
DESIRE IN THE DUST	TCF	1960
39 STEPS, THE	TCF	1960
MILLIONAIRESS, THE	TCF	1960
FRECKLES	TCF	1960
CIRCLE OF DECEPTION	TCF	1960
GODDESS OF LOVE, THE	TCF	1960
NORTH TO ALASKA	TCF	1960
LEGIONS OF THE NILE	TCF	1960

FILM	STUDIO	RELEASE YEAR
WIZARD OF BAGHDAD, THE	TCF	1960
TRAPPED IN TANGIERS	TCF	1960
UPSTAIRS AND DOWNSTAIRS	TCF	1960
SECRET OF THE PURPLE REEF, THE	TCF	1960
ESTHER AND THE KING	TCF	1960
FLAMING STAR	TCF	1960
MARRIAGE-GO-ROUND, THE	TCF	1961
LONG ROPE, THE	TCF	1961
SNIPER'S RIDGE	TCF	1961
SANCTUARY	TCF	1961
CANADIANS, THE	TCF	1961
DAYS OF THRILLS AND LAUGHTER, THE	TCF	1961
DESERT ATTACK	TCF	1961
FIERCEST HEART, THE	TCF	1961
ALL HANDS ON DECK	TCF	1961
TRAPP FAMILY, THE	TCF	1961
FERRY TO HONG KONG	TCF	1961
BIG SHOW, THE	TCF	1961
SILENT CALL, THE	TCF	1961
RETURN TO PEYTON PLACE	TCF	1961
RIGHT APPROACH, THE	TCF	1961
SNOW WHITE AND THE THREE STOOGES	TCF	1961
BATTLE AT BLOODY BEACH	TCF	1961
LITTLE SHEPHERD OF KINGDOM COME, THE	TCF	1961
MISTY	TCF	1961
20,000 EYES	TCF	1961
WILD IN THE COUNTRY	TCF	1961
FRANCIS OF ASSISI	TCF	1961
VOYAGE TO THE BOTTOM OF THE SEA	TCF	1961
MARINES, LET'S GO	TCF	1961
BIG GAMBLE, THE	TCF	1961
HUSTLER, THE	TCF	1961
PIRATES OF TORTUGA	TCF	1961
SEVEN WOMEN FROM HELL	TCF	1961
QUEEN'S GUARDS, THE	TCF	1961
COMANCHEROS, THE	TCF	1961
PURPLE HILLS, THE	TCF	1961
TWO LITTLE BEARS, THE	TCF	1961
TESS OF THE STORM COUNTRY	TCF	1961
SECOND TIME AROUND, THE	TCF	1961

FILM	STUDIO	RELEASE YEAR
INNOCENTS, THE	TCF	1961
MADISON AVENUE	TCF	1962
BACHELOR FLAT	TCF	1962
TENDER IS THE NIGHT	TCF	1962
SWINGIN' ALONG	TCF	1962
SATAN NEVER SLEEPS	TCF	1962
HAND OF DEATH	TCF	1962
STATE FAIR	TCF	1962
BROKEN LAND, THE	TCF	1962
LISA	TCF	1962
I LIKE MONEY	TCF	1962
CABINET OF CALIGARI, THE	TCF	1962
IT HAPPENED IN ATHENS	TCF	1962
WOMAN HUNT	TCF	1962
MR. HOBBS TAKES A VACATION	TCF	1962
AIR PATROL	TCF	1962
HEMINGWAY'S ADVENTURES OF A YOUNG MAN	TCF	1962
300 SPARTANS, THE	TCF	1962
FIREBRAND	TCF	1962
FIVE WEEKS IN A BALLOON	TCF	1962
LONGEST DAY, THE	TCF	1962
LOVES OF SALAMMBO, THE	TCF	1962
YOUNG GUNS OF TEXAS	TCF	1962
GIGOT	TCF	1962
LION, THE	TCF	1962
LAST DAYS OF SODOM AND GOMORRAH	TCF	1963
DAY MARS INVADED EARTH, THE	TCF	1963
HOUSE OF THE DAMNED	TCF	1963
MARILYN	TCF	1963
POLICE NURSE	TCF	1963
YELLOW CANARY, THE	TCF	1963
STRIPPER, THE	TCF	1963
CLEOPATRA	TCF	1963
CONDEMNED OF ALTONA, THE	TCF	1963
HARBOR LIGHTS	TCF	1963
LEOPARD, THE	TCF	1963
NINE HOURS TO RAMA	TCF	1963
YOUNG SWINGERS, THE	TCF	1963
OF LOVE AND DESIRE	TCF	1963

FILM	STUDIO	RELEASE YEAR
THUNDER ISLAND	TCF	1963
TAKE HER, SHE'S MINE	TCF	1963
MOVE OVER, DARLING	TCF	1963
SURF PARTY	TCF	1964
MAN IN THE MIDDLE, THE	TCF	1964
SHOCK TREATMENT	TCF	1964
THIRD SECRET, THE	TCF	1964
CURSE OF THE LIVING CORPSE, THE	TCF	1964
WHAT A WAY TO GO	TCF	1964
HORROR OF PARTY BEACH, THE	TCF	1964
HORROR OF IT ALL, THE	TCF	1964
WITCHCRAFT	TCF	1964
VISIT, THE	TCF	1964
NIGHT TRAIN TO PARIS	TCF	1964
APACHE RIFLES	TCF	1964
FATE IS THE HUNTER	TCF	1964
GUNS AT BATASI	TCF	1964
RIO CONCHOS	TCF	1964
MORO WITCH DOCTOR	TCF	1964
BACK DOOR TO HELL	TCF	1964
GOODBYE CHARLIE	TCF	1964
RAIDERS FROM BENEATH THE SEA	TCF	1964
ZORBA THE GREEK	TCF	1964
HUSH...HUSH, SWEET CHARLOTTE	TCF	1964
PLEASURE SEEKERS, THE	TCF	1964
DEAR BRIGITTE	TCF	1965
THANK HEAVEN FOR SMALL FAVORS	TCF	1965
SOUND OF MUSIC, THE	TCF	1965
WAR PARTY	TCF	1965
JOHN GOLDFARB, PLEASE COME HOME	TCF	1965
CURSE OF THE FLY, THE	TCF	1965
DEVILS OF DARKNESS	TCF	1965
FORT COURAGEOUS	TCF	1965
UP FROM THE BEACH	TCF	1965
HIGH WIND IN JAMAICA, A	TCF	1965
THOSE MAGNIFICENT MEN IN THEIR FLYING MACHINES	TCF	1965
CONVICT STAGE	TCF	1965
VON RYAN'S EXPRESS	TCF	1965
RAPTURE	TCF	1965

FILM	STUDIO	RELEASE YEAR
WILD ON THE BEACH	TCF	1965
EARTH DIES SCREAMING, THE	TCF	1965
MORITURI	TCF	1965
REWARD, THE	TCF	1965
SPACE FLIGHT IC-1	TCF	1965
AGONY AND THE ECSTASY, THE	TCF	1965
NANNY, THE	TCF	1965
RETURN OF MR MOTO, THE	TCF	1965
MURDER GAME, THE	TCF	1965
FLIGHT OF THE PHOENIX	TCF	1965
DO NOT DISTURB	TCF	1965
CAVERN, THE	TCF	1965
DRACULA -PRINCE OF DARKNESS	TCF	1966
PLAGUE OF THE ZOMBIES	TCF	1966
OUR MAN FLINT	TCF	1966
DANIEL BOONE - FRONTIER TRAIL RIDER	TCF	1966
RASPUTIN - THE MAD MONK	TCF	1966
REPTILE, THE	TCF	1966
CLOPORTES	TCF	1966
WEEKEND AT DUNKIRK	TCF	1966
STAGECOACH	TCF	1966
BLUE MAX, THE	TCF	1966
MODESTY BLAISE	TCF	1966
HOW TO STEAL A MILLION	TCF	1966
BATMAN	TCF	1966
SMOKY	TCF	1966
FANTASTIC VOYAGE	TCF	1966
BLUES FOR LOVERS	TCF	1966
BIBLE, THE	TCF	1966
THAT TENNESSEE BEAT	TCF	1966
WAY...WAY OUT	TCF	1966
I DEAL IN DANGER	TCF	1966
QUILLER MEMORANDUM, THE	TCF	1966
SAND PEBBLES, THE	TCF	1966
ONE MILLION YEARS B.C.	TCF	1966
DEVIL'S OWN, THE	TCF	1967
PREHISTORIC WOMEN	TCF	1967
FRANKENSTEIN CREATED WOMAN	TCF	1967
IN LIKE FLINT	TCF	1967
MUMMY'S SHROUD, THE	TCF	1967

FILM	STUDIO	RELEASE YEAR
HOMBRE	TCF	1967
TWO FOR THE ROAD	TCF	1967
CAPRICE	TCF	1967
GUIDE FOR THE MARRIED MAN, A	TCF	1967
ST. VALENTINE'S DAY MASSACRE	TCF	1967
FATHOM	TCF	1967
VIKING QUEEN, THE	TCF	1967
CAPETOWN AFFAIR, THE	TCF	1967
DAY THE FISH CAME OUT, THE	TCF	1967
FLIM FLAM MAN, THE	TCF	1967
JACKALS, THE	TCF	1967
INCIDENT, THE	TCF	1967
TONY ROME	TCF	1967
BEDAZZLED	TCF	1967
VALLEY OF THE DOLLS	TCF	1967
DOCTOR DOLITTLE	TCF	1967
ANNIVERSARY, THE	TCF	1968
PLANET OF THE APES	TCF	1968
FIVE MILLION YEARS TO EARTH	TCF	1968
EL GRECO	TCF	1968
FURTHER PERILS OF LAUREL AND HARDY, THE	TCF	1968
VENGEANCE OF THE SHE, THE	TCF	1968
PRUDENCE AND THE PILL	TCF	1968
DETECTIVE, THE	TCF	1968
BANDOLERO	TCF	1968
SWEET RIDE, THE	TCF	1968
LOST CONTINENT,THE	TCF	1968
SECRET LIFE OF AN AMERICAN WIFE, THE	TCF	1968
DEVIL'S BRIDE, THE	TCF	1968
CHALLENGE FOR ROBIN HOOD, A	TCF	1968
LEGEND OF CUSTER, THE	TCF	1968
DEADFALL	TCF	1968
BOSTON STRANGLER, THE	TCF	1968
DANGER HAS TWO FACES	TCF	1968
STAR!	TCF	1968
PRETTY POISON	TCF	1968
TOUCHABLES, THE	TCF	1968
JOANNA	TCF	1968
FLEA IN HER EAR, A	TCF	1968

FILM	STUDIO	RELEASE YEAR
LADY IN CEMENT	TCF	1968
MAGUS, THE	TCF	1968
DECLINE AND FALL OF A BIRDWATCHER	TCF	1969
GURU, THE	TCF	1969
PRIME OF MISS JEAN BRODIE, THE	TCF	1969
100 RIFLES	TCF	1969
HARD CONTRACT	TCF	1969
LAST SHOT YOU HEAR,THE	TCF	1969
VATICAN AFFAIR, THE	TCF	1969
CHAIRMAN, THE	TCF	1969
BOYS OF PAUL STREET, THE	TCF	1969
CHE!	TCF	1969
SECRET WORLD	TCF	1969
JUSTINE	TCF	1969
STAIRCASE	TCF	1969
FOOTPRINTS ON THE MOON - APOLLO 11	TCF	1969
WALK WITH LOVE AND DEATH, A	TCF	1969
BUTCH CASSIDY AND THE SUNDANCE KID	TCF	1969
UNDEFEATED, THE	TCF	1969
JOHN AND MARY	TCF	1969
HELLO, DOLLY!	TCF	1969
ONLY GAME IN TOWN, THE	TCF	1970
M*A*S*H	TCF	1970
KREMLIN LETTER, THE	TCF	1970
PATTON	TCF	1970
CHALLENGE, THE	TCF	1970
SICILIAN CLAN, THE	TCF	1970
GIRL WHO COULDN'T SAY NO	TCF	1970
BENEATH THE PLANET OF THE APES	TCF	1970
BEYOND THE VALLEY OF THE DOLLS	TCF	1970
MYRA BRECKINRIDGE	TCF	1970
HELLO-GOODBYE	TCF	1970
MOVE	TCF	1970
GAMES, THE	TCF	1970
FOUR CLOWNS	TCF	1970
TORA! TORA! TORA!	TCF	1970
COVER ME BABE	TCF	1970
GREAT WHITE HOPE, THE	TCF	1970
ESCAPE FROM THE PLANET OF THE APES	TCF	1971
MEPHISTO WALTZ, THE	TCF	1971

FILM	STUDIO	RELEASE YEAR
LITTLE MURDERS	TCF	1971
VANISHING POINT	TCF	1971
MAKING IT	TCF	1971
B.S. I LOVE YOU	TCF	1971
CELEBRATION AT BIG SUR	TCF	1971
WALKABOUT	TCF	1971
PANIC IN NEEDLE PARK, THE	TCF	1971
SEVEN MINUTES, THE	TCF	1971
MARRIAGE OF A YOUNG STOCKBROKER, THE	TCF	1971
FRENCH CONNECTION, THE	TCF	1971
DESPARATE MISSION, THE	TCF	1971
MADE FOR EACH OTHER	TCF	1971
WELCOME HOME, SOLDIER BOYS	TCF	1972
WITHOUT APPARENT MOTIVE	TCF	1972
CONCERT FOR BANGLADESH, THE	TCF	1972
CULPEPPER CATTLE COMPANY, THE	TCF	1972
HOT ROCK, THE	TCF	1972
OTHER, THE	TCF	1972
POSEIDON ADVENTURE	TCF	1972
STRANGE VENGEANCE OF ROSALIE, THE	TCF	1972
WHAT BECAME OF JACK AND JILL?	TCF	1972
CONQUEST OF THE PLANET OF THE APES	TCF	1972
TO KILL A CLOWN	TCF	1972
SALZBURG CONNECTION, THE	TCF	1972
SOUNDER	TCF	1972
DARWIN ADVENTURE, THE	TCF	1972
WHEN THE LEGENDS DIE	TCF	1972
DISCREET CHARM OF THE BOURGEOISIE, THE	TCF	1972
TROUBLE MAN	TCF	1972
VAMPIRE CIRCUS	TCF	1972
AND HOPE TO DIE	TCF	1972
SLEUTH	TCF	1972
HEARTBREAK KID, THE	TCF	1972
EFFECT OF GAMMA RAYS ON MAN-IN-THE-MOON MARIGOLDS	TCF	1972
KID BLUE	TCF	1973
GOSPEL ROAD	TCF	1973
ACE ELI AND RODGER OF THE SKIES	TCF	1973
EMPEROR OF THE NORTH POLE	TCF	1973
LEGEND OF HELL HOUSE, THE	TCF	1973
BATTLE FOR THE PLANET OF THE APES	TCF	1973
LAST AMERICAN HERO, THE	TCF	1973
NEPTUNE FACTOR, THE	TCF	1973
GORDON'S WAR	TCF	1973
HEX	TCF	1973
PAPER CHASE, THE	TCF	1973
LAUGHING POLICEMAN, THE	TCF	1973
SEVEN-UPS, THE	TCF	1973
CINDERELLA LIBERTY	TCF	1973
GREEN HORNET, THE	TCF	1974
ZARDOZ	TCF	1974
CONRACK	TC	1974
THREE MUSKETEERS, THE	TCF	1974
CLAUDINE	TCF	1974
DIRTY MARY CRAZY LARRY	TCF	1974
S*P*Y*S	TCF	1974
MAD ADVENTURES OF RABBI JACOB, THE	TCF	1974
TOGETHER BROTHERS	TCF	1974
HARRY AND TONTO	TCF	1974
99 AND 44/100% DEAD	TCF	1974
PHANTOM OF THE PARADISE	TCF	1974
11 HARROWHOUSE	TCF	1974
LACOMBE LUCIEN	TCF	1974
HOUSE ON SKULL MOUNTAIN, THE	TCF	1974
CRAZY WORLD OF JULIUS VROODER, THE	TCF	1974
PHANTOM OF LIBERTY, THE	TCF	1974
TOWERING INFERNO, THE	TCF	1974
YOUNG FRANKENSTEIN	TCF	1974
NICKEL RIDE, THE	TCF	1975
TERRORISTS, THE	TCF	1975
ROCKY HORROR PICTURE SHOW, THE	TCF	1975
FOUR MUSKETEERS, THE	TCF	1975
AT LONG LAST LOVE	TCF	1975
CAPONE	TCF	1975
FRENCH CONNECTION II	TCF	1975
W.W. AND THE DIXIE DANCEKINGS	TCF	1975
RACE WITH THE DEVIL	TCF	1975
DRAGON FLIES	TCF	1975

FILM	STUDIO	RELEASE YEAR	FILM	STUDIO	RELEASE YEAR
BLACK MOON	TCF	1975	HIGH ANXIETY	TCF	1977
PEEPER	TCF	1975	FURY, THE	TCF	1978
ROYAL FLASH	TCF	1975	UNMARRIED WOMAN, AN	TCF	1978
WHIFFS	TCF	1975	DRIVER, THE	TCF	1978
DOWN THE ANCIENT STAIRS	TCF	1975	DAMIEN - OMEN II	TCF	1978
DEVIL IS A WOMAN, THE	TCF	1975	WEDDING, A	TCF	1978
TAKE A HARD RIDE	TCF	1975	BOYS FROM BRAZIL, THE	TCF	1978
ADVENTURE OF SHERLOCK HOLMES' SMARTER BROTHER	TCF	1975	MAGIC	TCF	1978
LUCKY LADY	TCF	1975	QUINTET	TCF	1979
SCENT OF A WOMAN	TCF	1976	NORMA RAE	TCF	1979
NEXT STOP, GREENWICH VILLAGE	TCF	1976	PERFECT COUPLE, A	TCF	1979
I WILL, I WILL...FOR NOW	TCF	1976	DREAMER	TCF	1979
SKY RIDERS	TCF	1976	ALIEN	TCF	1979
DUCHESS AND THE DIRTWATER FOX, THE	TCF	1976	BUTCH AND SUNDANCE: THE EARLY DAYS	TCF	1979
BLUE BIRD, THE	TCF	1976	BREAKING AWAY	TCF	1979
END OF THE GAME	TCF	1976	LUNA	TCF	1979
MOTHER, JUGS AND SPEED	TCF	1976	NOSFERATU THE VAMPYRE	TCF	1979
LAST HARD MEN, THE	TCF	1976	AVALANCHE EXPRESS	TCF	1979
BREAKING POINT	TCF	1976	ROSE, THE	TCF	1979
SILENT MOVIE	TCF	1976	RUNNER STUMBLES, THE	TCF	1979
OMEN, THE	TCF	1976	ALL THAT JAZZ	TCF	1979
MOVING VIOLATION	TCF	1976	SCAVENGER HUNT	TCF	1979
ALEX AND THE GYPSY	TCF	1976	FATSO	TCF	1980
FIGHTING MAD	TCF	1976	INFERNO	TCF	1980
ALL THIS AND WORLD WAR II	TCF	1976	HEADIN' FOR BROADWAY	TCF	1980
SILVER STREAK, THE	TCF	1976	STAR WARS EPISODE V: THE EMPIRE STRIKES BACK	TCF	1980
WIZARDS	TCF	1977	BRUBAKER	TCF	1980
MR. BILLION	TCF	1977	STUNT MAN, THE	TCF	1980
RAGGEDY ANN AND ANDY	TCF	1977	OH, HEAVENLY DOG	TCF	1980
3 WOMEN	TCF	1977	MIDDLE AGE CRAZY	TCF	1980
STAR WARS EPISODE IV: A NEW HOPE	TCF	1977	WILLIE AND PHIL	TCF	1980
OTHER SIDE OF MIDNIGHT, THE	TCF	1977	HEALTH	TCF	1980
FIRE SALE	TCF	1977	MY BODYGUARD	TCF	1980
SUSPIRA	TCF	1977	TERROR TRAIN	TCF	1980
JULIA	TCF	1977	MAN WITH BOGART'S FACE, THE	TCF	1980
DAMNATION ALLEY	TCF	1977	KAGEMUSHA	TCF	1980
TURNING POINT, THE	TCF	1977	LOVING COUPLES	TCF	1980
THUNDER AND LIGHTNING	TCF	1977	CHANGE OF SEASONS, A	TCF	1980
WORLD'S GREATEST LOVER, THE	TCF	1977	TRIBUTE	TCF	1980

FILM	STUDIO	RELEASE YEAR
9 TO 5	TCF	1980
FORT APACHE, THE BRONX	TCF	1981
EYEWITNESS	TCF	1981
ON THE RIGHT TRACK	TCF	1981
FINAL CONFLICT, THE	TCF	1981
HARDLY WORKING	TCF	1981
DEATH HUNT	TCF	1981
SAVAGE HARVEST	TCF	1981
HISTORY OF THE WORLD, PART 1	TCF	1981
CANNONBALL RUN	TCF	1981
ZORRO, THE GAY BLADE	TCF	1981
CHU CHU AND THE PHILLY FLASH	TCF	1981
TATTOO	TCF	1981
WOMAN INSIDE, THE	TCF	1981
SOUTHERN COMFORT	TCF	1981
CHARIOTS OF FIRE	TCF	1981
SHOCK TREATMENT	TCF	1981
TAPS	TCF	1981
MODERN PROBLEMS	TCF	1981
SUZANNE	TCF	1981
VISITING HOURS	TCF	1982
QUEST FOR FIRE	TCF	1982
MAKING LOVE	TCF	1982
PORKY'S	TCF	1982
I OUGHT TO BE IN PICTURES	TCF	1982
AMATEUR, THE	TCF	1982
AUTHOR! AUTHOR!	TCF	1982
MEGAFORCE	TCF	1982
YOUNG DOCTORS IN LOVE	TCF	1982
SIX PACK	TCF	1982
PIRATE MOVIE, THE	TCF	1982
CHOSEN, THE	TCF	1982
EATING RAOUL	TCF	1982
I, THE JURY	TCF	1982
MONSIGNOR	TCF	1982
CLASS REUNION	TCF	1982
MAN FROM SNOWY RIVER, THE	TCF	1982
VERDICT, THE	TCF	1982
KISS ME GOODBYE	TCF	1982
THRESHOLD	TCF	1983

FILM	STUDIO	RELEASE YEAR
ENTITY, THE	TCF	1983
WITHOUT A TRACE	TCF	1983
KING OF COMEDY, THE	TCF	1983
BETRAYAL	TCF	1983
MAX DUGAN RETURNS	TCF	1983
HEART LIKE A WHEEL	TCF	1983
TO BEGIN AGAIN	TCF	1983
BILL COSBY, HIMSELF	TCF	1983
TOUGH ENOUGH	TCF	1983
STAR WARS EPISODE VI: RETURN OF THE JEDI	TCF	1983
PORKY'S II: THE NEXT DAY	TCF	1983
MR. MOM	TCF	1983
STAR CHAMBER, THE	TCF	1983
FIRE AND ICE	TCF	1983
CAREFUL, HE MIGHT HEAR YOU	TCF	1983
OSTERMAN WEEKEND, THE	TCF	1983
ALL THE RIGHT MOVES	TCF	1983
NIGHT IN HEAVEN, A	TCF	1983
SILKWOOD	TCF	1983
TWO OF A KIND	TCF	1983
REUBEN, REUBEN	TCF	1983
TO BE OR NOT TO BE	TCF	1983
ZIGGY STARDUST AND THE SPIDERS FROM MARS	TCF	1983
BICYCLES FOR SUMMER	TCF	1984
UNFAITHFULLY YOURS	TCF	1984
BLAME IT ON RIO	TCF	1984
ANTARCTICA	TCF	1984
ROMANCING THE STONE	TCF	1984
KIDCO	TCF	1984
STONE BOY, THE	TCF	1984
BUDDY SYSTEM, THE	TCF	1984
RHINESTONE	TCF	1984
BACHELOR PARTY	TCF	1984
GODS MUST BE CRAZY, THE	TCF	1984
REVENGE OF THE NERDS	TCF	1984
PHAR LAP	TCF	1984
ADVENTURES OF BUCKAROO BANZAI	TCF	1984
DREAMSCAPE	TCF	1984

FILM	STUDIO	RELEASE YEAR
IMPULSE	TCF	1984
GIMME AN 'F'	TCF	1984
PARIS, TEXAS	TCF	1984
GIVE MY REGARDS TO BROAD STREET	TCF	1984
JOHNNY DANGEROUSLY	TCF	1984
FLAMINGO KID, THE	TCF	1984
MISCHIEF	TCF	1985
TURK 182!	TCF	1985
PORKY'S REVENGE	TCF	1985
ALMOST YOU	TCF	1985
LADYHAWKE	TCF	1985
MOVING VIOLATIONS	TCF	1985
SECRET PLACES	TCF	1985
COCOON	TCF	1985
PRIZZI'S HONOR	TCF	1985
MAN WITH ONE RED SHOE, THE	TCF	1985
KEY EXCHANGE	TCF	1985
WARNING SIGN	TCF	1985
JOSHUA THEN AND NOW	TCF	1985
PLENTY	TCF	1985
COMMANDO	TCF	1985
DOCTOR AND THE DEVILS, THE	TCF	1985
LEGEND	TCF	1985
BAD MEDICINE	TCF	1985
JEWEL OF THE NILE, THE	TCF	1985
BRAZIL	TCF	1985
ENEMY MINE	TCF	1985
BOY IN BLUE, THE	TCF	1986
POWER	TCF	1986
STRIPPER	TCF	1986
VINDICATOR, THE	TCF	1986
DEATH OF AN ANGEL	TCF	1986
HIGHLANDER	TCF	1986
LUCAS	TCF	1986
SPACE CAMP	TCF	1986
MANHATTAN PROJECT, THE	TCF	1986
BIG TROUBLE IN LITTLE CHINA	TCF	1986
ALIENS	TCF	1986
BOY WHO COULD FLY, THE	TCF	1986
FLY, THE	TCF	1986
NAME OF THE ROSE, THE	TCF	1986

FILM	STUDIO	RELEASE YEAR
HALF MOON STREET	TCF	1986
JUMPIN' JACK FLASH	TCF	1986
STREETS OF GOLD	TCF	1986
MORNING AFTER, THE	TCF	1986
WISDOM	TCF	1986
BLACK WIDOW	TCF	1987
MANNEQUIN	TCF	1987
RAISING ARIZONA	TCF	1987
PROJECT X	TCF	1987
PREDATOR	TCF	1987
REVENGE OF THE NERDS II: NERDS IN PARADISE	TCF	1987
PICK-UP ARTIST, THE	TCF	1987
PRINCESS BRIDE, THE	TCF	1987
BIG SHOTS	TCF	1987
SICILIAN, THE	TCF	1987
LESS THAN ZERO	TCF	1987
WALL STREET	TCF	1987
BROADCAST NEWS	TCF	1987
SATISFACTION	TCF	1988
NIGHT IN THE LIFE OF JIMMY REARDON, A	TCF	1988
OFF LIMITS	TCF	1988
BAD DREAMS	TCF	1988
BLUE IGUANA	TCF	1988
BIG BLUE	TCF	1988
BIG	TCF	1988
LICENSE TO DRIVE	TCF	1988
DIE HARD	TCF	1988
YOUNG GUNS	TCF	1988
DEAD RINGERS	TCF	1988
ALIEN NATION	TCF	1988
COCOON: THE RETURN	TCF	1988
WORKING GIRL	TCF	1988
GLEAMING THE CUBE	TCF	1989
FLY II, THE: THE INSECT AWAKENS	TCF	1989
SKIN DEEP	TCF	1989
SAY ANYTHING	TCF	1989
HOW I GOT INTO COLLEGE	TCF	1989
GODS MUST BE CRAZY II, THE	TCF	1989
WEEKEND AT BERNIE'S	TCF	1989
ABYSS, THE	TCF	1989

FILM	STUDIO	RELEASE YEAR
MILLENIUM	TCF	1989
FABULOUS BAKER BOYS, THE	TCF	1989
WHEN THE WHALES CAME	TCF	1989
WORTH WINNING	TCF	1989
WAR OF THE ROSES, THE	TCF	1989
ENEMIES, A LOVE STORY	TCF	1989
DOWNTOWN	TCF	1990
NIGHTBREED	TCF	1990
NUNS ON THE RUN	TCF	1990
VITAL SIGNS	TCF	1990
SHORT TIME	TCF	1990
DIE HARD 2	TCF	1990
COUPE DE VILLE	TCF	1990
ADVENTURES OF FORD FAIRLANE, THE	TCF	1990
YOUNG GUNS II	TCF	1990
RENEGADES	TCF	1990
EXORCIST III	TCF	1990
MILLER'S CROSSING	TCF	1990
PACIFIC HEIGHTS	TCF	1990
MARKED FOR DEATH	TCF	1990
FRANKENSTEIN UNBOUND	TCF	1990
HOME ALONE	TCF	1990
PREDATOR 2	TCF	1990
EDWARD SCISSORHANDS	TCF	1990
COME SEE THE PARADISE	TCF	1990
SLEEPING WITH THE ENEMY	TCF	1991
CLASS ACTION	TCF	1991
FIVE HEARTBEATS	TCF	1991
MANNEQUIN 2: ON THE MOVE	TCF	1991
ONLY THE LONELY	TCF	1991
DYING YOUNG	TCF	1991
DICE RULES	TCF	1991
DUTCH	TCF	1991
HOT SHOTS!	TCF	1991
LIFE STINKS	TCF	1991
COMMITMENTS, THE	TCF	1991
BARTON FINK	TCF	1991
SUPER, THE	TCF	1991
29TH STREET	TCF	1991
FOR THE BOYS	TCF	1991

FILM	STUDIO	RELEASE YEAR
GRAND CANYON	TCF	1991
POINT BREAK	TCF	1991
NAKED LUNCH	TCF	1991
SHINING THROUGH	TCF	1992
BACK IN THE U.S.S.R.	TCF	1992
THIS IS MY LIFE	TCF	1992
MY COUSIN VINNY	TCF	1992
WHITE MEN CAN'T JUMP	TCF	1992
BAD INFLUENCE	TCF	1992
FERNGULLY: THE LAST RAINFOREST	TCF	1992
FOLKS	TCF	1992
ALIEN3	TCF	1992
UNLAWFUL ENTRY	TCF	1992
PRELUDE TO A KISS	TCF	1992
MAN TROUBLE	TCF	1992
BUFFY, THE VAMPIRE SLAYER	TCF	1992
RAPID FIRE	TCF	1992
STORYVILLE	TCF	1992
JUMPIN' AT THE BONEYARD	TCF	1992
LAST OF THE MOHICANS, THE	TCF	1992
NIGHT AND THE CITY	TCF	1992
LOVE POTION #9	TCF	1992
HOME ALONE 2: LOST IN NEW YORK	TCF	1992
USED PEOPLE	TCF	1992
TOYS	TCF	1992
HOFFA	TCF	1992
VANISHING, THE	TCF	1993
HEAR NO EVIL	TCF	1993
SANDLOT	TCF	1993
ONCE UPON A FOREST	TCF	1993
GOOD SON, THE	TCF	1993
HOT SHOTS, PART DEUX!	TCF	1993
ROOKIE OF THE YEAR	TCF	1993
ROBIN HOOD: MEN IN TIGHTS	TCF	1993
RISING SUN	TCF	1993
ONLY THE STRONG	TCF	1993
FREAKED	TCF	1993
BEVERLY HILLBILLIES, THE	TCF	1993
MRS. DOUBTFIRE	TCF	1993
GHOST IN THE MACHINE	TCF	1993

FILM	STUDIO	RELEASE YEAR
SUGAR HILL	TCF	1994
CHASE, THE	TCF	1994
BAD GIRLS	TCF	1994
P.C.U.	TCF	1994
SPEED	TCF	1994
BABY'S DAY OUT	TCF	1994
TRUE LIES	TCF	1994
AIRHEADS	TCF	1994
SCOUT, THE	TCF	1994
TRAPPED IN PARADISE	TCF	1994
MIRACLE ON 34TH STREET	TCF	1994
PAGEMASTER	TCF	1994
NELL	TCF	1994
FAR FROM HOME: THE ADVENTURES OF		
YELLOW DOG	TCF	1995
BYE BYE, LOVE	TCF	1995
KISS OF DEATH	TCF	1995
FRENCH KISS	TCF	1995
DIE HARD: WITH A VENGEANCE	TCF	1995
MIGHTY MORPHIN POWER RANGERS	Fox Animation	1995
NINE MONTHS	TCF	1995
BUSHWHACKED	TCF	1995
BROTHERS MCMULLEN	Searchlight	1995
WALK IN THE CLOUDS, A	TCF	1995
STRANGE DAYS	TCF	1995
WAITING TO EXHALE	TCF	1995
DUNSTON CHECKS IN	Fox Animation	1996
BROKEN ARROW	TCF	1996
DOWN PERISCOPE	TCF	1996
GIRL 6	Searchlight	1996
TRUTH ABOUT CATS & DOGS, THE	TCF	1996
GREAT WHITE HYPE, THE	TCF	1996
STEALING BEAUTY	Searchlight	1996
INDEPENDENCE DAY	TCF	1996
COURAGE UNDER FIRE	Fox 2000	1996
CHAIN REACTION	TCF	1996
SHE'S THE ONE	Searchlight	1996
THAT THING YOU DO	TCF	1996
LOOKING FOR RICHARD	Searchlight	1996
WILLIAM SHAKESPEARE'S ROMEO + JULIET	TCF	1996

FILM	STUDIO	RELEASE YEAR
SECRET AGENT, THE	Searchlight	1996
JINGLE ALL THE WAY	TCF	1996
CRUCIBLE, THE	TCF	1996
ONE FINE DAY	Fox 2000	1996
PICTURE PERFECT	TCF	1997
BLOOD AND WINE	Searchlight	1997
SMILLA'S SENSE OF SNOW	Searchlight	1997
TURBO: A POWER RANGERS MOVIE	Fox Animation	1997
LOVE AND OTHER CATASTROPHES	Searchlight	1997
INVENTING THE ABBOTTS	Fox 2000	1997
PARADISE ROAD	Searchlight	1997
VOLCANO	Fox 2000	1997
VAN, THE	Searchlight	1997
INTIMATE RELATIONS	Searchlight	1997
SPEED 2: CRUISE CONTROL	TCF	1997
RUBY CAIRO	TCF	1997
OUT TO SEA	TCF	1997
STAR MAPS	Searchlight	1997
FULL MONTY, THE	Searchlight	1997
CASPER, A SPIRITED BEGINNING	Fox Animation	1997
SOUL FOOD	Fox 2000	1997
EDGE, THE	TCF	1997
ICE STORM, THE	Searchlight	1997
LIFE LESS ORDINARY, A	TCF	1997
COLD AROUND THE HEART	TCF	1997
ANASTASIA	Fox Animation	1997
ALIEN RESURRECTION	TCF	1997
HOME ALONE 3	Fox Animation	1997
TITANIC	TCF	1997
OSCAR AND LUCINDA	Searchlight	1997
WHAT DREAMS MAY COME	TCF	1998
FIRESTORM	TCF	1998
GREAT EXPECTATIONS	TCF	1998
PRINCE VALIANT	TCF	1998
NEWTON BOYS	TCF	1998
OBJECT OF MY AFFECTION, THE	TCF	1998
TWO GIRLS AND A GUY	Searchlight	1998
SHOOTING FISH	Searchlight	1998
BULWORTH	TCF	1998
HOPE FLOATS	TCF	1998

FILM	STUDIO	RELEASE YEAR
COUSIN BETTE	Searchlight	1998
X-FILES, THE	TCF	1998
DR. DOLITTLE	TCF	1998
THERE'S SOMETHING ABOUT MARY	TCF	1998
POLISH WEDDING	Searchlight	1998
EVER AFTER: A CINDERELLA STORY	Fox Animation	1998
HOW STELLA GOT HER GROOVE BACK	TCF	1998
SLUMS OF BEVERLY HILLS	Searchlight	1998
IMPOSTORS, THE	Searchlight	1998
SIEGE, THE	TCF	1998
COOL DRY PLACE, A	Fox 2000	1998
WAKING NED DEVINE	Searchlight	1998
THIN RED LINE, THE	Fox 2000	1998
20 DATES	Searchlight	1999
OFFICE SPACE	TCF	1999
WING COMMANDER: THE MOVIE	Fox Animation	1999
RAVENOUS	Fox 2000	1999
AMONG GIANTS	Searchlight	1999
NEVER BEEN KISSED	Fox 2000	1999
PUSHING TIN	Fox 2000	1999
ENTRAPMENT	TCF	1999
WILLIAM SHAKESPEARE'S A MIDSUMMER NIGHT'S DREAM	Searchlight	1999
STAR WARS EPISODE I: THE PHANTOM MENACE	TCF	1999
LAKE PLACID	Fox 2000	1999
BROKEDOWN PALACE	Fox 2000	1999
BEST LAID PLANS	Fox 2000	1999
WHITEBOYS	Searchlight	1999
DRIVE ME CRAZY	TCF	1999
BOYS DON'T CRY	Searchlight	1999
FIGHT CLUB	Fox 2000	1999
DREAMING OF JOSEPH LEES	Searchlight	1999
ANYWHERE BUT HERE	Fox 2000	1999
LIGHT IT UP	Fox 2000	1999
BARTOK THE MAGNIFICENT	Fox Animation	1999
OLIVE, THE OTHER REINDEER	Fox Animation	1999
ANNA AND THE KING	Fox 2000	1999
TITUS	Searchlight	1999
BEACH, THE	TCF	2000
CLOSER YOU GET, THE	Searchlight	2000
SOFT FRUIT	Searchlight	2000
HERE ON EARTH	Fox 2000	2000
WHERE THE HEART IS	TCF	2000
BIG MOMMA'S HOUSE	TCF	2000
DANCER, THE	TCF	2000
TITAN A.E.	Fox Animation	2000
ME, MYSELF AND IRENE	TCF	2000
X-MEN	TCF	2000
WHAT LIES BENEATH	TCF	2000
SUNSET STRIP	Fox 2000	2000
WOMAN ON TOP	Searchlight	2000
BOOTMEN	Searchlight	2000
BEDAZZLED	TCF	2000
BLAIR WITCH 2	TCF	2000
LEGEND OF BAGGER VANCE, THE	TCF	2000
MEN OF HONOR	Fox 2000	2000
QUILLS	Searchlight	2000
DUDE, WHERE'S MY CAR	TCF	2000
CAST AWAY	TCF	2000
MONKEYBONE	Fox Animation	2001
SAY IT ISN'T SO	TCF	2001
SOMEONE LIKE YOU	Fox 2000	2001
KINGDOM COME	Searchlight	2001
MOULIN ROUGE	TCF	2001
SEXY BEAST	Searchlight	2001
DR. DOLITTLE 2	TCF	2001
DON'T SAY A WORD	TCF	2001
KISS OF THE DRAGON	TCF	2001
PLANET OF THE APES	TCF	2001
DEEP END, THE	Searchlight	2001
GLITTER	TCF	2001
JOY RIDE	TCF	2001
WAKING LIFE	Searchlight	2001
FROM HELL	TCF	2001
SHALLOW HAL	TCF	2001
NOVOCAINE	TCF	2001
BLACK KNIGHT	TCF	2001
BEHIND ENEMY LINES	TCF	2001
JOE SOMEBODY	Fox 2000	2001

FILM	STUDIO	RELEASE YEAR
KUNG POW: ENTER THE FIST	Fox Animation	2002
SUPER TROOPERS	Searchlight	2002
KISSING JESSICA STEIN	Searchlight	2002
ICE AGE	Fox Animation	2002
HIGH CRIMES	TCF	2002
LIFE, OR SOMETHING LIKE IT	New Regency	2002
UNFAITHFUL	Fox 2000	2002
STAR WARS EPISODE II: ATTACK OF THE CLONES	TCF	2002
MINORITY REPORT	TCF	2002
FIRST $20 MILLION IS ALWAYS THE HARDEST, THE	TCF	2002
LIKE MIKE	TCF	2002
ROAD TO PERDITION, THE	TCF	2002
GOOD GIRL, THE	Searchlight	2002
ONE HOUR PHOTO	Searchlight	2002
SWIMFAN	TCF	2002
BANGER SISTERS	Searchlight	2002
GARAGE DAYS	Searchlight	2002
TRANSPORTER, THE	TCF	2002
BROWN SUGAR	Searchlight	2002
SOLARIS	TCF	2002
DRUMLINE	Fox 2000	2002
ANTWONE FISHER	Searchlight	2002
JUST MARRIED	TCF	2003
DAREDEVIL	TCF	2003
DANCER UPSTAIRS, THE	Searchlight	2003
BEND IT LIKE BECKHAM	Searchlight	2003
GOOD THIEF, THE	Searchlight	2003
PHONE BOOTH	Fox 2000	2003
CHASING PAPI	Fox 2000	2003
X2	TCF	2003
DOWN WITH LOVE	Fox 2000	2003
L'AUBERGE ESPAGNOLE	Searchlight	2003
WRONG TURN	New Regency	2003
FROM JUSTIN TO KELLY	TCF	2003
28 DAYS LATER	Searchlight	2003
LEAGUE OF EXTRAORDINARY GENTLEMEN	TCF	2003
LUCIA, LUCIA	Searchlight	2003
LE DIVORCE	Searchlight	2003

FILM	STUDIO	RELEASE YEAR
THIRTEEN	Searchlight	2003
ORDER, THE	TCF	2003
RUNAWAY JURY	New Regency	2003
MASTER AND COMMANDER: THE FAR SIDE OF THE WORLD	TCF	2003
IN AMERICA	Searchlight	2003
STUCK ON YOU	TCF	2003
CHEAPER BY THE DOZEN	TCF	2003
NEVER DIE ALONE	Searchlight	2004
DREAMERS, THE	Searchlight	2004
CATCH THAT KID	Fox 2000	2004
WELCOME TO MOOSEPORT	TCF	2004
BROKEN LIZARD'S CLUB DREAD	Searchlight	2004
JOHNSON FAMILY VACATION	Searchlight	2004
GIRL NEXT DOOR, THE	New Regency	2004
MAN ON FIRE	Fox 2000	2004
DAY AFTER TOMORROW, THE	TCF	2004
GARFIELD	TCF	2004
NAPOLEON DYNAMITE	Searchlight	2004
DODGEBALL: A TRUE UNDERDOG STORY	TCF	2004
CLEARING, THE	Searchlight	2004
I, ROBOT	TCF	2004
GARDEN STATE	Searchlight	2004
ALIEN VS. PREDATOR	TCF	2004
PAPARAZZI	TCF	2004
FIRST DAUGHTER	New Regency	2004
I HEART HUCKABEES	Searchlight	2004
TAXI	TCF	2004
SIDEWAYS	Searchlight	2004
KINSEY	Searchlight	2004
FLIGHT OF THE PHOENIX	TCF	2004
FAT ALBERT	TCF	2004
PERFECT CREATURE	TCF	2007
NIGHT WATCH	Searchlight	2006
ELEKTRA	TCF	2005
HIDE AND SEEK	TCF	2005
BECAUSE OF WINN-DIXIE	TCF	2005
MILLIONS	Searchlight	2005
ROBOTS	Fox Animation	2005
MELINDA AND MELINDA	Searchlight	2005

FILM	STUDIO	RELEASE YEAR
GUESS WHO	New Regency	2005
FEVER PITCH	Fox 2000	2005
SANDLOT 2, THE	Fox Home Ent.	2005
KINGDOM OF HEAVEN	TCF	2005
STAR WARS EPISODE III: REVENGE OF THE SITH	TCF	2005
MR. AND MRS. SMITH	New Regency	2005
REBOUND	TCF	2005
FANTASTIC FOUR	TCF	2005
SUPERCROSS	TCF	2005
LITTLE MANHATTAN	New Regency	2005
TRANSPORTER 2	TCF	2005
SEPARATE LIES	Searchlight	2005
ROLL BOUNCE	Fox 2000	2005
IN HER SHOES	Fox 2000	2005
STAY	New Regency	2005
BEE SEASON	Searchlight	2005
WALK THE LINE	Fox 2000	2005
IN THE MIX	TCF	2005
FAMILY STONE, THE	Fox 2000	2005
CHEAPER BY THE DOZEN 2	TCF	2005
RINGER, THE	Searchlight	2005
GRANDMA'S BOY	TCF	2006
TRISTAN & ISOLDE	TCF	2006
IMAGINE ME AND YOU	Searchlight	2006
BIG MOMMA'S HOUSE 2	TCF	2006
BANDIDAS	TCF	2006
AQUAMARINE	Fox 2000	2006
HILLS HAVE EYES, THE	Searchlight	2006
THANK YOU FOR SMOKING	Searchlight	2006
ICE AGE THE MELTDOWN	Fox Animation	2006
PHAT GIRLZ	Searchlight	2006
SENTINEL, THE	TCF	2006
DR. DOLITTLE 3	Fox Home Ent.	2006
WATER	Searchlight	2006
JUST MY LUCK	New Regency	2006
X-MEN: THE LAST STAND	TCF	2006
LIKE MIKE 2	Fox Home Ent.	2006
OMEN, THE	TCF	2006
GARFIELD A TAIL OF TWO KITTIES	TCF	2006

FILM	STUDIO	RELEASE YEAR
DEVIL WEARS PRADA, THE	Fox 2000	2006
MY SUPER EX-GIRLFRIEND	New Regency	2006
LITTLE MISS SUNSHINE	Searchlight	2006
JOHN TUCKER MUST DIE	TCF	2006
IDIOCRACY	TCF	2006
TRUST THE MAN	Searchlight	2006
CONFETTI	Searchlight	2006
LAST KING OF SCOTLAND, THE	Searchlight	2006
MARINE, THE	TCF	2006
BEHIND ENEMY LINES II: AXIS OF EVIL	Fox Home Ent.	2006
FLICKA	Fox 2000	2006
BORAT: CULTURAL LEARNINGS OF AMERICA FOR MAKE BENEFIT GLORIOUS NATION OF KAZAKHSTAN	TCF	2006
GOOD YEAR, A	Fox 2000	2006
FAST FOOD NATION	Searchlight	2006
HISTORY BOYS, THE	Searchlight	2006
DECK THE HALLS	New Regency	2006
TURISTAS	Fox Atomic	2006
ERAGON	Fox 2000	2006
NIGHT AT THE MUSEUM	TCF	2006
NOTES ON A SCANDAL	Searchlight	2006
EPIC MOVIE	New Regency	2007
RENO 911!: MIAMI : THE MOVIE	TCF	2007
NAMESAKE, THE	Searchlight	2007
I THINK I LOVE MY WIFE	Searchlight	2007
HILLS HAVE EYES 2, THE	Fox Atomic	2007
FIREHOUSE DOG	New Regency	2007
SUNSHINE	Searchlight	2007
PATHFINDER	TCF	2007
LAKE PLACID 2	Fox Home Ent.	2007
SANDLOT 3, THE	Fox Home Ent.	2007
WAITRESS	Searchlight	2007
28 WEEKS LATER	Fox Atomic	2007
ONCE	Searchlight	2007
DAY WATCH	Searchlight	2007
FANTASTIC FOUR: RISE OF THE SILVER SURFER	TCF	2007
LIVE FREE OR DIE HARD	TCF	2007
JOSHUA	Searchlight	2007
SIMPSONS MOVIE, THE	Fox Animation	2007

FILM	STUDIO	RELEASE YEAR
DEATH SENTENCE	TCF	2007
DARJEELING LIMITED, THE	Searchlight	2007
SEEKER, THE: THE DARK IS RISING	TCF	2007
WRONG TURN 2	Fox Home Ent.	2007
COMEBACKS, THE	Fox Atomic	2007
HITMAN	TCF	2007
SAVAGES, THE	Searchlight	2007
JUNO	Searchlight	2007
ALVIN AND THE CHIPMUNKS	Fox 2000	2007
ALIENS VS. PREDATOR - REQUIEM	TCF	2007
27 DRESSES	Fox 2000	2008
JUMPER	TCF	2008
MEET THE SPARTANS	New Regency	2008
DR. DOLITTLE: TAIL TO THE CHIEF	Fox Home Ent.	2008
DR. SEUSS' HORTON HEARS A WHO	Fox Animation	2008
UNDER THE SAME MOON	Searchlight	2008
SHUTTER	New Regency	2008
NIM'S ISLAND	TCF	2008
YOUNG@HEART	Searchlight	2008
STREET KINGS	Searchlight	2008
DECEPTION	TCF	2008
ACE OF HEARTS	Fox Home Ent.	2008
WHAT HAPPENS IN VEGAS	TCF	2008
ONION MOVIE, THE	New Regency	2008
HAPPENING, THE	TCF	2008
MEET DAVE	TCF	2008
X-FILES: I WANT TO BELIEVE, THE	TCF	2008
MIRRORS	New Regency	2008
ROCKER, THE	Fox Atomic	2008
BABYLON A.D.	TCF	2008
CHOKE	Searchlight	2008
MAX PAYNE	TCF	2008
SECRET LIFE OF BEES, THE	Searchlight	2008
SLUMDOG MILLIONAIRE	Searchlight	2008
AUSTRALIA	TCF	2008
DAY THE EARTH STOOD STILL, THE	TCF	2008
WRESTLER, THE	Searchlight	2008
MARLEY & ME	Fox 2000	2008
BRIDE WARS	Fox 2000	2009
NOTORIOUS	Searchlight	2009

FILM	STUDIO	RELEASE YEAR
TAKEN	TCF	2009
STREET FIGHTER	TCF	2009
MISS MARCH	Fox Atomic	2009
12 ROUNDS	Fox Atomic	2009
DRAGONBALL: EVOLUTION	TCF	2009
X-MEN ORIGINS: WOLVERINE	TCF	2009
NIGHT AT THE MUSEUM: BATTLE OF THE SMITHSONIAN	TCF	2009
MY LIFE IN RUINS	Searchlight	2009
ICE AGE: DAWN OF THE DINOSAURS	Fox Animation	2009
I LOVE YOU, BETH COOPER	Fox Atomic	2009
500 DAYS OF SUMMER	Searchlight	2009
ADAM	Searchlight	2009
ALIENS IN THE ATTIC	TCF	2009
POST GRAD	Fox Atomic	2009
ALL ABOUT STEVE	Fox 2000	2009
JENNIFER'S BODY	Fox Atomic	2009
WHIP IT	Searchlight	2009
AMELIA	Searchlight	2009
GENTLEMEN BRONCOS	Searchlight	2009
FANTASTIC MR. FOX	Fox Animation	2009
CRAZY HEART	Searchlight	2009
AVATAR	TCF	2009
ALVIN AND THE CHIPMUNKS: THE SQUEAKQUEL	Fox 2000	2009
TOOTH FAIRY	TCF	2010
MY NAME IS KHAN	Searchlight	2010
PERCY JACKSON & THE OLYMPIANS: THE LIGHTNING THIEF	Fox 2000	2010
HOT SUMMER DAYS	Fox Int	2010
OUR FAMILY WEDDING	Searchlight	2010
DIARY OF A WIMPY KID	Fox 2000	2010
DATE NIGHT	TCF	2010
FLICKA 2	Searchlight	2010
JUST WRIGHT	Searchlight	2010
WIN/WIN	Fox Int	2010
MARMADUKE	TCF	2010
A-TEAM, THE	TCF	2010
ALIEN GIRL	Fox Int	2010
CYRUS	Searchlight	2010

FILM	STUDIO	RELEASE YEAR
KNIGHT AND DAY	TCF	2010
PREDATORS	TCF	2010
RAMONA AND BEEZUS	Fox 2000	2010
VAMPIRES SUCK	New Regency	2010
MACHETE	TCF	2010
NEVER LET ME GO	Searchlight	2010
WALL STREET: MONEY NEVER SLEEPS	TCF	2010
SPACE CHIMPS 2: ZARTOG STRIKES BACK	Fox Home Ent.	2010
CONVICTION	Searchlight	2010
MIRRORS 2	Fox Home Ent.	2010
BUTCHER, THE CHEF AND THE SWORDSMAN, THE	Fox Int	2010
127 HOURS	Searchlight	2010
UNSTOPPABLE	TCF	2010
LOVE & OTHER DRUGS	Fox 2000	2010
BLACK SWAN	Searchlight	2010
DOLPHIN: STORY OF A DREAMER, THE	Fox Home Ent.	2010
CHRONICLES OF NARNIA, THE: THE VOYAGE OF THE DAWN TREADER	Fox 2000	2010
YELLOW SEA	Fox Int	2010
GULLIVER'S TRAVELS	TCF	2010
DAAR...KE AAGE JEET HAI	Fox Int	2011
EARTHWORMS	Fox Int	2011
LOS MARZIANO	Fox Int	2011
TOMORROW NEVER AGAIN	Fox Int	2011
CHRONICLE	TCF	2012
CEDAR RAPIDS	Searchlight	2011
BIG MOMMAS: LIKE FATHER, LIKE SON	New Regency	2011
WIN WIN	Searchlight	2011
STREET KINGS 2: MOTOR CITY	Fox Home Ent.	2011
RIO	Fox Animation	2011
PARADISE LOST	Fox Int	2011
WATER FOR ELEPHANTS	Fox 2000	2011
TREE OF LIFE, THE	Searchlight	2011
MARLEY AND ME: THE PUPPY YEARS	Fox Home Ent.	2011
X-MEN: FIRST CLASS	TCF	2011
ART OF GETTING BY, THE	Searchlight	2011
MR. POPPER'S PENGUINS	TCF	2011
MONTE CARLO	Fox 2000	2011
SNOW FLOWER AND THE SECRET FAN	Searchlight	2011

FILM	STUDIO	RELEASE YEAR
ANOTHER EARTH	Searchlight	2011
RISE OF THE PLANET OF THE APES	TCF	2011
LOVE IN SPACE	Fox Int	2011
MISS BALA	Fox Int	2011
BUNKER	Fox Int	2011
WHAT'S YOUR NUMBER?	New Regency	2011
FORCE, THE	TCF	2011
MARGARET	Searchlight	2011
BIG YEAR, THE	Fox 2000	2011
WRONG TURN 4	Fox Home Ent.	2011
MARTHA MARCY MAY MARLENE	Searchlight	2011
IN TIME	New Regency	2011
DESCENDANTS, THE	Searchlight	2011
ICE AGE: A MAMMOTH CHRISTMAS	Fox Home Ent.	2011
SHAME	Searchlight	2011
SITTER, THE	TCF	2011
ALVIN AND THE CHIPMUNKS: CHIPWRECKED	Fox 2000	2011
WE BOUGHT A ZOO	TCF	2011
DARKEST HOUR, THE	New Regency	2011
WE ARE FAMILY	Fox Int	2012
SOUND OF MY VOICE	Searchlight	2012
THREE STOOGES, THE	TCF	2012
BEST EXOTIC MARIGOLD HOTEL, THE	Searchlight	2012
LOLA VERSUS	Searchlight	2012
PROMETHEUS	TCF	2012
ABRAHAM LINCOLN: VAMPIRE HUNTER	TCF	2012
BEASTS OF THE SOUTHERN WILD	Searchlight	2012
ICE AGE: CONTINENTAL DRIFT	Fox Animation	2012
MAGGIE SIMPSON IN "THE LONGEST DAYCARE"	Fox Animation	2012
RUBY SPARKS	Searchlight	2012
WATCH, THE	TCF	2012
DIARY OF A WIMPY KID: DOG DAYS	Fox 2000	2012
TAKEN 2	TCF	2012
SESSIONS, THE	Searchlight	2012
CHASING MAVERICKS	Fox 2000	2012
LINCOLN	TCF	2012
LIFE OF PI	Fox 2000	2012
HITCHCOCK	Searchlight	2012

FILM	STUDIO	RELEASE YEAR
CROW'S THUMB	Fox Int	2012
PARENTAL GUIDANCE	TCF	2012
SCHLUSSMACHER	Fox Int	2013
GOOD DAY TO DIE HARD, A	TCF	2013
STOKER	Searchlight	2013
TRANCE	Searchlight	2013
RUNNING MAN	Fox Int	2013
EPIC	Fox Animation	2013
EAST, THE	Searchlight	2013
INTERNSHIP, THE	TCF/NR	2013
HEAT, THE	TCF	2013
WAY, WAY BACK, THE	Searchlight	2013
PERCY JACKSON: SEA OF MONSTERS	Fox 2000	2013
SEPTIMO	Fox Int	2013
ENOUGH SAID	Searchlight	2013
BAGGAGE CLAIM	Searchlight	2013
RUNNER, RUNNER	New Regency	2013
12 YEARS A SLAVE	New Regency	2013
COUNSELOR, THE	Fox 2000	2013
BOOK THIEF, THE	Fox 2000	2013
BLACK NATIVITY	Searchlight	2013
WALKING WITH DINOSAURS	TCF	2013
SECRET LIFE OF WALTER MITTY, THE	TCF	2013
DEVIL'S DUE	TCF	2014
MONUMENTS MEN, THE	Fox 2000	2014
GRAND BUDAPEST HOTEL, THE	Searchlight	2014
DOM HEMINGWAY	Searchlight	2014
RIO 2	Fox Animation	2014
OTHER WOMAN, THE	TCF	2014
BELLE	Searchlight	2014
FOOD GUIDE TO LOVE, THE	Fox Int	2014
X-MEN: DAYS OF FUTURE PAST	TCF	2014
AMAPOLA	Fox Int	2014
FAULT IN OUR STARS, THE	Fox 2000	2014
PANDA EYES	Fox Int	2014
RICO, OSCAR AND THE DEEP SHADOWS	Fox Int	2014
DAWN OF THE PLANET OF THE APES	TCF	2014
I ORIGINS	Searchlight	2014
CALVARY	Searchlight	2014
LET'S BE COPS	TCF	2014

FILM	STUDIO	RELEASE YEAR
DROP, THE	Searchlight	2014
FINDING FANNY	Fox Int	2014
MAZE RUNNER, THE	TCF	2014
BANG BANG	Fox Int	2014
SLOW VIDEO	Fox Int	2014
GONE GIRL	TCF	2014
BIRDMAN	Searchlight	2014
BOOK OF LIFE, THE	Fox Animation	2014
TRINTA	Fox Int	2014
PYRAMID, THE	Fox Int	2014
WILD	Searchlight	2014
EXODUS: GODS AND KINGS	TCF	2014
NIGHT AT THE MUSEUM: SECRET OF THE TOMB	TCF	2014
TAKEN 3	TCF	2015
KHAMOSHIYAN	Fox Int	2015
KINGSMAN: THE SECRET SERVICE	TCF	2015
SECOND BEST EXOTIC MARIGOLD HOTEL, THE	Searchlight	2015
UNFINISHED BUSINESS	New Regency	2015
RAJATHANDHIRAM	Fox Int	2015
GUDDU RANGEELA	Fox Int	2015
LONGEST RIDE, THE	Fox 2000	2015
MR. X (3D)	Fox Int	2015
TRUE STORY	Searchlight	2015
FAR FROM THE MADDING CROWD	Searchlight	2015
LAILAA O LAILAA	Fox Int	2015
BOMBAY VELVET	Fox Int	2015
POLTERGEIST	Fox 2000	2015
ALOHA	TCF	2015
ME AND EARL AND THE DYING GIRL	Searchlight	2015
MISS TANAKPUR HAAZIR HO	Fox Int	2015
SPY	TCF	2015
PAPER TOWNS	Fox 2000	2015
SMOSH: THE MOVIE	TCF	2015
DRAGONBALL Z: RESURRECTION "F"	Fox Int	2015
FANTASTIC FOUR	TCF	2015
MISTRESS AMERICA	Searchlight	2015
BROTHERS	Fox Int	2015
HITMAN: AGENT 47	TCF	2015

FILM	STUDIO	RELEASE YEAR
DEMOLITION	Searchlight	2015
HE NAMED ME MALALA	Searchlight	2015
A BIGGER SPLASH	Searchlight	2015
MARTIAN, THE	TCF	2015
BRIDGE OF SPIES	Fox 2000	2015
BROOKLYN	Searchlight	2015
PEANUTS MOVIE, THE	TCF	2015

FILM	STUDIO	RELEASE YEAR
VICTOR FRANKENSTEIN	TCF	2015
YOUTH	Searchlight	2015
ALVIN AND THE CHIPMUNKS: THE ROAD CHIP	Fox 2000	2015
THE REVENANT	New Regency	2015
JOY	TCF	2015

BIBLIOGRAPHY

Adams, Nick. *The Rebel & The King.* WaterDancer Press, 2012.

Aherne, Brian assisted by George Sanders and Benita Hume. *A Dreadful Man.* New York: Simon and Schuster, 1979.

Alda, Alan. *Never Have Your Dog Stuffed and Other Things I've Learned.* New York: Random House, 2006.

Allvine, Glendon. *The Greatest Fox of Them All.* Secaucus: L. Stuart, 1969.

Allyson, June with Frances Spatz Leighton. *June Allyson.* New York: Berkley Books, 1983.

Ann-Margret with Todd Gold. *Ann-Margret: my story.* New York: GP Putnam's Sons, 1994.

Arce, Hector. *The Secret Life of Tyrone Power.* New York: William Morrow And Company, Inc., 1979.

Baker, Sarah. *Lucky Stars; Janet Gaynor & Charles Farrell.* Albany: BearManor Media, 2009.

Barrier, Michael. *Hollywood Cartoons; American Animation in its Golden Age.* New York: Oxford University Press. Inc., 1999

Behlmer, Rudy. *Henry Hathaway; A Directors Guild of America Oral History.* Lanham: The Scarecrow Press, Inc. 2001

Behlmer, Rudy. *Memo from Darryl F. Zanuck; The Golden Years At Twentieth Century-Fox.* New York: Grove Press, 1993.

Behlmer, Rudy. *Shoot the Rehearsal! Behind the Scenes with Assistant Director Reggie Callow.* Lanham: The Scarecrow Press, Inc. 2010.

Bergstrom, Janet. *William Fox Presents F.W. Murnau and Frank Borzage.* Twentieth Century Fox Home Entertainment, 2008.

Birchard, Robert S. *King Cowboy; Tom Mix and the Movies.* Burbank: Riverwood Press, 1993.

Black, Shirley Temple. *Child Star.* New York: McGraw-Hill Publishing Company, 1988.

Block, Alex Ben. *Outfoxed; Marvin Davis, Barry Diller, Rupert Murdoch, Joan Rivers, and the Inside Story of America's Fourth Television Network.* New York: St. Martin's Press, 1990.

Booker, Phil. *Jeanne Crain; the beautiful dreamer.* New York: Carlton Press, Inc., 1977.

Braun, Eric. *Deborah Kerr.* New York: St. Martin's Press, 1977.

Bronson, Fred. *The Sound of Music Family Scrapbook.* London: Carlton Books Limited, 2011.

Brown, David. *Let Me Entertain You.* New York: William Morrow and Company, Inc., 1990.

Carr, Charmian with Jean A.S. Strauss. *Forever Liesl; A Memoir of The Sound of Music.* New York: Penguin Books, 2000.

Castelli, Jean-Christophe. *The Making of Life of Pi; A Film A Journey.* New York: Harper Design, 2012.

Cartwright, Angela and Tom McLaren. *Styling the Stars; Lost Treasures from the Twentieth Century Fox Archive.* San Rafael: Insight Editions, 2014.

Chaplin, Saul. *The Golden Age of Movie Musicals and Me.* Norman: University of Oklahoma Press, 1994.

Chenoweth, Neil. *Rupert Murdoch; The Untold Story of the World's Greatest Media Wizard.* New York: Crown Business, 2001.

Christie, Ian and David Thompson. *Scorsese on Scorsese.* London: Faber and Faber Limited, 1989.
"Close-Ups" (studio newsletter), various years

Collins, Joan. *Past Imperfect.* New York: Simon and Schuster, 1978.

Cotton, Joseph. *Vanity Will Get You Somewhere; An Autobiography.* Lincoln: iUniverse, 2000.

Cronyn, Hume. *A Terrible Liar; A Memoir.* New York: William Morrow And Company, Inc., 1991.

Curtis, James. *Spencer Tracy.* New York: Alfred A. Knopf, 2011.

Daily Variety, various years

D'Arc, James V. *When Hollywood Came To Town.* Leyton: Gibbs-Smith, 2010.

Dahlquist, Marina. *Exporting Perilous Pauline; Pearl White and the Serial Film Craze.* Champaign: University of Illinois Press, 2013.

DiMaggio, June with Mary Jane Popp. *Marilyn, Joe & Me.* Roseville: Penmarin Books, 2006.

Dunne, John Gregory. *The Studio.* New York: Farrar, Straus, and Giroux, 1968.

Dunne, Philip. *Take Two; A Life in Movies and Politics.* New York: Proscenium Publishers Inc., 1992.

Eames, John Douglas. *The Paramount Story.* New York: Crown Publishers, Inc. 1985.

Ebsen, Buddy with Stephen Cox. *The Other Side of Oz.* Newport Beach: Donovan Publishing, 1993.

Eden, Barbara with Wendy Leigh. *Jeannie Out of the Bottle.* New York: Random House, 2011.

Edgerton, Gary R. *The Columbia History of American Television.* New York: Columbia University Press, 2007.

Elder, Jane Lenz. *Alice Faye; A Life Beyond the Silver Screen.* Jackson: University Press of Mississippi, 2002.

Eliot, Marc. *Cary Grant; a Biography.* New York: Random House, Inc., 2004.

Eliot, Marc. *Michael Douglas.* New York: Random House, Inc., 2012.

Elwes, Cary. *As You Wish; Inconceivable Tales From The Making of The Princess Bride,* New York: Touchstone, Inc., 2014.

Ephron, Henry. *We Thought We Could Do Anything; The Life of Screenwriters Phoebe and Henry Ephron.* New York: W.W. Norton & Company, 1977.

Epstein, Edward Z. *Portrait of Jennifer; A Biography of Jennifer Jones.* New York: Simon & Schuster, 1995.

Erengis, George P., "20th's Backlot Has Been Shorn Of Some of the Famous Sets Of U.S. Filmmaking," *Films in Review,* April 1962.

Evans, Linda with Sean Catherine Derek. *Recipes For Life; My Memories.* New York: Vanguard Press, 2011.

Eyman, Scott. *John Wayne; The Life and Legend.* New York: Simon & Schuster, 2014.

Eyman, Scott. *Print the Legend; The Life and Times of John Ford.* New York: Simon & Schuster, 1999.

Fahey, David and Linda Rich. *Masters of Starlight: Photographers in Hollywood.* New York: Ballantine Books, 1987.

Film Daily, various years

Fishgall, Gary. *Gregory Peck; A Biography.* New York: Scribner, 2002.

Fleischer, Richard. *Just Tell Me When To Cry; A Memoir.* New York: Carroll & Graf Publishing, Inc., 1993.

Focus on Fox (studio newsletter), various years

Fonda, Henry as told to Howard Teichmann. *Fonda; My Life.* New York: Penguin Group, 1982.

Fonda, Peter. *Don't Tell Dad.* New York: Hyperion, 1998.

Fox Folks (studio newsletter), various years

Fox, Susan and Donald G. Rosellini. *William Fox; A Story Of Early Hollywood 1915-1930.* Baltimore: Midnight Marquee Press, Inc., 2006.

Fricke, John. *Judy Garland; World's Greatest Entertainer.* New York: MJF Books, 1992.

Fuller, Samuel with Christa Lang Fuller and Jerome Henry Rudes. *A Third Face: My Tale of Writing, Fighting, and Filmmaking.* New York: Alfred A. Knopf, 2002.

Gabler, Neal. *An Empire of Their Own.* New York: Doubleday, 1988.

Garner, James and Jon Winokur. *The Garner Files.* New York: Simon and Schuster, 2011.

Golden, Eve. *Vamp; The Rise and Fall of Theda Bara.* New York: Emprise Publishing, Inc., 1996.

Grant, John. *A Comprehensive Encyclopedia of Film Noir; The Essential Reference Guide.* Milwaukee: Hal Leonard Corporation, 2013.

Gussow, Mel. *Don't Say Yes Until I Finish Talking; A Biography of Darryl Zanuck.* New York: Doubleday & Company, Inc., 1971.

Handelman, David Y. *"Twentieth Century Fox Film Corporation—A Brief History (1915-1990)"*

Harris, Marlys J. *The Zanucks of Hollywood.* New York: Crown Publishers, Inc., 1989.

Harrison's Reports, 1934-1935.

Harrison, Rex. *Rex; An Autobiography.* New York: William Morrow & Company, Inc., 1975.

Hart, Mother Dolores, OSB and Richard DeNeut. *The Ear of the Heart; An Actress' Journey from Hollywood to Holy Vows.* San Francisco: Ignatius Press, 2013.

Haver, Ron. *David O. Selznick's Hollywood.* New York: Knopf, 1980.

Havoc, June. *More Havoc.* New York: Harper & Row, Publishers, 1980.

Hearn, Marcus, and Alan Barnes. *The Hammer Story; The Authorized History of Hammer Films.* London: Titan Books, 2007.

Hirsch, Julia Antopol. *The Sound of Music; The Making of America's Favorite Movie.* Chicago: Contemporary Books, 1993.

Historic Context Statement; Film Production in Southern California: The Growth and Development of the Twentieth Century Fox Studio 1928-1950 Docent Handbook, Historic Resources Group, October 12, 1990.

Hollywood Herald, various years

Hollywood Reporter, various years

Hoopes, Roy. *When The Stars Went To War; Hollywood and World War II.* New York: Random House, 1994.

Huang, Yunte. *Charlie Chan.* New York: W.W. Norton & Company, 2010.

Huston, John. *An Open Book.* New York: Alfred A. Knopf, 1980.

Jenkins, Garry. *Empire Building; The Remarkable, Real-Life Story of Star Wars*. Secaucus: Carol Publishing Group, 1999.

Jensen, Richard D. *The Amazing Tom Mix*. Lincoln: iUniverse, 2005.

Johnson, Nunnally. *The Letters of Nunnally Johnson*. New York: Alfred A. Knopf, Inc., 1981.

Jones, Shirley, with Wendy Leigh. *Shirley Jones; A Memoir*. New York: Gallery Books, 2013.

Kasson, John F., *The Little Girl Who Fought The Great Depression; Shirley Temple and 1930s America*. New York: W.W. Norton & Company, 2014.

Katz, Ephraim with Ronald Dean Nolen. *The Film Encyclopedia*. New York: HarperCollins Publishers, 2012.

Kazan, Elia. *Elia Kazan; A Life*. New York: Alfred A. Knopf, 1988.

Kazanjian, Howard and Chris Enss. *The Young Duke*. Guilford: Morris Book Publishing, LLC., 2007.

Kellow, Brian. *The Bennetts; An Acting Family*. Kentucky: The University Press of Kentucky, 2004.

Ketchum, Robert M. *Will Rogers; His Life and Times*. New York: American Heritage Publishing Company, Inc., 1973.

Kobal, John. *People Will Talk*. New York: Alfred A. Knopf, 1985.

Lahue, Kalton. *Gentlemen to the Rescue*. New York: A.S. Barnes and Co., Inc., 1972.

Landis, Deborah Nadoolman. *Dressed; A Century of Hollywood Costume Design*. New York: HarperCollins Publishers, 2007.

LaPorte, Nicole. *The Men Who Would Be King; An almost epic tale of moguls, movies, and a company called DreamWorks*. New York: Houghton Mifflin Harcourt, 2010.

Lax, Eric. *Paul Newman; A Biography*. Atlanta: Turner Publishing, Inc., 1996.

Leaming, Barbara. *Marilyn Monroe*. New York: Three Rivers Press, 1998.

Leemann, Sergio. *Robert Wise On His Films; From Editing room To Director's Chair*. Los Angeles: Silman-James Press, 1995.

Leff, Leonard J. *Hitchcock and Selznick; The Rich and Strange Collaboration of Alfred Hitchcock and David O. Selznick in Hollywood*. Berkeley: University of California Press, 1987.

Lev, Peter. *Twentieth Century-Fox; The Zanuck-Skouras Years, 1935-1965*. Austin: University of Texas Press, 2013.

Levine, Josh. *David E. Kelley; The Man Behind Ally McBeal*. Toronto: ECW Press, 1999.

Levinson, Peter J. *Fred Astaire; Puttin' On The Ritz*. New York: St. Martin's Press, 2009.

Linet, Beverly. *Susan Hayward; Portrait of a Survivor*. New York: Atheneum Publishers, 1980.

Loy, Myrna and James Kotsilibas-Davis. *Myrna Loy: Being and Becoming*. New York: Alfred A. Knopf, Inc., 1987.

Mair, George. *The Barry Diller Story; The Life and Times of America's Greatest Entertainment Mogul*. New York: John Wiley & Sons, Inc., 1997.

MacLaine, Shirley. *My Lucky Stars; A Hollywood Memoir*. New York: Bantam Books, 1995.

Mankiewicz, Tom, and Robert Crane. *My Life As A Mankiewicz; An Insider's Journey Through Hollywood*. Kentucky: The University Press of Kentucky, 2012.

Marsh, Ed W. *James Cameron's Titanic*. New York: HarperCollins Publishers, Inc., 1997.

McBride, Joseph. *Searching For John Ford; A Life*. New York: St. Martin's Press, 2001.

McClelland, Doug. *Forties Film Talk; Oral Histories of Hollywood*. Jefferson: McFarland & Company, Inc., Publishers, 1992.

McGee, Tom. *Betty Grable; the Girl with the Million Dollar Legs*. New York: Welcome Rain Publishers, 1995.

McKinney, Devin. *The Man Who Saw A Ghost; The Life and Work of Henry Fonda.* New York: St. Martin's Press, 2012.

Merman, Ethel with George Eells. *Merman; An Autobiography.* New York: Simon and Schuster, 1978.

Miller, Eugene L. and Edwin T. Arnold. *Robert Aldrich Interviews.* Jackson: University Press of Mississippi, 2004.

Monroe, Marilyn, with Ben Hecht. *My Story.* New York: Taylor Trade Publishing, 2007.

Moore, Dick. *Twinkle, Twinkle, Little Star; but don't have sex or take the car.* New York: Harper & Row, Publishers, 1984.

Moseley, Roy with Philip & Martin Masheter. *Rex Harrison: The First Biography.* London: New English Library, 1987.

Mosley, Leonard. *Zanuck: The Rise And Fall Of Hollywood's Last Tycoon.* New York: McGraw-Hill Book Company, 1984.

Motion Picture Daily, various years

Motion Picture Herald, various years

Nollinger, Mark, "The Exit Files," *TV Guide,* Volume 50, Number 20, Issue #2564, May 18-24, 2002.

Nugent, Frank S.,"*Going Hollywood with Frank S. Nugent," Good Housekeeping,* July 1945.

O'Hara, Maureen, with John Nicoletti. *'Tis Herself; A Memoir.* New York: Simon & Schuster Inc., 2004.

O'Neal, Ryan with Jodee Blanco and Kent Carroll. *Both of Us; My Life With Farrah.* New York: Crown Archetype, 2012.

Parish, James Robert. *The Fox Girls; starring 15 beautiful vixens and one adorable cub.* New Rochelle: Arlington House, 1972.

Parton, Dolly. *Dolly; My Life and Other Unfinished Business.* New York: HarperCollins Publishers, 1994.

Pascale, Amy. *Joss Whedon; The Biography.* Chicago: Chicago Review Press, 2014.

Poitier, Sidney. *The Measure of a Man; a spiritual autobiography.* New York: HarperCollins Publishers Inc., 2000.

Poitier, Sidney. *This Life.* New York: Alfred A. Knopf, 1980.

Preminger, Otto. *Preminger; an Autobiography.* New York: Doubleday & Company, Inc., 1977.

Price, Shawn, "Exotic Malibu Creek area offers an easy jaunt—TRAIL GUIDE: The park, once used as a movie studio's back lot has a rich history," *The Orange County Register,* November 30, 2000.

Richardson, Frances C., "The Twentieth Century-Fox Research Library," *California Librarian.* April, 1967.

Riese, Randall. *The Unabridged James Dean; His Life and Legacy from A to Z.* Chicago: Contemporary Books, 1991.

Rogers, Betty. *Will Rogers; His Wife's Story.* Norman: University of Oklahoma Press, 1979.

Rogers, Ginger. *Ginger; My Story.* New York: HarperCollins Publishers, 1991.

Rooney, Darrell with Mark A. Vieira. *Harlow in Hollywood; The Blonde Bombshell in the Glamour Capital 1928-1937.* Santa Monica: Angel City Press, 2011.

Rose, Helen. *"Just Make Them Beautiful;" The Many Worlds of a Designing Woman.* Santa Monica: Dennis Landman publishers, 1976.

Sanders, George. *Memoirs of A Professional Cad.* New York: G.P. Putnam's Sons, 1960.

Schwarzenegger, Arnold, with Peter Petre. *Total Recall; My Unbelievably True Life Story.* New York: Simon & Schuster Inc., 2012.

Semenov, Lillian Wurtzel and Carla Winter. *William Fox, Sol M. Wurtzel and the Early Fox Film Corporation; Letters, 1917-1923.* Jefferson: McFarland & Company, Inc., Publishers, 2001.

Server, Lee. *Robert Mitchum; "Baby, I Just Don't Care."* New York: St. Martin's Griffin, 2002.

Sharaff, Irene. *Broadway & Hollywood: costumes designed by Irene Sharaff.* New York: Van Nostrand Reinhold Co., 1976.

Sikov, Ed. *On Sunset Boulevard; the Life and Times of Billy Wilder.* New York: Hyperion, 1998.

Silverman, Stephen M. *The Fox That Got Away; The Last Days of the Zanuck Dynasty at Twentieth Century-Fox.* Secaucus: Lyle Stuart Inc., 1988.

Sinclair, Upton. *Upton Sinclair Presents William Fox.* Los Angeles: published by the author, 1933.

Skouras, Spyros P., compiled and edited by Ilias Chrissochoidis. *Memoirs (1893–1953).* Stanford: Brave World, 2013.

Solomon, Aubrey, *The Fox Film Corporation, 1915-1935, A History and Filmography.* Jefferson: McFarland & Company, Inc., Publishers, 2011.

Solomon, Aubrey. *Twentieth Century-Fox: A Corporate and Financial History.* Metuchen: The Scarecrow Press, Inc., 1988.

Spelling, Aaron., with Jefferson Graham. *A Prime-Time Life; An Autobiography.* New York: St. Martin's Press, 1996.

Spoto, Donald. *The Dark Side of Genius; The Life of Alfred Hitchcock.* Boston: Little, Brown, 1983.

Spoto, Donald. *Enchantment; The Life of Audrey Hepburn.* New York: Three Rivers Press, 2006.

Spoto, Donald. *Marilyn Monroe; the Biography.* New York: Rowman & Littlefield Publishing Group, 1993.

Sragow, Michael. *Victor Fleming; an American Movie Master.* New York: Pantheon Books, 2008.

Stine, White & Bette Davis. *Bette Davis: Mother Goddam.* New York: Berkley Book/Hawthorn Books, 1974.

Strait, Raymond. *Mrs. Howard Hughes.* Los Angeles: Holloway House, 1970.

Strasberg, Susan. *Marilyn and Me; Sisters, Rivals, Friends.* New York: Warner Books, Inc., 1992.

Swanson, Gloria. *Swanson On Swanson; an autobiography.* New York: Random House, 1980.

Thomas, Bob. *Joan Crawford A Biography.* New York: Simon and Schuster, 1978.

Thomas, Tony. *The Dick Powell Story.* Burbank: Riverwood Press, 1993.

Thomas, Tony. *The Films of Olivia de Havilland.* Secaucus: Citadel Press, 1983.

Thomas, Tony and Aubrey Solomon. *The Films of 20th Century-Fox,* Secaucus: Citadel Press, 1979.

Tierney, Gene, with Mickey Herskowitz. *Self-Portrait.* New York: Simon and Schuster, 1979.

Time magazine, various years

Todd, Richard. *In Camera, an Autobiography continued,* London, Hutchinson, 1989.

Tornabene, Lyn. *Long Live The King.* New York: G.P. Putnam's Sons, 1976.

Truffaut, Francois. *Hitchcock.* New York: Simon and Schuster, 1984.

Turk, Edward Baron. *Hollywood Diva; A Biography of Jeanette MacDonald.* Berkeley: University of California Press, 1998.

Turner, Lana, *Lana. The Lady, The Legend, The Truth.* New York: Simon & Schuster, Inc., 1982.

Vargas, Alberto and Reid Austin. *Vargas.* New York: Harmony Books, 1978.

Variety, various years

Vogel, Michelle. *Gene Tierney: A Biography.* Jefferson: McFarland & Company, Inc., 2005.

Von Trapp, Agathe. *Memories Before and After The Sound of Music.* New York: HarperCollins, 2010.

Wagner, Robert J. and Scott Eyman. *Pieces of My Heart; a Life*. New York: HarperCollins, 2008.

Wagner, Robert J. and Scott Eyman. *You Must Remember This; Life and Style in Hollywood's Golden Age.*. New York: Viking, 2014.

Walsh, Raoul. *Each Man in His Time; The Life Story of a Director*. New York: Farrar, Straus and Giroux, 1974.

Wanamaker, Marc. *"A Chronology of the Fox Film Corporation: The Silent Years," Le Giornate del Cinema,* March, 1998.

Wanger, Walter and Joe Hyams. *My Life With Cleopatra*. New York: Random House, Inc. 2013.

Watkins, Mel. *Stepin Fetchit: the life and times of Lincoln Perry*. New York: Pantheon Books, 2005.

Webb, Clifton and David L. Smith, *Sitting Pretty, The Life and Times of Clifton Webb*. University Press of Mississippi, 2011.

Welch, Raquel. *Beyond The Cleavage*. New York: Weinstein Books, 2010.

Welles, Orson and Peter Bogdanovich. *This Is Orson Welles*. New York: Da Capo Press, 1998.

Wellman, William. *A Short Time for Insanity; an Autobiography*. New York: Hawthorn Books, Inc., 1974.

White, Pearl. *Just Me*. New York: George H. Doran Company, 1919.

Williams, Esther. *The Million Dollar Mermaid*. New York: Simon & Schuster, 1999.

Wolff, Michael. *The Man Who Owns The News; Inside the Secret World of Rupert Murdoch*. New York: Broadway Books, 2008.

Zanuck, Darryl F., *Tunis Expedition*, New York: Random House, 1943.

Zolotow, Maurice. *Marilyn Monroe*. New York: Bantam Books, 1960.

Zuckoff, Mitchell. *Robert Altman; The Oral Biography*. New York: Alfred A. Knopf, 2009.

DOCUMENTARIES

Becoming John Ford. 20th Century Fox Home Entertainment LLC, 1997.

Don't Say No Until I Finish Talking: The Story of Richard D. Zanuck, directed by Laurent Bouzereau, Amblin Television, 2013.

Murnau, Borzage, and Fox. 20th Century Fox Home Entertainment LLC, 2008.

Public Enemies; The Golden Age of the Gangster Film. Warner Bros. Entertainment, Inc. 2008.

Rothman, Tom, *Fox Legacy, The Fox Movie Channel episodes: Cleopatra, Die Hard, Tyrone Power, All That Jazz, How Green Was My Valley, Love is a Many-Splendored Thing, The Brothers McMullen, Waiting to Exhale, There's Something About Mary,* 2008–2012.

20th Century Fox: The First Fifty Years. produced by Van Ness Films, Inc. in association with Foxstar Productions, Twentieth Television and American Movie Classics, Directed by Kevin Burns, 1996.

20TH Century Fox: The Blockbuster Years. produced by Van Ness Films, Inc. in association with Prometheus Entertainment, Fox Television Studios, Foxstar Productions and American Movie Classics, Directed by Kevin Burns, 20th Century Fox, 2002.

INDEX